Human Capital Management and Competitive Advantage in Tourism

Mario Silic
Swiss School of Business and Management, Switzerland

Mahesh Luthia
Chetana's Institute of Management and Research, India

Faizan Ahmad
Cardiff Metropolitan University, UK

Partha Pratim Chakraborty
Chetana's Institute of Management and Research, India

IGI Global
Scientific Publishing
Publishing Tomorrow's Research Today

Vice President of Editorial	Melissa Wagner
Director of Acquisitions	Mikaela Felty
Director of Book Development	Jocelynn Hessler
Production Manager	Mike Brehm
Cover Design	Jose Rosado

Published in the United States of America by
IGI Global Scientific Publishing
701 East Chocolate Avenue
Hershey, PA, 17033, USA
Tel: 717-533-8845
Fax: 717-533-7115
Website: https://www.igi-global.com E-mail: cust@igi-global.com

Library of Congress Cataloging-in-Publication Data

Names: Silic, Mario, 1976- editor. | Luthia, Mahesh Srichand, 1971- editor. | Ahmad, Faizan, 1988- editor. | Chakraborty, Partha Pratim, 1977- editor.
Title: Human capital management and competitive advantage in tourism / edited by Mario Silic, Mahesh Luthia, Faizan Ahmad, Partha Chakraborty
Description: Hershey, PA : IGI Global Scientific Publishing, [2025] | Includes bibliographical references and index. | Summary: "The book aims to explore the role of sustainable human capital management in developing a competitive advantage for the Indian Tourism sector. The book attempts to present frameworks, tools and approaches by integrating theory and practice that can support human development in the sector through new age technology and contemporary human development approaches"-- Provided by publisher.i n tourism
Identifiers: LCCN 2024054368 (print) | LCCN 2024054369 (ebook) | ISBN 9798337300719 (h/c) | ISBN 9798337300726 (s/c) | ISBN 9798337300733 (ebook)
Subjects: LCSH: Tourism--India. | Personnel management--Environmental aspects--India. | Human capital--Management--India. | Tourism--Technological innovations--India. | Sustainability.
Classification: LCC G155.I4 H86 2025 (print) | LCC G155.I4 (ebook) | DDC 910.68/3--dc23/eng/20250111
LC record available at https://lccn.loc.gov/2024054368
LC ebook record available at https://lccn.loc.gov/2024054369
British Cataloguing in Publication Data
A Cataloguing in Publication record for this book is available from the British Library.

Editorial Advisory Board

Table of Contents

Detailed Table of Contents

wellbeing. Therefore, to reduce the impact of challenges on employee wellbeing, Organizational culture is the key.

The tourism sector is a pivotal contributor to economic growth, employment generation, and foreign exchange in India. Despite its substantial potential, the sector grapples with challenges such as high employee turnover, technological disruptions, and the demand for sustainable practices. This study examines the leadership challenges and opportunities within the tourism industry, emphasizing the role of transformational, adaptive, and sustainable leadership in achieving human capital excellence. It introduces the Integrated Leadership for Human Capital Excellence in Tourism (ILHCET) model, which aligns leadership with workforce optimization, technology integration, and sustainability.

This study explores the critical role of leadership in shaping sustainable growth and innovation within the tourism sector. It identifies key challenges such as skills gaps, resistance to change, and cultural barriers, proposing a tailored leadership framework that integrates human capital management, training, and lifelong learning. The research highlights the importance of fostering sustainability, adaptability, and workforce agility to align with emerging trends and global demands. By offering actionable recommendations for policymakers and industry stakeholders, the study aims to enhance leadership effectiveness, promote responsible tourism practices, and ensure long-term success and competitiveness in a rapidly evolving global landscape.

The need for collaboration of academia and Tourism industry has risen with the rise in inflow and outflow of tourist, not only domestic but international. This in turn has given a thrust to trained manpower for this service industry, as the tourist expectation is high on carrying back the best experience. It should be the aim of human resource to generate experiences providing a lasting impression. Hence, it has become mandatory to train the industry personnel on regular basis and also create skilled man power from the institutes. The objective of the chapter is to establish an understanding on how a collaboration can benefit both the academia and industry. It aims to skill, reskill, multi-skill and upskill the employee from time to time and make them relevant in the ever changing scenario of the most vibrant tourism industry. The Industry can take help of Institute for carrying out R&D and to solve any technical hurdles, and on the other hand the students & faculties get a chance to further hone their skills & knowledge

The Indian tourism sector is undergoing a transformative shift by integrating green skills and digital competencies into workforce strategies to align with sustainability goals and digital advancements. This research focuses on identifying essential green skills, such as resource conservation, environmental awareness, and community-centered social responsibility, to promote eco-friendly practices and preserve India's biodiversity and cultural heritage. Additionally, digital competencies, including AI-driven customer interaction tools, virtual engagement platforms, and data analytics, are explored to enhance smart tourism solutions and global appeal. The study aims to develop a comprehensive framework combining green and digital skills to address challenges such as workforce diversity, digital infrastructure gaps, and the need for sustainable practices in rural and eco-sensitive regions. Emphasizing inclusivity, the research will empower SMEs and local communities, enabling active participation in the tourism economy.

The tourism industry is highly sensitive and volatile, constantly being influenced by global trends and emerging technologies. One major change is the emergence of the metaverse, an extension of augmented reality, virtual reality, and 3D simulations. This digital innovation not only offers new ways to deliver tourism services but also offers significant potential to enhance human resource management within

This study employed bibliometric analysis to visualize global research trends and future research directions in sustainable tourism and its alignment with the Sustainable Development Goals (SDGs). The search strategy was designed to identify relevant literature by using specific keywords and search terms related to sustainable tourism and the SDGs Scopus database was selected to collect the data. A total of 380 documents were collected from the Scopus database. The search period was set from 2000 to 2024 to encompass recent developments. The subject area included Business, Management and Accounting, Economics, Econometrics and Finance, Social Sciences, and Arts and Humanities. By applying various filters and data cleaning process 230 documents were included in performing the final analysis.

Preface

The tourism sector serves as one of the major contributors to the economy. The diversity of tourism in India in terms of landscape, heritage, cuisines, wildlife, and adventure makes India one of the top preferred global tourist locations. With the recent shift towards medical, religious, and wellness tourism, eco-conscious travel, and immersive cultural experiences travelers to India seeking unique experiences and enhanced customer experience. Digital transformation of tourism has revolutionized the sector with new business models emerging and the adoption of technology in streamlining operations. New technologies such as new realities (AR/VR), artificial intelligence, and metaverse enable service providers, to personalize travel experience, facilitate destination management design customer service offerings, and promote sustainability leading the smart tourism.

The growth of smart tourism has resulted in new challenges of having a workforce that is more skilled with technological competence. The skill gap in India has resulted in in shortage of skilled workforce and limits the potential of the industry innovate and achieve a competitive advantage.

Human Resource Development can play a significant role in sustainably managing human resources. To address these issues, there is a need for innovative and contemporary human resource management and development practices that would contribute to the human capital in the sector. The most unique aspect of the book is, that it examines the role of human resources in the current dynamic context and adopts a futuristic approach.

This book, Human Capital Management and Competitive Advantage in Tourism is an attempt to examine sustainable human resource practices and trace emerging trends and the impact of technology on the workforce and promotion of Indian tourism. The book attempts to present frameworks, tools, and approaches by integrating theory and practice, that can support human development in the sector through new-age technology and contemporary human development approaches.

What sets this book apart is its interdisciplinary approach to not only explore contemporary HR practices but also examine emergent topics such as the role of digital transformation in tourism HRM, and resilient religious supply chain management in the context of post-pandemic religious tourism. The book contributes to enriching the existing literature of tourism management with a focus on leadership, strategy, and sustainability.

The chapters have been organized into three broad thematic areas to enable the readers to adopt a structured and coherent approach for an enhanced reading experience. Section 1, *Strategic Human Capital Management Practices in Tourism*, explores factors, challenges, and opportunities for medical tourism, and HRM challenges in the current changing environment. This section also illustrates leadership challenges and opportunities for excellence and tourism and the role of academia and Industry collaboration in tourism education for Sustainable Growth and Innovation.

Section 2, *Technology enabled Sustainable HCM Practices in Tourism*, delves into the integration of emerging technologies and sustainability-driven strategies in human capital development within the tourism sector. The chapters in this section highlight the convergence of green skills, metaverse and digital competencies and explore how also explores how virtual tourism and tech-driven innovations can enhance visitor experiences while promoting ecosystem conservation, inclusivity, and long-term sustainability in tourism workforce practices. The section how technology can contribute to developing digital leadership that is required in the digital era of tourism.

Section 3: *Emerging Paradigms in Tourism: Strategy, Sustainability, and Innovation*, presents a forward-looking perspective into the evolving dynamics of the tourism sector. The chapters examine internal marketing strategies, supply chain innovations in religious tourism, and the growing significance of wellness tourism. Additionally, the section analyses and maps global research trends in digital and sustainable tourism offering direction for future research and adopting sustainable practices

We hope that this book serves as a valuable resource for academics, practitioners, policymakers, and students on the role of human capital management strategies and digital technologies in developing a competitive advantage for Indian Tourism. We hope the book inspires us to adopt best practices and encourage dialogues between different stakeholders for strategic actions to build a sustainable and competitive tourism workforce in India.

Dr. Mahesh Luthia

Chapter 1
Competencies for Medical Tourism in India

Pankaj D. Kulkarni
https://orcid.org/0009-0003-4326-7100
Independent Researcher, India

ABSTRACT

India, the land of Susruta, "The Father of Surgery," boasts a rich history in medicine dating back to the Vedic era, with texts like the Atharvaveda blending religion, empiricism, and magic. This foundation evolved into advanced rational medicine by 1000 BC, leading to India's current prominence in global healthcare. As a leader in medical tourism, India attracts patients seeking affordable, high-quality treatments, from organ transplants to cosmetic surgeries and traditional therapies like Ayurveda and Yoga. Ranked 10th in the Medical Tourism Index (2020-21), India faces challenges like unstructured growth and regulatory gaps but leverages advancements like AI to improve care and streamline operations. With government support and strategic digitization, India can harness its cost advantage and skilled workforce to dominate the global medical tourism market. This paper explores India's competitive edge, stakeholder roles, and innovations needed to position it as a holistic healthcare destination, promoting economic growth and wellness tourism.

INTRODUCTION

> *"All in all Susruta must be considered the greatest surgeon of the pre medieval period." - A.O. Whipple*

DOI: 10.4018/979-8-3373-0071-9.ch001

It is aptly mentioned by A.O. Whipple the American surgeon on whose name the Pancreatic cancer surgery is named. India has a vast and ancient history of Medicine which can be traced to go back as far as remote antiquity.

The earliest of Indian medicines are found in the oldest sacred books of the Hindu religion, i.e. the 4 Vedas namely the Rigveda, Samveda, Yajurveda and Atharvaveda which were compiled in sanskrit between 3000 and 1000 B.C, Most of the early medicine compilation can be found in the Atharvaveda an amalgam or religion, empiric and magic, thus India can be considered as the birth place of medicine however the lack of knowledge of Sanskrit language may have led to the neglect of the Hindu medicine.

However, India was the birthplace of medicine and surgery, (H.H. Wilson,1823) & (J.F. Royle,1837) pioneered the study of Indian Medicine and gave it the recognition. Since then the medicine science has made tremendous advancement and from 19th century medicinal practice changed in view of the rapid advances done in science as well as the new approaches adopted by physicians, also the hospital doctors adopted a more systematic analysis of patients symptoms in their diagnosis. India has also been on the ascend in the field of medicine and today we have one of the best talent pool of medical professionals which are supported by excellent and world class infrastructure and today it is amongst the preferred destination for medical tourism.

It can be attributed to the fact that Liberalization of Indian economy in 1991 gave the way for the rise in consumption of consumer goods and services, along with this the service industry also had equal contribution in absorption of various business opportunities due to the formulation of new policies by the then government for the sustainable growth of Indian economy.

Along with the development of various industries, the health care industry also grew rapidly and the traces of the concept of Medical tourism existence can be found in the early 1990 whereby there were favourable policies to open the doors for International patients, thus hospitals found to use their existing facilities to provide specialized care to a new class of patients altogether.

Secondly in today's highly competitive business world, irrespective of whether the business is for Life caring or Lifesaving purposes it has become mandatory for hospitals to increase the patients base of treatment and care for survival through medical tourism.

Medical tourism can be defined as 'activities related to travel and hosting a foreign tourist who stays at least one night at the destination region for the purpose of maintaining, improving or restoring health through medical intervention' *(Ministry of Tourism, Government of India)*

The medical interventions can be classified into 3 categories

- Treatment for curative purposes - Organ Transplant, Knee replacement, Open heart Surgery etc.
- Treatment for Rejuvenation or for Aesthetic reasons- Cosmetic Surgery, Spas etc.
- Access to traditional systems of medicines such as (Ayurveda, Yoga & Naturopathy, Unani, Siddha, Homeopathy, AYUSH) Offering

Nowadays, the term "Medical tourism " is often referred to as Medical Value Travel as it captures the healthcare seeking behaviour of patients as well as the economic impact of such travel on the nation hosting them.

Besides India other countries like Greece, South Africa, Malaysia, Philippines, Thailand and Singapore are also promoting Medical tourism in a big way.

India has been ranked 10th in Medical Tourism Index (MTI) for 2020-21 out of 46 destinations of the world by Medical Tourism Association (Ministry of tourism, Govt of India), and though the market for Medical tourism is growing at CAGR of 15% it is still by and large unstructured comprising of small to medium sized hundreds of Medical tourism facilitators

Usually the term Medical Tourism only considers those who come to hospitals for treatment and it might be difficult in categorizing Yoga retreats, Meditation centers as medical tourism, however the reach of this India's healing arts cannot be ignored.

History tells us that ever since the advent of yoga 5000 years ago, India has enjoyed influx of medical travelers and spiritual learners hoping to learn and benefit from this alternative branch of medicine, hence India was one of the oldest medicine tourism destination, but now it is one of the world's most popular one.

The impetus on this alternative has been given now by the Government of India and it is considered as "Wellness Tourism ". In view of it the term Medical tourism term should have an expanded scope encompassing broader area than being limited.

FACTORS DRIVING MEDICAL TOURISM

In India the primary driver of the growth of medical tourism is the highly trained and knowledgeable medical fraternity who are very much adept in English (Crooks, et al., 2011), this tourism category falls under the services exports and is also one instrumental factor in earning foreign exchange for the nation as well as provide large employment opportunities for nation.

As the main objective of the medical tourists is getting good quality medical treatment at affordable costs, the healthcare hospitals which provide these have to adopt an approach of competitiveness on outward and an approach of operational excellence on inward to put the costs down.

The factors which make India an attractive destination are

Demand - In the western world there is long waiting lists which has resulted in patients considering other destinations
Affordability - The low costs with quality treatments in India makes it an attractive destination for consideration by the patients.
Accessibility - India has excellent connectivity via air routes with 50 International terminals connected to the various parts of the world as well internal connectivity via air, railways and roads is excellent.

Apart from the above the foreign exchange rate is favourable which makes it an economical viable destination. also the government of India has eased the visa rules as well as it issues e- visas for medical tourism purpose.

Communication skills - India having a basic English schooling facility available across the nation as well as the higher education across various disciplines, as such India also has a healthcare force which is good in English language communication.

Secondly with the digitization focus of the Indian government and an excellent Internet network with the advancement in telemedicine it enables the patients to get the follow up care, rehabilitative care after major surgery. As such this helps to avoid the need to have a follow up visit to the country.

However, there are some majorly considerations which are of prime importance for becoming a top destination in Medical tourism

Quality and Safety

These 2 variables are of prime consideration when one is to detail the importance of Medical tourism in India, these will be responsible for being a top reputation destination as a medical tourism hub.

Joint commission International (JCI) - a Global leader in Health care accreditation and National Accreditation Board for Hospitals and Healthcare providers (NABH) Accreditation by Quality council of India are the major agencies whose accreditation signifies that the standards conform to the norms set and they are satisfactory for International Patients to visit.

India has around 70000 hospitals (source: knight- frank global report,2023) out of which 63% are private, unlike in developed countries where the public sector healthcare is dominant, in India it is the private sector which is dominant.

Further a total of only 55 Hospitals in India are JCI accredited (source -https://www.jointcommissioninternational.org/) and 1426 are NABH accredited (Source: https://portal.nabh.co), out of the above 93 hospitals are either having their accreditation expired or not recommended for renewal or for other reasons and are now not under accreditation certifications.

The above figures inform that only around 0.13% of the hospitals out of the total can be considered for safe medical tourism which is extremely low and it needs to be improved.

Herein the Government of India can play an active role in where by the current status of the nation in Medical tourism can be improved.

LITERATURE REVIEW

Medical tourism in India has emerged as a significant sector, driven by the country's advanced healthcare facilities, cost-effectiveness, and the availability of diverse medical treatments. This literature review synthesizes key findings from various studies related to the competencies required for enhancing medical tourism in India.

Overview of Medical Tourism in India

India has positioned itself as a major destination for medical tourism, attracting patients from around the world seeking affordable and high-quality medical care.

According to a study by the Indian Institute of Tourism and Travel Management (Dr Monika Parekh, Tyagi& Devrath, 2011) the competence of healthcare professionals is a critical factor influencing medical tourists' decisions to seek treatment in India. The study emphasizes that patients prioritize the qualifications and skills of doctors, which significantly impacts their overall satisfaction with the services received

Core Competencies Required

The competencies required for effective medical tourism can be categorized into several key areas:

Healthcare Professional Competence: The skills and expertise of healthcare providers are paramount. Studies indicate that Indian doctors are often perceived as highly competent, with many holding international qualifications (Soveneshnhi Gunaselan, N.Kesavan, 2020)

Cultural Sensitivity: Understanding and addressing the cultural differences of international patients is crucial. Training for non-medical staff in cross-cultural communication can enhance patient experiences (Dr Jugal Kishore, Dr Panesar)
Operational Efficiency: Streamlining processes such as patient intake, treatment protocols, and post-operative care can improve service delivery. Efficient management practices are essential to meet the expectations of medical tourists (Shubham Varshney,2024)

Challenges Faced by Medical Tourists

Despite its advantages, the Indian medical tourism sector faces several challenges:

Expectation vs. Reality Gap: Research indicates that there is often a significant gap between what medical tourists expect and what they experience, particularly concerning facilitation and care during their stay (Brown, Johnson Rafferty, Barbera and Manoj Sharma, 2020).
Accreditation Issues: While many hospitals are accredited by organizations like JCI and NABH, there is still a lack of awareness among potential patients regarding these accreditations.
Policy and Infrastructure Development: The need for a cohesive national policy on medical tourism has been highlighted as essential for addressing issues such as visa regulations and quality assurance standards (Dr Abhay Sinha, 2022)

Future Directions

To enhance India's position in the global medical tourism market, several recommendations have been proposed:

Government Support: Increased collaboration between government bodies and healthcare providers is necessary to promote India effectively as a medical tourism destination (Dr Abhay SInha,Nov 2022, Kumar, Gowreesunkar Dec 2022)

Branding and Marketing: Developing a strong brand identity that emphasizes India's strengths in healthcare can attract more international patients (Dr Abhay Sinha, 2022)

Research and Data Analysis: Improved data collection on medical tourists can help tailor services to meet their needs better and identify emerging trends within the sector

CHALLENGES IN MEDICAL TOURISM

- Lack of Government regulation for MVT Sector

Currently no regulations to govern the MVT sector, which has resulted in the sector being unorganised and lacking any monitoring of the quality of service by the stakeholders namely - MVT facilitators and Service Providers. There needs to be more support from the Government for regulation, facilitating and promoting the nation as a Medical Value travel destination.

- Lack of Nodal agency to control the Medical Value travel

No nodal agency exists to head the Medical Value travel and also there is low coordination among the stakeholders like Airlines, Hospital & Hotels

- Heal in India

The Heal in India needs to be promoted aggressively by the government to imbibe in minds of foreign nationals that India be considered as a preferred destination for Medical tourism.

- Lack of awareness of NABH accreditation at International Level.

India has the accreditation which is very much robust through the National Accreditation Board for Hospitals and Healthcare. However, the awareness of it is not there among the foreign countries and hence the International patients still give greater consideration and value to JCI accreditation.

- Pricing policies

No uniform Pricing Policies across various hospitals due to which there is no consistency in pricing across the hospitals, due to this the MVT facilitators overcharge the patients sometimes which creates a ripple effect on the industry in a negative way.

- Perception as an unhygienic country

While India is one of the popular country for foreign tourists there is general perception about the country being not very hygienic. This has some impact on the choice of India being considered as a MVT destination.

- Medical Insurance

Non availability of Medical Insurance portability as well as non-coverage of traditional systems of medicine under the Medical Insurance policies at an International Level impacts the country being chosen as a MVT destination.

- Unorganized MVTF

The MVT facilitators have an important role in promoting the Medical tourism, NABH has a system of the accreditation for the facilitators but the same is not effective. This also gives the opportunity for the Middlemen i.e. MVT Facilitators to exploit the visiting patients, symptom of which is a negative image about the sector as well as the nation as a whole.

- Non-Coverage of Medical Insurance for Overseas patients

This factor makes the Medical Value travel less attractive as the patients will have to incur all the total costs i.e. travel, stay costs along with the Medical treatment costs .

While the above mentioned are some of the challenges faced by the Medical tourism industry and the thought of scope to be widened to include the wellness industry as well in the MVT concept like an addendum so that the nation's image as a Medical tourism is enhanced can be only possible if the challenges faced by wellness industry are overcome as albeit the demand for the wellness industry products and services is high the challenges are as below

Dearth of Good training institutes -

There has to be training institutes having standardized and accredited courses which are still not there .The vocational programmes which are present impart theoretical knowledge with almost nil or limited hands on training, another challenge is retention of skilled manpower in the wellness area as the skilled professionals available in the area are few in numbers and hence their lies a huge demand for them.

Lack of well-defined and structured framework -

There is no defined framework which will define the conduct for this industry

This creates a low entry barrier to enter, the advantage of which is taken by the small and unskilled players who might not adhere to hygiene requirements as well as lack the necessary infrastructure, transparent pricing and customer oriented approach, thus it leaves a vulnerable area which due to a single bad impression from any of the unskilled wellness provider might have a severe damaging effect on the entire industry and a collateral damage to the medical tourism industry to a certain extent.

Hence it essential to develop a legal framework which have a well-defined parameters of operations in the industry.

KEY STAKEHOLDERS IN INDIA IN MVT

The various stakeholders in the Medical tourism industry are

- Central Ministries
- State government
- Industry associations
- MVT facilitators
- Airlines and Hotels
- Healthcare industry

Central Ministries

Herein the below ministries are responsible

Ministry of Tourism

Ministry which is responsible for inbound tourism to the nation and can play a vital role in promoting the medical tourism industry abroad. It has set up Medical and wellness tourism board which governs as to act upon various aspects of Medical Value travel

Ministry of Commerce

Ministry which is responsible for framing policies of Service sector and identified Medical Value travel as one of the important aspect of contribution to the service sector. A suitable support by the ministry to Medical value travel will provide a big impetus to the MVT.

Ministry of Health.

Ministry for developing health care policy of the country in partnership with Private sector can support MVT by developing a regulatory framework in regards to safety of patients and develop trust in the Indian medical service industry.

Ministry of Ayush

Ayush can be distinctive offering from India, hence the ministry has to synergise the offering with other stakeholders to create India as a holistic destination for Medical travel

Ministry of External Affairs

The ministry and Indian Diplomatic Missions abroad in various countries can play a significant role in promoting India as a valuable MVT destination.

National Accreditation Board for Hospitals and HealthCare Providers

The framework developed by NABH is robust, however it needs to be promoted aggressively to convince that the standards are at par with International accreditation.

State Governments

State Governments have a crucial role in providing support in terms of ground infrastructure and can also be an enabler to the MVT for a destination in the state. It can cohesively act with the other stakeholders to enhance the MVT perception amongst the patients.

Healthcare Providers

Hospitals are the primary service providers for the patients and it is the point of first impression, hence it is absolutely essential to provide top quality healthcare services to the patients who are admitted to undertake the treatment in the hospital.

Industry Associations

Industry associations like FICCI, CII do work with other stakeholders to increase the awareness and highlight the issues related to MVT, in fact FICCI has been organizing annual MVT event on a global basis.

Association of MVT facilitators

These play a crucial role to bridge the gap between the medical value traveler and service provider.

Airlines and Hotels

These also have an important role to play in promotion of MVT, they have to coordinate with MVT facilitators and hospitals so that seamless experience can be provide to the patients.

Table 1. Shows the details of the tourists arrival for MVT purposes in India since 2020

Year	Medical Purpose (in thousand)
2020	183
2021	304
2022	475
2023 (*)	635

Source: Bureau of Immigration (BOI), *: Provisional

As can be seen from the above table there has been a rise in the arrival of patients for MVT purposes secondly as per Federation of Indian Chamber of Commerce and Industry, the Medical Value Travel in India is expected to grow at a CAGR of 21.1% from 2020-2027. The MVT market in India was estimated at around Rs 50,000 Crore (Approx. US$6 billion) in 2022 and is projected to increase to Rs 105,000 Crore (Approx. $13 billion) by 2026 .

The Medical Value Travel industry in India gets maximum patients for heart surgery, knee transplant, cosmetic surgery and dental care as the cost of treatment in India is considered to be the lowest in Asia, much lower than Thailand, Indonesia, Singapore and Hong Kong.

However Bangladesh, Iraq, Maldives, Afghanistan, Oman, Yemen, Sudan, Kenya, Nigeria and Tanzania account for about 88 per cent of the total international patients visiting India.

ADVANTAGE INDIA FOR MEDICAL TOURISM

Although the aforesaid challenges exists there are opportunities which provide a bright side to the sector. They are mentioned below

Excellent Connectivity In International Routes

India has excellent air connectivity at International level and also within the nation, hence it gives an opportunity to draw more people to the Medical Value travel.

Indian Diaspora Visiting India

There is huge population of Indian diaspora across the globe and the MVT can be tapped into this segment as the Indians abroad do visit the country at least minimum once in a year.

Long Waiting Period In Developed Countries To Get Access To Medical Facility

Table 2. Gives an idea of the waiting times in USA

Specialty	Average wait time	% change since 2017
Cardiology	26.6 days	+26%
Dermatology	34.5 days	+7%
Family medicine	20.6 days	-30%
Obstetrics/gynaecology	31.4 days	+19%
Orthopaedic surgery	16.9 days	+48%

Source: AMN /Merritt Hawkins' 2022 Survey of Physician Appointment Wait Times and Medicare and Medicaid Acceptance Rates.

The above table shows the opportunity India can have in terms of Medical treatment for foreign Patients

Lowest Cost for Treatment – India has one of the lowest cost of Treatments for various medical procedures which should be highlighted during promoting the MVT along with the accreditation standards

Table 3. Cost comparison of different treatments in various countries

Treatment Cost Comparison							
Procedures	USA ($)	Costa Rica ($)	India ($)	Korea ($)	Mexico ($)	Thailand ($)	Malaysia ($)
Heart Bypass	$144,000	$25,000	$5,200	$28,900	$27,000	$15,121	$11,430
Angioplasty	$57,000	$13,000	$3,300	$15,200	$12,500	$3,788	$5,430
Heart Valve Replacement	$170,000	$30,000	$5,500	$43,500	$18,000	$21,212	$10,580
Hip Replacement	$50,000	$12,500	$7,000	$14,120	$13,000	$7,879	$7,500
Hip Resurfacing	$50,000	$12,500	$7,000	$15,600	$15,000	$15,152	$12,350
Knee Replacement	$50,000	$11,500	$6,200	$19,800	$12,000	$12,297	$7,000
Spinal Fusion	$100,000	$11,500	$6,500	$15,400	$12,000	$9,091	$6,000

continued on following page

Table 3. Continued

Treatment Cost Comparison							
Procedures	**USA ($)**	**Costa Rica ($)**	**India ($)**	**Korea ($)**	**Mexico ($)**	**Thailand ($)**	**Malaysia ($)**
Dental Implant	$2,800	$900	$1,000	$4,200	$1,800	$3,636	$345
Lap Band	$30,000	$8,500	$3,000	N/A	$6,500	$11,515	N/A
Rhinoplasty	$8,000	$4,500	$4,000	$5,000	$3,500	$3,901	$1,293
Face Lift	$15,000	$6,000	$4,000	$15,300	$4,900	$3,697	$3,440
Hysterectomy	$15,000	$5,700	$2,500	$11,000	$5,800	$2,727	$5,250
Gastric Sleeve	$28,700	$10,500	$5,000	N/A	$9,995	$13,636	N/A
Gastric Bypass	$32,972	$12,500	$5,000	N/A	$10,950	$16,667	$9,450
Liposuction	$9,000	$3,900	$2,800	N/A	$2,800	$2,303	$2,299
Tummy Tuck	$9,750	$5,300	$3,000	N/A	$4,025	$5,000	N/A
Lasik (both eyes)	$4,400	$1,800	$500	$6,000	$1,995	$1,818	$477
Cornea (both eyes)	N/A	$4,200	N/A	$7,000	N/A	$1,800	N/A
Retina	N/A	$4,500	$850	$10,200	$3,500	$4,242	$3,000

Source:medicalindiatourism.com

The above table gives the picture that of all the countries India is the most economical destination in terms of cost for the various treatments mentioned. Hence there is no second thought that India should be the most preferred destination for medical tourism and all the stakeholders should make the efforts in that direction.

The ecosystem of the Medical and Wellness tourism includes various participants i.e. Hotels, Airlines, regulatory bodies and the Government Hence it is essential that a proper link be designed and developed to establish a connection or network link and understanding among the aforesaid participants of the responsibilities and roles they need to perform so as to forge partnership for promoting the Medical and wellness tourism sector.

MVT Facilitator's Registration

MVT facilitators play an important role in Medical and wellness tourism, and the real ones who are adept or have the necessary education, training, skills, and infrastructure should be encouraged and trained so that they promote the sectors in fair manner.

NABH has already set up the registration and accreditation so that it ensures that the non -clinical services provided are of certain quality standards and not adhoc or some quack service. It is important especially during the post-operative procedure whereby the patient might need accommodation and other services.

However it is noted that since last 7 years only 22 facilitators have applied for the registration and almost 50% of the applicant status shows the documents needed are still not received. The below table gives the needed information about the application by MVT facilitators for NABH Accreditation.

Table 4. Applications by MVT facilitators for NABH Accreditation

S.N.	Appl. ID	Name	Date of receipt of application	Present Status
1	MVTF-2017-0005	Medifriend Healthcare Private Limited, Delhi, Delhi, India	03-Feb-17	Application Closed
2	MVTF-2018-0015	Century Super Speciality Hospital Private Limited, Hyderabad, Telangana, India	19-Apr-18	Application Closed
3	MVTF-2018-0016	Sehat India Healthcare Services Private Limited, Mumbai, Maharashtra, India	06-Aug-18	Application Closed
4	MVTF-2018-0017	Aishani Internationals Medico-Tourism LLP, Noida, Uttar Pradesh, India	14-Aug-18	Application Closed
5	MVTF-2019-0022	Medobal A Part of Sansi Tourism Private Limited, Chennai, Tamil Nadu, India	02-Feb-19	Documents received
6	MVTF-2019-0027	Kenneth International Care and Medical Tourism Private Limited, Panaji (Panjim), Goa, India	19-Apr-2019	Application Closed
7	MVTF-2019-0028	Prayag Hospital and Research Centre, Noida, Uttar Pradesh, India	23-Nov-2019	Application Closed
8	MVTF-2020-0029	Heal Companion, Delhi, Delhi, India	05-Jan-2020	Documents not received
9	MVTF-2020-0030	NTP Healthcare NTP Tourism Affairs Ltd., Connaught Place, Delhi, Delhi, India	09-May-2020	Documents not received
10	MVTF-2022-0034	The Corporate Hospital, Amritsar, Punjab, India	07-Jul-2022	Documents not received
11	MVTF-2022-0038	AIG Hospitals (A Unit of Asian Institute of Gastroenterology Private Limited, Hyderabad, Telangana, India	22-Aug-2022	Documents received
12	MVTF-2023-0049	Treatment Traveller Private Limited, Noida, Uttar Pradesh, India	16-Aug-2023	Application closed
13	MVTF-2023-0050	MediGence Network Pvt. Ltd., New Delhi, Delhi, India	06-Sep-2023	Application closed
14	MVTF-2023-0051	World Health Dias Private Limited, Jungpura Extension, Delhi, India	20-Nov-2023	Documents Pending
15	MVTF-2023-0052	Intouch Healers, Delhi, Delhi, India	20-Dec-2023	Application closed
16	MVTF-2024-0054	I.M.S Medical Services Private Limited, Ahmedabad, Gujarat, India	09-Feb-2024	Application closed
17	MVTF-2024-0055	Heal Zone, Okhla, Delhi, Delhi, India	04-Mar-2024	Documents not received
18	MVTF-2024-0056	Healthy Hugs Healthcare, Palghar, Maharashtra, India	13-Mar-2024	Documents not received
19	MVTF-2024-0058	MED Access India Pvt. Ltd., Pune, Maharashtra, India	26-Mar-2024	Documents not received
20	MVTF-2024-0059	CROM Clinical Research & Medical Tourism Pvt. Ltd., North Goa, Goa, India	18-Oct-2024	Documents not received

continued on following page

Table 4. Continued

S.N.	Appl. ID	Name	Date of receipt of application	Present Status
21	MVTF-2024-0060	Al Afiya Healthcare Pvt Ltd, Delhi, Delhi, India	18-Oct-2024	Documents not received
22	MVTF-2024-0061	Crescent Meditours, Chennai, Tamil Nadu, India	04-Nov-2024	Documents not received

Source:https://nabh.co/applicantmvtf/

Table 5. Status of the empaneled MVT facilitators by NABH

S.N.	Reference No.	Name	Acc. No.	Valid From	Valid Upto	Remarks
1	MVTF-2016-0001	AAA+ Health Care Consultancy Services Private Limited, Mumbai, Maharashtra, India	MT-2016-0001	07-Mar-23	06-Mar-25	
2	MVTF-2016-0002	Magnus MediTourism Pvt. Ltd., Mumbai, Maharashtra, India	MT-2017-0002	18-Oct-22	17-Oct-24	
3	MVTF-2017-0003	Alshifa Healthcare Services Pvt Ltd, Delhi, Delhi, India	MT-2017-0003	01-Sep-22	31-Aug-24	
4	MVTF-2017-0004	Global Treatment Services Private Limited, Bangalore, Karnataka, India	MT-2017-0004	18-Oct-22	17-Oct-24	
5	MVTF-2017-0006	Anarghyaa Etech Solutions Pvt. Ltd., Bangalore, Karnataka, India	MT-2017-0005	02-Jul-17	01-Jul-19	Expired and not applied for Renewal empanelment
6	MVTF-2017-0008	HBG Medical Assistance (A Unit of Healthians Research Centre Private Limited), Gurgaon, Haryana, India	MT-2017-0006	07-Sep-22	06-Sep-24	
7	MVTF-2017-0007	medECUBE Healthcare India Private Limited, Gurgaon, Haryana, India	MT-2018-0007	07-Sep-20	06-Sep-22	Expired and not applied for Renewal empanelment
8	MVTF-2017-0009	Vaidam Health Pvt. Ltd., Gurgaon, Haryana, India	MT-2018-0008	18-Oct-22	17-Oct-24	
9	MVTF-2017-0010	eExpedise Healthcare Private Limited, Delhi, Delhi, India	MT-2018-0009	24-Feb-22	23-Feb-24	Expired and not applied for Renewal empanelment
10	MVTF-2017-0011	Medi Assist Healthcare Services Limited, Bangalore, Karnataka, India	MT-2018-0010	28-Aug-22	27-Aug-24	
11	MVTF-2017-0012	Konsult App Pvt. Ltd., Delhi, Delhi, India	MT-2018-0011	22-Jul-18	20-Jul-20	Expired and not applied for Renewal empanelment

continued on following page

Table 5. Continued

S.N.	Reference No.	Name	Acc. No.	Valid From	Valid Upto	Remarks
12	MVTF-2018-0013	Health Travellers Worldwide, Chennai, Tamil Nadu, India	MT-2018-0012	16-Sep-18	15-Sep-20	Expired and not applied for Renewal empanelment
13	MVTF-2018-0014	Mednexus Travel4Health Pvt. Ltd., Mayur Vihar - I, Delhi, Delhi, India	MT-2019-0013	13-Jan-19	12-Jan-21	Expired and not applied for Renewal empanelment
14	MVTF-2018-0020	INDHEAL Solutions Private Limited, Bangalore, Karnataka, India	MT-2019-0014	29-Apr-19	28-Apr-21	Expired and not applied for Renewal empanelment
15	MVTF-2018-0018	CROM Clinical Research And Medical Tourism Pvt. Ltd., North Goa, Goa, India	MT-2019-0015	27-Jul-19	26-Jul-21	Expired and not applied for Renewal empanelment
16	MVTF-2019-0024	Lyfboat Technologies Pvt. Ltd., Delhi, Delhi, India	MT-2019-0016	26-Aug-19	25-Aug-21	Expired and not applied for Renewal empanelment
17	MVTF-2018-0019	Ibex New Concepts Private Limited, Pune, Maharashtra, India	MT-2019-0017	26-Aug-19	25-Aug-21	Accreditation Expired & Application Closed
18	MVTF-2019-0025	VB Health Solutions Private Limited, Bangalore, Karnataka, India	MT-2019-0018	03-Nov-19	02-Nov-21	Expired and not applied for Renewal empanelment
19	MVTF-2019-0026	Curestay Services Private Limited, Delhi, Delhi, India	MT-2021-0019	06-Aug-23	05-Aug-25	
20	MVTF-2020-0031	MCS Consultancy Services (A Unit of Modern Concepts and Solutions LLP), Malappuram, Kerala, India	MT-2021-0020	06-Aug-23	05-Aug-25	
21	MVTF-2018-0021	Shinon Collaborative Consultancy Private Limited, Badli District, Delhi, Delhi, India	MT-2022-0021	24-Feb-24	23-Feb-26	
22	MVTF-2019-0023	Orioles Health India Pvt. Ltd., Faridabad, Haryana, India	MT-2022-0022	24-Feb-24	23-Feb-26	
23	MVTF-2021-0032	ORALCARE.CO.IN, Aurangabad, Maharashtra, India	MT-2022-0023	01-Nov-22	31-Oct-24	
24	MVTF-2022-0033	Sinodia Healthcare Private Limited, Delhi, Delhi, India	MT-2022-0024	01-Nov-22	31-Oct-24	
25	MVTF-2022-0036	Lavanya Medicare Solutions Pvt. Ltd., Gurgaon, Haryana, India	MT-2022-0025	01-Nov-22	31-Oct-24	Application Closed
26	MVTF-2022-0039	Digicore Technologies Private Limited, Raigarh, Mumbai, Maharashtra, India	MT-2022-0026	01-Nov-22	31-Oct-24	

continued on following page

Table 5. Continued

S.N.	Reference No.	Name	Acc. No.	Valid From	Valid Upto	Remarks
27	MVTF-2022-0037	Medijourn Solutions Private Limited, Hyderabad, Telangana, India	MT-2022-0027	11-Oct-22	10-Oct-24	
28	MVTF-2022-0035	Aadya Global Healthcare Private Limited, Delhi, Delhi, India	MT-2023-0028	11-Jan-23	10-Jan-25	
29	MVTF-2022-0042	Phasorz Technologies Private Limited (MediBuddy), Chennai, Tamil Nadu, India	MT-2023-0029	21-Feb-23	20-Feb-25	
30	MVTF-2022-0041	Globalspace Healthcare Technologies Pvt Ltd., Thane, Mumbai, Maharashtra, India	MT-2023-0030	21-Feb-23	20-Feb-25	
31	MVTF-2022-0040	Gomedii Technologies Pvt. Ltd., Delhi, Delhi, India	MT-2023-0031	07-Mar-23	06-Mar-25	
32	MVTF-2023-0045	Blue Line India Medical Tourism, Mumbai, Maharashtra, India	MT-2023-0032	23-May-23	22-May-25	
33	MVTF-2023-0043	Victor Hospital, Margao, Goa, India	MT-2023-0033	04-Jul-23	03-Jul-25	
34	MVTF-2023-0044	Justkare Technologies Pvt. Ltd., Kochi, Kerala, India	MT-2023-0034	18-Jul-23	17-Jul-25	
35	MVTF-2023-0047	Pristyn Care International Business (A Unit of GHV Advance Care Pvt. Ltd.), Gurgaon, Haryana, India	MT-2023-0035	26-Sep-23	25-Sep-25	
36	MVTF-2023-0048	Livonta Global Pvt. Ltd., Ahmedabad, Gujarat, India	MT-2023-0036	04-Oct-23	03-Oct-25	
37	MVTF-2023-0046	My Care India LLP, Delhi, Delhi, India	MT-2024-0037	16-Jan-24	15-Jan-26	
38	MVTF-2023-0053	Cikitsa India, Bangalore, Karnataka, India	MT-2024-0038	27-Feb-24	26-Feb-26	
39	MVTF-2024-0057	Bluedot Medical Assistance, Ernakulam, Aluva, Kerala, India	MT-2024-0039	11-Jun-24	10-Jun-26	

Source:- https://nabh.co/accreditedmvtf/

From the above table it can be concluded that although the NABH accreditation is well existing the MVT facilitators are not keen upon it.

Hence here in the importance of accreditation and the awareness of it should be undertaken by NABH as well as to make it mandatory if the business firm wants to operate in as a facilitator as Medical value travellers look to these facilitators to provide information about quality, safety and legal issues.

The facilitators also extend their services for accommodation, transport and medical VISA etc, hence an accreditation will enable act to serve as a quality standard service provider thus increasing confidence in the Medical and Wellness tourism sector of India.

The state governments have also realized the value importance of the medical tourism and efforts are being made to promote it, just in the month of October 2024 the Karnataka health Minister Mr. Dinesh Gundu Rao had a meeting with the representatives from the private hospitals and assured that the government will undertake all the necessary steps needed to promote the medical tourism in the state and also expresses his willingness to have more number of meetings in the coming times to discuss on the initiatives to be taken for promoting the Medical tourism .

Although the Government and Private sector hospitals are making efforts to put India on world map as a source of excellent medical tourism destination it is essential that a joint effort be made to highlight the strengths and the benefits a medical tourist will get when he chooses India for treatment apart just from the low cost factor .

The focus has to be on

Infrastructure and Digital Enablement

India has some of the hospitals which offer the best and latest treatment in the world, from eye, kidney problems, to eye to organ transplant, to orthopedics, cancer it provides the same at a very competitive rates as compared to the rest of the world which is depicted in table above.

It also has JCI accredited hospitals as well as NABH accredited hospitals that deliver care which meets or even exceeds the worldwide quality standards.

Trained Manpower

India has a large pool of talent in terms of doctors and nurses around 1308009 doctors are registered as of Dec 2023 as per the data of National Medical commission (source:- https://pib.gov.in/PressReleasePage.aspx?PRID=1985423) and around 2 million nurses as per the data of Respective state Nurses registration council (source:- https://pib.gov.in/PressReleasePage.aspx?PRID=1985423), also there are formally trained dentists and ayurvedic doctors which makes it a vast pool of available resource for class treatment as well as most of the doctors have received training and experience at most world's prominent medical institutions in USA, UK and other developed nations making them highly qualified and capable in their fields.

Care Quality

Apart from being an affordable and accessible destination for the health and clinical care, India also has a motto of "Aththi Devo Bhavo" i.e (Guest is God) philosophy which it embodies by providing care which is personal, compassionate and inclusive. The Medical workers in India strive to maintain highest standards by prioritizing needs and interests of patients with empathy and compassion.

Digital Enablement

The ministry of Commerce and Industry along with Services Export Promotion council (SECPC) have built a portal "Heal in India " for medical tourists from the world which serves as one stop information and shop point for hospitals, travel related information on India, however it can be made more significant by highlighting the JCI accreditation data as well as to create awareness about the NABH accreditation standard and the data of NABH Accredited Institutes which will garner confidence in the medical tourist to consider India as a top priority destination for medical tourism.

Apart from the above the website can also have a separate section tab which shall give a snap view of the tourist places to see in the state /city of treatment and can provide an external link to the tourism ministry of the respective state.

It shall provide a purpose of creating awareness of the tourist places of interest and also generate interest in the medical tourist of perhaps considering to visit after being cured. Thus it will also be an additional incentive to visit India.

Thus a conjoined efforts of the stakeholders under consideration will channelize towards a direction of making India a 1st consideration as destination in medical tourism.

Currently only certain regions and nations like Middle east, Bangladesh, GCC countries represent a key market for India's medical tourism industry, India being a diverse nations representing different race, religions and the availability of language interpreters and halal certified meals appeals India as a destination for medical tourism to this demographics, however as seen from the costs benefits the western nations and Latin America Markets should be targeted.

Awareness campaigns targeting the big economies in this continent and focusing on the cost benefits, the quality care India offers can enable to capture the target market audience, it should also explore if partnerships possibility with healthcare providers in Latin America as this will create a referral systems for patients to consider India as a Medical tourism top destination.

Further to the above, India can attract medical tourists from developed countries by promoting specialized treatments which are unavailable or which are ultra- expensive in their home nations

Also it can highlight the success stories of minimally invasive surgeries couple with the skilled medical professionals availability in certain treatment areas can be stresses on which will resonate with the target audience in Western

EXAMPLES OF INTERNATIONAL PATIENT CARE BY HOSPITALS

Kokilaben Dhirubhai Ambani Hospital

A state of the art JCI & CAP – USA NABH & NABL – India accredited hospital situated in Mumbai, with a range of departments catering to various illness including specialty care treatments and the only hospital in Mumbai having Full time specialist systems ensuring availability of dedicated specialists attached to the hospital. The accreditation stands as an testimony to the safety and quality healthcare access.

For promotion of Medical care to International patients is has a dedicated team and a webpage on its website which gives information on

-Compliance procedures to be followed by the patients,
-What to expect
-Why to choose the hospital
-Amenities
-Travel Partners
-Testimonials

The uniqueness of the Hospital is that it has tied up with Air Ethiopia and Air Tanzania who are the travel partners for patients from Africa, it gives discounts for airfare and also special tariff rates for treatments, and it also gives an opportunity to make payment in home currency at any office of Ethiopian Airline in Africa. Also they provide other facilities like accommodation, inland travel etc. which makes the patients comfortable as well as he has to have no reasonable worries.

Medanta City

One of the specialty state of the Art hospital chain in North India JCI and NABH accredited with presence across 5 cities, they have a dedicated section which takes care of the International Patients providing guidance in view of the needed documents, travel assistance, inland transport upon landing in India.

The uniqueness is that they have the Insurance partners located in Kenya, Rwanda, Uganda and Zambia which is a plus as the Insurance coverage for the treatment, they have plan your trip section which gives the directive to be followed.

Apollo Hospitals

One of the top state of the art hospital chain with JCI, NABH, NABL accredited and ISO 14001, ISO 22000-HACCP certified hospital chain with presence of around 50 hospitals across the nation. This is the most advantageous point as it can cater to more number of International patients as well as make available varied treatment procedures across multiple locations.

It has a special section dedicated to the International patients providing guidance for visa, appointments, documents, airport transfers as well as it has tie ups with various International Insurance for covering the treatment liability cost.

It has international promotion presence through 55 Medical facilitators spread across the globe which enable it to reach across various corners of the world.

ROLE OF AYUSH IN WELLNESS TOURISM

AYUSH (Ayurveda, Yoga, Unani, Siddha, and Homeopathy) gives India a unique advantage in the world for medical tourism. Kerala is well known as the "land of Ayurveda," It is the state which has an attraction globally and attracts thousands of international medical tourists who are seeking a holistic treatments for chronic conditions like relief from stress, lifestyle diseases, Ayurvedic treatments for Arthritis, yoga therapies for stress management etc. which are very widely sought after by various travelers across the globe especially Europe and Middle east,

Government of India's initiative such as the "Heal in India" campaign give emphasis on AYUSH as a very important core component for wellness tourism. Several wellness centers and retreats have several integrated packages which combine Ayurveda, yoga, and modern medical treatments.

Example, Soukya, an international wellness center in Bengaluru, has gained global recognition for its customized programs blending traditional and modern medicine.

India's AYUSH offerings can be a good choice catering to a growing global demand for alternative medicine, which will enable the country to position itself as a leader in holistic healing. The government has also prioritized standardizing AYUSH services and ensuring quality through accreditation systems like NABH, further boosting patient confidence.

Indian government also is promoting the same by including the AYUSH visa category which makes the travel simple for wellness tourist enabling the access to therapies like Panchkarma, Additionally state governments are also promoting the wellness tourism

India however needs to give a boost to AYUSH in order to make it an appeal on a global scale, it already has a MOU signed with 15 Universities in countries like Australia, Mauritius, Latvia, Hungary, Slovenia, Armenia, Russia, Malaysia, South Africa, Thailand, Bangladesh etc. It has established AYUSH academic chairs in these so as to promote AYUSH treatments

Also to promote AYUSH the Indian government every year allots 104 seats to students from foreign countries who come to learn Ayurveda, Yoga, Unani, etc., they are provided with scholarships, tuition fees, to and fro airfare etc. to study the AYUSH systems. At present 260 students from around 32 nations are taking Ayush education in different Institutes in India under the AYUSH fellowship Scheme, the students from below nations are studying AYUSH

Table 6. Countries from which students are studying AYUSH systems in India

S. No.	Countries	S. No.	Countries
1	Afghanistan	17	Mozambique
2	Armenia	18	Nepal
3	Austria	19	Netherlands
4	Bangladesh	20	Portugal
5	Bhutan	21	Russia
6	Brazil	22	South Korea
7	Bulgaria	23	Sri Lanka
8	Croatia	24	Suriname
9	Germany	25	Syria
10	Greece	26	Tanzania
11	Indonesia	27	Thailand
12	Iran	28	Turkey
13	Japan	29	Uganda
14	Kenya	30	USA

S. No.	Countries	S. No.	Countries
15	Malaysia	31	Venezuela
16	Mauritius	32	Vietnam

Source https://ayush.gov.in/#!/international

SOCIAL MEDIA AS A CHANNEL FOR MEDICAL TOURISM

Apart from the various avenues of Social Media should be also a top channel to promote Medical Tourism

Various media platforms like Facebook, Instagram, LinkedIn, Twitter, and YouTube definitely provide a cost effective and a wider reach tool to promote Medical tourism for India. It gives an opportunity for real time communication, personalization of Marketing and enable to disseminate any crucial information to Potential International medical tourists

The various social media platforms can showcase India's world-class hospitals, cost-effective treatments, and success stories, effectively bridging the gap between medical providers and patients abroad.

Various Social Media Channels for Promoting Medical Tourism

Facebook

With a global reach with more than billion active users it is an ideal platform for targeting global audience,

Hospitals can utilize stories and testimonies from various international patients who have received medical treatments in India as well as they can highlight the cost effectiveness and quality care made available to them during their visit.

Medical tourism or MVT facilitators can create Facebook groups for prospective patients to discuss their needs, share experiences, and build trust.

Instagram

This platforms emphasis on visual content will make it an ideal social media channel for showcasing state-of-the-art hospitals, beautiful wellness retreats, and varieties available in Indian tourist destinations.

It can be utilized to post high-quality images and videos of hospital facilities, advanced medical equipment, and patient care experiences so the prospects or general audience can have a virtual tour of the facilities available thus giving them an idea of what they can expect.

Can make use of reels to share patient journeys, from their arrival in India to their successful treatment and recovery.

They can also Partner with influencers and medical tourism ambassadors to promote India's medical and wellness services.

This platform can also be used to leverage hashtags like #HealInIndia, #MedicalTourismIndia, and #AYUSH Healing to improve discovery of India as a top choice medical tourism destination

YouTube

This offers a platform for long form content which will make it suitable for Medical expert's interviews, in depth patient testimonials and a walk through in thorough manner through the different medical procedures

This platform can be used to create video case studies which highlight successful treatments for surgeries and various advanced therapies. It can also be used to create content informing about the history of AYUSH

LinkedIn

Can be utilized for connecting with healthcare professionals across various geographies as well as insurance providers, and Facilitators

It can also be used to share thought leadership various articles by Indian healthcare experts, showcasing their global expertise. It can also be used to promote conferences, webinars, and workshops focused on medical tourism and wellness.

X (Formerly Twitter)

This is an excellent platform for sharing quick updates, news, and real-time interactions.

It can be used to post updates about new healthcare policies introduced, visa processes, and success stories in Indian medical tourism. It can also be used to hold chats with healthcare professionals to engage directly with potential medical patients

It can also be used to create global visibility.

Content Strategies for Social Media Success

Storytelling

This can be used to highlight real-life patient journeys to build trust and emotional connection.

Use before-and-after visuals to demonstrate the impact of treatments.

Localized Campaigns

Tailor content for different regions by using native languages and addressing specific healthcare challenges.

Collaborate with local influencers in target markets such as Africa, the Middle East, and South Asia.

Educational Content

Regularly post any articles, videos, and other info graphics on common medical procedures, recovery tips, and wellness practices also the social media channels can be used to have live sessions with doctors to answer frequently asked questions.

Partnerships with Influencers

Thought to be given for working with global health bloggers, travel influencers, and medical professionals to promote what India can offer.

Benefits of Leveraging Social Media for Medical Tourism

It enables the medical service providers with a global reach, thus social media reduces the geographical boundaries it can thus portray the benefits of India as a destination for not only medical tourism but wellness tourism destination as well.

Also it is very cost effective as compared to other channels like traditional advertising, thus it offers high return on investment if utilised strategically targeting the intended audience so as to reach in an effective manner, .

The social media channels also offer real time interaction by providing instant communication thus helping to address patient queries in less time resulting in quick response, it can be used as a tool for follow up nd also telemedicine .

The positive reviews, testimonials and various interactions on social media enhances trust among the prospects as well as the patients and when they will consider medical tourism India should be their 1st choice destination for it.

It thus will increase patients inflow into the country

Thus the social media channels can be considered as an opportunity to transform the position of India as a major player and preferred first choice destination for Medical tourism, the use of various social media platforms like Facebook, Instagram, youtube etc, the medical care facilities in India can showcase their advanced healtcare infrastructure, the different holistic offerings and the rich culture it has . A well defined, well planned and well executed social media strategy shall not only enable to attract more international Patients but also reinforce the nation's reputation s a compassionate and a competent destination for any healthcare treatment.

While the earlier quoted examples do give us the impetus placed by top hospitals about the parameters adopted for medical tourism a primary survey was conducted among healthcare and pharm professionals to know about the views regarding the factors which are to be considered for betterment of the same, the results are depicted in Figures as below

Figure 1. Indicating if there is need for availability of separate medical tourism department

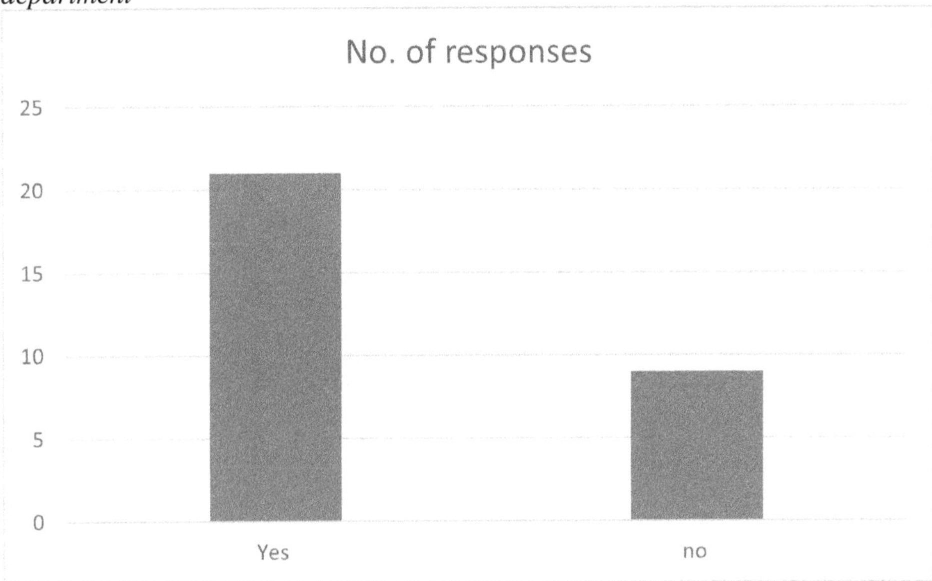

Analysis: The availability of dedicated departments for medical tourism is critical for streamlining processes, better coordination, and improved patient experience. If many hospitals lack such departments, it is an indication of a gap in organizational focus on this lucrative sector.

Figure 2. Indicating the regions distribution targeted to attract medical tourism

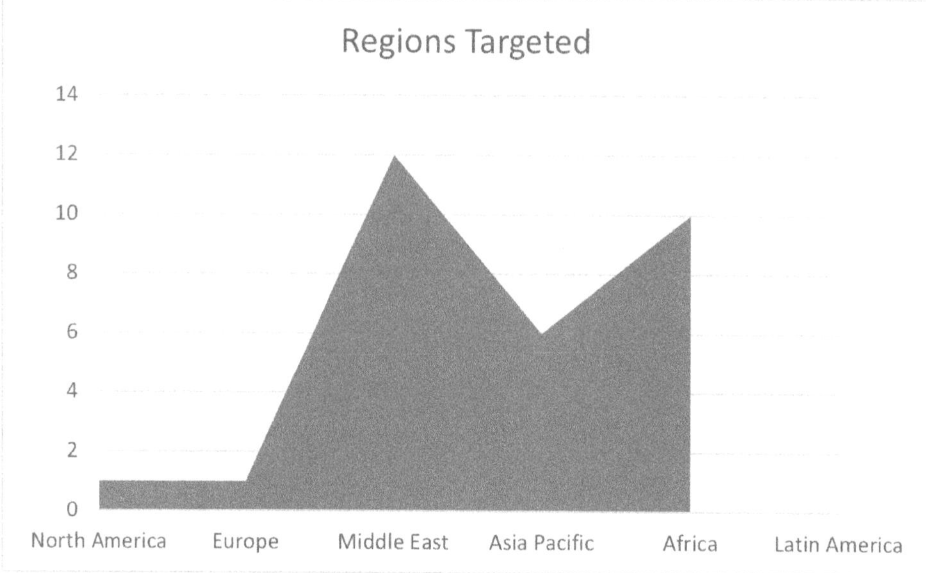

Analysis: Target regions highlight the regions for patient sourcing. Over-concentration in a few regions indicates a missed opportunity to tap into other lucrative markets

Figure 3. Indicating the treatments to be offered for medical tourism

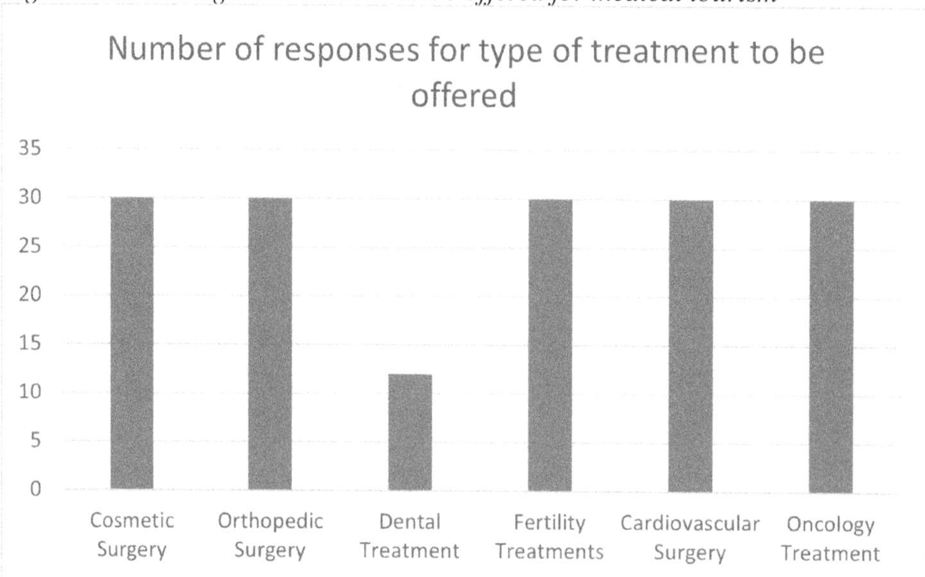

Analysis: Popular treatments for medical tourism seem include cosmetic surgeries, orthopedic procedures, and wellness therapies. The limited range could perhaps reduce competitveness,exploration of deeper areas like advanced oncology should be considered

Figure 4. Indicating whether a dedicated website should be there for medical tourism

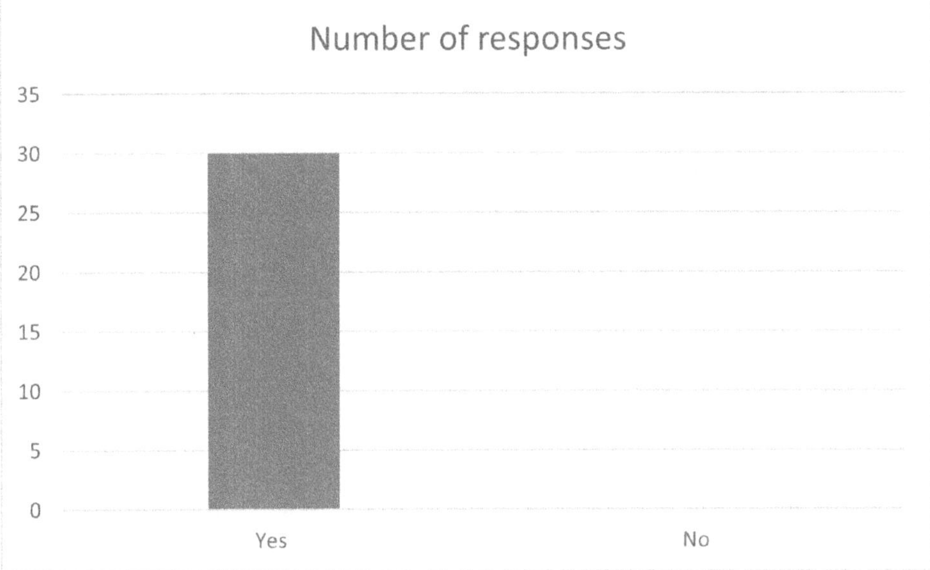

Analysis: A dedicated website will ensure visibility, accessibility of information, and develop trustworthiness for international patients. A lack of such a platform could reduce reach and also generate negative interest.

Figure 5. Responses for the type of channel to be used for promoting medical tourism

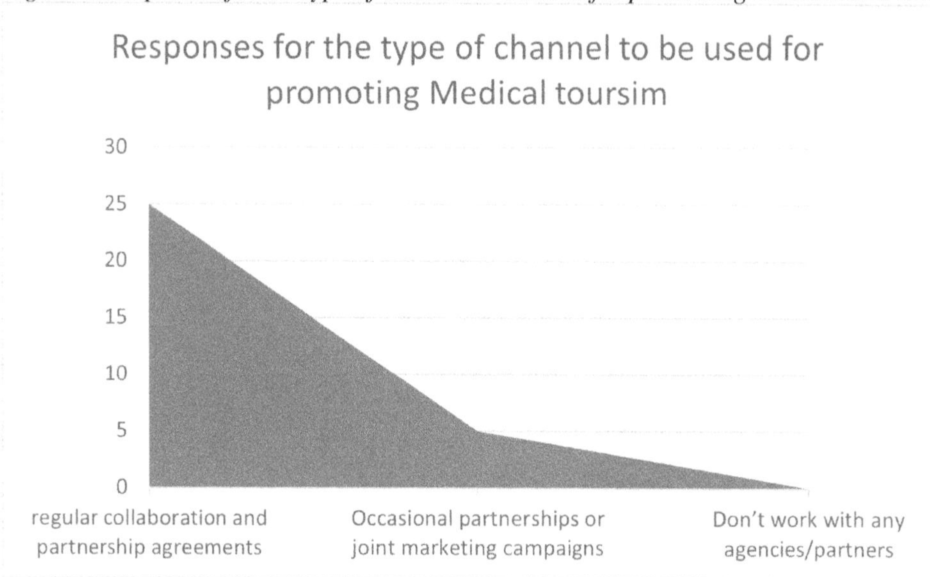

Analysis: Although the channels will act as a catalyst for getting the medical patients, digital marketing should be included, lack of it will sound outdated.

Figure 6. Responses for the services to be offered to make the experience memorable

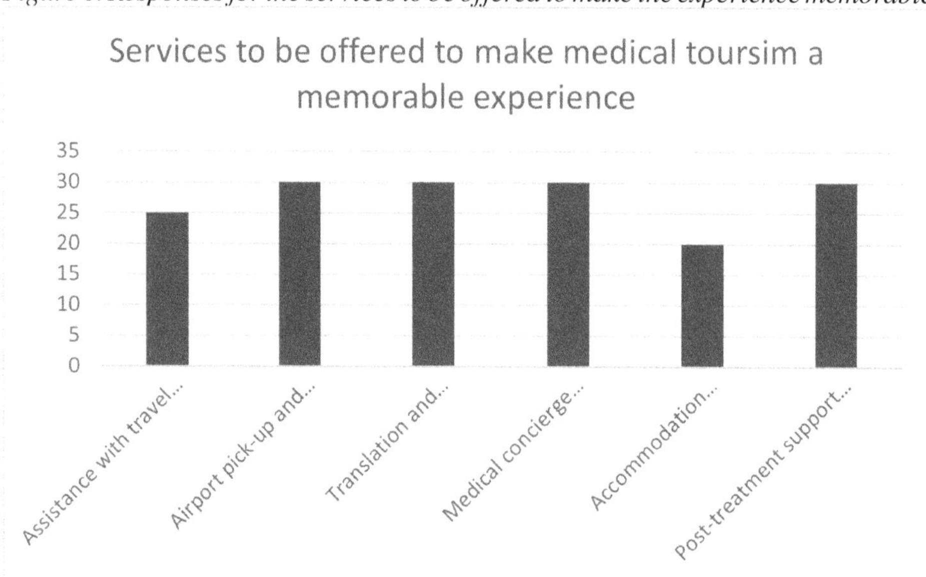

Analysis: Apart from the above service such as personalised care, concierge services should also be considered. Missing out on these services could perhaps impact patient satisfaction.

Figure 7. Responses for follow up care to be followed by hospitals

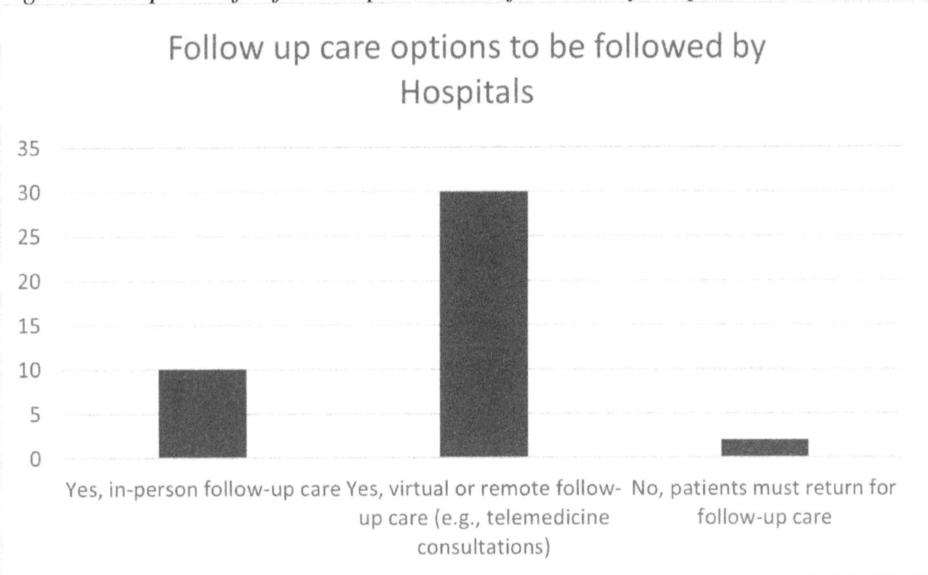

Analysis: Efficient follow-up care ensures better recovery and patient satisfaction. Inadequate follow-up mechanisms could result in negative feedback

Figure 8. Responses for hospitals to tie up with insurance providers to cover expenses during the medical trip

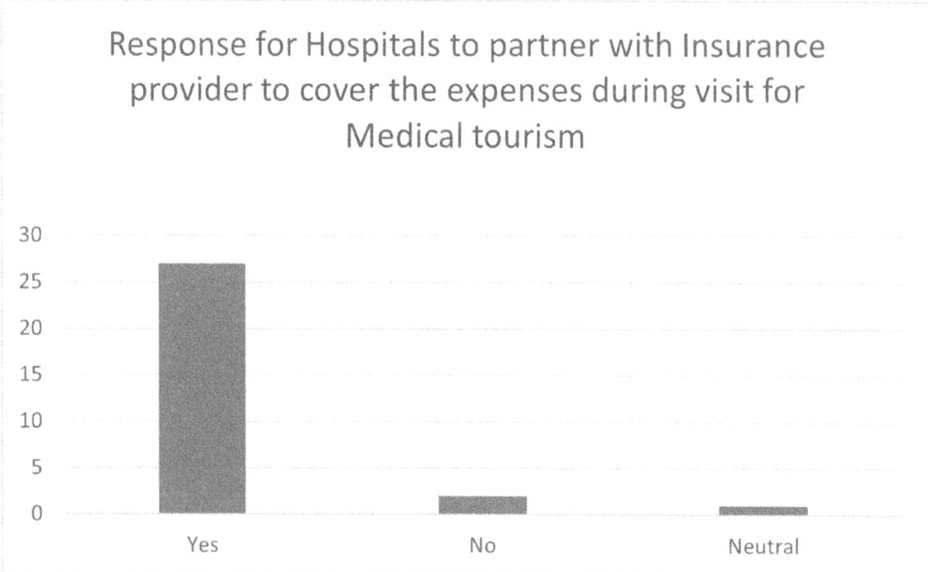

Analysis: Partnerships with insurance providers enhance affordability and will enable to attract more patients. A lack of such kind of partnerships might deter cost-sensitive patient

Figure 9. Responses for whether hospitals should participate in International Medical tourism exhibitions

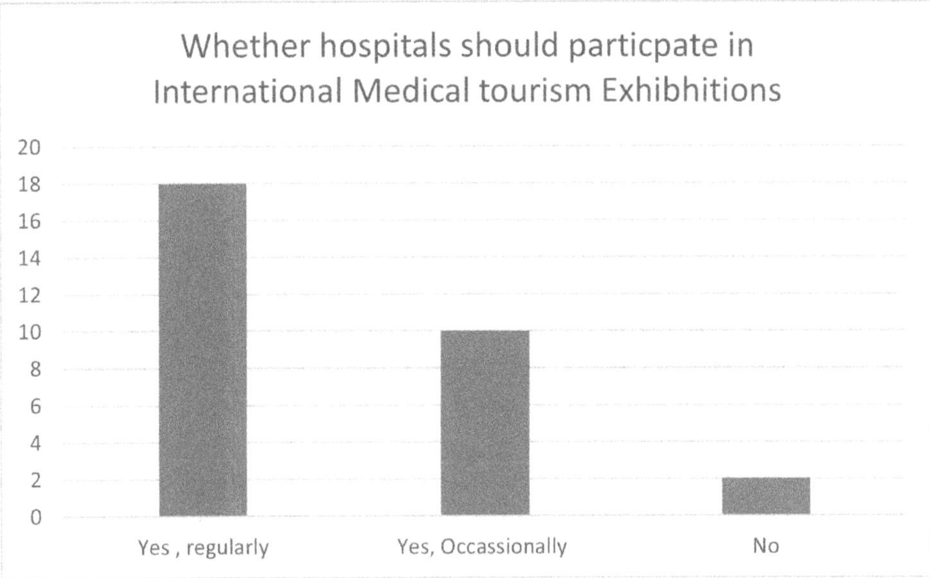

Analysis: Participation in exhibitions will increase brand visibility and networking opportunities and a limited or no participation might hinder growth.

Figure 10. Responses for whether hospitals tie up with travel and tourism companies for medical treatment.

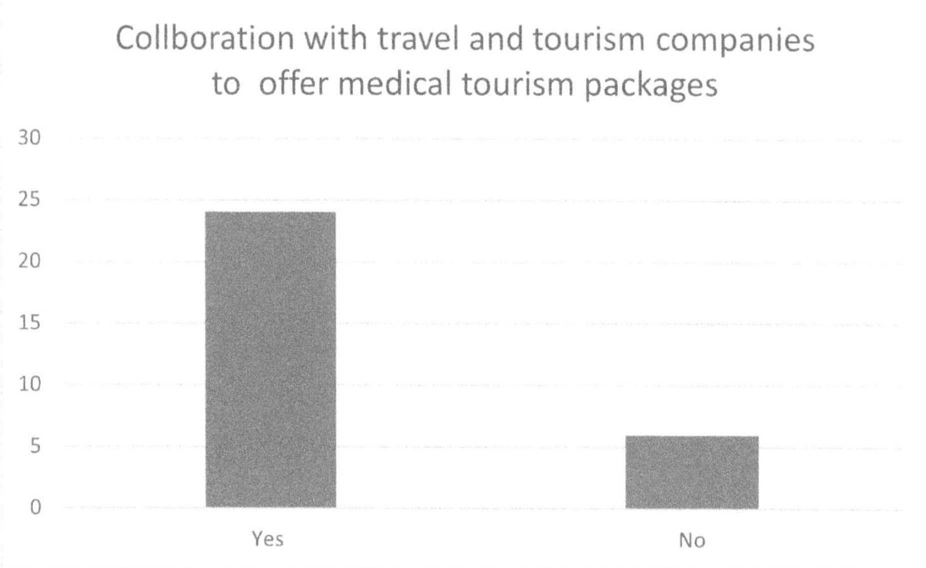

Analysis: Collaboration with travel companies will enable to enhance the patient journey by making provision of integrated services. A lack of such tie-ups might complicate logistics.

FINDINGS

From the details given one can get an extensive overview of the landscape of India's Medical tourism, which highlights the historical strengths, the challenges and its current positions.

The findings can be categorized as under.

Competitive Advantages

- Cost advantage as compared to other medical tourism destinations
- Highly Skilled and trained healthcare professionals with International Qualifications
- A rich heritage of traditional medicine systems (AYUSH).
- Robust connectivity through air routes and a growing digital presence.

Challenges

- Lack of formal and structured regulatory framework for the MVT Sector.
- Limited awareness of Indian accreditation (NABH) compared to international accreditations like JCI.
- Perceptions among foreign nationals with regards to hygiene and infrastructure
- Inconsistent pricing policies and not much regulated MVT facilitators.

Emerging Trends

- Increasing in number of patients for procedures such as heart surgeries, orthopedic surgeries, and cosmetic treatments.
- Digital advancements, including the "Heal in India" portal, are promising but it is underutilized.

Stakeholders and Integration

- Central ministries, state governments, hospitals, facilitators, airlines, and hotels play pivotal roles.
- A Limited collaboration among these stakeholders which might act as a bottleneck

RECOMMENDATIONS

Enhancement of Accreditation and Awareness

- Promote NABH accreditation aggressively to international audiences, emphasizing its parity parameters with JCI.
- Make and Mandate accreditation for MVT facilitators to ensure quality and transparency which will create confidence

Development of a Regulatory Framework

- Establish a nodal agency to oversee and regulate the medical tourism sector.
- Implement uniform pricing policies to prevent overcharging by facilitators and hospitals.

Expand Services and Specializations

- Introduce niche treatments such as advanced oncology and rare surgeries
- Adopt Bundling principle and offer traditional medicine services (AYUSH) with modern treatments to create a holistic wellness package.

Leveraging Digital Platforms

- Strongly promote and enhance the "Heal in India" portal with detailed information about accredited hospitals, facilitators, and tourist destinations as well as the facilities available at various centers.
- Offer virtual consultations and post-treatment follow-ups through telemedicine platforms.

Strengthen International Partnerships

- Collaborate with global insurance providers to cover treatment costs for international patients.
- Partner with airlines and travel agencies to offer all-inclusive medical tourism packages.
- Develop targeted marketing campaigns for untapped regions and diaspora communities.

SUGGESTIONS FOR FUTURE DIRECTION

Data-Driven Decision Making

- Utilise Data analytics to understand the patient demographics, preferences, and feedback.
- Use AI- tools in order to streamline administrative processes and enhance patient care.

Integrate Wellness Tourism along with Medical tourism

- Adopt the positioning strategy as a holistic destination by combination of traditional & Modern medicine.
- Focus on developing state-wise wellness tourism hubs - focusing on Ayurveda, yoga, and naturopathy with trained and skilled staff to take care.

REFERENCES

Akhter, F. (n.d.). India has competence advantage to take lead in medical tourism. LinkedIn. https://www.linkedin.com/pulse/india-has-competence-advantage-take-lead-medical-tourism-akhter

American Academy of Family Physicians. (n.d.). Wait times. https://www.aafp.org/pubs/fpm/blogs/inpractice/entry/wait-times.html

Apollo Hospitals. (n.d.). Table. https://www.apollohospitals.com/apollo_pdf/table.pdf

Arulmozhi, S. J., Praveenkumar, K., & Vinayagamoorthi, G. (2019). Medical tourism in India. International Journal of Recent Technology and Engineering (IJRTE), 8(2S10). https://www.ijrte.org/wp-content/uploads/papers/v8i2S10/B11230982S1019.pdf

Asopa Hospital. (n.d.). History of Indian medicine and surgery. https://asopahospital.in/history-of-indian-medicine-and-surgery/

Bagga, T., Vishnoi, S. K., Jain, S., & Sharma, R. (2020). Medical tourism: Treatment, therapy and tourism. *International Journal of Scientific and Technology Research*, *9*(3), 4447–4453. https://www.researchgate.net/publication/340117037_MEDICAL_TOURISM_TREATMENT_THERAPY_TOURISM

Beena, K. S., & Raju, V. (2018). A case study on medical tourism in Chennai city. [IJCIET]. *International Journal of Civil Engineering and Technology*, *9*(5), 984–991. https://iaeme.com/MasterAdmin/Journal_uploads/IJCIET/VOLUME_9_ISSUE_5/IJCIET_09_05_109.pdf

Bies, W., & Zacharia, L. (2007). Medical tourism: Outsourcing surgery. *Mathematical and Computer Modelling*, *46*(7–8), 1144–1159. https://www.sciencedirect.com/science/article/pii/S0895717707000933. DOI: 10.1016/j.mcm.2007.03.027

Brown, J., Johnson, J., Ozan-Rafferty, M. E., Sharma, M., & Barbera, S. (2020). Internet narratives focused on health travelers' experiences in India: Qualitative analysis. *Journal of Medical Internet Research*, *22*(5), e15665. https://www.jmir.org/2020/5/e15665/. DOI: 10.2196/15665 PMID: 32406860

Business Standard. (2024, November 11). Medical tourism revenue takes a hit after govt stops visas for Bangladeshis. https://www.business-standard.com/industry/news/medical-tourism-revenue-takes-a-hit-after-govt-stops-visas-for-bangladeshis-124111100831_1.html

Business Standard. (2024). Medical tourism revenue takes a hit after govt stops visas for Bangladeshis. https://www.business-standard.com/industry/news/medical-tourism-revenue-takes-a-hit-after-g;ovt-stops-visas-for-bangladeshis-124111100831_1.html

Business Today. (2024, August 8). India's medical tourism grew 33% in 2023 to surpass pre-pandemic level in 2024: ICRA. https://www.businesstoday.in/india/story/indias-medical-tourism-grew-33-in-2023-to-surpass-pre-pandemic-level-in-2024-icra-440692-2024-08-08

Crooks, V. A., Turner, L., Snyder, J., Johnston, R., & Kingsbury, P. (2011). Promoting medical tourism to India: Messages, images, and the marketing of international patient travel. *Social Science & Medicine*, *72*(5), 726–732. DOI: 10.1016/j.socscimed.2010.12.022 PMID: 21310519

Dania Medicare. (n.d.). The role of artificial intelligence in medical tourism: Enhancing patient experience. https://www.daniamedicare.com/blogs/the-role-of-artificial-intelligence-in-medical-tourism-enhancing-patient-experience

Federation of Indian Chambers of Commerce & Industry (FICCI). (n.d.). Medical value travel. https://www.ficci.in/api/sector_details/133

Future Market Insights. (n.d.). India medical tourism market. https://www.futuremarketinsights.com/reports/india-medical-tourism-market

. Government of India. (n.d.). National strategy and roadmap for medical and wellness tourism.

Gunaseelan, S., & Kesavan, N. (2020). A review on medical tourism in India. *Indian Journal of Public Health Research & Development*, *11*(1), 562–565. DOI: 10.37506/v11/i1/2020/ijphrd/193882

Hindustan Times. (2024). Millionaire Bryan Johnson shares photos of his age-reversing transformation. https://www.hindustantimes.com/business/millionaire-bryan-johnson-shares-photos-of-his-age-reversing-transformation-over-6-years-my-face-id-is-confused-101712729535622.html

Indian Institute of Tourism and Travel Management. (n.d.). A study of problems and challenges faced by medical tourists visiting India. https://tourism.gov.in/sites/default/files/2020-04/Med.pdf

Joint Commission International. (n.d.). Accredited organizations. https://www.jointcommissioninternational.org/who-we-are/accredited-organizations/#sort=%40aoname%20ascending&f:@aocountry=India

Kaur, M., & Kapoor, S. (n.d.). Medical tourism in India: A SWOT analysis. https://www.srcc.edu/system/files/Pg%2085-103%20Mandeep%20Kaur%20%26%20Samriti%20Kapoor%2C%20Medical%20Tourism%20in%20India%3B%20a%20SWOT%20analysis.pdf

Kishore, J., & Panesar, S. (n.d.). Concept note on preparation of standard operating procedure for medical tourism in India. Indian Medical Association. https://www.ima-india.org/ima/left-side-bar.php?pid=503

Kokilaben Hospital. (n.d.). International patients – Travel partners. https://www.kokilabenhospital.com/patients/internationalpatients/travel_partners.html

Kumar, S., & Gowrisunkar, V. G. B. (2022). Delving medical tourism in India: Insights and challenges. *Journal on Tourism and Sustainability*, *6*(1). https://www.researchgate.net/publication/371835112

Medanta. (n.d.). https://www.medanta.org

Medical Buyer. (2024). India's medical tourism on rise: 7.3M MVTs expected to visit in 2024. https://www.medicalbuyer.co.in/indias-medical-tourism-on-rise-7-3m-mvts-expected-to-visit-in-2024

Medical India Tourism. (n.d.). Treatment cost. https://www.medicalindiatourism.com/treatment-cost.html

Ministry of AYUSH, Government of India. (n.d.). https://www.ayush.gov.in

National Accreditation Board for Hospitals & Healthcare Providers. (n.d.). Accredited hospitals list. https://portal.nabh.co/frmViewAccreditedHosp.aspx#gsc.tab=0

Nimble, O. J., & Chinnaswamy, A. V. (2021). Health tourism: A case study of Narayana Health, Bangalore. Parikalpana - KIIT. *Journal of Management*, *17*(1). Advance online publication. DOI: 10.23862/kiit-parikalpana/2021/v17/i1/209035

Press Information Bureau, Government of India. (n.d.). https://pib.gov.in/PressReleaseIframePage.aspx?PRID=2036816

Raju, V. K. (2003). Susruta of ancient India. *Indian Journal of Ophthalmology*, *51*(2), 119–122. https://journals.lww.com/ijo/fulltext/2003/51020/susruta_of_ancient_india.2.aspx PMID: 12831140

Sagar, R., & Latha, P. V. (2014). Medical tourism – An emerging industry in India. *Journal of Medical Sciences Research*, *2*(3), 169–177. DOI: 10.17727/JMSR.2014/2-031

The Commonwealth Fund. (2017). Expanding access to low-cost, high-quality tertiary care. https://www.commonwealthfund.org/publications/case-study/2017/nov/expanding-access-low-cost-high-quality-tertiary-care

The Hindu. (2024). Health department working on promoting medical tourism: Health minister. https://www.thehindu.com/news/national/karnataka/health-department-working-on-promoting-medical-tourism-health-minister/article68773679.ece

. Varshney, S. (2024). Competency required by medical travel facilitators in medical tourism industry. Paripex - Indian Journal of Research, 13(6). DOI: 10.36106/paripex/4004052

Chapter 2

HRM Challenges and Employee Wellbeing in the Tourism Industry: Moderating Role of Organizational Culture

Neenu Antony
https://orcid.org/0009-0002-5192-9867
Christ University, India

Joby Thomas
https://orcid.org/0000-0002-4493-1048
Christ University, India

ABSTRACT

The current study aims to understand the Challenges faced by Tourism sector employees and its effect on employee well being. Also the moderating effect of Organizational culture is measured. Staff members of airlines, hotels, and travel agencies provided the main data used in this quantitative analysis. A total of 122 individuals were deemed suitable for the study according to the Kregcie-Morgan table. Using the HRM Challenges, Employee Wellbeing, and Organizational Culture measure as a starting point, a carefully crafted questionnaire was developed. Gaskins' master validity table was used to evaluate the reliability and validity of the questionnaire. Analysis of the data was done using SPSS for factor analysis and confirmatory factor analysis with. The findings show that there is a negative impact of HRM challenges on the employee wellbeing. But when organization culture is introduced as a moderator, it dampens the effect of challenges on employee wellbeing. Therefore, to reduce the impact of challenges on employee wellbeing,

DOI: 10.4018/979-8-3373-0071-9.ch002

Organizational culture is the key.

1. INTRODUCTION

Among India's most dynamic economic areas, the tourism industry is expanding at a rapid pace. Not only does the sector have a multiplier effect on the success of connected businesses, but it also has a substantial influence on employment and regional development. More than $59 billion would be earned by India's tourist and hospitality sector by the year 2028. Also, by 2028, the number of foreign tourists is expected to reach 30.5 million. (Sattigeri, 2023).

The Ministry of Tourism has declared 2023 as the 'Visit India Year' to encourage tourists to go to India in honor of the country's G20 Presidency and the India at the 75th Azadi ka Amrit Mahotsav festivities. The Prime Minister has laid out a 25-year plan to boost tourism during Amrit Kaal, with a focus on mission mode. Tourism has great potential, but this is the industry which suffered the most during the Pandemic. The whole industry was at a standstill position and the employees suffered. (Oromjonovna & Eshnazarovna, 2023).

Thus the tourism industry in India is gradually expanding in India, because an increasing number of foreign and domestic tourists visit the country's attractions and unique views and historical landmarks. Government has also been very keen in marketing the tourism sector for instance through the 'Incredible India' promotion, which has played a big role in revealing the beauty of the various states. That is why a large number of new hotels, resorts and tourism sites are being constructed to meet the demand and stimulate the economy through provision of employment (Chahal & Devi, 2024).

Human management resource is one of the most essential factors of any industry, more especially in the tourism industry whereby the employees are a central factor to the achievement of any venture (Ginting, Rismawati & Aisyah, 2024). A good recruitment process, staff development and management of human resources should be adopted in this dynamic industry. Besides, the HR managers in the Tourism Industry also have the challenge of improving the work environment and also increasing levels of employees' engagement in order to reduce cases of employee turnover. In this way, companies in the context of the Tourism Industry have the potential to benefit both their staff members and their financial outcomes and market image (Bansal et al., 2025).

Companies in the Tourism industry, who rely on customer service and other people-related services as part of their USP (Unique Selling Proposition), have human resource management as one of their most important components or functions (Arshad et al., 2023). Because hotels, tour operators, restaurants, and vacation resorts all rely on their staff to provide a unique competitive edge, human resource management may be considered the most important job in the hospitality industry (Al-Twal et al., 2024). As a result, successful human resource management is crucial for the Tourism industry's businesses. It is critical for human resource managers in the Tourism industry to address challenges like intercultural management, people empowerment, and people enabling so that their staff can carry out their responsibilities effectively and give exceptional customer service. (Jatav, 2023).

Some of the most common HRM Challenges encountered by employees working in the tourism sector include struggles with a high turnover rate owing to being seasonal, lack of career development opportunities, and inadequate training and development programs as well(Faeni, et al., 2023). Another key issue often faced by the tourism industry is struggles to maintain a diverse and inclusive labor force and address the unique needs and expectations of employees from different backgrounds (Kristiana et al., 2021). All these HRM Challenges are critical to overcome for the future success and long-term sustainability of the tourism sector. Furthermore, the human resource of the Tourism industry faced more challenges during Covid-19 like managing remote work, Implementing new health and safety protocols, and dealing with mass layoffs and furloughs (Abbas et al., 2021). As a result, these are difficult challenging times that have called upon the tourism industry's human resource to swiftly adapt to the conditions on the ground to save their businesses (Agarwal, 2021). However, despite these challenges, the HRM practices can enable the tourism industry to become stronger and more resilient. Thus the implementation of HRM practices that focus on employee work-Creating a sustainable work culture that responds appropriately to the need likelihood of change will adapt flexibly and effectively to a future characterized by uncertainty (Ngoc, et al., 2023).

Human resource management is all about Employee wellbeing. Since employee well being is critical for any organization. Organizations that take care of the well-being of the employee, normally get more work done, get less cases of employees changing companies and most of the employees are satisfied with their job. This paper will highlight the role, which organizations can take in improving well-being of workers and subsequently increase productivity of the firm through policies like work schedule, mental health assistance, and professional development (Dalkhjav et al., 2024). Finally, it can be restated that any company that is looking to not only do the right thing, but also to see business benefits, should consider investing in the well-being of its employees. Employee wellbeing is another common issue for human resources managers in the Tourism industry. (Hsu, 2019) The high prevalence of burnout in the industry is a direct result of the high stress levels of most professions in the field. Human resource managers in the field need to be creative and imaginative if they want to keep their personnel engaged and prevent high turnover rates caused by stress and exhaustion (Bohdanowicz & Zientara, 2009). Because the job is always going and shifts are always changing to keep service going, HR managers have to be as fair as possible when assigning responsibilities to workers so that the same people don't have to work the night shift all the time and get stressed out from past experiences.

On the other hand, organization culture has a more extended influence for impacting the employee wellbeing as well as job satisfaction. Engagement can be defined as an organisational value within which a positive and inclusive culture provides support to employees, thereby stimulating high levels of motivation (Salem et al., 2024). On the other hand, a toxic or an unhealthy culture is likely to have negative impacts on the wellbeing of the employee as well as his productivity level. Hence the need to ensure that organizations pay special attention to aspects of culture that enhance the health of the human resource. In Tourism Industry, organizational culture as defined could be shaped by customer service culture, teamwork culture or the culture that encourages innovation and inclusive culture can foster a sense of belonging and support among employees, leading to higher levels of engagement and motivation. Conversely, a toxic or unhealthy culture can have detrimental effects on employee mental health and productivity (Salem et al., 2024). Therefore, it is crucial for organizations to prioritize building a positive and supportive culture in order to promote the well-being of their employees. In Tourism Industry, organizational culture could be characterized by a strong emphasis on customer service, teamwork, and innovation. Such a culture could foster a fruitful work culture with employees responding positives to customer through positive service delivery.

Nowadays, human capital management (HCM) is one of the key success factors for tourism organizations in the face of growing competition in the market. It is, therefore, evident that the problems of HRM's within this sector are many, inclusive of the high turnover beyond. These challenges need to be tackled in managing human resources in tourism that is associated with the overall health of employees to improve the level of satisfaction, productivity and the turnover of employees. It is rather challenging to overemphasize the importance of the organizational culture to counteract the presented problem; if the culture in the organization is strong and positive, many of the HRM issues can be effectively managed due to the supportive climate that respects employees and takes care of their mental and emotional health. Employee support in the organization increases when the culture of the willing organization is in place and this makes the employees deliver quality services, which is very important in the tourism sector. Besides, such a culture fosters acquisition of knowledge and development with employees able to enhance knowledge and change services delivery based on new changes in the industry. Hence, the utilization of organizational culture in the enhancement of HRM initiatives for the improvement of employee conditions should be regarded significant to tourism businesses that planning to manage their people as their competitive advantage. It is, therefore, possible to indicate that by winning at HRM, companies embrace respect, inclusion, and professional growth as the key solutions instead of the challenges above-discussed, companies are in a better position to compete effectively at the global level.

With this background the current study aims to study the HRM Challenges and Employee wellbeing in Tourism Industry when Organizational Culture is a moderating variable. Five sections are adopted in this chapter. The first part is the introduction to the study which concerns itself with the challenges in human resource management, employee health or welfare, and organization culture. The second is the review of literature: regarding the three main themes of the study. The third section of the study describes the research method to be employed in the study, tools of data collection and the analytical tools to be used. The fourth section discusses the results of the study with focus on the emerging patterns and patterns. The last part is a practical one providing recommendations for organizations that would like to enhance positive organizational culture and overcome human resource issues.

2. REVIEW OF LITERATURE

The study focused Human resource management challenges, the wellbeing of the employee and organisational culture: a literature review. The review was sequential, with first phase being the identification of the studies and articles (100 articles). The second process entailed reviewing of the collected data and identification of themes and the results from the literature (86 articles). The third and last level comprised of integrating the knowledge collected to establish conclusions as well as to offer implications for the subsequent studies (60 studies). In general, the task of the systematic review offered a wealth of information regarding the multifaceted associations between the issues of human resource management, employee health, and culture. The databases used in the current study are Elsevier, Sage, Science Direct, Academcia, Web of Science etc. These databases were selected mainly due to their vast indexing of scientific publications in different fields. Further, they give a subject to access a number of peer reviewed journals and academic publications thus ensuring that findings from the study is credible and up to date.

2.1 HRM Challenges

Challenges in HRM in Tourism industry include: high turnover rates, skilled personnel who often defect and the seasonal nature of the business, making the challenges faced particularly difficult (Sharma & Gursoy, 2018). As a result, many companies in this industry can find it hard to provide consistent high-quality service for customers (Kumar & Abraham, 2019). Beyond that, with the diverse workforce in this industry, intercultural communication also poses problems (Kaushal & Srivastava, 2021). At the same time these challenges are what make HR management so crucial for companies in the tourism business. The challenges such as performance challenges, task challenges, occupational challenges, health challenges, and family challenges are most prelevant in Tourims industry (Babu & Eimani, 2014). The reasons for such challenges are often related to the fast-paced and constantly changing nature of the industry, as well as the high level of competition. (Dhiman & Dahiya, 2016).

In addition to facing high turnover rates and staffing shortages, tourism companies also face occupational challenges (Jauhari & Rishi, 2012). Health challenges such as stress and employee burnout can further compound these issues (Tomcíková et al.,2021). For example, family-related problems like balancing work schedules with personal commitments may also affect employee morale and productivity (Cizrelioğulları et al., 2024). Therefore, overall, it is critical for the survival and sustainable growth of companies in the tourism sector to combat these challenges through effective HR management strategies. (Gigauri, 2020).

Kaushal & Srivastava, (2021) asserted that The already-fragile tourist and hotel sector has faced unprecedented challenges because to the COVID-19 pandemic. Novel coronaviruses, which are extremely contagious, pose major threats to the sector and its continued existence. Two primary issues are covered by the research. The first is the state of the hotel and tourist sector and the significant problems it is facing right now. The second is the lessons that the industry can learn from these difficulties. Fifteen people with executive roles in the hotel sector and in tourism and hospitality education services participated in the interviews that formed the basis of the study. Using content analysis, we were able to distill 27 sub-themes from the interviewees' responses into 4 overarching themes. A more robust understanding of the importance of sanitation, hygiene, and related standard operating procedures (SOPs), a positive outlook on the industry's potential for recovery, the media's involvement, and the necessity for improved crisis preparedness were the most prominent subthemes that arose from the qualitative investigation. "Concerns," "Continuity," "Health and Hygiene," and "Human Resource Management" were the next subsequent overarching themes. In light of the current arguments presented in the literature, the study analyzes key themes and considers their consequences for decision makers. The study's main takeaways are a set of topics that contribute to the growing body of knowledge on the COVID-19 epidemic and the tourist and hospitality sector, as well as some managerial suggestions for dealing with a myriad of problems and making the most of the lessons learned from the present situation. We also talk about the potential limitations and areas of further investigation.

Sun et al., (2017) expressed that although improving organizational productivity has always been the end aim of human resource difficulties, the focus now is on people. Labor costs and the millennial workforce are two of the most current issues in human resources. The scarcity of workers, however, is the most pressing human resource issue confronting China's tourist sector right now. This study employs focus group interviews to delve into the concerns surrounding human resource challenges in the Chinese environment, namely in Guangdong province in the southern region. In addition to outlining the problems and their causes, this report offers suggestions for how to fix them in the areas of governance, staffing, employee development, and compensation.

2.2 HRM Challenges and Employee Well Being

Challenges of HRM in the tourism industry and its effect on employee well-being stem from high employee turnover rates because of seasonal employment (Ross, 2017). Jobs that can vanish entirely in the off-season, the demanding nature of the industry and a general lack of job security make up additional hurdles (Hsu, 2019) (Bohdanowicz & Zientara, 2009). These challenges can lead to increased stress, burnout (Kimbu, et al., 2023), and overall reduced job satisfaction among employees companies can create a positive and sustainable work environment for their employees (Berbekova & Uysal, 2021). Companies that are in tourism need to cope with these HRM challenges in order to guarantee employee well-being as well as retention (Joseph Sirgy, 2019). By offering more permanent positions or a combination thereof, adequate training and support, and closer attention to work-life balance. (Uysal et al., 2016).

Sarwar et al., (2020) stated that Among the organization's top brass, you'll find a plethora of unethical practises, including but not limited to: taking credit where credit is due, showing favouritism, and making a big deal out of unethical leadership mistakes. Few studies have focused on issues outside of corporate ethics research, such as employee well-being, despite the fact that there has been research on ethical culture, especially on the causes and impacts of ethical-decision. Consequently, the purpose of this research was to examine how ethical leadership, employee engagement, well-being, and performance are mediated by organizational ethical culture.

According to Tuzovic & Kabadayi, (2021) Many people's lives and means of subsistence have been profoundly affected by the current coronavirus disease 2019 (COVID-19) pandemic. Concerns about the welfare of service workers are heightened by the fact that service organizations must decide whether to go into hibernation or keep running. This paper presents a conceptual framework for studying the effects of social distancing practices on service hibernation or continuation in the face of the COVID-19 pandemic on many aspects of employees' subjective well-being

Salas-Vallina (2021) expressed that there are significant knowledge gaps about the mediating function of employee well-being in the HRM-performance relationship, despite the fact that this subject continues to be of interest. Studies also need to delve further into leaders' HRM practices, since most studies either cover HRM or leadership, and even fewer examine the interplay between the two in determining the success or failure of an organization's workforce.

Tien et al., (2021) expressed that both in theory and practice, the "Economics of happiness" is becoming an increasingly hot topic in modern society, particularly in the fields of management science and economics. In particular, there is mounting evidence in the form of publications published in prominent and respected journals about the topic of subjective well-being.

According to Sharma et al., (2021) The travel and tourism sector was hit hard by the COVID-19 pandemic. According to researchers, if the tourist industry adopts an inclusive resilience strategy, it has the potential to usher in a new global economic order that prioritizes sustainable practices, social welfare, climate action, and community engagement. Moreover, we provide avenues for further study in this field.

Digby et al., (2021) examined the effects on staff health of working during the early stages of the COVID-19 pandemic. Concerns regarding patient care were the first of seven highlighted themes, followed by adaptations to new working conditions, the challenges of adapting to a hospital setting, the effects of the pandemic, feelings of isolation and uncertainty, management and leadership, and the necessity for supplementary resources for employees. A

2.3 Moderating Role of Organizational Culture

A healthy organizational culture reduces the impact of HRM issues on employee well-being. A good, fair and inclusive organizational culture can provide support, colleagues able to help, and suitable systems of work that they may never even have dreamed of (Sanpakdee, et al.,2019). This grants them chances for success by providing the resources and encouragement they need. It leads to greater feelings of job satisfaction and lower turnover rates. Maintaining a good organizational culture is key to keeping HRM issues at bay, leading to a more involved and productive workforce (Tsaur, et al., 2012). Workers who dwell in a culture that values their welfare and fosters an environment that is conducive to growth are more likely motivated to work. This positive atmosphere can also lead to better communication and cooperation among employees. Ultimately, a strong organizational culture can help to create a more harmonious and successful workplace where employees feel valued and are able to thrive. (He, Z., & Hao, X., 2022).

Novitasari et al., (2022) The study's overarching goal is to dissect the interplay between various facets of innovative work behavior and its effects on job satisfaction, organizational citizenship behavior and its effects on job performance, and innovative work behavior and its effects on job performance via job satisfaction. The results of the study conducted by SmartPLS indicate that creative and original work practices have a substantial impact on job satisfaction and performance. These practices also have a substantial impact on organizational citizenship and performance.

Li et al., (2021) Researchers demonstrate that companies having a robust corporate culture continue to beat their non-cultured counterparts, even while COVID-19 has a significant detrimental effect on their operations. These businesses also outperform their competitors when it comes to community involvement, digital transformation, and product innovation. The business culture is an intangible asset that may be used to deal with unexpected situations as they come up, researchers conclude.

Sapta et al., (2021) Technology has a crucial part in the ongoing COVID-19 pandemic; without it, no activity can proceed. Specifically during a pandemic, this study shows that technology, organizational culture, and job happiness might motivate rural banks in Bali to improve their performance. Work motivation serves as an intermediary between the dependent variable (employee performance) and the independent factors (organizational culture, technology, and job happiness). A technique based on components or variance, with Partial Least Square applied, is used in this study to model structural equations. Technology, job satisfaction, and company culture all play a role in inspiring workers to do their best, according to the research. Culture in the workplace, however, does not affect productivity in a good or even indirect way. Business initiatives that aim to boost employee performance in a competitive setting and boost a bank's credibility can be informed by the study's findings.

2.4 Research Gap

The reviewed literature identified many articles and studies examining the HRM challenges experienced by the employees of the Tourism sector. These factors are increasingly high attrition and turnover rates, lack of career advancement opportunities and training, as well as difficulties with maintaining a work-life balance. However, considering the impact that these problems have on employee satisfaction, productivity, and overall organizational success, these variables were brought up during the discussion (Sun et al., 2017; Mohotti et al., 2013 ; Gruescu et al., 2008 ; Costa, 2004; Baum, 2012). In addition, a strong body of literature paired with the reviewed information included the role of organizational culture within the Tourism sector. Many recent studies on the tourism industry addressed this variable and stressed the importance of behaving and acting to achieve the desired engagement and long-lasting relationships with employees (Tepeci, 2005 ; Kyriakidou & Gore, 2005 ; Ratnasari, et al., 2020; Filipova, 2015 ; Gamage & Tajeddini, 2022). . Many researchers conducted studies to conclude that an organization that values its employees and sustains a supportive culture will continue attracting and maintaining high-quality staff, which is especially critical today within the competitive sector of tourism . To conclude, there are very few studies that have demonstrated the moderating impact of organizational culture on work culture and employee well-being. This gap is addressed in the current study.

2.5 Research Objectives

1. To identify HRM challenges faced by employees in Tourism Industry
2. To analyse the impact of HRM challenges on employee well being in Tourism Industry
3. To examine the moderating role of Organization culture on the relationship between HRM Challenges and Employee well being

2.6 Proposed Framework

The conceptual model developed for studying the research questions the following three goals: first, the definitions of the specific HRM challenges, second, the effects of the challenges on the employee, and third, the moderation of the organizational culture. This framework is sequential as well as integrative; the first step in this visualization includes identification, which entails both qualitative and quantitative data collection for systematically stating the specific perceived challenges in HRM among the employees in the tourism sector. These can cause some challenges in the organization such as lower job security, high turnover, lack of proper training and poor work life balance. The second stage includes an evaluation that considers how the mentioned challenges impact the welfare of the employees. This is in terms of psychological and sociological variables that measures its effects on employee's well-being, well-being at work and work engagement. The last step of the framework involves the investigation of the role of organizational culture as the moderation variable. This comprises of the assessment of moderating roles played by other factors like leadership practices, communication and organizational culture which either amplify or reduce impacts of the emerging issues in HRM on the employees.

It is important to discuss HRM challenges if one has to operate the sector because of several factors that have been noted as follows; Seasonal fluctuations, Human Contact, Guest Relation Emphasis. The following is a holding pattern in developing this model that shields or offers direction in handling these challenges in order to improve the Human resource practices and strategies. When specific HRM issues have been identified in the organizations, solutions can be designed to enhance employee satisfaction and retention, which are vital factors for consideration in the tourism industry, given that there are very many cases of employees' turnover. Further, it is important for organizations to comprehend the effects of these challenges on employees since it influences general overall worker health and satisfaction in the workplace. Solving such problems is not only provides benefits for the employees but also for improving the organizational service, which increases customer satisfaction and profitability.

Analyzing organizational culture as a moderator is crucial because it either enhances or reduces the effects of the revealed HRM challenges. However, when these challenges are within an organization, positive organizational culture promoted by strong leadership, communication, and empowement of employees may serve to reduce their impact, thus creating a more robust staff. This element of the framework emphasizes accelerating the warmth and flexibility of the organizational climate sufficient to deal with the ever-existing problems of the tourism sector. Through organizational culture, tourism organizations can attain a stable and better workforce so as to improve on the growth of the business and establish a competitive advantage in the market.

3. RESEARCH METHODS

The following research methods are used for the study

The research philosophy under consideration is positivism. The research philosophy of positivism is congruent with the theories on HRM Challenges, Employee well being and Organizational culture.. (Alharahsheh & Pius, 2020).

The research approach employed in this study is a deductive approach. The deductive technique is frequently employed in positivist research due to its reliance on formulating a hypothesis derived from preexisting theories, followed by empirical testing through data gathering and subsequent analysis. (Casula et al., 2021).

Research Methodology – Mono method quantitative analysis. The study focuses on Tourism sector employees in Bangalore city, employing a quantitative analysis approach. In order to acquire quantitative data, the researchers sent out surveys to Tourism sector employees in Airlines, Hotel and Travel sectors. Using this strategy, researchers were able to collect detailed data on the Tourism sector employees. (Manzoor, 2020).

The researcher employs the Survey method as a study strategy to gather data from Tourism sector employees. The survey comprises inquiries pertaining to the HRM Challenges, employee wellbeing and moderating role of organization culture. A well-structured questionnaire was prepared by referring to the previous articles. (Dawson, et al., 2011).

The present investigation pertains to a cross-sectional research design. The survey was done by the researcher over a duration of four months in order to collect data from educators in Bangalore city. The chosen timeframe provides an ample sample size and enables the researcher to effectively capture any potential fluctuations in app usage that may be influenced by seasonal factors. (Wang & Cheng,2020). (Xie et al., 2022).

The size of the sample used in the study involves the selection of a sample of 122 Tourism sector employees from Bangalore city, utilizing the Cochran formula to determine the sample size required for a 7.5% margin of error and a 95% confidence level.

The unit of analysis for this study are the Tourism sector employees who in the Tourism field for atleast 5 years. The Tourism employees who were interested to take a brief session on the topic and give their valuable insights were considered for the study.

The sample technique employed in this study is non-probability sampling, specifically convenience sampling. The utilization of convenience sampling was justified due to its ability to provide researchers with convenient access to a substantial pool of possible Tourism sector employees across Bangalore

The validity and reliability of data-gathering tool utilized in this study was conducted.

Gliem and Gliem, (2003) provide the following rules of thumb: "_ > .9 – Excellent, _ > .8 – Good, _ > .7 – Acceptable, _ > .6 – Questionable, _ > .5 – Poor, and _ < .5 – Unacceptable". The scores for reliability for all constructs in the educators' research instrument were above .9 and below .95 indicating excellent reliability. The inter item correlations between the constructs is tested using the confirmatory factor analysis. The Pearson correlation r value is 0.522 which is well within the criteria to affirm internal consistency. Convergent validity is the assessment of the degree of correlation among various concept indicators that show agreement. The indicator's factor loading, composite reliability (CR), and average variance extracted (AVE) must all be considered in order to determine convergent validity (Hair Jr & et al., 2017). The values are between 0 and 1. It is important for the AVE value to exceed the cutoff point of 0.50 in order to guarantee convergent validity. MaxR(H) - Maximum reliability > than MSV; CR - Composite reliability > than 0.70 (0.898); AVE - Average Variance explained > than 0.50 (0.762); MSV - Maximum shared square variance > than AVE. The Fornell-Lacker criterion is used to assess discriminant validity when applying the second criterion (Fornell, Cha, & Bagozzi, 1994) (Farrell & Rudd, 2009). This method compares the correlation of latent constructs with the square root of the average variance extracted (AVE) (Hair Jr & et al., 2017). A latent construct's ability to explain variance in its own indicators is predicted to be greater than its ability to explain variance in indicators of other latent constructs. Hair et al. (2017) state that it is expected that the correlations with other latent constructs will be lower than the square root of the average variance extracted (AVE) for each construct. The Tourism employees questionnaire was deemed valid and reliable in the current model since all dimensions have been verified and all constructs meet the validity criteria. The reliability and validity of the questionnaire was tested using the master validity tool by Gaskins and was affirmed. (Shia et al, 2023).

The study utilized SPSS Version 22 and AMOS Version 22 software for data analysis. Thakkar and Thakkar (2020). Andrew Hayes process macros was used for Moderation analysis

4. RESULTS AND DISCUSSION

4.1 Demographic Profile Of The Respondents

It is important for the analysis and interpretation of the responses to capture demographic variables. This allows researchers to discern potential biases or differences in opinion based on variables like age, gender, ethnicity, income and resource allocation and education,. This survey found that whereas 53.2% of HR professionals are men, 46.8% are female. Based on these results, it seems that the gender ratio in human resources is around average. Having said that, there may still be gender gaps in the HR department depending on the position or seniority level in question. To promote gender equality in human resources and understand the causes of the current gender gap, further studies are required. Of those surveyed, 29% were in the under-30 age bracket, 47% were in the 31–40 age bracket, and 24% were in the 41–60 age bracket. Based on this demographic data, it appears that age is another factor contributing to the gender gap in human resources. There may be more women in entry-level roles since fewer people their age are entering the workforce. The gender gap at senior levels may be exacerbated by the fact that more people are over the age of 41, which might be an indication that women do not have enough opportunities to advance in HR. To further understand and resolve these inequities, additional study should explore the confluence of gender and age within the HR profession. The survey found that 70.6% of HR personnel have postgraduate degrees. Given the significant number of postgraduates working in human resources, it seems that furthering one's education might be necessary to climb the corporate ladder in this sector. But we must investigate whether this stipulation adds to the gender disparities by affecting women more than males. While 28.4% of HR staff are unmarried, 66.1% are married. Of the HR staff, 15.6% had fewer than two years of experience, 22.0% had two to five years, and 49.5% had eight years or more. In the tourist sector, HR managers make up 44% of the HR workforce, executives account for 15.6%, while sole proprietors and small business owners make up the remaining 6%. Among human resources professionals, 66.7% had experience with one to two tourist firms, while 33.3% had experience with more than two. The airline business accounts for 21.1% of HR personnel, the hotel and resort industry for 31.2%, and the travel agency and tour operator sector for 47.7%.

4.2 Item Analysis for HRM Challenges, Employee Wellbeing and Organizational Culture

Item analysis refers to the process of understanding the mean, standard deviation, skewness and Kurtosis of the data. It is important to conduct item analysis since they give insight into the quality and reliability of the measurement instrument that is being used. They help in determining if the items are working effectively, if they able to measure what they are supposed to measure and if they function together. It also helps in identifying items that are not performing effectively and need to be revised or dropped to yield a more valid and reliable measurement instrument.

Item analysis is aimed at the overall quality of research findings and publications and at providing a reliable and valid measuring instrument for future research. HRM challenges were gauged in terms of five factors: performance challenges, task challenges, occupational challenges, health challenges, and family challenges. The mean score for the challenges was higher than 4.000. So people are very concerned about the challenge. The most highly ranked challenge was performance challenges, with a mean score of 4.500. This goes to show just how overwhelmed employees feel by the demands on them to be productive on the job. But for task challenges as well, the mean score of 4.200 rated only slightly lower, indicating there's also a lot that employees struggle with in the volume and complexity of their daily tasks. All these results serve to emphasize the detrimental effect of these challenges on employees' wellbeing and work performance in any organization.

Employee wellbeing consisted of psychological wellbeing, social wellbeing, workplace wellbeing, and Subjective Wellbeing. The mean score for well-being items is less than 3.50, indicating that workers in the tourist sector have poor well-being. These low scores for well-being hint at high levels of stress and dissatisfaction in the lives of staff in the tourism sector, this in turn, could be a source of their problems about job expectations and meeting task challenges. It is absolutely essential for the tourism sector to deal with these happiness problems in order to enhance employees' satisfaction and productivity. Providing support for employee wellbeing, such as mental health resources, work-life balance initiatives, and programs for managing stress at work could greatly improve the working environment for all employees.

4.3 Testing of Hypothesis

H1- There is an impact of HRM Challenges on employee well being
Step -1 Exploratory Factor analysis (Challenges)

- Barlett's Test of Sphericity (with a significance threshold of 5%), as well as the KMO measure of sample adequacy (0.878), are both statistically significant. With 127 degrees of freedom and a significant value less than 0.05, a chi-square value of 30209.750 for the Bartlett test indicates that the correlation matrix is not an identity matrix and appears to be factorable.
- The communalities for the stress items ranged from 0.487 to 0.879, which is over the recommended threshold of 0.300 for all items' extraction values.
- Roughly 83.37% of the initial loadings remain after removing all squared loadings. When applied to the social sciences, a cumulative Rotation Sum of Squared Loadings more than 50% is deemed satisfactory. The study found that when using the Factor Analysis technique, five components were found.
- No items were removed from the study as a result of adequate factor loadings, as shown by the rotated component matrix.

Step 2 – Model Fit

Within the reasonable range of 3 (more precisely, 2.876), the chi-square divided by degrees of freedom ($\chi 2$ / df) is acceptable. Compared to the suggested characteristics, the actual Goodness of Fit rating (0.826) is superior. The RMR comes out to be 0.048 according to the boundary estimation. Not only does this model have good fit metrics, but it has also received a lot of praise from academics.

Figure 1. SEM Analysis representation - impact of HRM Challenges on employee well being

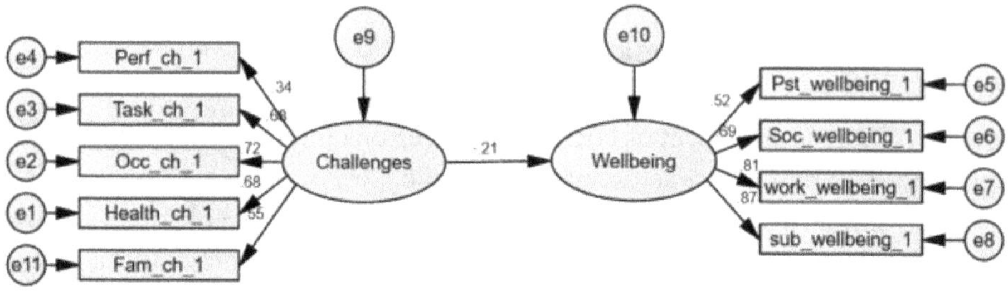

Table 1. Estimates for impact of HRM Challenges on employee well being

			Unstd Estimate	Std Estimate	P
Wellbeing	<---	**Challenges**	**-0.145**	**-0.205**	***
Health_ch_1	<---	Challenges	1	0.68	
Occ_ch_1	<---	Challenges	1.163	0.718	***
Task_ch_1	<---	Challenges	1.043	0.678	***
Perf_ch_1	<---	Challenges	0.545	0.341	***
Pst_wellbeing_1	<---	Wellbeing	1	0.517	
Soc_wellbeing_1	<---	Wellbeing	1.243	0.688	***
work_wellbeing_1	<---	Wellbeing	1.71	0.809	***
sub_wellbeing_1	<---	Wellbeing	1.788	0.869	***
Fam_ch_1	<---	Challenges	0.883	0.547	***

The HRM challenges have a significant negative impact on the Employee wellbeing and this relationship is statistically significant at (B= -0.145, b= -0.205. p=0.000). So it stands to reason that worker well-being worsens as HRM challenges worsen. Such an ill effect can result in inferior job satisfaction, higher stress levels, and decreased workplace productivity. Organizations must address and lessen HRM challenges in order to put their employees' welfare and happiness above everything else. HRM challenges were evaluated along five dimensions- performance, task, occupational, health, and family. Each of them affects employee well-being as well as overall job performance. Only by pinpointing and dealing with these challenges can organizations create a more positive and nurturing work environment for the whole staff. This yields higher levels of job satisfaction and less stress in the long run. Then, and only then, will productivity grow. Organizations must take action using strategies and resources to effectively manage HRM challenges and these actions should focus on safeguarding the well-being of their employees. Indeed, only by addressing these challenges can organizations provide a healthy and productive workplace for their employees.

They can help organizations create a healthier, more productive workplace by implementing strategies to improve aspects of human resource challenges--such as improving communication, giving effective training and support, or creating a favourable work environment. Moreover, dealing with HRM challenges will raise the morale, loyalty, and commitment of their employees--which is good news for any company. By prioritizing the well-being of employees, companies not only enhance individual job satisfaction and performance. It is also a sign of positive company culture and success. Then everyone benefits.

> H2- There is a moderating role of Organizational culture in dampening the effect of HRM Challenges

Table 2. Moderation analysis for role of organizational culture in dampening the effect of HRM challenges

Model : 1
Y : Emp_well
X : Challenges
W : Org_Culture
Sample
Size: 122
****
OUTCOME VARIABLE:
Org_Culture
Model Summary
R R-sq MSE F df1 df2 p
.3130 .0980 1.0212 15.7880 3.0000 436.0000 .0000
Model
coeff se t p LLCI ULCI

constant 2.9896 .3359 8.9008 .0000 2.3294 3.6497
Challenges -.0496 .1200 .4134 .6795 -.1862 .2854
Org_Culture .3800 .0940 4.0410 .0001 .1952 .5648
Int_1 .0695 .0332 -2.0907 .0371 -.1348 -.0042
Product terms key:
Int_1 : Challenges x Org_Culture
Test(s) of highest order unconditional interaction(s):
R2-chng F df1 df2 p
X*W .0090 4.3710 1.0000 436.0000 .0371

Figure 2. Regression line - role of organizational culture in dampening the effect of HRM challenges

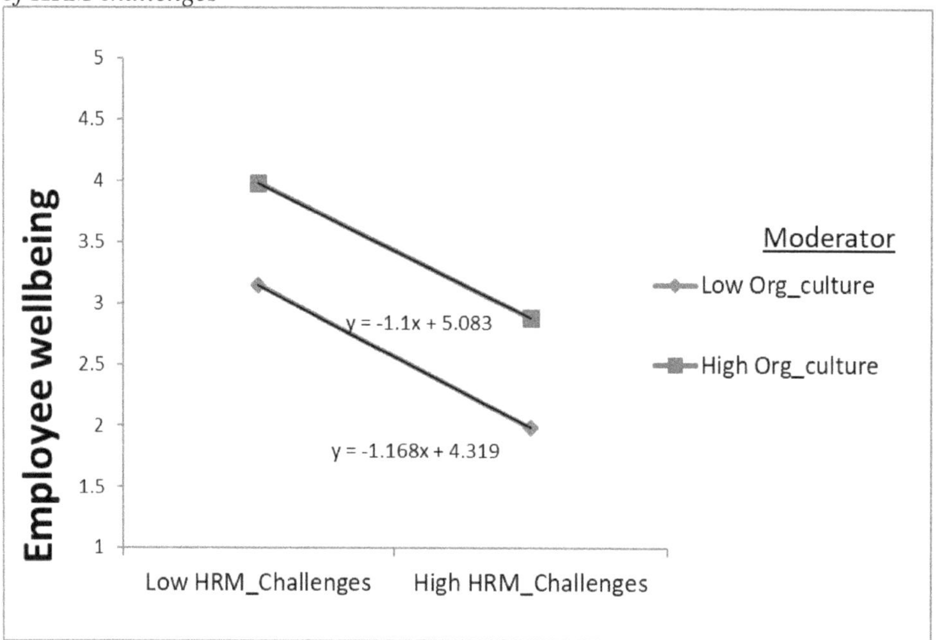

Y: Employee wellbeing indicates the independent variables, X: Challenges indicates the dependent variables and W: Organization culture indicates the moderating variables. The Interaction value of 0.0695 is statistically significant indicating the effect of moderating variable. The R square change of 0.0090 is also significant at p=0.005 as seen in Table 2.

The line Graph as seen in Figure 2 indicates that with organization culture, the effect of HRM Challenges can dampen. The equation of y = -1.1x + 5.083 shows that the effect of relationship moves inverse indicating that Organization culture acts as a catalyst to dampen the effects of HRM Challenges. This implies that HRM challenges lose their bite as organizational culture strengthens. It becomes clear from the negative coefficient on this regression equation that disseminating strong organizational culture depresses overall effects of HRM challenges: in other words, for each increase in HRM challenges correspondingly decreases the overall effect by a given amount. This relationship seems to suggest that creating a positive, supportive culture can make the difficulties associated with human resources management less challenging. By establishing such a strong organizational culture, companies can better deal with barriers like high levels of staff turnover rates or low employee satisfaction as well as conflicts in the workplace. A positive culture creates a sense of solidarity, trust, and shared values that eventually lead to higher levels of employee involvement and output. In short, a solid organizational culture provides the organization with a solid protective facades against the detrimental effects of HRM challenges, enabling it to live and prosper.

5. CONCLUSION

Perhaps, the human resource management is one of the significant departments of a firm, which also holds true for the Tourism industry. In the Tourism industry, HR is responsible for the selection and training of customers' service staff, handling of employee relations and implementing employee engagement plans to retain such staff in a highly competitive environment. Because of fluctuating employment rates of the industry, there is also the need to properly manage staffing and succession to reduce disruptions. In fact, the management of human resources can be preached as one of the most key success factors for any Tourism organization.

On the other hand organization culture play's a great role in enhancing employee wellbeing through minimizing challenges of HRM and promoting the organizational citizenship behaviours. Specifically, SHRM practitioners can enhance the organizational culture by fostering its positivity, as well as employee job satisfaction which would result in escalation of organizational performance, particularly with retention of talent. Also, unique organizational culture help attract employees and gives a tourism organization a competitive edge over the other similar organizations. As such, while human resource management tasks include only administrative assignments within the tourism industry, it is a vital component essential for creating or destroying organizational success and brand image.

The findings of the study imply that HRM Challenges have a significant negative influence on the psychological health of the employee. More specifically, employees subjected to HRM Challenges experienced higher levels of stress, burnout, and low morale. Therefore, it is essential to address and resolve the HRM Challenges to facilitate a conducive work environment that would promote the health and psychological wellbeing of employees. This could be achieved by fostering and promoting meaningful HR practices that would alleviate the adverse impact of the challenges on employees. Additionally, employees' resilience to the stressors is modulated by organizational culture, and the findings of the study implied such a dampening effect. Organizational culture orients employees to perceive and react to the stressful HRM challenge. A positive organizational culture makes employees feel supported and valued, hence reducing the impact of the challenge. This is achieved through the creation of effective communication, trust, and collaboration. Thus, investing in an effective HR practice and encouraging a positive organizational culture is critical to create a conducive work environment for employees.

In conclusion, human resources managers in the Tourism industry confront a plethora of problems, and the success or failure of their initiatives is dependent on how they tackle these problems through the use of effective organization culture. By fostering a positive work culture, human resources managers in the hotel industry can improve employee satisfaction, productivity, and retention rates. This will not only benefit the employees themselves but also contribute to a positive reputation for the organization as a whole. Additionally, a positive work environment can help to attract new employees who are looking for a company that prioritizes employee well-being and growth. Ultimately, investing in creating a positive work culture can have a significant impact on the overall success and longevity of the organization.

The current study is limited to the interviews of HR managers in the tourism industry at Bangalore. In the future, the empirical model can also address the viewpoint of the Tourism employees. Thus, the HR perspectives of the managers and the employees will offer a clear view of the challenges and opportunity of HRM in the tourism industry of the nation. The data analysis will be quantitative analysis and considering a large sample size for more statistical significance. Hence, a clear trend and pattern that present in the industry will be addressed. The research can also compare the HRM practices at the tourism sector in various cities of India with the sample size taken for the same, in order to analyse the regional differences. This study could also be extended to examining the primary differences among the cities. This comprehensive study will useful to the policy implementers and the industry professionals.

REFERENCES

Abbas, J., Mubeen, R., Iorember, P. T., Raza, S., & Mamirkulova, G. (2021). Exploring the impact of COVID-19 on tourism: Transformational potential and implications for a sustainable recovery of the travel and leisure industry. *Current Research in Behavioral Sciences, 2*, 100033. DOI: 10.1016/j.crbeha.2021.100033 PMID: 38620720

Agarwal, P. (2021). Shattered but smiling: Human resource management and the wellbeing of hotel employees during COVID-19. *International Journal of Hospitality Management, 93*, 102765. DOI: 10.1016/j.ijhm.2020.102765 PMID: 36919177

Al-Twal, A., Gammoh, L. A., & Zureikat, M. (2024). An Exploration of the Role of HR Departments in Optimizing Employee Mental Wellness in the Face of Organizational Risks. *The International Journal of Organizational Analysis*. Advance online publication. DOI: 10.1108/IJOA-07-2024-4648

Alharahsheh, H. H., & Pius, A. (2020). A review of key paradigms: Positivism VS interpretivism. *Global Academic Journal of Humanities and Social Sciences, 2*(3), 39–43.

. Arshad, M. O., Khan, S., Haleem, A., Mansoor, H., Arshad, M. O., & Arshad, M. E. (2023). Understanding the impact of Covid-19 on Indian tourism sector through time series modelling. *Journal of tourism futures, 9*(1), 101-115.

Babu, M. R., & Eimani, A. (2014). Human resource management: A challenging scenario in the Indian context. *Afro Asian Journal of Anthropology and Social Policy, 5*(1), 45–50. DOI: 10.5958/2229-4414.2014.00183.5

Bansal, A., Mukherjee, S., & Prayag, G. (2025). From crisis to care: Redesigning work and jobs for employee well-being in hospitality and tourism. *Tourism and Hospitality Research*, •••, 14673584251321038. DOI: 10.1177/14673584251321038

Baum, T. (2012). Human resource management in tourism: A small island perspective. *International Journal of Culture, Tourism and Hospitality Research, 6*(2), 124–132. DOI: 10.1108/17506181211233054

Berbekova, A., & Uysal, M. (2021). Wellbeing and quality of life in tourism. In *Tourist health, safety and wellbeing in the new normal* (pp. 243–268). Springer Singapore. DOI: 10.1007/978-981-16-5415-2_10

Bohdanowicz, P., & Zientara, P. (2009). Hotel companies' contribution to improving the quality of life of local communities and the well-being of their employees. *Tourism and Hospitality Research, 9*(2), 147–158. DOI: 10.1057/thr.2008.46

Casula, M., Rangarajan, N., & Shields, P. (2021). The potential of working hypotheses for deductive exploratory research. *Quality & Quantity*, *55*(5), 1703–1725. DOI: 10.1007/s11135-020-01072-9 PMID: 33311812

Chahal, H., & Devi, S. (2024). Drivers of service ecosystem: Moderating role of organizational culture in North Indian hotels. *International Journal of Quality and Service Sciences*, *16*(2), 295–323. DOI: 10.1108/IJQSS-07-2023-0099

Dalkhjav, B., Munkhuu, B., & Sukhragchaa, A. S. (2024). Enhancing job performance in the hospitality sector: Exploring the role of employee engagement, multitasking, organizational culture, and recruiting practices. *Journal of Tourism, Sustainability and Well-being*, *12*(2), 188–205.

Dawson, M., Abbott, J., & Shoemaker, S. (2011). The hospitality culture scale: A measure organizational culture and personal attributes. *International Journal of Hospitality Management*, *30*(2), 290–300. DOI: 10.1016/j.ijhm.2010.10.002

Faeni, D. P., Puspitaningtyas Faeni, R., Alden Riyadh, H., & Yuliansyah, Y. (2023). The COVID-19 pandemic impact on the global tourism industry SMEs: A human capital development perspective. *Review of International Business and Strategy*, *33*(2), 317–327. DOI: 10.1108/RIBS-08-2021-0116

Farrell, A. M., & Rudd, J. M. (2009). Factor analysis and discriminant validity: A brief review of some practical issues. In Australia and New Zealand Marketing Academy Conference 2009. Anzmac.

Filipova, M. K. (2015). Relationship between corporate culture and competitive power of the companies in the tourism industry. *Tourism & Management Studies*, *11*(1), 98–103.

Fornell, C., & Cha, J. (1994). *Partial Least Squares. Advanced Methods of Marketing Research*. RP Bagozzi.

Gamage, T. C., & Tajeddini, K. (2022). A multi-layer organizational culture framework for enhancing the financial performance in tourism and hospitality family firms. *Tourism Management*, *91*, 104516. DOI: 10.1016/j.tourman.2022.104516

Gigauri, I. (2020). Implications of COVID-19 for human resource management. *International Journal of Economics and Management Studies*, *7*(11), 25–33. DOI: 10.14445/23939125/IJEMS-V7I11P104

Ginting, Y. M., Rismawati, R., & Aisyah, S. (2024). The Moderating Role of Work Environment in the Relationship Between Organisational Culture, Employee Motivation, Performance Appraisal, and Job Satisfaction in Bali's Hotel Industry. *The South East Asian Journal of Management*, *18*(2), 6. DOI: 10.21002/seam.v18i2.1775

Gliem, J. A., & Gliem, R. R. (2003). *Calculating, interpreting, and reporting Cronbach's alpha reliability coefficient for Likert-type scales*. Midwest Research-to-Practice Conference in Adult, Continuing, and Community Education.

Gruescu, R., Nanu, R., & Pirvu, G. (2008). Human resource management in the tourism industry. *Bulletin UASVM. Horticulture*, *65*(2), 168–173.

Hair, J. F.Jr, Matthews, L. M., Matthews, R. L., & Sarstedt, M. (2017). PLS-SEM or CB-SEM: Updated guidelines on which method to use. *International Journal of Multivariate Data Analysis*, *1*(2), 107–123. DOI: 10.1504/IJMDA.2017.087624

He, Z., & Hao, X. (2022). Emotional labor and employee well-being in cross-cultural contexts: A Disney frontline staff's autoethnography. *Tourism Management*, *91*, 104518. DOI: 10.1016/j.tourman.2022.104518

Hsu, F. S., Liu, Y. A., & Tsaur, S. H. (2019). The impact of workplace bullying on hotel employees' well-being: Do organizational justice and friendship matter? *International Journal of Contemporary Hospitality Management*, *31*(4), 1702–1719. DOI: 10.1108/IJCHM-04-2018-0330

Jatav, S. (2023). Current Trends in Sustainable Tourism in the Indian Context. In *Handbook of Research on Sustainable Tourism and Hotel Operations in Global*

Joseph Sirgy, M. (2019). Promoting quality-of-life and well-being research in hospitality and tourism. *Journal of Travel & Tourism Marketing*, *36*(1), 1–13. DOI: 10.1080/10548408.2018.1526757

Kaushal, V., & Srivastava, S. (2021). Hospitality and tourism industry amid COVID-19 pandemic: Perspectives on challenges and learnings from India. *International Journal of Hospitality Management*, *92*, 102707. DOI: 10.1016/j.ijhm.2020.102707 PMID: 33024348

Kimbu, A. N., Adam, I., Dayour, F., & de Jong, A. (2023). COVID-19-induced redundancy and socio-psychological well-being of tourism employees: Implications for organizational recovery in a resource-scarce context. *Journal of Travel Research*, *62*(1), 55–74. DOI: 10.1177/00472875211054571 PMID: 36605829

Kristiana, Y., Pramono, R., & Brian, R. (2021). Adaptation strategy of tourism industry stakeholders during the COVID-19 pandemic: A case study in Indonesia. *The Journal of Asian Finance, Economics and Business*, *8*(4), 213–223.

Kumar, C. R., & Abraham, S. (2019). Challenges in Implementing Latest HR Polices in the Hospitality Sector. *Think India Journal*, *22*(14), 4071–4079.

Kyriakidou, O., & Gore, J. (2005). Learning by example: Benchmarking organizational culture in hospitality, tourism and leisure SMEs. *Benchmarking*, *12*(3), 192–206. DOI: 10.1108/14635770510600320

Li, K., Liu, X., Mai, F., & Zhang, T. (2021). The role of corporate culture in bad times: Evidence from the COVID-19 pandemic. *Journal of Financial and Quantitative Analysis*, *56*(7), 2545–2583. DOI: 10.1017/S0022109021000326

Manzoor, A. (2020). Designs of mixed method research. In Cognitive Analytics: Concepts, Methodologies, Tools, and Applications (pp. 95-121). IGI Global. DOI: 10.4018/978-1-7998-2460-2.ch007

Ngoc, N. M., Tien, N. H., Hieu, V. M., & Trang, T. T. T. (2023). Sustainable Integration in Vietnam's Tourism Industry. *World Review of Entrepreneurship, Management and Sustainable Development*, *3*, 1–16.

Novitasari, D., Asbari, M., & Purwanto, A. (2022). Tourist satisfaction and performance of tourism industries: How the role of innovative work behaviour, organizational citizenship behaviour? *Journal of Industrial Engineering & Management Research*, *3*(1).

Oromjonovna, O. S., & Eshnazarovna, M. S. (2023). Economic Development in Tourism Industry. *EUROPEAN JOURNAL OF BUSINESS STARTUPS AND OPEN SOCIETY*, *3*(2), 60–64.

Ratnasari, S. L., Susanti, E. N., Ismanto, W., Tanjung, R., Darma, D. C., & Sutjahjo, G. (2020). An experience of tourism development: How is the strategy? *Journal of Environmental Management and Tourism*, *11*(7), 1877–1886. DOI: 10.14505//jemt.v11.7(47).26

Ross, G. F. (2017). Tourism industry employee workstress–A present and future crisis. In *Tourism crises* (pp. 145–160). Routledge.

Salas-Vallina, A., Alegre, J., & López-Cabrales, Á. (2021). The challenge of increasing employees' well-being and performance: How human resource management practices and engaging leadership work together toward reaching this goal. *Human Resource Management*, *60*(3), 333–347. DOI: 10.1002/hrm.22021

Salem, E. Z. A., Al-Dubai, M., & Bardai, B. (2024). The Moderating Role Of Organization Culture On The Relationship Between Human Resources Management Practices And Knowledge Economy In Jordanian Telecom Company. *Calitatea*, *25*(202), 269–280.

Sapta, I., Muafi, M., & Setini, N. M. (2021). The role of technology, organizational culture, and job satisfaction in improving employee performance during the Covid-19 pandemic. *The Journal of Asian Finance, Economics and Business*, *8*(1), 495–505.

Sarwar, H., Ishaq, M. I., Amin, A., & Ahmed, R. (2020). Ethical leadership, work engagement, employees' well-being, and performance: A cross-cultural comparison. *Journal of Sustainable Tourism*, *28*(12), 2008–2026. DOI: 10.1080/09669582.2020.1788039

. Sattigeri, M. V. (2023). Tourism and Economic Growth in India. *An Approach towar Paradigm Shift*, 58.

Sharma, B., & Gursoy, D. (2018, June). HRM practices in hospitality and tourism industry: A review of the literature. In *8th Advances in Hospitality and Tourism Marketing and Management (AHTMM) Conference* (Vol. 28).

Sharma, G. D., Thomas, A., & Paul, J. (2021). Reviving tourism industry post-COVID-19: A resilience-based framework. *Tourism Management Perspectives*, *37*, 100786. DOI: 10.1016/j.tmp.2020.100786 PMID: 33391988

Shia, T. H., Mansor, R., & Majid, N. A. (2023). Confirmatory Factors Analysis of Scale Measuring Secondary School Students'. *Learning & Behavior.*

Sun, S., Liu, Z., Law, R., & Zhong, S. (2017). Exploring human resource challenges in China's tourism industry. *Tourism Recreation Research*, *42*(1), 72–83. DOI: 10.1080/02508281.2016.1253199

Tepeci, M. (2005). The dimensions and impacts of organizational culture on employee job satisfaction and intent to remain in the hospitality and tourism industry in Turkey. *Journal of Travel and Tourism Research*, *5*(1/2), 21–39.

. Thakkar, J. J., & Thakkar, J. J. (2020). Applications of structural equation modelling with AMOS 21, IBM SPSS. Structural Equation Modelling: Application for Research and Practice (with AMOS and R), 35-89.

Tien, N. H., Anh, D. B. H., Duc, L. D. M., Trang, T. T. T., & Ngoc, P. B. (2021). Subjective well-being in tourism research. *Psychology and Education*, *58*(5), 3317–3325.

Tomcíková, L., Svetozarovová, N., Coculová, J., & Danková, Z. (2021). The impact of the global Covid-19 pandemic on the selected practices of human resources management in the relationship to the performance of tourism companies. *Geo Journal of Tourism and Geosites*, *35*(2), 525–530. DOI: 10.30892/gtg.35233-680

Tsaur, S. H., & Tang, Y. Y. (2012). Job stress and well-being of female employees in hospitality: The role of regulatory leisure coping styles. *International Journal of Hospitality Management*, *31*(4), 1038–1044. DOI: 10.1016/j.ijhm.2011.12.009

Tuzovic, S., & Kabadayi, S. (2021). The influence of social distancing on employee well-being: A conceptual framework and research agenda. *Journal of Service Management*, *32*(2), 145–160. DOI: 10.1108/JOSM-05-2020-0140

Uysal, M., Sirgy, M. J., Woo, E., & Kim, H. L. (2016). Quality of life (QOL) and well-being research in tourism. *Tourism Management*, *53*, 244–261. DOI: 10.1016/j.tourman.2015.07.013

Wang, X., & Cheng, Z. (2020). Cross-sectional studies: Strengths, weaknesses, and recommendations. *Chest*, *158*(1), S65–S71. DOI: 10.1016/j.chest.2020.03.012 PMID: 32658654

Xie, C., Zhang, J., Chen, Y., & Morrison, A. M. (2022). Hotel employee perceived crisis shocks: Conceptual and scale development. *Journal of Hospitality and Tourism Management*, *51*, 361–374. DOI: 10.1016/j.jhtm.2022.04.005

Chapter 3
Navigating Leadership Challenges and Opportunities:
A Strategic Framework for Excellence in Tourism

Partha Pratim Chakraborty
https://orcid.org/0000-0002-6425-7564
Chetana's Institute of Management and Research, India

ABSTRACT

The tourism sector is a pivotal contributor to economic growth, employment generation, and foreign exchange in India. Despite its substantial potential, the sector grapples with challenges such as high employee turnover, technological disruptions, and the demand for sustainable practices. This study examines the leadership challenges and opportunities within the tourism industry, emphasizing the role of transformational, adaptive, and sustainable leadership in achieving human capital excellence. It introduces the Integrated Leadership for Human Capital Excellence in Tourism (ILHCET) model, which aligns leadership with workforce optimization, technology integration, and sustainability.

LEADERSHIP CHALLENGES AND OPPORTUNITIES FOR EXCELLENCE IN TOURISM

Tourism is a potential economic powerhouse for the country contributing significantly to its Gross Domestic Product (GDP), Employment Generation and Foreign Exchange Earnings. India is one of the fastest-growing tourism market in the world

DOI: 10.4018/979-8-3373-0071-9.ch003

with several millions of domestic and worldwide visitors yearly as India has a lot to offer from cultural heritage attractions to natural attractions to historical places.

Contribution to GDP: Tourism had been a major contributor to the GDP of India. The WTTC (World Travel & Tourism Council) stated that in 2017, the sector contributed 9.4% of Indian GDP, further emphasizing the significance of travel and tourism at the national economy level (WTTC, 2018). This contribution includes both direct impacts from travel services, as well as indirect effects through related industries such as hospitality and transportation.

Employment Generation: Tourism sector is one of the largest employment generators in India. In 2017, it directly contributed to roughly 41.6 million jobs, or 8% of total employment in the country (WTTC, 2018). This includes both direct employment in hotels, travel agencies, airlines and other passenger services, and indirect employment in sectors such as food production or retail.

Foreign Exchange Earnings: Tourism industry is one of the main sectors of India contributing to Foreign Direct Investment. Tourism receipts remained an important source of income, contributing US$21.07 billion to the country in 2015, highlighting the important role tourism plays in augmenting the nation's foreign reserves (WTTC, 2018). This influx helps to offset the national current account deficit and stabilizes the economy.

Regional Development: In less industrialized areas tourism will encourage infrastructure improvements by providing access to wholesale regional goods and services, construction stages, and many more economic opportunities. It promotes retention of cultural/natural heritage resulting in sustainable community development. Tourism, for example, has some Indian states such as Kerala and Rajasthan taken advantage of both the local economy and local infrastructure (Singh, 2019).

Challenges and Opportunities: To some measure, however, problems remain which —rumbling beneath the fore and bet you would be well-acquainted with — have militate against growth in the Indian tourism sector, including there cannot matches as far as infrastructure goes, environmental things, and our relatively-poor recall rate of human resource. On the other hand, programs such as the promotion of sustainable tourism, as well as niche tourism products (medical and eco-tourism) are opportunities for expansion and diversification (Ministry of Tourism, 2020).

Leadership excellence can be integrated into the tourism sector using the dynamics of technology, sustainability, and cross-sector collaboration. Technological advancements, including AI and analytics, greatly enhanced the processes of recruiting employees, workforce management, and operational efficiency. Chakraborty (2024) notes that these technologies provide essential assistance for sustainable tourism practices within organizations by ensuring operational efficiency and meeting changing consumer demands. Ethical implementation of these technologies is also critical. According to Chakraborty (2025), ethical dimensions need to be incorporated into AI development, stressing transparency and trust as foundational coordinates to look for to deliver responsible AI in decision-making.

Digital platforms have also been used strategically impacting tourism leadership. To illustrate, Chakraborty (2024) highlights the influence of social media in shaping travel choices, thus underlining the necessity for digital engagement in tourism marketing algorithms. Even lessons from other industries show how digital tools can empower leadership. In Chakraborty (2024), we look at how social media and podcasts serve as powerful mobilization tools for political campaigns to reach stakeholders. Drawing from this body of knowledge, the context highlights that tourism leaders are what is shaping the future of the industry in terms of innovation, resilience and sustainability through the alignment of technology, ethics and stakeholder engagement.

ROLE OF LEADERSHIP IN SHAPING HUMAN CAPITAL FOR A COMPETITIVE EDGE.

Human capital, which refers to the skills, knowledge, and abilities of employees, plays a critical role in the success of organizations competing in dynamic markets. There is an undeniable link between leadership-transformation and people, aligning human capital and strategic objectives, creating an organizational spirit of innovation and sustainable differentiation. Herein is an investigation of leadership and its impact on the development of human capital, anchored by salient academic perspectives.

The interplay between leadership and your most vital asset: human resources

Human capital has been recognized as a fundamental resource that enables the attainment of competitive advantage (Barney, 1991). Leadership is the accelerator that makes the best use of this resource. Leaders influence the organization culture, foster a culture of learning, and match the potential of employees to the changing needs of the dynamic business environment(Becker, 1994).One of the most powerful ways to improve human capital is using transformational vs. transactional leadership — transformational leadership focuses on getting followers excited with a vision and motivation. Studies show that this is a type of leadership that enhances employee engagement and growth significantly and positively (Wang et al., 2011). Likewise, servant leadership, which emphasizes the welfare of employees, fosters trust and commitment to the workforce (Greenleaf, 1977).

SKILLS DEVELOPMENT AND EDUCATION

Level Up Your Skills Continuously "Skill building is important to adapt to the changing requirements of the market. Employee Growth: Leaders committed to employee growth facilitate opportunities for upskilling and innovation leading to a more competitive organization (Noe et al., 2017).

ENGAGEMENT AND INNOVATION

Innovative and high-performing employees are more engaged. Employees are more creative work with leaders that support their autonomy and acknowledge their accomplishments, creating a culture of innovation and creativity (Albrecht et al., 2015).

CHALLENGES AND IMPLICATIONS

Although using leadership for optimizing human capital is promising, it is challenging. Individual and collective resistance to change, a lack of relevant skills, short-term focus, and leaders who rely on inconsistent practices can be roadblocks to making progress (Day et al., 2014). Moreover, the application of technology requires leaders with both the capacity to accommodate digital transformation and the touch to incorporate the human aspect for sustainable growth (Stone et al., 2015).

Emerging Challenges In Managing Tourism's Dynamic Environment

The tourism industry is a time-sensitive environment where changes driven through technology, consumer expectations and global competition demand an ever-improving and adaptive sector. In this dynamic environment, leaders in this sector are challenged with aligning their workforce to the digital age, with emerging technologies — AI, big data, automation — fundamentally shifting how services are delivered. Investing in training and development is essential to ensure that employees have the skills necessary to take advantage of these technologies. But, on the other hand, digitalization has not only given the opportunity to the traveller to ask for a customizable and sustainable experience, leaving a dot of pressure on leaders to reform and relieve the creativity and adaptiveness on their team to meet the expectations of the customers (Sigala, 2020).

Environmental sustainability has also become an emphasis, creating new complexities in tourism leadership. In light of the growing consciousness towards climate change and its consequent effects on the planetary ecosystems, travellers are constantly looking for environmentally sustainable travel options, which in turn has forced organizations of all kinds to adopt more eco-friendly practices. On the business side, however, these environmental concerns should be balanced with the need to maximize return and this often means striking unique variables in the search of integrating sustainability within operational frameworks to generate profits. Moreover, compliance with regulatory changes and international climate agreements requires leadership to promote, through human capital, not only higher standards of efforts dedicated to service delivery but also broader environmental goals (Baum & Hai, 2020).

Unexpected disasters like the COVID-19 pandemic have proven the vulnerability of the tourism business and the necessity of agile and resilient leadership. The pandemic unveiled vulnerabilities in workforce management, from sudden layoffs to the psychological burden on employees. For their part, leaders should now help nurture organizational resilience by building supportive environments focused on employee well-being and mental health. Additionally, recovery efforts necessitate strong leadership to restore confidence of consumers and sustain existing market positions whilst preserving morale of remaining workforce. These challenges underscore the need for leadership to navigate through uncertainties and work to maintain human capital as a source of competitive advantage in changing times (Sigala, 2020; Baum & Hai, 2020).

OBJECTIVES OF THE CHAPTER

- To identify and address key leadership challenges in tourism.
- To explore opportunities for leveraging leadership to achieve human capital excellence.

DATA, TRENDS, AND STATISTICS SUPPORTING LEADERSHIP OBJECTIVES IN TOURISM

Key Leadership Challenges in Tourism

High Employee Turnover

The national turnover is one of the highest labor turnover across all industries with seasonal employment, shifting work hours, and few career advancement opportunities driving attrition. In the Indian hotel industry, turnover rates of 25–30% per year are commonplace, particularly among frontline employees (Mishra & Mahapatra, 2022). Internationally, hospitality turnover can be as high as 30–70% (Baum, 2019), making leadership strategies an important area of research into employee retention.

Lack of Diversity in Leadership

And women hold only 20% of tourism's leadership positions, despite making up over half of its workforce (Segovia-Pérez et al., 2019). In the same vein, ethnic minorities account for less than 10% of leadership positions across Europe's hospitality industry (WTTC, 2021). To close these gaps, leaders need to put inclusive hiring and mentorship systems in place.

Technological Lag

Despite fast-paced technological advancements, a considerable skills gap remains in the tourism labor force. Exploring the balance between "traditional" tourism and technology services continues to be the challenge for leaders to integrate AI, big data, and automation while still not ignoring the human nature of service delivery (Buhalis & Sinarta, 2019)

Crisis Management Deficiencies

The COVID-19 pandemic laid bare the weaknesses in tourism, from a lack of preparedness to respond to unforeseen disruptions. Instability among the workforce, mental health issues, and financial losses highlighted the need for agile and resilient forms of leadership (Sigala, 2020).

Opportunities for Leveraging Leadership to Achieve Human Capital Excellence

Economic Contribution of Tourism

In 2017, the tourism sector accounted for 9.4% of India's GDP, underscoring its economic importance (WTTC, 2018). Furthermore, effective leadership can also help fine-tune such contribution with respect to operational efficiency and productivity of the workforce.

Employment Generation

In 2017, tourism directly supported 41.6 million jobs in India, comprising 8% of total employment (WTTC, 2018). Hence, the appropriate leadership could maximise this potential coupling with skill enhancement, employee engagement and innovation.

Technology Integration

Recruiting, Onboarding & Training: Leafing Through HR 4.0 Scrolls: AI & Analytics Transforming Human Capital Management On the other hand, platforms like Hire Vue employ technologies such as natural language processing (NLP) and facial recognition to create a more efficient recruitment process (Stone et al., 2015). Likewise, adaptive learning systems customize training modules to suit individual employee requirements, which improves knowledge retention and skills development (Noe et al., 2017).

Sustainability Initiatives

Modern tourism is increasingly built on a foundation of sustainability. Such sustainable initiatives, such as Kerala's Responsible Tourism Mission and Taj Hotels' EARTH program, showcase how sustainability leadership can establish eco-tourism, minimize carbon footprints, and involve local communities (Singh, 219, Baum, 2019).

Retention Strategies

Employee engagement programs created by AccorHotels were successful in reducing turnover by creating career development and wellness programs (Bennett et al., 2019). Leaders who take similar measures can counteract instability in the workforce.

Diversity and Inclusion

Results from Marriott International's mentorship programs yielded a 13% increase in leadership diversity over a 5-year period- an impressive demonstration that inclusive practices such as these allow for innovation and engagement in the workplace (Segovia-Pérez et al., 2019).

Crisis Resilience

Building proactive leadership frameworks such as crisis simulation exercises and employee wellness programs can fortify organizational resilience. A case-in-point to this, is the establishment of the UNWTO's Global Tourism Crisis Committee (Sigala, 2020).

Conclusion

The data and trends highlight the dual challenges and opportunities in tourism leadership. By addressing high turnover rates, integrating technology, promoting diversity, and building resilience, leaders can align human capital strategies with organizational goals to drive sustainable growth. These insights underscore the critical role of leadership in shaping the future of the tourism industry.

CHALLENGES IN LEADERSHIP FOR TOURISM

Workforce Challenges

High Turnover And Lack Of Skilled Manpower.

High turnover rates remains a perennial challenge in the tourism industry, with service delivery and operational efficiency suffering the consequences. Employee turnover in the hospitality sector is among the highest of any sector and can exceed anywhere of 30%–70% (Baum, 2019). Factors include trends of seasonal employment, inconsistent working hours, and low prospects for career progression. This sets off a cycle of recurring recruitment and retraining resulting in escalating costs and decreasing stability in the organization. In fact turnover rate in the Indian hotel industry is high around 25-30% every year (Mishra & Mahapatra, 2022), especially front-line of employees. These challenges need to be managed by leaders who can either invest more in professional development programs or provide more exciting pathways. AccorHotels is an excellent example; the company managed to reduce turnover rates by also implementing targeted "people engagement initiatives" such as career development and wellness programs (Bennett et al., 2019).

Tourism sector is a rapidly evolving domain which grapples with high employee turnover, perpetually leading to service challenges and operational inefficiencies. Within the hospitality industry, turnover is one of the highest of any sector, sometimes even ranging from 30%–70%. This is driven by a myriad of factors - trends of seasonal employment, inconsistent working hours and low chances of career progression. This leads to a vicious cycle of constant recruitment and retraining, with costs soaring and organizational stability crumbling. Actually, in the Indian hotel industry, the turnover rate is quite high, nearly 25-30% annual turnover specifically for front-line employees.

In order to overcome these issues, those at the top of the hospitality industry must do more to reinvest in professional development programs or offer more lucrative career paths. The company AccorHotels is one that has significantly decreased turnover rates through targeted "people engagement initiatives" like career development and wellness programs (Gom et al., 2021).

The high turnover populating the hospitality sector is documented (Gom et al. 2021), it is with parallel dimensions, at the sector level, almost double than the average number for all remaining sectors. Prior studies have demonstrated that leaders with transformational leadership traits can greatly affect employee behaviour and demeanour, which are important for providing quality service to hotel guests. Sustainable human resource management practices, including adopting strategies and practices that ensure evidence of achievement of long-term economic, social and environmental gains.

Need for Diversity And Inclusion In Tourism Leadership

Despite its global character, tourism industry leadership is often poor in diversity, and this is challenged as tourism serves for an increasingly multicultural customer segment. Segovia-Pérez et al. (2019) finds that globally women account for less than 20% of those in leadership roles in tourism, even though they represent over 50% of the workforce. There are similar gaps for other underrepresented groups, such as minorities and people with disabilities. For example, The World Travel and Tourism Council (WTTC, 2021) previously stated that in the European hospitality sector, people from ethnically diverse backgrounds occupied less than 10% of executive roles. Closing these gaps demands that leaders not only to put inclusive hiring and promotion practices in place, but also to create a workplace culture that embraces diversity. For example, Marriott International has introduced mentorship programs for both woman and minority employees contributing to a 13 percent increase in diversity at the leadership level over five years (Marriott, 2022).

While tourism has a global character, diversity at tourism industry leadership levels is routinely lacking, and this is problematized as tourism caters for a growing multicultural consumer segment. Segovia-Pérez et al. finds that the global leadership in tourism is less than 20% for women, even though they make up more than 50% of the global workforce. There are similar gaps for other underrepresented groups, like minorities and people with disabilities. For instance The World Travel and Tourism Council previously noted that in the European hospitality space less than 10% of executive chairs were occupied by people from ethnically diverse backgrounds. Closing these gaps requires leaders to not only implement inclusive hiring and promotion practices, but also cultivate a place of work culture where diversity is welcome. Marriott International, for example, has created mentorship programs for woman and minority employees, which have yielded a 13 percent increase in leadership diversity over a five-year period. In addition to developing diverse talent, leaders can also implement targeted recruitment strategies to access a more diverse candidate pool, pursue unconscious bias training for people involved in hiring, and periodically review compensation and promotions (Baum, 2019; Mishra & Mahapatra, 2022).

The tourism and hospitality industry has a severe problem with high turnover rates, which affects service delivery and operational efficiency. Turnover rates in the hospitality industry rank among the highest of any industry, and in some areas can surpass 30%–70%. This is partly due to the trends of seasonal staffing, unstable working hours, and the lack of career progression in the industry. This leads to an endless process of recruiting and retraining, in turn creating American enterprises to work harder (Kim, 2006). The turnover rate in the Indian hotel industry is around 25–30% each year, particularly at the front desk (Walmsley, 2004)(Kim, 2006)(Gom et al., 2021)

Leaders have to navigate through those challenges either with more money going towards the professional development or more exciting route. For example, the hotel chain AccorHotels was able to lower its turnover rates through implementing targeted "people engagement initiatives" like career development and wellness programs for its staff . By implementing better practices in these areas, hospitality companies can reduce turnover rates and build a more sustainable workforce.

LITERATURE REVIEW: LEADERSHIP CHALLENGES AND OPPORTUNITIES IN THE DEVELOPMENT OF HUMAN CAPITAL FOR EXCELLENCE IN TOURISM

The dynamic nature of the tourist sector, with its rapid technological advances, changing consumer interests, and questions of environmental sustainability, has made tourism industry leadership an important focus area. These challenges, however, can be surmounted, and human capital can be a source of competitive advantage with effective leadership. The literature on corporate leadership, however, has significant gaps when it comes to understanding how leadership would be able to not just cope with but leverage these transformations. The present review summarizes the main research on it concerning leadership challenges and opportunities in tourism and maps its findings to identify leadership challenges in tourism to investigate opportunities for attaining human capital excellency. conservations of natural resources, the management of tourism industry has become a critical issue. (Abson, 2017) (Colocassides, 2022) (Fowler et al., 2022)

One major challenge faced by tourism providers is their employee turnover rates. The hospitality industry experiences one of the highest turnover rates of any field, often ranging from 30%–70% on average per year1 as follows of employees leave for reasons like seasonal engagement, irregular hours, limited advancement opportunities. This manifests in a vicious cycle of hiring and retraining, with ever-increasing costs and continually diminishing organizational stability. This problem is especially noted in India's hotel industry, where the turnover rate, especially among the frontline employees, is estimated to be around 25-30% per annum. (2019), Baum et al., 2020, Vargas-Sevalle et al.

To combat this issue, investment into professionalisation and structured career pathways for employees is essential in order to attract and retain existing talent. Hilton Hotels realized a substantial turnover reduction with a targeted "people engagement initiative", offering career development and wellness programs (Bennett et al., 2019; Mishra & Mahapatra, 2022; Baum, 2019).

Transformational leadership approaches are consistently seen as an imperative to effectively lead human capital in the tourism industry sustainably. References: Transformational leadership is found to have positive relationships with employees' attitudes and behaviours resulting in improved quality of service and financial performance. They are an important aspect in ensuring the tourism industry adopts sustainable human resource management practices, allowing for the realization of long-term economic, societal and ecological objectives as well. (Gom et al., 2021)

Leadership Issues in Tourism

Volatility of the Workforce And Retention

Leaders face a challenging dynamic of high employee turnover respective to seasonal employment patterns in the tourism industry. Previous studies revealed that the talent retention was becoming a challenge due to the limited career growth opportunities and burnout, especially for high pressure job roles such as hospitality and travel services (Baum, 2019). Leadership approaches that do not consider these systemic concerns further create workforce instabilities where there are shortages of skills and a patchy service offer (Janta et al., 2011).

Gap: Despite a number of studies using local or business-cases to identify work-force related challenges in tourism, there has been little written about leadership tactics that would help the industry deal with and benefit from these challenges, especially in the context of engagement and retention of employees.

Technological Disruption, and Adaptation

The emergence of digital technology, to include artificial intelligence (AI), big data, and automated processes, has established a new era in the tourism sector, which requires new competencies by leaders and employees. Leaders are challenged to embrace these technologies, without losing a people-focused approach to service delivery. Tech has advanced quickly, but studies by Buhalis and Sinarta (2019) highlight that this rapid growth in tech does not correlate with the industry having a workforce prepared to respond, which leads to a lag in the required digital skills and a lack of readiness within organizations.

Research Gap: As realistic and effective for bridging skill gaps and preparing for a culture of adaptability in digitalisation in tourism, the vast majority of studies are focused on technology, however falling short to explain the associated leadership approach.

Information on Crisis and Resilience Management

The tourism industry has become increasingly aware of its vulnerabilities during global crises such as the COVID-19 pandemic. While trying to balance cost-cutting with employee well-being, morale and productivity naturally declined (Sigala, 2020).

Of course, the industry also faced compounding issues of not preparing or rehearsing for crises and also not training their leadership in helping navigate through crisis.

Gap Identified: Despite documentation of tourism's vulnerabilities, there should be better recommendations regarding leadership models that focus on resilience and proactive crisis management approaches to tourism (primaries, protest and tourism after the most recent catastrophe of: economic degradation).

Leadership Opportunities in Human Capital Excellence

Encouraging Constant Learning and Growing

Transforming for Continuous Learning by Leadership on Skills of the Workforce Research indicates that transformational and adaptive styles of leadership have important influence on employee learning and innovation (Wang et al., 2011). Lifelong learning and development is one of the managers who plan for up skilling ad reskilling techniques empower staff to compete in a industry which changes rapidly (Noe et al., 2017).

Identified Gap: While prior studies have focused on the positive facets of learning-oriented leadership, not much has been found on the application of scalable and inclusive skill development strategies, by the Tourism leaders, in conformance with the diverse workforce requirements.

The first step to becoming a great global leader in sustainability

Leaders are able to take the opportunity to lead the way when it comes to environmental sustainability and social responsibility with sustainable tourism on the rise. As noted by Bramwell & Lane (2011), organizational practices that align with sustainability goals gained more trust from their employees and customers through ethical leadership. Transformational leaders leveraging sustainable human capital practices are also innovation and longterm competitiveness leaners.

Gap Addressed: While it is recognized that there is a relationship between leadership and sustainability, research on the actual strategies that integrate sustainability with human capital in the context of tourism store is limited.

When the Human Capital Get Hierarchical, an Investing Decompounded By Technology

Advancements in technology allow leaders to enhance human capital by enabling the use of artificial intelligence in recruiting and development platforms and performance metrics. Research by Stone et al. (2015) highlights how technology facilitates improved decision-making and enhanced productivity of the workforce.

But to do this effectively fufilling tools must align with organizational culture and employee needs through the leaders' lens.

Gaps Summary: Prior literature does not provide leaders in tourism with useful frameworks for effective integration of technology and human capital management while still keeping pace with traditional service values.

Synthesis and Gaps Addressed

Existing literature reviewed highlights the great role of leadership in addressing issues of workforce retention, technology adaptation, and crisis resilience along with opportunities for talent management, sustainability, and technology adoption. But there are major gaps still:

Tourism-Specific Leadership Models: Many existing leadership studies are generalized, and often overlook the sector-specific challenges (such as seasonal employment, and high staff turnover) that the tourism industry continues to struggle with.

Aligning Tech with Human-Centric Leadership: Research tends to consider technology and human capital development separately, leaving limited opportunities to decipher how leaders can interlink the dynamics of both aspects effectively.

Crisis Leadership in Tourism: Although crisis management frameworks are abundant, few authors outline proactive and adaptive leadership frameworks tailored to tourism (e.g., Becken 2019).

These voids are closely related to the goals of this study to ensure that these leadership gaps are addressed to elevate human capital excellence in tourism in light of the challenges and opportunities that the industry faces.

THEORETICAL FOUNDATIONS: INTEGRATED LEADERSHIP FOR HUMAN CAPITAL EXCELLENCE IN TOURISM (ILHCET) MODEL

Figure 1. Framework of the model

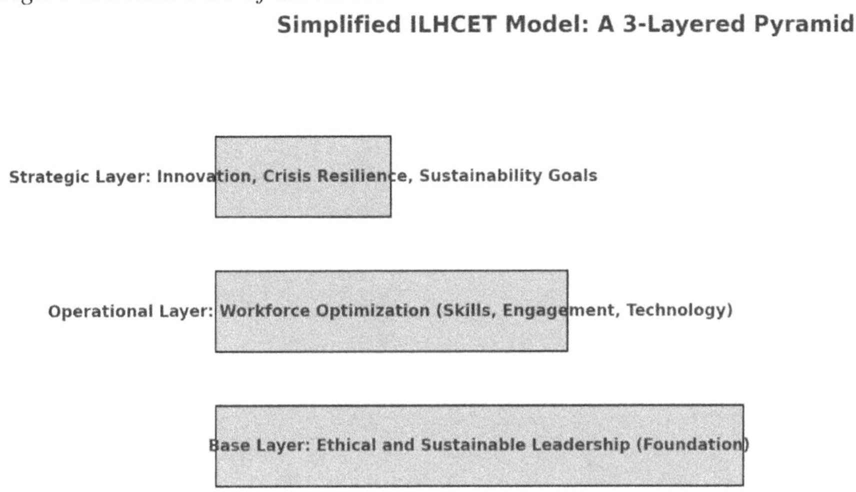

The model of ILHCET works with three interconnected layers:

Base Layer: Organizational values led by ethical and sustainable leadership

Operational Layer: Workforce optimization through tech integration, skill development, & engagement practices.

Strategic Layer: Realigns leadership with broader goals of crisis, innovation and sustainability.

Key Features of the Model

Integrative: Marries traditional leadership theories with modern-day imperatives, like digital transformation and sustainability.

Flexibility: Adjusts to the specific circumstances of the tourism sector, characterized by seasonal jobs and significant staff turnover.

Scalability: Fits for organizations of all sizes and market orientations, e.g. local tourism operators; global hospitality chains.

Proposed Detailed Model: Integrated Leadership for Human Capital Excellence in Tourism (ILHCET)'

Based on the synthesis of the literatures, the ILHCET model offers an innovative approach to integrating the leadership challenges and opportunities in tourism. It emphasises on the alignment of leadership styles, readiness to adopt technology, lifestyle engagement of employees and sustainability practice, thus providing an actionable model specific to the tourism industry.

Figure 2. Integrated Leadership for Human Capital Excellence in Tourism (ILH-CET) detailed model

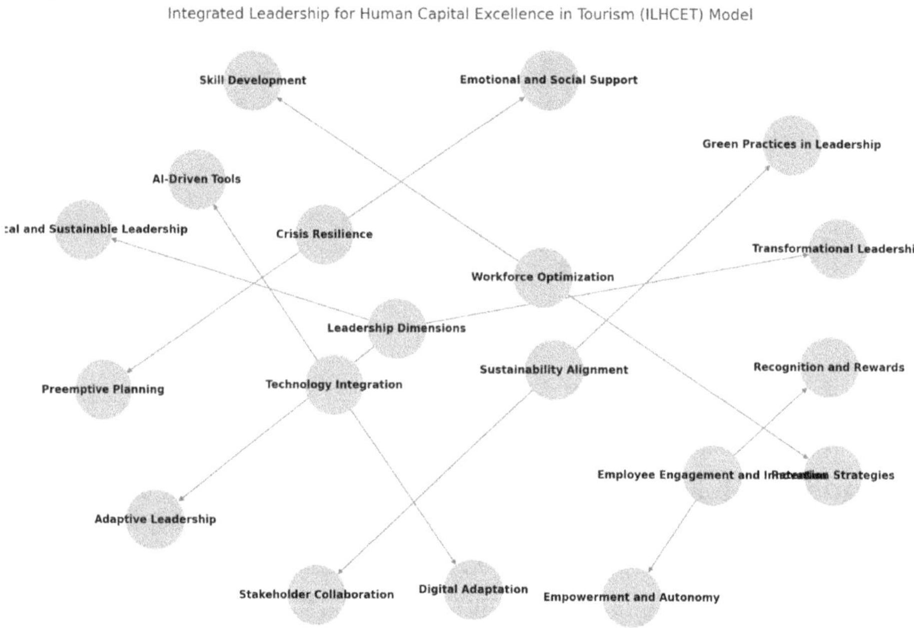

THE ILHCET MODEL Components

Strategic Approaches to Excellence in Tourism — Leadership Dimensions

The nature of tourism leadership is multidimensional and must be a blend of styles and strategies that are appropriate for the specific challenges and opportunities within the sector. ILHCET model emphasizes upon the need of the hour for leaders to maintain the balance between optimized work force, Integration of Technology and alignment to sustainability.

Leadership Dimensions

Transformational Leadership

Transformational leadership is about challenging and inspiring your followers to achieve their goals through the goals of the organization. As a result, this dynamic form of internal knowledge mobility promotes innovation and organizational development, and is especially pronounced in high-paced industries such as tourism (Wang et al., 2011).

Adaptive Leadership

However, adaptive leadership facilitates organizations with agile and responsive to change to embrace turbulence and crises. Within this framework, leaders inspire resilience and adaptability that are critical in maintaining operations in an ever-evolving marketplace (Heifetz et al., 2009).

Sustainable and Ethical Leadership

Which establishes this dimension of embedding sustainability into leadership, the trust with the team, and a conscious culture of sustainability and ethics where everyone has ownership. This type of leaders are often interested in long-term value creation in accordance with environmental and social purposes (Bramwell & Lane, 2011).

Workforce Optimization

Skill Development

Leaders are leaning into creating a continuous learning and upskilling culture with attention to technology emergence and market shifts. These efforts help employees adjust to the future of work and ensure the organization's competitiveness (Noe et al., 2017).

Retention Strategies

It is vital to develop programs that cultivate a conducive atmosphere and diminish the attrition rate. Strategies include employee engagement initiatives, wellness programs, and clear pathways for career progression (Baum, 2019).

Technology Integration

AI-Driven Applications

Using AI for recruitment, onboarding and performance monitoring streamlines operations. However, good leaders will ensure that these technologies will fit within the existent workflows (Stone et al., 2015).

Digital Adaptation

Leaders need to cultivate readiness to embrace and adopt emerging technologies. These may include investing in training to use digital tools and aligning technological advancements with organizational aims.

Crisis Resilience

Advance Arrangements

For workforce stability and continuity, proactive crisis management strategies are essential. Leader should create the structure on how to effectively manage the emergency so that will make the effect is lesser (Sigala, 2020).

Emotional and Social Support

Tackling mental health and promoting employee well-being in times of crisis serve to not only keep productivity and morale up. There are supports that leaders can put in place that start to create a culture in which conversations about mental health are normal and pathways to recovery are visible.

Specialization, Growth, and Skills Development

By motivating autonomy in every tier of the organization, we grant our employees the opportunity to step outside their comfort zones, facilitating a culture of both innovation and ownership (Deci & Ryan, 2000).

Recognition and Rewards

Better donor accountabilities tap to improve motivation and engagement. This strategy reinforces the alignment of individual performance and organizational objectives (Eisenberger et al., 2020).

Sustainability Alignment

Leadership Green Behavior

Sustainable practices integrated into human capital strategies speak to an organizations commitment to fulfilling environmental and social goals. Such practices are promoted by leaders (Bramwell & Lane, 2011).

Stakeholder Collaboration

Working together with academia and government, collaboration in this context multiplies impact. The need to partner in order to respond to complex issues and draw on diverse skills and experience.

The ILHCET-Model Implementation

The proposed model will require tourism leaders to take a multi-faceted approach that includes leadership transformation, technology integration, cultural development, and strategic planning. First, leaders must have transformational, adaptive and ethical leadership skills that can drive transformation, align the objectives of the workforce with those of the organisation and cultivate resilience in challenging environments. Funny enough, Human Capital Management boils down to these againt tech integration; utilizing AI and analytics can make contactless recruiting a possibility, upgrade on training programs and work engagement through facts on data.

Additionally, creating a culture that encourages learning and innovation is paramount for sustained growth. Leaders to create dedicated portals for continuous workforce learning and collaborative platforms to facilitate the co-creation of solutions to industry challenges. Finally, creating comprehensive playbooks is key to preparing for crises and enabling sustainability. They should offer frameworks for leaders that help to strategically approach crisis management in advance of lockdowns and layoffs, as well as facilitate sustainable steps the leaders and their organizations can take in lockstep while in lock-down mode, as well as after a lock-down concludes. When these strategies combine, tourism leaders can shape and translate excellence and adaptability throughout their organizations.

OPPORTUNITIES FOR EXCELLENCE IN TOURISM LEADERSHIP: LEVERAGING TECHNOLOGY FOR HUMAN CAPITAL DEVELOPMENT

AI, Analytics, And Digital Platforms For Recruitment, Training, And Workforce Management.

Each industry is observing the adoption of these technologies, and significant changes can be seen also in the field of human capital, most important for the tourism sector, integrating artificial intelligence (AI), analytics, and digital platforms. From hiring and training to workforce management, these technologies have allowed organizations to improve operational efficiency and employee engagement by simplifying recruitment and refining employee training.

AI And Analytics- Recruitment And Its Optimization

Candidates can be screened and selected with the help of Artificial Intelligence-based solutions, which have greatly improved recruitment processes. Machine learning algorithms are trained on vast amounts of candidate data (Stone et al., 2015) such as resumes and the social media activity to find the candidates that best fit particular roles. In addition, predictive analytics aid in anticipating hiring requirements, minimizing time taken to fill positions, and ensuring alignment with organizational objectives. As an example, AI tools such as Hire Vue utilize natural language processing (NLP) and facial recognition to evaluate candidate competencies, enabling data-driven hiring.

Training and Skills Development

AI and digital platforms can offer tailor-made training experiences by reviewing personal styles and preferences. Adaptive learning encompasses systems that deliver training modules customized to employees' needs, increasing knowledge retention and skills improvement (Noe et al., 2017). In the tourism sector, gamified e-learning platforms mimic real-world scenarios in which workers can refine their problem-solving skills without any risk in a controlled environment.

Workforce Management Which Is Efficient

Digital platforms strengthen workforce management through analytics and AI. Tasks like performance tracking, employee scheduling and engagement surveys get automated — Box average managers can now refocus on strategic assignments.

With advanced analytics tools, actionable insights into workforce productivity are available to leaders for making strategic decisions. AI-enabled analytics are used by platforms such as Workday to facilitate the allocation of resources, monitor staff development, and pinpoint where focus is needed, keeping the workforce in alignment with organizational goals (Stone et al., 2015).

Examples of Successful Technology Integration in Tourism Leadership

AI-Powered Recruitment at Marriott International

For example, Marriott International has implemented an AI-powered recruitment platform to facilitate its hiring process. So, when candidates boast their experiences, the platform matches candidate profiles against what the jobs demand through machine learning algorithms and saves the time consumed by manual screening. In addition to improving the candidate experience, and hence reducing the cost of recruiting talents, Sigala (2020) suggests that this technology has also aided Marriott in attracting top talent whilst ensuring operational efficiencies.

Gamified Training Programs at Hilton Hotels

An example from this is Hilton Hotels, who capitalized on gamified e-learning platforms to boost employee training. These digital environments recreate real-world situations typical of hotel operations, where workers can acquire and enhance skills in areas such as customer service and conflict management. The initiative was not only effective in improving employee performance but also in increasing engagement and job satisfaction (Buhalis & Sinarta, 2019).

Workforce Analytics at the TUI Group

TUI Group, European tourism operator, implemented workforce analytics to enhance employee scheduling and workforce performance management. With data on employee productivity, customer feedback, and operational needs, TUI was able to build a dynamic scheduling system that flows for the best staffing. It has allowed for improved operational efficacy with increased customer satisfaction (Baum & Hai, 2020).

Leadership Development Programs: Strategies for nurturing future tourism leaders.

How We Can Develop the Next Generation of Industry Leaders

Effective leadership is crucial to ensuring the long-term success and sustainability of the tourism sector. Tourism is a fast-paced and customer-oriented field and therefore, requires leaders who have both technical as well as strategic and people skills. Some approaches have been suggested to cultivate future tourism leaders.

Leadership Development Based on Competencies

The Development of Tourism Leadership 2.0 = Confronting Concerns found in tourism leadership needs their contemporary program models. According to Day et al. competency-based approaches tailor leadership development to the unique requirements of the institution (2014). For example, programs that include simulations of real-world tourism challenges, like managing customer expectations or responding to a crisis, prepare leaders to succeed in high-pressure situations.

Integrated Leadership Frameworks

Integrated frameworks are adopted for leadership development, meaning there is a recognition of the technical, operational, and ethical dimensions of leadership. Research has demonstrated that these types of frameworks enhance effectiveness in leadership development by creating clear paths for skills development (Noe et al., 2017). This is especially important in an area like tourism, where leaders need to juggle having an efficient operation while delivering a memorable customer experience.

Teaching Across Cultures And Together With Others

The global nature of tourism means cross-cultural understanding is a vital asset for future leaders. Culturally Aware and Globally Collaborative Leadership Development Programs Lead to Inclusion (Buhalis & Sinarta, 2019) Some of these programs integrate exchange opportunities or associations with international institutions to help leaders experience varied operational contexts.

Skills for Technical and Digital Leadership

They will need to be able to use technology to improve all aspects of operations too. The widespread use of technologies — such as AI for customer engagement and big data for strategic decision-making — has led to the rise of training programs centered around digital transformation (Stone et al., 2015).

Importance of Mentorship And Experiential Learning.

Significance of Mentorship & Experiential Learning

Personalized mentorship, as well as experiential education, are two key resources that can lead to more effective leadership training in this sector in the long run, beyond the offered theoretical knowledge.

Importance of Guidance for Developing Leaders

Mentorship should be built on a formal framework for learning and development. One way effective leaders show up is by mentoring and guiding emerging leaders as they navigate the complexities of the industry and equipping them with valuable insights and best practices. As described in Albrecht et al. (2015), research shows that mentorship improves the confidence, decision-making ability and career advancement of the mentees, while also developing a culture of continuous learning in the organization. For example, mentorship programs at companies like Marriott International have played a key role in creating a more diverse talent pipeline — including underrepresented groups within the tourism workforce (Sigala, 2020).

Gaining Practical Insights through Experiential Learning

Experiential learning allows students to transition from theory and knowledge to application and practice. In the case of tourism professionals, this translates into a variety of experiential learning opportunities including on-the-job-training, internship experiences, and simulation exercises. According to Kolb's experiential learning theory, leaders who learn through experiences can develop skills such as critical thinking and problem-solving (Kolb, 2015). AccorHotels for instance, builds experiential learning into its leadership programs so trainees have to manage small-scale operations themselves thereby practicing leadership in kn controlled environment.

Shadowing and Peer Learning

Opportunity to Shadow Senior Leaders And Learning through Peers– this hands-on form of shadowing senior leaders in the organization give aspirants opportunity to observe them closely thereby learning form the different set of various leadership styles & approaches Through such activities, the participants learn how decision-making works at different levels, how teams operate, and how interpersonal relations get built.

BUILDING SUSTAINABLE AND ETHICAL PRACTICES

Role of leadership in driving sustainability and ethical tourism practices.

Leaders in the tourism business play a critical role in promoting sustainability with ethical practices. Great leaders apply the tenets of environmental, social and governance (ESG) principles to the organization and business to do what is right while creating sustainable regional tourism. This is especially true when transformational, ethical, and adaptive organizational leadership styles are utilized to operationalize these values in thought and practice.

Intermediate Concepts The Provision of Basic Instincts

Leadership plays a critical role in creating a culture of sustainability. Transformational leaders encourage employees to act in accordance with the organization's sustainability objectives, fostering waste reduction, energy efficiency and green practices (Bramwell & Lane, 2011). Another example of sustainable travel is organizations who implement green policies and practices that minimize their ecological footprint as well as attract eco-friendly travelers.

Ethical Tourism Practices

Ethical decision-making is the responsibility of leaders in the organization. This entails treating employees fairly, communicating transparently with stakeholders, and interacting ethically with local communities. Tourism organizations trust and collaborate with ethical leadership that delivers on entire legal and social responsibility (Becken, 2019). Such practices are essential for tackling problems such as overtourism, cultural appropriation and exploitation of labour within the tourism industry.

Engagement and empowerment of things in their community

Sustainable tourism leader does a community driven economic development This helps create jobs, boost local businesses, and preserve cultural traditions. Community focused governance facilitates equitable distribution of tourism benefits, further enhancing the sector's resilience and sustainable longevity (Baum & Hai, 2020).

Examples from Indian and Global Contexts

Eco-Tourism in Kerala

A state that has taken the lead in eco-tourism led by the Kerala Tourism Department, Kerala or "God's Own Country" has long been at the forefront of working towards sustainable tourism practices in the state. With the programme "Responsible Tourism" we promote eco-friendly practices, like community-based tourism, organic farming and waste management. This initiative has highlighted stakeholders working together to engage local communities, private actors and government agencies (Singh, 2019).

Taj Hotels' EARTH Initiative

IHCL has taken forward its sustainability practices across its properties under the "EARTH" initiative. The leadership also carries out efforts to reduce carbon emissions, conserve water and eliminate single-use plastics. IHCL has also started initiatives to train and hire members of local communities, though ethical practices in the tourism operations are also emphasized (Baum, 2019).

Global Context

Model for Sustainable Tourism in Costa Rica

Costa Rica is at the forefront of sustainable tourism in the world, with the government and private sectors expressing real personal leadership in environmental conservation. With policies that encourage renewable energy, biodiversity protection and eco-certifications, Costa Rica is an example of ethical tourism practices. Leadership in this context is visible in the introduction of sustainability objectives at each tier, from local efforts to federal legislation (Buhalis & Sinarta, 2019).

Marriott International's Environmental Initiatives

As part of its "Serve 360" initiative, Marriott International has made a promise to reduce its environmental footprint. The program deals with sustainable hotel operations, community empowerment, and ethical sourcing. Marriott holds these aspirations by involving employees, suppliers, and guests in all aspects of sustainability from energy conservation to the support of local artisans (Sigala, 2020).

RECOMMENDATIONS FOR STAKEHOLDERS – INDUSTRY, ACADEMICS AND POLICY MAKERS

For Industry Practitioners

Practical Steps To Address Workforce Challenges

Solving Workforce Challenges — Practical Steps

The tourism industry deals with frequent turnover, skill shortages, and various modes of employment. If not managed properly these issues can have an impact on operational efficiency and quality of services. These challenges can be addressed by industry practitioners through some practical strategies.

Syndicate This Posts Implementing Comprehensive Retention Programs

High turnover rates are detrimental to any firm; therefore, retention strategies are crucial. Organizations must create an atmosphere of participation and growth by being the facilitator of career pathways, establishing mentorship connections, and wellness initiatives. One such company was AccorHotels, which managed to lower turnover by implementing specific employee engagement programs, including employment training programs and well-being support systems (Baum, 2019).

Building up Competences via Education and Development

With continuous employee development, we can fill the skill gaps. Personalized training programs tailored to industry requirements provide employees with the skills to adapt to changing customer expectations and technological trends. For example, Marriott International has adopted strong training modules that cover both technical and soft skills, enabling employees to thrive in a competitive tourism environment (Sigala, 2020).

Opting for Technology For Improvement of Workforce

Workforce analytics and scheduling platforms are then used to allocate resources to improve productivity. Predictive analytics is another area where organizations are employing AI-driven solutions to help forecast and streamline workforce requirements. For example, Tui Group adopted workforce analytics, a data-informed decision-making approach that improved efficiencies and lowered labour costs (Buhalis & Sinarta, 2019).

Fostering Diversity and Inclusion

Developing a workplace that encourages diversity and inclusivity can increase employee morale and draw in talent from different backgrounds. This means having blind recruitment practices, equal opportunity for growth, and a culture of inclusivity. For instance, Marriott's diversity mentorship programs, which led to a 13% increase in diverse leadership representation, demonstrate the positive outcomes of such programs (Segovia-Pérez et al., 2019).

Emphasis on Continuous Leadership Development.

The importance of leadership in overcoming workforce challenges and driving organizational success cannot be understated. Ongoing development creates a group of leaders still growing and evolving to meet changing trends in the industry.

Leaders to Become Lifelong Learners

Skills including adaptability, emotional intelligence, and strategic thinking used to efficiently lead organizations should be prioritized in leadership training programs. These traits help leaders with the intricacies of the tourism industry, from putting together diverse teams to handling crises. One great example of how certain types of leadership can create a more positive environment is transformational leadership, which has been shown to create significantly higher levels of employee engagement and innovation (Wang, et al., 2011).

Creating a Leadership Pipeline

Focus on successor planning—Identifying high-potential employees and preparing them for leadership. You can help create a solid leadership pipeline through structured mentorship programs and experiential learning opportunities. For example, Hilton Worldwide has implemented programs that groom mid-level managers for executive roles to ensure leadership continuity and business resilience (Noe et al., 2017).

Technology in Leadership Development

Examples include agile talent and skill tools which can provide real-time feedback and access to courses, although - we can help you with a bespoke version of just some of them. AI-powered learning tools can evaluate a leader's skills and shortcomings and then generate personalized recommendations for self-betterment. For example, Workday's leadership development solutions leverage AI to provide insights that are actionable and improve effectiveness of leaders (Stone et al., 2015).

Infusing Ethical and Sustainable Leadership

It means training the leadership development programs to include ethics decision making and sustainability practices. What leaders need to know to optimize their organisation to be more valuable to both their customers at a time when customers increasingly care about organizations engaging in environmentally and socially responsible practices. Research indicates that ethical leaders promote trustworthiness among employees, and create alignment between corporate goals and societal directions (Bramwell & Lane, 2011).

For Academicians and Researchers

Future Research Directions In Leadership And Human Capital Management

Leadership and human capital management (HCM) are two major streams of study in the context of management sciences, in particular dynamic industries like tourism characterized by rapid technological changes, increasing diversity of workforce as well as global crises. Theoretical frameworks provide conceptual lenses through which to enhance leadership strategies and human capital.

Leadership Approaches in the Technology-Driven Environment

Integrating AI in Leadership Decision-Making

Further studies could explore the use of ai by leaders in the context of strategy and human capital. The limited research that does exist on this topic tends to focus on the various uses of AI in recruitment and effectiveness but not much on how leaders can harness AI-based insights to predict future workforce trends, boost employee engagement or enhance team dynamics (Stone et al., 2015). Researchers could also study the ethics of AI in leadership, including bias, transparency and employee trust.

Digital Transformation Thought Leadership

As more businesses are utilising digital platforms, the need for leadership is expanding to incorporate digital fluency. Research may clarify which competencies leaders need to lead successful digital transformations, especially in tourism organizations. Digital leadership and organizational culture: Research may also explore the intersection of digital leadership and organizational culture, examining how leaders balance efficiency with human-centric values (Buhalis & Sinarta, 2019).

How to Address and Combat Workforce Diversity and Inclusion

Inclusive Leadership in Multicultural Environments

The tourism sector serves a diverse clientele, hence the need of leadership that reflects and supports multiculturalism. Also, they can study how inclusive leadership affects workforce productivity, such as, employee satisfaction and organizational success. Examples of areas of focus are gender diversity, representation of under-represented groups, or inclusion of people with disabilities into leadership roles (Baum, 2019).

Strategies for Leadership in an Intergenerational Workplace

With more generations in the workforce than ever, leaders are challenged to accommodate the different needs and expectations of employees spanning multiple age groups. Future studies could explore leadership practices that engage collaboration and knowledge transmission across generational cohorts with an emphasis on developing technology as a way to bridge generational divides (Noe et al., 2017).

For Policy Makers

Policy Recommendations For Enabling Leadership Excellence In Tourism.

Sustainable tourism post-COVID-19: The importance of hive(5) leadership Strategic initiatives by policymakers to create an enabling environment and policy-driven reforms synergizing industry requirements in sync with global trends can also be the missing piece in the leadership puzzle. With this trailer in mind, here are some policy recommendations intended to help tourism leaders, organizers and tourism organizations scale their operational and talent management capabilities to world-class levels.

Implement Leadership Development Programs

To address the unique challenges of the tourism sector, policymakers must create conducive environment for specialized leadership development interventions. These programs could include developing skills in strategic thinking, digital transformation, and crisis management for leaders. Public–private partnerships (PPPs) can ensure access to high-quality training resources and a shared platform for exchanging what is learned (Baum, 2019). Examples like the SkillsFuture program introduced by Singapore Tourism Board as a government-backed initiative, have effectively led to upskilling tourism leaders and workforce while fostering an ethos of continuous learning and adaptability (Sigala, 2020).

Incentivize Leadership Digital Transformation

Policymakers can also incentivize technology adoption, with tools ranging from tax benefits to grants or subsidies for organizations investing in AI and analytics tools for leadership and upskilling the workforce. Policies should also promote the development of digital literacy programs to prepare leaders for technology-driven decision-making. In this context, one of the examples is the Digital Tourism initiative, which serves as an initiative of the European Union to endorse small and medium-sized enterprises (SMEs) to transform their traditional activities to include digital tools that can improve their competitiveness in the global marketplace (Buhalis & Sinarta, 2019).

Encouraging Diversity and Inclusion in Leadership

Tourism ethical policy should dictate the need for diversity in leadership positions that should represent the nature of the industry, which has a global and multicultural scope. Examples of this can be seen in targeted initiatives, such as quotas to cover women and underrepresented groups in leadership roles and funding for mentorship schemes, that focus on diversifying (Segovia-Pérez et al., 2019).. For instance, implementing a global diversity program, as practiced in Marriott International, can strengthen diversity at the leadership level by ensuring more diverse decision-making, ultimately making the decision-making process in teams more representative and innovative (Baum & Hai, 2020).

Adopt the Frameworks of Crisis Leadership

Policy makers should make it a requirement that industry develop crisis leadership frameworks that improves resilience. These structures should encompass protocols for pre-crisis preparation, employee wellness programs, and recovery plans. It can be institutionalized, with regular crisis simulation exercises that prepare leaders for unanticipated disruptions. One notable initiative here is the UNWTO's Global Tourism Crisis Committee, an effort to develop common plans to address global crises such as pandemics and climate-related disasters (Sigala, 2020).

Policymakers should reward leaders for integrating sustainability principles into their operating strategies. They help support sustainable tourism practices by offering incentives for green certifications and recognizing leaders in sustainability among organizations. Policies such as the Eco-Tourism Policy of India highlight the importance of responsible tourism practices that are integrated with environmental conservation and community development priorities (Bramwell & Lane, 2011).

Encourage Cooperation Across Multiple Sectors

Policymakers must also facilitate collaboration among academia, government, and private industry to leverage synergies for leadership excellence. This will cause difficulties and can lead to broad solutions in workforce shortages or technology implementations by working together. The example of programs such as Australia's Tourism Employment Plan Initiative showcases the success of collaborations between multiple stakeholders to tackle workforce and leadership challenges (Buhalis & Sinarta, 2019)

Make Leadership Metrics and Recognitions Part of the Normal Process

To leverage this potential, policymakers can set benchmarks and KPIs to évaluate and reward effective tourism leadership. Annual awards or certifications can serve as a carrot for leaders and organizations in the pursuit of continuous improvement. At the same time, the World Travel & Tourism Council (WTTC) have also been awarding winners annually the Tourism for Tomorrow Awards that showcase leadership excellence in sustainability and innovation, inspiring others to take best practices (WTTC, 2021).

SUMMARY OF KEY INSIGHTS

Reinforcement of leadership's role in sustainable human capital management.

Key Takeaways: Emphasizing Leadership Responsibility of Sustainable Human Capital Management

The tourism industry is a vibrant sector with a huge economic potential and an important contribution to GDP, employment creation, and foreign currency earnings. It is leadership that drives this potential towards success through aligning human capital strategies with sustainable and competitive business practices.

Leadership in Human Capital Development: A Strategic Imperative

Leadership is stipulate to be a primary driver of the tourism human asset development and maintenance. They have argued that transformational and adaptive leadership styles are more effective, particularly in inspiring innovation, establishing a culture of continuous learning, and aligning employee skills with organizational needs. It is arguably most important in an industry driven by service quality and customer satisfaction (Wang et al., 2011; Noe et al., 2017) that leaders create an atmosphere within which employees can flourish in an ever-evolving and competitive market place.

The Intersection of Technology and Ethical Leadership

53Emerging tools like AI, analytics, and digital platforms are transforming the recruitment, training, and management of the workforce in the tourism ecosystem. Leaders need to ensure the ethical adoption of these technologies, but transparency, trust, and equitable use must remain at the forefront of this process (Stone et al., 2015; Chakraborty, 2025). Moreover, elements like corporate social responsibility and sustainability are paramount ethical issues that seep into how companies are perceived by consumers and stakeholders alike.

Sustainability and Resilience

Sustainability is at the very heart of modern-day tourism leadership. Be rooted in the environmental and social goals of the organization as a whole, promoting energy and material resource efficiency, waste reduction, and community engagement throughout its human capital strategies — from recruitment to retention strategies to reward mechanisms to employee communications. At the same time, crises such as the COVID-19 pandemic highlight the need for resilient leadership. Creating crisis management frameworks and fostering employee well-being during and beyond emergencies is crucial to sustaining morale and operations and ensuring business longevity (Sigala, 2020; Baum & Hai, 2020).

Workforce Issues and Opportunities

These perennial issues of high employee turnover and skills shortages are highly relevant for the tourism industry. These challenges can be addressed with effective leadership through retention strategies, increasing diversity and inclusion, and providing the career development opportunities employees seek. For example mentorship programs and learning modules specific to industry (Baum, 2019; Segovia-Pérez et al., 2019) have proven effective in addressing attrition and improving work stability.

Co-Creative and Inclusive Leadership

These challenges are complex, and the tourism industry leaders must play a role as facilitators of collaboration among academia, the government, and the private sector. This collaborative teamwork not only fosters creativity and innovation, but a no- one-size-fits-all strategy that reflects that each employee and consumer demographic is different and that leadership practices that are inclusive.

Conclusion

These insights highlight that leadership in tourism needs to be dynamic, ethical and inclusive for sustainable human capital management. Transitioning to transformational and adaptive leadership, responsibly implementing technology, and nurturing a sustainability-focused and innovative culture will help tourism leaders guarantee the industry's resilience and sustainable development moving forward. By re-affirming these principles of leadership, the tourism industry can be well placed to address future challenges but also continue to play a key role in economy and community development.

VISION FOR THE FUTURE

Vision for the Future: Strategic Pathways for Fostering Leadership Excellence in Indian Tourism The tourism industry in India plays an integral role in driving economic growth and contributes prominently to GDP, employment, and cultural sustainability. However, the fluid and rapidly evolving nature of this sector, characterized by changing consumer demands, technological disruptions, and global trends, requires strategic pathways for fostering leadership excellence. Indeed, a visionary approach to leadership is critical to building resilience, stimulating innovation, and ensuring sustainable growth. Strengthening Leadership Development Frameworks Competency-Based Leadership Programs. Develop leadership programs targeted at critical and emerging competencies such as strategic thinking, digital fluency, and crisis management. Additionally, design programs that meet the unique needs of tourist sector leaders with issues including high staff turnover, diversity management, and customer engagement and quality. Partnering with institutions including the Indian Institute of Tourism and Travel Management (IITTM) can support such programs. Experiential Learning and Mentorship. Offer learning experiences through internships and simulations, supported by a structured mentorship program to prepare future leaders for the malaise of the job market. Leading industry players such as Taj Hotels and Oberoi Group can serve as mentors to foster a culture of sharing and learning. Cross-Cultural and Global Leadership. Including training on cross-continental communication dynamics and attracting global tourist traffic. Establish collaborations with recognized international organizations and universities to improve learning and experience. Leveraging Technology for Leadership Excellence Digital Leadership Development Platforms. Utilize artificial-intelligence-based platforms to provide personalized leadership training. These platforms offer continuous real-time feedback, track progress, and recommend learning pathways for leaders based on needs and performance. Data-Driven Decision Making. Encourage leaders to use big data analytics platforms for making decisions. Platforms such as Tableau and Power BI can help leaders analyse behavioural trends, forecast market dynamics, and optimize resource allocations.

Use of Technology in Staff Management

For example, train leaders in recruiting, training, and performance monitoring using technology, such as AI and automation. Reducing resource commitment In its best manifestation, for instance, Workday and SAP SuccessFactors ensures that HR processes become streamlined, enabling leaders to focus on strategic action rather than operational execution.

Incorporating Sustainability Through Leadership Practices

Sustainable Tourism Policies

In order to chunk these numbers and to get a sense of how they translate in terms of action, the focus of leadership should be on driving sustainable tourism practices, be that local communities, eco-tourism, carbon foot prints or just action. Examples such as Kerala's Responsible Tourism Mission can be a guide.

Paraphrased Version Energy Transition ESG Integration

Empower leaders to align corporate objectives with ESG Values. These can include sustainable resource management, ethical labour practices, and transparent governance.

Incentives Recognition on Social Media

Award and certify leaders who show exceptional commitment to sustainability. Initiatives like the Earth Check Certification can encourage leaders to operate greener.

Promoting Resilience and Emergency Preparedness

Crisis Leadership Frameworks

Build structured paths for anticipatory crisis engagement, putting workforce stability front and centre, along with business continuity. For instance, among many things, leaders ought to be trained in scenario planning and recovery strategies.

Mental Health and Well-Being

Ensure you have training about how to deal with employee mental health and maintaining a supportive work environment, especially during crises. Wellness programs and counselling services are examples of initiatives that can cultivate resilience in the workforce.

Learning from Past Crises

Use case studies from the COVID-19 pandemic to teach leaders how to navigate uncertainty as they head into recovery, as well as how to rebuild trust with consumers and keep their operations sustainable.

Developing People with Diversity and Inclusion in Leadership

Inclusive Hiring Practices

Policies have to be design, so that diverse representatives are included in leadership roles, whether they are women, minorities, or differently- abled. For example, blind recruitment techniques can help reduce unconscious bias.

Dealing with Diversity in Multicultural Groups

Train leaders to effectively leverage diversity to build inclusion across teams. Leadership programs can include modules on cultural sensitivity and equity.

PPP (Public–Private Partnership)

Encourage partnerships between governmental organizations, private sector, and academic institutions to co-design and implement leadership initiatives. Such as the recent IITTM and FICCI (Federation of Indian Chambers of Commerce and Industry) partnerships.

Cross Sector Education Sharing

Hold forums and workshops to share best practices across industries This can include lessons learned on technology adoption, crisis management, and sustainable practices, to name a few.

Global Collaborations

Trent with other travel-related bodies of other nations to incorporate best practices and new models of leadership.

Identifying Leadership Metrics and Recognition

Testing Your Metal Performance Benchmarks for Leaders

Formulate key performance indicators (KPIs) that measure exemplary leadership in innovation, employee engagement and sustainability.

Annual excellence awards for leadership

Honor outstanding leadership with tourism sector awards. These could be along the lines of awards for innovation, sustainability, and crisis management.

Transparent Assessment Mechanisms

Implement a fair and transparent leadership performance evaluation with the help of technology to improve accountability and motivation in the workplace.

Together Policies that Support Leadership Development

The National Leadership Development Agenda

Make sure government funding and support initiatives, part of the National Tourism Policy for Leadership Development.

Reimbursement for Leadership Training

Provide tax incentives and grants to corporations for investing in human leader-based capacity programs in least developed areas.

Bringing to Mind Sustainable Tourism Frameworks

More broadly, require leadership training and organizational strategies to include sustainable practices and align with environmental objectives at the national and global levels.

Conclusion

Developing Leadership Excellence in Tourism in India – This need a well thought Strategic Approach As a result, the sector will be able to navigate challenges and maximize opportunities well through enhanced leadership development frameworks, utilizing technology, embedding sustainability strategies, advancing inclusivity, and encouraging resilience. A combination of multi-stakeholder collaboration and government support will enable entrepreneur leaders of the future who can help the tourism industry innovate and transition to a new sustainable and resilient model – paving the way for India to achieve its goal of becoming a global leader in the tourism sector.

REFERENCES

Albrecht, S. L., Bakker, A. B., Gruman, J. A., Macey, W. H., & Saks, A. M. (2015). Employee engagement, human resource management practices, and competitive advantage: An integrated approach. *Journal of Organizational Effectiveness: People and Performance, 2*(1), 7–35. DOI: 10.1108/JOEPP-08-2014-0042

Barney, J. (1991). Firm resources and sustained competitive advantage. *Journal of Management, 17*(1), 99–120. DOI: 10.1177/014920639101700108

Baum, T. (2019). Hospitality employment 2033: A backcasting perspective. *International Journal of Hospitality Management, 76*, 45–52. DOI: 10.1016/j.ijhm.2018.06.027

Baum, T., & Hai, N. T. T. (2020). Hospitality, tourism, human resource management and the impact of COVID-19. *International Journal of Contemporary Hospitality Management, 32*(8), 2397–2415. DOI: 10.1108/IJCHM-03-2020-0242

Becken, S. (2019). Decarbonising tourism: Mission impossible? *Tourism Recreation Research, 44*(4), 419–433. DOI: 10.1080/02508281.2019.1598042

Becker, G. S. (1994). *Human capital: A theoretical and empirical analysis, with special reference to education* (3rd ed.). University of Chicago Press.

Bramwell, B., & Lane, B. (2011). Critical research on the governance of tourism and sustainability. *Journal of Sustainable Tourism, 19*(4–5), 411–421. DOI: 10.1080/09669582.2011.580586

Buhalis, D., & Sinarta, Y. (2019). Real-time co-creation and nowness service: Lessons from tourism and hospitality. *Journal of Travel & Tourism Marketing, 36*(5), 563–582. DOI: 10.1080/10548408.2019.1592059

Chakraborty, P. P. (2024). *The role of technology in enhancing sustainable tourism practices*. IGI Global Scientific Publishing., DOI: 10.4018/979-8-3693-5903-7.ch011

Eisenberger, R., Malone, G. P., & Presson, W. D. (2020). *Optimizing perceived organizational support to enhance employee engagement*. Society for Human Resource Management and Society for Industrial and Organizational Psychology.

Greenleaf, R. K. (1977). *Servant leadership: A journey into the nature of legitimate power and greatness*. Paulist Press.

Hjalager, A. M. (2010). A review of innovation research in tourism. *Tourism Management, 31*(1), 1–12. DOI: 10.1016/j.tourman.2009.08.012

Janta, H., Brown, L., Lugosi, P., & Ladkin, A. (2011). Migrant networks, learning and tourism employment. *Annals of Tourism Research, 38*(4), 1322–1343. DOI: 10.1016/j.annals.2011.03.004

Marriott International. (2022). Diversity and inclusion report: Elevating leaders from underrepresented groups. Retrieved from https://marriott.com/diversity

Ministry of Tourism. (2020). *India tourism statistics at a glance 2020*. Government of India.

Noe, R. A., Clarke, A. D. M., & Klein, H. J. (2017). Learning in the twenty-first-century workplace. *Annual Review of Organizational Psychology and Organizational Behavior, 4*, 245–275. DOI: 10.1146/annurev-orgpsych-032516-113326

Segovia-Pérez, M., Figueroa-Domecq, C., Fuentes-Moraleda, L., & Muñoz-Mazón, A. (2019). Incorporating a gender approach in the hospitality industry: Female executives' perceptions. *International Journal of Hospitality Management, 76*, 184–193. DOI: 10.1016/j.ijhm.2018.05.008

Sigala, M. (2020). Tourism and COVID-19: Impacts and implications for advancing and resetting industry and research. *Journal of Business Research, 117*, 312–321. DOI: 10.1016/j.jbusres.2020.06.015 PMID: 32546875

Singh, S. (2019). Tourism in India: Potential, problems, and prospects. *Journal of Tourism and Hospitality Management, 7*(1), 1–14.

Stone, D. L., Deadrick, D. L., Lukaszewski, K. M., & Johnson, K. M. (2015). The influence of technology on the future of human resource management. *Human Resource Management Review, 25*(2), 216–231. DOI: 10.1016/j.hrmr.2015.01.002

Wang, H., Oh, I. S., Courtright, S. H., & Colbert, A. E. (2011). Transformational leadership and performance across criteria and levels: A meta-analytic review of 25 years of research. *Group & Organization Management, 36*(2), 223–270. DOI: 10.1177/1059601111401017

World Travel & Tourism Council. (2018). *Travel & tourism economic impact 2018 India*. WTTC.

WTTC. (2021). *Gender representation in tourism leadership: Insights for advancing diversity*. Retrieved from https://wttc.org

WTTC. (2021). *Tourism for Tomorrow Awards*. Retrieved from https://wttc.org

Chapter 4
Leadership in the Tourism Sector: Strategies for Sustainable Growth and Innovation

Raed Awashreh
https://orcid.org/0000-0002-2252-0299
A'Sharqiyah University, Oman

ABSTRACT

This study explores the critical role of leadership in shaping sustainable growth and innovation within the tourism sector. It identifies key challenges such as skills gaps, resistance to change, and cultural barriers, proposing a tailored leadership framework that integrates human capital management, training, and lifelong learning. The research highlights the importance of fostering sustainability, adaptability, and workforce agility to align with emerging trends and global demands. By offering actionable recommendations for policymakers and industry stakeholders, the study aims to enhance leadership effectiveness, promote responsible tourism practices, and ensure long-term success and competitiveness in a rapidly evolving global landscape.

INTRODUCTION

The tourism sector represents a dynamic and transformative force, offering unparalleled opportunities for individuals and nations alike. Beyond its role in providing entertainment and cultural enrichment, tourism encompasses a vibrant tapestry of landmarks, religious sites, breathtaking landscapes, diverse markets, world-class restaurants, and immersive travel experiences. This sector has become a cornerstone of national economies worldwide, generating substantial revenues,

DOI: 10.4018/979-8-3373-0071-9.ch004

showcasing cultural diversity, and exemplifying renowned hospitality. However, as the industry evolves in response to global trends and shifting traveler expectations, the need for effective leadership has never been more critical (Stolz, 2024).

Leaders in the tourism sector face multifaceted challenges, ranging from bridging skills gaps and overcoming resistance to change to navigating cultural and regulatory complexities. Addressing these challenges is essential for elevating service quality, fostering innovation, and advancing sustainable practices (Mouazen et al., 2024). Despite its immense potential, the sector continues to grapple with a significant leadership gap, which impedes its ability to maximize opportunities, sustain competitiveness, and align with global sustainability goals (Onifade et al., 2024).

This chapter aims to address this pressing issue by exploring and proposing a comprehensive leadership framework tailored to the tourism industry's unique needs. By doing so, it seeks to unlock the sector's potential for sustainable growth, innovation, and workforce agility. This chapter is guided by the following objectives:

1. **Examine Leadership Challenges**: Identify the leadership challenges confronting the tourism industry, including skills shortages, resistance to change, and cultural and organizational barriers.
2. **Develop a Leadership Framework**: Design a tailored leadership framework for the tourism sector, integrating best practices in human capital management, training, and development.
3. **Foster Sustainability and Innovation**: Investigate how effective leadership can drive sustainability, innovation, and agility within the tourism workforce to meet emerging trends and demands.
4. **Provide Practical Recommendations**: Present actionable strategies for policymakers and industry stakeholders to enhance leadership effectiveness and promote responsible growth within the sector.

The central chapter Question focal around: How can a comprehensive leadership framework be developed to address the challenges in the tourism sector and promote sustainable growth, innovation, and workforce agility?

This chapter introduces a comprehensive framework for effective leadership in the tourism sector. The framework emphasizes the integration of best practices in human capital management with a strong focus on training, development, and lifelong learning. Leveraging technology and fostering collaboration between public and private sectors are essential components of this approach, enabling leaders to cultivate an agile and skilled workforce equipped to adapt to emerging trends and demands.

A key pillar of this framework is prioritizing human capital management to build a resilient workforce that balances economic growth with sustainability (Prayag, Muskat, & Dassanayake, 2024). Strong leadership is instrumental in promoting sustainable tourism practices that align economic goals with environmental conservation and cultural preservation. Leaders must articulate a clear vision, inspire stakeholders to embrace sustainability, and foster a culture of innovation and adaptability across the workforce. By focusing on leadership development and nurturing a culture of continuous learning, the tourism sector can empower employees to remain ahead of industry trends and technological advancements. This, in turn, enhances the industry's global competitiveness while supporting long-term sustainability (Afridi et al., 2023).

This chapter underscores the critical role of leadership in shaping the future of the tourism sector. By addressing leadership challenges and opportunities, it provides strategies for cultivating resilient and agile leaders capable of driving sustainable growth. Through actionable recommendations, this research equips policymakers and industry stakeholders with the tools to enhance leadership effectiveness, foster innovation, and promote responsible growth, ensuring the tourism sector's enduring success and relevance in a rapidly evolving global landscape. It structured as follows: it begins with a literature review on leadership and its roles in the tourism sector, examining key concepts such as transformational leadership. This is followed by the methodology, and then the proposed framework for effective leadership. Next, the chapter focuses on challenges and opportunities in the tourism sector using case studies. It then presents the expected outcomes, alongside theoretical implications. The chapter concludes with a discussion on societal, individual, and institutional implications, and offers suggestions for further research.

LITERATURE REVIEW

The literature review explores leadership's role in enhancing efficiency, workforce engagement, and sustainability in tourism. It examines transformational, servant, and digital leadership, focusing on innovation and growth. The review highlights global best practices for fostering sustainability, community empowerment, and workforce development, with an emphasis on adapting leadership to industry challenges.

Role of Leadership

The role of leadership in the tourism sector has been a focal point of research, particularly in enhancing operational efficiency, workforce engagement, and sustainability. Leadership plays a pivotal role in driving innovation, adaptability, and service excellence, especially in dynamic and competitive environments (Awashreh & Mohamed, 2024). This section examines how various leadership models and theories contribute to overcoming industry challenges and achieving sustainable growth.

Transformational leadership is particularly emphasized for its ability to inspire teams, foster creativity, and adapt to changing market demands. Leaders adopting this style encourage innovation and prioritize organizational goals, enhancing employee satisfaction and service quality (Gumusluoglu & Ilsev, 2009). Recent studies indicate that transformational leadership also plays a crucial role in promoting sustainable tourism initiatives, particularly by integrating environmental responsibility into organizational strategies (Jun & Lee, 2023). Similarly, servant leadership has proven essential in the tourism industry, where service quality and stakeholder satisfaction are paramount. By focusing on the well-being of employees and fostering a collaborative environment, servant leaders create a culture of trust and loyalty, resulting in higher employee engagement and customer satisfaction (Bavik, 2020).

While these leadership styles are widely discussed, there is limited empirical evidence on their direct impact on tourism business performance and sustainability outcomes. Future research should explore how transformational and servant leadership influence key performance indicators such as revenue growth, employee retention, and customer loyalty in tourism enterprises (Holston-Okae, 2018).

In addition to leadership styles, the development and management of human capital are critical to addressing skill shortages and embracing technological advancements. Digital leadership and AI-driven management have emerged as essential elements of workforce development, enabling leaders to leverage data analytics, automation, and personalized customer experiences to remain competitive in the evolving tourism landscape (Pawar, S., & Dhumal, 2024). Training and leadership development programs empower employees with the skills needed to thrive in a rapidly evolving industry, contributing to sustainable tourism practices and improved organizational performance (Awashreh & Sayyad, 2023).

Sustainability is a core theme in tourism leadership. Leaders must balance economic growth with environmental and cultural preservation to meet the growing demand for responsible travel. Sustainability-focused leadership emphasizes eco-friendly practices, community engagement, and long-term value creation. Distributed leadership, which empowers employees across organizational levels, aligns well with this goal by encouraging innovation and accountability, particularly in frontline operations (Zada et al., 2025). However, sustainability efforts often remain at the conceptual level without clear implementation strategies. Empirical studies on the effectiveness of sustainability leadership frameworks in tourism businesses are needed to bridge this gap.

Furthermore, leadership theories such as situational, authentic, transactional, and democratic leadership offer diverse perspectives on addressing the unique challenges of the tourism sector. Situational leadership, for instance, underscores the importance of flexibility and adaptability in navigating peak seasons, crises, or technological disruptions (Awashreh & Hamid, 2025). Crisis leadership has become particularly relevant post-pandemic, as tourism businesses must develop resilience strategies to recover from external shocks such as economic downturns, natural disasters, and geopolitical conflicts. Authentic leadership, rooted in transparency and ethical behavior, fosters trust and loyalty, essential for building lasting customer relationships (McCleskey, 2014).

Finally, comparative studies highlight the need for strategic collaboration and cross-cultural learning in tourism leadership. A growing body of research emphasizes the role of leadership in fostering community-based tourism, where local stakeholders actively participate in decision-making to ensure equitable benefits (Krittayaruangroj, Suriyankietkaew & Hallinger, 2023). Global best practices, such as public-private partnerships and workforce development programs, provide valuable insights for creating a resilient and sustainable tourism industry. However, the over-reliance on case studies from high-profile destinations such as Costa Rica and New Zealand limits the global applicability of these findings. Expanding the scope to include underrepresented regions such as Africa, Southeast Asia, and South America would provide a more comprehensive understanding of leadership dynamics in diverse tourism contexts (Graci, 2012).

Global Best Practices in Leadership and Tourism Development

In the global tourism sector, several best practices have emerged as critical in enhancing leadership effectiveness, workforce development, and sustainable tourism initiatives. These practices, drawn from diverse international experiences, provide valuable insights into overcoming challenges and maximizing the potential of tourism destinations. As tourism continues to evolve, it is essential for destinations to focus on sustainability, community empowerment, and innovation to stay competitive and responsive to market demands (Khizar et al., 2023).

For example, leading tourism destinations like Costa Rica and New Zealand have demonstrated the importance of sustainability as a foundational pillar of their tourism strategies. By integrating environmental conservation into policy frameworks, these countries have fostered eco-friendly practices among businesses and communities. Such approaches include implementing eco-certifications for hotels and tour operators to incentivize sustainable tourism practices (Dangi & Jamal, 2016). In this regard, other destinations can adopt similar strategies by focusing on environmental stewardship, showcasing their natural beauty, and preserving cultural heritage to attract environmentally conscious travelers. However, further research is needed to assess the long-term impacts of these eco-certification schemes on local economies and their actual effectiveness in reducing carbon footprints. These efforts can enhance a destination's reputation and align with long-term sustainability goals (Baena & Cerviño, 2024).

Furthermore, the success of community-based tourism in regions like Bhutan underscores the value of engaging local residents in decision-making processes. This approach ensures that local communities benefit economically while preserving their culture and environment. Recent studies have highlighted the need for more robust evaluation metrics to assess the economic and social impacts of community-based tourism, particularly in remote or underdeveloped regions (Jackson, 2025). As such, other tourism destinations can replicate these practices by fostering collaboration with local stakeholders, promoting cultural traditions, crafts, and culinary experiences, and ensuring that tourism activities generate shared benefits. This not only enriches visitor experiences but also strengthens the cultural identity and economic resilience of communities, creating a more inclusive and sustainable tourism model (Wanie, Ahmad & Sha, 2022).

In parallel, countries like Singapore and Germany have recognized the critical role of workforce training and development in delivering exceptional service. These nations have invested in building a skilled workforce that can adapt to the evolving demands of the tourism sector. The effectiveness of these training programs in addressing labor shortages and improving service delivery needs further empirical validation, particularly in the context of high-demand tourist seasons (Clemens, 2015). Tourism destinations looking to enhance service quality can benefit from establishing comprehensive training programs that focus on hospitality, cultural sensitivity, and technological adaptation. Collaborations with educational institutions to develop tailored programs will ensure employees are well-equipped to meet the challenges of an ever-changing tourism landscape, ultimately improving organizational performance and sustainability (Baporikar et al., 2011).

As technology continues to shape the tourism sector, destinations such as Japan and South Korea have successfully leveraged digital tools and smart tourism initiatives to enhance visitor experiences and operational efficiency. These countries have integrated real-time mobile applications and innovative technologies to engage visitors more effectively. To remain competitive, destinations must not only implement smart tourism solutions but also address privacy and data security concerns that may arise with the use of these technologies (Topsakal, Icoz & Icoz, 2022). Other tourism destinations can follow suit by investing in digital marketing strategies, developing apps for navigation and personalized recommendations, and creating immersive experiences that incorporate emerging technologies. This technological integration not only attracts a tech-savvy audience but also enriches the overall tourist experience (Leong, Leong & Leong, 2024). In addition, countries like Australia and Canada have demonstrated the importance of robust leadership development programs within their tourism sectors. These initiatives aim to equip leaders with the skills and capacity to drive change, foster innovation, and build resilience in their organizations. To cultivate effective leadership, tourism destinations can implement mentorship programs, collaborative projects, and workshops that empower emerging leaders to adopt global best practices. These efforts promote continuous improvement and adaptability, ensuring long-term growth and success in the sector (Hussein et al., 2024).

Equally important, Italy and Spain highlight the significance of cultural heritage and authenticity as key differentiators in the competitive tourism market. These countries focus on curating cultural festivals, heritage trails, and immersive experiences that showcase local history and traditions (Galli, 2024). However, ensuring the authenticity of these experiences is increasingly challenging due to the pressures of mass tourism. Future research should investigate how tourism can maintain cultural integrity while accommodating large volumes of visitors. Destinations can replicate these strategies to create unique offerings that deepen the connection between tourists and communities. By emphasizing authenticity, destinations not only attract visitors but also foster meaningful engagement that enhances the overall visitor experience and ensures long-term sustainability (Eck, Zhang & An, 2023).

Lastly, successful tourism destinations, like Iceland, emphasize the importance of collaboration among diverse stakeholders, including governments, private businesses, and local communities. Through partnerships, Iceland has been able to develop sustainable tourism initiatives that balance environmental preservation with economic growth. However, the success of these partnerships often relies on strong regulatory frameworks and political will, which can be difficult to achieve in certain regions (Helgadóttir et al., 2019). Other destinations can adopt similar collaborative frameworks by encouraging dialogue among stakeholders, addressing shared challenges, and leveraging collective resources to create innovative and sustainable solutions. This collaborative approach will help destinations tackle complex issues while building resilience and ensuring sustainability (Shahirah et al., 2020).

By adapting these global best practices to their unique contexts, tourism destinations can strengthen their leadership capabilities, enhance workforce skills, and implement sustainable practices that align with cultural values and respect for natural resources. These strategies not only improve the overall visitor experience but also ensure that tourism contributes positively to local communities, drives economic growth, and preserves the environment for future generations (Bindawas, 2025).

METHODOLOGY

The research will employ qualitative methods to gain a deeper understanding of effective leadership practices in the tourism sector, relying heavily on secondary data and thorough secondary data analysis. By utilizing existing literature, reports, and case studies, the study aims to uncover key themes and insights related to leadership dynamics within tourism organizations (Ruggiano & Perry, 2023). This approach allows for a comprehensive examination of both established practices and emerging trends, offering a nuanced understanding of how leadership influences various aspects of the tourism experience. Recent research indicates that effective leadership can lead to long-term success in tourism organizations, particularly through strategic decision-making and fostering a culture of innovation (Müller et al., 2022). The analysis will focus on identifying patterns and correlations that highlight the characteristics of successful leaders and their impact on workforce performance, customer satisfaction, and organizational sustainability. Through this process, the research will aim to fill gaps in the existing knowledge base and propose targeted strategies for enhancing leadership capabilities within the tourism sector (Tromp et al., 2021).

In addition to secondary data analysis, the research will incorporate case studies and real-world examples to illustrate effective leadership practices in diverse tourism contexts. By examining specific instances where leadership has led to significant improvements in operational efficiency, employee engagement, and sustainability, the study will offer practical insights that can be adapted to various tourism environments. For instance, recent case studies have shown that adaptive leadership in response to global challenges, such as the COVID-19 pandemic, has enabled tourism destinations to recover quickly and innovate their service models (Lee & Kim, 2023). These case studies will draw from both local and international examples, highlighting a wide range of leadership styles and strategies that have effectively addressed common challenges in the tourism industry. This multifaceted approach will not only enrich the research findings but also provide actionable recommendations for leaders in the sector, stressing the importance of adaptability, collaboration, and innovation in fostering a resilient and successful tourism industry (Al Dhaheri, 2024). Furthermore, by incorporating emerging leadership models, such as those focused on digital transformation, the research aims to provide a forward-looking perspective on the future of leadership in the tourism sector (Zhao et al., 2024). Ultimately, the integration of qualitative methods with real-world insights will provide a robust framework for understanding the critical role of leadership in driving excellence within the tourism sector (Piwowar-Sulej & Iqbal, 2023).

In developing this chapter, a strategic balance was maintained between recent studies and foundational research. A total of 70 references were used, with 54 cited from 2020 and beyond, reflecting the latest trends, challenges, and innovations in the tourism sector. These recent sources provide valuable insights into leadership models, sustainability practices, and the evolving needs of the industry in a rapidly changing global context. The remaining 16 references, drawn from 2019 and earlier, offer foundational theories and classic models that continue to shape the understanding of leadership in tourism. This combination ensures that the chapter remains both current and rooted in established academic frameworks.

PROPOSED FRAMEWORK

The proposed framework for analyzing leadership challenges and opportunities in the tourism sector will adopt a systematic approach aimed at improving leadership effectiveness. The first step will involve identifying key leadership challenges, such as workforce skill gaps, resistance to change, and external factors like economic fluctuations and environmental concerns (Awashreh & Hamid, 2024). Through qualitative methods, including interviews and focus groups with industry stakeholders, the framework will gather valuable insights into the challenges faced by leaders. Additionally, a review of relevant literature and case studies will help contextualize these challenges within the broader global tourism landscape (Al Harrasi et al., 2024). Martin et al (2023) highlighted the significant role that external factors, such as climate change and geopolitical instability, play in shaping leadership challenges in tourism.

Once challenges are identified, the framework will assess current leadership practices by evaluating leadership styles, organizational structures, and decision-making processes within the tourism sector. By analyzing secondary data and case studies, the framework will assess how different leadership approaches impact workforce engagement, operational efficiency, and sustainability efforts (Al Maghribi, Awashreh & Al Naqbi, 2023). This evaluation will highlight areas where current practices align with industry best practices and pinpoint gaps that offer opportunities for improvement (Khairy, Baquero & Al-Romeedy, 2023). Further research has shown that adaptive leadership, which emphasizes flexibility in decision-making and responsiveness to external pressures, has been particularly effective in addressing current leadership gaps (Fayolle et al., 2022).

Following this, the framework will explore opportunities to enhance leadership effectiveness by focusing on trends such as technological advancements and shifting consumer preferences. By examining these trends, the framework will provide insights into how leaders can adapt their strategies to better align with the evolving tourism landscape. It will also investigate potential leadership development avenues, such as training programs, mentorship, and collaboration between public and private sectors, offering strategies to strengthen leadership capabilities (Kremer, Villamor & Aguinis, 2018). The growing importance of digital transformation in tourism leadership cannot be overstated, with technology offering solutions to enhance decision-making, improve customer experiences, and drive sustainability (Leung et al., 2023).

Building on the insights from challenges and current practices, the framework will provide actionable recommendations to enhance leadership in the tourism sector. These recommendations, based on successful global case studies, will be tailored to the specific context of the tourism industry. Suggested strategies may include fostering a culture of continuous learning, investing in technology-driven solutions, and encouraging greater community involvement in tourism initiatives (Dimanche & Andrades, 2024). The primary goal will be to equip leaders with practical tools and strategies to drive sustainable tourism and improve organizational performance. Global examples of destination resilience, such as the recovery strategies implemented in Greece and Iceland post-crisis, provide valuable lessons for creating robust and adaptable leadership frameworks (Peterson & Andrews, 2023). Finally, the framework will emphasize the importance of continuous evaluation and adaptation of leadership practices. By establishing metrics to measure the effectiveness of implemented strategies, leaders can assess their impact and make necessary adjustments. This iterative process will ensure that leadership in the tourism sector remains responsive to changing dynamics, fostering resilience and long-term sustainability (Kremer, Villamor & Aguinis, 2018). Recent studies emphasize the value of regular performance reviews and real-time data analysis to continuously improve leadership practices (Li & Zhang, 2024). By integrating these components, the framework will offer a structured approach to analyzing leadership challenges and opportunities, contributing to the sustainable development of tourism. Below is simple table (1) summarizing the proposed framework for analyzing leadership challenges and opportunities in the tourism sector

Table 1. Proposed framework for analyzing leadership

Step	Description	Methods/Approach	References
1. Identify Leadership Challenges	Identify key challenges such as workforce skill gaps, resistance to change, and external factors (economic fluctuations, environmental concerns).	Qualitative methods: Interviews, focus groups with industry stakeholders; literature review and case studies.	Awashreh & Hamid, 2024; Al Harrasi et al., 2024
2. Assess Current Leadership Practices	Evaluate leadership styles, organizational structures, and decision-making processes. Assess impact on workforce engagement, operational efficiency, and sustainability.	Secondary data and case studies analysis to evaluate leadership effectiveness and identify gaps for improvement.	Khairy, Baquero & Al-Romeedy, 2023
3. Explore Opportunities for Enhancement	Identify trends such as technological advancements and shifting consumer preferences. Examine leadership development strategies (e.g., training programs, mentorship, public-private collaboration).	Analysis of emerging trends and leadership development avenues; provide strategies for adapting to tourism landscape changes.	Kremer, Villamor & Aguinis, 2018
4. Provide Actionable Recommendations	Offer recommendations to enhance leadership, tailored to the tourism sector context. Suggest strategies such as continuous learning, technology investment, and community involvement.	Drawing on global case studies to develop specific strategies for improving leadership effectiveness in the tourism sector.	—
5. Continuous Evaluation & Adaptation	Emphasize the importance of continuous evaluation and adapting leadership practices. Measure effectiveness of implemented strategies and make necessary adjustments.	Develop metrics to track effectiveness and facilitate ongoing adaptation of leadership practices.	Kremer, Villamor & Aguinis, 2018

This table provides a clear overview of the framework's steps, methods, and objectives in analyzing leadership challenges and opportunities in the tourism sector. (Developed by the Author, 2024)

OVERCOMING LEADERSHIP BARRIES

The tourism sector faces significant leadership challenges, including cultural barriers, skill gaps, and resistance to change. Overcoming these obstacles requires fostering collaboration, embracing technology, and investing in continuous learning. Public-private partnerships and leadership innovation are essential to driving sustainability, improving service delivery, and positioning the industry for long-term success.

Leadership Challenges

Cultural and organizational barriers present significant challenges to effective leadership in the tourism sector. These barriers often create silos within organizations, hindering collaboration and communication among teams. As a result, a lack of shared vision and commitment to sustainable practices may emerge, which ultimately affects the overall growth and resilience of the industry. When departments prioritize their own goals over organizational objectives, particularly regarding sustainability, the potential for innovative solutions diminishes, and efforts to achieve environmental stewardship become fragmented (Bogers et al., 2022). Furthermore, silos foster competition rather than cooperation, leading to misunderstandings and reduced morale. Recent studies have emphasized the increasing importance of cross-cultural collaboration within international tourism organizations, highlighting how effective communication can bridge organizational gaps and improve overall performance (Wang et al., 2023). To address these challenges, leaders must promote a culture of collaboration and open communication. By breaking down silos and encouraging interdepartmental relationships through cross-functional projects and regular collaborative meetings, organizations can foster a sense of unity and shared purpose. This, in turn, enhances commitment to sustainability and innovation, driving the industry forward and ensuring a more cohesive and adaptive tourism landscape (Gerges, E., 2021).

Another critical issue the tourism sector faces is the considerable skill gap that undermines the workforce's effectiveness in delivering high-quality services. The shortage of trained professionals hampers the industry's ability to meet the increasing demands from both domestic and international travelers. Additionally, the lack of skilled personnel limits the sector's capacity to embrace new technologies essential for enhancing the visitor experience (Recuero-Virto, 2023). Without a sufficiently skilled workforce, tourism businesses struggle to implement innovative practices and maintain service standards, which can lead to declines in customer satisfaction and competitiveness. Recent studies underscore the need for targeted training programs that focus not only on technical skills but also on emotional intelligence and adaptability, which are crucial for delivering superior customer service in dynamic tourism environments (Lee & Chen, 2023). To address this issue, investing in training and professional development initiatives is imperative. Equipping employees with the necessary competencies will not only improve service delivery but also foster a resilient and adaptive tourism sector capable of thriving in a dynamic market landscape. Such efforts will ensure the industry is better positioned to meet evolving challenges and opportunities (Al Shanfari, 2024).

In addition to skill gaps, resistance to change and innovation poses a significant challenge for leaders in the tourism sector. This resistance often stems from deeply ingrained practices, where employees grow accustomed to routine processes and familiar workflows. While these comfort zones create a sense of stability, they can also breed fear of the unknown when new strategies or innovations are introduced. This fear can manifest as passive resistance, where employees outwardly comply but remain disengaged, or as active opposition, where new initiatives are openly challenged (Jalo & Pirkkalainen, 2024). The roots of this resistance are multifaceted, often arising from a lack of understanding or awareness regarding the need for change. Employees may perceive existing methods as sufficient, leading them to view new approaches as unnecessary or even harmful. Additionally, concerns about job security or status can contribute to a protective mindset, where individuals resist shifts that might threaten their roles (Jalo & Pirkkalainen, 2024). Recent studies suggest that fostering an organizational culture that emphasizes the positive aspects of change—such as personal growth and professional advancement opportunities—can mitigate resistance and encourage more proactive engagement from employees (Nguyen et al., 2022).

Moreover, the implementation of new strategies frequently requires significant investments of time and resources, which can heighten employee anxiety. Without immediate tangible benefits to demonstrate, skepticism often grows, causing team members to question the motivations and potential outcomes of the changes. This uncertainty can foster a fear of failure, which becomes a major deterrent to embracing innovation. To overcome these challenges, leaders must adopt a proactive approach that emphasizes open communication, education, and engagement (Al Ghunaimi & Awashreh, 2025). By involving employees in the change process and clearly articulating the rationale behind new initiatives, leaders can help demystify transitions and alleviate fears. Studies indicate that involving employees in pilot phases and gathering their feedback can build trust and show the real-time impact of changes (Hsu & Wei, 2023). Opportunities for feedback and input foster a sense of ownership, making employees feel valued and more inclined to support change. Providing training and support during implementation is also critical, as it equips staff with the skills needed to adapt to new technologies or processes, thereby facilitating smoother transitions (Tao et al., 2022).

Building a culture that embraces change requires sustained effort and commitment from leadership. Leaders should model adaptability themselves, demonstrating a willingness to learn and evolve in response to challenges. Recognizing and celebrating small wins during the change process can help build momentum and encourage further innovation (Maley, 2024). Additionally, creating an environment where experimentation is encouraged and failures are viewed as learning opportunities can gradually shift the organizational mindset towards valuing continuous improvement.

While resistance to change is a common challenge, it is not insurmountable. By addressing employees' fears and fostering open dialogue, leaders can cultivate more adaptive organizations. This transformation enhances the capacity to implement new strategies effectively and positions the organization for long-term success in a rapidly evolving tourism landscape (Mouazen et al., 2024).

Opportunities for Excellence

Leveraging technology for training and development offers transformative opportunities for the tourism sector, enabling organizations to elevate their initiatives and create more accessible and engaging learning experiences for their workforce. By integrating e-learning platforms and virtual training programs, companies can deliver essential skills and knowledge crucial for success in an increasingly digital landscape. These technological solutions facilitate flexible learning schedules and cater to diverse learning styles, ensuring that all employees benefit from tailored educational resources (Zamiri & Esmaeili, 2024). Moreover, recent advancements in augmented and virtual reality (AR/VR) provide immersive experiences that simulate real-world scenarios, enabling employees to gain hands-on experience in a controlled environment. Such innovations are particularly effective in training staff for high-touch service roles, where real-time feedback can dramatically enhance performance and learning retention (Smith & Choi, 2023). This technology-enhanced training allows for real-time updates and interactive content, fostering a dynamic learning environment that encourages continuous improvement and innovation. This approach equips employees with the competencies needed to meet the demands of modern tourism while cultivating a culture of lifelong learning within organizations. Consequently, prioritizing technological integration in training and development enhances workforce capabilities, drives operational efficiency, and enables the sector to deliver exceptional service that aligns with the evolving expectations of travelers (Zamiri & Esmaeili, 2024).

Fostering a culture of continuous learning is equally vital for empowering employees to engage in ongoing professional development and adaptability. Establishing an environment where learning is prioritized enables the workforce to embrace change and drive innovation, which is particularly crucial in the fast-paced tourism sector. This commitment not only enhances individual skill sets but also instills a strong sense of ownership and responsibility among employees, motivating them to contribute actively to organizational objectives (Dao, 2024). Furthermore, the integration of micro-learning modules—bite-sized learning content designed for quick consumption—can significantly enhance knowledge retention and support the fast-paced nature of tourism service delivery. A culture of continuous learning has profound impacts on service quality and operational efficiency. When employees are encouraged to acquire new knowledge and skills, they become better equipped to meet evolving customer needs and respond effectively to industry trends. This proactive approach nurtures creativity and problem-solving capabilities, enabling teams to develop innovative solutions that elevate the visitor experience. By prioritizing continuous learning, organizations position themselves for long-term success, maintaining a competitive edge in a rapidly changing landscape while consistently delivering exceptional service. Investing in workforce development not only enhances operational capabilities but also fosters a more resilient and adaptable tourism industry (Radu, 2023).

In addition, collaborations between the public and private sectors play a crucial role in driving advancements in the tourism industry by facilitating the pooling of resources, expertise, and innovative ideas. These partnerships enable the development of comprehensive training programs that equip the workforce with the essential skills required to excel in a competitive environment. By leveraging the unique strengths of both sectors, collaborations also contribute to enhancing infrastructure, ensuring that tourism facilities effectively meet the diverse needs of visitors and local communities (Ekstrom, 2023). Moreover, cross-sector collaborations are critical for establishing global standards for service excellence and sustainability practices in tourism, ensuring that best practices are shared and adopted widely (Gonzalez & Baker, 2024). Public-private partnerships are pivotal in promoting sustainable tourism practices that benefit the entire ecosystem. By working together, stakeholders can implement initiatives that prioritize environmental conservation, cultural heritage preservation, and community engagement. Such efforts not only enrich the visitor experience but also contribute to the long-term sustainability of tourism destinations. Ultimately, fostering these partnerships establishes a foundation for a more resilient and adaptive tourism sector, capable of responding effectively to emerging challenges and seizing new opportunities. This synergy between public and private entities strengthens the industry while ensuring alignment with broader societal goals, promoting a more sustainable and inclusive future for tourism (Juniarmi, 2024).

Leadership Innovation in Tourism

The following short case studies in the tourism sector highlight innovative solutions for leadership challenges. These cases emphasize the critical role of leadership development, collaboration, and technological integration in overcoming industry challenges. A hotel chain created a tailored training program, enhancing employee engagement and guest satisfaction. A public-private partnership promoted sustainable tourism, benefiting local economies. A travel agency adopted a digital learning platform to boost skills and customer service, while a tour operator fostered continuous learning for innovation and loyalty. Lastly, a tourism agency improved interdepartmental collaboration, aligning objectives and enhancing sustainability (Lv et al., 2020). These examples showcase effective strategies for elevating leadership and success in the tourism industry.

For instance, a prominent hotel chain identified a critical gap in leadership skills within its management team, which negatively impacted both service quality and employee morale. This gap also contributed to operational inefficiencies and high turnover rates, undermining guest satisfaction. To address these challenges, the hotel partnered with a well-respected local educational institution to develop a comprehensive and tailored leadership training program. This program included a variety of components, such as immersive workshops, personalized mentorship opportunities, and hands-on practical experiences (Fouad, 2019). The curriculum was designed to enhance key competencies like emotional intelligence, strategic decision-making, and cultural awareness, enabling leaders to navigate the complexities of the tourism industry more effectively. The program's content was also specifically tailored to the challenges faced by the hospitality industry, incorporating case studies and real-life scenarios that leaders could directly apply. Following the program's implementation, the hotel reported a significant increase in employee engagement and guest satisfaction, as leaders became more adept at managing challenges, fostering teamwork, and implementing innovative service solutions. This holistic approach not only enhanced the hotel's reputation but also set a benchmark for leadership development in the hospitality sector (Al-Balushi, 2017).

In a different context, a public-private partnership was formed in response to concerns about environmental degradation and cultural preservation in a popular coastal region. The partnership, which involved local government agencies, tourism operators, and community organizations, aimed to promote sustainable tourism practices. This collaboration led to the development of a long-term sustainability framework, which integrated environmental, cultural, and economic goals into a cohesive strategy (Tamakloe et al., 2020). It resulted in a series of initiatives, including eco-friendly tours and community-based cultural experiences, which helped protect the region's natural and cultural resources while providing economic benefits to local communities. Training sessions for local guides emphasized the importance of sustainable practices and equipped them with the necessary knowledge to enhance visitor experiences. This collaborative effort resulted in increased awareness and participation in sustainable tourism, a rise in tourist numbers, and the preservation of environmental and cultural heritage sites (Üzülmez et al., 2023). The partnership also created a model for future collaborations, demonstrating how sectors can work together to ensure long-term sustainability in tourism. This case illustrates how public and private sectors can work together to create a sustainable tourism model that benefits both the community and the environment (Al Mahrizi et al., 2024).

Additionally, a mid-sized travel agency recognized the challenges it faced in keeping its workforce updated with technological trends and customer service practices, which impacted its competitiveness in the tourism industry. Acknowledging the need for ongoing technological advancements, the agency decided to integrate AI-based tools to further personalize customer interactions and streamline service delivery (Adaghe & Barakat, 2023). In response, the agency adopted a digital learning platform, providing employees with access to online courses, webinars, and virtual training sessions on emerging technologies and customer service techniques. This platform facilitated flexible learning, allowing employees to upskill at their convenience. The transition to this technology-driven training model led to increased employee confidence, job satisfaction, and improved customer service, which in turn boosted sales and enhanced the agency's position in the market. Moreover, the agency integrated data analytics to monitor employee progress and adjust training content to meet specific needs. This case highlights the transformative impact of leveraging technology for workforce development in the tourism industry (Giannoukou, 2024).

Moreover, a leading tour operator recognized the importance of fostering a culture of continuous learning to remain competitive in the tourism sector. The organization introduced regular training workshops, knowledge-sharing sessions, and encouraged employees to participate in external certification programs. By prioritizing continuous learning, leadership demonstrated a strong commitment to professional development, resulting in increased employee engagement and creativity (Mishra & Painoli, 2024). These initiatives were designed to align with changing consumer preferences, empowering employees to develop unique and personalized experiences for clients. Employees developed innovative tour packages that resonated with customer preferences, leading to improved customer satisfaction and loyalty. This focus on a learning culture not only benefitted employees but also contributed to the organization's success and reputation in the competitive tourism landscape (Abdelfattah et al., 2024).

In another case, a tourism agency faced significant challenges due to internal silos that hindered collaboration and communication between departments. These silos led to inefficiencies and misalignment in service delivery, undermining the organization's overall objectives. To address these cultural and organizational barriers, the agency implemented initiatives such as cross-functional teams working on specific projects and regular team-building activities (de Waal, et al., 2019). These efforts improved communication, collaboration, and alignment across departments, leading to enhanced service delivery and a unified approach to challenges. The cultural shift also strengthened the agency's commitment to sustainable tourism practices and made the organization more agile and responsive to the evolving needs of the sector. This transformation in organizational culture helped the agency not only address internal challenges but also better meet the expectations of its clients. (Manta & Mansi, 2024). These case studies illustrate various approaches to addressing leadership challenges and enhancing the effectiveness of the tourism sector, demonstrating the potential for positive outcomes through strategic initiatives.

EXPECTED OUTCOMES

The development of a comprehensive framework for leadership in the tourism sector is expected to yield significant outcomes that enhance the industry's overall effectiveness and sustainability. By providing a structured approach to leadership challenges, this framework aims to equip leaders with the necessary tools and strategies to navigate the complexities of the tourism landscape. Incorporating a multi-dimensional approach, the framework draws upon best practices from both local and global contexts, ensuring that it is both relevant and adaptable to the unique challenges faced by the tourism sector in various regions (Byrd, 2007). It will address key issues such as skill gaps, resistance to change, and cultural barriers, which can impede progress in tourism organizations. This systematic approach will empower leaders to cultivate an organizational culture that prioritizes sustainability and innovation, enabling them to foster collaboration across departments and implement targeted initiatives (Hussein et al., 2024). Furthermore, the framework will emphasize the importance of continuous learning and adaptability, equipping leaders to manage the rapidly evolving dynamics of the industry. Ultimately, this approach will not only strengthen leadership effectiveness but also contribute to the sustainable development and resilience of the tourism sector as a whole (Roxas et al., 2020).

Building on this framework, practical recommendations for policymakers and industry stakeholders focus on addressing workforce skill gaps through targeted training programs and professional development initiatives. In line with the framework, these recommendations stress the importance of developing a skilled workforce capable of adapting to technological advances and shifting market demands (Oeij et al., 2024). By investing in education and enhancing workforce capabilities, organizations can build a more competent and adaptable team to meet the evolving demands of the tourism sector. In parallel, fostering collaboration between the public and private sectors is emphasized as a key strategy for driving sustainable growth. Collaborative efforts can facilitate resource pooling, enhance innovation, and support the development of sustainable tourism practices that balance economic growth with environmental and cultural preservation. Such partnerships can facilitate knowledge sharing, resource pooling, and joint initiatives, effectively addressing shared challenges. Moreover, supportive policies that encourage eco-friendly practices, cultural preservation, and innovation are vital for ensuring alignment between tourism development and broader economic and environmental objectives. These recommendations collectively provide a roadmap for enhancing leadership effectiveness while promoting sustainable growth and resilience in the tourism industry (Papageorgiou, Marneros & Efstathiades, 2024).

In addition, this study contributes to the body of knowledge on sustainable tourism management by highlighting the critical role of leadership in driving positive outcomes. By examining the dynamics of leadership within the tourism sector, the research offers valuable insights and frameworks that can be adapted to various regional and global contexts facing similar challenges. These frameworks serve as practical tools for leaders aiming to foster a culture of sustainability and innovation while navigating the complexities of the industry (Martinez-Martinez, 2022). The research also emphasizes the need for a proactive approach to leadership, one that is future-focused and able to respond to emerging trends such as digitalization and the growing demand for sustainable tourism. Furthermore, the study underscores the importance of resilience and adaptability, providing strategies to help organizations remain competitive in a rapidly changing environment. By sharing best practices and lessons learned, the study further enriches the understanding of sustainable tourism management, contributing to the development of a more robust industry. Ultimately, this research serves as a resource for policymakers, industry stakeholders, and academic researchers committed to advancing sustainable tourism practices globally, ensuring long-term success and growth (Martínez-Martínez, Cegarra-Navarro & García-Pérez, 2022).

The theoretical implications of this work extend to the broader understanding of leadership in complex industries. The frameworks proposed offer an opportunity to advance leadership theory by integrating sustainability and innovation as core principles in leadership models for the tourism sector. These frameworks can be integrated into existing leadership theories to enhance their applicability within the tourism sector, particularly in terms of addressing the dynamic challenges of sustainability and innovation. These theoretical insights can also inform leadership development programs, making them more contextually relevant and aligned with industry needs. However, while these frameworks offer valuable guidance, there are limitations to their immediate application. The diverse nature of global tourism markets, coupled with varying institutional capacities, may pose challenges in implementing these frameworks universally. In addition, disparities in cultural, political, and economic contexts across regions may require tailored approaches to leadership that are more context-specific. Moreover, regional differences in cultural and economic contexts may require customized approaches, thus limiting the generalizability of some recommendations.

Furthermore, there is an urgent need for further research to explore the longitudinal impacts of leadership interventions in tourism and their effects on both organizational outcomes and community well-being. Future studies could investigate how different leadership styles influence sustainability practices in tourism across different regions and identify best practices that could be universally applied. By fostering interdisciplinary collaboration among academia, industry, and government, such research can provide a comprehensive understanding of how leadership can best contribute to the long-term resilience of the tourism sector. Additionally, research focusing on the role of digital technologies and sustainable practices in leadership within tourism could provide a deeper understanding of the evolving dynamics in the sector. This collaborative approach will help shape a dynamic leadership landscape that not only responds to current challenges but also anticipates future changes, ensuring the sector remains adaptable and competitive in an increasingly complex global environment. Ultimately, these efforts will reinforce the tourism industry's role in economic development, community enhancement, and environmental stewardship, securing its long-term success and growth.

CONCLUSION

Effective leadership is paramount in the pursuit of excellence within the tourism sector, acting as a powerful catalyst for innovation, talent development, and the promotion of sustainable practices. Strong leaders in tourism possess the ability to craft a compelling vision that aligns diverse stakeholders while fostering a shared sense of purpose and commitment across the organization. By inspiring and empowering their workforce, these leaders enable employees to deliver exceptional experiences that consistently meet and exceed visitor expectations. This alignment between leadership and employees is crucial for fostering a unified culture that drives both individual and organizational success. It not only enhances customer satisfaction but also elevates the overall reputation of the industry, facilitating both growth and long-term sustainability. When employees feel valued and motivated, they are more likely to go above and beyond in their roles, leading to memorable interactions that encourage repeat visits and positive word-of-mouth referrals.

Moreover, effective leadership is the backbone of a resilient and adaptive tourism sector. In an industry that faces constant change—whether due to economic fluctuations, shifting consumer preferences, or environmental challenges—strong leaders cultivate an agile environment that can quickly respond to new opportunities and challenges. They prioritize sustainability, ensuring that the tourism sector not only thrives economically but also contributes positively to the communities and ecosystems it impacts. This resilience is increasingly important as the industry navigates pressing global challenges such as climate change, economic instability, and evolving travel demands. Ultimately, the impact of effective leadership in tourism transcends individual organizations; it shapes the industry as a whole. By investing in the development of their teams and fostering collaboration among stakeholders, leaders contribute to creating a vibrant and sustainable tourism landscape. This holistic approach not only secures a competitive edge in the market but also enriches the experiences of visitors while fostering a brighter future for the industry.

The implications of effective leadership within tourism extend beyond organizational success and have significant societal impacts, benefiting travelers, communities, and institutions alike. From a societal perspective, strong leadership can ensure that tourism contributes positively to local communities, providing economic opportunities while respecting cultural heritage and environmental sustainability. Leaders who champion these values can create tourism models that prioritize inclusivity and long-term well-being, aligning economic growth with responsible practices. Travelers benefit from this approach by gaining access to more meaningful and authentic experiences that resonate with their values, such as eco-tourism and culturally sensitive travel options. Institutional implications involve the need for both private and public sector collaboration to establish policies and frameworks that encourage sustainable tourism practices, resource-sharing, and long-term growth. Leaders who promote cross-sector partnerships foster a more cohesive, adaptable, and resilient tourism sector. By encouraging collaboration, they can help address global challenges such as climate change, economic disparities, and the degradation of natural resources.

However, while the potential benefits of effective leadership are clear, several limitations should be considered. One of the most significant challenges is balancing the competing demands of economic growth, environmental sustainability, and community interests. Leaders must also navigate institutional inertia, where deeply entrenched practices within organizations may resist innovative or sustainable changes. Furthermore, varying levels of readiness for innovation or sustainability across different regions or sectors of the tourism industry may pose barriers to the widespread adoption of progressive leadership strategies. These challenges highlight the need for context-sensitive leadership approaches that are adaptable to diverse regional realities and organizational capacities.

To address these challenges, further research is needed to explore best practices in leadership development and sustainability within the tourism sector. Future studies could investigate how leadership can be more deeply integrated into organizational culture and how leadership training programs can be customized to suit the diverse cultural, economic, and political contexts within which tourism operates. Additionally, collaborative research efforts involving academia, industry leaders, and government bodies will be crucial in developing actionable insights and recommendations that can be applied on a global scale. Such interdisciplinary collaborations will ensure that leadership strategies are informed by both academic rigor and practical experience, facilitating the development of policies and practices that can be widely adopted across the sector. By fostering these partnerships, we can promote a tourism industry that is not only economically viable but also socially responsible and environmentally sustainable. Ultimately, this approach will contribute to the creation of a more resilient, adaptive, and inclusive tourism sector capable of navigating future challenges while enhancing broader societal well-being.

REFERENCES

Abdelfattah, F., Salah, M., Dahleez, K., Darwazeh, R., & Al Halbusi, H. (2024). The future of competitive advantage in Oman: Integrating green product innovation, AI, and intellectual capital in business strategies. *International Journal of Innovation Studies*, *8*(2), 154–171. DOI: 10.1016/j.ijis.2024.02.001

Adaghe, W., & Barakat, A. (2023). What are the impacts of digitalization in travel agencies' business models in Sweden? A qualitative study on the role of physical travel agencies in Sweden. *ResearchGate*. DOI: 10.13140/RG.2.2.18534.40001

Afridi, S. A., Javed, A., Ali, S. Z., Zafar, S., & Haider, M. (2023). Cultivating sustainability: The role of generative leadership, green passion, and green work behavior in Pakistan's tourism industry. *Sustainability (Basel)*, *15*(19), 14139. DOI: 10.3390/su151914139

Al-Balushi, M. (2017). Issues affecting Omanization of the hotel sector. *Journal of Tourism and Hospitality Management*, *6*(2), 14. Advance online publication. DOI: 10.15640/jthm.v6n2a14

Al Dhaheri, D. A. (2024). The role of effective leadership strategy in enhancing employee performance: Analysing the hospitality sector for economic growth in UAE. *Journal of Hospitality and Tourism*, *4*(1), 19–34. DOI: 10.47672/jht.1883

Al Ghunaimi, H., & Awashreh, R. (2025). Enhancing sustainability and competitiveness of self-funded SMEs: The hotel model. *International Journal of Innovative Research and Scientific Studies*, *8*(1), 1806–1817. Advance online publication. DOI: 10.53894/ijirss.v8i1.4805

Al Harrasi, N., Al Balushi, B., Al Khayari, S., & al Rashdi, M. M. (2024). Human resource management practices in Oman: A systematic review and synthesis for future research. *Cogent Business & Management*, *11*(1), 2337053. Advance online publication. DOI: 10.1080/23311975.2024.2337053

Al Maghribi, A., Awashreh, R., & Al Naqbi, S. (2023). The impact of strategic planning governance process on employee performance at the Ministry of Social Development. *Journal of Namibian Studies: History Politics Culture*, *35*, 1027–1041. DOI: 10.59670/jns.v35i.3657

Al Mahrizi, A. S. K., Gray, T., Gregory-Smith, D., & Stead, S. M. (2024). The role of stakeholder participation in Oman's tourism planning system. *Tourism Planning & Development*, *21*(6), 1–36. DOI: 10.1080/21568316.2024.2379904

Al Shanfari, S. A. (2024). Exploration on job mismatch with job placement: Employers' perspective in the Sultanate of Oman. *International Journal of Academic Research in Business & Social Sciences, 14*(1). Advance online publication. DOI: 10.6007/IJARBSS/v14-i1/20471

Awashreh, A., & Sayyad, N. A. (2023). Leadership programs: Framework for creating real leaders. *Migration Letters : An International Journal of Migration Studies, 20*(S11), 1001–1013. DOI: 10.59670/ml.v20iS11.6030

Awashreh, R., & Hamid, A. (2024). *Understanding Wise Leadership: Employees' perspective in Oman's Government Sector*. South Africa Journal of Human Resources Management., DOI: 10.4102/sajhrm.v22i0.2747

Awashreh, R., & Hamid, A. (2025). The role of entrepreneurial leadership in driving employee innovation: The mediating effect of knowledge sharing. *Cogent Business & Management, 12*(1), 1–18. DOI: 10.1080/23311975.2025.2466812

Awashreh, R., & Mohamed, Y. (2024). A Comparative Study of Leadership Perceptions in Government and Education Sectors: Insights from the UAE and Oman. Journal of Leadership and Organization Development. *The International Journal of Organizational Diversity, 24*(2), 109–123. Advance online publication. DOI: 10.18848/2328-6261/CGP/v24i02/109-123

Baena, V., & Cerviño, J. (2024). Tourism in the era of social responsibility and sustainability: Understanding international tourists' destination choices. *Sustainability (Basel), 16*(19), 8509. DOI: 10.3390/su16198509

Baporikar, N., Ordóñez de Pablos, P., Tennyson, R., & Zhao, J. (2011). Emerging trends in the tourism industry in Oman. In *Global hospitality and tourism management technologies* (pp. 1–16). Business Science Reference., DOI: 10.4018/978-1-61350-041-5.ch008

Basit, S. A., Gharleghi, B., Batool, K., Hassan, S. S., Jahanshahi, A. A., & Kliem, M. E. (2024). Review of enablers and barriers of sustainable business practices in SMEs. *Journal of Economy and Technology, 2*, 79–94. DOI: 10.1016/j.ject.2024.03.005

Bavik, A. (2020). A systematic review of the servant leadership literature in management and hospitality. *International Journal of Contemporary Hospitality Management, 32*(1), 347–382. DOI: 10.1108/IJCHM-10-2018-0788

Bindawas, A. M. (2025). Promoting sustainable tourism through employee skills: Contextualizing quality education and the human resource management perspective (SDG-4). *Sustainability (Basel), 17*(2), 748. DOI: 10.3390/su17020748

Bogers, M., Biermann, F., Kalfagianni, A., Kim, R. E., Treep, J., & de Vos, M. G. (2022). The impact of the Sustainable Development Goals on a network of 276 international organizations. *Global Environmental Change*, *76*, 102567. DOI: 10.1016/j.gloenvcha.2022.102567

Byrd, E. T. (2007). Stakeholders in sustainable tourism development and their roles: Applying stakeholder theory to sustainable tourism development. *Tourism Review*, *62*(2), 6–13. DOI: 10.1108/16605370780000309

Clemens, M. A. (2015). Global Skill Partnerships: A proposal for technical training in a mobile world. *IZA Journal of Labor Policy*, *4*(2), 2. Advance online publication. DOI: 10.1186/s40173-014-0028-z

Dangi, T., & Jamal, T. (2016). An integrated approach to "sustainable community-based tourism.". *Sustainability (Basel)*, *8*(5), 475. DOI: 10.3390/su8050475

Dao, H. A. (2024). Impact of human resource management on organizational commitment of higher education lecturers: A case study at local universities in the Northern Midlands-and-Mountainous Region of Vietnam. *Asian Development Perspectives*, *15*(1), 24–43. DOI: 10.22681/ADP.2024.15.1.24

de Waal, A., Weaver, M., Day, T., & van der Heijden, B. (2019). Silo-busting: Overcoming the greatest threat to organizational performance. *Sustainability (Basel)*, *11*(23), 6860. DOI: 10.3390/su11236860

Dimanche, F., & Andrades, L. (2024). Tourism trends: Current challenges for tourism destinations management. In Andrades, L., Romero-Dexeus, C., & Martínez-Marín, E. (Eds.), *The Spanish model for smart tourism destination management* (pp. 1–20). Springer., DOI: 10.1007/978-3-031-60709-7_1

Eck, T., Zhang, Y., & An, S. (2023). A study on the effect of authenticity on heritage tourists' mindful tourism experience: The case of the Forbidden City. *Sustainability (Basel)*, *15*(10), 7756. DOI: 10.3390/su15107756

Ekstrom, S. (2023). Collaboration is key in tourism education. *LEarn Tourism*. https://blog.learntourism.org/collaboration-is-key-in-tourism-education

Fouad, M. (2019). Impact of leadership style on employee job satisfaction in the hospitality industry. *International Journal of Heritage Tourism and Hospitality*, *13*(1), 1–12. DOI: 10.21608/ijhth.2019.35101

Galli, A. (2024). Effect of cultural heritage on tourism development in Italy. *International Journal of Modern Hospitality and Tourism*, *4*(2), 54–65. DOI: 10.47604/ijmht.3061

Gerges, E. (2021). Citizenship education in neoliberal times [Dissertation in practice, Western University]. Western University. https://ir.lib.uwo.ca/cgi/viewcontent.cgi?article=1250&context=oip

Giannoukou, I. (2024). Revolutionizing hospitality: Strategic integration of innovation management embracing technological innovation for enhanced customer experiences. *Technium Business and Management*, *7*, 24–39. DOI: 10.47577/business.v7i.10585

Graci, S. (2012). Collaboration and partnership development for sustainable tourism. *Tourism Geographies*, *15*(1), 1–18. DOI: 10.1080/14616688.2012.675513

Gumusluoglu, L., & Ilsev, A. (2009). Transformational leadership and organizational innovation: The roles of internal and external support for innovation. *Journal of Product Innovation Management*, *26*(3), 264–277. DOI: 10.1111/j.1540-5885.2009.00657.x

Helgadóttir, G., Einarsdóttir, A. V., Burns, L., & Matthíasdóttir, J. M. E. (2019). Social sustainability of tourism in Iceland: A qualitative inquiry. *Scandinavian Journal of Hospitality and Tourism*, *19*(4), 1–18. DOI: 10.1080/15022250.2019.1696699

Holston-Okae, B. L. (2018). The effect of employee turnover in the hospitality industry: Quantitative correlational study. *International Journal of Learning and Development*, *8*(1), 156. DOI: 10.5296/ijld.v8i1.12513

Hussein, H., Albadry, O. M., Mathew, V., Al-Romeedy, B. S., Alsetoohy, O., Abou Kamar, M., & Khairy, H. A. (2024). Digital leadership and sustainable competitive advantage: Leveraging green absorptive capability and eco-innovation in tourism and hospitality businesses. *Sustainability (Basel)*, *16*(13), 5371. DOI: 10.3390/su16135371

Jackson, L. A. (2025). Community-based tourism: A catalyst for achieving the United Nations Sustainable Development Goals one and eight. *Tourism and Hospitality*, *6*(1), 29. DOI: 10.3390/tourhosp6010029

Jalo, H., & Pirkkalainen, H. (2024). Effect of user resistance on the organizational adoption of extended reality technologies: A mixed methods study. *International Journal of Information Management*, *75*, 102731. DOI: 10.1016/j.ijinfomgt.2023.102731

Jun, K., & Lee, J. (2023). Transformational leadership and followers' innovative behavior: Roles of commitment to change and organizational support for creativity. *Behavioral Sciences (Basel, Switzerland)*, *13*(4), 320. DOI: 10.3390/bs13040320 PMID: 37102834

Juniarmi, I. (2024). Public-private partnerships in sustainable tourism development: A review of best practices and policy implications. *Journal of Tourisma, 1*(1), 1–8. https://nawalaeducation.com/index.php/JT/article/view/509

Khairy, H. A., Baquero, A., & Al-Romeedy, B. S. (2023). The effect of transactional leadership on organizational agility in tourism and hospitality businesses: The mediating roles of organizational trust and ambidexterity. *Sustainability (Basel), 15*(19), 14337. DOI: 10.3390/su151914337

Khizar, H. M. U., Younas, A., Kumar, S., Akbar, A., & Poulova, P. (2023). The progression of sustainable development goals in tourism: A systematic literature review of past achievements and future promises. *Journal of Innovation & Knowledge, 8*(4), 100442. DOI: 10.1016/j.jik.2023.100442

Kremer, H., Villamor, I., & Aguinis, H. (2018). Innovation leadership: Best-practice recommendations for promoting employee creativity, voice, and knowledge sharing. *Business Horizons, 62*(1), 53–65. DOI: 10.1016/j.bushor.2018.08.010

Leong, W. Y., Leong, Y. Z., & Leong, W. S. (2024). Smart tourism in ASEAN: Leveraging technology for sustainable development and enhanced visitor experiences. *International Journal of Social Sciences and Artistic Innovations, 4*(3), 18–31. DOI: 10.35745/ijssai2024.v04.03.0003

Lv, X., Li, N., Xu, X., & Yang, Y. (2020). Understanding the emergence and development of online travel agencies: A dynamic evaluation and simulation approach. *Internet Research, ahead-of-print*. https://doi.org/DOI: 10.1108/INTR-11-2019-0464

Maley, J. F. (2024). Operationalising employee capabilities post-pandemic crisis: A sustainable HR approach. *Review of Managerial Science, 18*(12), 3575–3596. DOI: 10.1007/s11846-024-00726-4

Manta, O., & Mansi, E. (2024). The impact of globalization on innovative public procurement: Challenges and opportunities. *Administrative Sciences, 14*(4), 80. DOI: 10.3390/admsci14040080

Martínez-Martínez, A., Cegarra-Navarro, J. G., & García-Pérez, A. (2022). Sustainability knowledge management and organisational learning in tourism: Current approaches and areas for future development. *Journal of Sustainable Tourism, 31*(4), 895–907. DOI: 10.1080/09669582.2022.2086560

McCleskey, J. A. (2014). Situational, transformational, and transactional leadership and leadership development. *Journal of Business Studies Quarterly, 5*(4), 117–130. https://www.researchgate.net/publication/272353199

Mishra, J. K., & Painoli, G. K. (2024). Learning and development initiatives: Adapting human resources practices to upskill higher education institution employees in a pandemic. *The International Journal of Interdisciplinary Organizational Studies*, *19*(1), 1–XX.

Mouazen, A. M., Hernández-Lara, A. B., Abdallah, F., Ramadan, M., Chahine, J., Baydoun, H., & Bou Zakhem, N. (2024). Transformational and transactional leaders and their role in implementing the Kotter change management model ensuring sustainable change: An empirical study. *Sustainability (Basel)*, *16*(1), 16. DOI: 10.3390/su16010016

Oeij, P., Lenaerts, K., Dhondt, S., & Warhurst, C. (2024). A conceptual framework for workforce skills for Industry 5.0: Implications for research, policy, and practice. *Journal of Innovation Management*, *12*(1), 205–233. DOI: 10.24840/2183-0606_012.001_0010

Onifade, M., Zvarivadza, T., Adebisi, J. A., Said, K. O., Dayo-Olupona, O., Lawal, A. I., & Khandelwal, M. (2024). Advancing toward sustainability: The emergence of green mining technologies and practices. *Green and Smart Mining Engineering*, *1*(2), 157–174. DOI: 10.1016/j.gsme.2024.05.005

Papageorgiou, G., Marneros, S., & Efstathiades, A. (2024). Predicting career success in the hospitality industry of Cyprus: A competency-based approach. *Journal of Teaching in Travel & Tourism*, *24*(3), 236–268. DOI: 10.1080/15313220.2024.2341616

Pawar, S., & Dhumal, V. (2024). The role of technology in transforming leadership management practices. *Multidisciplinary Reviews*, *7*(4), 2024066. DOI: 10.31893/multirev.2024066

Piwowar-Sulej, K., & Iqbal, Q. (2023). Leadership styles and sustainable performance: A systematic literature review. *Journal of Cleaner Production*, *382*, 134600. Advance online publication. DOI: 10.1016/j.jclepro.2022.134600

Prayag, G., Muskat, B., & Dassanayake, C. (2024). Leading for resilience: Fostering employee and organizational resilience in tourism firms. *Journal of Travel Research*, *63*(3), 659–680. DOI: 10.1177/00472875231164984

Radu, C. (2023). Fostering a positive workplace culture: Impacts on performance and agility. In *Human Resource Management - An Update* [Working Title]. https://doi.org/DOI: 10.5772/intechopen.1003259

Recuero-Virto, N. (2023). Tourism talent shortage in the fourth industrial revolution. In *International Handbook of Skill* (pp. 1–12). Education, Learning, and Research Development in Tourism and Hospitality., DOI: 10.1007/978-981-99-3895-7_8-1

Roxas, F. M. Y., Rivera, J. P. R., & Gutierrez, E. L. M. (2020). Mapping stakeholders' roles in governing sustainable tourism destinations. *Journal of Hospitality and Tourism Management*, *45*(16), 387–398. DOI: 10.1016/j.jhtm.2020.09.005

Ruggiano, N., & Perry, T. E. (2019). Conducting secondary analysis of qualitative data: Should we, can we, and how? *Qualitative Social Work: Research and Practice*, *18*(1), 81–97. DOI: 10.1177/1473325017700701 PMID: 30906228

Shahirah, N., Shariffuddin, N. S. M., Adzim, W. M., & Zain, W. M. (2020). Collaborative challenges among stakeholders on tourism destination competitiveness. *International Journal of Innovation, Creativity and Change*, 13(1), 454–466. www.ijicc.net

Stolz, R. (2024, July 12). Tourism in the GCC: A comparative country by country analysis. Roland Berger. https://www.rolandberger.com/en/Insights/Publications/Tourism-in-the-GCC.html

Tamakloe, G., Xiao, Z., Siueia, T. T., & Tettey, I. (2020). Developing sustainable tourism through public-private partnership to alleviate poverty in Ghana. *Tourist Studies*, *21*(1), 146879762095525. DOI: 10.1177/1468797620955250

Tao, W., Lee, Y., Sun, R., Li, J. Y., & He, M. (2022). Enhancing employee engagement via leaders' motivational language in times of crisis: Perspectives from the COVID-19 outbreak. *Public Relations Review*, *48*(1), 102133. Advance online publication. DOI: 10.1016/j.pubrev.2021.102133 PMID: 36570417

Topsakal, Y., Icoz, O., & Icoz, O. (2022). Digital transformation and tourist experiences. In *Handbook of Research on Digital Communications, Internet of Things, and the Future of Cultural Tourism* (1st ed.). IGI Global., DOI: 10.4018/978-1-7998-8528-3.ch002

Üzülmez, M., Ercan İştin, A., & Barakazı, E. (2023). Environmental awareness, ecotourism awareness, and ecotourism perception of tourist guides. *Sustainability (Basel)*, *15*(16), 12616. DOI: 10.3390/su151612616

Wanie, M. D., Ahmad, Z., & Sha, S. A. (2022). The impact of community empowerment on sustainable tourism development and the mediation effect of local support: A structural equation modeling approach. *Community Development (Columbus, Ohio)*. Advance online publication. DOI: 10.1080/15575330.2022.2109703

Weber, K., & Ladkin, A. (2010). Developing effective tourism leadership. *Journal of China Tourism Research*, *6*(4), 410–427. DOI: 10.1080/19388160.2010.527578

Zada, M., Erkol Bayram, G., Contreras-Barraza, N., Kaptangil, K., & Aylan, S. (2025). Integrating social media-driven service innovation and sustainable leadership: Advancing sustainable practices in tourism and hospitality. *Sustainability (Basel)*, *17*(2), 399. DOI: 10.3390/su17020399

Zamiri, M., & Esmaeili, A. (2024). Methods and technologies for supporting knowledge sharing within learning communities: A systematic literature review. *Administrative Sciences*, *14*(1), 17. DOI: 10.3390/admsci14010017

Chapter 5
Collaboration of Academia and the Tourism Industry to Produce Skilled Human Resources

Urvashi Yashroy
https://orcid.org/0009-0005-9001-6552
Tuli Group of Educational Institutions, India

ABSTRACT

The need for collaboration of academia and Tourism industry has risen with the rise in inflow and outflow of tourist, not only domestic but international. This in turn has given a thrust to trained manpower for this service industry, as the tourist expectation is high on carrying back the best experience. It should be the aim of human resource to generate experiences providing a lasting impression. Hence, it has become mandatory to train the industry personnel on regular basis and also create skilled man power from the institutes. The objective of the chapter is to establish an understanding on how a collaboration can benefit both the academia and industry. It aims to skill, reskill, multi-skill and upskill the employee from time to time and make them relevant in the ever changing scenario of the most vibrant tourism industry. The Industry can take help of Institute for carrying out R&D and to solve any technical hurdles, and on the other hand the students & faculties get a chance to further hone their skills & knowledge

DOI: 10.4018/979-8-3373-0071-9.ch005

1. INTRODUCTION

The collaboration between industry (the practical world) and academia (the theoretical domain of knowledge) play an important role in enhancing competencies of graduates that would benefit all stakeholders in both sectors. Aligning skillsets for student employability in higher education with industry requirements offers valuable insights into the practical dimensions of various projects.

Academic-industry collaboration provides an excellent platform for learning new skills and gaining hands-on experience through teamwork. It enables individuals to engage in projects that might not be feasible independently and helps build a professional network comprising industry experts and academic mentors—connections that can be beneficial for future opportunities.

Government involvement in this Collaboration, will improve the opportunities for innovation and economic development. Academia-industry-government collaboration will strength the association and create a more complete ecosystem to skill the workforce, and contribute to the sector. These partnerships improve the global competitiveness of regions by creating a positive ecosystem for innovation.

This type of collaboration can also inspire academic research, resulting in increased creativity and innovation. Not just academic knowledge, but meaningful progress. Academia can bring research and new understanding to potential emerging skills. This allows the industry to learn, use and practice these results, affirming the importance and necessity of the academic contributions. Industry, therefore, provides an active domain for researchers where practitioners can provide their real-life experiences, thus inscribing research. The collaboration between academia and industry will ensure that the research carried out is relevant and meaningful.

1.1 Industry Overview

The tourism industry in India has shown remarkable growth and has become a significant contributor to the country's economy. It is recognized as the largest service industry in India, contributing substantially to GDP and employment. The sector's growth is driven by India's rich cultural heritage, diverse geographical attractions, and increasing global interest in its historical landmarks. The economic impact of tourism is profound, with the industry being a major source of foreign exchange earnings and employment. Looking forward, the future potential of tourism in India is promising, with expectations of continued growth and development, provided that strategic planning and policy interventions are effectively implemented. The Compound Annual Growth Rate (CAGR) for the tourism sector has been positive, indicating a steady increase in economic contributions and foreign tourist arrivals(Mahour, 2024)

According to the World Travel and Tourism Council (WTTC), the travel and tourism sector in India contributed approximately USD 199.6 billion to the national economy in the year 2022. The Indian travel and tourism sector is projected to exhibit an annual growth rate of 7.1%. In the WTTC's Economic Impact Report for the year 2023, the contribution of India's Travel and Tourism to the Gross Domestic Product (GDP) experienced an increase of 5.9%.

In 2021, the GDP contribution by the travel and tourism sector was USD 178 billion; this figure is anticipated to escalate to USD 512 billion by the year 2028. The tourism sector generated 7.6 million jobs in the fiscal year 2023, and by 2029, it is forecasted to account for approximately 53 million jobs. Within India, contribution of the tourism industry to the GDP is projects to growth annually at from 7% to 9% during the period from 2019 to 2030. The Medical Tourism sector is forecasted to expand at a compound annual growth rate (CAGR) of 21.1% from the years 2020 to 2027. The government of India has projected that India will achieve a market size comprising 1.2 million cruise visitors by the year 2030-31. India stands as the most digitally advanced nation for travelers concerning the utilization of digital tools for the planning, booking, and experiencing of journeys. The growth of domestic and outbound tourism has been bolstered by the rise of India's middle class and an increase in disposable income.

The industry has a multiplier effect on the economy, promoting infrastructure development and regional economic integration. By 2030, India is projected to become the third-largest economy globally, with tourism playing a vital role in achieving this milestone (Sivaprasad, 2024).

While the growth indicators are very positive, the sector poses a huge gap in terms of skilled manpower equipped to handle the growth and international customers. Despite the sector's significant contribution to India's GDP and employment, the industry struggles to find adequately skilled workers, which hampers its growth and competitiveness.

1.2 Skill Gap Challenge

The Indian education system produces a large number of graduates annually, yet only a small percentage are deemed employable due to a lack of practical and soft skills, namely critical thinking, communication, and collaboration (Bhat & Gupta, 2024; "Skill Building", 2023).

In addition to the technological advancement, the Indian hospitality industry is increasingly adopting eco-friendly practices, with eco hotels becoming more prevalent. These hotels focus on sustainable operations, such as conservation of water and energy, reduction of waste, and adoption of eco-friendly materials (Shanmugapriya, 2022). The Indian government has formulated a National Strategy for Sustainable Tourism, aiming to foster resilient, inclusive, and resource-efficient tourism while preserving natural and cultural assets (Chopra, 2017). Sustainable tourism in India is not only an environmental imperative but also an economic opportunity. The sector is expected to grow significantly, by creating new jobs, develop new infrastructure, and increate foreign exchange earnings for India (NUC, 2022; Lal, 2024).

1.3 The Missing Skill Gap

The fast pace of technological adoption has resulted in demand for new skills, particularly in emerging technologies, digitization, and data management. The tourism industry requires employees who are proficient in these areas, yet there is a notable gap in digital skills among the workforce. The integration of technology in tourism operations necessitates a workforce that is adept at using digital tools, which is currently lacking due to insufficient training and education in these areas (Singh & Sharma, 2014; Singh & Hassan, 2024). The rapid technological change an industry often results in higher education institutions leading behind in their curricula and delay in integrating new technologies into educational programs (Manta et al., 2023). Academia often focuses on theoretical knowledge and intellectual challenges, while industries prioritize practical skills and technology transfer for commercial success(Han et al., 2022).

In India only 2.3% of the workforce has undergone formal skill-based training, indicating a significant gap in vocational education and training (VET) systems. The Skill India initiative aims to address this by training 300 million people by 2022, but the current infrastructure and investment are insufficient to meet the industry's demands (Dixit & Mawroh, 2019). Vocational education programs often suffer from outdated curricula and limited industry collaboration, which restricts their ability to equip students with relevant skills for the tourism sector(Syafruddin et al., 2025). Graduates face difficulties in transitioning from academic environments to the corporate world due to a lack of practical skills and industry readiness(Alamgir et al., 2021). They lack practical experience and soft skills, essential for a career in the tourism sector. This is partly due to insufficient **internship opportunities** and **practical training** within educational programs (Tushabe & Murimi, 2024).

There is a significant gap in collaboration and communication between educational institutions and industry stakeholders, which hinders the design of relevant and practical curricula (Avornyo, 2014; Tushabe & Murimi, 2024). Many educational programs have not kept pace with the evolving needs of the tourism industry, resulting in a curriculum that does not adequately prepare students for current market demands (Syafruddin et al., 2025). There is a huge gap between industry and academia where a student's learning is concerned. It is also sometimes called the Performance Gap or Employability Gap. Lack of communication and collaboration between higher educational institutions (HEIs) in tourism results in the gap between skills developed among learners. Most of the academia doesn't frequently interact with the industries. The lack of collaboration between faculty of higher institutions and industry is a multifaceted issue that affects innovation, economic growth, and employment opportunities. Academic institutions often prioritize intellectual challenges and theoretical research, while industries focus on technology transfer and revenue generation. This divergence in goals creates a fundamental barrier to collaboration(Han et al., 2022).

The Indian tourism industry is undergoing rapid digital transformation, demanding a workforce equipped with contemporary skills in technology, sustainability, and customer engagement. However, a significant skills gap persists due to outdated curricula, limited industry-academia collaboration, and insufficient practical training. Graduates fail to demonstrate the digital competencies and soft skills that the sector, and employers in general, are now seeking, leading to a gap between what contributes to the end result of education and what will contribute to employment in the industries. Higher education institutions must joint hands with Industry to prepare a future-ready tourism workforce. This will also help the industry to grow and attract tourism from different parts of world. Tourism education is significant for developing capable and competent workforce being inducted into the tourism sector.

Specialised training and education provided by Higher education institutions as per industry needs can fulfil the demand of industry and cultivate upskilled workforce. Positive outcomes of successful interactions between industry and academia can be innovation, economic progress and greater employment opportunities. To realize these outcomes, however, we must overcome underlying barriers, including differing objectives, bureaucratic obstacles, and constraints in communication. By implementing policy reforms and fostering a culture of collaboration, both academia and industry can work together to create a more symbiotic relationship that benefits society. Collaboration between higher educational institution and industry could build a robust and relevant tourism education system, improve economic performance of the sector and contribute to creating skills workforce.

The chapter aims to identify the key contemporary skills required in the Indian tourism industry, with a focus on digital proficiency, sustainability, and customer-centric competencies.

The chapter also proposes an Academic-Industry Collaboration framework (AICF) based on the Triple Helix model, outlining strategies for effective of collaboration between higher education institutions, industry and the government contributing to joint curriculum design, vocational training, and academia-oriented internships and projects to develop a future-ready and employable tourism workforce.

Academic collaborations can take for forms of research collaboration, academic collaboration between higher education institutions and industrial collaboration. The focus of this chapter is industrials collaboration and its role in creating a skilled workforce, foster exchange of knowledge, support technology transfer and provide better employment opportunities to students in the tourism education.

2. LITERATURE REVIEW

Collaboration can be defined as a collective efforts by individuals or groups with a common purpose and direction in an common environment integrating physical, intellectual, digital and virtual resources (Shelbourn et al., 2012). It facilitates sharing of information and knowledge based on the awareness of the environment. It involves effective co-ordination and taking effots of creating positive change to achieve the common vision.

Academic collaboration is a complex and essential aspect of modern research, involving partnerships between academics, library staff, and industry. Effective collaboration can enhance research outcomes and ensure industrial relevance (Wohlin et al., 2011).

Governments play a very important role in fostering collaboration between academia and industry through policies and funding (Etzkowitz, 2003). Through the facilitation of synergies among governmental entities, industrial sectors, and academic institutions, nations can ascertain the adaptability, resilience, and preparedness of their labour force for future employment opportunities. Henderson (2018) advocates that collaboration must take place with industry stakeholders to develop curricula that is aligned with the needs of the marketplace. Consortia examples in the industry, tourism enterprises, and destination management entities set up partnerships with educational institutions to help integrate experiential learning, case studies, and internships into curriculum, which ultimately prepares students for employment and a trained workforce. Smith & Jones (2012) highlight the need for education programs to integrate more hands-on, practical learning opportunities and for universities to take an active role in collaborating with industry to ensure education programs are aligned with labor market demands. Educational institutes can ensure that their degree programs align better with the need which in return will elevate overall program performance in terms of employability and readiness (Philips, 2023) through building partnerships with tourism businesses, destination management organizations and other consortia of the industry.

2.1 Academic Collaboration

Academic collaboration is a multifaceted process involving joint intellectual efforts to produce scholarly work and achieve shared goals (Naik, 2020). It encompasses research, academic, and industry partnerships, offering benefits such as knowledge sharing, resource exchange, and enhanced performance for institutions and individuals (Sharma & Kaushik, 2022).

Long-term collaboration between Industry and Academia can take place in three strategic form contributing to skill workforce development, namely research collaboration, academic collaboration and industrial collaboration. Research collaboration facilitates joint research and projects including Ph.D guidance and exchange of scientific publication. Collaboration between academic partners support faculty and student exchange programs, joint conferences, curriculum development and capacity building programs. Industrial Collaboration facilitates skill skills development of students through various interventions such as value-added training programs, visits to the industry, internship and placement opportunities. Such collaboration helps transfer of knowledge, insights into latest technological changes, innovation and understanding of contemporary industry practices. Industry and academic can co-create knowledge and improve the overall quality of tourism education. (Garcia et al., 2020; Sharma and Kaushik, 2022)

2.2 Academic – Industry Collaboration

Academica-Industry collaboration can play an important role in developing skilled workforce for the industry. Academia-industry collaboration will help in developing industry-relevant skills in the workforce. This partnership is important to align the educational outcomes of tourism education with the evolving needs of the industry, ensuring that graduates possess the necessary skills to thrive in their careers. Such collaborations not only benefit students by providing practical experience and exposure to real-world challenges but also help industries by creating a pipeline of skilled workers who are ready to meet current and future demands (Sharma and Kaushik, 2022)

Both academia and industry benefit from collaborations. Universities gain access to cutting-edge technologies and industry problems, while industries receive skilled workers with specialized expertise. Such collaborative efforts can help higher education institutions to develop industry-relevant skills through practical training and sharing of specialized expertise. Such association is very important to develop new technologies and promote innovation in an industry leading to skilled employees (Kossifos & Ollett, 2024).

Collaboration aids student in understanding industry dynamics, expectations and latest trends, in turn improving their job prospects. It helps students develop professional networks, interactions with industry experts and professionals during collaborative projects expand students' professional networks and knowledge. A strong Industry-Academic linkage provides opportunities for research and development based on industry problems.

2.3 Contemporary Skill Requirements in the Tourism Industry

Tourism education in India is crucial for enhancing the travel and tourism sector, which significantly contributes to foreign exchange earnings and job creation. The focus is on equipping professionals with the skills to serve clients traveling for leisure or business. This involves understanding travelers' needs and guiding them in selecting optimal travel options. (Majeed, 2023).

Currently Tourism education in India is evolving to adapt the new environment and offer a blend of professional, academic and practical components. This approach provides a wide range of skills to graduates helping them secure jobs in the tourism industry (Dighliya & Dahiya, 2023). However, post pandemic there has been a shift in the way the tourism sector operates. There is increasing digitalisation of process and changing customer expectations resulting in the demand for new skills. This transition has underscored the importance of digitalization and the need for educators to enhance their proficiency in utilizing new technologies(Wan et al., 2024). There is also a need for a paradigm shift in human resource development, focusing on enhancing competencies and creating opportunities for professional growth and certification (Polimenov, 2022).

2.2.1 Digital Skills

The essential generic skills required in the Indian tourism sector, as identified in the literature review, include communication skills, problem-solving skills, decision-making skills, social skills, people skills, and leadership skills. Additionally, impression management, relaxation, motor, manual, mood management, stress management, goal management, time management, and conflict management skills are crucial. These skills can be developed through continuous focused efforts by employees and training provided by the learning and development department within the hospitality industry (Frantz & Misal, 2016).

The digital transformation of India's tourism industry is crucial for its future competitiveness and growth. Research indicates a significant gap between current and future digital skill needs in the sector, with organizations recognizing the importance of digital competencies but acknowledging that much work remains to be done (Zaragoza-Sáez et al., 2021). The adoption of technologies like artificial intelligence, big data, mobile apps, social media, and virtual/augmented reality is reshaping the travel experience and streamlining business processes (Kumar et al., 2022). Digital skills beyond oral and written communication skills are are gaining importance in the tourism sector (Cuic Tankovic et al., 2023). While traditional skills such as communication, interpersonal, and language skills remain vital, digitalization of tourism has created the need to develop digital skills among the workforce (Modi, 2023). Understanding and using various IT tools such as booking systems, CRM and social media are very important skills required by graduates in the tourism sector. With customer using online portals for booking and checking customer reviews, there is a huge amount of data pertaining to travel trends and preferences emerging that needs to be analysed for making service offering decisions and improving customer experience. It is time for higher education to adapt to the changes to modify their curriculum as per the changing patterns.

2.2.2 Customer Centric Competencies

Indian tourism industry should concentrate on enhancing critical customer-centric capabilities that can empower it to compete effectively on a global stage. Such competencies are critical to satisfy customers and improve service quality and customer experience quality in unique competitive and dynamic global tourism context. This includes training a workforce to consistently provide quality services, highlighting the changing dynamics of customer expectations (Maikhuri, 2024).

Communication skills are important for setting up and nurturing strong relationships with tourists. Good communication skills, helps to build relationships, trust and overall satisfaction of the customer. Communication skills helps to understand different customer needs and create a positive experience. Tourism is a form of personal selling whose sales role relies heavily on communication skills. These skills enable interaction and provide value to the customer and aid in building trust and satisfaction. Empahsis must be laid on how to improve communication across different cultures including sub-cultures. (Sanda, 2015; Luthia & Strid, 2020).

Training programs that focus on emotional intelligence development, such as those employing Transformative Learning theory, can enhance these skills among tourism employees(Kallou et al., 2022). Emotional intelligence influences the problem-solving capabilities of tourism graduates. Problem solving has direct relation with emotional intelligence which can be improved through culture and art leisure activities. Yet, emotional regulation does not matter that much when it comes to solving problems (Kim, 2023). Such competencies allow graduates to communicate with various cultures, apply critical thinking in solving complex issues, and manage feelings in a fast-paced working atmosphere.

Customer experiences can be enhanced by integrating digital innovations like AI, automation, and IOT. These technologies can be used for hyper-personalized services in order to enhance service delivery (Maikhuri, 2024) This article is a contribution to the development of emotional intelligence in tourism education, with particular emphasis on the role of digital technologies. These technologies offer new approaches to teaching and learning, playing an instrumental role in the advancement of higher-order emotional skills as indicated by Kallou et al. (2021).

2.2.3 Sustainability Skills

This means you have to be sensitive to sustainability; as a tourism graduate it is a complex topic needed to be addressed in light of the environmental knowledge, attitudes and educational experiences of the graduates. Tourism students have been reported as generally displaying moderate to high pro-environmental behavioral intentions, which are strongly affected by environmental knowledge and sensitivity. The fact environmental management is integrated into tourism education is vital for sustainability problems in the tourism field to be addressed among graduate students. This means preparing students with knowledge, attitudes, and skills to take environmentally friendly practices into whatever jobs they will have.

Environmental knowledge is one of the key factors in predicting pro-environmental behavioral intentions of tourism students. It also acts to bolster their sensitivity toward and responsibility for the environment, which enhances their act of environmental protection(Pan et al., 2018). The role of education in tourism in improving students' sensitivity to the environment In order to better prepare students to face environmental challenges in their future careers, educators can incorporate environmental education as part of the tourism curricula (Fuchs, 2023).

In terms of sustainability sensitivity, it is also a determinant of sustainable tourism experiences as culture sensitivity influences students' perceptions and interactions over various cultural settings that ultimately determine their sustainable sensitivity (Baran, 2024). Sustainability education is slowly becoming recognized as a pivotal element in preparing graduates for the new opportunities in risk-sensitive industries such as hospitality and tourism which is undergoing transformations towards more environmentally conscious practices(Sulkowski et al., 2024). As environmental concerns become a more pressing issue for the travel industry, tourism graduates must have a wide variety of skills to address the issues. This includes strategic, tactical, and operational skills that must be performed to implement certain environmental management practices in tourism enterprises(Veliverronena et al., 2024). Differences in educational strategies and priorities regarding environmental consideration within the tourism sector across regions and schools also point to the need for a more systematic integration of environmental education in tourism.

3. MODELS FOR COLLABORATIONS

Industry-academic collaboration models are essential frameworks that facilitate the integration of academic research with industrial applications, fostering innovation and addressing real-world challenges. These models vary in structure and focus, but they all aim to bridge the gap theoretical knowledge imparted in educational institutions and their practical application in the Industry.

3.1 Statist Model

In this model, Government will give some project to be executed in collaboration with govt. the rules to be framed by govt. agency only. and must be adhered to strictly. The model promotes the Government to leads the industry and academia collaborations with a lead role. Govt. provides a lot of project initiatives and data sources to execute project. So one way is a model where a crucial role of the government is to stimulate and coordinate cooperation between universities and industries. This model is characterized, most commonly, by government funding, policy initiatives, and regulations aimed at encouraging research, development, and innovation.

3.2 Laissez Faire Model

The Laissez Faire model of academic collaboration — minimal interventionism + high degree of autonomy — translates into the dissemination of knowledge in academia by supporting the idea that researchers should be free to explore their interests and collaborate organically as borne out by their own curiosity. In the laissez-faire relationship model, the role of the government is limited to a regulator and a customer. In contrast, this model is much less structured, as in the case of the Triple Helix, where government could be seen as a major broker in the means of bringing together these different communities. The Laissez Faire is a model that gives freedom and autonomy to researchers to not only have self-guided tours but to ensure that no one person is supervising or influencing the research results. This flexibility results in creative research outcomes, as scholars are not hamstrung by straitjacket institutional mandates. Universities and industries interact according to market demand and opportunity, with partnerships often based on commercial interest. The Laissez Faire model enables collaborations to emerge spontaneously through market forces, enabling institutions to innovate in order to gain a competitive edge(Nawaz & Koç, 2020). Nevertheless, one major issue with the model is that in the absence of a central coordinating entity, collaborations will likely not be in line with national or regional innovation strategies. On a smaller scale, smaller institutions or industries can face difficulties in competing against larger ones resulting in inequitable opportunities for collaboration.

3.3 Triple Helix Model

The transition from a Laissez Faire model to more integrated systems like the Triple Helix reflects a shift towards recognizing the importance of structured collaboration for innovation and economic development. The Triple Helix model significantly influences the relationship between academia, industry, and government by fostering a collaborative environment that enhances innovation and economic development. This model, conceptualized by Etzkowitz and Leydesdorff (2000), emphasizes the interdependence of these three sectors, promoting a dynamic interaction that leads to the capitalization of knowledge and the creation of new technologies and enterprises.

Triple Helix of University-Industry-Government Relations" (TH) brings industrial innovation closer to public R&D that supports joint research by government or industry, transfer of technology and designing programs and policies strategically. The model suggests that innovation require mutual co-operation between Business, Government and Industry for a mutually beneficial relationsip (Leydesdorff and Ivanova, 2016).

The Triple Helix model facilitates the transfer of knowledge and technology between universities and industries, leading to the development of spin-offs and start-ups that drive economic growth. Universities play a crucial role as entrepreneurial entities, contributing to socio-economic development through patent registrations and the commercialization of research (Jiménez & Dittmar, 2019). The model also addresses the skills mismatch between graduates and industry demands by encouraging collaborative efforts to align educational programs with market needs (Sulasula, 2023). The Triple Helix model is instrumental in promoting innovation by aligning the strategic goals of academia, industry, and government, leading to sustained economic growth(Razak & White, 2015). The Triple Helix model introduces a more active government role, facilitating and supporting collaborations through policies and funding. This model seeks to balance the roles of universities, industries, and government, creating a more integrated and supportive ecosystem for innovation.

Collaboration between academia, industry, and government can lead to the development of competencies necessary for addressing various sectoral challenges, including those in tourism, by creating a workforce equipped with relevant professional, technical, and managerial skills essential for economic and social transformation (Kawimbe and Muya, 2023).

The T-Hub, an incubator in India is a classic example that demonstrate how the collaboration between local government, academic institutions, and industry has fostered entrepreneurial activity in Hyderabad. This model can be replicated in the context of tourism education. This transition highlights the evolving nature of these relationships and the importance of adapting to changing economic and societal contexts.

Key roles and responsibilities of stakeholders in the Triple Helix Model

Academia

- Knowledge generation and research
- Intellectual Capital Development
- Technology transfer and commercialisation
- Collaborative research and partnership

Industry

- Commercialisation and market application
- Innovation and entrepreneurship
- Industry academia collaboration
- Corporate social responsibility and societal impact

Government

- Policy making and regulation
- Funding and investment
- Supportive ecosystem and infrastructure
- Education and workforce development

Figure 1.

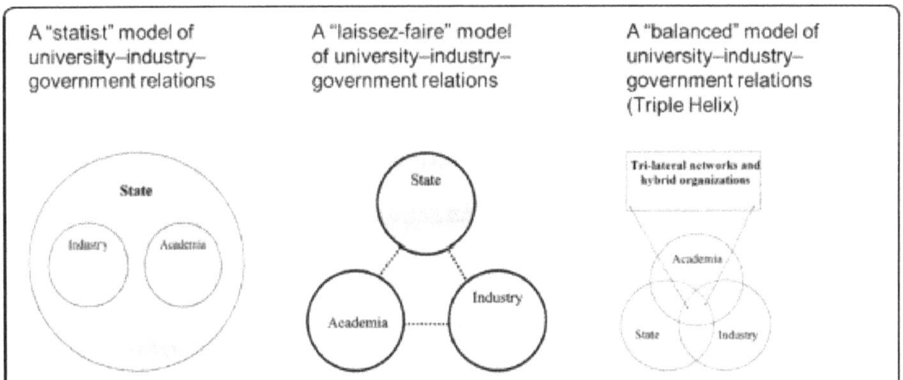

Etzkowitz & Leydesdorff, 2000; Ranga & Etzkowitz, 2013

Fig. 1 Three models for relations between academia-industry-government. Three possible models have been presented concerning relations between the public sector, industry and academia. These comprise a statist model, a laissez-faire model and a triple helix model

4. ACADEMIA-INDUSTRY COLLABORATION FRAMEWORK (AICF) IN TOURISM EDUCATION

As discussed above the Triple Helix Model (THM) supports open innovation. The model explains the inter-relation between practioners (Industry), regulators (government) and knowledge repository (universities) to facilitate innovation. The interaction among them, help each other to over shortcoming in each stakeholder. Higher education institutions can benefit from this interaction by providing academicians insights on practical problems of the industry to apply knowledge.

As the relationship between academia and industry is influenced by the triple helix model, covering the working relationship between those three actors (the academic, industry, and government), it creates a synergy between these actors to bridge the education-business gap. It helps align educational programs with what industry needs, drives policy development that supports skill enhancement, and promotes innovation through collaboration. The model encourages collaboration between governmental entities, academia, and industry professionals to capitalize on their individual strengths, which it believes will foster a workforce better suited to meet the needs of tourism, as cited by the 3rd edition of the World Tourism Forum in 2023.

According to the THM (triple helix model), and based on the findings of Ahmed et al., (2022), the framework proposed Academia-Industry Collaboration (AICF) can create a strong collaborative arrangement between education insititions, industry and the government. It combines processes, methods, and tools to facilitate collaboration. It provides a roadmap for partnerships and enabling innovation. This model stresses the significance of processes, suitable approaches for implementation (Ahmed et al., 2022) and adequate tools to improve collaboration results.

The model reflects both the collaborative roles of universities, industries and governments creating and applying knowledge in ways that improve tourism service and education are the focus. The combination of these three kinds of sectors through the Triple Helix encourages formulating tourism policies, forming unique tourism products, and improving education programs according to the needs of the tourism business.

HEI's can improve their curriculum leading to a trained workforce as per industry standards. Active collaboration with industry can help students to pursue projects that are relevant to the industry and contribute to developing their employability skills. The collaboration will not just help them to develop skills required by the industry but also secure placement opportunities. The industry can involve their trained professionals to teach, guide and mentor students providing them practical insights to real-world situations and problems.

Within the AICP model each stakeholder has a significant role to bridging the skills gap and developing a skilled workforce as indicated in Figure 2.

4.1 Role of Higher Education Institutions

Industry partnerships, and increased investment in training infrastructure is crucial for aligning vocational education with current market demands and sustainability goals. Institutions are encouraged to align their curriculum as per industry demands, to ensure that graduates have the skills required by employers. This involves updating educational programs to include relevant technical, behavioural and soft skills, such as hospitality management and cultural sensitivity, which are crucial for the tourism sector. Vocational education significantly contributes to bridging the skills gap in the sustainable tourism sector by developing both technical skills, comprising of hospitality management and ecotourism operations, and soft skills, including communication and cultural sensitivity. (Sulasula, 2023; Syafruddin et al., 2025). HEIs play a very important role in aligning the curriculum to meet industry needs to develop a skilled workforce that is employment ready. This is the starting point to ensure that their graduates are employed.

Higher educational institutions can benchmark their curriculum, adapt teaching pedagogy and assessments to global practices to make their graduates employed globally. Developing a curriculum that incorporates environmental, social, and economic sustainability is vital for future-proofing the workforce. Encouraging lifelong learning as part of organizational strategy ensures that both individuals and companies remain competitive in the face of technological advancements. Promoting continuous learning platforms and integrating digital skills into education can help address workforce challenges and maintain competitiveness. This multifaceted approach will contribute to up-skilling and re-skilling existing workforce in the tourism sector. This partnership ensures that the workforce is has the relevant skills and knowledge, fostering a more competent and adaptable labor pool.

This collaboration ensures that educational course and programs are in-line with industry requirements, equipping the learners with relevant competence. The model also supports the creation of competency frameworks that define the skills required for various roles in the tourism sector, ensuring that training programs are targeted and effective (Sugiama, 2013; Friedman, 2019). The process of offering vocational training, aligning programs to meet industry needs will result in an improve curriculum that would be designed in collaboration with industry thought leaders.

Educational institutions that are a primary source of research and innovation can enhance their capability of providing the foundational knowledge necessary for tourism development. They engage in research that informs policy-making and the creation of new products and services in the tourism sector. (Sugiama, 2013).

Employees in the tourism sector, are subject to work related stress. With increasing focus on mental well-being, higher institutions must focus on providing support on mental health to create a sustainable workforce. Besides technical and soft skill training the employee also needs calming activity. They should be able to understand their own personality and then act accordingly. Meditation should be made a mandatory part of training. A psychologist should be involved in the learning and development program of the team, who can guide them to understand their personalities positive and negative aspects The aim is to nurture the positives and ignore the negatives till the positives become part of their daily personality trait.

4.2 Role of Industry

The industry plays a crucial role by collaborating with academic institutions to provide real-world insights and opportunities for students. This collaboration can take the form of internships, apprenticeships, and joint research projects, that can help students to experience practical application of theories, frameworks and practices (Sulasula, 2023; Ferreira & Steenkamp, 2015). These inputs can contribute towards making the curriculum more industry relevant. Industries can initiate training programs and workshops that focus on specific skills required in the tourism sector. These initiatives help ensure that the workforce is continuously updated with the latest industry trends and practices (Syafruddin et al., 2025). The Industry can provide students with opportunities for Work Integrate learning (WEL).

Work Integrated learning Sattler (2011) suggests the integration of real-world work experience with academic study. Participatory with potential linking to real life applications, it elevates students' practical skills while solving industry gaps. This method allows for enhanced collaboration, which includes preparation, engagement, and reflection stages, making sure that thorough learning occurs for students and meaningful participation in output for industry partners (Nuuyoma et al., 2024). Collaborative projects between the industry and academia can enable intern and in-place training programs. Such leadership experiences go a long way in closing the gap between the academic knowledge and the industry mandate. Such programs give students experiential knowledge that improves employability and career prospects (Thakur et al., 2024).

Internships bridged the essential gap between academic academia of requirements and practicality. They provide students the opportunity to engage with the realities of business and try out classroom theories in the real world. Internships are an integral part of tourism education both on an academic as well as industry basis. Besides exposing students to hands-on experience, these internships help in honing their management skills while boosting the employability in the tourism and hospitality industries. Internships should be integrated into tourism education programs given its importance of industry-connected skills and competencies development.

This bridging of the gap between academia and industry serves as practical insights and real-world applications for academic research, thereby keeping educational programs updated and in line with market needs (Attas et al., 2020). Collaborations with academia help industries to get the latest researches and advances of technology, which can be utilized for better tourism service and products.

The substantial growth of the tourism sector in India is reinforced by government programs such as "Skill India" that are in line with the Triple Helix concept to improve the skill set of the workforce and the competitiveness of industries (Singh, 2018). This helps to improve the overall quality of workforce which is one of the critical factors accounting for growth and competitiveness of the Indian tourism sector. It could also attract foreign students to do tourism education in India.

4.3 Role of Government

Policies that promote skills development in the tourism sector must be created by governments. These include funding educational programs, increasing the incentive system for collaboration between industry-academia, and establishing labor market information systems to improve the match between skills and job opportunities. However, through investment in infrastructure and technology as well as creating a friendly ecosystem and enabling innovation and skills in this sector, governments can promote the growth of the sector (Etzkowitz & Zhou, 2017; Sulasula, 2023). Governments develop policies and allocate funding via grants that enable and incentivise co-operation between academia and industry. Such assistance is vital for the promotion of the tourism infrastructure and for new tourism policies (Sugiama, 2013).

The academic programs are significantly influenced by the government. The NEP 2020 (Indian National Education Policy) also aims to strengthen the quality of tourism education through a comprehensive reform in education to make sure that what is being taught in schools and colleges meets industrial requirements. Its focus on developing skills, engaging with industry, and integrating technology into the curriculum is critical to the tourism industry. These efforts aim to create a workforce that is both knowledgeable and skilled in a more applied way, ready to enter the tourism and hospitality market.

However government can boost tourism in a country which can make it more attractive for international visitors and can have a wide-spread impact in terms of demand and supply of skilled workforce. Recent initiatives such as "Swadesh Darshan 2.0" for sustainable destinations, promotion of "Dekho Apna Desh" for domestic travel and " PRASHAD Technology to rejuvenate pilgrimage sites etc. are classic examples of how government can promote tourism.

The research carried out by academia and industry can be funded by government through grants and also patent support can be provided by means of financial assistance or reimbursement for expenses incurred for filing patents. This will ensure protection on intellectual property jointly created through the academic-industry collaboration.

Figure 2. Academia-Industry Collaboration framework (AICF) for tourism education

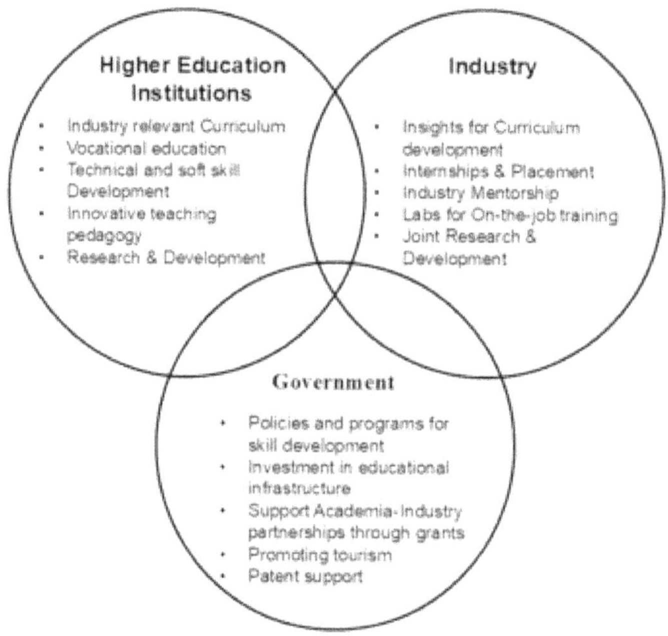

The above figure 2 exhibits the AIC framework for tourism education that can strengthen collaboration between Educational Institutions, Industry and Government based on the Triple Helix model. The model encourages synergistic discussions among the three partners to solve problems and formulate effective tourism policies. This collaborative approach ensures that all stakeholders are aligned in their efforts to address the skills gap (Sugiama, 2013). The integration of smart tourism strategies, which involve the use of technology to improve the tourist experience, is a key area where the Triple Helix model can make a significant impact. It requires joint efforts to develop intelligent services and value propositions that meet consumer expectations.

4.4 Framework Activity to Implement AICF

The success of the above AIC framework for tourism education is contingent of effective communication between the key partners. It is important to outline a framework activity that would lead to collaboration, improve communication and foster the extended relationship for sharing of resources, knowledge and capabilities.

Successful collaboration between Academic Institutions, Industry and government is crucial to foster innovation, enhancing employability. The 3C's of collaboration—Communication, Cooperation, and Coordination (Kempf et al., 2023) are pivotal in ensuring the success of such partnerships.

Communication: Both parties should have a clear understanding of their goals and expectations. What does each partner hope to achieve from the collaboration? Defining objectives is the first step to ensuring a successful partnership.

Regular and open communication is vital for addressing issues promptly and ensuring that all parties are on the same page. This includes both formal meetings and informal interactions. Clearly defining the roles and responsibilities of each party helps in avoiding conflicts and ensures that all stakeholders are aware of their contributions to the collaboration. Teams must communication in a cohesive manner, seek clarification, share feedback, and support each other to resolve conflicts and encourage each other in right direction. Meetings, presentations, emails, and messages are important communications

Cooperation: Providing motivation and incentives for participants can enhance cooperation and commitment levels, ensuring that both parties remain engaged and productive. Working towards the common goal defined through mutual co-operation is very important. Teams need agreed methods and common tools for working on shared tasks. Creating content with other teams or working together on group projects. Effective communication is essential. Regular meetings, updates and feedback sessions keep the collaboration on track and allow for adjustments as needed. Trust is the cornerstone of any successful partnership. The stakeholder must respect each other's expertise and contributions. A collaborative mind-set is key.

Co-ordination: In the Increasing complex environment, the stakeholder must maintain smooth co-ordination among themselves. Understanding barriers of co-ordination and overcoming them are very important. A structured system must be placed for smooth co-ordination and ensure that each other's progress is visible and recognised. Ongoing cross-team processes, or updating information that tracks a project's progress. These are building blocks of any collaboration and team building.

Agile leadership: Agile leadership emphasizes continuous communication and collaboration, which are vital for the success of industry-academia projects. This approach ensures that all stakeholders are aligned and informed, reducing misunderstandings and fostering a collaborative environment. agile approach allows for flexibility and responsiveness, enabling teams to pivot and adjust project goals and methods in response to new information or changing circumstances, which is crucial in the fast-paced environment of collaborative research. hese leadership qualities motivate individuals and facilitate collaboration among geographically distributed teams, addressing common challenges in industry-academia research collaborations (IARCs). (Guillot et al., 2017; Luthia, 2023). Agile leadership in higher education, industry and governments will support effective communication and collaboration creating and collaborative environment. Academic leaders will be more flexible and responsive to lead change and adapt the changing environment.

5. PRACTICAL AND MANAGERIAL IMPLICATIONS

Academia–industry partnerships are increasingly focusing on upskilling, multi-skilling and reskilling existing employees. The tri-party collaboration will enable institutions to align their academic programs and projects to the industry requirements and government policies. Institutions would get support from Industry and government to carry out sponsored research. Government guidelines as National Education Policy (NEP) 2020, Skill India Mission(SIM) will provide a framework on vocational training, development of digital skills and flexibility of taking courses by learners. Through the National Skill Development Council and programs such as Pradhan Mantri Kaushal Vikas Yojna (PMVY) certificate programs can be offered to students through educational institutions in association of hotel groups and industry partners. Through the Government supported schemes such National Apprenticeship Promotion Scheme (NAPS), Industry can design internship apprenticeship or on-the job training programs leading to skill development, upskilling and re-skilling of workforce.

The NSQF (National Skills Qualification Framework) developed in consultation with the industry and academia can support competency framework development to training graduates and equip them with the required skill sets. The AICF can further promote skill development through Government or industry sponsored tourism hackathons and innovation grants. Finally joint monitoring and evaluation of the academic programs can improve the quality leading to more skilled workforce.

6. CONCLUSION

The Indian tourism gaining global attention and there is a huge growth opportunities. Focus on digital transformation, sustainability practices, and higher customer orientation is gaining importance. There is a need to bridge the skill gap in the tourism sector to achieve growth and develop a competitive advantage. Tourism education can play a significant role in training workforce for an industry that has a major contribution to India's GDP.

While NEP 2020 presents a comprehensive framework for improving tourism education, it is essential to consider the broader context of educational reforms in India. The Academia-Industry Collaboration Framework (AICF) can create an ecosystem to improve the overall quality of Tourism education in India. It will foster a environment of knowledge sharing, improve skills among the workforce, and make research relevant. The Triple Helix model remains a valuable approach for fostering innovation and addressing skills gaps in various sectors, including tourism. While academia-industry-government collaborations offer significant benefits, they also require careful management to overcome inherent challenges. Through Communication, Cooperation, and Coordination these challenges and barriers can be overcome. Agile leadership in academia, industry and government will foster such collaboration that would help the parties achieve the common goal.

By promoting a culture of continuous learning and adaptation, the tourism sector can better meet the evolving demands of the global market. Tourism industry is a service industry and the skill of handling the customer is of great importance. Service industry creates an experience for the guest every second and that experience is, what the guest carries as the remembrance. Service sector is very versatile and tests the skills of the employee at every step. Careful consideration of the employee's action is done, and the next learning is based on the previous action. Learning and development are a regular aspect of the service sector and industry can depend upon academia to design the program according to the inputs received from the industry with support from the government.

7. REFERENCES

Attas, A., Risal, M., & Aqsa, M. (2020).. . *The Role of Government, Academia, and Private Sector Using Triple Helix Approach in Tourism Development in East Luwu Regency, 79–82*. Advance online publication. DOI: 10.2991/assehr.k.201017.018

Baran, Z. (2024). Cultural Sensitivity and Respect in Sustainable Tourism. *Advances in Hospitality, Tourism and the Services Industry (AHTSI) Book Series*, 63–84. DOI: 10.4018/979-8-3693-3150-7.ch004

Bhat, I. H., & Gupta, S. (2024). *A Study of the 21st Century 4Cs Skill Gap in the Indian Private Sector*. Emerald Publishing Limited., DOI: 10.1108/S1569-375920240000112A014

Cuic Tankovic, A., Kapeš, J., & Benazić, D. (2023). Measuring the importance of communication skills in tourism. *Economic research-. Ekonomska Istrazivanja, 36*(1), 460–479. DOI: 10.1080/1331677X.2022.2077790

Etzkowitz, H. (2003). Innovation in innovation: The triple helix of university-industry-government relations. *Social Sciences Information. Information Sur les Sciences Sociales, 42*(3), 293–337. DOI: 10.1177/05390184030423002

Frantz, A., & Misal, A. (2016). Essential Generic Skills for Human Resources in Hospitality: A Literature Review. *International Journal of Business, 2*(5), 124–128. https://ideas.repec.org/a/apa/ijbaas/2016p124-128.html

Garcia, R., Araújo, V., Mascarini, S., Santos, E. G., & Costa, A. R. (2020). How long-term university-industry collaboration shapes the academic productivity of research groups. *Innovation (North Sydney, N.S.W.), 22*(1), 56–70. DOI: 10.1080/14479338.2019.1632711

Guillot, I., Paulmani, G., Kumar, V., & Fraser, S. N. (2017). *Case Studies of Industry-Academia Research Collaborations for Software Development with Agile*. Springer., DOI: 10.1007/978-3-319-63874-4_15

Han, B., Chen, J., Guo, T., Lee, S.-J., Swaminathan, V., & Venieris, S. I. (2022). Guest Editorial: Bridging the Gap Between Industry and Academia for Networking Research. *IEEE Network, 36*(1), 8–9. DOI: 10.1109/MNET.2022.9740650

Kawimbe, S., & Muya, C. (2023). Emerging Role of Universities in Collective Impact Initiatives for Business and Community Benefit: the Tripple Helix Model. *International Journal of Research and Innovation in Social Science*. DOI: 10.47772/IJRISS.2023.71025

Kempf, C., Hellwig, I., Bastian, A., Ritzer, K., & Albers, A. (2023). *Success Factors and Barriers in Industry-Academia Collaborations - A Descriptive Model.* DOI: 10.1115/IMECE2023-112574

Leydesdorff, L., & Ivanova, I. (2016). "Open innovation" and "triple helix" models of innovation: Can synergy in innovation systems be measured? *Journal of Open Innovation, 2*(3), 1–12. DOI: 10.1186/s40852-016-0039-7

Luthia, M. (2023). Agile leadership in managing human capital in Industry 4.0. In *Agile Leadership for Industry 4.0* (pp. 79–95). Apple Academic Press. DOI: 10.1201/9781003314615-5

Luthia, M., & Strid, J. E. (2020). Communication Skills and Relational Outcomes: The Mediating Impact of Customer Orientation. [IJM]. *International Journal of Management, 11*(8).

Majeed, A. (2023). Tourism Education in India. *International Journal for Research in Applied Science and Engineering Technology, 11*(8), 1238–1240. DOI: 10.22214/ijraset.2023.55351

Modi, N. (2023). *Knowledge, Skills, and Attitudes: Competencies for Sustainable Tourism.* Springer Nature., DOI: 10.1007/978-981-99-3895-7_48-1

Sanda, G. (2015). Customer relationships in tourism-a very important sector of this industry. *Annals - Economy Series, 1*, 462–467. https://ideas.repec.org/a/cbu/jrnlec/y2015v6specialp462-467.html

Sharma, D. (2023). *The Triple Helix Concept: Examining the Interplay between Academia.* Industry, and Government in Driving Innovation and Societal Impact.

Sharma, D. K., & Kaushik, H. (2022). A Study of Role and Importance of Academic Collaborations/Memorandum of Understanding in Higher Education Institutions. *2022 10th International Conference on Reliability, Infocom Technologies and Optimization (Trends and Future Directions) (ICRITO)*, 1-8.

Shelbourn, M., Sheriff, A., Bouchlaghem, D., El-Hamalawi, A., & Yeomans, S. (2012). Collaboration: key concepts. In *Collaborative working in construction* (pp. 6-25). Routledge.

Singh, A., & Hassan, S. C. (2024). *Identifying the Skill Gap in the Workplace and Their Challenges in Hospitality and Tourism Organisations.* Emerald Publishing Limited., DOI: 10.1108/S1569-37592024000112B006

Singh, M., & Sharma, M. (2014). Bridging the Skills Gap: Strategies and Solutions. *The IUP Journal of Soft Skills*, *8*(1), 27. https://www.questia.com/library/journal/1P3-3349429571/bridging-the-skills-gap-strategies-and-solutions

Sivaprasad, K. I. (2024). *Role of the tourism sector in carving out a better india.* EPRA International Journal of Environmental, Economics, Commerce and Educational Management., DOI: 10.36713/epra15458

Sugiama, A. G. (2013). *KERANGKA KERJA PENGEMBANGAN ASET PARIWISATA DARI MODEL TRIPLE HELIX Hubungan Akademia-Industri-Pemerintah. 10*(5). https://jurnal.polsri.ac.id/index.php/admniaga/article/view/463

Sulasula, J. (2023). Government-university-industry Nexus: a Triple Helix Review of Employment Options for College Graduates in Zamboanga City, Philippines. *Social Science Research Network.* DOI: 10.2139/ssrn.4519513

Suprabha, K. R., & Prasad, K. (2017). *Labour Intensity and Skill Gap in the Hospitality Sector: A Study in South India. 23*(1), 84–110. https://doi.org/DOI: 10.21571/pehyj.2017.2301.04

Thakur, R., Chavan, M., Vasoya, A., Kasturiwale, H., Ghosh, S., & Mishra, S. (2024). *Bridging Academia And Industry: A Study On The Skill Development Effects Of Internships And On-The-Job Training Programs.* DOI: 10.53555/kuey.v30i4.2276

Viken, A., Höckert, E., & Grimwood, B. S. (2021). Cultural sensitivity: Engaging difference in tourism. *Annals of Tourism Research*, *89*, 103223. DOI: 10.1016/j.annals.2021.103223

Waters, S. (1996). Travel industry world year book.

Wohlin, C., Aurum, A., Angelis, L., Phillips, L., Dittrich, Y., Gorschek, T., Grahn, H., Henningsson, K., Kagstrom, S., Low, G., Rovegard, P., Tomaszewski, P., van Toorn, C., & Winter, J. (2011). The success factors powering industry-academia collaboration. *IEEE Software*, *29*(2), 67–73. DOI: 10.1109/MS.2011.92

Yen, H. R., Pham Thi, H., Li, E. Y., & Li, E. Y. (2021). Understanding customer-centric socialization in tourism services. *Service Business*, *15*(4), 1–29. DOI: 10.1007/s11628-021-00463-8

Zaragoza-Sáez, P. D., Marco-Lajara, B., & Úbeda-García, M. (2021). Digital skills in tourism. A study from the Next Tourism Generation (NTG) Alliance. *Measuring Business Excellence.*

ADDITIONAL READING

Chhom, C., Vy, S., Chheav, R., Bou, D., Kheuy, S., & Sam, R. (2024). The Laissez-Faire Leadership Style in Higher Education Institutions: A Systematic Literature Review. *European Journal of Contemporary Education and E-Learning*, *2*(6), 140–168. DOI: 10.59324/ejceel.2024.2(6).09

López Jiménez, D., & Dittmar, E. C. (2019). *Triple helix model of innovation: university, industry and government interactions*. 2570–2574. DOI: 10.21125/edulearn.2019.0705

Chapter 6
Fostering Sustainable Workforce Development in the Indian Tourism Sector:
Integrating Green Skills and Digital Competencies for Competitive Advantage

Archan Mitra
https://orcid.org/0000-0002-1419-3558
Amity University, Mumbai

Sanchita Paul
https://orcid.org/0009-0006-6437-3991
Neil Patel Digital India, India

ABSTRACT

The Indian tourism sector is undergoing a transformative shift by integrating green skills and digital competencies into workforce strategies to align with sustainability goals and digital advancements. This research focuses on identifying essential green skills, such as resource conservation, environmental awareness, and community-centered social responsibility, to promote eco-friendly practices and preserve India's biodiversity and cultural heritage. Additionally, digital competencies, including AI-driven customer interaction tools, virtual engagement platforms, and data analytics, are explored to enhance smart tourism solutions and global appeal. The study aims to develop a comprehensive framework combining green and digital skills to address

DOI: 10.4018/979-8-3373-0071-9.ch006

challenges such as workforce diversity, digital infrastructure gaps, and the need for sustainable practices in rural and eco-sensitive regions. Emphasizing inclusivity, the research will empower SMEs and local communities, enabling active participation in the tourism economy.

1. INTRODUCTION

1.1 Overview of India's Tourism Sector and Its Contribution to the Economy

India's tourism industry is a critical pillar of the nation's economy, contributing significantly to employment generation and GDP. According to the World Travel and Tourism Council (WTTC), the tourism sector accounted for 6.9% of India's GDP in 2021, generating approximately 32 million jobs, a figure expected to rise with focused development initiatives. The sector's potential extends beyond economic contributions, influencing cultural preservation and social development. Key government programs, such as *Incredible India 2.0* and *Swadesh Darshan*, aim to enhance the global competitiveness of Indian tourism through innovation and sustainability-focused policies. However, as the industry grows, so does its responsibility to align with global sustainability and environmental goals, presenting unique challenges and opportunities for workforce development (WTTC, 2022).

1.2 Emerging Trends in Sustainable and Smart Tourism

The paradigm shift towards sustainable tourism is gaining momentum worldwide, with India following suit. Sustainable tourism emphasizes reducing the ecological footprint of travel while preserving cultural heritage and promoting local economies. Simultaneously, the advent of smart tourism, powered by digital transformation, introduces innovative tools such as artificial intelligence (AI), data analytics, and virtual platforms to enhance customer experiences and operational efficiencies (Nabila, 2023). These twin trends—sustainability and smart tourism—are reshaping the landscape of the industry, making it imperative for India to adapt. Integrating these elements requires a workforce proficient in green skills, such as environmental responsibility, and digital competencies, such as familiarity with AI-driven customer interaction tools. However, achieving this integration is fraught with challenges, particularly in a country as diverse and resource-intensive as India (UNWTO, 2023).

1.3 Challenges Faced in Aligning Workforce Skills with Sustainability and Technological Advancements

Despite its economic significance, the Indian tourism workforce often lacks the skills needed to navigate this dual transition effectively. Green skills, including resource conservation and ecological awareness, are either underdeveloped or absent in many workforce training programs (Al-Romeedy & Alharethi, 2024). Moreover, the pace of digital adoption in the sector remains uneven, with significant gaps in the understanding and implementation of emerging technologies. Rural and small-scale tourism enterprises, which form the backbone of the sector, are particularly disadvantaged due to limited access to training and resources (Mantay, 2021). These deficiencies hinder India's ability to position itself as a leader in sustainable and smart tourism, leaving a crucial gap that this research seeks to address (Ministry of Tourism, 2022).

1.4 Problem Statement

As the global tourism industry transitions towards sustainability and smart solutions, the Indian tourism workforce faces critical skill deficits. The absence of robust green skills training has resulted in unsustainable practices that threaten ecological conservation efforts, particularly in environmentally fragile destinations like the Himalayas and Western Ghats. Simultaneously, inadequate digital competencies limit the sector's ability to leverage technological advancements, such as AI-powered booking systems and virtual engagement platforms. These gaps not only undermine India's competitive edge but also jeopardize the long-term sustainability of the sector. The research identifies these deficits as a pressing problem and aims to propose actionable solutions to bridge them.

1.5 Research Objective

The primary objective of this research is to develop a comprehensive framework for integrating green skills and digital competencies into India's tourism workforce. This framework aims to:

- Enable the workforce to align with sustainability goals and technological advancements.
- Foster inclusive economic growth by promoting equitable opportunities across rural and urban tourism enterprises.
- Advance environmental conservation by embedding eco-friendly practices into workforce training programs.

By achieving this, the study seeks to support India's vision of becoming a global leader in responsible tourism while addressing the sector's evolving demands.

1.6 Significance of the Study

The study holds significant implications for multiple stakeholders. For policymakers, it provides actionable insights into creating training policies and incentive structures that promote the adoption of green skills and digital competencies across the tourism sector. By addressing skill gaps, the research supports national and international sustainability goals, such as the United Nations' Sustainable Development Goals (SDGs), particularly Goal 8 (Decent Work and Economic Growth) and Goal 12 (Responsible Consumption and Production).

HR managers within the tourism industry can use the proposed framework to design workforce training programs that are adaptive to environmental and technological shifts. For instance, integrating eco-tourism modules and digital engagement tools into training curricula can enhance employee readiness and operational efficiency. Similarly, educators in tourism management programs can incorporate the findings into their syllabi, preparing future professionals to navigate the challenges of sustainable and smart tourism.

At the sectoral level, the research strengthens India's position as a responsible tourism destination, attracting environmentally conscious travelers and investors. By fostering a workforce skilled in green and digital competencies, the study enables tourism enterprises to adapt rapidly to global trends, enhancing their resilience and competitive advantage. The integration of these skills also benefits local communities, promoting equitable economic growth and social inclusivity (Ministry of Tourism, 2022).

2. LITERATURE REVIEW

2.1 Human Capital Development in Tourism

The concept of human capital, defined as the stock of skills, knowledge, and social attributes contributing to economic productivity, plays a pivotal role in tourism. Existing research emphasizes that workforce development is crucial for enhancing service quality and meeting the dynamic needs of tourists. Baum (2015) argues that the tourism industry is inherently labor-intensive, relying heavily on human interactions, which necessitates continuous investment in workforce development to improve service standards and customer satisfaction. Similarly, Nickson (2013) highlights the importance of skills training in hospitality and tourism, emphasizing that human capital significantly impacts the visitor experience and overall competitiveness of destinations.

However, workforce development in tourism is often fragmented, with limited focus on holistic skill-building. McKercher (2018) critiques conventional training models for being too focused on technical skills, neglecting broader competencies like environmental awareness and technological adaptability, which are increasingly relevant in a globalized, sustainability-driven tourism industry. This gap underscores the need for integrated training approaches that prepare the workforce for modern challenges.

2.1.1 Role of Human Capital in Achieving Sustainability and Competitive Advantage

Human capital is not only a driver of economic productivity but also a crucial force for achieving sustainability in tourism. According to Koundinya and Singh (2019), an educated and skilled workforce is essential for implementing sustainable practices, such as waste management and energy conservation, in tourism operations. Furthermore, stakeholders recognize that investing in workforce sustainability enhances a destination's reputation, attracting environmentally conscious travelers and generating competitive advantage (Gössling & Hall, 2019, Alsheref et al., 2024).

Competitive advantage in tourism is increasingly linked to a destination's ability to adapt to changing market demands. Porter (1985) explains that destinations leveraging human capital to innovate and adopt sustainable practices can differentiate themselves in the global tourism market. For instance, destinations that train their workforce in green and digital skills are better positioned to attract high-value tourists and meet international sustainability standards (UNWTO, 2023).

2.2 Green Skills and Sustainability in Tourism

Green skills refer to the knowledge, abilities, and attitudes required to support environmental sustainability. These include resource conservation, waste reduction, and social responsibility. According to Strietska-Ilina et al. (2011), green skills are crucial for transitioning towards sustainable practices across various industries, including tourism. In the tourism context, these skills manifest in activities such as implementing eco-friendly accommodations, reducing carbon footprints in transportation, and promoting sustainable consumption among tourists (Srivastava, 2024).

For example, sustainable hospitality initiatives like LEED-certified hotels rely on employees trained in energy efficiency and waste management (Velaoras et al., 2024). Similarly, tour operators offering eco-tourism packages depend on guides knowledgeable about biodiversity and cultural preservation. These examples illustrate the practical application of green skills in advancing sustainability within tourism (Dodds & Butler, 2019).

2.2.1 Successful Green Initiatives in Tourism

One notable example of successful green initiatives is Kerala's Responsible Tourism Mission, which trains local communities in sustainable tourism practices, including organic farming, waste management, and cultural preservation. This initiative not only enhances the economic well-being of communities but also promotes Kerala as a responsible tourism destination (Kerala Tourism, 2022, Markose et al., 2022).

Another example in the South Asia is the Bhutan Tourism Board's "High-Value, Low-Impact" policy, which mandates training programs on environmental conservation for all tourism stakeholders (Choegyal, 2022). The policy's success in maintaining Bhutan's pristine environment underscores the critical role of green skills in sustainable tourism (UNDP, 2021). These cases provide actionable insights for integrating green skills into India's tourism workforce.

2.3 Digital Competencies for Smart Tourism

2.3.1 Importance of Digital Tools in Modern Tourism

Digital transformation is reshaping the tourism industry, enabling innovative solutions for enhanced customer engagement and operational efficiency. AI-powered tools, virtual platforms, and data analytics are becoming indispensable for managing tourism enterprises (Kannan, 2024). Buhalis and Amaranggana (2015) note that smart tourism destinations utilize digital platforms to integrate real-time data, offering personalized services to visitors and improving resource management.

Virtual platforms, such as virtual reality (VR) tours, allow potential tourists to experience destinations remotely, influencing their travel decisions (Fan et al., 2022). Data analytics, meanwhile, enables businesses to predict consumer behavior, optimize marketing strategies, and improve service delivery (Tussyadiah et al., 2020). These tools require a workforce skilled in digital competencies, highlighting the need for targeted training programs.

2.3.2 Challenges in Digital Adoption within the Indian Context

Despite the potential of digital tools, their adoption in India's tourism sector faces significant hurdles. According to the Ministry of Tourism (2022), the lack of digital literacy among the workforce is a critical barrier. Rural tourism enterprises, in particular, struggle to access and implement digital solutions due to limited infrastructure and financial resources. Moreover, resistance to technological change among older employees further impedes progress (World Bank, 2021).

Addressing these challenges requires an inclusive approach that bridges the digital divide. Training programs must be tailored to different levels of digital proficiency, ensuring that all segments of the workforce can benefit from technological advancements.

2.4 The Need for a Dual Approach Combining Green Skills and Digital Competencies

While existing literature extensively discusses green skills and digital competencies independently, there is limited research on their integration within the tourism workforce. Gössling and Hall (2019) emphasize the importance of green skills for sustainability, and Buhalis (2020) highlights the transformative potential of digital tools in tourism. However, few studies explore the synergies between these skill sets and their combined impact on workforce development.

This gap is particularly evident in the Indian context, where the tourism workforce faces dual challenges of sustainability and technological adaptation. Addressing this gap requires a comprehensive framework that simultaneously fosters green and digital competencies, aligning with India's unique socio-economic and environmental landscape. This research aims to fill this void, providing actionable insights for policymakers, HR managers, and educators.

3. RESEARCH METHODOLOGY

The research methodology for this study is designed to address the objective of developing a comprehensive framework for integrating green skills and digital competencies into India's tourism workforce. The methodology employs a mixed-methods approach to provide both qualitative and quantitative insights, ensuring a holistic understanding of the issue.

3.1 Research Design

A mixed-methods research design combines qualitative and quantitative techniques to explore the multifaceted nature of workforce development in the tourism sector. This approach is appropriate for:

- Understanding the specific green and digital skills required in the tourism workforce.
- Analyzing the barriers to skill integration.
- Developing actionable strategies to overcome these barriers.

3.2 Data Collection Methods

3.2.1 Primary Data Collection

1. **Surveys**

Structured surveys will be administered to stakeholders, including tourism employees, HR managers, policymakers, and educators. The survey questions will focus on:

- o Awareness and implementation of green skills and digital competencies.
- o Perceived barriers to skill development and integration.
- o Suggestions for improving workforce training programs.

The survey will employ a Likert scale to gauge responses, allowing for quantitative analysis of perceptions and readiness levels across different stakeholder groups.

3.2.2 Secondary Data Collection

- **Literature Review**: Analysis of academic journals, industry reports, and government publications to understand existing frameworks for workforce development, green skills, and digital competencies in tourism.
- **Case Studies**: Examination of national and international best practices, such as Kerala's Responsible Tourism Mission and Bhutan's "High-Value, Low-Impact" policy.
- **Policy Documents**: Review of government initiatives like *Swadesh Darshan* and *Digital India* to contextualize the research within existing policy frameworks.

3.3 Sampling Techniques

3.3.1 Target Population

The study targets a diverse group of stakeholders involved in the tourism sector, including:

- Tourism workforce (both urban and rural).
- HR managers and training facilitators.
- Policymakers and government officials.
- Academics and educators in tourism and sustainability studies.

3.3.2 Sampling Method

A purposive sampling technique will be employed to ensure that participants with relevant expertise and experiences are included in the study. Additionally, stratified random sampling will be used for survey distribution to represent various segments of the tourism workforce.

3.3.3 Sample Size

- **Surveys**: Approximately 500 participants across five key Indian tourism regions (North, South, East, West, and Northeast).

3.4 Case Study Selection Criteria

The selection of case studies for this framework was guided by specific criteria to ensure relevance, diversity, and applicability to the objectives of integrating green skills and digital competencies into India's tourism workforce.

1. **Relevance to Green Skills and Digital Competencies**:

Case studies were chosen based on their emphasis on workforce development in green practices (e.g., resource conservation, biodiversity preservation) and digital innovations (e.g., GIS, AR/VR) (Fan et al., 2022). Examples like Kerala's *Responsible Tourism Mission* and Madhya Pradesh's AR-driven heritage tours demonstrate the integration of these elements in real-world scenarios.

2. **Geographical Diversity**:

To capture regional disparities and strengths, case studies were selected from various parts of India to highlight unique challenges and strategies across regions.

3. **Sustainability and Scalability**:

Initiatives were prioritized based on their demonstrated success in promoting sustainability and their potential for replication in other regions. For instance, Kerala's community-centric green tourism model is a scalable approach applicable to other rural areas.

4. **Policy Alignment**

Selected case studies align with existing government policies like *Swadesh Darshan* and *Digital India*, ensuring their relevance to national development goals.

This structured approach ensures that the case studies provide actionable insights and serve as replicable models for integrating green and digital competencies in India's tourism sector.

3.5 Data Analysis

3.5.1 Quantitative Data Analysis

1. **Descriptive Statistics**:
   - o Percentage distribution to understand the prevalence of green and digital skills.
   - o Mean and standard deviation to analyze the level of skill adoption and readiness.
2. **Inferential Statistics**:
   - o Regression analysis to assess the relationship between skill integration and perceived benefits (e.g., improved competitiveness, sustainability).
   - o Chi-square tests to explore differences in skill adoption across demographic groups.

3.5.2 Qualitative Data Analysis

1. Content Analysis:

Analyzing secondary data, such as policy documents and case studies, to extract insights on existing frameworks and their applicability to the Indian context.

3.6 Framework Development

The findings from the data analysis will inform the development of a comprehensive framework that:

- Identifies the specific green and digital skills required for sustainable and smart tourism.
- Proposes strategies for training and integrating these skills into the workforce.
- Includes implementation guidelines for policymakers, HR managers, and educators.

3.7 Ethical Considerations

- **Informed Consent**: Participants will be fully informed about the study's purpose and their rights, ensuring voluntary participation.
- **Confidentiality**: Data will be anonymized to protect participants' identities.

3.8 Limitations of the Methodology

- **Reliance on Self-Reported Data**: Surveys and interviews may introduce biases such as social desirability and recall inaccuracies, affecting data reliability.
- **Regional and Demographic Constraints**: Limited access to marginalized or rural workforce groups may result in uneven representation, particularly in remote or underserved areas.
- **Technological Barriers**: The digital divide and low digital literacy levels in rural areas may hinder participation in online surveys or virtual interviews.
- **Limited Generalizability**: Findings are specific to India's socio-economic and policy context and may not be directly applicable to other regions or countries.
- **Evolving Skill Definitions**: The dynamic nature of green and digital skills may create inconsistencies in understanding and reporting among participants.
- **Sectoral Diversity**: Variability in skill requirements across tourism sub-sectors could challenge the development of a universal framework.
- **Logistical and Financial Constraints**: Budget limitations and resource challenges may restrict comprehensive data collection, especially in geographically dispersed regions.
- **Temporal Constraints**: Rapid changes in tourism trends and policies may limit the study's long-term relevance.

4. CASE STUDIES

4.1 Kerala's Responsible Tourism Mission

Kerala has pioneered sustainable tourism practices through its widely acclaimed *Responsible Tourism Mission*. Launched in 2008, the mission aims to empower local communities by integrating them into the tourism value chain while ensuring environmental sustainability. This initiative has focused on skill-building in areas such as organic farming, waste management, and sustainable crafts. For instance, local artisans are trained to create eco-friendly souvenirs, reducing the dependence on non-recyclable materials. Similarly, homestay operators receive guidance on energy conservation and waste segregation, which align their operations with green practices (Kerala Tourism, 2022).

Additionally, the mission includes training sessions on biodiversity conservation, educating local guides and operators about the importance of preserving Kerala's backwaters and forests. These efforts have created a ripple effect, enhancing community livelihoods and promoting a more responsible form of tourism (Shetty et al., 2024). The program also incorporates digital platforms to market local products globally, further strengthening the connection between local communities and international tourists. The success of Kerala's Responsible Tourism Mission has set an exemplary benchmark for other Indian states to emulate.

4.2 The Ecotourism Model of Sikkim

Sikkim has emerged as a frontrunner in ecotourism, aligning its tourism strategy with its commitment to becoming a fully organic state. This Himalayan state integrates green skills training and modern technology to create a tourism model that is environmentally sustainable and economically inclusive. The government collaborates with local communities, particularly those involved in trekking and adventure tourism, to impart skills such as biodiversity conservation, waste management, and eco-friendly trekking practices (Lam, 2021, Chandel et al., 2024).

To complement these green initiatives, digital tools have been introduced to enhance the tourist experience. Mobile apps provide real-time information on trekking routes, weather conditions, and ecological guidelines, ensuring that visitors remain informed about sustainable practices during their stay. Additionally, the state uses Geographic Information System (GIS) technology to monitor tourist activities in sensitive ecological zones, preventing over-tourism and ensuring the preservation of natural resources (Sikkim Tourism, 2021).

This combined approach has not only attracted eco-conscious travelers but has also improved local employment opportunities, particularly for women and youth in rural areas. Sikkim's ecotourism model demonstrates the power of blending traditional ecological knowledge with modern digital tools.

4.3 Rajasthan's Desert National Park Initiatives

Rajasthan, known for its arid landscapes and rich biodiversity, has undertaken innovative steps to integrate green skills into its tourism sector through initiatives in the *Desert National Park*. This fragile ecosystem faces numerous challenges, including water scarcity and habitat degradation. To address these issues, the park authorities have launched training programs focusing on wildlife conservation, sustainable water management, and waste reduction. Local communities and park staff are trained to manage tourism activities in a way that minimizes environmental impact while educating visitors about the delicate desert ecosystem (Rajasthan Forest Department, 2020).

In addition to these green initiatives, the park has embraced digital transformation to enhance both conservation and tourism experiences. Virtual tours of the park allow tourists to explore its unique biodiversity without physically visiting, reducing ecological pressure on the area. Furthermore, AI-based monitoring systems are employed to track wildlife movements and detect illegal activities such as poaching (Tripathi, 2024). These technologies ensure the park's conservation goals are met while also offering tourists a modern, interactive experience.

The initiative has not only bolstered Rajasthan's reputation as a sustainable tourism destination but has also created new livelihood opportunities for local communities, making it a holistic model for eco-tourism development.

4.4 Madhya Pradesh's Heritage and Sustainable Tourism Project

Madhya Pradesh's *Heritage and Sustainable Tourism Project* integrates sustainable practices into the management of its UNESCO World Heritage Sites, including Khajuraho and Sanchi. Recognizing the environmental challenges posed by mass tourism, the project focuses on equipping local guides and service providers with green skills such as cultural preservation, waste management, and energy-efficient operations. These practices help reduce the ecological footprint of tourism while preserving the historical and cultural significance of the sites.

The project also leverages cutting-edge digital technologies to make heritage tourism more sustainable and accessible. Augmented Reality (AR) applications offer virtual tours of heritage sites, enabling visitors to experience their beauty and historical importance without overcrowding fragile structures. These tools have been particularly useful during the COVID-19 pandemic, when physical visits were restricted (Atsiz, 2021). The use of digital platforms has also increased the accessibility of these heritage sites to differently-abled tourists, promoting inclusive tourism (Madhya Pradesh Tourism Board, 2022).

This project demonstrates the transformative potential of combining digital innovation with sustainable tourism practices to achieve economic, social, and environmental benefits.

5. DATA ANALYSIS

The data analysis section provides a comprehensive examination of quantitative and qualitative insights to address the research objectives. It integrates descriptive statistics, inferential statistics, and content analysis to understand the prevalence, gaps, and perceived benefits of green and digital skills in India's tourism workforce.

5.1 Understanding Awareness, Gaps, and Benefits Across Regions

Descriptive statistics were used to summarize awareness levels, skill gaps, and perceived benefits for green and digital skills across regions. The awareness levels, skill gaps, and perceived benefits for green and digital skills vary significantly across India's regions.

Table 1. Regional statistics for awareness, gaps, and perceived benefits

Region	Green Skills Awareness (%)	Digital Competencies Awareness (%)	Skill Gap Green (%)	Skill Gap Digital (%)	Perceived Benefit Green (%)	Perceived Benefit Digital (%)
North	68	60	32	40	80	75
South	72	75	28	25	85	88
East	55	50	45	50	65	60
West	65	70	35	30	78	82
Northeast	50	45	50	55	60	58

Table 1 shows that the South region leads with the highest awareness levels (72% for green skills, 75% for digital competencies) and the lowest skill gaps (28% and 25% respectively). Whereas the Northeast region shows the largest deficits, with awareness at 50% (green) and 45% (digital), and skill gaps at 50% and 55%, respectively.

Figure 1. Skill gaps and perceived benefits

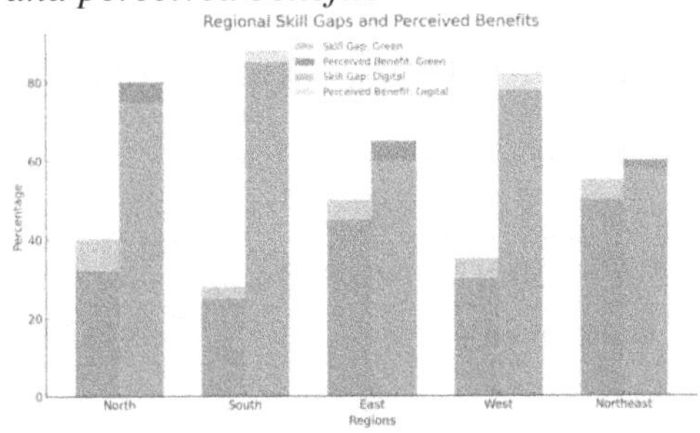

Figure 1 displays regional skill gaps and perceived benefits for green and digital competencies. The South region's performance highlights the importance of robust training programs and digital readiness. In contrast, the Northeast requires significant focus on awareness campaigns and infrastructure support.

5.2 Examining the Drivers of Perceived Benefits

Regression models were applied to understand the relationship between awareness levels and perceived benefits. To understand the relationship between skill awareness and perceived benefits, regression models were developed.

1. **Green Skills**: Awareness strongly predicts perceived benefits (R2=0.92R^2 = 0.92R2=0.92), indicating that a 1% increase in awareness improves perceived benefits by 0.64%.
2. **Digital Competencies**: A similarly strong relationship (R2=0.91R^2 = 0.91R2=0.91) was observed, with benefits increasing by 0.74% per unit of awareness.

Figure 2. Awareness vs perceived benefits

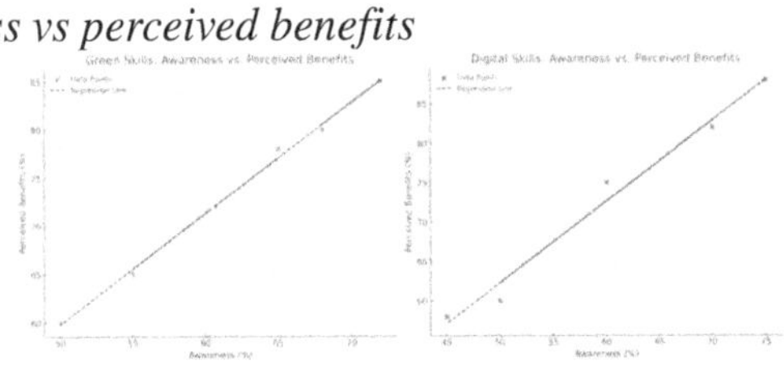

Figure 2 illustrates the relationships between awareness levels and perceived benefits for green and digital skills, showcasing the strength of these correlations.

5.3 Adoption Across Demographics

A comparison of skill adoption between urban and rural demographics revealed practical disparities:

Table 2. Adoption levels for urban and rural groups

Group	Green Skills Adoption (%)	Digital Skills Adoption (%)
Urban	80	75
Rural	60	50

Table 2 shows the percentage of adoption levels for urban and rural groups Chi-Square Test Results:

- **Statistic**: 0.12
- **P-Value**: 0.73

Figure 3. Adoption of green and digital skills in urban vs. rural areas

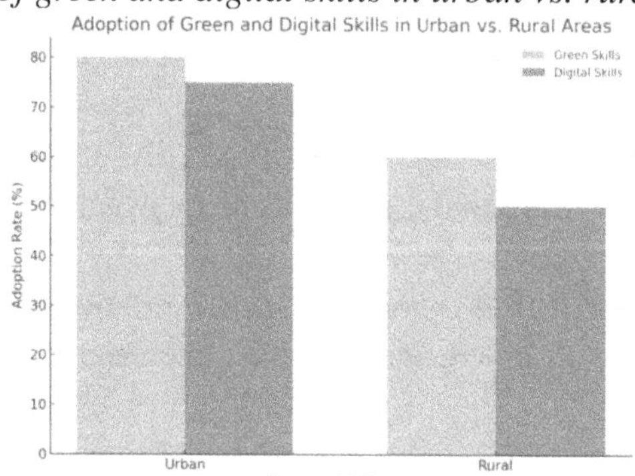

Figure 3 highlights the adoption rates of green and digital skills in urban and rural areas, emphasizing demographic disparities. It indicates that while statistically insignificant, the absolute differences point to practical challenges, such as limited access to training and infrastructure in rural areas.

5.4 Insights from Real-World Applications

An analysis of case studies revealed thematic insights into the application of green and digital skills in India's tourism sector:

Table 3. Combined insights from case studies

Case Study	Focus Area	Key Initiative	Outcome
Kerala's Responsible Tourism Mission	Community-driven	Sustainable crafts and e-commerce training	Enhanced livelihoods and eco-awareness
Sikkim's Sustainable Tourism Model	Eco-tourism	GIS monitoring and biodiversity training	Improved satisfaction and reduced ecological disruption
Rajasthan's Desert National Park	Wildlife conservation	Virtual tours and AI for wildlife tracking	Minimized interference and increased tourist engagement
Madhya Pradesh's Heritage Tourism	Cultural preservation	Augmented reality and heritage guide training	Improved accessibility and preservation of fragile sites

Table 3 summarizes crucial insights from four case studies. Recurring themes extracted from the analyzed policies and initiatives include:

1. **Community-Centric Approaches**: The success of Kerala and Sikkim demonstrates the importance of involving local communities in both green and digital skill-building efforts.
2. **Technological Integration**: Rajasthan and Madhya Pradesh show how digital tools can complement sustainability goals.
3. **Scalability and Replicability**: These models provide frameworks that can be adapted across regions, tailored to specific needs.

Figure 4. Effectiveness focus across case studies

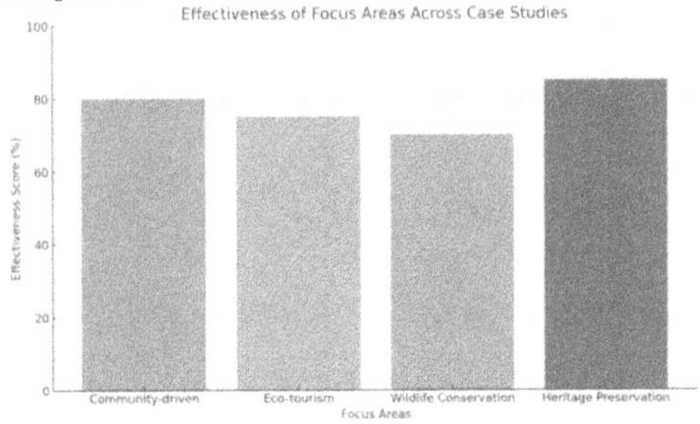

Figure 4 show represents the thematic focus distribution across the four case studies, showing how each focus area contributes to the overall analysis. These four case studies highlight successful models of integrating green and digital skills to address specific regional needs while fostering sustainability.

6. FINDINGS

The analysis reveals significant disparities in the awareness, adoption, and perceived benefits of green skills and digital competencies across India's tourism workforce. These findings highlight areas of strength and concern, offering valuable insights for policymakers, educators, and industry stakeholders.

6.1 Regional Disparities

- **Awareness Levels**: The South region leads with the highest awareness for green skills (72%) and digital competencies (75%). In contrast, the Northeast exhibits the lowest awareness levels, with only 50% for green skills and 45% for digital competencies.
- **Skill Gaps**: While the South has relatively low skill gaps (28% green, 25% digital), the Northeast faces significant challenges, with gaps of 50% for green and 55% for digital competencies. These disparities underline the need for region-specific training programs.

6.2 Relationships Between Awareness and Perceived Benefits

- Regression analysis indicates a strong positive correlation between awareness and perceived benefits for both green (R2=0.92R^2 = 0.92R2=0.92) and digital competencies (R2=0.91R^2 = 0.91R2=0.91).
- Regions with higher awareness levels, such as the South, also report greater perceived benefits, emphasizing the importance of awareness campaigns to enhance workforce engagement and value realization.

6.3 Adoption Across Demographics

- Urban areas report higher adoption rates for green skills (80%) and digital competencies (75%) compared to rural areas (60% and 50%, respectively).
- While the chi-square test shows no statistically significant differences between urban and rural groups, practical barriers like infrastructure and access to training resources remain critical concerns in rural regions.

6.4 Insights from Case Studies

- Successful integration of green skills in Kerala's Responsible Tourism Mission has enhanced community livelihoods and eco-awareness through sustainable practices.
- Sikkim's eco-tourism model demonstrates the effectiveness of combining biodiversity conservation training with GIS-based digital tools for monitoring.
- Rajasthan's use of virtual tours and AI for wildlife conservation highlights how technology can minimize human interference while improving visitor engagement.
- Madhya Pradesh's use of augmented reality in heritage tourism enhances accessibility and reduces the physical strain on fragile sites, showcasing the potential of digital tools in cultural preservation.

7. FRAMEWORK FOR INTEGRATING GREEN SKILLS AND DIGITAL COMPETENCIES INTO INDIA'S TOURISM WORKFORCE

India's tourism sector holds immense potential to contribute to sustainable development by integrating green skills and digital competencies into its workforce. These capabilities are critical for addressing environmental challenges, meeting technological demands, and improving the sector's global competitiveness. This framework presents a structured approach to bridge the skill gaps and align workforce capabilities with sustainability goals and smart tourism practices.

7.1 The Need for Green Skills and Digital Competencies

7.1.1 Importance of Green Skills

Green skills encompass capabilities that support environmental conservation, resource efficiency, and sustainability in tourism operations. The growing awareness of climate change and biodiversity loss makes these skills vital. For instance, the success of Kerala's *Responsible Tourism Mission* underscores the role of green skills in training local communities in waste management, organic farming, and energy efficiency, resulting in increased eco-awareness and livelihoods (Kerala Tourism, 2022).

Globally, sustainable tourism models like Bhutan's "High-Value, Low-Impact" policy demonstrate the transformative impact of such skills in reducing the carbon footprint and preserving fragile ecosystems (UNDP, 2021). Similarly, the International Labour Organization highlights green skills as a cornerstone for achieving the UN Sustainable Development Goals (ILO, 2011).

7.1.2 The Role of Digital Competencies

Digital tools and platforms revolutionize the tourism experience, from AI-driven personalization to augmented reality (AR) for heritage preservation. Sikkim's GIS-enabled trekking routes illustrate how digital tools can monitor tourist activities, promote safety, and minimize environmental disruption (Sikkim Tourism, 2021). Madhya Pradesh's AR-based virtual tours at heritage sites have successfully reduced physical strain on fragile monuments while increasing visitor engagement (Madhya Pradesh Tourism Board, 2022).

Moreover, integrating technologies like IoT and big data analytics into tourism operations enhances resource management and decision-making, as evidenced by smart tourism initiatives in destinations like Singapore and Dubai (Buhalis & Amaranggana, 2015).

7.2 Key Components of the Framework

7.2.1 Developing Green Skills

1. **Training in Sustainable Practices** o Programs should focus on resource conservation, energy efficiency, and waste management. For example, Kerala's eco-friendly homestays integrate green skills training to reduce waste and improve operational sustainability (Kerala Tourism, 2022). o Training modules can include case studies, on-ground workshops, and virtual simulations to deepen understanding.
2. **Community Engagement** o Engaging local communities in green initiatives ensures inclusivity and long-term sustainability (Rahman & Baddam, 2021). Rajasthan's Desert National Park trains local communities in wildlife conservation and eco-tourism, creating economic opportunities while protecting biodiversity (Rajasthan Forest Department, 2020).
3. **Eco-Certifications** o Introducing certification programs for green tourism skills enhances worker employability and ensures industry-wide standards (Yaghı, 2024). Certifications aligned with global benchmarks, such as those offered by the Global Sustainable Tourism Council (GSTC), can be adopted.

7.2.2 Promoting Digital Competencies

1. **Skill Development in Digital Tools** o Training programs should focus on AI, AR, VR, and GIS applications tailored for tourism (Lin et al., 2020). Madhya Pradesh's heritage sites have leveraged AR to offer virtual tours, making cultural heritage accessible to diverse audiences (Madhya Pradesh Tourism Board, 2022).
2. **Data Literacy and Analytics** o Equipping workers with data literacy enhances decision-making and enables personalized tourism experiences (Ercik & Kardaş, 2024). For instance, leveraging visitor data analytics helps operators tailor offerings to customer preferences, increasing satisfaction and revenue (Gössling & Hall, 2019).
3. **Digital Infrastructure Development** o Enhancing internet connectivity and providing access to digital tools in rural and remote areas ensures inclusivity. Sikkim's mobile apps for eco-tourism are a model for bridging technological divides (Sikkim Tourism, 2021).

7.3 Strategies for Implementation

7.3.1 Stakeholder Engagement

1. **Government Initiatives** o Programs like *Digital India* and *Swadesh Darshan* should integrate skill-building modules. For example, Swadesh Darshan's thematic circuits, such as the Northeast's eco-tourism circuit, can incorporate green and digital skills into project development (Ministry of Tourism, 2022).
2. **Private Sector Collaboration** o Partnerships with technology providers can facilitate access to the latest tools and training resources. Global examples like Google's *Grow with Google* initiative offer free training in digital skills that could be adapted to the tourism context (World Economic Forum, 2020).
3. **Academic and Training Institutions** o Collaborations with universities and vocational institutes can embed green and digital skills into tourism curricula. Research collaborations can also identify emerging industry trends and skill requirements (Nickson, 2013, Chen et al., 2022).

7.3.2 Regional Customization

It is crucial to tailor programs to regional needs ensures their relevance and impact. For instance:

1. **Northeast India**: Emphasize eco-tourism and biodiversity training to address the region's low awareness and high skill gaps (Sikkim Tourism, 2021).
2. **South India**: Build on existing digital readiness by offering advanced training in AI and data analytics (Gössling & Hall, 2019).
3. **Heritage-Rich Regions**: Focus on AR and VR technologies for heritage preservation in states like Madhya Pradesh (UNWTO, 2023).

7.4 Monitoring and Evaluation

7.4.1 Measuring Impact

To address the evolving challenges of talent management in the tourism sector, it is crucial to integrate adaptive performance measures and resilience-building strategies into workforce development, fostering employee collaboration, learning, and adaptability to navigate uncertain and complex environments (Luthia, 2022). In addition, performance metrics and annual audits can help enhance the impact of the programs.

1. **Performance Metrics**: Evaluate programs based on skill adoption rates, employability, and environmental impact (Strietska-Ilina et al., 2011). Metrics should include reductions in resource wastage and energy savings.
2. **Annual Audits**: Independent audits can assess the effectiveness and scalability of training programs (UNDP, 2021).

7.4.2 Feedback Mechanisms

1. **Real-Time Feedback**: Digital tools can collect feedback from trainees and employers, enabling continuous refinement of programs (World Travel and Tourism Council, 2021).
2. **Trainee Surveys**: Periodic surveys can gauge satisfaction and identify areas for improvement.

7.5 Expected Outcomes

7.5.1 Economic Gains

1. Enhanced employability of trained workers increases their competitiveness in global markets.
2. Sustainable tourism attracts high-value visitors, boosting revenue.

7.5.2 Environmental Benefits

1. Reduction in carbon footprint and resource wastage through sustainable practices.
2. Preservation of ecosystems and heritage sites through eco-friendly and tech-driven interventions.

7.5.3 Social Impact

1. Empowering marginalized communities with skills promotes equitable economic growth.
2. Strengthened community resilience through inclusive tourism models (UNWTO, 2023).

7.6 Addressing Challenges

7.6.1 Challenges

1. **Infrastructure Gaps**: Limited access to digital tools and internet connectivity in rural areas hinders training delivery.
2. **Resistance to Change**: Workers and employers may hesitate to adopt new practices due to lack of awareness or perceived risks.
3. **Funding Limitations**: Training initiatives require significant investment, which may strain resources.

7.6.2 Mitigation Strategies

1. **Infrastructure Investment**: Enhancing connectivity and digital literacy in underserved regions through public-private partnerships (World Economic Forum, 2020).
2. **Awareness Campaigns**: Educating stakeholders on the benefits of skill integration to reduce resistance and build enthusiasm (UNDP, 2021).
3. **Funding Models**: Encourage co-investment by government and private players, ensuring sustainability and scalability (Hossin et al., 2024).

8. DISCUSSION

The integration of green skills and digital competencies into India's tourism workforce represents a transformative opportunity to align the sector with global sustainability goals and technological advancements. This discussion synthesizes the framework's findings, explores its implications, and addresses the broader challenges and prospects of implementing such a framework.

8.1 Relevance of Green Skills and Digital Competencies

8.1.1 Sustainability as a Necessity

The increasing pressure on natural resources and fragile ecosystems necessitates the adoption of green skills in the tourism sector. Training programs focused on resource efficiency, waste management, and biodiversity conservation can significantly reduce tourism's ecological footprint. Kerala's Responsible Tourism Mission illustrates how community-driven initiatives can enhance eco-awareness while boosting local livelihoods (Kerala Tourism, 2022). This dual impact of environmental conservation and socio-economic development makes green skills indispensable for the sector's long-term viability.

8.1.2 Digital Transformation in Tourism

The role of digital competencies has expanded significantly in tourism, particularly in enhancing visitor experiences and operational efficiency. For example, augmented reality (AR) applications in Madhya Pradesh's heritage tourism not only protect fragile monuments but also offer immersive experiences to visitors (Madhya Pradesh Tourism Board, 2022). Similarly, Sikkim's GIS-enabled eco-tourism demonstrates how digital tools can balance visitor engagement with environmental protection (Sikkim Tourism, 2021). These examples underscore the transformative potential of technology in driving smart and sustainable tourism.

8.2 Implications for Policy and Practice

8.2.1 Bridging Regional Disparities

One of the key findings of this study is the stark disparity in skill levels and readiness across regions. The South leads in both awareness and perceived benefits, while the Northeast lags significantly. This gap highlights the need for region-specific interventions, such as focusing on eco-tourism and biodiversity training in the Northeast and advancing AI and data analytics capabilities in South India (Gössling & Hall, 2019). Policymakers must ensure equitable access to training resources, especially in underserved areas, to achieve balanced regional development.

8.2.2 Fostering Inclusivity

Inclusivity is critical for sustainable development. Marginalized communities often face barriers to accessing training programs due to infrastructure deficits, cultural biases, and financial constraints (Gillovic & McIntosh, 2020). Programs like Rajasthan's wildlife conservation training in Desert National Park show that involving local communities not only enhances skill adoption but also empowers them economically (Rajasthan Forest Department, 2020). Ensuring participation from women and marginalized groups can drive inclusive growth and foster resilience in local economies.

8.2.3 Strengthening Public-Private Partnerships

The role of public-private partnerships is pivotal in overcoming resource and infrastructure constraints (Hossin et al., 2024). Collaboration with technology providers can facilitate access to advanced tools, as seen in global initiatives like Google's Grow with Google program, which provides free digital skills training (World Economic Forum, 2020). The government's existing schemes, such as Digital India and Swadesh Darshan, can be leveraged to fund and scale these collaborations.

8.3 Challenges in Implementation

8.3.1 Infrastructure Deficits

The lack of adequate infrastructure, particularly in rural and remote areas, poses a significant challenge to implementing the proposed framework. Limited internet connectivity and access to digital tools hinder the adoption of digital competencies. For instance, while Sikkim's eco-tourism model has made strides in GIS-enabled monitoring, similar efforts in other regions are constrained by technological and infrastructural gaps (Sikkim Tourism, 2021).

8.3.2 Resistance to Change

Another barrier is the resistance to adopting new practices among workers and employers. Many stakeholders view the adoption of green and digital skills as disruptive, requiring significant behavioral and operational changes. Awareness campaigns that highlight the long-term benefits of skill integration, such as increased employability and revenue, are crucial for mitigating this resistance (Hussain et al., 2024).

8.3.3 Funding Limitations

Implementing large-scale training programs requires substantial financial investment, which may strain government budgets. Encouraging co-investment from private players and exploring alternative funding models, such as CSR initiatives and international grants, can address these constraints (Gössling & Hall, 2019).

8.4 Future Prospects

8.4.1 Scaling Success Stories

The success of Kerala's community-driven green initiatives and Madhya Pradesh's AR-based heritage tours provide replicable models for other states. Scaling such initiatives through policy support and cross-regional collaboration can accelerate the integration of green and digital skills into the workforce.

8.4.2 Leveraging Technology for Training

Technological advancements offer innovative ways to deliver training. Virtual reality (VR) simulations, for example, can provide practical training in wildlife management and eco-tourism without requiring trainees to travel to remote locations. Online learning platforms can further expand the reach of training programs, ensuring inclusivity and scalability (Buhalis & Amaranggana, 2015).

8.4.3 Global Alignment

Aligning India's tourism practices with global sustainability and technological standards enhances its competitiveness in international markets. Certifications aligned with the Global Sustainable Tourism Council (GSTC) and collaborations with international organizations like UNWTO can establish India as a leader in sustainable and smart tourism (UNWTO, 2023).

9. CONCLUSION

Integrating green skills and digital competencies into India's tourism workforce is essential for fostering a sustainable and competitive industry. This framework emphasizes equipping the workforce with the tools and knowledge needed to align with global sustainability and technological standards. By addressing skill gaps and leveraging regional strengths, the tourism sector can achieve greater inclusivity, efficiency, and environmental stewardship.

Green skills, such as resource conservation, waste management, and biodiversity preservation, are critical for reducing tourism's ecological footprint while promoting sustainable livelihoods. Similarly, digital competencies, including data analytics, GIS, and augmented reality, enhance operational efficiency and visitor experiences. Augmented reality (AR), in particular, offers a transformative potential by creating interactive and user-centered learning environments, enabling preliminary training and seamless simulation experiences while improving operational efficiency (Singh & Ahmad, 2024). These skills empower the workforce to adopt eco-friendly practices and capitalize on technology-driven opportunities.

The disparities in skill levels across regions, especially between the South and Northeast, highlight the need for tailored, region-specific interventions. Addressing these gaps requires strategic investments in infrastructure, targeted training programs, and collaborations with private and academic stakeholders. Public-private partnerships and initiatives like Digital India and Swadesh Darshan offer valuable platforms for scaling these efforts.

The successful integration of these competencies will yield multiple benefits: a skilled workforce, improved employability, increased tourism revenue, and the preservation of natural and cultural assets. Moreover, fostering inclusivity through the involvement of marginalized communities ensures equitable growth and strengthens local economies.

Looking ahead, India's tourism sector must continue to innovate and adapt by embracing global best practices and sustainability certifications. With strategic planning and a commitment to inclusive growth, India can position itself as a global leader in sustainable and smart tourism, contributing significantly to socio-economic and environmental progress. Through these efforts, the sector can not only meet immediate challenges but also build a resilient and thriving future.

REFERENCES

Al-Romeedy, B. S., & Alharethi, T. (2024). Sustainable Tourism Performance Through Green Talent Management: The Mediating Power of Green Entrepreneurship and Climate. *Sustainability (Basel)*, *16*(22), 9900. DOI: 10.3390/su16229900

Alsheref, F. K., Khairy, H. A., Alsetoohy, O., Elsawy, O., Fayyad, S., Salama, M., Al-Romeedy, B. S., & Soliman, S. A. E. M. (2024). Catalyzing Green Identity and Sustainable Advantage in Tourism and Hotel Businesses. *Sustainability (Basel)*, *16*(12), 5267. DOI: 10.3390/su16125267

Atsız, O. (2021). Virtual reality technology and physical distancing: A review on limiting human interaction in tourism. Journal of multidisciplinary academic tourism, 6(1), 27-35.

Baum, T. (2015). *Human Resource Management for Tourism, Hospitality, and Leisure*. Channel View Publications.

Buhalis, D. (2020). Technology in tourism: From information communication technologies to eTourism and smart tourism towards ambient intelligence tourism. *Tourism Review*. Advance online publication. DOI: 10.1108/TR-06-2019-0258

Buhalis, D., & Amaranggana, A. (2015). *Smart tourism destinations. Information and Communication Technologies in Tourism*. Springer.

Chandel, N., Dutta, K., & Bhujel, P. R. (2024). Eco-Tourism as a Driver for Sustainable Regional Development Amidst Climate Change Realities in the Eastern Himalayas: A Study of Sikkim in India. In *Climate Change and Regional Socio-Economic Systems in the Global South: Resilience Strategies for Sustainable Development* (pp. 373–394). Springer Nature Singapore. DOI: 10.1007/978-981-97-3870-0_18

Chen, M., Pei, T., Jeronen, E., Wang, Z., & Xu, L. (2022). Teaching and learning methods for promoting sustainability in tourism education. *Sustainability (Basel)*, *14*(21), 14592. DOI: 10.3390/su142114592

Choegyal, L. (2022). Tourism for Development in the Himalaya: Using Ecotourism to Improve Livelihoods. In Tourism and Development in the Himalaya (pp. 129-148). Routledge.

Dodds, R., & Butler, R. (2019). *Overtourism: Issues, Realities, and Solutions*. De Gruyter. DOI: 10.1515/9783110607369

Ercik, C., & Kardaş, K. (2024). Reflections of digital technologies on human resources management in the tourism sector. *Worldwide Hospitality and Tourism Themes*, *16*(5), 646–663. DOI: 10.1108/WHATT-09-2024-0208

Fan, X., Jiang, X., & Deng, N. (2022). Immersive technology: A meta-analysis of augmented/virtual reality applications and their impact on tourism experience. *Tourism Management*, *91*, 104534. DOI: 10.1016/j.tourman.2022.104534

Gillovic, B., & McIntosh, A. (2020). Accessibility and inclusive tourism development: Current state and future agenda. *Sustainability (Basel)*, *12*(22), 9722. DOI: 10.3390/su12229722

Gössling, S., & Hall, C. M. (2019). Sustainable tourism: A global perspective. *Tourism Management.*

Hossin, M. A., Alemzero, D., Abudu, H., Yin, S., Mu, L., & Panichakarn, B. (2024). Examining public private partnership investment in energy towards achieving sustainable development goal 7 for ASEAN region. *Scientific Reports*, *14*(1), 16398. DOI: 10.1038/s41598-024-66800-9 PMID: 39014008

Hussein, H., Albadry, O. M., Mathew, V., Al-Romeedy, B. S., Alsetoohy, O., Abou Kamar, M., & Khairy, H. A. (2024). Digital leadership and sustainable competitive advantage: Leveraging green absorptive capability and eco-innovation in tourism and hospitality businesses. *Sustainability (Basel)*, *16*(13), 5371. DOI: 10.3390/su16135371

. Kannan, R. (2024). Revolutionizing the Tourism Industry through Artificial Intelligence: A Comprehensive Review of AI Integration, Impact on Customer Experience, Operational Efficiency, and Future Trends. International Journal for Multidimensional Research Perspectives, 2(2), 01-14.

Kerala Tourism. (2022). *Responsible Tourism Mission Report*. Government of Kerala.

Koundinya, S., & Singh, M. (2019). Workforce sustainability in tourism: The role of human capital. *Tourism Economics*.

Lama, N. (2021). Community Based Eco-Tourism: Looking into the Government Policy Initiatives in Sikkim. [IJAEM]. *International Journal of Advances in Engineering and Management*, *3*(7), 1368–1377.

Lin, L. P. L., Huang, S. C. L., & Ho, Y. C. (2020). Could virtual reality effectively market slow travel in a heritage destination? *Tourism Management*, *78*, 104027. DOI: 10.1016/j.tourman.2019.104027

Luthia, M. (2022). Reimaging talent management through adaptive performance in the next normal. *SDMIMD Journal of Management, 13*, 113–124. DOI: 10.18311/sdmimd/2022/29708

Madhya Pradesh Tourism Board. (2022). *Heritage and Sustainable Tourism Project Report*. Government of Madhya Pradesh.

Mantey, I. (2021). SMALL AND MEDIUM SCALE ENTERPRISES (SMEs) IN THEDEVELOPMENT OF TOURISM IN THE GLOBAL SOUTH: THEIR ROLE AND CHALLENGES.

Markose, N., Vazhakkatte Tazhathethil, B., & George, B. (2022). Sustainability initiatives for green tourism development: The case of Wayanad, India. *Journal of Risk and Financial Management, 15*(2), 52. DOI: 10.3390/jrfm15020052

McKercher, B. (2018). *Contemporary Tourism Dynamics*. Oxford University Press.

Ministry of Tourism. (2022). *Tourism Statistics at a Glance*. Government of India.

Nabila, E. M. (2023). Digital transformation and AI in tourism: Trends, challenges, and successful experiences. *Economic Studies, 23*(01), 522–545.

Nickson, D. (2013). *Human Resource Management for Hospitality and Tourism*. Routledge. DOI: 10.4324/9780080966496

Porter, M. (1985). *Competitive Advantage: Creating and Sustaining Superior Performance*. Free Press.

Rahman, S. S., & Baddam, P. R. (2021). Community Engagement in Southeast Asia's Tourism Industry: Empowering Local Economies. *Global Disclosure of Economics and Business, 10*(2), 75–90. DOI: 10.18034/gdeb.v10i2.715

Rajasthan Forest Department. (2020). *Sustainable Practices in Desert National Park*. Government of Rajasthan.

Shetty, N. K., Kamath, S., Patil, A. A., Tejaswi, S. I., Bhat, M., Naik, S. R., & Samrajya, S. (2024). Creating Sustainable Experiential Tourism for Showcasing Tulunadu's Ecological Treasures. *Journal of Informatics Education and Research, 4*(1).

Sikkim Tourism. (2021). *Ecotourism Development Plan for Sikkim*. Government of Sikkim.

Singh, G., & Ahmad, F. (2024). An interactive augmented reality framework to enhance the user experience and operational skills in electronics laboratories. *Smart Learning Environments, 11*(1), 5. DOI: 10.1186/s40561-023-00287-1

Srivastava, P. (2024). Tourism's green lens: Navigating sustainable development from tourists' viewpoint. *International Journal of Services and Standards*, *14*(1), 28–50. DOI: 10.1504/IJSS.2024.140077

Strietska-Ilina, O.. (2011). *Skills for Green Jobs: A Global View*. International Labour Organization.

Tripathi, N. (2024). Innovation in Action Harnessing Technology for Wildlife Conservation in India.

Tussyadiah, I.. (2020). Virtual reality, presence, and attitude change: Empirical evidence from tourism. *Tourism Management*.

UNDP. (2021). *Bhutan's high-value, low-impact tourism*. UNDP Sustainable Development Reports.

UNWTO. (2023). *Sustainability and Digital Transformation in Tourism*. United Nations World Tourism Organization.

Velaoras, K., Menegaki, A. N., Polyzos, S., & Gotzamani, K. (2024). *The Role of Environmental Certifications in the Hospitality Industry: Assessing Sustainability*. Consumer Preferences and Economic Impact.

World Bank. (2021). *Digital Divide and Development: A Case for India*. World Bank Reports.

WTTC. (2021). *Economic Impact Report for India*. World Travel and Tourism Council.

Yaghı, L. (2024). Optimizing employee performance: Comparing the impact of different training methods in the travel and tourism industry of Lebanon (Master's thesis, İzmir Ekonomi Üniversitesi).

APPENDIX: SURVEY QUESTIONS

1. What is your role in the tourism industry?
   - o Employee
   - o HR Manager
   - o Policymaker
   - o Educator
   - o Other
2. What is your primary region of operation?
   - o North
   - o South
   - o East
   - o West
   - o Northeast
3. Are you based in:
   - o Urban area
   - o Rural area
4. Are you familiar with the concept of green skills in the tourism sector?
   - o Yes
   - o No
5. Which of the following green skills are you aware of?
   - o Resource conservation
   - o Biodiversity preservation
   - o Waste management
   - o Eco-friendly hospitality practices
6. Rate your awareness of green skills relevant to your role:
   - o 1 (Low)
   - o 2
   - o 3
   - o 4
   - o 5 (High)
7. Are you familiar with the concept of digital competencies in the tourism sector?
   - o Yes
   - o No
8. Which of the following digital tools are you familiar with?
   - o Data analytics
   - o Augmented/Virtual Reality (AR/VR)
   - o AI-powered customer interaction tools
   - o GIS and mapping technologies

9. Rate your awareness of digital competencies relevant to your role:
    - o 1 (Low)
    - o 2
    - o 3
    - o 4
    - o 5 (High)
10. Do you feel there is a gap between your current skills and the skills required to meet sustainability goals in tourism?
    - Yes
    - No
11. Which area do you feel the largest skill gap exists?
    - Green skills
    - Digital competencies
    - Both equally
12. Rate the impact of this skill gap on your ability to perform effectively:
    - 1 (Low)
    - 2
    - 3
    - 4
    - 5 (High)
13. How beneficial do you think integrating green skills into the tourism workforce would be for economic growth?
    - 1 (Low)
    - 2
    - 3
    - 4
    - 5 (High)
14. How beneficial do you think integrating digital competencies into the tourism workforce would be for efficiency and innovation?
    - 1 (Low)
    - 2
    - 3
    - 4
    - 5 (High)
15. What barriers do you face in accessing training for green skills and digital competencies?
    - Lack of awareness
    - Limited access to training resources
    - Cost of training
    - Resistance to change

16. Would you be interested in participating in workshops or training programs to enhance your green skills and digital competencies?
    - Yes
    - No

Chapter 7
Leveraging the Metaverse for Transformative Talent Management in the Tourism Industry

Aman Kabia
Central University of Himachal Pradesh, India

Gulab Kumar
https://orcid.org/0009-0002-7171-4062
Central University of Himachal Pradesh, India

Dipanker Sharma
https://orcid.org/0000-0003-0501-1473
Central University of Himachal Pradesh, India

ABSTRACT

The tourism industry is highly sensitive and volatile, constantly being influenced by global trends and emerging technologies. One major change is the emergence of the metaverse, an extension of augmented reality, virtual reality, and 3D simulations. This digital innovation not only offers new ways to deliver tourism services but also offers significant potential to enhance human resource management within the sector. Talent management (TM) is a significant challenge in tourism, and this chapter explores how the metaverse can be used to address this issue. It discusses the different types of metaverse, their relation to tourism, and their role in improving TM. The metaverse can also help address challenges such as data security, employee well-being, and work-life balance by creating immersive virtual environments. Additionally, chapter reviews how the metaverse has been applied in other industries

DOI: 10.4018/979-8-3373-0071-9.ch007

and identifies future opportunities for its use in tourism. Ultimately, it shows how virtual spaces can transform TM and strengthen the resilience of the tourism sector.

1. INTRODUCTION

American science fiction author Neal Stephenson originally used the word "metaverse" in his 1992 book "Snow Crash." (Faraboschi et al., 2022; Ioannidis &Kontis, 2023). The term Metaverse is a Greek word that is divided into two words "Meta" and "Verse"(Kye et al., 2021) suggesting that there is a reality outside of the one in which we all live (Ioannidis & Kontis, 2023). The World Economic Forum (2022) defined the term "metaverse," which forms the foundation of transforming consumer interaction and company processes., It creates new channels for communication between companies and clients, creating chances to offer distinctive goods or specialized, tailored services. One of the main sectors gaining from the use of the metaverse is the tourism and hospitality sector, which can be used to add a competitive advantage (Chi et al., 2024). The metaverse has implications in many different fields(Piñeiro-Chousa et al., 2024) including healthcare, engineering, education, finance, marketing, and the environment.

The idea of the Metaverse has drawn interest from the corporate, technological, and scientific communities in recent years (Kim, 2021). With the possibility for a virtual and technologically immersive world, the Metaverse is becoming a topic of research and investigation across several fields (Buhalis et al., 2023). The concept of the metaverse was first introduced in the book Machine Stops by E. M. Foster in 1909. An environmental catastrophe renders the world unusable, forcing nearly all people to live underground in separate pods, based on the brief science fiction narrative "Machine Stops". Every human need and want is met by an intricate global machine in Foster's hypothetical society, ranging from 75 fundamental demands (pure air, light, food, and shelter facilities) to more upscale desires (such as leisure, literature, melody, and social contact). When Facebook changed itself from Facebook to "Meta," a metaverse firm, the metaverse recently attracted renewed attention; about a century after the initial publication of the "machine stops" (Kim, 2021;Gursoy et al., 2022). Metaverse can be best described as the evolution of today's internet activities, this is something with which we are completely involved, and it's not something that we look at primarily but something in which we are completely immersed today.

The use of metaverse in the tourism industry has many potential benefits they may include:

1. Allowing tourism providers or agencies that facilitate journeys to tourists, to provide highly or completely customized experiences based on individual preferences.
2. Metaverse facilitates customers to interact with their tourist guides and locals virtually and provides the benefit of participating in various activities virtually.
3. Travelers can reduce their carbon impact by using the metaverse to transfer part of their activities to a virtual environment, and this will promote sustainable development.
4. Metaverse plays a vital role by making travel experiences more accessible and more reliable for individuals with disabilities so that they can enjoy various destinations virtually.
5. When it comes to safety, metaverse plays a vital role by providing customers with a safe environment before actually visiting the tourist destination and helps them gain proper knowledge about cultures, and local customs or deal with potential dangers in the destination.

Nonetheless, the involvement of the metaverse is not limited to customer relations; it also offers great potential in another key area of organizational relevance – human resource management (HRM). An organization's most significant assets, its people, are managed through a variety of tasks collectively referred to as HRM (Kumar et al., 2025). Some of the biggest issues affecting the industry involve talent management. The sector often has very high employee turnover rates, problems recruiting and retaining quality staff, and employees require constant training (Pencarelli, 2020). Due to the dispersed nature of human resources – managing employees geographically spread across hotels, airlines, tour operators, and other service providers becomes even more challenging. Metaverse presents itself as an antidote to this problem as various talent management processes can be conducted in an online space (Dutta et al., 2023). The metaverse has the ability to change HRM's conventional procedures into more engaging and dynamic ones. AI-driven metaverses in hiring not only reduce the amount of time needed to finish the process but also calculate many dynamics at scale to help with decision-making (Anshima et al., 2023). The way individuals are managed at work has changed as a result. Using the metaverse to manage people has become more successful than using traditional methods as the need for remote work and hybrid work grows (Bala et al., 2024b). Therefore, HRM practitioners must encourage and support innovation and its results for the future of work and workforce, particularly in the context of hospitality and tourist businesses (Bamber et al., 2017).

The next sections of the chapter are organized as follows: 2) The Metaverse 3) Talent Management and Metaverse 4) Tourism Industry and Metaverse 5) Future Opportunities of Metaverse in the Tourism Industry 6) Different uses of Metaverse for Tourism 7) Impact of Metaverse on Tourist Behavior, and 8) Conclusion.

2. THE METAVERSE

According to (Dwivedi et al., 2022), the metaverse engages individuals based on their innate desire provides psychological stability and emotional connection, and can assist in resolving real-world problems with societal inequity and prejudice. The metaverse can promote deep attachment and emotional connection through virtual immersive environments, and the avatars can assist in hiring employees virtually and in virtual training environments. Social engagement and participation can be carried out through the stability of avatars' emotions and psychology within the metaverse, independent of the physical presence. We observe one adaptation from a tourist technology company in managing talent learning. Metaverse knowledge, as an agent of technology, provides efficiency and flexibility in bringing about organizational structures, routines, and practices (Dutta et al., 2023). A three-dimensional (3D) virtual environment that prioritizes human interactions is referred to as the "metaverse," which was made feasible by Web 3.0. The metaverse is attracting interest from the hotel and tourism industry due to its potential to foster social connections as well as a sense of presence (Gursoy et al., 2022).

2.1 Evolution of Metaverse

In the vibrant roaring twenties, the idea of the metaverse first appeared. The term "Metaverse" was first used by an American novelist in 1992 in his best-selling book "Snow Crash" (Dutta et al., 2023). With the advent of this incredible digital world, an increasing number of tech businesses started to investigate the idea of virtual reality. When Microsoft launched the "Mesh" platform and Facebook renamed itself from Facebook to "Meta," the metaverse gained a lot of attention in 2021. As the trend persisted, new and improved virtual reality versions with increasingly complex hardware and software were released each year. Metaverse dates back to long time duration and has gained significance over time. Let's see how the term metaverse has changed over time and how it is applicable in various sectors like education, gaming, tourism, and military etc.

2.1.1 Metaverse in 90's (1992-1993)

Neal Stephenson, an American author of science fiction, used the term "Metaverse" in his book "Snow Crash". The foundation of Bitcoin was established by Israeli and American computer scientists Cynthia Dwork and Moni Naor, who created evidence of work methods to prevent denial-of-service attacks and spam (Dutta et al., 2023).

2.1.2 Metaverse During 2000's (2003-2010)

The term metaverse has gained immense importance during this time. Second Life is a 3D virtual environment introduced by Linden Labs. Users can explore, communicate with others, make things, and exchange virtual products using it. Users can develop and play massively multiplayer games made by other users on the online gaming platform ROBOX (Hung et al., 2024; Núñez et al., 2025), which was co-created by Roblox and Roblox. For mobile devices, Google Street View augmented maps allow visitors to investigate a virtual representation of the real environment. Satoshi Nakamoto introduced the first public blockchain using the proof-of-work method. When Konami released the mobile game Dragon Collection on Japan's social networking site, they used the Gacha model.

2.1.3 Metaverse During 2011-2016

Ernest C. Talin published his Ready Player One book in 2011, which was about the VR games that take place in 2044 (Maslin, 2011). Palmer Luckey, an American businessman, introduced "Oculus" on Kick-starter, the very first affordable 3D device for the general public. Facebook acquired Oculus and created a specialized 3D infrastructure to support it. Anil Dash, a software entrepreneur, and American artist Kevin Mccoy established the first NFT, a special cryptographically secured virtual asset. Ethereum is a decentralized blockchain application that was developed by Canadian programmer Vitalik Buterin and English computer scientist Gavin Wood (Wood, 2014). Early decentralized autonomous venture capital raising organization DAO debuts Ethereum blockchain. AR games overlaying the actual world were first made available by Pokémon GO.

2.1.4 Metaverse During 2018- Till Present

The Blockchain game named Axie Infinity was developed by the studio named Sky Mavis which is a Vietnam-based studio, which is also well-known for its Ethereum-based cryptocurrency in-game economy. Epic Games' "Fortnite" is also well-liked in the shared digital world, with more than 250 million active users.

Facebook's parent business changed its name to "Meta," which is a broad concept of the Metaverse. To create the Industrial Metaverse, Siemens and NVIDIA collaborated. "Vision PRO," a kind of head-mounted display for augmented reality as well as public relations events, was introduced by Apple under the name "Spatial Computing" (Bala et al., 2024a).

2.1.5 Metaverse in the Future

A digital realm where web-based technologies become more protected, decentralized, and integrated within fully immersive virtual environments is anticipated to be shaped by Web 3.0 technology, a revolutionary internet advancement that has just started to have an impact on our lives and is anticipated to be crucial in forming the future economy (Hanbay Tiryaki & Balaman, 2025).

Table 1. Evolution of metaverse

Year	Evolution
1992-1993	Cynthia Dwork and Moni Naor laid the foundation for Bitcoin with their proof-of-work method to combat spam and cyber-attacks, Neal Stephenson created the idea of the "metaverse" in "Snow Crash".
2003-2010	Inventions such as Satoshi Nakamoto's blockchain and the Gacha model in gaming have revolutionized digital experiences, with the metaverse developing with platforms such as Second Life, Roblox, and Google Street View, allowing virtual interaction and exploration.
2011-2016	Technological advancements include low-cost 3D devices such as Oculus, NFTs by Anil Dash and Kevin McCoy, Ethereum by Gavin Wood and Vitalik Buterin, and innovations such as DAOs on Ethereum and augmented reality games through Pokémon Go.
2018-Present	Siemens-Nvidia's industrial metaverse, Apple's Vision Pro for augmented reality, Meta's emphasis on the metaverse, Fortnite's massive user base, and Axie Infinity's Ethereum-based economy are just a few examples of virtual world innovations.

Source: Created by Authors

2.2 Component of Metaverse

2.2.1 Augmented Reality (AR):

AR is a key component of new industrial revolutions and one of the most prominent technologies of the twenty-first century. Researcher Thomas Caudell coined the term "augmented reality" in 1992 when he created an industrial AR program to see some assembly plans (Dutta et al., 2023). For users who experience virtual reality through these gadgets, navigation devices such as AR offer advantages like cost benefits, time savings, well-being, and security (Dutta et al., 2023; Pratisto et al., 2022). With assistance from components like a display, sensors, and a processor, AR made life easier for users by providing real-time experiences by assessing the existing state of the virtual world and the physical world and then displaying the virtual world in a manner that makes the user feel that the element of the virtual world is part and parcel of his or her physical world.

2.2.2 Virtual Reality (VR):

VR can reproduce real-life situations and even allow people to delve into a specially designed 3D environment composed by computer to simulate and act out a sequence of procedures using headsets, omnidirectional treadmills, as well as special gloves that stimulate our senses to generate an illusion of reality, the very concept has attracted major attention and even brought a paradigm shift in some training directions, primarily in the chemical, medical, and aviation industries. Virtual reality can revolutionize learner interaction and user experiences by simulation emotional and cognitive processes to enhance user-environment interaction and mimic the entire in-person classroom experience (Dwivedi et al., 2022). Although virtual tours, AR-delivered tours, and marketing campaigns based on VR are already widely used in the industry (Buhalis & Sinarta, 2019;Guttentag, 2010).

2.2.3 Mixed Reality:

Mixing both AR and VR, a technology is named Mixed Reality (MR). Users can also navigate through a computer-generated environment using a virtual reality headset. However, soon after the advent of AR, the lack of the essence of the real environment was replaced. This technology creates an augmented reality to further improve the user's perspective of the real environment by fusing human-generated information with it. This environment is such that, through the window between virtual and augmented worlds, it lets the user have an experience in a realistic scenario because real-world objects would be allowed to interact with virtual ones. There are three fundamental parts of any MR system: a procedure that combines virtual and real-world items, allows for real-time interaction, and maps to produce interactions (Bala et al., 2024a).

Figure 1. Components of metaverse

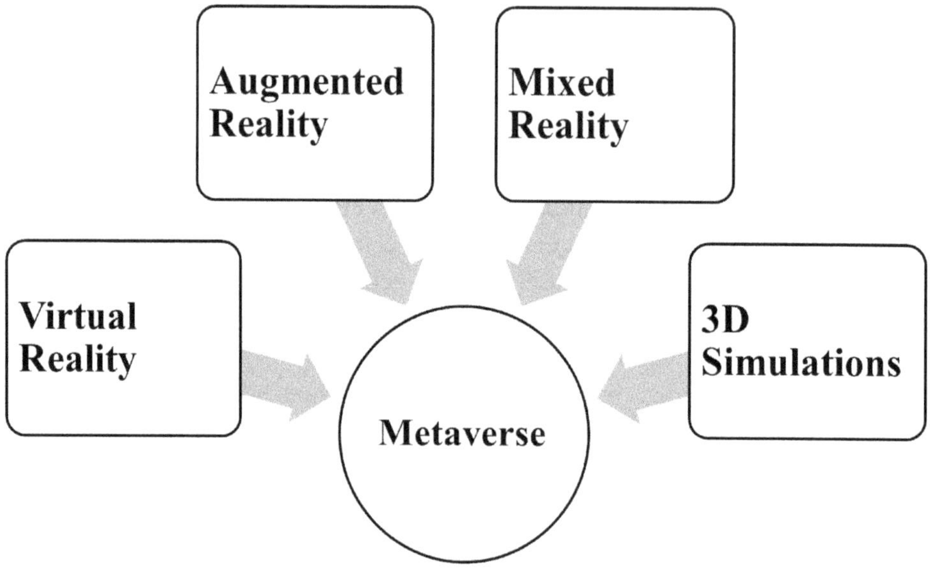

Source: Created by Authors

2.2.4 3D Simulations:

The artists can utilize the computer graphics technology referred to as 3D simulation when making fire, liquids, particles, and devastation appear as realistic as in life. A 3D model usually contains some vertices that can combine to form the mesh. One can manipulate each point to alter the shape of the model. It uses coordinate information to calculate the location of each point both in its vertical and horizontal position with respect to a reference point. Three-dimensional models use three-dimensional models, which are collections of points that exist in 3D space joined together by many geometric elements like triangles, lines, and curved surfaces. 3D models, collections of data in the form of points and other information, can also be generated through scanning or more algorithmic methods-procedural modeling entirely by hand; some use texture mapping to define surfaces of their models more saliently.

2.3 Application of Metaverse In Various Industries

2.3.1 Tourism:

As the metaverse has many of these opportunities, the hospitality industry will also have a chance to transform and create new marketing and operating strategies and designs for travel experiences for guests, which are interesting options for immersive tourism in this concept. The metaverse gives tourists a new and innovative experience of various tourist destinations by allowing the exploration of virtual worlds and their interactive exercises in real-life settings. Imagine visiting museums, historical sites, amusement parks, and natural wonders without ever leaving your house (Volchek & Brysch, 2023; Laachach et al., 2024).

2.3.2 Education:

Under dynamic settings in the metaverse, there is an allowance for immersed training and pedagogical experiences for students to learn. Over the past couple of years, virtual reality and augmented reality have gained popularity within education, and with AR and VR, students may engage in immersive digital experiences (Kumar et al., 2024). Most of the educational institutions adopted and embraced the online teaching and learning process. Metaverse learning has evolved traditional instruction for the production of more potent learning opportunities. However, fast change in online learning has very slowly made the students realize the gap between the fully involved, virtual in-class experiences and those that are real. The metaverse can help close that gap by using digital 3D virtual classrooms to connect them with teachers and classmates. This metaverse-enabled learning space allows students from anywhere to join in and do far more than they might in a traditional classroom.

2.3.3 Military:

In the military, it is considered an upbeat approach, with the entrance of a deep immersive, and engaging virtual environment, which may change the way commanders and military men and women would communicate, train, and make decisions in real-time. (Nedelcu & Petre, 2024). The Metaverse makes it possible to simulate military activities and combat situations realistically (Hajjami& Park, 2024). One can test and develop military technology, for example, autonomous vehicles, surveillance devices, as well as weapon systems. Such technologies may be tested as well as adjusted before they are implemented in the physical world to assess their effectiveness within the virtual setting (Nedelcu & Petre, 2024).

2.3.4 Healthcare:

The metaverse will highly influence the healthcare sector. Through technology, the use of telehealth and telemedicine removed geographical boundaries. You can talk to doctors while being thousands of miles away from them through video chats, phone calls, and video calls. Many people do not like visiting medical facilities and doctors' offices because they feel uneasy. Thanks to the metaverse, such virtual consultations are possible, and doctors can converse with patients from a 3D clinic. This would further help physicians record the emotional and physical reactions of the patients. There is development in simulation suites that train physicians and nurses. Continuous human contact with the patient is required for the detection of both physical as well as emotional reactions. That is to say, it had to be brought to this end with this pandemic, unfortunately. So, there are efforts to incorporate technologies like telehealth into the system of remote care by accessing digital information and communication technologies that provide medical services remotely.

Figure 2. Metaverse in various industries

Source: Created by Authors

2.3.5 Gaming:

The focus area of metaverse technology is mostly on the gaming sector. Several hundreds of millions use game consoles and PCs all around the world. Online role-playing games are a kind of games that are otherwise known as massively multiplayer online role-playing games or MMORPGs. Increasingly, people are getting drawn toward online role-playing games. The massively multiplayer online role-playing game users interact with each other in the virtual environment, create and manage avatars, give out the game theme, and encourage unstructured gameplay. Some of the examples of MMORPGs are as follows: Lords of the Rings Online, Eve Online, and World of War craft. That aside, money from virtual estate sales, game adverts, and the subscription fee, gaming companies also bring in revenue in the metaverse (Bala et al., 2024a).

3. TALENT MANAGEMENT AND METAVERSE

The term talent management (TM) is not a newly coined term; it was first put to paper in a 1957 American Management Association document (Ansar, 2018). As such, the field of talent management (TM) has captured both academic and practitioner imagination. Corporate needs are a necessary prerequisite for this academic interest in talent management (Gallardo-Gallardo et al., 2017). The term was first used in its current meaning in the 19th century. Talent management, or human capital management as it is known alternatively, encompasses the acquisition and recruitment of a firm's most treasured asset- people. It also encompasses the development, evaluation, and retention of them (Khatri et al., 2010). Integrated talent management can be perceived as not being a human resource (HR) form-based pay system, a recruiting system, or a performance appraisal system. This technically is a framework of closely related HR processes, allowing you to make informed decisions that will eventually lead towards the strategic objective of success and profitability (Kumar et al., 2025; Sharma et al., 2024).

The well-known paper by McKinsey, "The War for Talent," published way back at the turn of the 20th century in 1998, is credited with conceptualizing TM as it currently exists in the fields of corporate competitiveness and strategic management (Ansar, 2018). There exist varied scholarly opinions on the objective definition of talent management (TM); however, there is an established discipline that is increasingly becoming significant. In theory, management of the desired skill is hard and uncertain. A scrutiny of the existing literature on the current topic reveals that efforts to distinguish TM from its various sub-streams within HRM have been ineffective. Talent is usually denoted by a few related phrases that lead to further conceptual complications. To some, talent is not very scarce; talent is something that anyone can possess, and it can be used in numerous ways and situations. As there was no well-defined definition of the term, every author expressed his problem when he worked on talent management. It is therefore believable that talent may mean anything a business leader or writer wishes it to mean (Cappelli & Keller, 2014).

The metaverse calls for attention concerning matters of HRM in the hotel and tourist industry. There is a need for specific personnel attitudes, skills, and knowledge that face challenges such as virtual and augmented reality, artificial intelligence (AI), data utilization, simulation, gaming, and evolving profiles and practices of digital consumers. Training people with values acceptable for sustainability, diversification, collaboration, and technological development is still a major challenge in hospitality and tourism development. Future metaverse trends in talent management should be considered. Talent management means attracting, nurturing, and keep ready to offer workers some specialized knowledge, abilities, experiences, and dispositions. The applied future metaverse HRM trends inform the research work in luring, nurturing, and keeping ready-skilled or adaptable workers.

AI can be exploited to analyze employee data and find trends or patterns to enable HR professionals to make more informed decisions concerning pay, benefits, or training (Aydin et al., 2024). Another feature that AI has is the ability to analyze the data related to employee satisfaction about which areas are presently dissatisfying them. Changes can then be made within the workplace that increase employee satisfaction. AI is extremely helpful in monitoring employee satisfaction and pinpointing areas for development while giving tailored feedback. This can be really helpful for the organization especially HR professionals to build a better work environment for their employees. The most important benefits of using metaverse technologies in HR management were defined as remote working and global collaboration, as well as innovative and engaging training opportunities.

3.1 Contemporary Use of Metaverse in HRM

In distributed work, engagement of staff will be highly key to developing relationships among the employees and can be furnished by metaverse. Training in the metaverse can develop an immersive, fascinating, and memorable learning environment that will allow staff members to learn and grow at a pace acceptable to our constantly shifting, hybrid world. Some other applications of the metaverse include virtual meetings, hiring and recruitment interviews, onboarding, and learning and development. All these can help foster a sense of community on the part of staff members and the company, too. Several advantages are associated with introducing metaverse technology to HRs. It is possible to increase access and enhance the organizational atmosphere, and optimize resource usage. With this technology, onboarding, employee engagement, virtual meetings, hiring and recruitment interviews, and communication from anywhere are possible. AI work capability assessments, online competency testing, employment information exchange, and orientation of new employees can all be improved with the help of the metaverse by HR. The metaverse can also serve as a method to enrich the employee engagement experience, where employees are given an opportunity to work together, collaborate, share ideas, and craft projects. It can also be used in terms of training employees and allowing them to learn new skills, which would make the workplace exciting and interesting (Thakur et al., 2020). Employees can be taught and educated by their employer, guiding them through various scenarios in a virtual setting. Virtual reality training increases the productivity levels of employees by 70% (Aydin et al., 2024).

4. TOURISM INDUSTRY AND METAVERSE

Thus, this field of hospitality and tourism industry has huge potential for the metaverse, while on the other side, new technologies are tedious and a long process. According to(Komulainen & Nätti, 2023) everyone is in their own shoes where some would wait and take it slow, while others get impatient to be an early adopter. Business acceptance is slow on issues of governance and ethics (Monaco & Sacchi, 2023) as well as security and privacy issues (Buhalis et al., 2023; Ioannidis & Kontis, 2023; Chi et al., 2024). The application of the travel and tourism industry in various sectors that enhance marketing, customer experience, and operational efficiency is already being witnessed in many spheres. Today, the metaverse is used highly in the following key areas:

1. *Virtual Tours:* Travelers can now explore destinations before they arrive using virtual reality (VR) tours offered by destinations. Travelers can make well-informed decisions about their itinerary thanks to this immersive experience.
2. *Enhanced Booking Experience:* Augmented Reality (AR) capabilities are being used by travel agencies and platforms to provide interactive experiences during the reservation process. The ability to illustrate your stay and travel locations enhances the customer experience.
3. *Virtual Events and Experiences:* Tourism businesses can reach a larger audience by organizing virtual festivals, concerts, and cultural events accessible from anywhere in the world thanks to the metaverse.
4. *Training and Simulations:* Employees in the hospitality and tourism industries can receive training through simulations in a virtual setting. This enhances operational effectiveness and customer service capabilities without the need for physical presence.

5. *Social Interaction and Community Building:* By giving Travelers a place to meet others, exchange stories, and create groups centered around their travel interests, the metaverse can increase visitor happiness and engagement.
6. *Destination marketing*: Using the metaverse for marketing efforts, tourism boards and businesses are creating immersive advertising that lets potential tourists experience their products in a virtual setting.

4.1 Positive Impacts Of A Metaverse In The Tourism Industry

In light of these facts, which will bring appreciable long-term positive effects and add value to both visitor and business experiences, the metaverse has great transformative potential in every dimension of the travel and tourism industry. Some of the positive impacts brought by the uptake of the metaverse to the tourism industry include:

4.1.1 Immersion Experiences Prior To Travel

Virtual reality (VR) offers travelers a very immersive method to explore destinations. This enables them to digitally tour local landmarks, beaches, and attractions using 360-degree experiences. Travelers can make better decisions by seeing a place before they arrive, and modern technology can replicate real-world settings, giving users a better understanding of the atmosphere, customs, and activities of a place, which in turn fuels their desire to visit.

4.1.2 Availability

For those who may suffer from health, financial, or other disabilities that prevent them from traveling in the real world, the metaverse would unlock a new opportunity to do the impossible: travel around the world. Everyone can visit museums, historical monuments, and natural wonders by using virtual tours. Thus, one might develop more consciousness and respect for other cultures and live upon knowing that he or she could travel to other countries without leaving home.

4.1.3 Virtual Experiences And Tours

Museums and other cultural institutions can offer educational content through interactive exhibits in the metaverse, allowing deeper engagement with history and art. Tour operators can also offer virtual guided experiences, which allow travelers to communicate in real-time with tour guides and local experts, enhancing the experience with personal insights and storytelling.

4.1.4 Organizing Events And Involving The Community

Attendance is more accessible and reasonably priced because of the metaverse, which enables worldwide participation in conferences, trade exhibitions, and festivals without requiring travel. Increased networking opportunities and cross-border knowledge sharing may result from this. By connecting like-minded people who can exchange experiences, advice, and suggestions, virtual platforms can help create communities focused on travel interests.

4.1.5 Tailored Travel Arrangements

Travelers can use virtual environments to personalize their itineraries by choosing and experiencing possible activities and accommodations in real-time, and travel companies can use AI in the metaverse to offer personalized trip suggestions based on user preferences and behaviors, improving customer satisfaction and increasing sales.

4.1.6 Marketing Strategies

Virtual influencers can promote destinations within the metaverse by engrossing audiences with experiences that combine immersive content and storytelling, and tourism brands can create highly engaging marketing campaigns in the metaverse that enable prospective Travelers to interact with content and experience what a destination has to offer more compellingly.

4.1.7 Environmental Consciousness And Sustainability

The metaverse can lessen the environmental effects of travel, such as emissions from airplane travel and the use of physical resources, by promoting virtual tourism and experiences. Virtual platforms can also be used to launch campaigns that support sustainable practices, like conservation initiatives or the promotion of environmentally friendly travel destinations.

Increased client loyalty and engagement: Travel agencies can use gamification in the metaverse to improve customer loyalty by offering incentives for taking part in virtual tours or customized experiences. Businesses can modify and enhance their offers based on real-time data and customer input thanks to the metaverse's instantaneous customer feedback and interaction capabilities.

4.1.8 Social Interaction

Through the metaverse, it enables its users to link to social media websites that can resemble the real world. Users can make friends, create avatars, and participate in activities in VRChat. Social networks in the metaverse have taken a new trend; people are not limited to the earlier dimensions such as time and other barriers. They can reach anyone on Earth without roaming around the world. This metaverse plays a very important role these days because whenever it comes to connecting with people who live very far from us and we want to have real-life experiences, such as having fun with them, having professional meetings with them, or visiting places or celebrating any festival or anything else, the metaverse comes into play and helps users have such live experiences.

As discussed above in points, it can be easily reached to a conclusion that the coming of the metaverse in the tourism industry is very positive with positive actions in all possible ways to make the experiences of consumers more effective and lively, especially for those consumers who cannot visit a number of destinations for one or two reasons, such as some consumers cannot afford to visit the destination on account of heavy cost; it may take a lot of time, and metaverse saves a lot of time according to visiting at a destination.

4.2 Challenges in the Adoption of Metaverse

4.2.1 Technological Barriers

Therefore, it would have to integrate, coordinate, and collaborate without hitching diverse technologies in the production of for the user an integrative and immersive experience. That digital environment would require interoperability in different platforms where such interoperability would also enable the user to move their assets or even interact with one another by using multiple virtual environments. It recognizes AR and VR as some of the critical technologies that have enabled an immersive experience that happens to be defining the metaverse. Both AR and VR depend upon a robust infrastructure of cloud computing and high-speed internet to work (Poonkuzhali et al., 2023). The greatest challenge in its current implementation, however, remains technical problems (Buhalis et al., 2023; Z. Chen, 2023; Mosco, 2023). Even though the metaverse supports technologies like VR and AI, it doesn't provide templates is expensive to develop, and carries lots of risks. For most potential customers, the scope of access and participation to experiences in the metaverse will be limited because they are unlikely to own an essential technology, for instance, a VR headset or high-speed internet. This becomes particularly true in regions whose base technology infrastructure is less developed.

4.2.2 Data Security And Privacy

In addition, security along with privacy in the metaverse becomes important. It is the best collection of massive behavioral data in comparison to any other conventional one (Park & Kim, 2022). As the metaverse is controlled by third-party service providers, the customers along with the organizations are afraid of uncontrolled surveillance, misuse of data frauds, and cyber attacks (Mkedder & Das, 2024). The hotel and tourism industry, which handles private customer data like preferences, booking details, payment details, and relocation, is also affected by these issues (Yang & Wang, 2023). Of all the challenges that accompany the usage of metaverse technology in travel and hospitality assimilation, one of the massive impacts is the challenge that comes with data privacy. Virtual location data easily opens up personal preferences and even biometric data to possible massive misuse or unauthorized access.

4.2.3 Employee Well-Being And Work-Life Balance

Perhaps, metaverse technology will influence the work-life balance and well-being of employees, which helps an individual to live a prosperous and healthy life (Jaswal et al., 2024). In fact, a human loses the boundary between his personal life and professional life because VR and AR are very attractive and thus require more hours to work or need constant interaction that will make sure the rooms are immersive, thereby letting users lose the border of reality. In general, effectiveness as well as efficacy regarding the rollout of new technologies would be affected once it begins to make employees stressed or sick.

4.2.4 Cost and Return on Investment

The biggest challenge that comes with metaverse technologies is that they're pricey; these are pretty high-tech products (S. Chen et al., 2023;Wei, 2024). The cost of using these kinds of technologies within the hospitality and tourism industry is relatively very high. Quality virtual experiences are quite cost-prohibitive. All this garbage, starting from the software and VR headsets-something much more crucial above all that is that everything here would be frightfully expensive for the proper education of personnel. It is worth mentioning that most companies are afraid to take risks and they await a tangible effect before investing in such areas. Such a big investment will be there in the designing and programming of the hardware within the hospitality and tourism-specific metaverse because it is going to be tested for running; such investment will be there to sustain the metaverse (Koohang et al., 2023).

4.2.5 Adoption Resistance

The metaverse technology deployed into the hospitality and tourism sector will resist it on both organizational and individual grounds. Most of the employees and departments will also resist this system because they are used to the more conventional ways of running things. A phobic culture will emerge as people fear new technologies, uncertainty, and even loss of employment (Buhalis, Leung, et al., 2023). Therefore, with such resistance, good training, efficient change management strategies, and proper communication of how applications in the metaverse serve for better integration will be required (Gursoy et al., 2022).

Figure 3. Challenges in the adoption of metaverse

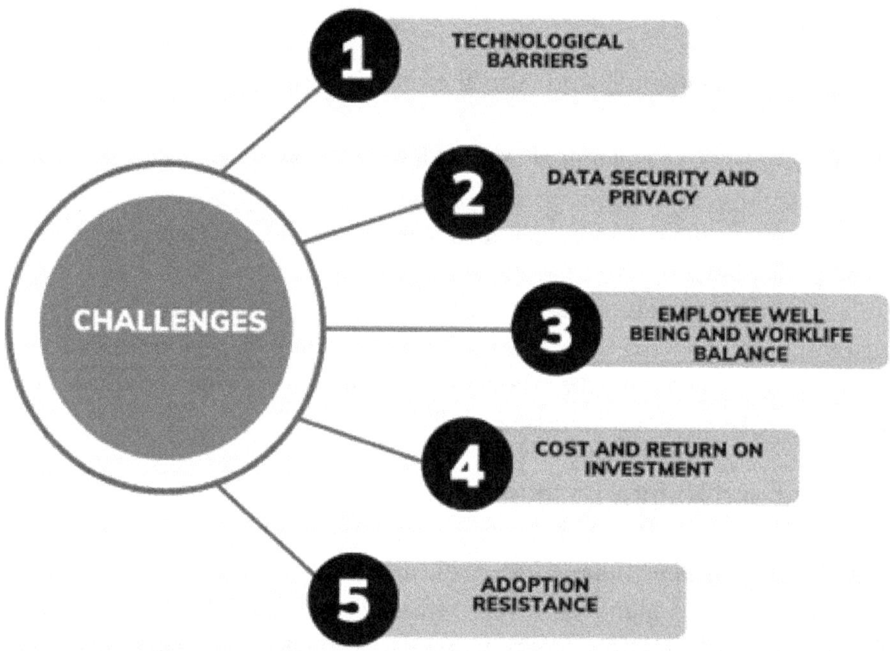

Source: Created by Authors

Collectively, these issues characterize the level of hardship hospitality and tourism would have to endure to pursue the metaverse's potential. Such challenges need to be addressed very often so that such advanced technologies can be well accepted and integrated into our world. Hospitality and tourism is one of the largest industries that can use the metaverse to acquire its competitive advantage in the market.

5. FUTURE OPPORTUNITIES OF METAVERSE IN THE TOURISM INDUSTRY

New and exciting opportunities open up in tourism with the metaverse. For them, journeying virtually to such a destination, landmark, or cultural site should be possible even from the comfort of their homes. The possibility might thus appear interesting for those who are in some way bound from traveling physically: financially, due to health, or out of other reasons. It may also facilitate better pre-travel planning as a result of having an even more immersive and realistic simulation of the pre-travel experience. Travelers might explore hotels, resorts, and other tourist destinations virtually to make better-informed travel choices.

It might be a way of managing the expectations of travelers and satisfying them with the destination they have chosen for their travel. Indeed, the metaverse can turn out to be a new business birth for the travel and tourism industry. There could be virtual tour operators and travel firms multiplying in number and providing vacations and tourist experiences.

5.1 Virtual Tourism Experiences

The metaverse allows companies to create fully immersive virtual tourism experiences, providing potential Travelers with the opportunity to explore their destinations before actually making a booking. Companies can develop 3D representations of local attractions and even let users virtually stroll through historic sites, natural parks, or an urban environment. Such a virtual tour will improve decision-making in Travelers while reducing uncertainty and raising conversion rates. Along with this, such experiences can be a successful marketing tool, attracting visitors who never even considered visiting the destination.

5.2 Hybrid Events and Meetings

The hospitality industry can, in the metaverse, redefine conferences, exhibitions, and other events by hybrid formats that combine a combination of physical presence with virtual participation, thus opening opportunities for event organizers to reach a larger audience as remote attendees participate in real-time interactions within a virtual space. Hotels and venues will have a better variety of bookings since they can accommodate in-person participants and virtual participants simultaneously. This trend is more relevant as most organizations have flexible work policies in place, hence more attractiveness to remote participation.

5.3 Enhanced Customer Engagement

Such engagement strategies may be more personalized and interactive with tourism businesses in the metaverse. Brands can, on avatars and virtual environments, market unique experiences that are tailored towards the interests of specific users through those forms of gamified experiences, virtual loyalty programs, and curate itineraries to enhance the customer journey. For example, a virtual concierge service would suggest a package of bespoke experiences, local dining, and attractions relevant to users' interests, thereby enhancing a travel experience before, during, or even after a trip.

5.4 Training and Workforce Development

It is something new both to the hospitality industry and to its future, concerning training. Virtual reality training allows employees to train in how to serve real customers in prepared, simulated conditions. This method would undoubtedly bring in better service quality and provide the employee with essential soft skills such as conflict resolution, customer relations, etc. More to that, onboarding new staff with immersive training also creates much faster learning curves, and therefore a more prepared workforce in a highly competitive industry.

5.5 Sustainability and Environmental Impact

Metaverse technology can help sustain tourism industries. The carbon footprints of transport and accommodations are reduced because tourism businesses can offer virtual experiences instead of actual trips. Destinations plagued by over-tourism can easily offer virtual alternatives where visitors can experience locales without placing an additional burden on the resources. The metaverse also encourages its users to be environmentally responsible through responsible tourism behaviors.

5.6 Dynamic Travel Experiences

Destinations may provide unique and fascinating experiences that beyond the norm by utilizing technology. Dynamic travel experiences may now be created with great effectiveness thanks to technologies like virtual reality and augmented reality. Travelers may be able to engage with virtual objects, virtually explore places, and even relive historical events in immersive worlds made possible by VR and AR. By taking consumers to different eras and locations, these technologies enable them to have an exciting and one-of-a-kind travel experience. Before making a reservation,

Travelers can use VR and AR to see the lodging, activities, and attractions, which enhances and improves their decision-making.

5.7 Intelligent Tourism

Most recently, (Buhalis & Sinarta, 2019), conceptualized intelligent tourism in exhorting the integration of intelligent technologies and data analytics in providing context-aware experiences tailored to individual travelers. Such a platform should evolve towards becoming the metaverse-one communal virtual environment in the next stage where people are provided with tailored recommendations by intelligent avatars while remaining abreast of the latest metaverse information based on location and preference. This is that technology and data integration might make the whole experience of tourism turn to become better as such customize it to meet the needs of every visitor and smooth interactions with the destination. Technology has also fast developed the world, changing how people travel and what research they have to possibly find destinations.

This way, it can reach customers on a much more profound level and address a far wider audience. The metaverse concept is gaining popularity as interest in such technologies, like virtual reality, augmented reality, extended reality, and mixed reality, which blur the lines between the two separate worlds-physical and real-continues to grow over time. It has been observed that many consider the metaverse as the next-generation internet and something ready to break human interaction with other people and with its environment in some radical ways (Cheng et al., 2022). In some ways, nothing like this has ever been seen in the metaverse, as it is offering something innovative, personal, and risk-reducing in the sense that it offers experiences unattainable hitherto, thereby paving the way for higher levels of customer interaction, engagement, and motivation (Ampountolas et al., 2024). The rate at which this metaverse technology is spreading to diverse industries, plus tourist and hospitality industries, has become substantial. In this scenario, it has become a huge influencer in changing the users' perception and thus perpetuating the wide diffusion of metaverse technology.

6. DIFFERENT USES OF METAVERSE FOR TOURISM

The metaverse is a limitless virtual environment that can increase accessibility to locations and other individuals at any time. Therefore, it can change and improve travel experiences before, during, and after travel by enabling users to interact with other users online. A summary of the possible effects of the Metaverse on traveler behavior and tourism enterprises is provided.

6.1 Uses Before Travel

By using the metaverse to virtually experience a destination firsthand, Travelers can do more than just imagine. Using the metaverse's immersive and lifelike environments, potential tourists can gain insight into their experiences before and during their trip, and assess whether a place can meet their needs and desires (Buhalis et al., 2023). As a result, Travelers can plan their route or select a destination by using the metaverse to realistically and interactively experience goods and services, which will encourage people to travel in person (Zhong et al., 2024). Prospective visitors can reduce their purchasing risks and finish Metaverse decision-making procedures, such as booking and payment, by using the information they find there. They can select suitable holiday destinations and items based on personality traits with the help of comprehensive pre-travel metadata (G et al., 2023) by analyzing the quality of services provided by different service providers such as hotels and restaurants (Buhalis & Sinarta, 2019). By doing this, users can prevent unpleasant surprises in the real services cape and unexpected cancellation rates can be reduced. Additionally, the persuasive power of this technology can be leveraged by tourism businesses to better market their offerings. The metaverse can increase brand awareness by isolating products and services from competitors in the market (Dwivedi et al., 2022).

6.2 Uses During Travel

Tourist experiences are no longer limited to in-person contacts and services. They can be expanded over both physical and virtual experience regions and supplemented by the metaverse, which can also act as a real-time interactive guide and provide a suitable environment for visitors to share user-generated content about the places they visit Cultural heritage places, for instance, can provide a forum where people can openly study historical material. Personalization is supported by the system's adaptability to each user's requirements and preferences. Travelling can therefore become more memorable and meaningful for visitors thanks to the Metaverse.

Metaverse can provide tourists with virtual restorations so they can visualize missing or damaged artifacts in a destination in their original state. Visitors are given a sense of the era through the virtual display of historical relics from ancient ruins and other cultural sites in the Metaverse. Instead of merely simulating historical communities, visitors can experience them as living museums. Therefore, via the use of illusion and immersion, visitors are successfully transported and given the sense that they are in the past. For example, they may perform actual religious rites in Egyptian pyramids or at the temple of Athena at the Acropolis of Athens (Dwivedi et al., 2022). The adventurers visit and have fun with many to get a thing or two from it. For example, eating places could utilize the Metaverse so their customers would experience Flavours of what they plan to be served for tastes, therefore retaining their characters as part of a display in virtual reality. The ingredients, production processes, preparation, and how it is prepared along are seen beyond the served meal (Rejeb et al., 2021).

It may complement or enhance the real experience of travel. Metaverse certainly will never replace the real experience of travel; however, the numerous benefits it has provided to users have been in the form of virtual opportunities to travel in more than just one way. Its metaverse allows those who can't travel physically because of their health conditions and those who cannot afford to travel physically but can attend events virtually. A customer might be able to find ways to communicate with others by choosing avatars, traveling in a preferred body, and engaging in activities. For instance, the beginning of 2022 saw Saudi Arabia report that it was working on a project in the Metaverse that would simulate a visit to the Muslim holy site Kaaba. So perhaps for those who cannot attain their religious obligations in the real world, Saudi Arabia could be an opportunity to do so in the Metaverse.

6.3 Uses After Travel

Following the trip, Travelers can utilize the metaverse to evaluate their experiences, exchange content about them, and even build their own content repository. Because they may effectively relive them in an immersive environment, Travelers may find experiences assisted by the metaverse more memorable. Additionally, Travelers can communicate in real-time with other Travelers, travel agencies, and destination marketing groups in the Metaverse. This can enhance their interaction with local resources tourism sites and organizations while they are traveling, resulting in life-changing experiences after they return. By recreating their travel experiences and sharing them in the Metaverse, Travelers can impact other Travelers' pre-trip stages and establish platforms where they can get the inspiration, information, and viewpoints that are essential for making travel decisions.

7. IMPACT OF METAVERSE ON TOURIST BEHAVIOR

Figure 4. Impact of metaverse on tourist behavior

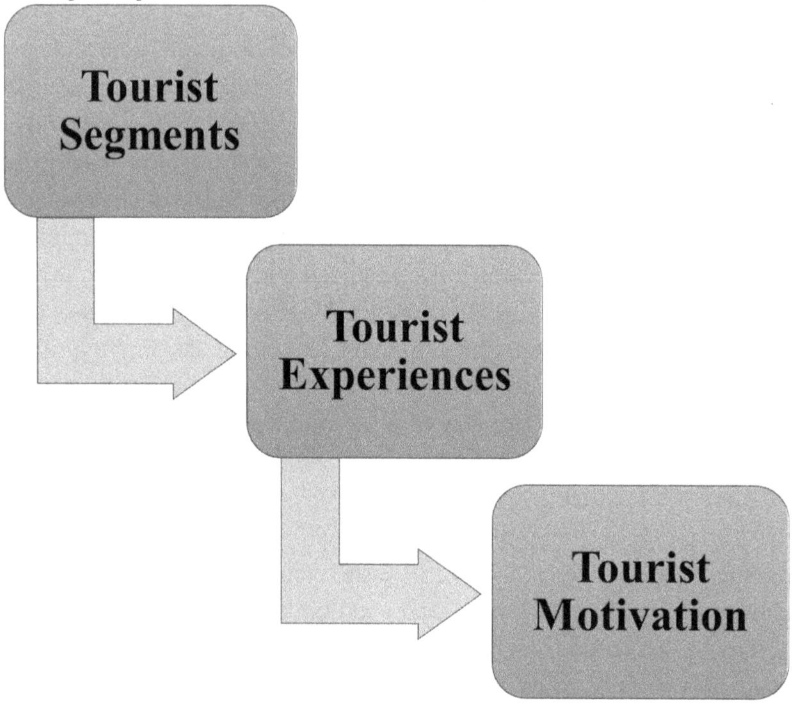

Source: Created by Authors

7.1 Tourist Motivation:

Tourist motivation refers to the underlying reasons and desires that inspire individuals to engage in travel and exploration. In the context of the metaverse's impact on tourist behavior, the concept of motivation is evolving as digital and virtual experiences become more sophisticated. By stimulating interest, the metaverse can persuade potential customers to try new things (Xu et al., 2016). The metaverse, a digital universe blending virtual reality (VR), augmented reality (AR), and other immersive technologies, offers new ways for tourists to experience destinations without physically being there. This shift towards virtual reality can impact traditional motivations for travel, such as the desire for novelty, adventure, and cultural exploration. Virtual experiences within the metaverse can fulfill some of these motivations by providing interactive and engaging simulations of real-world locations, allowing tourists to "travel" virtually to places they might not have been able to visit otherwise (Go & Kang, 2023).Generation Z is eager to share and show off their experiences in the Metaverse since they are fascinated by it. Is the Metaverse used for educational purposes? Yes, if you just want to learn about a place's history, reading books isn't enough, you can use metaverse for educational purposes, but the Metaverse can enhance cognitive function and offer a more vibrant environment (Wei, 2024).

7.2 Tourist Experiences:

The pre-, during-, and post-trip stages of the customer journey are experiences for Travelers.

7.2.1 Before Travel Experiences

Prospective Travelers can research and investigate destinations, places to stay, places to eat, transportation, and other important facilities. For example, people can use the Metaverse to visually check their plane seats before leaving for that place, providing a realistic trial experience (Koo et al., 2023). The metaverse enables "try before you buy," that is, "more stimulating experiences," which can enhance the pre-purchase and decision-making process. Similar to this, "we can see the places to visit and adjust our time and budget accordingly before we go to a country we will visit." While others highlighted the metaverse's educational value, one response explained that it will eventually become a center for information: "At the moment, we can only search for online reviews and read a text" but that's made clear by the metaverse.

7.2.2 During Travel Experience

Travelers use Metaverse to research every facet of their trip before departing, enabling them to make wise choices once they arrive. This could lead to a more enjoyable and stress-free journey. One suggestion was that the Metaverse "can be a good complement while traveling" and that it might be used as a smartwatch-like exercise tool. Metaverse technologies provide real-time on-site information on user preferences and experiences. Several respondents reiterated this: "For instance, I use Metaverse technology to determine what is best for me in this timeline when I am in Rome because I don't have time to see everything." It can therefore be used even when you get there.

7.2.3 After the Travel Experience

In exploring the Metaverse, can make experiences and memories meaningful and memorable. It makes it possible to have it all as a digital photo album, lets one improve the whole journey, and serves as a means of preserving and accessing memories. It helps people record and share travel experiences, inspires others to go, and increases the possibility that visitors will return. Other than this, the Metaverse will enable virtual exploration of the place in an immersive form whereby visitors can pre-explore sites or even create ways to have interactive relationships with historical and cultural information. This would further bond the traveler to places by improving possibilities in storytelling. The Metaverse would therefore easily transport both digital and physical experiences, bringing real-world travel to pair virtual upgrades to present tourists with new ways to creatively share their journey and beautifully communicate what they have experienced.

7.3 Tourist Segment:

Different tourist sectors use the mm in different ways, as demonstrated by differences in their lives, personalities, niche markets, and demographics. By applying this impact on tourist behavior in the metaverse, the tourist segment can be categorized by how people take up and engage with the technology. Early adopters incorporate the metaverse into their travel planning to explore destinations, cultural experiences, and tools' interaction. For these customers, the metaverse enhances satisfaction for a trip and encourages return intention. These are interested in having meaningful and unique experiences. They use the metaverse to experience multidimensional storytelling, to take virtual tours, and to re-enact historical events that broaden their views of destinations, which in turn influence their activity and location preferences. For other budget-conscious Travelers, the Metaverse is an affordable means of experiencing destinations they cannot afford to visit. This cohort finds virtual previews and virtual experiences useful to plan for travel and experience the same without considerable financial strain. Together, these segments reveal how the metaverse transforms behaviors around travel (G et al., 2023).

8. CONCLUSION

In essence, the concept infused into the tourism industry is in reality a revolutionizing change in how firms interact with clients and talent. The immersive technologies that include AR, VR, and MR are perhaps what allow the tourism industry to go beyond space accessibility and customer participation. This virtual evolution therefore not only opens up destinations in unprecedented detail before booking but also provides an environmentally sustainable and inclusive alternative, reducing impacts on the environment while increasing accessibility for all, whether physically challenged or having very limited financial budgets. The metaverse shall be used in industrial talent management, opening avenues for new training, employee development, and distant cooperation, thus a more flexible, skilled, and innovative workforce. As businesses operate in this same landscape, businesses may now use the metaverse to offer virtual tours, improved booking experiences, interactive customer engagement, and even hybrid events where both the physical and virtual realms blend together flawlessly. More than that, it provides brands the opportunity for more personable marketing and an immersive experience wherein a brand can connect with customers because of relevant virtual content. Immersive interactions thereby data-driven insights which may shape customer preferences and lead to further targeted offers and improved service standards. However, successful integration into metaverse technology depends on answers to some tough questions, including proper infrastructure, data privacy, security, cost, and the natural resistance of conventional business models to change. It is for this reason that as companies begin to invest in the metaverse, high-speed internet, VR-compatible devices, and strong cyber security are becoming increasingly important, especially in less technologically advanced areas. Besides, the proven real terms value of the metaverse-more customer satisfaction opportunities, better efficiency at operation levels, and employees' welfare-will remove skepticism at the industrial level. The future metaverse for the tourism industry is vast with innovative solutions that could change everything about the traveler's experience before visitation, during travels, and after return. It promises to redefine the flavor of customer experience, creating much deeper emotional connections and a sense of belonging within a space almost indistinguishable from reality but limitless in possibility. The metaverse offers an unparalleled opportunity for experiential learning and entertainment in allowing simulations, augmentations, and transcending the limitations of a physical world altogether in responding to the shifting expectations of a tech-savvy global audience. It will be the key enabler for a sustainable, inclusive, and personalized experience in travel; therefore, how tourism is expected to reshape its own future and redefine boundaries in terms of travel and experiences involved.

REFERENCES

Ampountolas, A., Menconi, G., & Shaw, G. (2024). Metaverse research propositions: Online intermediaries. *Tourism Economics*, *30*(1), 255–261. DOI: 10.1177/13548166231159520

Ansar, N. (2018). Talent and Talent Management: Definition and Issues. *IBT Journal of Business Studies*, *14*(2), 174–186. DOI: 10.46745/ilma.jbs.2018.14.02.14

Aydin, O., Karaarslan, E., & Narin, N. G. (2024). *Artificial Intelligence, VR, AR and Metaverse Technologies for Human Resources Management*. http://arxiv.org/abs/2406.15383

Bala, M., Bhardwaj, B., & Sharma, D. (2024a). *Eco-Metaverse Bridge*., DOI: 10.4018/979-8-3693-3985-5.ch016

Bala, M., Bhardwaj, B., & Sharma, D. (2024b). Innovative People Management Through Metaverse: An Emerging Dimension. In *Reference Module in Social Sciences*. Elsevier., DOI: 10.1016/B978-0-443-13701-3.00456-4

Bamber, G. J., Bartram, T., & Stanton, P. (2017). HRM and workplace innovations: Formulating research questions. *Personnel Review*, *46*(7), 1216–1227. DOI: 10.1108/PR-10-2017-0292

Bhardwaj, B., & Sharma, D. (2024). Artificial Intelligence: Shifting the Landscape of the Human Resource Ecosystem. In Leveraging AI and Emotional Intelligence in Contemporary Business Organizations (pp. 371-381). IGI Global Scientific Publishing.

Buhalis, D., Leung, D., & Lin, M. (2023). Metaverse as a disruptive technology revolutionising tourism management and marketing. *Tourism Management*, *97*, 104724. DOI: 10.1016/j.tourman.2023.104724

Buhalis, D., Lin, M. S., & Leung, D. (2023). Metaverse as a driver for customer experience and value co-creation: Implications for hospitality and tourism management and marketing. *International Journal of Contemporary Hospitality Management*, *35*(2), 701–716. DOI: 10.1108/IJCHM-05-2022-0631

Buhalis, D., & Sinarta, Y. (2019). Real-time co-creation and nowness service: Lessons from tourism and hospitality. *Journal of Travel & Tourism Marketing*, *36*(5), 563–582. DOI: 10.1080/10548408.2019.1592059

Cappelli, P., & Keller, J. R. (2014). Talent Management: Conceptual Approaches and Practical Challenges. In *Annual Review of Organizational Psychology and Organizational Behavior* (Vol. 1, pp. 305–331). Annual Reviews Inc. DOI: 10.1146/annurev-orgpsych-031413-091314

Chakraborty, D., Polisetty, A., Khorana, S., & Buhalis, D. (2023). Use of metaverse in socializing: Application of the big five personality traits framework. *Psychology and Marketing*, *40*(10).

Chen, S., Chan, I. C. C., Xu, S., Law, R., & Zhang, M. (2023). Metaverse in tourism: Drivers and hindrances from stakeholders' perspective. *Journal of Travel & Tourism Marketing*, *40*(2), 169–184. DOI: 10.1080/10548408.2023.2227872

Chen, Z. (2023). Beyond Reality: Examining the Opportunities and Challenges of Cross-Border Integration between Metaverse and Hospitality Industries. *Journal of Hospitality Marketing & Management*, *32*(7), 967–980. DOI: 10.1080/19368623.2023.2222029

Cheng, R., Wu, N., Chen, S., & Han, B. (2022). Will Metaverse Be NextG Internet? Vision, Hype, and Reality. *IEEE Network*, *36*(5), 197–204. DOI: 10.1109/MNET.117.2200055

Chi, M., Chen, Y., Xu, Y., & Wu, Y. (2024). Modelling barriers to metaverse adoption in the hospitality and tourism industry. *Information Technology & Tourism*, *26*(4), 711–743. Advance online publication. DOI: 10.1007/s40558-024-00298-9

Dutta, D., Srivastava, Y., & Singh, E. (2023). Metaverse in the tourism sector for talent management: A technology in practice lens. *Information Technology & Tourism*, *25*(3), 331–365. DOI: 10.1007/s40558-023-00258-9

Dwivedi, Y. K., Hughes, L., Baabdullah, A. M., Ribeiro-Navarrete, S., Giannakis, M., Al-Debei, M. M., Dennehy, D., Metri, B., Buhalis, D., Cheung, C. M. K., Conboy, K., Doyle, R., Dubey, R., Dutot, V., Felix, R., Goyal, D. P., Gustafsson, A., Hinsch, C., Jebabli, I., & Wamba, S. F. (2022). Metaverse beyond the hype: Multidisciplinary perspectives on emerging challenges, opportunities, and agenda for research, practice and policy. *International Journal of Information Management*, *66*, 102542. DOI: 10.1016/j.ijinfomgt.2022.102542

Faraboschi, P., Frachtenberg, E., Laplante, P., Milojicic, D., & Saracco, R. (2022). Virtual Worlds (Metaverse): From Skepticism, to Fear, to Immersive Opportunities. *Computer*, *55*(10), 100–106. DOI: 10.1109/MC.2022.3192702

Gallardo-Gallardo, E., Thunnissen, M., & Scullion, H. (2017). Special issue of International Journal of Human Resource Management. A contextualized approach to Talent Management: Advancing the field. *International Journal of Human Resource Management, 1–4*, 1–4. Advance online publication. DOI: 10.1080/09585192.2016.1275292

Go, H., & Kang, M. (2023). Metaverse tourism for sustainable tourism development: Tourism Agenda 2030. *Tourism Review, 78*(2), 381–394. DOI: 10.1108/TR-02-2022-0102

Gursoy, D., Malodia, S., & Dhir, A. (2022). The metaverse in the hospitality and tourism industry: An overview of current trends and future research directions. *Journal of Hospitality Marketing & Management, 31*(5), 527–534. DOI: 10.1080/19368623.2022.2072504

Guttentag, D. A. (2010). Virtual reality: Applications and implications for tourism. *Tourism Management, 31*(5), 637–651. DOI: 10.1016/j.tourman.2009.07.003

Hajjami, O., & Park, S. (2024). Using the metaverse in training: Lessons from real cases. *European Journal of Training and Development, 48*(5/6), 555–575. DOI: 10.1108/EJTD-12-2022-0144

Hanbay Tiryaki, S., & Balaman, F. (2025). Web 3.0 and the Metaverse: Transformative Impacts on Education. *International Journal of Contemporary Educational Research, 12*(1), 102–122. DOI: 10.52380/ijcer.2025.12.1.756

Hung, H.-Y., Kumar, A., Kumar, V., Lin, C.-C., & Tan, K. H. (2024). Exploring player cocreation dynamics on the gaming platform: Interplay of goal fulfillments, orchestration actions, and platform affordances. *International Journal of Research in Marketing*. Advance online publication. DOI: 10.1016/j.ijresmar.2024.12.003

Ioannidis, S., & Kontis, A.-P. (2023). Metaverse for tourists and tourism destinations. *Information Technology & Tourism, 25*(4), 483–506. DOI: 10.1007/s40558-023-00271-y

Jaswal, N., Sharma, D., Bhardwaj, B., & Kraus, S. (2024). Promoting well-being through happiness at work: a systematic literature review and future research agenda. In *Management Decision* (Vol. 62, Issue 13, pp. 332–369). Emerald Publishing. DOI: 10.1108/MD-08-2023-1492

Khatri, P., Gupta, S., Gulati, K., & Chauhan, S. (2010). Talent Management in HR. *Journal of Management and Strategy, 1*(1). Advance online publication. DOI: 10.5430/jms.v1n1p39

Kim, J. (2021). Advertising in the Metaverse: Research Agenda. *Journal of Interactive Advertising, 21*(3), 141–144. DOI: 10.1080/15252019.2021.2001273

Komulainen, R., & Nätti, S. (2023). Barriers to blockchain adoption: Empirical observations from securities services value network. *Journal of Business Research, 159*, 113714. DOI: 10.1016/j.jbusres.2023.113714

Koo, C., Kwon, J., Chung, N., & Kim, J. (2023). Metaverse tourism: Conceptual framework and research propositions. *Current Issues in Tourism, 26*(20), 3268–3274. DOI: 10.1080/13683500.2022.2122781

Koohang, A., Nord, J. H., Ooi, K.-B., Tan, G. W.-H., Al-Emran, M., Aw, E. C.-X., Baabdullah, A. M., Buhalis, D., Cham, T.-H., Dennis, C., Dutot, V., Dwivedi, Y. K., Hughes, L., Mogaji, E., Pandey, N., Phau, I., Raman, R., Sharma, A., Sigala, M., & Wong, L.-W. (2023). Shaping the Metaverse into Reality: A Holistic Multidisciplinary Understanding of Opportunities, Challenges, and Avenues for Future Investigation. *Journal of Computer Information Systems, 63*(3), 735–765. DOI: 10.1080/08874417.2023.2165197

Kumar, G., Sharma, D., & Bhardwaj, B. (2024). Artificial Intelligence in Education. In *Reference Module in Social Sciences*. Elsevier., DOI: 10.1016/B978-0-443-13701-3.00483-7

Kumar, G., Sharma, D., & Bhardwaj, B. (2025). Artificial Intelligence as Disruptive Technology in Human Resource Management. In *Handbook of Disruptive Technologies* (pp. 38–58). CRC Press., DOI: 10.1201/9781032700953-4

Kye, B., Han, N., Kim, E., Park, Y., & Jo, S. (2021). Educational applications of metaverse: Possibilities and limitations. *Journal of Educational Evaluation for Health Professions, 18*, 32. DOI: 10.3352/jeehp.2021.18.32 PMID: 34897242

Laachach, A., Mumtaz, S., & Andaloussi, B. Z. (2024). Unveiling opportunities and challenges of the metaverse in the tourism and the hospitality sector: A qualitative investigation. *Tourism and Hospitality Management, 30*(4). Advance online publication. DOI: 10.20867/thm.30.4.1

Maslin, J. (2011). *A Future Wrapped in 1980s Culture*. The New York Times. https://www.nytimes.com/2011/08/15/books/ready-player-one-by-ernest-cline-review.html

Mkedder, N., & Das, M. (2024). Metaverse integration challenges: An in-depth ISM and MICMAC analysis. *Journal of Retailing and Consumer Services, 77*, 103684. DOI: 10.1016/j.jretconser.2023.103684

Monaco, S., & Sacchi, G. (2023). Travelling the Metaverse: Potential Benefits and Main Challenges for Tourism Sectors and Research Applications. *Sustainability (Basel)*, *15*(4), 3348. DOI: 10.3390/su15043348

Mosco, V. (2023). Into the Metaverse: Technical Challenges, Social Problems, Utopian Visions, and Policy Principles. *Javnost - The Public, 30*(2), 161–173. DOI: 10.1080/13183222.2023.2200688

Nedelcu, A.-A., & Petre, I. (2024). Rolul Metaversului în domeniul militar. *Revista Română de Informatică i Automatică*, *34*(3), 79–90. DOI: 10.33436/v34i3y202406

Núñez, J. G., Bolognesi, M., & Godbehear, J. (2025). Creators at the Core: How Second Life and Roblox Empowered Creators in the Post-COVID Era. *IEEE Engineering Management Review*, •••, 1–23. DOI: 10.1109/EMR.2025.3555501

Park, S.-M., & Kim, Y.-G. (2022). A Metaverse: Taxonomy, Components, Applications, and Open Challenges. *IEEE Access : Practical Innovations, Open Solutions*, *10*, 4209–4251. DOI: 10.1109/ACCESS.2021.3140175

Pencarelli, T. (2020). The digital revolution in the travel and tourism industry. *Information Technology & Tourism*, *22*(3), 455–476. DOI: 10.1007/s40558-019-00160-3

Piñeiro-Chousa, J., López-Cabarcos, M. Á., VittoriRomero, V., & Pérez-Pérez, A. (2025, January). VittoriRomero, V., & Pérez-Pérez, A. (2024). Evolution and trends of the metaverse in business and management: A bibliometric analysis. *Review of Managerial Science*, *19*(1), 197–222. Advance online publication. DOI: 10.1007/s11846-024-00741-5

Poonkuzhali, S., Archana, J. S., & Anand, T. P. P. (2023). *Metaverse 3C: Concept*. Components, and Challenges in Travel and Tourism Sector., DOI: 10.1007/978-981-99-1767-9_51

Pratisto, E. H., Thompson, N., & Potdar, V. (2022). Immersive technologies for tourism: A systematic review. *Information Technology & Tourism*, *24*(2), 181–219. DOI: 10.1007/s40558-022-00228-7

Rejeb, A., Keogh, J. G., Simske, S. J., Stafford, T., & Treiblmaier, H. (2021). Potentials of blockchain technologies for supply chain collaboration: A conceptual framework. *International Journal of Logistics Management*, *32*(3), 973–994. DOI: 10.1108/IJLM-02-2020-0098

Sharma, D., Salehi, W., Bhardwaj, B., Chand, M., & Salihy, H. (2024). Dovetailing the human resource management with the cloud computing in the era of industry 4.0: A review. *Frontiers in Management and Business*, *4*(2), 340–351. DOI: 10.25082/FMB.2023.02.004

Thakur, D. J., Verma, P., & Sharma, D. (2020). Demographic analysis of Ethical Leadership Style and Employee Performance. *Journal of Xi'an University of Architecture & Technology*, *12*(03), 5645–5651.

Volchek, K., & Brysch, A. (2023). *Metaverse and Tourism: From a New Niche to a Transformation* (pp. 300–311). DOI: 10.1007/978-3-031-25752-0_32

Wei, W. (2024). A buzzword, a phase or the next chapter for the Internet? The status and possibilities of the metaverse for tourism. *Journal of Hospitality and Tourism Insights*, *7*(1), 602–625. DOI: 10.1108/JHTI-11-2022-0568

Wood, G. (2014). Ethereum: A secure decentralised generalised transaction ledger. *Ethereum Project Yellow Paper*, 1–32.

Xu, F., Tian, F., Buhalis, D., Weber, J., & Zhang, H. (2016). Tourists as Mobile Gamers: Gamification for Tourism Marketing. *Journal of Travel & Tourism Marketing*, *33*(8), 1124–1142. DOI: 10.1080/10548408.2015.1093999

Yang, F. X., & Wang, Y. (2023). Rethinking Metaverse Tourism: A Taxonomy and an Agenda for Future Research. *Journal of Hospitality & Tourism Research (Washington, D.C.)*. Advance online publication. DOI: 10.1177/10963480231163509

Zhong, L., Xu, Z., Morrison, A. M., Li, Y., & Zhu, M. (2024). Metaverse customer journeys in tourism: Building viable virtual worlds. *Tourism Review*, *79*(8), 1409–1426. DOI: 10.1108/TR-07-2023-0492

Chapter 8
Untapping AI-Driven Solutions for Virtual Tourism:
Congruent Visitor Experience and Ecosystem Conservation

Bhupinder Singh
https://orcid.org/0009-0006-4779-2553
Sharda University, India

Saurabh Chandra
https://orcid.org/0000-0003-4172-9968
Bennett University, India

ABSTRACT

AI technologies that bring virtual tourism to life are genuinely changing the way in which we explore our planet, with augmented experiences designed not only as a substitute for live traveling but also aimed to support ecosystem conservation. With the help of virtual reality (VR) and artificial intelligence (AI), destinations can offer visitors immersive, real-life-like experiences to areas that are far away from them tour sites, cultural places or natural wonders all without leaving home. This helps make the industry more available even to a wider public, and is also set up as a climate-friendly parallel trade digital travel interrupts carbon emissions at least in conjunction with environmental impact of mass tourism. The amalgamation of technology and tourism extends an exclusive approach towards traveling more sustainably by using a local environmental friendly built environment, allowing travelers to see the global destinations at lift-off while also reducing their carbon footprint thus ensuring double benefit over perspectives.

DOI: 10.4018/979-8-3373-0071-9.ch008

1. INTRODUCTION

Artificial intelligence improves the visitor experience by suggesting a personal tour, optimizing walking route or providing real-time exhibition translations. It can also help save the planet, as it takes pressure off both living species dependent on very limited environments and buried treasures like pre-historical sites that cannot be revealed to thousands of pairs of hiking boots per year without them suffering irreparable damage. AI-Driven Solutions to Activate Virtual Tourism for a Sustainable Visitor Experience and Conservation of Ecosystem These powerful tools that have transformed and made disruptions in virtually every industry is the rise of Artificial Intelligence (AI) where tourism has not been exempted. A particularly promising area for AI-based transformation is virtual tourism by offering an amalgamation of a realistic tour with easier conservation practices. Incorporating AI in combination with virtual reality (VR) and augmented reality (AR), the idea of the "virtual tourism" empowers travelers to discover places from their living rooms, reducing environmental footprints while improving ease of access as well for customization. This method is now increasingly regarded as a viable long-term solution to save our environment and culture while changing the patterns of how we spend leisurely hours.

1.1 Immersive Experience Powered by Artificial Intelligence

The power of AI in Virtual tourism- Because it caters to providing a realistic, immersive and personalized experience. AI, when using VR and or AR technologies can build real-world destination environments with desired precision to the point that a user may explore tourist sites; museums; natural landscapes locations, as well as previously remote or restricted areas. AI-enhanced lifelike scenarios of travel environments make it possible for virtual tourists to virtually stroll through landmark cities, visit ancient ruins, or take a dive in coral reefs all from the comfort of their home. What makes virtual tourism truly appealing is AI the technology that can offer real-time responses, respond to user actions and personalise a trip based on preferences.

For instance, machine learning algorithms can study things like user behavior, past interactions and preferences in order to tailor virtual tours or recommend destinations or cultural activities. User engagement boosts with AI that use natural language processing (NLP) to have real-time conversations through virtual guides, avatars, or chatbots and elaborate on landmarks history & cultural aspects. This sort of content-based, in real-time translation enables to experience aspects of different cultures without the language barrier which can make this new genre inclusive across languages and broadly accessible globally. AI can also mimic real-world environments like weather, soundscape or seasons to improve the experience of virtual reality. Powered by AI, now visitors can interact with the environment rather than just look at it to have an entertaining and educating experience. For example, an AI can provide the same experience as standing in front of Eiffel Tower at Paris or watching sunset on Grand Canyon cliffs or feeling those energetic streets of Tokyo everything within high fidelity interactive virtual environment.

1.2 Accessibility and Inclusivity in Tourism

AI technology enables virtual tourism explore some of the most exciting ways AI-powered virtual travel innovations will increasingly allow you to travel wherever in the world with just your imagination. It also extends the possibility of making some places accessible to individuals who would not otherwise have had access to traditional travel. AI modifies experiences according to each single wish, democratizing tourism application is the voice-guided virtual tour guide for sightless travelers and simplified navigation aid designed for users with mobility issues. With a massive democratization of tourism, global travel opens up to new horizons and provides access to different experiences which are beneficial in terms of sightseeing around the globe. AI-powered virtual tourism offers an economic value to local communities by digitally transmitting their culture, history as well nature & civilization beauty across globe. Remote or underserved regions can attract virtual travellers, with the resulting interest in visiting their area and increased tourism without immediate environmental/infrastructural strain through virtual tourism (Lavuri & Akram, 2023).

1.3 AI-Driven Virtual Tourism for Ecosystem Conservation

Virtual tourism helps decrease the carbon footprint related to physical travel by reducing the necessity for transportation, accommodation as well as other activities connected with tourism. This is even more so the case for long distance or ecologically sensitive areas such as the Galápagos Islands or Antarctica. AI can support the simulation of environments that humans might not venture to or places where it is potentially risky for them including deep-sea habitats and remarkable wildlife reserves yielding a counter-ethical counterpart from conventional tourism ways (Kacprzak & Hensel, 2023).

AI reinforces the educational component of virtual tourism by educating tourists on environmental conservation. AI-driven storytelling, users are made aware of the significance of conservation efforts and thus their loves for environment is reinstated as well ensuring that they work towards conserving it further to pass on a healthy planet. AI-driven tools can also help conservationists analyze ecosystem data to better understand biodiversity, climate patterns and human effects within these environments.

1.4 Economic and Social Benefits

AI-powered virtual tourism can offer the advantages of both economic and social while crawling over travelers, host communities. For the traveler, virtual tourism provides a cheap way to visit new places. This is eliminating travel, accommodation and food costs for a wide range of possible tourists. AI tailors the experience to each individual by suggesting content suitable for that user based on their personal interests, preferences and past behaviour resulting in higher levels of satisfaction & engagement. On a local scale, and especially for those communities trying to keep their heads above the water with tourism revenue during demystification what virtual means is an alternative way of presenting cultural heritage (arts) or locally produced goods. They offer rich virtual discovery experiences that can be used as a promotional tool to drive in-person traffic once you reopen your site, while also providing opportunities for 'virtual attendence' revenue through donations or locally crafted goods. Using AI-powered platforms, indigenous communities and local culture will have a place to give representation that is bombarded globally.

1.5 Ethical and Technological Hurdles

While the possibilities of virtual travel AI are life-changing, it also has its challenges. We may even question the authenticity in such virtual experiences as it lacks sensory richness of actual physical travel. As AI-driven platforms gather massive amounts of information, data privacy and security issues also emerge. In addition, technology such as VR headsets, high speed internet and AI driven platforms are too restricted at global scale. Overcoming these issues will be vital to the future of virtual tourism. Solutions are emerging in technology infrastructure and data protection modalities, as well as innovations such sensory experiences which will break down existing barriers impeding the widespread adoption of AI-driven tourism.

An AI-based global virtual tourism, will presents a solution for providing an immersive and customized travel experience as well helping world in terms of nature reservation and cultural heritage preservation. Artificial intelligence helps shift sustainable tourism towards an eco-friendly industry by decreasing physical travel. Virtual tourism will soon be the future of travel and a great middle ground to strike for tourists, as well as their impact on our planet that is bound to make this world a better place for all (Vinaykarthik, 2022).

Figure 1. Shares the dimensions of introduction section

(Source- Self Prepared- Original)

2. ROLE OF AI IN TRANSFORMING TOURISM: KEY FEATURES OF VIRTUAL TOURISM: VR, AR, AND 360-DEGREE VIDEOS

Artificial Intelligence (AI) and Immersive technologies are as transforming the Tourism Industry With traditional tourism coming up against increasing hurdles such as environmental sustainability, overcrowding and the type of inclusivity required; virtual tourism proposes an innovative solution that in turn combines state-of-the-art technologies like virtual reality (VR), augmented reality (AR) and 360-degree videos. These experiences are further improved by AI, which enables personalized, cost-effective and green alternatives to conventional physical travel. With AI-powered virtual tourism, people can experience destinations that were previously impossible to access- all without harming the environment further and promoting sustainable economic development while preserving culture.

With help of AI, virtual tourism has transformed into more interactive, lifelike and even adaptive experience. It permits the development of much personalised virtual tourism matches individual tastes, and gives real-time feedback with directions. Using AI-driven algorithms, the platform processes this massive amount of data together with user behavior and preferences as well as past trips to create tailored virtual tours that feel very personal (Kamal & Himel, 2023). This local touch combined with the immersive capabilities of VR, AR and 360-degree videos provides an incredibly appealing package that improves engagement user experience leading to a genuine virtual tourism prospect. AI-powered virtual tourism platforms can provide real-time translations, multilingual support and interactive guides which will help engage a larger audience create global travel experiences.

AR, VR and 360-videos As the name suggests– AI driven Virtual Tourism consists of three main elements which are AR- Augmented Reality and VR-Virtual Realiy along with 320-degree videos without this there can be no successful concept to drive tourism through a virtual process using an algorithm. All of these technologies has its own unique benefits and when coupled with AI can deliver a comprehensive virtual travel experience. Gerber points to virtual reality (VR) as likely the most immersive and innovative of all digital tourism technologies. The use of computer-generated imagery to create a simulated environment allows users to experience real-world scenarios in VR, giving the impression they are travelling from one location to another without ever stepping out of their home. Artificial intelligence enhances the experience by providing a personalized journey through virtual experiences with customized content and enabling users to have interactive experiences that simulate real-world scenarios (Ahmed, 2022).

These ways is how AI analyses information on that can include natural and cultural landscape conditions, as well as local weather fit to recreate a life-like appearance of the destination in VR-based tourism. Users, for instance, can tour virtually the Louvre Museum in Paris and have AI-driven guides relay data about artwork significance or tell tales of historical & architectural importance instantly. Incorporating machine learning algorithms allows VR platforms to understand what users want and personalize the experience showing, for example, certain types of art or historical periods that might align with a particular user's interests.

VR tourism is also good for sustainability purposes as well, since it allows tourists to see ecologically delicate areas without disturbing the environment. Virtual tourism allows people to explore destinations such as the Galápagos Islands, coral reefs and Amazon rainforest in a more sustainable way without overcrowding or polluting sites and destroying habitats typically associated with conventional vacations (Vuong & Mai, 2023). VR removes the physical limitations associated with traditional tourism and is even accessible to those who are disabled or who have difficulty moving. AI can enable VR systems to come with adapted interfaces and guided tours that cater specially for those individual needs. This new found inclusivity opens a much larger group to access for tourism creating social and cultural links that ignore physical country limits.

There are further, concerns with virtual tourism inspired to the concept of augmented reality (AR) which is a digital layer over the real world. This is because VR places users entirely in a digital world, whereas AR adds virtual components onto the real physical things around them. AI is key to AR for real-time data processing, object recognition and context-aware information delivery on-the-go. In Tourism AR enables users to interact with the surroundings while overlays relevant information via smartphones, tablets or even through AR glasses. For example, tourists can experience a reconstructed image of ancient ruins on the site and overlay them in real-time with an existing landscape. AI can deliver a set of descriptions about those sites, historical contexts and interactives as videos, 3D models so that the tour takes on an educational impact.

2.1 Potential Benefits and Risks

AI-powered AR can also help tourists get around foreign cities. For instance, AI could soon be used to analyze GPS data and provide real-time recommendations on things such as nearby tourist attractions or restaurants. Combining artificial intelligence and augmented reality, tourists can tap into custom tips based on their personal preferences for instance where they like to eat, but also get real-time notifications about what's going down in a locale or keep up with the forecast. Not only that, AR also offers a great degree in cultural conservation and in publicizing hidden treasures. AI-driven AR applications will also enable visitors elsewhere to see these remote or threatened sites without going in person, further aiding preservation efforts. This helps to conserve a nation's history from the wear and tear of mass tourism, while also introducing emerging generation tourists to cultures and traditions that may otherwise die out.

360-degree videos are a perfect backdrop to take users on an immersive visual journey that allows them to visit destinations with panoramic views. Unlike 2-dimensional video, which lets viewers scan a file visually from one side to the other and sit back, maybe listen in stereo sound; "That's versus this potential thing that steps out of your context. And with the integration of AI, 360-videos combine all their power into personalized and user-driven experiences based on each viewer's interest. The AI improves the 360-degree experience by deducing personal tastes and offerings a predetermination suggestion on which scenes or destinations to pounce up next. As an instance if a user like adventure tourism, AI can suggest 360-degree videos of hiking in the Himalayas, Dive at Great Barrier Reef or journey into Amazon rainforest. This keeps the audience engaged and interested from start to finish in an AI-driven made-for-you virtual tour (Auttri et al., 2023).

AI can be used for those immersive 360-degree video tours to offer real-time information including the background of different landmarks or historical insights or even recommendations on what future travel plans should look like. AI-driven voice assistants or virtual guides can interact with visitors by answering questions and providing more information about respective location being visited. 360-degree and virtual reality videos are gradually becoming ways to promote locations without transporting masses of people. Powered by cutting-edge 360 video technology, their software makes it possible to travel the world from home – providing an alternative solution that prevents overcrowding at tourist hotspots while easing pressure on endangered ecosystems and cultural landmarks. This not only helps to protect the natural environment, it also presents a very attractive option for attracting virtual tourists from all over the world and thus promoting an even distribution of tourism income throughout regions that do not usually receive many visits.

2.2 Personalization and Accessibility Powered by AI

Virtual tourism offers the advantage of enabling AI to provide hyper personalized experiences. Through user data like previous trips, any interests or behaviors in the online realm AI-driven algorithms tailor virtual tours for personalized experiences. The personalization is valid for all aspects of virtual tourism, from the choice of destinations to the degree of interactivity and type/format using in content delivery (Zaki, 2022). AI can recommend places users have never visited before based off their travel history and even advice similar destinations or ask you to try out something new according to your interests in the region. The ML algorithms keep updating these recommendations to show the users tactics increasingly consistent with their tastes. In addition, AI enables virtual tours to serve information in a personalized manner and users can choose the level of description they would like based on the user's background or interest for one in topic.

In virtual tourism, accessibility can be improved with the help of AI to accommodate solutions for disabled people as well. AI-powered voice recognition can provide audio-guided tours for blind people and AI-translation services can be a bridge to help international travelers. With being as inclusive as this, virtual experiences are made available to a wider audience democratizing tourism in a manner that regular physical visits cannot. Talking about the tourism sector, AI is making a gigantic change by promoting virtual tourism experiences via VR (Virtual Reality), AR (Augmented Reality) technologies or 360-degree videos. This offers an eco-friendly and cost-effective alternative to travelling; decreasing the carbon footprint by giving games even more personalized, interactive experiences. As AI technology advances, the future of virtual tourism is bright and promises to revolutionize our approach to experiencing the world restoring travel as a more accessible activity with minimal environmental footprint (Soliman & Al Balushi, 2023).

3. AI-POWERED VIRTUAL TOURISM: TRANSITION TO AI-ENHANCED VIRTUAL EXPERIENCES

The impact of AI on different fields is evident, and one such field that has seen a complete transformation in the light of rapid advancement in Artificial Intelligence (AI), is tourism. AI enables virtual tourism to be the cornerstone of a conservation ethic comfort and become something that draws you fully into any place without leaving your home (Bhatnagar, 2022). Adopting AI-empowered virtual experiences simply responds to a technological evolution, it is also partly driven by the need for greener-living (eco-conscious); on-demand and personal travel options (P2X) as well social inclusion goals. With the further evolution of AI, virtual tourism will change and revolutionize the travel industry in ways that can make us experience different things while staying indoors and never leave one spot.

3.1 AI Is Revolutionizing Virtual Tourism Across the World

Use of AI in virtual tourism to recreate travel experiences at home and explore tourist spots as though the user has themselves visited these locations. Using AI, these virtual experiences can be taken to the next level by adding more advanced algorithms that offer better personalization of content and provide real-time information interactively giving users a tour of destinations. This personalized link is essential to the commercial success of AI-driven virtual tourism, since it can reflect personal preferences, interest profile and past behaviors. AI can analyze the history of travel or online search habits and give virtual tours to certain places, areas according to their interests. If a user likes cultural heritage sites, adventure tourism or food fairs, AI will personalize the virtual tour accordingly. What is more, AI systems can change on the fly themselves and learn as they are called by using all of this that exists during a tour.

This provides AI the mechanism to deliver real-time data as well, such is the case with any system. The tourists meanwhile, can get real-time updates of the weather or any events happening in a particular place. Take the AI in customer service, it can predicts the questions of user and displays contextual information based on virtual guides or chatbots with machine learning algorithms (Henke & Jacques Bughin, 2016). Blending cultures and physically traveling further to learn about them in-depth as much through our taste buds make this experience yet even more interactive while ensuring everyone gets a hands-on feel of it thus making us realise how travelling not so far has got nearer with virtual ones.

3.2 Current AI Technologies in Virtual Tourism

Key technologies give the user an entire view from different viewpoints; It's almost as if they were actually on a tour of the destination as AI empowers all three of these categories, providing something for everyone.

Virtual Reality (VR): VR is possible by stimulating our senses with visual and auditory stimuli, which allow for life-like sensations of noise-canceling gaming. Artificial Intelligence augments VR by building such vivid and interactive virtual tours. This means, users can VR-headset walk through the ancient city of Machu Picchu while AI-powered guide walked alongside providing real-time comments and history. All of this is made more immersive through the personalization capabilities AI offers, enabling users to concentrate on ideas that most resonate with them.

Augmented Reality (AR): While VR immerses users in an entirely virtual world, AR overlays digital information onto the real-world. Usage of Artificial Intelligence would expect, artificial intelligence is a core-function necessary to enable augmented reality by assisting in the analysis of data and developing real-time interaction with various aspects surrounding users. AR could even add another layer of information during a real-world visit to the site in tourism. Tourists in Rome are able to see what ancient ruins would have looked like originally thanks to AI-powered AR apps, providing the experience with historical context (Kaushal & Yadav, 2023).

360-Degree Videos: This next best thing to being there is the visual impressions through 360-degree videos that gives its viewers a sight of locations from every corner angles. AI helps to enrich these videos by individualizing content to each watcher and making it interactive with the help of some functions like narration powered by AI or personalized recommendation. Be it a narrated visual trip through the Amazon rainforest or virtual flyby of Eiffel Tower, AI keeps thing engaging yet informative.

AI-enabled virtual tourism could be an environmentally friendly substitute for many forms of traditional travel. Physical tourism causes challenges for the environment like over-tourism, pollution and damage to both natural and cultural sites. It is impossible to visit all of these destinations, but by practicing virtual tourism instead users can start having a better experience the beauty this world has without harming it. AI-powered virtual landscapes perfectly simulate the ambience of a spot to cut off constant travelling and as means for sustainability. AI for accessibility in tourism It allows people who otherwise could not afford to travel, as well as those with issues around mobility and geography to have that experience. People with physical disabilities or without the money to afford international travel, can virtually experience global locations through AI-powered virtual tours. The AI powered solutions will provide multilingual support as well to let you understand what others are talking and voice recognition systems, which makes it more inclusive.

Virtual tourism powered by AI makes a remarkable breakthrough in the industry, being an intersection between technology and sustainability seen through lens of accessibility. Through the development of virtual tourism, AI will also increasingly involve itself in providing a more personalized and better travel experience as well as to open it up for everyone. Integrating AI-powered solutions like VR, AR and 360-degree videos, the tourism industry can provide engaging hands-on experiences that will appeal to a broad range of individual preferences while simultaneously fostering environmental-friendly practices and global cultural harmony (King, 2022).

4. MACHINE LEARNING, NATURAL LANGUAGE PROCESSING (NLP) AND COMPUTER VISION IN VIRTUAL TOURISM

The incorporation of latest technologies such as deep learning skills, natural language grammar and computer interpretation makes virtual tourism more ubiquitous. Together, these technologies improve user experience in an interactive and personalized way when taking virtual tours so that users can explore global destinations more closely without needing to travel. Taking us to unprecedented heights of virtual tourism, each one is a key facilitator (Sadowski, 2023). When it comes to virtual tourism, machine learning can be a great asset whereby systems will run based on the algorithms of this technique and improve themselves over time by processing data. ML algorithms learn user preferences, behavior and feedbacks in the virtual tourism platforms to provide personalized recommendations for tours attractions or activities. ML which through the analysis of interests in cultural heritage tourism, nature or adventure on a user can make an adaptation bases with those tastes for virtual experience. The recommendation engine creates a more personal, dynamic experience and serves users content right up their alley.

ML will make virtual environments more life-like and interactive based on the predictive analytics, ML can capable of predicting user behavior and at that time it can adjust flow for virtual tour dynamically. Like when a user is spending more time on some artifacts in one of the virtual museums, it can suggest similar exhibits or historical facts. These are adaptive tools that help maintain user attention, thus providing a more intuitive and fun virtual tourism experience. When it comes to virtual tourism, NLP is instrumental in helping the users interact with AI-driven virtual guides through natural language. But the NLP also helps to induce multilingual support into virtual tourism platforms promising a wider audience. With NLP, languages can be processed and translated in real time so people with different language backgrounds might want to go on the same tour but experience it in their local tongue thus enabling accessibility. This tech also enhances the precision of voice commands and makes for more seamless interactions between users using vocal input to ask their virtual guides questions (Sharma & Singh, 2022).

There is a large focus on using computer vision to create visually immersive and interactive virtual tourism experiences. Virtual tourism sites can use computer vision to capture and interpret visual data from real-world environments through image recognition, deep learning algorithms. It provides the means to map destinations in full 3D, and thus generate photorealistic virtual worlds which users can explore (Mashood et al., 2023). Consider the example of computer vision which may help to stitch together high-resolution images into a panoramic, 360-degree view so that users can look around themselves and interact within their environment in real-time. It can also pin-point objects of interest on a route and name and describe them as they are approached, all using with increasing levels of detail with each generation still imagery gathered by the car itself. This even get to explore virtually natural and historic scenes for computer vision that makes these virtual places still feel real.

The implementation of technologies like machine learning, NLP (Natural Language Processing), and a computer vision are the primary factor that is shaping this trend in virtual tourism. Collectively, they deliver uniquely tailored interactive and engaging experiences, making virtual travel as an appealing and accessible option to its physical counterpart (Gao & Liu, 2022). As these technologies continue to advance, so too will the ability of virtual reality tourism to bring more nuanced and inclusive experiences; opening up new doors on how we travel in this world.

5. ENHANCING VISITOR EXPERIENCE THROUGH AI: ROLE IN ENHANCING INTERACTIVITY AND PERSONALIZATION

Artificial intelligence (AI) is changing tourism completely unlocking the potential for a more interactive and personalized visitor experience that we have come to expect as it defines modern travel. The power of AI to sift through reams of information and anticipate what users would like provides a game-changing element whereby travelers interact with destinations both virtually now, but ultimately physically (Rajamannar, 2021). AI is present throughout the entire path, from immersive virtual tours and personalized suggestions to dynamic experiences tailored for individual interests.

5.1 AI-Driven Interactivity

The interactive nature of tourism experience could be bolstered through AI that boosts the interactivity making more engaging and reaction to user interactions. These AI-powered virtual tours offer real-time, dynamic interactions with destinations. A user could, for instance, walk through a museum in VR and the instant they look at any piece of art an AI system knows all about it. Powered by AI, chatbots and virtual assistants can respond to specific questions with personal flavor adding additional interest points related to historical or cultural context making the tour appear more intimate & engaging.

Also, AI-based systems can help develop dedicated experiences with the assistance of technologies like virtual reality (VR) and augmented reality (AR). When boosted by AI, these technologies enable immediate feedback and live interaction. But then AR apps can place reconstructed versions into your actual view of landmarks, and AI makes sure the context-specific detail matches what you probably want. This not only makes discovering a new place informative yet also more engaging (Ancillai et al., 2019).

5.2 Personalization Through AI

Personalisation is a key element in tourism today, and AI has the ability to provide customised experiences according to your travel choices. Machine learning algorithms make sense of the user data which includes your travel history, browsing patterns and even social media feeds to suggest personalized itineraries or activities in some cases virtual tours too. For instance, if someone types in search for adventure tourism information on a regular basis, the system will provide virtual hikes or mountain treks AI can promote it similar.

AI also personalizes in-the-moment experiences as the user interacts with it. While a user interacts with an AI powered virtual platform, the system can simultaneously learn from their behavior and adapt its content or focus areas to align more effectively with other areas of interest for them. This ensures a personalized, engaging experience for the users as they will feel that the tour has been created just for them. Even journeys in the physical space are aided by AI technology, which provides personalized dining and activity suggestions for each individual traveler. AI is transforming the visitor experience through enhanced interactivity and personalization of destinations, virtually as well as physically (George, 2023).

6. PROMOTING ECOSYSTEM CONSERVATION WITH VIRTUAL TOURISM

Advances in virtual tourism are turning this niche into a powerful engine for helping preserve ecosystems by conducting travel experiences that replicate the carbon emissions of actual journeys (Wind & Hays, 2016). With natural environments and cultural heritage sites more at risk than ever before due to over-tourism, pollution and habitat destruction, virtual tourism offers an eco-friendly alternative that allows the world explorer in us all come alive whilst also safeguarding these fragile ecosystems.

6.1 Eco-Footprint Reduction

The environmental impact of physical travel is without a doubt one of the most important advantages that, due to its very nature relating to virtual reality, can give us. The nature, tourism is responsible for large amounts of carbon emissions in the form of transportation as most typically air travel and tourist storage creates pressure on natural resources at popular destinations (Kuusinen, 2019). Virtual tours enabled with VR (virtual reality) are experience-able to an extent without leaving your room as virtual world of AR or Augmented Reality. Physical footfall in places of interest will be reduced by letting individuals 'visit' from the comfort and safety without triggering habitat degradation, waste creation or resource depletion for developing experiences.

6.2 Preserving Fragile Ecosystems

The ecosystems must be among the most important in human history, coral reefs and tropical rainforests have been just as high regards to conditions where they are highly sensitive being altered by humans. The answer is virtual tourism, which not only can ease the burden of visitors on these natural wonders but also allows them to stay a while without disturbing this vulnerable harmony. Virtual tours of conservation sites, for example the Galápagos Islands or Great Barrier Reef, allow people to explore those ecosystems in a way that is educational and non-disruptive. The wildlife and their habitats are themselves conserved, but also gives rise to awareness about why we should conserve these.

6.3 Training and Awareness Opportunities

Virtual Tourism and Environmental Education Immersive experiences provide information on the ecological importance of each location, threats faced by them and conservation efforts that are ongoing. Use of Virtual intelligence operated guides, which would provide in real-time information on the key sustainability points as well interactive elements for users to be more enganged. The providing of a more engaging way of showcasing his locations, virtual tourism motivates people less motivated to help conservation efforts and take up better practices in the real world travel. Virtual tourism provides new avenues in promoting eco-conservation by providing sustainable alternatives to traditional forms of entertainment which helps raise awareness towards the beauty of conserving what mother nature has gifted us in order for future generations to enjoy (Naji et al., 2024).

7. ECONOMIC AND SOCIAL IMPACTS OF AI-DRIVEN VIRTUAL TOURISM

Virtual tourism powered by artificial intelligence (AI) is creating a new economic and social landscape, challenging the status quo of never-ending modern tourist life while also addressing existing problems faced within traditional forms of tourism. With advances in technology like virtual reality (VR), augmented reality (AR) and machine learning, have seen virtual tourism be introduced as a valid substitute to actually travelling for some time now. Such a shift has wide ramifications for economies, communities and tourism experience as well bringing with it the opportunities involved and challenges (Wheeler, 2023).

7.1 Economic Impacts

The biggest as-yet unseen economic effect of AI led virtual tourism is the segmentation and growth in demand within a broader market for travel. Destinations that once required time-consuming and expensive travel, can now easily bring their experience to a global audience by providing an immersive virtual. Virtual tourism provides businesses, museums and heritage sites with new revenue streams such as charging users for virtual tours or exclusive content an/or even interactive experiences. That is an opportunity for smaller or less well-known locations to get a far higher profile and appeal to broader market without the necessity of expensive infrastructure or being on mass tourist's wish list.

As well as, virtual tourism reduces their dependence on seasonal tourism as many regions suffer from this problem. It can help to avoid reliance on peak season which will lead every travel business owner at the risk and mercy of off-peak periods. But virtual tourism is year-round and represents the opportunity for destinations to bring in consistent income. This stability can help businesses to remain robust during global crises when travelling physically get disrupted due to pandemics and natural calamities. AI-enabled virtual tourism can offset the economic cost in destinations that are over-touristed. Overcrowding is placing environmental and infrastructural stress on popular tourist destinations such as Venice, Machu Picchu or Barcelona. Virtual tourism provides a sustainable alternative, allowing such destinations to conserve their cultural and natural heritage while still getting some revenue from sightseers (Sedkaoui, 2018).

7.2 Social Impacts

AI-driven virtual tourism fundamentally changes our society is just as important. First and foremost is the democratization of travel. The experience of virtual tourism alleviates many aspects that are normally associated with travel such as cost, difficulty in mobility or barriers arising from geography. What this means is that global destinations can now be accessed by individuals who dong have the financial wherewithal or may not even be put too-fared ball physically travel through AI-powered virtual platforms. All of this has fostered an environment that contributes to sharing cultures and making more educational or cultural experiences available, which before was often so unattainable (Neuwirth, 2023).

While it gives access, AI-driven virtual tourism also directly contributes to cultural preservation and appreciation. In this case, virtual tourism can serve as a tool to both preserve the sites and display them without adding more damage. This way, communities can share their cultural practices with the world wide audience if ever they wish to and not at risk of damaging wear tear from footfall. Artificial Intelligence and Virtual Tourism experiences also provide opportunities for communities to start communicating with visitors in a new form. Features like access to native guides and storytellers leading virtual tours for live insights, personalized real-time experiences from local people as well (Schaeffer, 2017). It creates meaningful relationships amongst tourists and local folks, transferring cultural without being harmful to the environment moving physically. Aside from these, AI-enabled platforms can also help in aiding local economies to share locally produced goods and services virtually many through virtual markets or integrated e-commerce functionalities.

8. CHALLENGES AND CONSIDERATIONS

AI driven virtual tourism poses several challenges that need to be solved. One of the major concerns is potential job displacement in existing tourism. If virtual tourism picks up, the demand for real-world equivalents tour guides, hospitality workers, transport services etc. At the same time, it directly opens up new spaces in digital tourism content creation, virtual tour concept development and AI implementation to partially compensate for these losses. There is also the challenge of a digital divide, making virtual tourism inaccessible to people in areas where internet infrastructure or digital literacy are lacking. Making virtual tourism widely available will require investment in digital infrastructure and literacy, especially for those residing in the underserved regions.

Virtual tourism powered by AI is shaping the face of modern tourism world economically and socially. It has the power to change how people explore the world, offering new ways for cultural and economic exchange that also allows authentic heritage preservation. Yet it is important to meet the demands of job displacement and digital access in order for all people have a fair shake at enjoying this exciting, new phenomenon (Venkatesh, 2021).

Figure 2. Illuminates the challenges and considerations

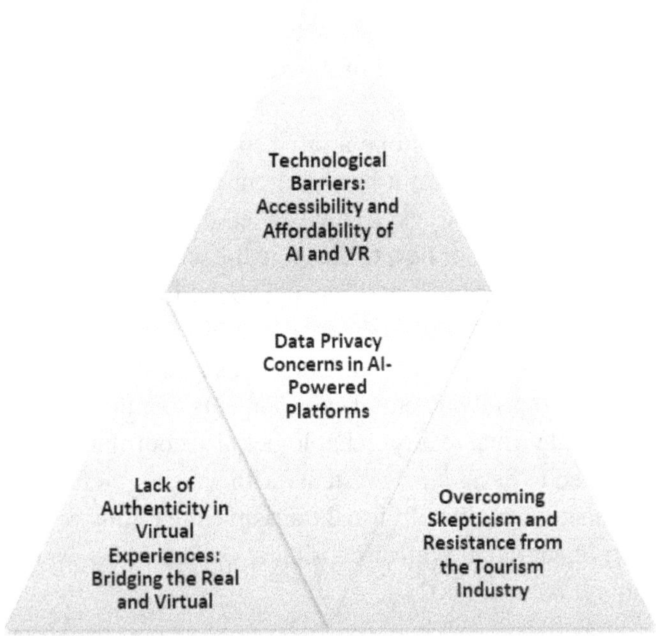

(Source- Self Prepared- Original)

9. ETHICAL CONSIDERATIONS IN AI-DRIVEN VIRTUAL TOURISM

The use of AI for virtual tourism provides exciting new immersive travel experiences, but it is important to consider relevant ethical issues in ways that comport with responsible and diverse uses. As virtual tourism platforms are relying more on artificial intelligence (AI), concerns of privacy, accessibility and cultural representation so too do questions about environmental sustainability. The processing of user data is the key ethical issue related to AI-driven virtual tourism (Reviglio della Venaria, 2020). These virtual tourism tools are also nothing to sneeze at in terms of data aggregation, however they glean an incredible amount of personal information and biometric readings. It is important for app developers to take the necessary steps to secure users from data theft and misuse. Transparent data collection and better control over user's own data is an absolute must to solve most of these problems. Virtual tourism powered by AI provides the opportunity to present rich cultures and heritage sites worldwide. Yet, it should be done carefully when representing these milk cultures. Misrepresentation or worse, commodification of cultural objects can quickly lead to racial stereotyping, oppressive expoliation. Any tourism experience must involve a responsive approach with the local stakeholders and communities represented, showing that their cultural heritage is shared in an appropriate way at all times mindful of how they see themselves and what rights belong to them (Duan, et al., 2024).

Although virtual tourism could be a ramp to equalize the opportunity for everyone having travel experiences; it has been put in difficulty of digital divide as well. Those who do not have access to high-speed internet and a digital device, or those without the knowledge of how to navigate the web are left out from engaging in such experiences thereby indirectly causing social inequalities. When it comes to ethical virtual tourism initiatives, the focus should be on expanding access and providing this tech for underserved populations. This type of virtual tourism certainly has a much smaller footprint on natural environments, but the energy consumption required to run AI and virtual reality technologies also contribute carbon emissions. Developers also need to design their systems with an energy-efficiency in mind so that the environmental benefits of virtual tourism can be fully realized. AI-driven virtual tourism is beneficial, ethical considerations must be overcome by these solutions (Tzampazaki et al., 2024).

10. CONCLUSION, FUTURE DIRECTIONS AND INNOVATIONS

Leveraging AI-powered virtual tourism can be a game-changer for visitor experience enhancement as well as ecosystem conservation. With the increasing prevalence of artificial intelligence, virtual reality or augmented reality are set to grow in use with storytelling similar to how interactive movies began using VR technology 30 years ago and will be enhanced through new techniques that bring a deeper level of interaction for emotional engagement along cognitive depth. Utilizing this two-pronged approach not only democratizes travel but also illustrates the need to protect vulnerable habitats.

Potential future innovations might offer better personalization through algorithms that use machine learning to tailor experiences based on user behavior and preferences, or real-time environmental data can inform visitors of ecological impacts on their surroundings. As such, collaborative platforms that link local communities with virtual tourists can facilitate cross-cultural meeting points and sustainable economic practices that ensure the latter make it to where they are needed most.

In the future, it is probable that continued progress with immersive technologies will offer even more lifelike and affordable experiences which bridge between virtual tourism to physical destinations. So, as long ethical concerns are prioritized, and inclusivity taken into deep consideration the future of AI for tourism will inevitably lead to a sustainable and exciting way forward balancing both exploration joys with the conservation needs of our ecosystems. There is so much potential for AI-powered virtual tourism to disrupt the bad way in which travel works today, and open up a new future where both people as individuals, and us as part of planet earth are truly enriched by being present on it.

REFERENCES

Ahmed, A. (2022). Marketing 4.0: The Unseen Potential of AI in Consumer Relations. *International Journal of New Media Studies: International Peer Reviewed Scholarly Indexed Journal*, *9*(1), 5–12.

Ancillai, C., Terho, H., Cardinali, S., & Pascucci, F. (2019). Advancing social media driven sales research: Establishing conceptual foundations for B-to-B social selling. *Industrial Marketing Management*, *82*, 293–308. DOI: 10.1016/j.indmarman.2019.01.002

Auttri, B., Chaitanya, K., Daida, S., & Jain, S. K. (2023). Digital Transformation in Customer Relationship Management: Enhancing Engagement and Loyalty. [EEL]. *European Economic Letters*, *13*(3), 1140–1149.

. Babet, A. (2020). Utilization of personalization in marketing automation and email marketing.

. Bhatnagar, S. (2022). Digital Disruptions and Transformation of Bank Marketing.

Duan, W., Khurshid, A., Khan, K., & Calin, A. C. (2024). Transforming industry: Investigating 4.0 technologies for sustainable product evolution in china through a novel fuzzy three-way decision-making process. *Technological Forecasting and Social Change*, *200*, 123125. DOI: 10.1016/j.techfore.2023.123125

. Gao, Y., & Liu, H. (2022). Artificial intelligence-enabled personalization in interactive marketing: a customer journey perspective. *Journal of Research in Interactive Marketing*, (ahead-of-print), 1-18.

George, A. S. (2023). Future Economic Implications of Artificial Intelligence. *Partners Universal International Research Journal*, *2*(3), 20–39.

. Henke, N., & Jacques Bughin, L. (2016). The age of analytics: Competing in a data-driven world.

Kacprzak, A., & Hensel, P. (2023). Exploring online customer experience: A systematic literature review and research agenda. *International Journal of Consumer Studies*, *47*(6), 2583–2608. DOI: 10.1111/ijcs.12966

Kamal, M., & Himel, A. S. (2023). Redefining Modern Marketing: An Analysis of AI and NLP's Influence on Consumer Engagement, Strategy, and Beyond. *Eigenpub Review of Science and Technology*, *7*(1), 203–223.

Kaushal, V., & Yadav, R. (2023). Learning successful implementation of Chatbots in businesses from B2B customer experience perspective. *Concurrency and Computation*, *35*(1), e7450. DOI: 10.1002/cpe.7450

King, K. (2022). *AI Strategy for Sales and Marketing: Connecting Marketing, Sales and Customer Experience*. Kogan Page Publishers.

. Kuusinen, M. (2019). Scenarios for digital marketing: a Delphi-based analysis for 2028.

Lavuri, R., & Akram, U. (2023). Role of virtual reality authentic experience on affective responses: Moderating role virtual reality attachment. *Journal of Ecotourism*, •••, 1–19.

Mashood, K., Kayani, H. U. R., Malik, A. A., & Tahir, A. (2023). ARTIFICIAL INTELLIGENCE RECENT TRENDS AND APPLICATIONS IN INDUSTRIES. *Pakistan Journal of Science*, *75*(02). Advance online publication. DOI: 10.57041/pjs.v75i02.855

Naji, K. K., Gunduz, M., Alhenzab, F., Al-Hababi, H., & Al-Qahtani, A. (2024). A Systematic Review of the Digital Transformation of the Building Construction Industry. *IEEE Access : Practical Innovations, Open Solutions*, *12*, 31461–31487. DOI: 10.1109/ACCESS.2024.3365934

Neuwirth, R. J. (2023). Prohibited artificial intelligence practices in the proposed EU artificial intelligence act (AIA). *Computer Law & Security Review*, *48*, 105798. DOI: 10.1016/j.clsr.2023.105798

Rajamannar, R. (2021). *Quantum marketing: mastering the new marketing mindset for tomorrow's consumers*. HarperCollins Leadership.

. Reviglio della Venaria, U. (2020). Personalization in Social Media: Challenges and Opportunities for Democratic Societies.

Sadowski, J. (2023). Total life insurance: Logics of anticipatory control and actuarial governance in insurance technology. *Social Studies of Science*, •••, 03063127231186437. PMID: 37427796

Schaeffer, E. (2017). *Industry X. 0: Realizing digital value in industrial sectors*. Kogan Page Publishers.

Sedkaoui, S. (Ed.). (2018). *Big data analytics for entrepreneurial success*. IGI Global.

Sharma, A., & Singh, B. (2022). Measuring Impact of E-commerce on Small Scale Business: A Systematic Review. *Journal of Corporate Governance and International Business Law*, *5*(1).

Soliman, M., & Al Balushi, M. K. (2023). Unveiling destination evangelism through generative AI tools. *ROBONOMICS: The Journal of the Automated Economy*, *4*(54), 1.

Tzampazaki, M., Zografos, C., Vrochidou, E., & Papakostas, G. A. (2024). Machine Vision—Moving from Industry 4.0 to Industry 5.0. *Applied Sciences (Basel, Switzerland)*, *14*(4), 1471. DOI: 10.3390/app14041471

Venkatesh, D. N. (2021). *Winning with employees: Leveraging employee experience for a competitive edge*. SAGE Publishing India.

Vinaykarthik, B. C. (2022, October). Design of Artificial Intelligence (AI) based User Experience Websites for E-commerce Application and Future of Digital Marketing. In *2022 3rd International Conference on Smart Electronics and Communication (ICOSEC)* (pp. 1023-1029). IEEE.

Vuong, N. A., & Mai, T. T. (2023). Unveiling the Synergy: Exploring the Intersection of AI and NLP in Redefining Modern Marketing for Enhanced Consumer Engagement and Strategy Optimization. *Quarterly Journal of Emerging Technologies and Innovations*, *8*(3), 103–118.

Wheeler, J. (2023). *The Digital-First Customer Experience: Seven Design Strategies from the World's Leading Brands*. Kogan Page Publishers.

Wind, Y. J., & Hays, C. F. (2016). *Beyond advertising: Creating value through all customer touchpoints*. John Wiley & Sons.

Zaki, H. O. (2022). The Impact Of Artificial Intelligence On Content Marketing. *Journal of Strategic Digital Transformation In Society*, *2*(3).

Chapter 9
Sustainable Tourism in the Digital Age: Leveraging Technology for Enhanced Practices, Experiences, and Sustainability Challenges

Tanusree Chakraborty
https://orcid.org/0000-0003-0322-3990
Administrative Staff College of India, India

V. S. Sharada
https://orcid.org/0009-0006-7378-2949
Administrative Staff College of India, India

Nandita Mishra
https://orcid.org/0000-0003-1140-3991
Chetana's Institute of Management and Research, India

ABSTRACT

Sustainable tourism management is a critical issue in the modern tourism industry, focusing on maximizing benefits to local communities, minimizing negative environmental impacts, and preserving natural and cultural heritage. This chapter explores the integration of sustainability principles into tourism practices, emphasizing the role of technology in enhancing sustainable tourism experiences and addressing challenges. The chapter begins by discussing the concept of sustainable tourism management and its importance in achieving long-term environmental, social, and economic goals.

DOI: 10.4018/979-8-3373-0071-9.ch009

1. INTRODUCTION TO SUSTAINABLE TOURISM MANAGEMENT

Sustainability is the latest concept in tourism industry and environment friendly tourism is believed to be the only way to minimise negative impacts (Miller and Spoolman, 2016). Sustainable tourism management refers to the process of managing tourism in a way that maximizes the benefits to local communities, minimizes negative impacts on the environment, and promotes the conservation of natural and cultural heritage. Sustainable Tourism is a sustainable approach to the tourism industry, aiming to minimize negative impacts and maximize positive ones. It involves the integration of sustainability principles into all aspects of tourism development and operations. Any travel that serves the needs of current visitors and the community while safeguarding the intent of the future travellers is sustainable tourism (Edgell, 2019). To guarantee that, tourism can be sustained throughout time, it entails the careful management of all resources, including natural, cultural, and human resources (Murphy & Price, 2012). The capacity of sustainable tourism management to maintain natural and cultural resources, boost regional economies, and advance social welfare makes it crucial (Streimikiene et al., 2021). Destinations may attract environmentally and socially concerned travellers, strengthen their competitive edge, and help the world accomplish its sustainability goals by incorporating sustainability concepts into its tourism policies.

Technology is essential to sustainable tourism management because it helps destinations operate more efficiently, improve guest experiences, and perform better environmentally (Loureiro & Nascimento, 2021). Digital technologies are becoming key enablers of sustainable tourism development, providing new opportunities for improving destination management, enhancing visitor experiences (Polishchuk et al., 2023). Technologies that can be used to track and control the effects of tourism, encourage sustainable behavior, and include visitors in sustainability projects include information and communication technology (ICT), big data analytics, and the Internet of Things (IoT). In general, sustainable tourism management is necessary to guarantee that tourism can minimize adverse effects on the environment and society while continuing to benefit destinations, communities, and tourists (Ali et al., 2020). By incorporating technology into sustainable tourism practices, travel destinations can provide more responsible and pleasurable travel experiences while still achieving their sustainability goals (Sharma & Kumar, 2024).

Table 1. Various strategies to implement sustainability in tourism

S No.	Aspect	Examples of Implementation
1.	Sustainable Accommodation	Eco-friendly hotels using renewable energy sources Lodges with sustainable construction practices
2.	Sustainable Transportation	Electric vehicle (EV) tours Bicycle rentals for eco-friendly exploration
3.	Waste Management	Recycling programs at tourist sites Composting food waste in hotels
4.	Conservation and Biodiversity	Protected area visits with guided tours to raise awareness Wildlife conservation projects supported by tourism
5.	Community Engagement	Homestay programs where tourists stay with local families Community-led tours showcasing local culture and traditions
6.	Cultural Preservation	Heritage tours promoting traditional arts and crafts Cultural events and festivals highlighting local traditions and practices
7.	Sustainable Food and Dining	Restaurants serving locally sourced, organic food Cooking classes using traditional, sustainable ingredients
8.	Education and Awareness	Guided tours explaining local ecosystems and conservation efforts Workshops on sustainable living practices for tourists and locals
9.	Water Conservation	Hotels and resorts using water-saving fixtures and practice Educational programs on water conservation for tourists and staff
10.	Renewable Energy	Tourist attractions powered by solar or wind energy Eco-lodges using solar panels for electricity
11.	Green Certification Programs	Hotels and tour operators obtaining certifications like EarthCheck or Green Globe Participation in eco-labeling schemes for sustainable tourism
12.	Sustainable Souvenirs	Gift shops selling locally made, eco-friendly products Artisanal crafts made from recycled materials
13.	Responsible Tour Operators	Tour companies offering low-impact tours and responsible wildlife viewing practices Carbon offset programs for tour activities
14.	Carbon Offsetting	Hotels and tour operators offering carbon offset options for travellers Planting trees to offset carbon emissions from travel

Sustainable tourism practices are being promoted through the use of information and communication technology (ICT) in many ways (Rattanamanee, 2024). For instance, ICT tools are being used by Destination Management Organizations (DMOs) to inform travellers about sustainability initiatives, like highlighting eco-friendly travel options and activities. Additionally, ICT is being used to gather and examine data on visitor behavior and preferences, which enables destinations to modify their offers to satisfy sustainability objectives. Big data analytics, which offers insights into visitor trends and behavior, is assisting destinations in managing tourism more sustainably (Gupta et al., 2024). Destinations can find opportunities to enhance sustainability practices by analyzing huge amounts of data. For example, they might manage tourist flows to prevent crowding in sensitive regions or optimize transportation routes to lower carbon emissions (Luo et al., 2024). Through the utilization of linked devices, the Internet of Things (IoT) is enabling destinations to embrace sustainable practices. IoT sensors, for instance, can be used to track water and energy usage in hotels, enabling more effective resource management. To reduce conflicts between people and animals, IoT devices can also be used to follow the movements of wildlife in protected areas (Babu et al., 2024).

With this background, it can be understood that there is an increasing importance of sustainable tourism in today's world. As tourism continues to grow, there is a pressing need to ensure that it is managed in a way that minimizes negative impacts on the environment, supports local communities, and preserves cultural heritage. Technology plays a crucial role in achieving these goals by providing tools and solutions that can enhance sustainable practices in the tourism industry. The research gap that leads to this chapter is the lack of comprehensive understanding and analysis of how various technologies are being utilized in sustainable tourism. While there is some literature available on the topic, it often focuses on specific technologies or applications, rather than providing a holistic view of the role of technology in sustainable tourism. This chapter aims to bridge this gap by providing a comprehensive overview of the various technologies used in sustainable tourism and their applications.

The novelty of this chapter lies in its comprehensive approach to the topic. By exploring a wide range of technologies and their applications in sustainable tourism, it provides valuable insights for researchers, practitioners, and policymakers alike. Additionally, by including examples of companies and portals/apps where these technologies can be accessed, the chapter offers practical information that can help stakeholders in the tourism industry implement sustainable practices more effectively.

The current chapter has the following research questions:

- How can the use of information communication technology (ICT) be optimized to promote sustainable tourism practices, including the dissemination of information about eco-friendly accommodations and activities?
- What are the most effective strategies for online booking platforms to integrate sustainability criteria into their systems and promote sustainable tourism choices among travellers?
- How can digital marketing strategies be tailored to effectively communicate genuine sustainability efforts and combat greenwashing in the tourism industry?
- What are the key challenges and opportunities in integrating technology for sustainable tourism, including cost considerations, digital divide issues,

data privacy concerns, and the need for stakeholder awareness and skills development?

The chapter unfolds with an introduction to Sustainable Tourism Management, setting the stage for a comprehensive exploration of the role of technology in this field. It progresses through distinct sections: the Role of Technology in Sustainable Tourism, Information and Communication Technology (ICT) in Sustainable Tourism, Digital Marketing for Sustainable Tourism, Virtual Reality (VR) and Augmented Reality (AR) in Sustainable Tourism, Challenges and Opportunities in Integrating Technology for Sustainable Tourism, and Impacts of Sustainable Tourism Management. These sections probe into the overarching role of technology in shaping sustainable tourism practices, highlighting its potential to enhance visitor experiences, conserve natural and cultural heritage, and support local communities. They examine how ICT tools and platforms are leveraged to disseminate information about sustainable practices, facilitate communication between stakeholders, and enhance the overall tourism experience. The chapter also discusses the role of digital marketing strategies in promoting sustainable tourism, including the use of social media, online booking platforms, and targeted advertising to raise awareness and drive sustainable travel choices. It further explores the transformative impact of VR and AR technologies, highlighting how they create immersive experiences that educate and inspire travellers about sustainability and conservation efforts. Additionally, the chapter considers the various challenges, such as cost, digital divide, and data privacy, along with the opportunities presented by technology integration in sustainable tourism management. Finally, it evaluates the overall impacts of sustainable tourism management, considering its effects on the environment, local communities, and the tourism industry as a whole. Together, these sections provide a comprehensive overview of the role of technology in sustainable tourism, highlighting its potential to drive positive change and enhance the overall sustainability of the tourism industry.

2. ROLE OF TECHNOLOGY IN SUSTAINABLE TOURISM

The role of technology in sustainable tourism is multifaceted, encompassing digital marketing, virtual reality (VR), augmented reality (AR), and mobile applications (Samaddar & Mondal, 2024). These technologies play a crucial role in promoting sustainable practices and destinations, enhancing the visitor experience, and improving resource management. Digital marketing is instrumental in communicating with environmentally conscious travellers and spreading awareness about sustainability programs (Talawar et al., 2024). Through social media platforms, tourism organizations can engage directly with visitors, inspiring them to support eco-friendly projects and make responsible travel choices (Clark et al., 2023). Online booking platforms also play a role by showcasing sustainable lodging options and encouraging travellers to make informed decisions that prioritize sustainability (Nicola-Gavrilă, 2023).

VR and AR technologies are revolutionizing the way travellers experience destinations. VR allows tourists to explore natural wonders and cultural attractions virtually, while AR enhances their understanding of the environment by superimposing digital data on the real world.

These technologies can be used to educate visitors about conservation efforts, highlight sustainable practices, and raise awareness about environmental and cultural issues. Mobile applications are another key tool in sustainable tourism, providing travellers with up-to-date information about eco-friendly lodging options, sustainable tourist destinations, and ethical tour operators. These apps also offer virtual tours, audio guides, and interactive maps, enhancing the overall visitor experience (Table 2).

Table 2. Applications of technology in sustainable tourism and examples of companies using them

Application	Examples of Companies Using Them
Online Booking Platforms	Booking.com: Offers filters for eco-friendly accommodations
	Airbnb: Highlights sustainable stays and experiences for conscious travellers
	Expedia: Features eco-certified hotels and activities
VR and AR Technologies	Google Expeditions: Offers virtual tours of iconic landmarks and natural wonders
	Oculus VR: Provides immersive travel experiences through VR
	AR City: Enhances city tours with augmented reality features
Mobile Applications	Eco Companion: Provides information on sustainable travel options
	FairTrip: Offers a platform for discovering and booking sustainable experiences
	HappyCow: Helps find vegan and vegetarian-friendly restaurants worldwide
IoT (Internet of Things)	GreenWave: Monitors energy usage and environmental conditions in hotels
	Smart Parks: Uses sensors to manage visitor flows and protect wildlife
	CleanRobotics: Offers waste management solutions using AI and IoT

Source: Compiled by authors

Table 3 provides a summary of key features found in eco-friendly travel apps, highlighting how these apps help travellers make sustainable choices. Carbon footprint tracking allows users to understand the environmental impact of their travel activities, while green accommodation options promote eco-friendly lodging. Public transport guidance encourages the use of sustainable transportation, and recommendations for local and sustainable dining support environmentally conscious food choices. Waste reduction tips help minimize environmental impact, and community engagement features facilitate connections with local communities. Educational resources raise awareness about sustainable tourism practices, empowering users to make eco-conscious decisions while traveling.

Table 3. A Summary of key features found in eco-friendly travel apps

S. No.	Feature	Description
1	Carbon Footprint Tracking	Allows users to track and understand the carbon footprints during the transport, travel, accommodation and regular activities.
2	Green Accommodation Options	Provides information on environmentally friendly accommodation options such as hotels, hostels, or alternative lodging with eco-friendly practices.
3	Public Transport Guidance	Offers comprehensive guides and information on public transport systems in various destinations to encourage the use of sustainable transportation options.
4	Local and Sustainable Dining	Highlights restaurants and eateries offering locally sourced, organic, and sustainable food options to support local communities and reduce environmental impact.
5	Waste Reduction Tips	Provides tips on minimizing waste generation during travel, including reducing single-use plastics, proper waste disposal, and supporting circular economy initiatives.
6	Community Engagement	Facilitates connections between travelers and local communities, promoting responsible tourism through cultural exchange, volunteering, or supporting conservation efforts.
7	Educational Resources	Includes educational materials to raise awareness about the environmental impact of travel, empowering users to make eco-conscious choices and contribute to sustainable tourism.

In the quest for sustainable travel, a new breed of mobile applications is revolutionizing how we explore the world while minimizing our environmental impact. These eco-friendly travel apps offer a range of features designed to help travellers make greener choices, from offsetting carbon emissions to finding locally sourced food and supporting fair-trade businesses. Table 4 explores some of the top apps that are leading the way in sustainable tourism:

Table 4. A Summary of top apps that are leading the way in sustainable tourism

S.No.	App Name	Description
1	Glooby	Provides cross- references across multiple bookings in flights and hotels, making it easy to go green and wallet-friendly. Includes all taxes and fees in price quotes.
2	TripIt	Besides storing travel information and forwarding reminders, TripIt tracks carbon emissions and offers options to offset flight effects, using the "Greenhouse Gas Protocol" for accurate data.
3	Localvore	Helps users explore farmers markets and local produce restaurants, promoting sustainable food choices and reducing waste.
4	Klima	Aims to reduce daily carbon footprint through investments in natural, technological, and social environmental solutions, offsetting pollution.
5	Closca Water	Provides in-app maps to find eco-friendly water refill stations, helping eliminate single-use plastic bottles while offering rewards to users.
6	HappyCow	Helps users find vegetarian, vegan, and eco-friendly restaurants worldwide, promoting a diet that reduces greenhouse-gas emissions and supports better land management.
7	Helsinki City	Helsinki's app guides visitors to low-impact hotels, activities, and transportation, part of the city's aim to be carbon-neutral by 2035. Other cities like Barcelona are also launching similar apps for sustainable tourism.
8	Bikemap	For cyclists, offering a platform to discover and plan cycling routes worldwide, with detailed maps, elevation profiles, and user reviews for a greener way to explore.
9	Komoot	Catering to hikers and cyclists, Komoot provides detailed insights into outdoor adventures, including offline maps, route tracking, and user-generated recommendations, promoting sustainable exploration.
10	BlaBlaCar	Connects drivers with empty seats to passengers heading in the same direction, encouraging car-sharing and reducing individual vehicle use for cost-effective and eco-friendly travel.
11	BookDifferent	Empowers users to book eco-friendly accommodations by providing information on sustainable hotels worldwide, helping travellers make informed choices for a greener stay.
12	FairTrip	Connects users with sustainable and responsible travel experiences, offering eco-friendly accommodations, ethical tours, and local businesses prioritising social and environmental responsibility for a more sustainable travel experience.

While technology offers many benefits for sustainable tourism, there are also challenges, such as the cost of implementation, the digital divide, and concerns about data security and privacy. However, the integration of technologies like IoT sensors and data analytics can lead to increased resource efficiency and improved visitor experiences. On the whole, it can be seen that, technology has the potential to transform sustainable tourism by promoting cooperation, accountability, and resilience in tourist locations.

3. INFORMATION AND COMMUNICATION TECHNOLOGY (ICT) IN SUSTAINABLE TOURISM

ICT is essential for encouraging sustainable tourist practices. ICT refers to a broad array of technologies, such as the internet, mobile devices, social media, and software applications. These technologies are used to enhance tourism experiences, increase operational efficiency, and minimise environmental effects. Studies has demonstrated that Information and Communication Technology (ICT) can have a substantial influence on the growth of tourism, particularly in places such as Africa. The connection between ICT, infrastructure, and tourism has been analysed in these regions using dynamic panel models (Adeola & Evans, 2019). ICT plays a crucial role in destination management, which is a key area for promoting sustainable tourism. Digital platforms and mobile applications offer travellers up-to-date information regarding destinations, activities, and local services, empowering them to make well-informed choices that reduce their impact on the environment. For instance, tourists have the ability to utilise smartphone applications to retrieve public transit timetables, pinpoint environmentally friendly lodging options, and uncover sustainable dining choices. According to Zhu et al., (2021), the use of ICT, such as laptops and smartphones, has been shown to enhance the involvement of rural inhabitants in tourism. This highlights the significance of ICT in broadening tourism prospects. ICT enables effective communication and collaboration among players in the tourism business. Online platforms and social media networks facilitate the sharing of best practices, coordination of efforts, and promotion of sustainable tourism projects by corporations, governments, and NGOs. The cooperation is crucial for the implementation of sustainable tourism policies and initiatives at both the local and global scales. Moreover, ICT empowers tourism enterprises to enhance their operational efficiency and minimise resource consumption. ICT plays a significant role in smart tourism for small- and medium-sized tourism firms, since it helps rebalance competition and supports the achievement of sustainable development goals (O'Connor, 2023). Hotels can employ energy management systems and intelligent technology to oversee and regulate energy consumption, water usage, and trash production. This not only decreases expenses but also mitigates the ecological consequences of tourism activity. Moreover, the utilisation of Information and Communication Technology (ICT) in rural community-based homestays has been recognised as crucial for sustainable tourist marketing strategies, where possessing ICT proficiency is considered a great advantage for gathering and analysing data (Janjua et al., 2022). Ultimately, ICT has the capacity to revolutionise the tourism sector through the promotion of sustainable practices and the improvement of the overall tourist experience. Through the utilisation of information and communication technology (ICT) tools and platforms (Table 5), individuals and organisations involved in the tourist sector may collaborate to establish a tourism business that is both environmentally sustainable and socially responsible, ensuring its longevity for future generations.

Table 5. Use of various Information and Communication Technology (ICT) in sustainable tourism

S. No.	Technology	Use in Sustainable Tourism	Examples of Companies	Portals/Apps
1.	**Website Development**	Create websites to promote sustainable tourism practices and destinations, provide information to travellers.	Sustainable Travel International, Responsible Travel, Ecotourism Australia	sustainabletravel.org, responsibletravel.com, ecotourismaustralia.com
2.	**Social Media**	Use platforms like Facebook, Twitter, and Instagram to engage with travellers, promote eco-friendly travel strategies.	Airbnb, Booking.com, TripAdvisor	Airbnb app, Booking.com app, TripAdvisor app
3.	**Online Booking**	Offer sustainable lodging options, showcase eco-certified accommodations, enable travellers to make sustainable choices.	Airbnb, Booking.com, Expedia	Airbnb app, Booking.com app, Expedia app
4.	**Mobile Applications**	Provide up-to-date information on sustainable tourism options, offer virtual tours, audio guides, and interactive maps.	National Geographic, Lonely Planet	National Geographic app, Lonely Planet app
5.	**Data Analytics**	Analyze visitor behavior and preferences to tailor sustainable offerings, manage tourist flows for environmental conservation.	Visit.org, Green Key Global	Visit.org website, Green Key Global website
6.	**Internet of Things**	Track and control the effects of tourism, monitor resource usage in hotels for efficient management.	Hilton, Marriott International	Hilton Honors app, Marriott Bonvoy app

continued on following page

Table 5. Continued

S. No.	Technology	Use in Sustainable Tourism	Examples of Companies	Portals/Apps
7.	**Virtual Reality**	Create immersive experiences to educate travellers about conservation efforts, simulate 8environmental impacts of travel.	Conservation International, The Ocean Agency	Conservation International website, The Ocean Agency website
8.	**Augmented Reality**	Enhance visitors' understanding of their surroundings by superimposing digital data on the real world.	Google, Apple	Google Lens app, Apple ARKit

4. DIGITAL MARKETING FOR SUSTAINABLE TOURISM

In order to promote sustainable tourism practices and destinations, digital marketing is essential. Now, tourism organizations can communicate with environmentally conscious travellers, spread the word about sustainability programs, and encourage responsible travel by utilizing digital media. Social media sites are excellent resources for promoting eco-friendly travel strategies. Social media can be used by tourism organizations to disseminate information about sustainable tour operators, eco-friendly lodging, and responsible travel advice. By providing alternatives that prioritize sustainability, online booking platforms can encourage the use of sustainable tourism practices. Booking websites, for instance, can showcase lodging options with carbon offset plans or eco-certifications. Platforms have the opportunity to assist travellers in making more sustainable and informed decisions by including sustainability criteria into their booking systems.

Digital marketing is an influential tool for marketing sustainable tourism practices and destinations. This platform facilitates the ability of tourist enterprises and locations to connect with a worldwide audience, promote consciousness regarding sustainability efforts, and foster responsible travel conduct. The inclusion of digital marketing tactics in the tourism sector has been acknowledged as a catalyst for the advancement of sustainable tourism (Aman & Papp-Váry, 2022). A crucial element of sustainable tourism's digital marketing strategy is the art of storytelling. Marketers may attract environmentally conscious travellers who are seeking unique and meaningful experiences by crafting captivating stories that showcase the natural beauty, cultural diversity, and sustainability initiatives of a place. Moreover, digital marketing has been identified as the most efficient and sustainable promotional strategy for reaching new and larger target audiences in rural tourism (Aman & Papp-Váry, 2022). Destinations may effectively demonstrate their dedication to sustainability and motivate travellers to adopt responsible behaviours by utilising visually captivating content, including videos, blogs, and social media posts. Digital marketing is essential for teaching travellers about sustainable tourism practices. Marketers can assist travellers in making environmentally conscious choices by offering details on eco-friendly lodging, responsible wildlife encounters, and sustainable transportation alternatives. The significance of social media in promoting sustainable tourism has been highlighted, as firms actively adopt internet and social media technologies to effectively represent themselves as environmentally friendly and sustainable (Thirumaran et al., 2021). In addition, digital marketing can be utilised to highlight sustainable tourism certifications and labels, such as Green Globe or Earth Check, that aid travellers in identifying businesses and places that conform to sustainability criteria. In the era of the "new normal," there is a growing interest in utilising digital marketing strategies to improve the performance of tourism businesses and implementing digital innovations in the tourism industry to ensure sustainable business practices. This highlights the significance of digital marketing in adapting to evolving circumstances (Deb, 2022) Moreover, digital marketing empowers tourist enterprises to contact with travellers in a personalised and engaging manner. Businesses may encourage sustainable travel choices by utilising data analytics and customer relationship management (CRM) systems to customise marketing messages based on individual interests and behaviour. Businesses can, for instance, create eco-friendly trip packages, advertise low-impact activities, or offer advice on minimising carbon footprint during travel. Furthermore, a study has examined the utilisation of digital marketing in promoting sustainable tourism in tourist villages, highlighting the capacity of digital marketing to enhance sustainable tourism on a community level (Wibawa et al., 2022). Ultimately, the literature emphasises the crucial impact of digital marketing on advancing sustainable tourism. This includes improving the operations of tourism enterprises, preserving tourism resources, and effectively and efficiently reaching new target demographics. Social media has been recognised as a beneficial instrument for promoting tourism growth in the post-COVID-19 age, by showcasing tourist destinations and aiding in the long-term viability of the tourism industry (Wahyuni et al., 2021). Utilising digital marketing is an invaluable resource for promoting sustainable tourism practices and destinations. Through the strategic utilisation of digital platforms, the tourism sector can effectively communicate captivating narratives, provide informative guidance to travellers, and establish meaningful connections with them on an individual basis. By doing so, the industry can promote conscientious travel, conduct and actively contribute to the safeguarding of both natural and cultural heritage for the benefit of future generations.

5. VIRTUAL REALITY (VR) AND AUGMENTED REALITY (AR) IN SUSTAINABLE TOURISM

Virtual Reality (VR) and Augmented Reality (AR) are cutting-edge technologies that are transforming the way sustainable tourism is encountered and advertised. These technologies provide engaging and interactive experiences that help educate and motivate travellers to make more environmentally friendly decisions while improving their overall tourist experience. Through VR, tourists can see natural wonders and cultural attractions without physically being there. Contrarily, AR superimposes digital data on the actual world to improve visitors' comprehension of their surroundings. VR and AR can be used in sustainable tourism to tell visitors about conservation efforts, highlight sustainable practices, and bring attention to environmental and cultural issues. For instance, while AR apps can tell users about the local flora and fauna during nature hikes, virtual reality experiences can replicate the consequences of climate change on natural environments. Another effective technique for improving the visitor experience in sustainable tourism is a mobile application. These apps can give travellers up-to-date information about eco-friendly lodging options, sustainable tourist destinations, and ethical tour operators. To improve tourists' experiences, they can also include virtual tours, audio guides, and interactive maps.

Beck et al., (2019) emphasised the effect of VR on both the supplier side of tourism and tourists themselves, highlighting the increasing influence of emerging technologies in the tourism industry. Destination marketing is a significant use of VR and AR in sustainable tourism. Through the creation of virtual tours, individuals can conveniently experience various areas without the need for physical travel, hence minimising the environmental consequences typically connected with such journeys. Additionally, these virtual tours can showcase sustainable practices and attractions, such as environmentally-friendly lodging, wildlife preservation endeavours, or renewable energy programmes, motivating travellers to select areas that prioritise sustainability. According to Putra et al. (2022), the use of VR in educational materials can make a significant contribution to promoting tourism sustainability in regional development. This is especially true in the areas of ecotourism and rural sustainability. VR and AR have the potential to augment the educational significance of travel experiences. Virtual reality simulations have the ability to replicate historical events or natural occurrences, allowing travellers to gain a more profound comprehension of the cultural and environmental importance of a site. Augmented reality apps have the capability to superimpose instructional content onto real-world surroundings, providing interactive learning opportunities that captivate and educate travellers about sustainable practices and local conservation initiatives. Ebinger et al., (2022) emphasised the significance of AR and VR technologies in delivering educational information on sustainable development. They underlined the ability of these technologies to imitate real-world events and offer immersive learning formats. This highlights the capacity of virtual reality (VR) and augmented reality (AR) to not only improve visitor experiences, but also to advance sustainable development by means of educational programmes in the tourism industry. During the COVID-19 pandemic, virtual and augmented reality applications have facilitated virtual tourism experiences, offering a safer option for travellers who are unable to physically visit destinations (Yerden & Uydaci, 2022). This exemplifies the versatility of VR and AR technologies in tackling obstacles within the tourism sector, such as travel limitations and safety apprehensions during pandemics. Ultimately, VR and AR possess the capacity to revolutionise the sustainable tourism sector through the provision of immersive and instructive encounters that encourage conscientious travel conduct. By utilising these technologies to promote sustainable destinations, increase knowledge about environmental and cultural preservation, and enhance the educational aspect of tourism experiences, the tourism sector can contribute to a more sustainable and responsible future for tourism.

6. CHALLENGES AND OPPORTUNITIES IN INTEGRATING TECHNOLOGY FOR SUSTAINABLE TOURISM

We are in an age of technology and every aspect of our lives is affected whether it's travelling, tourism or exploring the world. Technology has transferred the industry and today it relies heavily on unique and immersive experiences. Advanced transportation technologies such as GPS navigation, real-time traffic monitoring, and ride-sharing apps, optimize travel routes, reduce congestion and enhance the efficiency of transportation networks. However, the challenges in integrating technology in tourism are many. Several factors influence the adoption of technology, these factors range from social and demographic factors to the political and legal framework and the economic conditions that shape tourism behaviour. (Gkilias, 2024)

Human Resource and Skills Challenges- Small businesses will lack the knowledge and skills required for digitalisation. Training staff is a continuous process and requires time, resources and capital investment. (Melovic, et al, 2023). The tourism industry being seasonal is based on temporary staff and small family-run businesses don't want to invest in technology as the investments are huge and the staff are temporary. With the increasing demand for integrating technology in all aspects of business, this is one area of focus and development of the skills required in the tourism industry. Tourism stakeholders, including businesses, employees, and destination management organizations, lack the requisite digital skills and expertise to effectively utilize technology. Training and capacity-building programs are needed to bridge the digital skills gap

Uncertainty of Returns on Investment- The crucial challenge for all businesses is the ROI. Technology comes with a high cost and the returns on investment (ROI) may not be commensurate with the cost of the projects. Such projects also have a huge gestation period, so small businesses avoid investing in digital innovations (Cheng et al.,2023). Implementing technological solutions often requires significant investment in infrastructure, hardware, software, and training. modest and medium-sized enterprises (SMEs) in the tourism sector, particularly those in development regions, may struggle to pay the upfront costs of technology adoption. Disparities in the basic infrastructure facilities further increase the cost of the projects in remote locations.

Availability of Internet Facilities- Businesses as well as tourists located in remote areas lack infrastructure as well as poor internet connectivity. Integrating digital services is a challenge in the absence of regular electricity supply and secured internet services. A combination of strategies like low-bandwidth technology, mobile-based apps and public-private partnerships often are not available for remote tourist destinations leaving the place poorly developed.

Ever-Changing Consumer Demand and Behaviour- Consumer demands are constantly changing and ever-increasing. There is always a possibility of technology becoming obsolete and being replaced by futuristic technology. This becomes a challenge for small players and travel organizations. Small travel organizations find it difficult to understand how to keep the personal touch in business and upgrade the requirement of technology in tourism. (Sharma et al., 2020) Financial challenges become significant in the travel industry. The sector goes through loss during off- seasons and it becomes difficult to cope with the economic conditions of businesses, the poor performance of travel businesses makes it challenging to integrate expensive technology.

Data Privacy and Security- The vulnerability of data is a critical concern. Tourism industry data is very sensitive and always at risk. Travel companies collect and store verified personal data including passport numbers, credit card information, addresses and names. The challenge is in processing such huge data sets and still keeping the clients' data confidential. The use of electronic payment methods depends on online payment facilities. If the system is hacked the entire data leak can affect the image and business of the travel company. Firms find the integration of technology expensive as the system is continuously evolving. Data breaches, hacking and phishing attacks are constant threats. Employing robust cyber security such as encryption, firewalls and regular audits can protect against these threats. Accidental data deletion or server failures are huge challenges that negatively impact tourism. Regular backups and strong data storage systems can handle data loss and data threats. In the spree to make travel booking easy and accessible, travel companies go for weak authentication mechanisms and this poses a big challenge to the system. Regularly updating security measures and keeping updated on cyber security trends can help organizations adapt to data privacy and confidentiality.

The Digital Divide- The digital divide is one of the competitive issues facing any industry based on technology. There is an unequal distribution of information which can lead to digital and social exclusion. ICT readiness pillars comprise of eight indicators; ICT use for business-to-business transactions, internet use for business-to-consumer transactions, internet users, broadband users, mobile telephone subscribers, quality of electricity supply, network and telecommunication infrastructure and digital applications. Apart from technology challenges in the digital divide, factors like digital literacy, technical skills, language barriers and cultural norms can affect people's ability to effectively use digital tools and services. The skill divide along with the income divide plays a significant role in shaping the digital divide. Disparities in ICT infrastructures and connectivity vary in different geographies. Addressing the digital divide requires multi-faceted approaches that involve infrastructure development, policy interventions, community engagement, education and training. (Reverte, et al, 2022)

Environmental Degradation: Tourism contributes to greenhouse gas emissions through excessive transportation, accommodation and other activities. Tourism emerges out of travelling long distances, burning fuels and emitting CO2. The biggest challenge is to control pollution from vehicles and prevent environmental degradation. Implementing eco-friendly transportation and energy-efficient infrastructure is necessary for sustainable tourism. While technology has supported sustainability initiatives it has also contributed to environmental degradation through more carbon emissions due to tourism growth. Tourism electronic wastes from obsolete devices and huge energy consumption from data centres and digital infrastructure have led to environmental degradation. Addressing this issue can resolve the challenge technology poses to the environment.

Addressing these challenges requires collaboration and cooperation among stakeholders, including governments, local communities, and NGOs, along with creating awareness among tourists. Managing sustainable tourism is the key to ensuring that tourism can continue to thrive while preserving the planet for future generations

7. IMPACTS OF SUSTAINABLE TOURISM MANAGEMENT:

Managing sustainable tourism involves balancing, economic, social and environmental factors to minimize negative impacts while maximizing the benefits for local communities and ecosystems. Sustainable tourism guidelines and practices apply to all forms of tourism including the high-end and niche segments. Tourism can be effectively managed with policies for safe mobility, crisis management, inclusiveness, green practices and policies regarding investment and infrastructure.

7.1 Ensuring the Safety of Travellers

Working with industry and international partners to provide and share information on travel policy and follow common policies for international travellers encourages tourists to visit. Creating awareness and providing information regarding inbound and outbound border restrictions come in handy for travellers. Providing accessible, consistent, clear and updated information to travellers, will facilitate travel planning and journey.

7.2 Crisis Management

Tourism can become sustainable by maintaining and improving the connectivity, safety and sustainability of the transport system. A crisis management strategy should be in place for all stakeholders. Countries with strict tourism policies, clear communication, and strategies for do's and don'ts make decision-making faster for authorities and help in good brand and image building.

7.3 Inclusiveness

By promoting legislations, regulations and good practices that include, women, youth, minorities and representatives from all groups, ecotourism can be achieved. If tourism is developed with the local supply chains, local entrepreneurs and local capacity builders, it becomes sustainable.

7.4 Infrastructure and Investment

Ecotourism should build capacity and coordinate actions along with the government to support sustainable tourism. With ESG gaining importance, financing and investment practices should embrace eco-tourism. Investment partners and financiers fund firms and companies that focus on the principles of ESG. Hence companies should prepare action plans and costings focusing on sustainable tourism. Ecotourism strongly supports ESG thereby.

7.5 Green Transformation

Government and industry bodies support and incentivise tourism businesses that pursue sound environment management and adopt models of green practices. Industry experts and consultants should work on specific initiatives to reduce environmental issues arising out of tourism. Voluntarily, monitoring and measurement of continuous improvement in the sustainability process should be planned. Strategies to mitigate water crisis, climate challenges and environmental degradation should be encouraged and supported. Digital transition and transformation, as is happening at a fast rate will support green transformation and save the planet by reducing the use of paper.

7.6 Managing Tourists

Impression about a tourist place to large extent is determined by way in which tourists and traffic are handled. Managing the tourist zones, and diverting traffic by designing proper strategies is highly recommended in tourist management. Codes of conduct are often employed to educate tourists and mandatory regulations are effective when enforced. Apart from this, strategies ensuring proper facilities and infrastructure alignment to the demand is the most practical approach to promote sustainable tourism. Every tourist spot must have a survey of the load generated and the load-bearing capacity. By capping the tourist number, strategies can become very doable and desirable. Knowledge of the location, square feet, height, Floor Space Ratio (FSR), Floor Area Ratio (FAR), and minimum distance between landscape and the infrastructure play a central role in sustainable tourism practices.

Managing eco-tourism plays a pivotal role as it contributes towards economic growth and development. Proper management facilitates proper growth. Tourism if managed effectively can reduce poverty, promote economic growth, preserve local communities and maintain social integrity

8. CONCLUSION AND FUTURE PROSPECTS

In conclusion, there are many advantages and difficulties to the use of technology in sustainable tourism management. First of all, technology is essential for encouraging sustainable practices because it makes it possible to share knowledge about eco-friendly solutions and aids in the development of sustainable tourist projects. Second, new technologies like ICT, big data analytics, and IoT are transforming sustainable tourism by giving us new tools for tracking visitors, managing resources effectively, and keeping an eye on the environment. Thirdly, in order to ensure that tourists make responsible and well-informed decisions, internet marketing and promotion are essential for spreading the word about sustainability and battling greenwashing. Fourthly, technology improves visitor experiences by offering immersive and instructive virtual and augmented reality experiences that support cultural awareness and sustainability. Cost issues, the digital divide, data privacy worries, technological obsolescence, and the requirement for stakeholder knowledge and skill development are some of the difficulties that come with integrating technology. The tourism industry must address these issues and take use of the opportunities that come with technological integration if it is to grow sustainably.

REFERENCES

Adeola, O., & Evans, O. (2019). Ict, infrastructure, and tourism development in africa. *Tourism Economics*, *26*(1), 97–114. DOI: 10.1177/1354816619827712

Ali, A., Rasoolimanesh, S. M., & Cobanoglu, C. (2020). Technology in tourism and hospitality to achieve sustainable development goals (SDGs). *Journal of Hospitality and Tourism Technology*, *11*(2), 177–181. DOI: 10.1108/JHTT-05-2020-146

Aman, E. E., & Papp-Váry, Á. (2022). Digital marketing as a driver for sustainable tourism development. Multidiszciplináris Kihívások. *Sokszínű Válaszok*, (2), 3–33. DOI: 10.33565/MKSV.2022.02.01

Babu, V., Pineda, R. F., Bizan, M., Wojak, A., Wierzowiecki, S., Gervásio, J., & Di Carlo, A. (2024). Perovskite Solar Module Enabled IoT Asset Tracking for Wildlife Conservation. *IEEE Journal of Photovoltaics*, *14*(2), 337–343. DOI: 10.1109/JPHOTOV.2024.3355406

Beck, J., Rainoldi, M., & Egger, R. (2019). Virtual reality in tourism: A state-of-the-art review. *Tourism Review*, *74*(3), 586–612. DOI: 10.1108/TR-03-2017-0049

Cheng, X., Xue, T., Yang, B., & Ma, B. (2023). A Digital Transformation Approach in Hospitality and Tourism Research. *International Journal of Contemporary Hospitality Management*, *35*(8), 2944–2967. DOI: 10.1108/IJCHM-06-2022-0679

Clark, M., Kang, B., & Calhoun, J. R. (2023). Green meets social media: Young travelers' perceptions of hotel environmental sustainability. *Journal of Hospitality and Tourism Insights*, *6*(1), 36–51. DOI: 10.1108/JHTI-03-2021-0062

Deb, S. K., Nafi, S. M., & Valeri, M. (2022). Promoting tourism business through digital marketing in the new normal era: A sustainable approach. *European Journal of Innovation Management*, *27*(3), 775–799. DOI: 10.1108/EJIM-04-2022-0218

. Ebinger, F., Buttke, L., & Kreimeier, J. (2022). Augmented and virtual reality technologies in education for sustainable development: an expert-based technology assessment. TATuP - Zeitschrift Für Technikfolgenabschätzung in Theorie Und Praxis, 31(1), 28-34. https://doi.org/.DOI: 10.14512/tatup.31.1.28

Edgell, D. L.Sr. (2019). *Managing sustainable tourism: A legacy for the future*. Routledge.

Gkilias, T. (2024). *Challenges and Trends of Digital Innovation in the Tourism Sector: Contemporary Literature Review*. Business School, University of Macedonia., DOI: 10.4236/ojbm.2024.121013

Gupta, Y., Khan, F. M., Kumar, A., Luthra, S., & Queiroz, M. M. (2024). Mobilising big data analytics capabilities to improve performance of tourism supply chains: The moderating role of dynamic capabilities. *International Journal of Logistics Management, 35*(2), 649–679. DOI: 10.1108/IJLM-03-2022-0125

Janjua, Z., Krishnapillai, G., & Rehman, M. (2022). Importance of the sustainability tourism marketing practices: An insight from rural community-based homestays in malaysia. *Journal of Hospitality and Tourism Insights, 6*(2), 575–594. DOI: 10.1108/JHTI-10-2021-0274

Loureiro, S. M. C., & Nascimento, J. (2021). Shaping a view on the influence of technologies on sustainable tourism. *Sustainability (Basel), 13*(22), 12691. DOI: 10.3390/su132212691

Luo, J., Zhuo, W., Liu, S., & Xu, B. (2024). The optimization of carbon emission prediction in low carbon energy economy under big data. *IEEE Access : Practical Innovations, Open Solutions, 12*, 14690–14702. DOI: 10.1109/ACCESS.2024.3351468

Melovic, M., Baynazoglu, M. E., & Seric, N. (2023). Family Businesses in Tourism—The Use of Digital Technologies in Times of Uncertainty and Crisis. *Journal of Family Business Management, 13*(1), 185–209. DOI: 10.1108/JFBM-06-2022-0086

Miller, G. T., & Spoolman, S. E. (2016). *Environmental Science* (15th ed.). Cengange Learning.

Murphy, P. E., & Price, G. G. (2012). Tourism and sustainable development. In *Global tourism* (pp. 167–193). Routledge.

Nicola-Gavrilă, L. (2023). Empirical Approaches Regarding Interdependency between Technology and Sustainable Tourism. [JEMT]. *Journal of Environmental Management and Tourism, 14*(4 (68)), 2140–2147. DOI: 10.14505/jemt.v14.4(68).25

O'Connor, P. (2023). Small- and medium-sized tourism enterprises and smart tourism: Tourism agenda 2030 perspective article. *Tourism Review, 78*(2), 339–343. DOI: 10.1108/TR-09-2022-0431

Polishchuk, E., Bujdosó, Z., El Archi, Y., Benbba, B., Zhu, K., & Dávid, L. D. (2023). The Theoretical Background of Virtual Reality and Its Implications for the Tourism Industry. *Sustainability (Basel), 15*(13), 10534. DOI: 10.3390/su151310534

Putra, A. K., Islam, M. N., Hilmi, R., Khairunisa, T., & Huda, I. A. S. (2022). *Geography virtual reality for learning about ecotourism and rural sustainability*. KnE Social Sciences., DOI: 10.18502/kss.v7i16.12176

Ramlavat, M. (2023) Is Technology Revolutionizing or Hindering the Tourism Industry, https://syndelltech.com/is-technology-revolutionizing-or-hindering-travel-industry/

Rattanamanee, K. (2024). Future Perspectives on Communication Management for Promoting Tourism in Chachoengsao Province (2024-2027). *International Journal of Professional Business Review: Int.J. Prof. Bus. Rev.*, *9*(1), 33.

Reverte, F. G., & Luque, P. D. (2022). Digital Divide in E-Tourism. In Xiang, Z., Fuchs, M., Gretzel, U., & Höpken, W. (Eds.), *Handbook of e-Tourism*. Springer., DOI: 10.1007/978-3-030-48652-5_109

Salnikova, E., Strizhakova, Y., & Coulter, R. (2022). Engaging Consumers with Environmental Sustainability-Initiatives: Consumer Global-Local Identity and Global Brand Messaging. *JMR, Journal of Marketing Research*, *59*(5), 983–1001. Advance online publication. DOI: 10.1177/00222437221078522

Samaddar, K., & Mondal, S. (2024). AR and VR-based travel: A responsible practice towards sustainable tourism. *International Journal of Tourism Cities*, *10*(1), 105–128. DOI: 10.1108/IJTC-05-2022-0135

. Sharma, A., Sharma, S. and Chaudhary, M. (2020). Are small travel agencies ready for digital marketing? Views of travel agency managers. *Tourism Management*, [online] 79, p.104078. doi:https://doi.org/.DOI: 10.1016/j.tourman.2020.104078

Sharma, R., & Kumar, S. (2024). The Impact of Technology on Educational Sustainability in the Tourism Industry. In *Revolutionizing the AI-Digital Landscape* (pp. 138–150). Productivity Press. DOI: 10.4324/9781032688305-10

Streimikiene, D., Svagzdiene, B., Jasinskas, E., & Simanavicius, A. (2021). Sustainable tourism development and competitiveness: The systematic literature review. *Sustainable Development (Bradford)*, *29*(1), 259–271. DOI: 10.1002/sd.2133

Talawar, A., Suresh, S., & Alathur, S. (2024). Assessing the moderating effects of involvement on tourist attitudes and intentions through virtual reality applications. *Journal of Hospitality and Tourism Insights*.

Thirumaran, K., Jang, H., Pourabedin, Z., & Wood, J. (2021). The role of social media in the luxury tourism business: A research review and trajectory assessment. *Sustainability (Basel)*, *13*(3), 1216. DOI: 10.3390/su13031216

UNEP and UNWTO. (2005), Making Tourism More Sustainable: A Guide for Policy Makers, https://www.e-unwto.org/doi/epdf/10.18111/9789284408214

Wahyuni, H., Purnomo, E. P., & Fathani, A. T. (2021). Social media supports tourism development in the covid-19 normal era in bandung. [Indonesian Journal of Communications Studies]. *Jurnal Studi Komunikasi*, *5*(3), 600–616. DOI: 10.25139/jsk.v5i3.3805

Wibawa, I. P. A., Astawa, I. P., Sukmawati, N. M. R., Arjana, I. W. B., & Sutarma, I. G. P. (2022). Digital marketing and sustainable tourism for tourist villages in bangli regency. *International Journal of Glocal Tourism*, *3*(2), 88–99. DOI: 10.58982/injogt.v3i2.209

Yerden, N. K., & Uydaci, M. (2022). Covid 19 pandemi̇ süreci̇nde desti̇nasyon pazarlamasi bağlaminda müzelerde sanal tur uygulamalarina yöneli̇k karşilaştirmali anali̇z. *Journal of Research in Business*, *7*(1), 229–248. DOI: 10.54452/jrb.1062407

Zhu, Z., Ma, W., & Leng, C. (2021). Ict adoption and tourism consumption among rural residents in china. *Tourism Economics*, *28*(6), 1669–1675. DOI: 10.1177/13548166211000478

Chapter 10
Digital Accessibility at the Nexus of Barriers of Accessible Tourism

L. N. Harsha Vardhini
Amrita School of Business, Coimbatore, India

Sandhya Srinivasan
Amrita School of Business, Coimbatore, India

Madhan Kumar
https://orcid.org/0000-0002-6664-2124
Prin. L.N. Welingkar Institude of Management and Research, India

Nimmi P. Mohandas
https://orcid.org/0000-0002-8750-6500
Amrita School of Business, Coimbatore, India

ABSTRACT

Accessible tourism aims to provide inclusive travel experiences for individuals with disabilities by offering accommodations, transportation, and attractions that cater to their needs. Imrie et al. (1998) and Escudero's et al. (2021) conducted studies on disabled people's experiences with access in the built environment and the decision-making process when organizing a tourist experience. They found that disabled people's needs are poorly met in the design and development of the built environment, and regulatory controls overseeing disabled people's access are weak. The study also found that tourist experiences significantly impact the perspective of disabled people in their daily lives, with independence being a crucial aspect. Kim et al. (2011) investigated service failures experienced by disabled tourists,

DOI: 10.4018/979-8-3373-0071-9.ch010

identifying three dimensions of service failures: service delivery failure, unfulfilled special requests, and unsolicited employee conduct.

INTRODUCTION

Tourism is inherently complex and multifaceted, influencing the economy and requiring input from economic, social, cultural, and environmental resources, which contributes to its intricate and multi-dimensional nature (Lickorish et al., 2007; Cabral & Dhar.,2019; Cabral, C & Jabbour.,2020). It depends on natural settings as part of its attractions, leading to a considerable environmental impact; however, it can also aid in conservation efforts (Buckley., 2011). The tourism sector is a significant, multi-trillion-dollar industry that facilitates and enhances a unique form of human engagement (Buckley.,2011; Suban et al.,2021). Closely linked with industries such as transportation, lodging, entertainment, and food and beverage services, tourism is embedded in global economic systems through the consumption behaviours of travellers (Lafferty et al., 2001). Despite its beneficial economic influence and vital role in bolstering global economies, tourism can also lead to economic, social, and ecological challenges (Erol et al., 2022; Suban et al.,2021). In the context of economic globalization, tourism presents a natural environment for corporate consolidation (Lafferty et al., 2001).

In 2019, tourism contributed 5.5 percent of global GDP and supported 272 million jobs, marking it as one of the world's most crucial industries. Before the COVID-19 pandemic, the tourism sector was responsible for creating one out of every four new jobs within a five-year span (Erol et al., 2022). The primary advantage of tourism for a region or nation lies in its economic benefits, providing opportunities for job creation and generating income at various levels—international, national, regional, and local. Being a labour-intensive service industry, tourism serves as a key source of employment (Zaei & Zaei., 2013). It employs a diverse workforce and offers a broad array of jobs, ranging from unskilled labour to highly specialized roles (Zaei & Zaei., 2013). Revenue from tourism flows into both urban and rural communities, stimulating the emergence of new businesses and enhancing the public image of those areas. Consequently, the economic effects of tourism are significant factors in state, regional, and community planning and economic growth. There is a growing interest among businesses and public entities in understanding these economic effects at national, state, and local levels. Acknowledging the economic importance of tourism grants the industry increased recognition among business leaders, government officials, and the general population (Stynes., 1997).

The Sustainable Development Goals (SDGs) are a collection of 17 global objectives set forth by the United Nations to steer initiatives towards sustainable development. The core meaning of sustainability is "that which can be upheld over time." Hence, a sustainable society would be capable of maintaining itself for many centuries (Heinberg & Lerch, D., 2010; Kaul & Gupta.,2009). Sustainable development is characterized as "development that fulfils the needs of the present without hindering the capacity of future generations to fulfil their own needs" (Scoones., 2007; Kaul & Gupta.,2009). These goals were developed by an open working group under the UN General Assembly and include 169 specific targets aimed at tackling global issues such as poverty, inequality, climate change, environmental degradation, peace, and justice. Introduced with an initial group of 330 indicators in March 2015, the SDGs build on the foundation of the Millennium Development Goals while integrating innovative objectives to form a more holistic framework for sustainable development (Hak et al.,2016).

The United Nations Sustainable Development Goals seek to promote healthier and more equitable societies, yet their advancement has been sluggish and inconsistent due to inadequate coordination across sectors. The challenges and opportunities associated with these goals, highlighting the necessity for improved alignment in conceptualization, implementation, and evaluation processes (Saxena et al., 2021). By synchronizing philosophical, strategic, and operational efforts with a dialectical approach, the SDG initiative can more effectively integrate outcomes with the broader aspirations of the SDGs to catalyse transformative societal change (Saxena et al., 2021). The authors' analyses how responsibility is portrayed in key UN documents regarding the Sustainable Development Goals, emphasizing three aspects of responsibility: cause, obligation, and accountability. The primary focus is on responsibility as an obligation, which is limited by national sovereignty and often leaves the duties of non-governmental entities ambiguous (Mathew et al., 2024, Mathew, 2022). Accountability, measured through quantitative indicators, may inadvertently show that responsibility within these documents remains centred on the state, allowing for national sovereignty and self-regulation, while also emphasizing that these three aspects of responsibility are interconnected, thus laying the groundwork for further investigation into accountability and implementation of the SDGs (Easterly et al.,2015). Sustainable Tourism seeks to reduce negative impact and increase positive benefit for the environment, economy and local communities.

It involves practices to ensure long term growth without harming nature and cultural resources. (Bulter et al., 1999). Accessible Tourism when included with Sustainable tourism not only focuses on the environment but also on the social and economic sustainability of travel. The removal of barriers that might prevent individuals with disabilities from enjoying tourism experiences. By integrating sustainability with accessibility, tourism can provide a more equitable, inclusive, and responsible travel experience to both the environment and travellers (Berry et al., 1997).

Sustainable tourism aims to balance social, environmental and financial sustainability, which is known as the Triple Bottom Line (TBL). Accessible tourism aligns well with all three aspects. By promoting social inclusion and equity in tourism experiences it creates positive impact on the societal aspect. As accessible tourism represents a growing and significant industry by making the offerings more accessible, tourism businesses improve their financial performance (Darcy et al.,2010). Both sustainable and accessible tourism emphasize collaboration between various stakeholders, suggesting a holistic approach to tourism development (Sisto et al.,2021).

Accessible tourism is an emerging segment that emphasizes tourism in public spaces free from barriers - architectural, cultural, attitudinal, informational. Accessibility is crucial for any sustainable tourism policy and strategy from a business competitiveness standpoint (Dickson et al., 2009; Darcy et al., 2010). Accessible tourism aims to provide an inclusive travel experience for an individual with a disability by offering, accommodation, transportation, and attractions that cater to their needs. Accessible tourism refers to the practice of providing tourism experience to all individuals including people with disabilities. This approach ensures that the tourism experience is accessible to everyone aimed at fostering equality and enhancing the travel experience for all individuals (Dickson et al., 2009; Darcy et al., 2010). This paper focuses on tourism accessibility for people with disabilities highlighting the importance of understanding and overcoming obstacles that hinder their tourism experiences.

LITERATURE REVIEW

Accessible tourism remains a critical yet often neglected segment of the travel industry, posing numerous challenges for individuals with disabilities (Cabral & Dhar.,2019; Cabral & Jabbour.,2020). Both sustainable and accessible tourism focuses on the long-term perspective and puts emphasis on designing products and infrastructure that are used by everyone regardless of their ability i.e. universal design. Sustainable tourism focuses on responsible resource management and accessible tourism can contribute to this by ensuring effective utilisation (Polat et al.,2016; Cabral & Dhar.,2019; Cabral & Jabbour.,2020). Studies reveal significant gaps in the built environment's design and regulatory oversight negatively impacting disabled people's experiences (Imrie et al 1998; Escudero et al 2021).

They found that disabled people's needs are met poorly in the design and development of built environment and regulatory control overseeing disabled people's access is weak. The study also found that the tourist experience significantly impacts the perspective of disabled people in their daily lives. The high pricing of tourism products, as highlighted for further restricts access (Dobransky et al 2006; Wu et al 2014) further restricts access. Additionally, psychological barriers hinder disabled tourist participation, underscoring the need for comprehensive strategies to enhance their travel experience. Here, through a comprehensive literature review, we look at the different factors that hinder accessible tourism.

1. Unprofessional Customer Service

The Author highlights the growing significance of accessible tourism, focusing on two key objectives: evaluating the tourism industry's ethical behaviour in relation to international legal mandates and conventions promoting the rights of individuals with disabilities, and introducing accessible tourism (AIT) as a broader concept relevant to diverse population groups, including senior citizens, pregnant women, and individuals following special diets (Sotiroula et al.,2017).

The study also explores the experiences of disabled tourists, emphasizing their decision-making processes when organizing trips. Factors influencing these decisions include limited negotiating scope, the necessity of care assistance, language barriers at destinations, and the availability of state aid. Investigated service failures experienced by disabled tourists, identifying three key areas: failures in service delivery, unmet special requests, and inappropriate employee conduct. These findings offer valuable insights for practitioners, enabling them to better cater to this underserved market segment and improve the overall tourism experience for individuals with disabilities. Addressing these specific concerns can significantly enhance inclusivity within the tourism sector (Kin et al.,2011).

Tour guides play a pivotal role in creating inclusive tourism experiences. According to study tour guides can transform ordinary trips into inclusive experiences through their knowledge, ability to interpret attractions, and flexible communication and customer service techniques. However, they face challenges such as unclear career pathways, reliance on unpredictable income, and varying levels of professionalism, which hinder true inclusivity. In highly competitive markets, professional service standards are crucial, particularly in destinations striving to implement accessible tourism. Drawing lessons from Hong Kong, suggest improving training, monitoring programs, and support structures to prepare tour guides for accommodating diverse visitor needs. These efforts are essential to enhancing inclusion and sustainability in the travel industry while raising the professional standards of tour guides worldwide (AP et al.,2001).

The Study emphasize the importance of bridging the customer service gap in accessible tourism by providing comprehensive, easily navigable information about accessible accommodations. Poor customer service often stems from a lack of understanding of the complex needs of travellers with disabilities, leaving them excluded and dissatisfied. The study highlights the value of detailed information, including digital photographs, floorplans, and textual descriptions, which help foster transparency and trust among customers. Tourist operators can improve service quality by adopting these practices, thereby increasing customer satisfaction and advancing diversity. Neglecting these requirements risks perpetuating negative perceptions of accessibility in the travel industry and undermines efforts toward social sustainability (John et al.,2001).

Unprofessional customer service has a significant impact on the evaluation of service encounters, particularly for individuals with disabilities who rely on inclusive and seamless interactions Poor communication, inadequate accommodations, or disrespectful behaviour can lead to negative attributions and lower satisfaction levels. suggest that service providers can improve customer evaluations in accessible tourism by prioritizing professional, compassionate responses, offering clear explanations during service disruptions, and implementing compensation measures when issues arise. By addressing these concerns and fostering inclusive environments, accessible travel services can enhance customer experiences and restore trust even in challenging situations (Simon et al.,2010).

Unethical behaviours, such as insufficient accommodations, discriminatory actions, or inaccessible facilities, often contribute to unprofessional customer service for individuals with disabilities. These factors lead to lower satisfaction and a negative ethical perception of the service provider. argue that while ethical and inclusive practices are often taken for granted, their absence disproportionately affects individuals with disabilities, reinforcing barriers to fair service experiences. (James et al., 2002; Scott et al.,2002)

Finally, inadequate documentation and marketing of accessible accommodation information exacerbate unprofessional service for disabled travellers. The study emphasizes the need for detailed, accurate, and accessible information, including visual aids and clear descriptions, as these factors play a critical role in the decision-making process for individuals with disabilities. A failure to provide such information leads to frustration, exclusion, and eroded trust, undermining social sustainability and fair access to services.

2. High Pricing Of Tourism Products

Pricing determines the value created for a particular product or service, reflecting its perceived worth. It plays a crucial role in the marketing mix by signalling the monetary value at which consumers can purchase the product or service (Bagwell & Riordan., 1991). Defining the price is the first step in the selling process and is one of the key factors influencing a company's revenue (Dolgui & Proth, 2010;

Cabral & Dhar.,2019). Pricing strategy involves adjusting prices to achieve objectives such as profit maximization or increased sales volume. However, a premium price is effective only if it aligns with the customers' perceived value of the product; otherwise, it may result in commercial failure (Dolgui & Proth, 2010). The best price at any point in time is achieved when marginal revenue equals marginal cost (Rao., 1984). A suitable pricing approach in tourism involves striking a balance between the value of the product or service and the price consumers are willing to pay (Moussaa et al., 2020; Cabral & Dhar., 2019).

Affordability is often considered a relationship between the cost-of-service delivery and the consumer's income. Accessibility, in this context, depends on travel costs and related factors such as time and effort. In its narrowest sense—potential accessibility—it refers to the ease with which an individual can undertake desired journeys and the quality of the facilities they can access (Gwilliams., 2017; Cabral & Dhar.,2019). Destinations rely on their primary tourism products as the main pull factors motivating tourists to visit. These products, which include the experiences themselves, are central to tourist choice and satisfaction. Developing primary tourism products within destinations is complex, involving tangible components like natural features and infrastructure, as well as intangible elements such as cultural meanings and symbols (Benur & Bramwell., 2015; Cabral & Dhar.,2019). Diversifying these products can broaden the experiences of current tourists or attract new visitors by offering a wider range of options (Benur & Bramwell., 2015).

Price is a critical factor influencing tourists' purchasing decisions, closely tied to their financial ability and income levels. Tourists are more likely to purchase products priced within their spending capacity, making price a competitive factor in their decision-making process (Moussaa et al., 2020; Cabral & Dhar.,2019). Properly organizing and delivering tourism products allows consumers to fulfil their travel aspirations within their financial means (Moussaa et al., 2020). However, high prices remain a significant barrier for people with disabilities. Research highlights disparities in the willingness and ability of disabled individuals to access online services, reflecting broader challenges in accessible tourism (Dobransky et al., 2006; Wu et al., 2014).

To address these issues, (Wu et al.,2014) propose an accessible tourism platform based on the principles of the long tail theory. This platform aims to empower travel agents to design packages tailored to the needs of disabled travellers, emphasizing high-quality experiences and services. By focusing on niche markets, this approach seeks to enhance accessibility while raising the standard of the overall tourism experience. The platform underscores the importance of personalized services in transforming the travel industry to accommodate every traveller's needs.

Further research into accessible accommodations reveals that areas with more luxury accommodations also offer more accessible facilities (Ivica et al., 2017). An analysis of administrative regions, including accommodations, dining facilities, tourist routes, and UNESCO sites, found that only 11% of accommodations and 12% of dining establishments are barrier-free. However, national parks were identified as the most accessible areas (Ivica et al., 2017). Despite these findings, accessible tourism services remain scarce, highlighting the need for further development in this field (Ivica et al., 2017).

3. Lack of Mobility Infrastructure

It highlights Italy's National Plan for Tourist Mobility, which emphasizes accessibility as a key driver for investment in tourism infrastructure. IT explore the service needs of passengers with reduced mobility (PRMs) and identify significant barriers to air travel. Key challenges include terminals, aircraft embarkation, and disembarkation points, which create obstacles at the ground–air interface. The reliance on third-party assistance at airports compromises a passenger's autonomy, violating their rights. (Sofia et al.,2016).

The study concludes that improvements in airport services and facilities, including better-designed terminals, efficient boarding processes, and comprehensive staff training, are essential to enhance air transport accessibility for PRMs.

These studies collectively stress the importance of comprehensive and inclusive approaches to tourism and transportation, emphasizing that addressing the needs of disabled individuals through national investment plans or targeted sector-specific improvements promotes both accessibility and social equity. Furthermore, note that individuals with severe disabilities face the most barriers, with younger disabled people reporting challenges due to inadequate equipment and older individuals experiencing social obstacles. (Kaganek et al.,2017) and (Mayor et al.,2019)

The study argue that mobile applications can revolutionize accessibility in the travel and tourism industry, particularly for individuals with impairments. Such applications, leveraging advanced technologies, can address specific needs and preferences of disabled travellers beyond basic information or location-based suggestions. By incorporating customized interaction methods, these solutions have the potential to create more inclusive and barrier-free travel experiences. (Ribeiro et al.,2018)

It provides an overview of current mobile applications designed to facilitate accessible travel, discussing their features, challenges, and areas for improvement .Two critical issues highlighted include the necessity of user-friendly interfaces and the integration of accessibility elements. Positive features, such as the applications' ability to enhance convenience and inclusivity, are also noted. (Siva et al., 2018)

To address existing constraints, propose a customized and cooperative system framework aimed at improving assistance for disabled individuals during travel. This framework emphasizes the formal design, development, and testing of prototype systems to promote accessibility and sustainability in the travel industry. (Arlindo et al., 2018)

Accessibility is a fundamental human right, as highlighted explore its role in promoting inclusive travel. Their study focuses on a digital platform that offers detailed information about the accessibility of roads, public spaces, and points of interest, aiming to position the Pieria region of Greece as an accessible tourist destination. The platform enables users to design safe travel routes by aggregating data on accessibility infrastructure, including sidewalks, ramps, and culturally significant sites (Achillas et al., 2024).

Preliminary results from the Platamonas region demonstrate the platform's efficacy, documenting 68 points of interest and 97 routes. These initiatives not only improve travel accessibility for tourists but also contribute to social inclusion and regional economic development. By enhancing accessibility, Pieria establishes itself as a leader in inclusive and sustainable tourism (Dimitrios et al., 2024).

It analyses the challenges in developing tourism infrastructure for individuals with impairments. Using qualitative methods and descriptive analyses of data from sources such as the BPS and UNWTO, the study identifies major shortcomings, including inadequate legislation, financial constraints, and insufficient employee training. The authors propose a disability-friendly tourism infrastructure model that focuses on staff training, accessible physical design, and easily navigable information. They emphasize the need for collaboration among government, the tourism industry, and civil society to create an inclusive tourism environment (Putri et al., 2024).

It examines the significant transportation and mobility constraints faced by individuals with disabilities in middle- and low-income nations. These challenges are exacerbated by factors such as geography, socioeconomic status, and policy gaps. While transportation is often cited as a primary barrier to inclusion, there is a lack of empirical data measuring its impact on the daily lives of disabled individuals in these regions. The study advocates for rethinking "special" transportation provisions, focusing on lived experiences, and shifting the discourse from mere access to meaningful inclusion. Key areas for further research include addressing behavioural and experiential issues, creating equitable legislation, and understanding transportation usage patterns. By identifying knowledge gaps, obstacles, and potential solutions, this research aims to promote inclusive and equitable transportation systems that actively incorporate the needs of individuals with disabilities. (Maria et al.,2019)

4. Lack of Information And Communication

People with disabilities require clear, accurate, and accessible information about their travel options, particularly online (Buhalis et al., 2011). It is crucial to cater to the unique needs and preferences of individuals, which cannot always be achieved through traditional market segmentation based on broad categories. To address this, destinations can offer personalized services that promote participation, aligning with the principles of the social model of disability (Buhalis et al., 2011; Pühretmair et al., 2006).

However, shortcomings such as high fragmentation and limited geographical reach often result in incomplete or inaccessible information. These limitations hinder the implementation of five key components essential to meeting the needs of disabled tourists: a customer-focused strategy, dependable and detailed information, easy access to relevant sources, and user-friendly communication tools (Eichhorn et al., 2007). Furthermore, entrepreneurial stakeholders and policy brokers face challenges due to the limited number of actors involved in granting accessibility to disabled tourists (Bianchi et al., 2020).

A promising solution lies in using technology-driven models that provide objective and detailed accessibility information tailored to individuals' needs. Such models can significantly enhance accessibility (Kołodziejczak, 2019).

It examines the needs of travellers with impairments and the challenges of developing accessible tourism information systems. The study identifies essential criteria, such as minimal accessibility prerequisites, detailed accessible pathways, and door-to-door access maps, derived from focus groups and interviews. (Best et al.,2012).

Technical challenges like interoperability, content integration, and personalization are highlighted. The report concludes with recommendations for overcoming these barriers and improving services for tourists with disabilities (Eleni et al., 2012).

It explores accessibility schemes as communication tools to meet the informational demands of travellers with impairments, drawing on information search theory. The study identifies critical components such as information richness, reliability, appropriate sources, communication tools, and customer-oriented services. While these schemes partially meet national and regional coverage needs, they fall short of fully satisfying the informational requirements of disabled travellers. The study underscores the importance of understanding diverse needs and improving information sources to enhance accessibility in tourism.

The lack of critical scholarly discourse on the terminology and language used in accessible travel literature. The study emphasizes how language shapes identities and has the potential to support or challenge prevailing beliefs about disability. Content analysis reveals inconsistent, interchangeable, and euphemistic usage of phrases, often stemming from incorrect interpretations. The study argues that academics have a responsibility to use liberating language that reconstructs societal perceptions of disability, rather than reinforcing oppression. (Ana et al.,2023)

It investigates how people with visual impairments participate in tourism, focusing on the factors influencing their travel choices. Using in-depth interviews, the study highlights that tourism engagement is an ongoing, interactive process affected by social, personal, and disability-related factors. It identifies trends in barriers, facilitators, and negotiation strategies. These strategies include personal and interpersonal methods, as well as adjustments in trip planning, enabling sustained participation in tourism despite obstacles (E. Devile et al., 2020).

5. Lack of Digital Accessibility

The availability of technological products, resources, and services across hardware and software platforms is referred to as digital accessibility (Kulkarni, 2019). A key component of digital accessibility is web accessibility, which involves removing barriers to accessing the web so that online content is accessible to all users. The primary goal of digital accessibility is to create an inclusive environment that enables people with disabilities to actively participate in education, employment, and political activities (Kulkarni, 2019). However, digital accessibility benefits everyone, not just individuals with disabilities. While accessibility was initially designed for specific groups, its advantages extend far beyond those groups (Kulkarni, 2019).

Digital accessibility is no longer just a technical requirement; it has become a legal necessity. Organizations that prioritize accessibility not only comply with legal standards but also demonstrate social responsibility (Kulkarni, 2019). Understanding digital accessibility as a chain of dependencies—including training, hardware, software, content, and standards—provides a comprehensive view of the system. These elements must function cohesively to ensure effective digital accessibility (Botelho, 2021).

While digital technology has long supported people with disabilities, accessibility is not automatic or guaranteed. Instead, it must be treated as an ongoing, evolutionary process (Botelho, 2021). Similar to architectural standards for physical accessibility, technical standards for digital accessibility must guide the selection and design of software and hardware (Botelho, 2021). Without placing accessibility at the forefront, market dynamics and technological developments can inadvertently limit equal access for people with disabilities (Botelho, 2021).

One key takeaway is that ignoring even one element of the accessibility process can undermine inclusion efforts for people with disabilities. Despite progress in wealthier nations, awareness of digital accessibility remains underdeveloped, with free assistive technologies often underutilized due to limited training and guidance.

Additionally, outdated or incomplete information can hinder effective use (Botelho, 2021).

Language barriers, especially for sign language users or those speaking minority languages, further restrict access to technical information. Physical interfaces, such as buttons and touchscreens, also present challenges for older adults or individuals with motor or visual impairments, making technology less accessible for these groups (Botelho, 2021).

The 5A's model provides a heuristic for analysing barriers to inclusive technology access, focusing on five dimensions: availability, affordability, awareness, ability, and agency.

- **Availability** assesses who can or cannot access a particular technology (Roberts & Hernandez, 2019).
- **Affordability** highlights that even if technology is available, it may still be financially out of reach (Roberts & Hernandez, 2019).
- **Awareness** addresses the knowledge gap that can prevent the effective use of affordable, accessible technology (Roberts & Hernandez, 2019).
- **Ability** emphasizes the importance of digital literacy and skills, even when the first three dimensions are addressed (Roberts & Hernandez, 2019).
- **Agency** reflects an individual's capacity to make decisions and take actions, existing along a spectrum rather than as a binary concept (Roberts & Hernandez, 2019).

Technology can enhance tourism accessibility for people with disabilities (Cassia et al., 2020; Vila et al., 2024). Tools like navigation and virtual reality applications offer new opportunities, while a digital ecosystem promoting collaboration and information sharing among tourism stakeholders could significantly improve accessibility. Inclusive design plays a pivotal role in achieving these goals (Cassia et al., 2020).

However, significant barriers remain in achieving full digital accessibility in tourism. An assessment of accessible tourism websites revealed that none achieved a perfect score, with many failing to meet the WCAG 2.0 standards set by the W3C (Fernández-Díaz et al., 2023; Silva et al., 2020). These findings underscore the need for consistent improvements in digital accessibility. Additionally, online forums and focus groups have identified a lack of representation of people with disabilities in discussions about travel technology. This absence has limited understanding of their perspectives and needs (Ali et al., 2023; Stankov et al., 2024). Recent studies have developed new models to enhance technology use among people with disabilities, offering recommendations for more accessible designs and emphasizing collaboration to improve travel experiences (Ali et al., 2023; Stankov et al., 2024).

6. Psychological Barriers

The psychology of disability emphasizes the psychosocial tension and stress arising from social relations associated with disability rather than focusing on impairment itself. This perspective aligns closely with the psychological-emotional impact of disability (Reeve., 2006). Disability can be understood as an act of social oppression, wherein society imposes restrictions on the activities of impaired individuals and contributes to the degradation of their psycho-emotional well-being (Reeve., 2006). A comprehensive social model of disability incorporates both structural and psycho-emotional elements, providing a foundation for a psychology of disability rather than a focus on psychopathology (Reeve., 2006).

Emotional health plays a critical role in successful self-management (Skinner., 2004). In the context of disability, fear often reflects an inability to act due to imposed restrictions, resulting in feelings of inadequacy. Scholars identify fear of inadequacy, fear of making mistakes, and fear of the unknown as factors that hinder learning. Anxiety, characterized by subjective feelings of worry or tension, can lead to mental disorganization. Similarly, low motivation, often linked to a lack of self-confidence, manifests as a lack of interest, energy, or enjoyment in learning. Signs of low motivation include perceiving learning as lacking value and avoiding asking questions (Wulandari et al., 2018). Symptoms of emotional distress, such as fear, mood swings, anger, low self-confidence, poor concentration, and "going blank," are prevalent among individuals with disabilities (Wulandari et al., 2018).

Psychological barriers significantly hinder people with disabilities in various domains, including transportation. These barriers extend beyond physical access to include personal, psychological, and social factors that impede mobility (Koppa et al., 1998). Among these, fear is paramount. Individuals with disabilities may experience anxiety about potential assaults, falling, exhaustion, or being without assistance. Fear of unfamiliar environments or new ideas further compounds reluctance to use public transport (Koppa et al., 1998). Coupled with the stigma of being labelled as "disabled," the lack of social support and awareness of available transport facilities exacerbates these barriers. Other challenges include the unpredictability of travel, such as disruptions or delays, which can be overwhelming for those who are emotionally unstable or cognitively impaired. Addressing these barriers requires more than financial investment or infrastructure changes; it calls for a deeper understanding of the emotional and cognitive experiences of individuals with disabilities (Koppa et al., 1998).

Stigma, closely linked to communication challenges, represents one of the most complex social problems faced by children and young people with disabilities. Emotional self-isolation is a common consequence of stigma (Overchuk, 2019). Physical and psychological barriers restrict individuals with disabilities from achieving fulfilling social and professional lives. Disabilities complicate interactions with the environment, limit community participation, and negatively affect personal development. These experiences often lead to fear, low self-confidence, and inferiority complexes, potentially resulting in egocentrism or asocial behaviour (Overchuk., 2019). Disability-related stigma, a critical socio-cultural issue, further hinders communication and motivation. Emotional barriers affect both parties: non-disabled individuals may respond with guilt, anxiety, or pity, while individuals with disabilities may anticipate pity or blame others for their circumstances (Overchuk., 2019). Discrimination and stigmatization remain pervasive, creating significant obstacles in social and professional contexts for individuals with disabilities (Overchuk., 2019).

A primary reason for reluctance among individuals with disabilities to engage in fitness and recreational activities is the perception of these environments as unwelcoming (Rimmer., 2004). This perception is often accompanied by reports of hostile attitudes from staff and non-disabled patrons. Emotional and psychological barriers such as fear of the unknown, fear of needing help, and lack of family and social support further discourage participation (Rimmer., 2004). Additional challenges include self-consciousness, unfamiliarity with the environment, and fear of making mistakes. Collectively, these barriers highlight the need for more inclusive and supportive recreational spaces (Rimmer., 2004).

Travel participation among people with disabilities is a complex phenomenon influenced by situational, personal, and environmental factors. Continuous engagement in travel involves overcoming various constraints, often through negotiation techniques, including travel arrangement strategies and personal or interpersonal adaptations (Devile et al., 2020). Most barriers to travel are intrinsic, such as lack of confidence, negative perceptions of disability, and fear of burdening others (Allan et al., 2015). Fear of losing independence or increasing reliance on caregivers further contributes to travel reluctance. External factors, including societal norms and previous negative travel experiences, can intensify anxiety about being observed or judged (Kaganek et al., 2017). Addressing these barriers is essential for developing accessible products and services that cater to the needs of the accessible tourism market (Qiao, 2022).

METHODOLOGY

The main focus of this research is on the tourism sector, specifically on accessible tourism. We employed a purposive sampling method to choose respondents who possess knowledge about and understanding of accessible tourism. To analyse and understand the impact of barriers on accessible tourism, we developed a closed-ended questionnaire for factor-by-factor comparisons. Fifteen experts with substantial experience and expertise in accessible tourism were chosen. Their insights on barriers to accessible tourism were sought, updated, and confirmed through face validation of the questionnaire. TISM, or Transitive Interrelation and Interpretive Structural Modelling, is a decision modelling approach aimed at constructing a robust theoretical framework. Its objective is to elucidate the transitive connections and logical reasoning underlying the relationships among identified factors. Utilizing TISM allows for the development of a contextual relationship-based conceptual model, which represents an advancement over traditional ISM methods. Through TISM, specific relationships can be interpretively modelled based on the factors involved. This methodology effectively addresses the research question "How, What, and Why", by transforming fragmented mental models into well-organized frameworks, thereby facilitating a deeper understanding of the significance and impact of the identified factors (Albi and Suresh, 2023).

FINDINGS

Figure 1. Digital accessibility

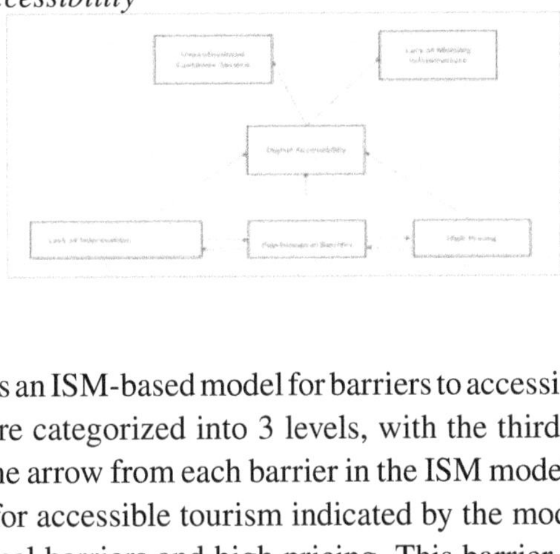

Figure 1 provides an ISM-based model for barriers to accessible tourism in tourist places. 6 barriers are categorized into 3 levels, with the third level indicating the topmost priority. The arrow from each barrier in the ISM model indicates the same. The main barriers for accessible tourism indicated by the model are lack of information, psychological barriers and high pricing. This barrier is highly significant as it forms the basis of the ISM hierarchical model. While the digital accessibility is situated at Level 2 highlights the need for digital devices in tourist destinations. Lack of mobility infrastructure and unprofessional customer service are crucial barrier on accessible tourism and it forms the top of the ISM hierarchy.

Figure 2. Mic Mac analysis

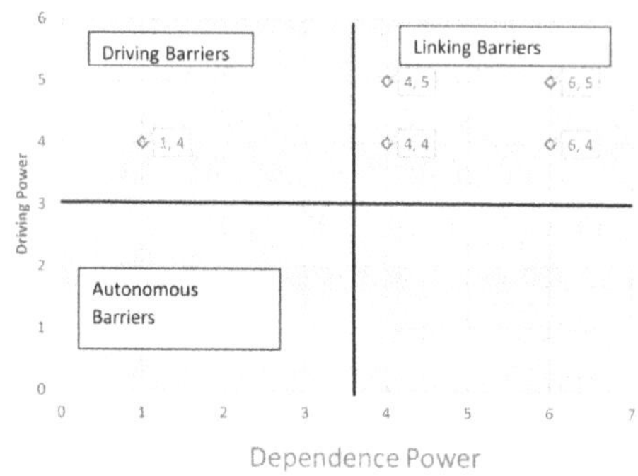

Autonomous Barriers

The autonomous barriers have weak dependence and driving power. These barriers have barely any links with other barriers. In this study, there are no autonomous barriers.

Dependent Barriers

This cluster represents barriers having strong dependence power but weak driving power. In this study, there are no dependent barriers.

Linkage Barriers

The linkage barriers have strong dependence and driving power. They are highly volatile in nature. Resultantly, a small change in the linkage barriers can have a multiplier effect on other tourism barriers. There are five linkage barriers in this study such as Unprofessional customer service, Lack of Information, Psychological Barriers/Resistance, High pricing and Digital Accessibility.

Independent or Driving Barriers

This cluster presents barriers having weak dependence power but strong driving power. Key barriers restricting accessible tourism are present in this cluster. The barrier possessing high driving power is lack of mobility infrastructure.

Level 1 Barriers

Unprofessional Customer Service refers to the failure of service providers to meet the expectations and needs of their customers, leading to dissatisfaction and negative experiences. This Practice Highlights the need for practitioners to address these concerns to better serve disabled individuals and improve their overall tourism experience. Lack of mobility infrastructure refers to inadequate facilities provided to disabled people. It highlights the economic significance of accessible tourism for better infrastructure. It identifies specific barriers for disabled passengers. To address these issues substantial improvements are necessary. These studies underscore the importance of developing comprehensive and inclusive mobility infrastructure to enhance accessibility, promote social equity and support the economic benefits of accessible tourism. Addressing unprofessional customer service and lack of mobility infrastructure is important for encouraging tourism experience for the disabled. Unprofessional customer service leads to dissatisfaction and negative experiences Highlighting the need for service providers to better meet expectations and needs of disabled individuals. Substantial Improvement in these areas is essential to develop comprehensive and inclusive mobility infrastructure enhancing accessibility promoting the economic benefits of accessible tourism.

Level 2 Barriers

Information accessibility is essential for ensuring everyone's ethical right to travel, regardless of their disability. Making tourism information and services accessible is a social responsibility that ensures everyone can participate in tourism activities. Digital tools can bridge the information gap for tourists with disabilities, allowing them to plan and participate in tourism activities. Accessible tourism is a growing market segment that can contribute to economic development. Smart tourism service providers need to consider digital accessibility alongside physical accessibility to achieve an inclusive experience. Tourism websites need to create a positive user experience for all visitors, including those with temporary or permanent disabilities, as difficulty in accessing information on these websites can lead to digital exclusion. That would mean that other tourist service providers will have a competitive advantage, enhanced reputation and wider reach by attracting a wider range of tourists by providing them with better opportunities to travel. So, utmost importance should be given to usable and understandable design and features like ease of use and comprehension should be considered in travel technology design for a positive technology experience. It is also essential to check compliance with the Web Content Accessibility Guidelines (WCAG). The guidelines, published by the Web Accessibility Initiative of the World Wide Web Consortium, aim to improve access to information for people with disabilities and the elderly. There is a wide information gap in accessible tourism so technology can be a solution for travel challenges faced by some individuals with disabilities. This in turn empowers people with all disabilities to travel as accessible digital tools can help them research destinations, book services, and navigate their trips, leading to a more enjoyable and inclusive experience. By prioritizing digital accessibility, the tourism industry can unlock the potential of a vast and diverse travel market, promote social good, and create a more enriching experience for all.

Level 3 Barriers

The first barrier in level 3 points out the lack of information available to people with disability, which affects their successful tourism prospects. The availability of information is scarce, unreliable and not accessible to people with disabilities. Information is not available through mainstream channels with no customer service provisions. Added to this is the fragmentation of information across different sources, ultimately resulting in less traffic from this market to the suppliers of destination and tourism. These factors discourage people with disability from planning trips and prevent them from travelling altogether. As one of the solutions improved exchange of information among stakeholders can not only help in better compliance and execution but also in the creation of policies for accessible tourism. The second barrier of level 3 discusses the psychological barrier and its significance in preventing people with disabilities from enjoying travelling. The main intrinsic motivation for people to travel is to relax and enjoy the travel and the main constraint that prevents them from travelling is also intrinsic. They might have a fear of failure leading to a lack of confidence regarding their physical limitations. They might face anxiety while navigating unfamiliar places and might feel out of place at tourist destinations leading to social isolation. People with a disability might also feel isolated when being excluded from mainstream tourism offerings and forced into a segregated category. The third barrier of level 3, is high pricing. People with disability may face difficulty in affording the necessary assistive technology needed to use computers and the Internet. The financial restrictions can limit travel opportunities for people with disabilities

DISCUSSION

The key finding of the paper highlights the importance of digital accessibility in enabling people with disabilities to access tourism facilities. Stakeholders must consider how to effectively reach disabled individuals and explore innovative ways to connect with them. Governments should establish platforms where disabled people can interact with genuine service providers. Additionally, NGOs can play a vital role in raising awareness among people with disabilities about how to access places and websites for leisure activities. Most importantly, disabled individuals should be empowered with the knowledge and tools to understand and utilize the support available to them. (

Overcoming Psychological Barriers

People with disability can adopt numerous techniques to mitigate and cope with the psychological constraints of traveling and tourism and, as such, have a greater control over their overall experience of travel. The common constraints include the fear of unknown situations, fear and anxiety, lack of confidence in themselves, and stigma that surround them (Reeve, 2006). There is the need to explore and understand such emotional challenges for a person who could then take proactive action and improve resilience and self-efficacy. Gradual exposure to the travel environment forms an effective approach. The ease with which this is achieved starts with small outings in the same environments in which they are to travel, giving PWD familiarity with the processes of travel. With increased experience in positive travel conditions, people start to be comfortable with progressively challenging travel situations (Koppa et al., 1998). Overcoming the emotional and psychological barriers demands a strong support system. The encouragement, practical assistance as well as emotional reinforcement derived from family, friends, and peer groups diminish the fear of isolation or of being burdensome (Overchuk, 2019). In addition, peer support provides valuable shared experiences and coping strategies.

Acquisition of practical skills like planning itineraries, doing research on accessible destinations, and learning different forms of transportation boosts preparedness and control and diminishes anxiety greatly (Devile et al., 2020). Technologies, including apps that specifically assist in navigation for PWD, provide instant support and information. Cognitive maturation techniques will help the practitioner in anxiety management and boosting self-confidence. Such techniques include positive self-talk, visualization, and mindfulness and help in re-framing a negative thought to allow for stress relief (Wulandari et al., 2018). For example, visibility in their minds of successful travel creates a positive mental image, which serves to enhance motivation and combat fear or anxiety. Engaging in any confidence-building activities, including volunteering, participating in community organizations, or developing hobbies, raises self-confidence in travel settings (Skinner, 2004). Counselling or other forms of therapy would also provide specific ways of dealing with gravely intense phobias and will provide an ordered framework in which to work through feelings and feeling management. Thus, self-advocacy, coupled with the education of their rights and available accommodations, must be undertaken. The knowledge of the accommodations and rights available enables PWD to appropriately take up the issues needed, reduces discomfort, and maximizes inclusion in travel experiences (Kaganek et al., 2017). Exercise, healthy eating, good sleep, and relaxation help lessen anxiety and ulcers. Then, this lays an emotional background for the persons with disabilities, allowing them to cope effectively with travel challenges. This way, it creates a positive emotional base for the persons with disabilities, which, in turn, lets them even better cope with the challenges of travel. A self-care routine is a sturdy structure for resilience during travel. With these mechanisms in hand, PWD are dismantling these psychological barriers and the movement beyond being a daunting prospect toward a more vital realm of individual growth. Allowing PWD to face these barriers internally means fostered independence, broadened travel experiences, and eventually the moving of travel toward greater accessibility and inclusion.

INITIATIVES FROM GOVERNMENT FOR ACCESSIBLE TOURISM FOR PERSONS WITH DISABILITIES AND SUGGESTIONS FOR IMPROVEMENT

Tourism is an integral part of cultural exchange and economic development; however, tourism services are often inaccessible to PWD. The government has an important role to play in bringing down those barriers to create an inclusive environment wherein all PWD can enjoy their right to travel in tourism. Tackling all physical, transportation, and digital challenges, as well as helping them in encouraging inclusive policies and infrastructure, can help governments create a more equitable and sustainable tourism sector.

The important and main problem in accessible tourism is the lack of physical infrastructure. Provision of wheelchair-accessible trains, vehicle, buses and airports are a much needed and crucial factors in enhancing on physical infrastructure. Governments can also put in the effort to ensure whether the tourist attraction sites, hotels, restaurants, public buildings and other most visited places have ramps or elevators as they help in the mobility for PWD. Apart from these the government has the huge responsibility in making the pedestrian infrastructure on the country accessible to people with disability. They can do so by laying down spacious wide pathways which is smooth and well-maintained. They can also install audio signals for visually impaired tourists which can greatly ensure their safety. Studies show that only a few percent of accommodations and restaurants are fully accessible, but areas with luxury accommodations have more accessible facilities (Ivica et al., 2017). National parks have been considered the most accessible environments. However, the general lack of accessible tourism services underlines a major need for structural improvements. Governments are held responsible to impose strict accessibility standards that demand barrier-free designs for new constructions as well as in existing buildings. Encouraging businesses to hold an older building to such standards will ensure that accessibility becomes a business norm rather than the exception.

Transport, which is key in tourism, presents difficulties to persons with disabilities, especially in the middle- and low-income group countries. Geographical and policy gaps compounded the problems that persons with disabilities face generally usable. Governments must ensure that professionals in the tourism industry are appropriately trained by providing special training for tourism staffs and assist then on awareness about disability so that they can understand and meet the needs of PWDs, thereby reducing attitudinal problems and enhancing service quality. They can also collaborate and help in the provision of customized packages for touring which caters to different disabilities. For example, provision on sign language interpretation services to deaf tourist can help them in participating in the travel actively. The policies must promote synergies among the government, the tourism sector toward a systemic switch toward inclusivity (Ali et al., 2023; Stankov et al., 2024).

Governments places a number of policies to help people with disability for their rights in society. In India through tax breaks and disability pension government try to help people with physical challenges. Government tries to help people with disability by upgrading infrastructure by providing opportunities for skill development and by providing free education. Create campaigns for awareness. Government also collaborates with private institutions and NGO to expand their opportunities.

Government helps people with disability by enforcing provisions and acts for their rights and also provide financial assistance and social security programmes and also provide free health care facilities and rehabilitation services at lowest cost provide scholarship and fee concession for children with physical disability and also provide employment opportunities to them. Government also encourages them to take part in cultural and sports events, theatres plays and musical events etc. This enhances their mental wellbeing, builds confidence and build stronger community.

How NGO Helps people with Disability

In order to empower people with disability and solve their obstacles with the help of non-governmental organisation are important. Nonprofit ensures that individual with disability have access to social life, work, Health care and education as part of their aim to build an inclusive society. In addition to these people's quality of life their work advances and equality is also taken care by NGO. (Lang et al ., 2000)

Increasing awareness about the rights of those with disability has become one of the important functions of NGO. They fight against social injustice push for policy changes and they also make sure that business and government put people with disability as their first choice. NGO frequently collaborate with local government and international organisations to implement policies for disability people. A lot of NGOS provide access to free education to kids (special kids) so that financial limitations do not stop them from education. They provide scholarships and also offer skill development program that cater to the interest of these children. By teaching them the means to succeed in workforce and live independent life (Baranauskiene et al, 2011).

Disability leads to low self-esteem and feeling of loneliness to solve this problem NGO has established community centres and support group where people interact with each other more comfortably. This platform ensures a secure place to talk about their experiences their difficulties in life get emotional support. NGO often face challenges like limited funding, no proper infrastructure facility. They depend on donations and partnership and support from government to continue their work. NGO put efforts to work towards inclusive and equitable world for people with disability. They provide all opportunities to people with disability so that they can live an independent life.

CONCLUSION

To summarize, it is a necessity to understand the needs and opinions of people with disabilities to provide better service to them. The major barriers to accessible tourism are unprofessional customer service, lack of accessibility in physical environments, high pricing of tourism products, lack of mobility infrastructure, lack of information and communication, lack of digital accessibility, psychological barriers resulting in both physical and digital barriers which greatly discourages people with disability from participating in tourism. These barriers can be overcome with the formulation of models using the help of technology. Collaboration among stakeholders also plays a crucial role as barriers can be overcome by the combined efforts of various stakeholders like government agencies, tourism businesses, digital accessibility groups and technological developers. Focusing on continuous improvements is a must as technology perception and definition of disability evolve in our society. This is because there is an immense need for the tourism industry to continuously strive to improve its new offerings and remove new emerging barriers in the accessible tourism industry. By creating a more inclusive tourism industry, stakeholders of tourism can tap into a vast and growing market, fostering economic growth and enriching the travel experience for all.

REFERENCES

Achillas, C., Aidonis, D., Folinas, D., Kostavelis, I., Tsolakis, N., Triantafyllou, D., . . . Dimou, V. (2024, May). Digital platform for strengthening accessibility of tourist destinations in the Pieria Region. In Olympus International Conference on Supply Chains (pp. 99-106). Cham: Springer Nature Switzerland.

Achillas, C., Aidonis, D., Tsampoulatidis, I., Folinas, D., Kostavelis, I., Tsolakis, N., Triantafyllou, D., Vlachokostas, C., Kelemis, A., & Dimou, V. (2024). Empowering Tourism Accessibility: A Digital Revolution in Pieria, Greece. *Applied Sciences (Basel, Switzerland)*, *14*(23), 11136. DOI: 10.3390/app142311136

Ali, F., Cain, L., Legendre, T. S., & Wu, L. (2023). The intersection of technology, accessible tourism, and tourists with intellectual disabilities: Proposing a novel conceptual framework. *Journal of Hospitality & Tourism Research (Washington, D.C.)*, *47*(4), NP76–NP90. DOI: 10.1177/10963480221142499

Allan, M. (2015). Accessible tourism in Jordan: Travel constraints and motivations. *European Journal of Tourism Research*, *10*, 109–119. DOI: 10.54055/ejtr.v10i.182

Ap, J., & Wong, K. K. (2001). Case study on tour guiding: Professionalism, issues, and problems. *Tourism Management*, *22*(5), 551–563. DOI: 10.1016/S0261-5177(01)00013-9

Bagwell, K., & Riordan, M. H. (1991). High and Declining Prices Signal Product Quality. *The American Economic Review*, *81*(1), 224–239. https://www.jstor.org/stable/2006797

Baranauskienė, I., Gerulaitis, D., & Radzevičienė, L. (2011). Social empowerment and participation of people with disabilities through NGO activities. *Social Welfare: Interdisciplinary Approach*, *1*(1), 15–26. DOI: 10.15388/SW.2011.28311

Battams, S., & Johnson, A. (2009). The influence of service users and NGOs on housing for people with psychiatric disability. *Health Sociology Review*, *18*(3), 321–334. DOI: 10.5172/hesr.2009.18.3.321

Benur, A. M., & Bramwell, B. (2015). Tourism product development and product diversification in destinations. *Tourism Management*, *50*, 213–224. DOI: 10.1016/j.tourman.2015.02.005

Berry, S., & Ladkin, A. (1997). Sustainable tourism: A regional perspective. *Tourism Management*, *18*(7), 433–440. DOI: 10.1016/S0261-5177(97)00053-8

Best, K., & Butler, S. (2012). Disability and communication: A consideration of cross-disability communication and technology. *Disability Studies Quarterly*, *32*(4). Advance online publication. DOI: 10.18061/dsq.v32i4.3290

Bianchi, P., Cappelletti, G. M., Mafrolla, E., Sica, E., & Sisto, R. (2020). Accessible tourism in natural park areas: A social network analysis to discard barriers and provide information for people with disabilities. *Sustainability (Basel)*, *12*(23), 9915. DOI: 10.3390/su12239915

Bitner, M. J. (1990). Evaluating service encounters: The effects of physical surroundings and employee responses. *Journal of Marketing*, *54*(2), 69–82. DOI: 10.1177/002224299005400206

Botelho, F. H. (2021). Accessibility to digital technology: Virtual barriers, real opportunities. Assistive Technology, 33(sup1), 27-34.

Buckley, R. (2011). Tourism and environment. *Annual Review of Environment and Resources*, *36*(1), 397–416. DOI: 10.1146/annurev-environ-041210-132637

Buhalis, D., & Darcy, S. (Eds.). (2010). Accessible tourism: Concepts and issues.

Buhalis, D., & Michopoulou, E. (2011). Information-enabled tourism destination marketing: Addressing the accessibility market. *Current Issues in Tourism*, *14*(2), 145–168. DOI: 10.1080/13683501003653361

Butler, R. W. (1999). Sustainable tourism: A state-of-the-art review. *Tourism Geographies*, *1*(1), 7–25. DOI: 10.1080/14616689908721291

Cabral, C., & Dhar, R. L. (2019). Green competencies: Construct development and measurement validation. *Journal of Cleaner Production*, *235*, 887–900. DOI: 10.1016/j.jclepro.2019.07.014

Cabral, C., & Dhar, R. L. (2019). Ecotourism research in India: From an integrative literature review to a future research framework. *Journal of Ecotourism*, *19*(1), 23–49. DOI: 10.1080/14724049.2019.1625359

Cabral, C., & Jabbour, C. J. C. (2020). Understanding the human side of green hospitality management. *International Journal of Hospitality Management*, *88*, 102389. DOI: 10.1016/j.ijhm.2019.102389

Cassia, F., Castellani, P., Rossato, C., & Baccarani, C. (2020). Finding a way towards high-quality, accessible tourism: The role of digital ecosystems. *The TQM Journal*, *33*(1), 205–221. DOI: 10.1108/TQM-03-2020-0062

Coppola, P., Carbone, A., Aveta, C., & Stang Herlin, P. (2020). Assessing transport policies for tourist mobility based on accessibility indicators. *European Transport Research Review, 12*(1), 56. DOI: 10.1186/s12544-020-00444-4

Darcy, S. (2010). Inherent complexity: Disability, accessible tourism, and accommodation information preferences. *Tourism Management, 31*(6), 816–826. DOI: 10.1016/j.tourman.2009.08.010

Darcy, S., Cameron, B., & Pegg, S. (2010). Accessible tourism and sustainability: A discussion and case study. *Journal of Sustainable Tourism, 18*(4), 515–537. DOI: 10.1080/09669581003690668

Darcy, S., Cameron, B., Pegg, S., & Packer, T. (2008). *Developing business case studies for accessible tourism.* Sustainable Tourism for Cooperative Research Centre.

Darcy, S., & Dickson, T. J. (2009). A whole-of-life approach to tourism: The case for accessible tourism experiences. *Journal of Hospitality and Tourism Management, 16*(1), 32–44. DOI: 10.1375/jhtm.16.1.32

Debeljak, M., Vidmar, G., Matjačić, Z., & Burger, H. (2020). Information and communication technology used by people with lower limb loss in Slovenia. *International Journal of Rehabilitation Research. Internationale Zeitschrift fur Rehabilitationsforschung. Revue Internationale de Recherches de Readaptation, 43*(2), 188–191. DOI: 10.1097/MRR.0000000000000405 PMID: 32106175

Devile, E., & Kastenholz, E. (2020). Accessible tourism experiences: The voice of people with visual disabilities. In *Social Tourism at the Crossroads* (pp. 84–104). Routledge. DOI: 10.4324/9780429290077-6

Dobransky, K., & Hargittai, E. (2006). The disability divides in internet access and use. *Information Communication and Society, 9*(3), 313–334. DOI: 10.1080/13691180600751298

Dolgui, A., & Proth, J. M. (2010). Pricing strategies and models. *Annual Reviews in Control, 34*(1), 101–110. DOI: 10.1016/j.arcontrol.2010.02.005

Easterly, W. (2015). The SDGs should stand for senseless, dreamy, garbled. *Foreign Policy, 28*, 1–5.

Ee Kim, S., & Lehto, X. Y. (2012). The voice of tourists with mobility disabilities: Insights from online customer complaint websites. *International Journal of Contemporary Hospitality Management, 24*(3), 451–476. DOI: 10.1108/09596111211217905

Eichhorn, V., Miller, G., Michopoulou, E., & Buhalis, D. (2007). Enabling disabled tourists? Accessibility tourism information schemes. *Annals of Tourism Research.*

Eichhorn, V., Miller, G., Michopoulou, E., & Buhalis, D. (2008). Enabling access to tourism through information schemes? *Annals of Tourism Research*, *35*(1), 189–210. DOI: 10.1016/j.annals.2007.07.005

Erol, I., Neuhofer, I. O., Dogru, T., Oztel, A., Searcy, C., & Yorulmaz, A. C. (2022). Improving sustainability in the tourism industry through blockchain technology: Challenges and opportunities. *Tourism Management*, *93*, 104628. DOI: 10.1016/j.tourman.2022.104628

Fernández-Díaz, E., Jambrino-Maldonado, C., Iglesias-Sánchez, P. P., & de las Heras-Pedrosa, C. (2023). Digital accessibility of smart cities-tourism for all and reducing inequalities: Tourism agenda 2030. *Tourism Review*, *78*(2), 361–380. DOI: 10.1108/TR-02-2022-0091

Gaspar, S. R. D. S. (2016). Airport accessibility and mobility: Infrastructures, services, and perception of passengers with reduced mobility (Doctoral dissertation).

Gonda, T. (2023). The importance of infrastructure in the development of accessible tourism. Journal of Infrastructure, Policy and Development, 8(2).

Gwilliams, K. (2017). Transport pricing and accessibility.

Hák, T., Janoušková, S., & Moldan, B. (2016). Sustainable Development Goals: A need for relevant indicators. *Ecological Indicators*, *60*, 565–573. DOI: 10.1016/j.ecolind.2015.08.003

Heinberg, R., & Lerch, D. (2010). What is sustainability. *The Post Carbon Reader*, *11*, 19.

Imrie, R., & Kumar, M. (1998). Focusing on disability and access in the built environment. *Disability & Society*, *13*(3), 357–374. DOI: 10.1080/09687599826687

Jones, P., Hillier, D., & Comfort, D. (2016). Sustainable tourism and corporate social responsibility: A review and critique. *International Journal of Economic Practices and Theories*, *6*(3), 278–288.

Kaganek, K., Ambroży, T., Mucha, D., Jurczak, A., Bornikowska, A., Ostrowski, A., Janiszewska, R., & Mucha, T. (2017). Barriers to participation in tourism in the disabled. *Polish Journal of Sport and Tourism*, *24*(2), 121–129. DOI: 10.1515/pjst-2017-0013

Kaul, H., & Gupta, S. (2009). Sustainable tourism in India. *Worldwide Hospitality and Tourism Themes*, *1*(1), 12–18. DOI: 10.1108/17554210910949841

Kett, M., Cole, E., & Turner, J. (2020). Disability, mobility, and transport in low- and middle-income countries: A thematic review. *Sustainability (Basel)*, *12*(2), 589. DOI: 10.3390/su12020589

Khetarpal, A. (2014). Information and communication technology (ICT) and disability. *Review of Market Integration*, *6*(1), 96–113. DOI: 10.1177/0974929214560117

Kołodziejczak, A. (2019). Information as a factor of the development of accessible tourism for people with disabilities. *Quaestiones Geographicae*, *38*(2), 67–73. DOI: 10.2478/quageo-2019-0014

Koppa, R., Davies, B., & Rodriguez, K. (1998). Barriers to use of transportation alternatives by people with disabilities.

Kulkarni, M. (2019). Digital accessibility: Challenges and opportunities. *IIMB Management Review*, *31*(1), 91–98. DOI: 10.1016/j.iimb.2018.05.009

La Placa, V., & Knight, A. (2018). The role of ICT in enabling accessible tourism. In *Inclusive Tourism: Improving the Accessibility of the Tourist Offer* (pp. 53–67). Springer.

Langvinienė, N., & Daunoravičiūtė, I. (2015). Factors influencing the success of business model in the hospitality service industry. *Procedia: Social and Behavioral Sciences*, *213*, 902–910. DOI: 10.1016/j.sbspro.2015.11.503

Langvinienė, N., Zagrabskaite, R., & Bazinaitė, D. (2015). The digitalization of Lithuanian tourism: Trends and perspectives. *Procedia: Social and Behavioral Sciences*, *213*, 757–761.

Laws, E. (1995). *Tourism destination management: Issues, analysis, and policies*. Routledge.

Lehto, X. Y., Lin, Y. C., Park, J., & Jang, S. C. (2012). Visitors with disabilities: A tourism market segment untapped by businesses. *Journal of Business Research*, *65*(4), 396–402.

Mathew, P. V. (2022). Sustainable tourism development: Discerning the impact of responsible tourism on community well-being. *Journal of Hospitality and Tourism Insights*, *5*(5), 987–1001.

Mathew, P. V., Cabral, C., & Mohandas, N. P. (2024). Influence of responsible tourism practices on the destination perceptions of tourists. *International Journal of Tourism Research*, *26*(4), e2692. DOI: 10.1002/jtr.2692

Mazanec, J. A., & Ritchie, J. B. (Eds.). (2020). *The handbook of tourist behavior: Theory & practice*. Routledge.

McKercher, B., Packer, T. L., Yau, M. K., & Lam, P. (2003). Travel agents as facilitators or inhibitors of travel: Perceptions of people with disabilities. *Tourism Management, 24*(4), 465–474. DOI: 10.1016/S0261-5177(02)00107-3

Michopoulou, E., & Buhalis, D. (2008). Information provision for challenging markets: The case of the accessibility requiring market in the context of tourism. *Information & Management, 45*(4), 241–249.

Mikulić, J., Gregori, N., Crnogaj, K., & Barac, D. (2021). Examining the gap between tourist perceptions and expectations of sustainable tourism: Evidence from Croatian protected areas. *Tourism Management, 83*, 104235.

Murphy, P. E. (2013). *Tourism: A community approach.* Routledge. DOI: 10.4324/9780203068533

Napolitano, F., & Ragni, M. (2008). A model of tourism carrying capacity in protected areas. *Tourism Analysis, 13*(3), 193–206.

Navarro, J. P., & Avellaneda, C. N. (2021). Tourism, political accountability, and the mediation of digital accessibility. *Tourism Management, 85*, 104318.

O'Neill, M. A., & Palmer, A. (2003). An exploration of the effects of experience on consumer perceptions of the service quality construct. *Managing Service Quality, 13*(3), 187–196. DOI: 10.1108/09604520310476454

O'Neill, M. A., & Palmer, A. (2004). Importance-performance analysis: A useful tool for directing continuous quality improvement in higher education. *Quality Assurance in Education, 12*(1), 39–52. DOI: 10.1108/09684880410517423

Oliver, M. (1996). *Understanding disability: From theory to practice.* Macmillan International Higher Education. DOI: 10.1007/978-1-349-24269-6

Park, J., & Jang, S. C. (2012). Visitors with disabilities: A tourism market segment untapped by businesses. *Journal of Business Research, 65*(4), 396–402.

Pike, S., & Page, S. J. (2014). Destination marketing organizations and destination marketing: A narrative analysis of the literature. *Tourism Management, 41*, 202–227. DOI: 10.1016/j.tourman.2013.09.009

Pineda, V. (2010). Enabling Justice: Spatializing Disability in the Built Environment. *Environment & Planning A, 42*(11), 2748–2767.

Poria, Y., Reichel, A., & Brandt, Y. (2009). Accessible tourism–tourism for all through information technologies.

Russo, A. P., & van der Borg, J. (2002). Planning considerations for cultural tourism: A case study of four European cities. *Tourism Management, 23*(6), 631–637. DOI: 10.1016/S0261-5177(02)00027-4

Sadykova, A., & Gali, Y. (2021). The involvement of ICT in accessible tourism. *Turizm Akademik Dergisi, 8*(2), 255–264.

Salvatore, D., & Scipioni, A. (2022). A new conceptual framework for accessible tourism: Overcoming barriers and promoting inclusivity. *International Journal of Tourism Research, 24*(6), 1082–1094.

Scarpi, D. (2012). Work and fun on the internet: The effects of utilitarianism and hedonism online. *Journal of Interactive Marketing, 26*(1), 53–67. DOI: 10.1016/j.intmar.2011.08.001

Smith, M. K. (2015). *Issues in cultural tourism studies*. Routledge. DOI: 10.4324/9781315767697

Smith, R. W. (1987). Leisure of disabled tourists: Barriers to participation. *Annals of Tourism Research, 14*(3), 376–389. DOI: 10.1016/0160-7383(87)90109-5

Son, H., Lee, J., Kim, S., & Lee, J. (2021). Information communication technologies for accessible tourism in cultural heritage sites: A case study in Korea. *Sustainability, 13*(21), 11895.

Suban, S. A., Madhan, K., & Shagirbasha, S. (2021). A bibliometric analysis of Halal and Islamic tourism. *International Hospitality Review, 37*(2), 219–242. DOI: 10.1108/IHR-05-2021-0038

Takano, T., & Nakamura, K. (2001). An analysis of health levels and various indicators of urban environments for healthy cities projects. *Journal of Epidemiology and Community Health, 55*(4), 263–270. DOI: 10.1136/jech.55.4.263 PMID: 11238582

Teixeira, L. R., Neves, L. F., & Rebelo, F. (2019). Accessible tourism in the mobile era: Exploring the role of mobile applications in promoting inclusivity. *Disability & Society, 34*(4), 571–589.

Thomas, J. L., Vitell, S. J., Gilbert, F. W., & Rose, G. M. (2002). The impact of ethical cues on customer satisfaction with service. *Journal of Retailing, 78*(3), 167–173. DOI: 10.1016/S0022-4359(02)00062-3

Tielmann, B., & Locher, D. (2017). Exploring the potential of mobile applications to enhance accessible tourism. In *HCI in Business, Government and Organizations. Supporting Business* (pp. 24–37). Springer.

Tsolakis, N., Triantafyllou, D., & Koukouvinou, E. (2022). A systematic literature review on digital and sustainable development in the tourism sector. *Journal of Hospitality and Tourism Technology*, *13*(4), 507–527.

Vella, K. (2023). Factors influencing participation in sports and physical activity for people with disabilities. *Sport Management Review*, *16*(1), 42–58.

Walker, J., Stubbins, J., & McDonnel, J. (1996). Accessible tourism: A review of definitions, concepts, and challenges. *Journal of Vacation Marketing*, *2*(3), 222–234.

Yau, M. K., McKercher, B., & Packer, T. L. (2004). Traveling with a disability: More than an access issue. *Annals of Tourism Research*, *31*(4), 946–960. DOI: 10.1016/j.annals.2004.03.007

Zhang, X., Cole, S. T., & Fan, D. X. F. (2020). Accessibility and inclusivity: The case of Hong Kong's tourism industry. *Asia Pacific Journal of Tourism Research*, *25*(1), 36–49.

Chapter 11

Fostering the Metaverse to Drive Digital Leadership, Productivity, and an Inclusive Work Environment

Saed Adnan Mustafa
https://orcid.org/0000-0002-3099-7230
The American University of Kurdistan, Iraq

Mahesh Luthia
https://orcid.org/0000-0002-6114-6463
Chetana's Institute of Management and Research, India

Ruqiya Jaber Al Darwashi
Independent Researcher, Oman

ABSTRACT

Globally the tourism sector is going through digital transformation. The develop a sustainable competitive advantage, the Indian tourism sector will have adopted emerging technologies for better customer experience and overall operational efficiency. Metaverse is emerging as a transformative force in the Indian tourism industry that can develop digital skills among leaders, help them improve employee performance and contribute to building an inclusive work culture. The chapter adopts a pragmatic and futuristic approach and aims to enable the readers to examine the role, strategies and actionable insights for leveraging metaverse as a virtual workspace by developing digital leadership, optimising performance management

DOI: 10.4018/979-8-3373-0071-9.ch011

systems and creating an inclusive work environment in the Indian Tourism sector. The chapter provides a broad framework of actionable recommendations that can be used to leverage the metaverse technology. Ethical issues and risks are examined so that organisations are aware of the risks of adopting these new age technologies.

1. INTRODUCTION

Digital transformation is the emerging paradigm in the Indian tourism sector through adoption of new technologies. These technologies have helped the service provides to keep pace with changes such as online booking, enriched travel experience and multiple point of contacts with customers for better satisfaction and interaction. Some of the technologies that have impacted the tourism sector are artificial intelligence, big data, mobile applications, virtual and augmented realities and the metaverse technology. The Metaverse has been emerging as a transformative force in the Indian tourism industry, offering new ways to enhance tourist experiences and reshape how destinations are marketed and consumed. It allows an immersive and interactive experience that can significantly impact how tourists engage with destinations, both virtually and physically. While integration of metaverse technology in tourism at a nascent stage in India, it envisaged to transform the tourism industry. The following sections explore the various roles and impacts of the metaverse in Indian tourism.

Metaverse offers many avenues for Indian tourism leaders to pioneer digital strategies that integrate virtual experiences with traditional tourism offerings, creating a hybrid model that can attract a global audience. By leveraging the Metaverse, tourism leaders can enhance destination awareness and strategic positioning, thus strengthening brand presence in a competitive market. Effective digital leadership is essential for creating sustainable businesses within the Metaverse. Leaders in this space must possess a complete understanding of the technology driving the Metaverse, along with the social and cultural dynamics influencing its evolution. They should proactively anticipate shifts in the digital landscape and craft strategies that prioritize agility and adaptability to navigate this rapidly changing environment. The technology can help leaders develop to create and inclusive work environments by removing physical boundaries and fostering accessibility. Metaverse facilitates efficient coordination and management through digital twins, which can simulate real-world environments for planning and operational purposes. While the technology has a great transformative potential there are limited applications providing evidence of its application in the tourism industry.

Background

India has also undergone great development, including creating its digital infrastructure, which has gained speed thanks to better internet access and mobile connectivity (Latta & Sarkar, 2021). For these reasons, the metaverse finds an ideal environment for deployment here. However, it's in the Indian tourism industry is still not explored empirically, with considerable unrealized potential to reshape how visitors experience the destination and its functioning.

India's VR and AR market are growing fast, aided, in particular, by rising demand for gaming, which, in turn, benefits tourism by offering better virtual tours and experiences. According to market research, the market was estimated at around $ 1.69 billion in the year 2021 and is expected to touch around $ 9.28 billion by 2028, with a CAGR of 28% during this period (2021-2028) (blueweaveconsulting.com, 2022). *(Refer Figure: 01)*

In addition to improving the overall customer experience Metaverse offers revolutionary tools for Human Resource Development (HRD) within the tourism sector. By leveraging AR/VR for training and development, tourism professionals can gain practical and hands-on experience in an environment that is risk-free and controlled (Raji et al. 2024). This is particularly advantageous for preparing staff in high-stakes roles such as customer service and emergency management, where real-world experience is important but challenging to simulate safely and cost-effectively.

With digital transformation becoming an integral part of business today, leaders must adopt new technologies as it is important for managing change and influencing employee performance. Lack of understanding the role of digital leadership with limit the ability of an organisation to keep pace with change, create digital awareness in the organisation and create a culture supporting communication and collaboration and innovation contributing to employee performance. This collaboration and communication can facilitate access to digital resources, timely feedback and help employees achieve their full potential by adoption of new technologies (Turyadi et al., 2023). Hence the authors aim to examine how new technologies such as the metaverse can influence development of digital leadership skills, which will help improve employee performance and create and inclusive workplace.

The chapter adopts a pragmatic and futuristic approach and aims to enable the readers to examine the role, strategies and actionable insights for leveraging metaverse as a virtual workspace by developing digital leadership, optimising performance management systems and creating an inclusive work environment in the Indian Tourism sector. The chapter starts with providing an overview of the metaverse technology with specific focus on the tourism sector followed by discussing the role of the technology in developing digital leadership, creating an inclusive work environment and improve overall productivity for travel planning and decision-making, in virtual environment. Challenges and risks related to adopting the metaverse are examined. The chapter concludes by providing a set of actionable recommendations.

2. LITERATURE REVIEW

2.1 Understanding the Metaverse

The concept of Metaverse can be defined by a set of key components that collectively create an immersive, interconnected virtual environment. These components are required for the OTS effective functionality and its potential to transform different sectors, such as entertainment, education, and commerce.

MCKinsey defined metaverse *as one of the emerging 3-D-enabled digital space that integrates virtual and augmented realities with advanced internet technologies* (Hanafizadeh et al., 2011).

Metaverse includes many virtual worlds, layered environments, or interactive features that combine into an integrated and interconnected universe. This evolution of the internet turns the internet into an all-in-one homogenous space in which users are able to communicate with others in real-time through digital objects. Navigating within this complex digital Eco vortex is possible through advanced virtual reality (VR), AR technologies, and other such means such that participants are able to experience a virtual panorama of rich interactions and connections that begin to blur the borders between the physical and virtual. Metaverse, helps users to explore, collaborate, and create in an engaging, persistent, dynamic environment defining digital content and social connectivity (Mystakidis, 2024).

The metaverse encompasses Virtual and Augmented reality (VR and AR), and artificial intelligence (AI) technology to set-up an immersive and interactive virtual environment (Rane et al. 2023). This is particularly important in the tourism sector, where experience quality plays an important role. Given the current global tourism trends, these technologies are increasingly integrated to improve visitor experiences and operations and broaden marketing strategies. *(Refer Image 02)*

Metaverse can be referred as an expansive virtual immersive shared collective space expanding a seamless AR integration and enhanced physical realities. The integration of Virtual Reality with Metaverse are transforming the digital space. In VR technology, users are engaged in a digital environment through headsets such as Oculus Rift or HTC Vive. Other technology is then used to essentially cloak the user's peripheral vision for a more immersive experience in the metaverse.

2.2 Metaverse in Tourism

VR and AR technology adoption by the Tourism Industry in India is increasing at a tremendous rate, corroborating the larger digital transformation in the sector (Samaddar & Mondal, 2024).

AR superimposes digital details on top of the real world by shining them on smartphones or AR glasses and enhancing the real environment with a variety of more information. This technology bridges the virtual and the real world, required for real-time interaction in the Metaverse environment. Everything from non-player character behavior to natural language processing and machine learning all sits on top of AI in order to power those complex interactions and behaviors in Metaverse (Fadhel et al. 2024)

Metaverse has made it possible by means of decentralized and secure transactions other than blockchain technology. This enables a trustable economy in a virtual environment by also verifying asset ownership and exchange. With these technologies becoming a reality in practical applications, these are being used to enhance a visitor's experience via immersive previews of destinations, interactive historical narratives, and more personalized engagement. For example, potential customers can explore accommodations virtually through a virtual hotel tour using VR (Bwhotelier.com, 2024). In turn, AR provides digital information about cultural monuments and historical facts, which overlays in real-time during tours, giving travel an educational and interactive tone. In addition, the Indian Government and private sector players increasingly recognize the use of such technologies as a strategic tool to enhance tourism competitiveness and innovation (Tourism.gov.in, 2024). This is indicative of a broader understanding that digital tools, such as VR and AR, make the consumer's experience better as well as make business operations and marketing more efficient.*(Referfigure 3)*

VR is being used by tourism companies to build very detailed virtual tours of destinations to train guides and travel agents. It also enables them to get and learn about destinations remotely, so they're more able to communicate a tour or location's features effectively when marketing them to prospects. For instance, the Ministry of Tourism in India introduced a series of virtual reality experiences in key tourist destinations, like the Taj Mahal and Varanasi, on its Incredible India platform (ndtv.com, 2024). By presenting a realistic image of these sites, this initiative contributes to training tour operators and guides on how to enrich tourists with fine, detailed, and engaging information. ***(ReferFigure 4)***

Research Gaps

There is a need for a clear definition and understanding of digital leadership within the Metaverse. Current literature suggests that digital leadership involves vision motivation, digital empowerment, and innovation, but how these translate into the Metaverse context remains underexplored (Lin, 2024; Beil etal., 2025). Current research indicates a lack of comprehensive performance metrics tailored to the metaverse environment. Traditional KPIs may not be applicable, necessitating the development of new metrics to evaluate avatar performance and productivity in virtual workspaces (Tsappi & Papageorgiou, 2023). While the metaverse can potentially promote diversity, equity, and inclusion (DEI), there are few frameworks and empirical evidences of its implementation. Although metaverse offers numerous possibilities for creating an inclusive high-performing workforce, it also presents challenges that need to be addressed through targeted research.

3. DEVELOPING DIGITAL LEADERSHIP THROUGH METAVERSE

The metaverse provides a platform for leaders to engage with teams in virtual environments, enhancing collaboration and communication (Kaur et al., 2024). The metaverse is emerging as a powerful tool for developing digital skills and leadership across various domains. In education, it can enhance soft skills like communication, creativity, and critical thinking for ESL learners (Alshammari, 2023). Effective digital leadership is essential for creating sustainable businesses within the Metaverse. Leaders in this space must possess a comprehensive understanding of the technologies driving the Metaverse, along with the social and cultural dynamics influencing its evolution. They should proactively anticipate shifts in the digital landscape and craft strategies that prioritize agility and adaptability to navigate this rapidly changing environment (Sandu, 2023)

Mihardjo et al., 2019 defined digital leadership as 'a combination between digital culture and digital competence' (p. 1750; Mihardjo et al., 2019).

3.1 Key Traits - Digital Leadership

Agility, ability to adapt, and foresight around where strategy heads are the key traits of digital leaders in the Metaverse. As technological change accelerates and the Metaverse becomes a more central part of digital strategy, these qualities are becoming even more important.

Agility

Digital leadership is, in a sense, reliant on it because it needs to adopt the new tools quickly while adapting to changes in the digital environment. Digital leaders also need to have an innate ability to pivot and just embrace a new tool or platform as it comes up in the chaotic world of the metaverse (Radanliev, 2024). It is about reacting quickly to events and being proactive in looking ahead to see what's coming next. Leaders are now able to place their organizations in a good place to compete in an ever-shifting digital world by effectively embracing these emerging trends into business strategy.

Adaptability

The early stages of metaverse development require that it can be adaptable; metaverse is still in development. Leaders must learn how to manoeuvre around this perpetual changing landscape. This means being willing to embrace a cornucopia of new technologies and ready to try a multitude of new and unique ways to engage customers and employees. Success in these dynamic virtual environments will be very dependent on fostering engaging experiences that ring true with their users.

Strategic Foresight

In this fast-changing world, it is imperative to understand and take hold of future trends. As leaders, one must go past what is happening now technologically and think of how the metaverse could change their industry. To embrace foresight, a process of deep understanding of current innovations and a strategic decision-making process, managing the current business tactics and objectives in the context of current business tactics and progressive ones is required. Moreover, leaders are required to have a certain flexibility so that they can make an unexpected change in this ever-changing environment more quickly (Akbar et al. 2024).

Insights from statistics indicate a reasonably broad business leader's understanding of and cautious approach to the Metaverse. They see potential, and they recognize how challenging that will be with interoperability and strategic integration into business models. In numerous industry discussions, people are talking about encouraging companies to approach Metaverse technologies with critical thought about the applications that would benefit them and customer engagement strategies rather than a one-size-fits-all.

As such, it is up to these metaverse leaders to manage the innovative risk that a metaverse must take in order to succeed. The key to this balance will be vital as companies attempt to use the new digital frontier to enhance competitive edge and operational efficiency.

3.2 Metaverse-Based Leadership Training Programs

The richness and embedded immersion of the metaverse platforms are an effective way to practice real-world challenges and scenarios in the leadership training process (Jagatheesaperumal et al. 2024). These are advanced programs that can be thoughtfully designed with a wide range of challenging problem-solving tasks for leaders to solve creatively and critically thought through. In this virtual setting, participants can try crisis management simulations that approximate such high-stress situations and provide an opportunity to practice responses and develop essential skills to deal with real crisis situations.

These platforms can also embed strategic decision-making exercises to make leaders experiment with their critical decisions in a controlled, realistic setting. The experience is real-time and helps them deep dive into the leadership dynamics. Organizations use the metaverse as a safe space for leaders to practice and improve their skills, try out strategies that won't get them fired in real life, and encourage teamwork, all while uncovering valuable learnings for their professional environments.

These can also be large and global in scale, with leaders from around the world working and talking together in one virtual world. It develops and refines communication, cross-cultural management, and overall, an enhanced understanding of global business dynamics. Leaders having the critical skills which are empathy, adaptability, and proactive thinking, would be trained together through this training.

3.3 Role of Gamification in Leadership Development

Deterding et al, 2011 defined as application of game principles and design elements to a non-game situation. It is used to create engaging training content. In leadership development, companies can use gamification to make learning more engaging and remembered (Mohanty & Christopher, 2024). It has elements of play, such as point scoring, other players playing against, rules and play, and character development, which helps to motivate players and keep them more interested and more engaged.

For example, leaders manage virtual resources under time constraints to achieve specific objectives with gamification, i.e., by teaching resource management. It could actually model a resort budget manager that has to invest money in each of the departments, create unexpected expenses, and be able to respond to the consequences of its choice on customer and business results.

Gamification in leadership development is beneficial because it has been found to improve retention of information, help participants develop problem-solving skills, and motivate those participating (Saleem et al. 2022). Applying these skills in their professional roles is more dynamic and interactive and likelier to happen from leaders when learning becomes a process. Besides, gamification allows learners to get immediate feedback on the consequences of the decision made and modify the strategy appropriately.

Both metaverse-based training and gamification are a complete way of developing leaders who are better suited to the business situation in the modern age. The first set of strategies addresses the technical skills required for leadership, and the second set focuses on interpersonal and strategic thinking skills that are so needed in the digital age. With these immersive and interactive techniques, leadership development gains greater effectiveness and engagement and matches the requirements of a rapidly changing business environment.

Using the Metaverse requires digital leadership. Metaverse technology offers opportunities for tourism sector leaders to champion and adopt strategies that embed the technology into operations for efficient operations and customer engagement (Ersoy, 2024). Digital leadership is linked to improved organizational performance through the development of digital skills and capabilities, which are essential for navigating digital transformations

In addition, the Metaverse can also help create more inclusive work environments as they get rid of the physical hindrances of work needed for employment and let a diverse workforce work together in ways never possible before. Such a culturally diverse and geographically dispersed nation like India desperately needs it.

4. METAVERSE FOR PERFORMANCE MANAGEMENT

In addition to using the metaverse for training purposes, it has a huge potential to be integrated with artificial intelligence (AI) and knowledge management (KM), system to enhance employee performance. The metaverse is revolutionizing workplace performance management by introducing new KPIs for avatar performance, which differ from traditional metrics. This shift necessitates new strategies for managing virtual work environments (Tsappi & Papageorgiou, 2023).

4.1 Performance Simulation and Assessment

Complex guest interactions are simulated using VR for performance assessment. Managers have the opportunity to evaluate staff through the challenge of delivering service in different, often uncomfortable, scenarios in order to assess performance and provide feedback without any real stakes. Luxury resorts in Goa use VR to enable performance evaluation of guest interactions, for example (bwhotelier.com, 2024). It is important for the luxury tourism sector to maintain the high standard of service expected. However, this can be very difficult to do if management is unaware of how their staff deals with different service scenarios and cannot assess this. For tours or events, tourism staff using AR glasses could receive real-time information with prompts or corrective suggestions on demand. This technology improves our capability to do so across experiences.

The metaverse can improve the motivation to perform by offering immersive virtual environments that facilitate interactive learning and skill acquisition. The virtual reality technologies, employees can participate in engaging training sessions and collaborative projects, leading to improved teamwork and productivity. The metaverse can be integrated into performance management systems to provide real-time 360-degree feedback, gamified learning experiences, and personalized goal-setting, all of which contribute to increased employee engagement and motivation.

4.2 Immersive Learning and Development

One of the most unique features of metaverse platform is the ability to create immersive learning experiences for employees. Through simulated real-life scenarios, employees can gain hands experience and develop their skills in an environment that is risk-free. This helps in better performance and employee engagement. Virtual spaces within the metaverse can be tailored for specific learning objectives, allowing for personalized and adaptive learning experiences that cater to individual employee need. By creating virtual spaces for collaboration, organizations can break down geographical barriers and foster a more inclusive and diverse work environment, further enhancing employee engagement (Lim et al., 2023; Karadayı et al., 2024). Most importantly, organisations can leverage these tools to identify training needs of their remote employees to offer more personalised training plans that can customised and personalised depending on their role. Some of the key areas that metaverse can be used to train employees to improve their performance are:

- VR simulation is used by hotels and resorts to train staff in customer service, management, and tasks from the operations. For example, Marriott has used VR to train staff on room setup and customer interaction simulations, creating controlled simulations that employees can become brilliant at before talking to customers (medium.com, 2024).
- With VR platforms staff is able to participate in emergency response drills in a virtual environment replicating hotel, resort, or other tourist environments.

Teaching staff to handle real-life emergencies is a form of training that is critical in ensuring quick, safe reactions to emergencies.

- Language learning and cultural training in the tourism industry are used to help staff with barriers to interactions with tourists from different cultures by using AR and VR. Immersive experiences that mimic real experiences of interacting with foreign tourists have allowed these technologies to improve skills for communication and the understanding of cultures (Li et al. 2024).

Metaverse has the potential to offer real-time feedback and performance tracking, which are critical components of effective performance management. The integration of HR analytics with metaverse technologies can provide valuable insights into employee performance and engagement, enabling organizations to make data-driven decisions to enhance workforce productivity (Rathi & Prabhash, 2024). The metaverse also has the transformative power of creating an inclusive workforce. It can be utilized to enhance engagement and participation of disabled individuals in the metaverse. This approach emphasizes the importance of involving disabled individuals in the design and development of metaverse platforms to promote inclusivity (Radanliev et al., 2023). *(ReferFigure 6)*

The metaverse trains highly interactive and engagement-rich experiences. Virtual reality, for example, can be used to create precise scenarios requiring hotel or travel agency operations, such as working as a customer service attendant, crisis manager, or even day-to-day operations of the hotel or travel agency. An advantage of this is that it creates a safer place for employees to practice skills and get immediate feedback, which makes the learning experience so much richer and productive (Saeed et al. 2024).

5. ROLE OF METAVERSE IN CREATING AN INCLUSIVE WORKFORCE

The metaverse presents opportunities for creating inclusive work environments by removing physical boundaries and fostering accessibility (Parker et al., 2024; Parker et al., 2023). It can enhance diversity, equity, and inclusion (DEI) efforts through fairer performance assessments and improved employee experiences, particularly regarding gender and race. The responsible implementation of AI-driven metaverse capabilities is crucial to avoid potential negative DEI outcomes and privacy concerns (Marabelli & Lirio, 2024). One practical application is the development of metaverse-based softbot tutors to support and train impaired operators in Industry 5.0 settings, promoting more human-centric and inclusive industrial workplaces (Zambiasi et al., 2023).

5.1 Inclusive Participation

Metaverse can support meaningful participation of disabled creatives, ensuring that their needs are considered in the design and development processes. The metaverse provides a platform for co-creation, allowing individuals to collaborate and innovate in immersive environments. This can eliminate knowledge and experience boundaries, enabling diverse teams to work together effectively (Kim et al., 2023). It creates Metaverse to generate several scenarios for addressing the needs of tourists with disabilities. Virtual training in these environments helps staff learn how best to interact with and help guests with different accessibility needs.

Different cultural situations in a tourist population can be presented to staff within virtual environments, where sensitivity and understanding can be sensitively increased. Interaction with people from different cultural backgrounds is normal in global tourism. Therefore, this training is very important. For instance, the Indian Tourism industry predicates its immersive VR experiences on cultural practices and tourist expectations of tourists from different countries to educate their staff (Prayag et al. 2020). This initiative also leads to increasing cultural sensitivity and customer satisfaction.

5.2 Virtual Accessibility

Built, the metaverse can be completely accessible and feature voice-to-text, text-to-speech, and customizable avatars to fit any physical ability. Avatar-based interaction (ABI) is a power tool in the metaverse that enables individuals from diverse background to represent people in the virtual space. ABI can promote inclusiveness through personalised representation and create an equitable environment. A Virtual reality-based system was created for communication that would reflect gestures, facial expressions, and speech of people from different cultures. This can help organisations integrate the virtual and physical worlds and use it with block chain technology for security and protection. Various 2D, 3D and VR avatars can be used for interaction. Digital humans' avatars can be used to represent real-life humans and historical figures (Yoon et al., 2022)

Virtual Avatar-based interaction can also be used on the customer side. For example, people with mobility impairments could have access to virtual tours of heritage sites so that they might experience and explore those that are physically inaccessible to them (Murugkar et al. 2024). Virtual tours can be design with higher emotional engagement, to increase travel intention, specially among older travellers, building confidence and reducing stress (Hao et al., 2025).

Metaverse offers many opportunities to overcome challenges faced by people with disabilities. It limits access and exposure and access to career opportunities (Zallio and Clarkson, 2022).

The metaverse would also provide training programs, for instance, training staff to interact with tourists as disparate as possible in backgrounds and needs. With these programs, this can immerse staff in a world of customer service situations involving people across cultures, languages, and disabilities and ensure your staff is ready and sensitive to the variations of customer interactions with tourists. Virtual reality has the potential to further cultural education by delivering rich, culturally diverse environments within which to immerse users. People can celebrate different festivals like Diwali, Eid, or Christmas in Metaverse, where people around the globe can participate and learn about these traditions in such a deeply engaging manner (linkedin.com, 2023). So, it teaches and helps stimulate respect and appreciation for cultural diversity._*(Referfigure 5)*

6. CHALLENGES AND ETHICAL CONSIDERATIONS

While metaverse technologies have been adopted in Indian tourism, there are several barriers that could, in fact, prevent inputs from being integrated and made workable. The technology infrastructure needed to run metaverse platforms is one of the great barriers. While internet access and the computing hardware required for "VR and AR technologies" continue to thrive, access to high-speed internet and such computing hardware is not uniform across all regions of the Indian subcontinent (Kedia et al. 2020). As a result, unbalanced access to metaverse-based tourism experiences may arise, especially in less developed areas of disadvantaged rural or less economically developed regions.

The other problem is that creating and developing metaverse environments has a cost. VR and AR systems can be quite expensive in terms of the initial investment in software and user equipment (Dargan et al. 2023). On the other hand, the financial outlay involved may prevent digital technology installation in small and medium-sized enterprises in the tourism sector that may not have the finances to invest in such advanced technology. Additionally, the metaverse has a cultural and perceptual barrier to penetration (El Emary, 2024). Although not all stakeholders will accept the idea of virtual tourism, they may like the traditional tourism idea. Furthermore, there is resistance to change from within the industry, where conventional ways and means of doing things are embedded at a very deep level.

There are privacy and security concerns for virtual environment data, which would hinder wider uptake (Jha et al. 2022). Users and providers trust that the platform is secure and won't leak their personal and financial information to cyber threats. Hurdles to metaverse adoption in the Indian tourism sector are identified, and ways to overcome these through strategic planning, education, and policy changes are prescribed.

The metaverse is multifaceted in its trust: trust in the technology providers, trust in the content of the metaverse and trust in the security of transactions within this virtual space. Virtual tourism experiences can be misrepresented or incorrectly represented, which can cause mistrust and scepticism on the part of the users. For example, if a virtual tour says it provides an experience that is far beyond its physical reality. If this is the case, it erodes the trust in the specific service provider and the virtual tourism ecosystem (Ioannidis & Kontis, 2023). Furthermore, deep fakes or content manipulation can tip the trust aspects in their favor, quite possibly cherry-picking users and distorting cultural heritage.

However, the effects of long exposure to virtual environments on an individual's psyche are becoming appreciable. Mild symptoms such as nausea and dizziness commonly called VR sickness can occur (Chattha et al. 2024). In immersive environments, however, the biostable lines between real and virtual over time can lead to confusion and even identity dissociation. Such potential effects may be understood little by users in India, where digital literacy is varied, and it is difficult to obtain informed consent. At the same time, the social implications are huge, with the Metaverse having the ability to change significantly how people interact with each other socially on a personal (isolate people) or global (change traditional social norms) level.

As a new frontier for digital interaction, the metaverse presents many challenges in terms of inclusivity and equity. The digital divide is one primary concern. Metaverse technologies are not provided to every person who has high-speed internet, and proper hardware cannot go well (Wang et al. 2023). This applies to India in particular because here there is a huge gap between how the urban and rural people get access to digital infrastructure. The ability to represent and access this metaverse can exclude the disabled. Most virtual environments are not built with accessibility in mind, effectively shutting out people with many physical abilities.

Many HR challenges are facing the Indian tourism industry, which directly impacts its growth and operational efficiency. However, these shortages, skills gaps, and barriers to adopting advanced technologies are key among these challenges. To support an inclusive culture metaverse must be designed keeping social equity and inclusion in mind (Zallio and Clarkson, 2022).

As the Indian tourism sector is provide to significant contributor to the nation's Gross Domestic Product and employment, the sector faces a huge shortage of skilled professionals for running sustainable tourism in the country. Not only is that gap true for high-demand roles, but it's true across the board in the industry. The report by Tourism and Hospitality Skill Council, there is a huge skill gap in the entire sector and the need for training and education to make workers in the industry cope with the changing job requirements. The vast number of graduates aside, employability is still a key issue. Employability rates are relatively uniform across different tiers of colleges, with Tier-1 at 46 percent, Tier-2 at 44 percent, and Tier-3 at 43 percent, pointing to a pronounced skills gap that permeates many colleges, India Brief reported (timesofindia.indiatimes.com, 2024) . It means fitting to the new consumer preferences, such as participating in adventure and eco-tourism, which demand the absence of expertise and skills in the workforce.

7. FRAMEWORK FOR LEVERAGING THE METAVERSE IN INDIAN TOURISM HR

There exist revolutionary opportunities in the Indian tourism sector for transforming human resources (HR) practices in the Metaverse. Through the use of Metaverse tools, this sector can improve training, recruitment, and worker engagement, which are essential dimensions in the resolution of issues and offering of service today. Metaverse offers a huge potential to develop digital leadership in organizations to support digital transformation and leverage the integrated tools such as artificial intelligence, mixed realities and blockchain technology.

Training and development is one of the most profound advantages of the metaverse. This immersive virtual environment is used to enable employees to engage in dynamic and realistic simulations simulating real-world scenarios. For example, they can use the service to practice customer service, go through complicated customer questions, and solve problems efficiently in a managed environment. Additionally, the metaverse provides chances for the employees of the tourism industry to handle emergencies like natural disasters or medical emergencies, which lets employees of the tourism industry build important response skills without the true world risks involved in such situations (Johri et al. 2024).

These new training methods rely on experiential learning, so participants are more active learners rather than passive. Staying lost in the virtual world also allows employees to practice in a safe setting and gain confidence and competence if they are being challenged in a real-world setting. Moreover, this solution provides a more inclusive solution to the different types of learners. In the end, the Metaverse digitizes training for employees, delivering an immersive experience that gives employees practical skill sets to be successful at their jobs.

7.1 Actionable Recommendations

Metaverse has the capability to improve digital dexterity and develop digital leadership skills through immersive platforms for leadership development. It can provide new tools to set performance standards, measure performance and reward employees. Virtual environments, when integrated into the metaverse, can act as a means of transformation in performance management. Through these immersive settings, HR managers can provide dynamic, real-time feedback and detailed performance tracking based on real-time tracking of employee tasks. Simulations that replicate real-world challenges can enable organizations to provide employees with a more engaging and realistic experience. Metaverse contributes to social equity and diversity through new social interactions heuristics, creating a sense of equity among different communities and contributing to psychological safety.

Based on the above, Table 1, outlines a set of actionable strategies that can be implemented for effective utilization of metaverse to develop digital leadership skills, improve employee performance and create an inclusive workplace

Table 1. Actionable recommendations for stakeholders

Objective	Outcome	Strategy
Digital leadership	leadership Capabilities of Agility, Adaptability and Strategic Foresight	Embed immersive platforms through VR-based training that simulate crisis scenarios, change management, and strategic decision-making.
	Problem Solving and emotional intelligence and digital dexterity	Adopt gamification in leadership development
Performance Management	Enhanced overall motivation and key performance indicators	Interactive and immersive learning and skill acquisition; Provide 360° feedback in virtual environments with avatars; Tracking of KPIs
	Skill Development and Career Management	VR simulation for employee training in safe and risk - free environments, Virtual emergency response drills; AI-powered virtual assistants for career path planning
Inclusive Workforce	Inclusive participation through Cross Cultural Communication skills	Virtual training; Language learning and cultural training
	Cohesive team spirit and inclusivity	Metaverse-based collaboration zones; cross-functional avatar-based interaction (ABI); reduce physical accessibility barriers and cultural biases

7.2 Contribution to Human Capital Management

The study draws attention on how organisations and employees can use the power of the metaverse for developing human capital. The metaverse is increasingly influencing human capital management by transforming traditional HR practices into more dynamic, immersive, and efficient processes. The metaverse provides immersive training environments that can simulate real-world scenarios, allowing employees to practice skills in a risk-free setting. It can is particularly beneficial for complex or challenging environments like tourism where it may not be possible to employees to be physically present (Hajjami & Park, 2023). Metaverse facilitate remote work and virtual collaboration, enabling teams to work together seamlessly regardless of geographical location. The metaverse introduces new key performance indicators (KPIs) tailored to virtual work environments, allowing HR professionals to better assess and manage employee performance. These metrics focus on avatar performance and other digital interactions, providing a more comprehensive view of employee contributions (Tsappi & Papageorgiou, 2023). The integration of metaverse technologies into HRM requires organizations to adapt their strategies and processes to accommodate digital transformation.

8. CONCLUSION

The Indian tourism sector has the enormous transformative potential of the Metaverse through its Human Resource Development (HRD), training, recruitment, and enhancement of employee engagement. The Metaverse enhances training environments to give learners and professionals better environments to develop skills faster and retain them better as they immerse themselves in simulations that realistically depict real life. Virtual reality innovations in recruitment and onboarding make it possible for potential employees to get a more in-depth idea of what it is like to work for the company, increasing the fit and reducing early turnover.

Recent literature widely suggests that hybrid work models significantly enhance employee productivity. However, while certain tasks may be well-suited to the metaverse, not all types of work can be effectively conducted in this virtual environment. Successfully implementing the metaverse requires organizations to adopt digital leadership, foster innovation, introduce policy adjustments, and incorporate gamification into employee development. the full realization of the metaverse faces technological challenges and raises concerns about privacy, trust, and psychological impacts. Despite these challenges, the metaverse has the potential to transform various aspects of work, including marketing, education, and healthcare. As organizations explore metaverse adoption, they must consider its implications for digital leadership, work ethics, and employee management in this evolving virtual landscape (Dwivedi et al., 2022; Lim et al., 2023; Rozak et al., 2023).

The metaverse will be applied to these goals of smoothing operations, lowering expenses, and increasing employee engagement and retention by offering exceptional solutions and technologies to enhance the office. The Indian tourism industry can gain significant innovation, competitive advantage, and resiliency to stay relevant on a global platform by adopting the metaverse.

Real-time feedback and deep analytics in a virtual scenario have value to performance management by enabling precise skill assessment and developmental feedback. The Metaverse also contributes to employee engagement, enabling people in the same team, especially when remote, to collaborate and grow bonds to develop a well-knit organizational culture. According to these insights, the application of Metaverse technologies would greatly reduce the procedures employed in HR practices, increase service quality, and improve the global competitiveness of tourism services.

However, the adoption of metaverse technologies in HRD would provide transformational outcomes in the Indian tourism sector. The metaverse also makes training methodologies more immersive virtual environments which advances to more interactive and interesting training. Because of this, it is crucial to effectively deal with the real skills gap in the industry by giving employees engaging and dynamic required competencies in a timely manner. In addition, tools in the Metaverse facilitate recruitment and onboarding of staff, providing new employees with a virtual rather than real experience of the organizational culture and the type of work required, which can thereby potentially lower turnover and increase job satisfaction.

Virtual environments are equally beneficial to performance management since they allow real-time employee performance monitoring and evaluation in order to provide real-time personalized feedback and more efficient improvement tracking. Also, the Metaverse can increase employee engagement, which becomes increasingly important among remote or dispersed teams, through community and collaboration through virtual interactions. All the innovations taken together can improve service quality and operational efficiency and reinforce the competitive position of Indian tourism on a global scale.

Opportunities for Further Research

There are many opportunities for further research in integrating the metaverse into HR practices in Indian tourism, primarily because of the scarcity of literature on the usage of AR/VR for enhancing HR practices in tourism. There is a need to assess the impact of such metaverse–based training interventions on employee performance and retention. The skill development could be studied over a period of time to determine how virtual training shapes it in comparison to a traditional approach to training. The other viable research topology is the ROI of Metaverse technology that include cost savings and productivity gains versus the total cost of the investment. Further, a study of the degree to which Metaverse tools are culturally adaptive can assist in identifying ways in which regions in India react to and value Web-based spaces and could inform more granularized and effective implementations.

Also, research on data privacy and data security in the metaverse might be conducted with recommendations on how to keep sensitive information safe in the virtual world. Finally, there are also possibilities of studies of virtual environments' psychological impacts on people who are in the tourism field and have been exposed for a long time to virtual environments because they might provide guidelines for developing healthier digital working environments. Such research areas will enable the stakeholders to better understand the practical issues, challenges or barriers, and benefits associated with the adoption of Metaverse technologies in the tourism sector and its approach to managing human capital.

REFERENCES

Akbar, S., Pranajaya, S. A., Nurkadarwati, N., Hoesny, R., & Mutmainnah, I. (2024). Leadership Dynamics in The Era of Educational Transformation: Integrating The Concept of Adaptable Leadership in Sustainable Educational Administration. *International Journal of Teaching and Learning*, *2*(1), 223–235.

Alshammari, A. F. (2023). Digital transformation, environmental protection, and technology competence: An integrated analysis of sustainability preferences. *Amazonia Investiga*, *12*(72), 145–158. DOI: 10.34069/AI/2023.72.12.13

Beil, B., Freyermuth, G. S., Hamm, I., & Ossa, V. (2025). *Gaming the Metaverse*. Transcript Verlag.

Blueweaveconsulting.com. (2022). India Augmented Reality And Virtual Reality Market. Retrieved on: 24th March 2025, from: https://www.blueweaveconsulting.com/report/india-augmented-reality-and-virtual-reality-market

Bwhotelier.com. (2024). Treehouse Hotels launches 'Aura' VR Wellness experience at Goa property. Retrieved on: 24th March 2025, from: https://bwhotelier.com/article/treehouse-hotels-launches-%E2%80%98aura%E2%80%99-vr-wellness-experience-at-goa-property-536321

Chattha, U. A., Janjua, U. I., Anwar, F., Madni, T. M., Cheema, M. F., & Janjua, S. I. (2020). Motion sickness in virtual reality: An empirical evaluation. *IEEE Access : Practical Innovations, Open Solutions*, *8*, 130486–130499. Retrieved March 24th, 2025, from https://ieeexplore.ieee.org/iel7/6287639/6514899/09133071.pdf. DOI: 10.1109/ACCESS.2020.3007076

Dargan, S., Bansal, S., Kumar, M., Mittal, A., & Kumar, K. (2023). Augmented reality: A comprehensive review. *Archives of Computational Methods in Engineering*, *30*(2), 1057–1080. DOI: 10.1007/s11831-022-09831-7

Deterding, S., Sicart, M., & Nacke, L. o'hara, K., & Dixon, D. (2011). Gamification. Using game-design elements in non-gaming contexts. In *CHI'11 extended abstracts on human factors in computing systems* (pp. 2425-2428).

Dwivedi, Y. K., Hughes, L., Baabdullah, A. M., Ribeiro-Navarrete, S., Giannakis, M., Al-Debei, M. M., Dennehy, D., Metri, B., Buhalis, D., Cheung, C. M. K., Conboy, K., Doyle, R., Dubey, R., Dutot, V., Felix, R., Goyal, D. P., Gustafsson, A., Hinsch, C., Jebabli, I., & Wamba, S. F. (2022). Metaverse beyond the hype: Multidisciplinary perspectives on emerging challenges, opportunities, and agenda for research, practice and policy. *International Journal of Information Management*, *66*, 102542. DOI: 10.1016/j.ijinfomgt.2022.102542

El Emary, I. M. (2024). Assessing the adoption of Metaverse platforms: A structural equation modeling approach with mediating effects of switching costs. *International Journal Research on Metaverse, 1*(3), 236–263. DOI: 10.47738/ijrm.v1i3.14

Ersoy, A. (2024). Entrepreneurship in the Era of Metaverse: Understanding Critical Success Factors from the Perspective of Hospitality Industry Professionals. *Gümüşhane Üniversitesi Sosyal Bilimler Dergisi, 15*(2), 544–555.

Fadhel, M. A., Duhaim, A. M., Albahri, A. S., Al-Qaysi, Z. T., Aktham, M. A., Chyad, M. A., Abd-Alaziz, W., Albahri, O. S., Alamoodi, A. H., Alzubaidi, L., Gupta, A., & Gu, Y. (2024). Navigating the metaverse: Unraveling the impact of artificial intelligence—a comprehensive review and gap analysis. *Artificial Intelligence Review, 57*(10), 264. DOI: 10.1007/s10462-024-10881-5

Gadekallu, T. R., Huynh-The, T., Wang, W., Yenduri, G., Ranaweera, P., Pham, Q. V., . . . Liyanage, M. (2022). Blockchain for the metaverse: A review. *Arxiv preprint arxiv:2203.09738.*

Hajjami, O., & Park, S. (2023). Using the metaverse in training: Lessons from real cases. *European Journal of Training and Development*. Advance online publication. DOI: 10.1108/EJTD-12-2022-0144

Hanafizadeh, P., & Ravasan, A. Z. (2011). A mckinsey 7S Model-Based Framework for ERP Readiness Assessment. *International Journal of Enterprise Information Systems, 7*(4), 23–63. DOI: 10.4018/jeis.2011100103

Hao, F., Back, K. J., & Chon, K. K. S. K. S. (2025). Age-inclusive hospitality and tourism: Navigating the metaverse travel with avatar. *International Journal of Contemporary Hospitality Management, 37*(2), 482–501. DOI: 10.1108/IJCHM-03-2024-0323

Ioannidis, S., & Kontis, A. P. (2023). Metaverse for tourists and tourism destinations. *Information Technology & Tourism, 25*(4), 483–506. DOI: 10.1007/s40558-023-00271-y

Jagatheesaperumal, S. K., Ahmad, K., Al-Fuqaha, A., & Qadir, J. (2024). Advancing education through extended reality and internet of everything enabled metaverses: Applications, challenges, and open issues. *IEEE Transactions on Learning Technologies, 17*, 1120–1139. DOI: 10.1109/TLT.2024.3358859

Jha, D. N., Lenton, G., Asker, J., Blundell, D., & Wallom, D. (2022). Trusted platform module-based privacy in the public cloud: Challenges and future perspective. *IT Professional, 24*(3), 81–87. DOI: 10.1109/MITP.2022.3147968

Johri, A., Sayal, A., Chaithra, N., Jha, J., Aggarwal, N., Pawar, D., & Gupta, A. (2024). Crafting the techno-functional blocks for Metaverse-A review and research agenda. *International Journal of Information Management Data Insights*, *4*(1), 100213. DOI: 10.1016/j.jjimei.2024.100213

. Karadayı, Z., Özdem, M., Karaceylan, İ. B., & Duman, Z. Y. (2024). *Establishing the Future of Work and Collaboration through Institutional Metaverse*. DOI: 10.1109/IWCMC61514.2024.10592490

Kaur, S., Goel, D., Yadav, B., & Devi, S. (2024). The metaverse as India's next-generation internet : Opportunities and challenges. *Journal of Information and Optimization Sciences*, *45*(6), 1607–1621. DOI: 10.47974/JIOS-1637

Kedia, M., Sekhani, R., & Katiyar, T. (2020). *The Role of Standards in Diffusion of Emerging Technologies Internet of Things (iot)* (No. 20-r-04). Indian Council for Research on International Economic Relations (ICRIER), New Delhi, India.

Kim, D. Y., Lee, H. K., & Chung, K. (2023). Avatar-mediated experience in the metaverse: The impact of avatar realism on user-avatar relationship. *Journal of Retailing and Consumer Services*, *73*, 103382. DOI: 10.1016/j.jretconser.2023.103382

Kinseng, R. A., Kartikasari, A., Aini, N., Gandi, R., & Dean, D. (2022). COVID-19 and the emergence of virtual tourism in Indonesia: A sociological perspective. *Cogent Social Sciences*, *8*(1), 2026557. DOI: 10.1080/23311886.2022.2026557

Latta, A., & Sarkar, D. (2021). Imperative role of Digitalization in the Indian economy During COVID-19. *People*, *2*(3), 164–178. DOI: 10.48175/IJARSCT-V2-I3-329

. Li, Q., Liu, Q., Jiang, M., & Wang, R. (2024). Virtual reality as a bridge: enhancing intercultural learning and communication skills among international students. *International Communication of Chinese Culture*, 1-27.

Lim, D. H., Lee, J. Y., & Park, S. (2023). The Metaverse in the Workplace: Possibilities and Implications for Human Resource Development. *Human Resource Development Review*. Advance online publication. DOI: 10.1177/15344843231217174

. Lin, X. (2024). A metaverse of Chinese traditional folk villages and houses with great aesthetic pleasure: A virtual world dedicated to the enthusiasts of life with art, culture, history and architectures.

Linkedin.com, 2023. Deepavali in the Metaverse: A New Dimension of Celebration.

Marabelli, M., & Lirio, P. (2024). AI and the metaverse in the workplace: DEI opportunities and challenges. *Personnel Review*. Advance online publication. DOI: 10.1108/PR-04-2023-0300

Medium.com, (2024). Virtual Reality and AI in Hotel Marketing: A Heavenly Synergy?

Mihardjo, L., Sasmoko, S., Alamsjah, F., & Elidjen, E. (2019). Digital leadership role in developing business model innovation and customer experience orientation in industry 4.0. *Management Science Letters*, *9*(11), 1749–1762. DOI: 10.5267/j.msl.2019.6.015

Mohanty, S., & Christopher, B. P. (2024). The Role of Gamification Research in Human Resource Management: A PRISMA Analysis and Future Research Direction. *SAGE Open*, *14*(2), 21582440241243154. DOI: 10.1177/21582440241243154

. Murugkar, K., Kashyap, A., & Mullick, A. (2020). Examining the Experience, Barriers and Enabling Measures for Visually Impaired Visitors in Heritage Sites—A Study in the Indian Context to Enhance Accessibility and Inclusion. *Disability Studies in India: Interdisciplinary Perspectives*, 295-318.

Mystakidis, S. (2022). Metaverse. *Encyclopedia*, *2*(1), 486–497. DOI: 10.3390/encyclopedia2010031

Ndtv.com, (2024). Kashi Vishwanath Temple In UP Introduces Virtual Reality Darshan.

Parker, C., Yoo, S., Fredericks, J., Tran, T. T. M., Williamson, J. R., Lee, Y., & Woo, W. (2024). Building a metaverse for all: Opportunities and challenges for future inclusive and accessible virtual environments. In *Extended Abstracts of the CHI Conference on Human Factors in Computing Systems* (pp. 1-5).

Parker, C., Yoo, S., Lee, Y., Fredericks, J., Dey, A., Cho, Y., & Billinghurst, M. (2023). Towards an inclusive and accessible metaverse. In *Extended Abstracts of the 2023 CHI Conference on Human Factors in Computing Systems* (pp. 1-5). DOI: 10.1145/3544549.3573811

Prayag, G., Gannon, M. J., Muskat, B., & Taheri, B. (2020). A serious leisure perspective of culinary tourism co-creation: The influence of prior knowledge, physical environment and service quality. *International Journal of Contemporary Hospitality Management*, *32*(7), 2453–2472. DOI: 10.1108/IJCHM-10-2019-0897

Radanliev, P. (2024). The rise and fall of cryptocurrencies: Defining the economic and social values of blockchain technologies, assessing the opportunities, and defining the financial and cybersecurity risks of the Metaverse. *Financial Innovation*, *10*(1), 1. DOI: 10.1186/s40854-023-00537-8

Radanliev, P., De Roure, D., Novitzky, P., & Sluganovic, I. (2023). *Accessibility and Inclusiveness of New Information and Communication Technologies for Disabled Users and Content Creators in the Metaverse*. /arxiv.2308.01925DOI: <ALIGNMENT.qj></ALIGNMENT>10.48550

Raji, M. A., Olodo, H. B., Oke, T. T., Addy, W. A., Ofodile, O. C., & Oyewole, A. T. (2024). Business strategies in virtual reality: A review of market opportunities and consumer experience. *International Journal of Management & Entrepreneurship Research*, *6*(3), 722–736. DOI: 10.51594/ijmer.v6i3.883

. Rane, N., Choudhary, S., & Rane, J. (2023). Enhanced product design and development using Artificial Intelligence (AI), Virtual Reality (VR), Augmented Reality (AR), 4D/5D/6D Printing, Internet of Things (iot), and blockchain: A review. *Virtual Reality (VR), Augmented Reality (AR) D, 4*.

Rathi, S., & Prabhash, K. (2024). *Role of Human Resource (HR) Analytics and Metaverse in Employee Engagement and Turnover Intention*. IGI Global., DOI: 10.4018/979-8-3693-5868-9.ch006

Rozak, H. A., & Fachrunnisa, O., Sugiharti, Taswan, & Fitriati, I. R. (2023, August). Metaverse and Modification Needs of Human Resources Management Practices and Policies: An Overview. In International Conference on Intelligent Networking and Collaborative Systems (pp. 285-294). Cham: Springer Nature Switzerland.

Saeed, A., Ali, A., & Ashfaq, S. (2024). Employees' training experience in a metaverse environment? Feedback analysis using structural topic modeling. *Technological Forecasting and Social Change*, *208*, 123636. DOI: 10.1016/j.techfore.2024.123636

. Salama, A. F. (2024). The Impact of AI Applications (Virtual Reality and Augmented Reality) in the Hospitality Industry: Opportunities and Challenges. *Journal of Association of Arab Universities for Tourism and Hospitality*.

Saleem, A. N., Noori, N. M., & Ozdamli, F. (2022). Gamification applications in E-learning: A literature review. *Technology. Knowledge and Learning*, *27*(1), 139–159. DOI: 10.1007/s10758-020-09487-x

Samaddar, K., & Mondal, S. (2024). AR and VR-based travel: A responsible practice towards sustainable tourism. *International Journal of Tourism Cities*, *10*(1), 105–128. DOI: 10.1108/IJTC-05-2022-0135

. Sandu, M. (2023). Metaverse Sustainability Through Integrated Digital Leadership and Resilient Entrepreneurship. *Geopolitical perspectives and technological challenges for sustainable growth in the 21st century*, 462-473.

Timesofindia.indiatimes.com. (2024). Degree vs. Skill: Why is India producing graduates with low. Retrieved on: 24th March 2025, from: https://timesofindia.indiatimes.com/articleshow/114615522.cms?Utm_source=contentofinterest&utm_medium=text&utm_campaign=cppst

Tourism.gov.in. (2024). Ministry of Tourism launches Incredible India Content Hub and Digital Portal. Retrieved on: Retrieved on: 24th March 2025, from: https://tourism.gov.in/sites/default/files/2024-09/PIB2059426.pdf

. Tsappi, E., & Papageorgiou, G. Z. (2023). *Towards Deriving Organizational Key Performance Indicators in a Metaverse Workplace: A Systematic Literature Review*. DOI: 10.1145/3594806.3594835

Turyadi, I., Zulkifli, Z., Tawil, M. R., Ali, H., & Sadikin, A. (2023). The role of digital leadership in organizations to improve employee performance and business success. *Jurnal Ekonomi*, *12*(02), 1671–1677.

Wang, H., Ning, H., Lin, Y., Wang, W., Dhelim, S., Farha, F., Ding, J., & Daneshmand, M. (2023). A survey on the metaverse: The state-of-the-art, technologies, applications, and challenges. *IEEE Internet of Things Journal*, *10*(16), 14671–14688. Retrieved December 24th, 2024, from https://arxiv.org/pdf/2111.09673. DOI: 10.1109/JIOT.2023.3278329

Yoon, H., Lee, Y., & Shin, C. (2022). Avatar-based metaverse interactions: A taxonomy, scenarios and enabling technologies. *Journal of Multimedia Information System*, *9*(4), 293–298. DOI: 10.33851/JMIS.2022.9.4.293

. Zallio, M., & Clarkson, P. (2022). Inclusive Metaverse. How businesses can maximize opportunities to deliver an accessible, inclusive, safe Metaverse that guarantees equity and diversity.

Zambiasi, L. P., Rabelo, R. J., Zambiasi, S. P., & Romero, D. (2023). Metaverse-Based softbot tutors for inclusive industrial workplaces: Supporting impaired operators 5.0. In *IFIP International Conference on Advances in Production Management Systems* (pp. 662-677). Cham: Springer Nature Switzerland. DOI: 10.1007/978-3-031-43662-8_47

APPENDIX

Figures

Figure 1. India augmented reality and virtual reality market

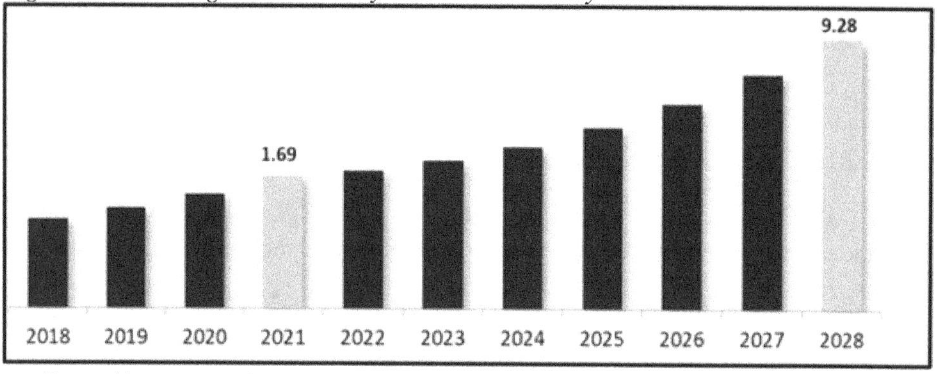

(Source: blueweaveconsulting.com, 2022)

Figure 2. Functioning of the metaverse

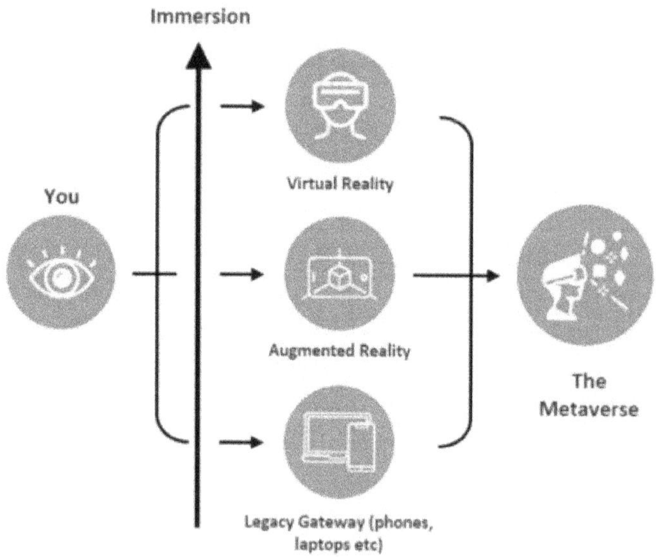

Adapted from Aranca website, https://www.aranca.com/knowledge-library/articles/investmentresearch/metaverse-the-future-of-internet, accessed April 01, 2025."

Figure 3. "A blockchain consists of blocks that are linked together using their unique hash codes."

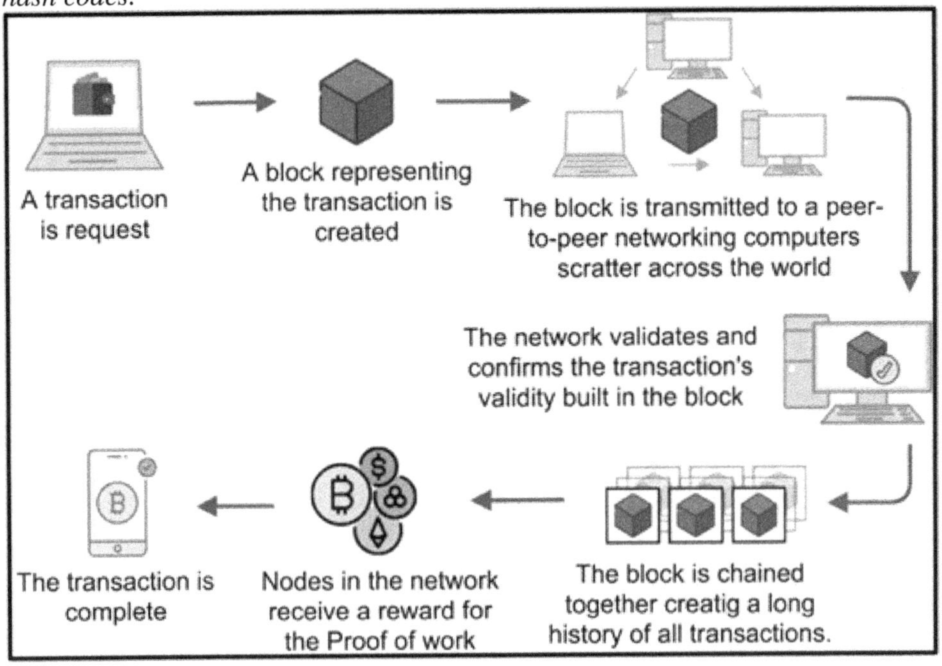

(Source: Gadekallu et al. 2022)

Figure 4. Concept of virtual tours

(Source: Kinseng et al. 2022)

Figure 5. "Concept of metaverse in hospitality training"

(Source: Salama, 2024)

Figure 6. "Advantages of metaverse in training"

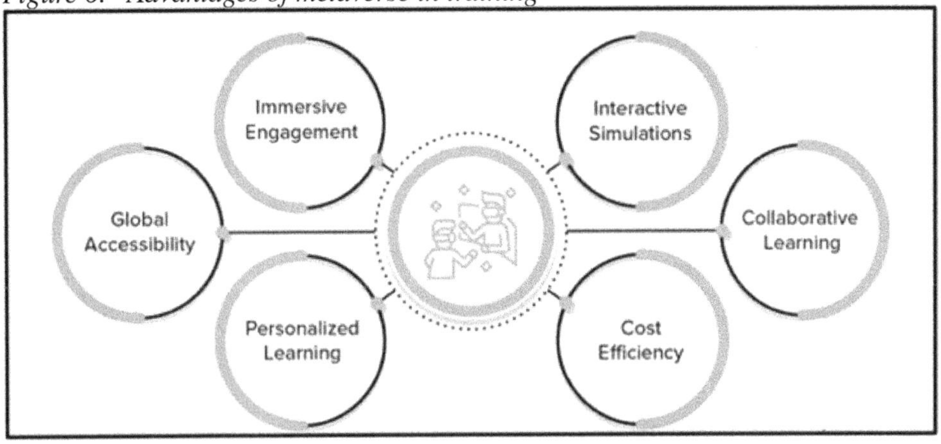

(Source: Saeed et al. 2024)

Chapter 12
Endomarketing and Internal Marketing Management Tourism Contexts:
Preliminary Insights

Daniela Marques Cardoso
Polytechnic University of Cávado and Ave, Portugal

Bruno Barbosa Sousa
https://orcid.org/0000-0002-8588-2422
Polytechnic University of Cávado and Ave (IPCA), Portugal & Applied Management Research Unit (UNIAG), Portugal & Centro de Investigação, Desenvolvimento e Inovação em Turismo (CiTUR), Portugal

ABSTRACT

The concept of Human Resources Management constitutes the most effective and productive approach to managing these precious assets. The objective of the present study, based on an extensive literature review, is to analyze how internal marketing is applied in companies in the tourism sector, more specifically in the Quadrilátero do Minho (Portugal). The conclusions allow us to assess the long road that remains to be covered regarding the effective implementation of human resources management and talent management practices in this sector. Internal marketing is not always seen as a strategic business factor in the medium and long-term planning process.

DOI: 10.4018/979-8-3373-0071-9.ch012

INTRODUCTION

Tourism, in addition to being an economic phenomenon, is a set of social and human manifestations related to needs and motivations. Furthermore, it depends above all on the human and professional quality of Human Resources (HR) who, throughout the cycle of the tourism product, are responsible for providing the services that comprise it (Salgado, 2016). According to the same author, the behavior of tourism professionals is a result of their social and cultural level, a function of the general or basic education received, the specific education, the training they have received and, also, the working conditions. As a basis for research, this report aims to study the following theme - "Endomarketing and Management in Tourist Contexts: Study Applied to the Minho Quadrangle. Assuming that the tourism industry, like other service industries, is mainly based on intensive labor in its various sectors, the management of companies in the tourism sector faces the problem of ensuring superior performance by their HR (Nankervis, 1995). This is a very challenging sector where atypical working hours and a high rate of staff turnover are traditionally prevalent (Costa, 2005). The lack of knowledge and implementation of a department or employee dedicated to HRM often results in poor management of employees, who end up not feeling fulfilled or valued in their workplace. This factor is one of the consequences that causes the exponential increase in the lack of employees interested in working in the area (Salgado, 2016). This staff turnover represents a cost for organizations, regardless of their size, in terms of time management, which has to be spent on recruitment and selection, loss of interest in training and the consequent reduction in the level of service that can be offered to customers (Wood, 1996). Internal marketing is therefore an essential differentiation, since in order to retain the best talents in a work team and ensure that the business gets the best out of them, management needs to understand the complexity of human behavior and specialize in each of the functions that make up the HRM process, from recruitment to selection, through to training and motivation (Kusluvan, 2010).

Motivational theories are particularly important for managers in the tourism industry, which traditionally employs a large number of unskilled workers, with low salaries, but who are of paramount importance due to their interaction with the customer (Martins, 2018). In order to carry out the proposed work, a systematic work plan was drawn up. The first part provides a comprehensive approach to the concept of Internal Marketing, which is essential for the continuation of this study. The following section presents a literature review based on specialized research, namely scientific articles and journals. Specifically, the labor market in the sector is characterized, namely, the specificities of the sector, the relevance of human capital in tourism, the consequences of staff turnover and, finally, the importance of talent management. The remaining chapters refer to the empirical study carried out in this chapter. First, the research methodology is presented. This is followed by an analysis of the results obtained through four interviews with representatives of the four tourism units under study in the Quadrilátero do Minho. The results obtained are then discussed and the conclusions are presented.

THEORETICAL BACKGROUND

ENDOMARKETING IN AN ORGANIZATIONAL CONTEXT

In the 21st century there have been great advances and changes in the area of technology and information that have been reflected above all in organizations, the what influenced the opinion of the managers what no prioritized just machines, but to the people, which are the main asset of an organization because productivity and obtaining results depend on it (Puccio, et al., 2020). The remote work model was prioritized above all, and it became even more important that communication with employees be constant and as close as possible, and the organization must provide channels and resources for digital communication and collaboration (Ecklebe & Sarah, 2021).

For this dynamic to be effective, it is necessary to correctly manage the difficulties that remote work brings to employees within organizations. When formal internal communication is inefficient, rumors – known as informal communication and which can cause mental and emotional discomfort in employees – appear as the best source of information about what is happening in the company, since the organization does not perform this role adequately (Charoensukmongkol & Puyod, 2021). In this sense, it is possible to note the intrinsic relationship between internal communication and employee satisfaction with communication. Thus, an effective communication plan, which presents information clearly, directly and consistently, encourages employees to become more intensely and genuinely involved with work and the company. However, for this relationship between internal communication and employee satisfaction to work, it is necessary to have trust as a basis, hence the importance of transparency on the part of the organization, which, in a hybrid work model, with a strong influence of remote work and physical distancing, becomes an even greater point of attention in the company-employee relationship. The organization's vision and positioning must be clear, precise and properly communicated to employees in order to generate trust and increase the company's credibility in relation to professionals, especially in times when face-to-face contact and sensory appeals are limited, making employee engagement even more difficult (Santos, 2023). The efficiency of internal communication is an important indicator of organizational success. The values generated by good communication aimed at employees are generally future-oriented, with the potential to generate growth opportunities for the corporation. As companies have come to recognize the importance of employees who are strongly involved in the business – reflected in results derived from good performance, innovation and productivity –, employee recruitment has emerged as an essential concept that affects organizational effectiveness and competitiveness. In order to effectively encourage employee recruitment, it is necessary for them to be truly involved and motivated by the company's purpose. In addition to financial rewards – which carry the risk of creating weak, vulnerable and ineffective bonds – employees need to feel valued in their professional and personal lives, see meaning in what they do, be fulfilled by their contributions and feel that they are part of the organization's identity and achievements. In this way, treating employees as customers, paying attention to their needs, communicating appropriately and offering support so that their career path is the best possible, tends to make people more satisfied and emotionally involved in their roles and in the company they work for (Brum & Medeiros, 2005). Thus, internal marketing aims to seek out and understand the desires of employees in their role in the company, strengthen the relationship with them and develop actions to add value to their organizational experience (*employee experience*), through an experience with which employees identify and feel welcomed, included and integrated by the company (Brum A. d., 2007).

Internal marketing aims to bring the organization and employees closer together, so that they feel encouraged to become more deeply involved with the company's goals and purpose, through the creation of systems and benefits that help meet the needs of employees, thus stimulating a healthy, productive and long-term relationship between employees and the company (Brum & Medeiros, 2005). Furthermore, it favors an exchange relationship between internal customers and the company, in which internal marketing actions should be seen as an investment that drives the generation of new revenue, encouraging employees to propose new ideas, as well as improving their performance and productivity (Brum A. d., 2007). Internal marketing is a process whose focus is to tune and synchronize, to implement and operationalize the marketing structure of the company or organization that aims to act on the market. Its objective is to facilitate and carry out exchanges, building relationships with the internal public, sharing the goals of the company or organization. This perspective of value creation, focuses on the company-employee exchange, and how each of these parties can affect or be affected for the execution of the your own purposes. Identify the importance and role of employees requires that managers consider them as representatives of the first the organization's market, its functions represent internal products that must be developed according to with your needs (Aberje, 2022).

Therefore, an organization that is clear about this scenario and adopts internal marketing strategies appropriately tends to have more committed and involved employees, contributing to the creation of a deep feeling of connection between the employee and the company. This type of procedure will help stimulate the company's growth, retain talent, reduce turnover and allow it to benefit from the marketing that a satisfactory employee experience can provide to the organization.

Considering the work context that has been imposed since the Covid-19 pandemic, prioritizing hybrid work – which has gained preference among most professionals in recent years – and increasing the physical distance between people and companies, internal communication presents itself as a key mechanism to foster the employee-organization relationship, becoming an important point of connection between both (Einwiller & Stranzl, 2021). In the organizational environment, internal communication arose from the need for companies to communicate with their employees, especially in a context in which the absence of a single, coherent and consistent message poses the risk of an image crisis, which can even have a direct impact on the results of organizations, thus demonstrating that the internal public is one of the most important and highly credible actors in the corporate communication process (Cappellano, 2010). Misinformed, dissatisfied and unmotivated employees have the potential to cause serious damage to the reputation and performance of companies because they are more capable of expressing authentically, more than any other *stakeholder, the negative aspects of an institution's organizational culture* . Thus, internal communication has become a strategic area that goes far beyond informing employees about organizational events and decisions (Bueno, 2005). Internal marketing should be interpreted as a strategic management philosophy for the development and recognition of internal processes, highlighting that its main focus is knowing how to gain and retain consumer awareness in and of the employee (Grönroos, 1990). The concept of internal marketing was patented by Bekin in 1991 and is synonymous with internal marketing. On the other hand, this position is contested by Inkotte who considers that the positioning of the customer differentiates the terms: in internal marketing, the customer is outside the organization; while in internal marketing the target audience is inside the organization (Silva, 2012). This differentiation of concepts is not consensual, thus culminating in one of the obstacles to research in this area. However, starting from the observation that "internal marketing" does not appear in the Anglo-Saxon bibliography – which is why the keyword "internal marketing" was used to find and help find an approach to internal marketing.

RELEVANCE OF HUMAN CAPITAL IN TOURISM

The tourism industry depends on a set of service activities, which determine a complex phenomenon, which includes cultural, economic, political, social and technological variables. Because it is a sector that is constantly changing and altering, the tourism sector is forced to follow market trends, including a vast set of knowledge that, in this way, creates a differentiation in the training of professionals at two levels (Salgado & Lemos, A importância da Gestão Turística no Ensino Superior em Portugal, 2016): top management – direction and/or administration and the person responsible for the development and implementation of policies and action plans for each area/department. Thus, the qualification and training of human resources is considered an added value for all areas of study. It is therefore important that those responsible for the sectors work accordingly so that it is possible to invest regularly in the qualifications necessary for the activity in question. However, and in the segment of this analysis, the tourism sector has been showing a deficit, caused by the reduction in the labor market, thus causing a shortage in the workforce and specific qualifications (Salgado & Lemos, A importância da Gestão Turística no Ensino Superior em Portugal, 2016). According to Martins (2018), in order to increase the quality of service, it is necessary to develop human resource management practices, thus enabling the recruitment and selection of competent professionals who are prepared to achieve the organization's objectives (Martins, Áreas que geram mais emprego têm falta de trabalhadores qualificados, 2018). In our country, Portugal, there is a competent public body called "Turismo de Portugal", whose main objective is to encourage and develop a policy for training human resources in tourism and the technical-pedagogical research associated with it (Portugal, 2017). This entity coordinates, implements and recognizes courses and professional training actions in the tourism sector, thus ensuring that students acquire the professional skills necessary to practice the profession they will perform in the future. Therefore, Turismo de Portugal invests in training young people and professionals in the sector, through its extensive network of knowledge and hotel and tourism schools, present throughout the country. Given all the dilemmas facing the tourism sector, Turismo de Portugal (2017) decided to draft a strategy entitled "Tourism Strategy 2027", which includes the five challenges for the next ten years, encouraged by an online public survey. According to the responses, the five challenges were:

- Combating seasonality;
- Enhancement of Heritage and Culture;
- Deconcentration of demand;
- Qualification and appreciation of human resources;
- Stimulating innovation and entrepreneurship.

Considering that the tourism sector is driven by people and their services, it is challenging to obtain an innovative and personalized service. However, investing in qualified labor is crucial for the sector, with the main objective of human evolution (Portugal, 2017). With the data acquired by this research, we observe the fragility demonstrated in the sector, due to the low level of qualification and income of tourism professionals, assuming direct and indirect disadvantages for the same. (Portugal, 2017). In this sense, skills are sought, derived from technical and professional experiences, that is, experiences obtained through the exercise of work.

The concept of skills has been increasingly referenced due to its importance in human resources management, as well as its role in the use of tools to prepare human capital for a competitive market (Cascão, 2014). Some skills do not require changes, while others require constant updates to keep up with the progress of the sector and promote organizational strategies. To support technical skills, transversal skills are added to these, which are skills not related to training in a specific area of study. Transversal skills are characterized by personality traits, objectives, preferences and reasons for action; compared to technical skills, these skills are more difficult to observe and evaluate (Swiatkiewicz, 2014). The author Swiatkiewicz (2014) divides technical skills into two distinct aspects, "hard skills" and "soft skills". "Hard skills" are identified as skills of a technical nature, acquired through professional, academic or experience training. Thus, it is stated that studying technical skills is necessary for the student, but this does not guarantee that the student will become a good professional. "Soft skills" are transversal skills such as general, critical, universal, human and non-academic skills. It is also essential to align human resources management tools with those of the company itself, so that the most relevant skills can be identified at any given time (Swiatkiewicz, 2014). This recognition of skills makes it possible to assess capabilities, identifying strengths and areas for development, and in the same way, preventing and reducing potential problems in the company (Rego, et al., 2015). To assist in this process, planned and developed skills maps were created, enabling the correct implementation of recruitment, selection, professional training, performance management and rewards processes. Employees are then able to access these maps, where the company states what it values and expects from them. According to the author Ruschmann (2008), it is essential to analyze the key role of tourism human capital in the competitive strategy of the international framework, as a basic and differentiating element capable of indicating competitive advantages for the tourism sector. Tourism human capital therefore corresponds to the amount of technical knowledge and qualifications that employees in the sector have, as a result of investments in formal education and job training (Ruschmann, 2008).

METHODOLOGY AND CONTEXT

This chapter is described as an exploratory descriptive study and presents a qualitative methodology, analyzing the impact of internal marketing on tourism organizations in the Minho Quadrilateral. According to Snyder, conducting research and relating it to existing knowledge is the cornerstone of all academic research activities (Snyder, 2019). The research methods that can be applied to respond to the problems presented and the proposed objectives for this study to be more assertive and rigorous must be qualitative, since they do not focus on numerical magnitudes, that is, they do not evaluate cause-effect relationships on the topic, but rather collect, evaluate and interpret existing discourses, thus obtaining descriptive data through a possible diversity of methods. Furthermore, in a qualitative study the answers to the questions are not direct and vary from organization to organization, hence the interpretation of the results obtained is more demanding and laborious, since it gathers saturated and highly detailed reports from the participants that will later be selected, compared and analyzed. Another relevant aspect in qualitative research is the sample size, which in these cases tends to be smaller (Batista & Moreira, 2012). Therefore, this chapter uses exploratory and bibliographical research, with a qualitative approach, through conducting semi-structured interviews with managers of certain organizations in which they work and then conducting a focus group with the intervention of 1 to 2 elements from each organization to talk a little about the company's behaviors in relation to the topic discussed in the interviews (Batista & Moreira, 2012). The target of this research are entities in the tourism sector in the Northern Region of Portugal. It is a qualitative approach sample and generally consists of a small number of people, within the context of the study and who are studied in depth. Researchers using this methodology employ theoretical or intentional sampling models, rather than random ones, looking for groups, environments and individuals with whom the processes under study are most likely to occur (Denzin, 2018).

The author also highlights the five main characteristics of qualitative research. However, he believes that it is not necessary to have all of them to be recognized as qualitative. The five characteristics can be systematized as follows:

1. In qualitative research, the direct source of data is the natural environment. The researcher is the main instrument.
2. Qualitative research is descriptive. The data collected are in the form of words or images, not numbers. The data include interview transcripts, field notes, photographs, videos, personal documents, memos, and other official records. The data are analyzed in all their complexity.
3. Qualitative researchers care more about the process than the results. Situations during the research are extremely relevant to the analyses.

4. They tend to examine data inductively. As observations are grouped together, they check whether the hypotheses are confirmed or not.
5. Meaning is of paramount importance in the qualitative approach. Researchers respect the way in which subjects give meaning to their experiences and their lives, and how they perceive their social world.

In this sense, the sampling technique used in this research is theoretical sampling, which consists of identifying those who have the greatest capacity to help meet the intended objectives. Thus, the interviews are aimed at *stakeholders* of the destination and businesspeople in the sector in the destination, who constitute the study sample, as it is considered that these are the stakeholders with the greatest knowledge in the approaches of internal marketing with organizational happiness. Based on the Program Strategic of Cooperation (2008), to the Chambers Municipal of Barcelos, Braga, Guimarães and Vila Nova de Famalicão considered that the POLIS XXI Cities Policy, in its axis for Networks Urban to the Competitiveness and the Innovation, constitutes a great opportunity to work in set, in order to project this urban network created by these four municipalities at an international level (Quadrilátero Urbano, 2008). These four municipalities belonging to the district of Braga are divided into two NUT III subdivisions. Braga and Barcelos belong to Cávado, while Guimarães and Vila Nova de Famalicão are included in Ave.

Braga is the most populous municipality, followed by Guimarães, Vila Nova de Famalicão and finally Barcelos. Of these four municipalities, only Braga has shown population growth, while Vila Nova de Famalicão and Guimarães have shown a not very significant loss. Barcelos is considered the municipality that has lost the most inhabitants in relation to the others. In general, all municipalities have lower numbers of young people and higher numbers of elderly people, which represents an ageing population, which is increasingly noticeable when experiencing the streets of these cities.

The Strategic Cooperation Program (2008), the principles established by POLIS XXI, of cooperation between cities and actors urban, aims to specify some strategic objectives:

- Add to the intra-urban dimension, which was the focus of previous programs, a broad vision that includes the development of cities within the framework of both the national and international urban networks in which they are located and the region in which they are integrated, thus strengthening their connection;
- Put physical interventions at the service of a more integrative policy for transforming cities into spaces of cohesion, competitiveness and environmental quality;

Encourage new forms of governance, based on greater participation by citizens and various urban stakeholders, while also encouraging flexible mechanisms of cooperation between cities and surrounding areas (Quadrilátero Urbano, 2008). The «Minho Quadrilateral» represents approximately 10.5% of the area of NUTS II North, the municipalities that make it up total around 600 thousand inhabitants, based on the data published by INE, based on the 2021 Census, Braga has around 193,349 inhabitants, Barcelos 116,766 inhabitants; Guimarães 156,849, and finally, Vila Nova de Famalicão, with 133,574 inhabitants. According to updated INE data for the year 2020, the large volume of business in cities is notable. quadrilateral, and the your strong presence us several sectors of activity economic. Braga thus stands out from the cities under analysis, with a turnover much higher than the others (€8,211,227,360), with construction being the major driver of the economy in this city. Other economic activities that the city is involved in highlights they are the business the retail, the transport and storage, the education, among others. Although it is not a city that has industries focused on extraction activities, in electricity, gas, steam, hot and cold water and cold air, the results obtained demonstrate that it has a strong economic dynamism. Regarding the remaining cities, we can say that the cities of Guimarães and Vila Nova de Famalicão have the highest business volume, with very close values, €5,383,986,414 and €5,327,737,650, respectively. These cities have a presence in all economic activities mentioned by INE. The city of Barcelos does not have businesses in the extractive industries as previously mentioned in the city of Braga, as well as in the information and communication activities, and even having a lower turnover than this and considerable for the local economy.

FINAL CONSIDERATIONS

This chapter presents the main conclusions reached through the theoretical and empirical research developed during this study. The aim is to present the results of four companies in the tourism sector located in the Quadrilátero do Minho, in the application of internal marketing. The main contributions of the study, the limitations found and some proposals for future research are also presented. The relationship between tourism and internal marketing is undoubtedly a topic that should be addressed in scientific articles more regularly, given its importance. The main objective of this report was to verify how internal marketing was present in the daily management of the four selected companies. It was found that, despite the limitations of the study, this research brought satisfactory conclusions, considering the objectives initially proposed. Through this research it was possible to identify some relationships between tourism and knowledge of what internal marketing is. There are several questions that are established as a starting point for this study, these being related to the importance given to the Human Resources function and the most important HRM practices for the sector. Based on the literature review, we were able to perceive that the tourism companies studied in the Quadrilátero do Minho adopt some endomarketing strategies, but in an empirical way, without carrying out major planning and in-depth knowledge of the available instruments.

From the analysis carried out on the data collected, it is possible to observe that in general and in the majority, with only one case contradicting this statement, the interviewees feel satisfied with the leadership system, and it can be concluded that they feel satisfied with the management and the measures implemented by them. In order to assess the view of each of these businesses, semi-structured interviews were conducted with each representative by the HRM or the work team. The script was structured with several questions, initially focused on the strategies implemented and defined by the companies, from the recognition of good workers to rewards or productivity bonuses. Next, questions focused on communication between both parties and how this communication was carried out, and finally, it ended with two questions that reflected on how these measures had an effect and motivated employees. It is possible to conclude that attracting and retaining talent is not a difficult task for these companies, as they are able to meet the individual needs of each person and thus motivate them to remain in the organization. These companies demonstrate an interest in working on employee satisfaction and encourage the involvement of everyone who is part of the organization.

However, it is clear that this is still a topic that has not been fully developed or studied. We therefore hope that this article can contribute to the development of new research in this area. It is essential that organizations understand the importance of internal marketing and are able to implement their strategies so that competitiveness in the tourism sector is achieved through the satisfaction of internal employees. A favorable internal environment makes it possible to offer a service that meets the demands of tourism demand. An organization's success with its external audience is intrinsically linked to a satisfactory work environment. The research presented followed an entirely qualitative methodological approach, namely using semi-structured interviews. However, it would have been important to analyse the perceptions of employees through the creation of a focus group, which unfortunately was not possible due to their lack of availability. Therefore, we also felt the need to undertake a quantitative approach in the future that would allow us to collect more robust data and, consequently, improve the quality of the results obtained. Furthermore, the fact that it was not possible to interview a tourism company in Famalicão, despite several attempts to contact them, ended up being a shortcoming in this research, as there were no terms of comparison between this municipality and the others.

Internal marketing, as verified in this research, is a very important tool in the management of human capital in organizations, and unfortunately it is a topic that, although it has gained some dimension in recent decades, is still neglected. Like many other studies already carried out, some limitations were identified that are important to reference for a better understanding of this research. Firstly, we begin by characterizing the sample. The selected sample was somewhat small, given that there was little flexibility in the companies in this specific sector in participating in this study, which led to a relatively small study. In this sense, other studies could be developed with a larger number of organizations, in order to try to understand whether there is greater agreement in the data. In addition, the companies' lack of flexibility made the data collection process very difficult, as responses took longer and made the process slower.

REFERENCES

Argenti, P. A. (2006). How technology has influenced the field of corporate communication. *Journal of Business and Technical Communication*, *20*(3), 357–370. DOI: 10.1177/1050651906287260

Azevedo, J. (2012). *Internal Communication and Organizational Culture.* Casa das Musas.

Bahia, J. (2008). *Introduction to business communication.* Mauad Editora Ltda.

Bekin, S. F. (2004). *Internal marketing: how to practice it successfully.* Prentice Hall.

Boella, M. J. (1992). *Human Resource Management in the hospitality Industry* (5th ed.). Stanley Thornes Ltd.

Braga, M. (2024). Strategic Plan for the Economic Development of Braga 2014-2026.

Brambilla, R. (2005). Conceptual Approach to Internal Marketing. *Electronic Journal*, 1-56.

Brum, A. d. (2007). *Internal Marketing from A to Z.* Editora Dora Luzzatto.

Bueno, W. d. (2005). *Business communication in Brazil: A critical reading.* All Print.

Bulchand-Gidumal, J., William Secin, E., O'Connor, P., & Buhalis, D. (2024). Artificial intelligence's impact on hospitality and tourism marketing: Exploring key themes and addressing challenges. *Current Issues in Tourism*, *27*(14), 2345–2362. DOI: 10.1080/13683500.2023.2229480

Cascão, F. (2014). *Skills, Knowledge and Talent Management: The State of the Art of Theory and Best Practices in People Management.* Sílabos.

Puyod, J. V., & Charoensukmongkol, P. (2021). Effects of workplace rumors and organizational formalization during the COVID-19 pandemic: A case study of universities in the Philippines. *Corporate Communications*, *26*(4), 793–812.

Costa, C. (2005). Tourism and culture: Assessment of cultural theories and practices in the tourism sector. *Analise Social*, •••, 279–285.

Cunha, MD (2016). *Staff turnover in hotel units: the role of human resource management practices.*

Daymon, C., & Holloway, I. (2010). *Qualitative research methods in public relations and marketing communications.* Routledge.

Deb, S. K., Nafi, S. M., & Valeri, M. (2024). Promoting tourism business through digital marketing in the new normal era: A sustainable approach. *European Journal of Innovation Management, 27*(3), 775–799. DOI: 10.1108/EJIM-04-2022-0218

Denzin, N. K. (2018). *The qualitative manifesto: A call to arms*. Routledge. DOI: 10.4324/9780429449987

Dias, Á., Camal, C., Sousa, B., & Pereira, L. (2024). The Role of Incubators in Promoting Innovation Ambidexterity Among Start-Ups in the Tourism and Hospitality Industry. *Tourism and Hospitality Management, 30*(4), 569–579. DOI: 10.20867/thm.30.4.10

Ecklebe, S., & Löffler, N. (2021). A question of quality: Perceptions of internal communication during the Covid-19 pandemic in Germany. *Journal of Communication Management (London), 25*(3), 214–232.

Einwiller, S., Ruppel, C., & Stranzl, J. (2021). Achieving employee support during the COVID-19 pandemic–the role of relational and informational crisis communication in Austrian organizations. *Journal of Communication Management (London), 25*(3), 233–255.

Fernandes, B. (2013). *Strategic People Management with a Focus on Competence*. Elsevier Publishing Ltd.

Grönroos, C. (1990). Relationship Approach to Marketing in Service Contexts: The Marketing and Organizational Behavior Interface. In *Journal of Business Research* (pp. 3–11). Elsevier Saence Publishing Co, Inc. DOI: 10.1016/0148-2963(90)90037-E

INE. (2024). Resident Population by Place of Residence. National Institute of Statistics. Delloite Insights. (2023). *D. Global Human Capital Trends 2023* .

Kusluvan, S. K. (2010). The human dimension: A review of human resources management issues in the tourism and hospitality industry. 171-214.

Liu-Lastres, B., Wen, H., & Okumus, F. (2024). Exploring the impacts of internal crisis communication on tourism employees insights from a mixed-methods study. *Tourism Management, 100*, 104796. DOI: 10.1016/j.tourman.2023.104796

Martins, R. (2018). *Areas that generate more jobs have a lack of qualified workers*. Jornal Público.

Nankervis, A. R., & Debrah, Y. (1995). Human resource management in hotels: A comparative study. *Tourism Management, 16*(7), 507–513. DOI: 10.1016/0261-5177(95)00068-Y

Pires, A. R. (2010). *Quality Management Systems: Environment, Safety*. Silabo Editions.

Portugal, T. d. (2017). *Tourism Strategy 2027*. Retrieved from https://www.turismodeportugal.pt/

Praça, FS (2015). Scientific research methodology: structural organization and challenges in writing the final paper. *Electronic Journal "Academic Dialogues"*, 72-87.

Puccio, B., & Acan, Y. (2020). Creative problem solving in small groups: The effects of creativity training on idea generation, solution creativity, and leadership effectiveness. *The Journal of Creative Behavior*, *54*(2), 453–471. DOI: 10.1002/jocb.381

Quesado, P. R., Duarte, M., & Sousa, B. B. (2024). The Human Resource Balanced Scorecard (HRBSC) and Internal Marketing Management in (Post) Pandemic Tourism Contexts. In *Human Relations Management in Tourism* (pp. 225-235). IGI Global.

Ruschmann, D. (2008). *Competency-based training in tourism: analysis of the model proposed by the hospitality institute*. SeminTur.

Sackey, B. B., Yang, J., Quansah, P. E., Ekumah, C. A., Arboh, F., & Boadu, B. (2024). Internal marketing orientation and employee innovative behaviour: the mediating role of workforce agility and moderating role of psychological empowerment. *Journal of Hospitality and Tourism Insights*.

Salgado, L. &. (2016). The importance of Tourism Management in Higher Education in Portugal.

Santos, AL (2023). The influence of internal marketing on employee engagement in the hybrid model.

Silva, J. C. (2012). *Internal marketing: a strategic tool in the communication mix*. Cândido Mendes University.

Sorcaru, I. A., Muntean, M. C., Manea, L. D., & Nistor, R. (2024). Entrepreneurs' perceptions of innovation, wine tourism experience, and sustainable wine tourism development: The case of Romanian wineries. *The International Entrepreneurship and Management Journal*, *20*(2), 901–934. DOI: 10.1007/s11365-023-00918-6

Swiatkiewicz, O. (2014). *Transversal, technical or moral skills: An exploratory study on competences*.

Tang, A. D., Luu, T. T., Chen, W. K., & Liu, S. C. (2024). Internal corporate social responsibility and customer-oriented organizational citizenship behavior: The mediating roles of job satisfaction, work-family facilitation, life satisfaction, and the moderating role of organizational tenure. *Journal of Sustainable Tourism*, *32*(5), 986–1007. DOI: 10.1080/09669582.2023.2195134

Tosun, P., Uslu, A., & Erul, E. (2024). Connecting through chatbots: Residents' insights on digital storytelling, place attachment, and value co-creation. *Current Issues in Tourism*, •••, 1–24.

Wang, Q., Sun, N., Hon, A. H., & Zhu, Z. (2024). Linking organizational justice to tourism and hospitality employees' service orientation: The roles of Confucian values and relationship quality. *International Journal of Contemporary Hospitality Management*, *36*(6), 2107–2124. DOI: 10.1108/IJCHM-10-2022-1269

Wood, T. (1996). *Strategic Compensation - The New Competitive Advantage*. University of Chicago Press.

ADDITIONAL READING

Awad, A. H. I., Elnaggar, M. K., Abd, A. A. E. K. G., Ahmed, M. F. A. E. L., & Wahba, S. A. M. (2024). The Moderating Role of Internal Marketing on the Relationship Between Organizational Trust and Job Engagement: Evidence From Hotels and Travel Agencies. *Geo Journal of Tourism and Geosites*, *53*(2), 554–563. DOI: 10.30892/gtg.53219-1231

Kaplan, R. S. (2017). Internal Marketing and Internal Branding in the 21st Century Organization. IUP Journal of Brand Management,, 14.

Neves, M. S., Gonçalves, J. S., Sousa, B. B., & Veloso, C. M. (2024). The Importance of Internal Marketing in Achieving Job Satisfaction and Organizational Success. In Popescu, C., Martínez-Falcó, J., Marco-Lajara, B., Sánchez-García, E., & Millán-Tudela, L. (Eds.), *Building Sustainable Human Resources Management Practices for Businesses* (pp. 254–274). IGI Global., DOI: 10.4018/979-8-3693-1994-9.ch016

Ružić, M. D. (2015). Direct and indirect contribution of HRM practice to hotel company performance. *International Journal of Hospitality Management*, *49*, 56–65. DOI: 10.1016/j.ijhm.2015.05.008

Scale, P. (2020). Winning The Juggling Act: How Strategic Compensation Attracts And Retains Top Talent in a Tightening Labor Market.

KEY TERMS AND DEFINITIONS

Business: an organization or enterprising entity engaged in commercial, industrial, or professional activities. A business can be described as an organization or enterprising entity that engages in professional, commercial or industrial activities.

Competitive Advantage: an attribute that allows an organization to outperform its competitors. A competitive advantage is anything that gives a company an edge over its competitors, helping it attract more customers and grow its market share.

Internal Marketing: is the promotion of a company's objectives, products and services to employees within the organization. The purpose is to increase employee engagement with the company's goals and foster brand advocacy.

Human Resources Management: or HRM, involves coordinating, managing, and allocating human capital, or employees, in ways that move an organization's goals forward. HRM focuses on investing in employees, ensuring their safety, and managing all aspects of staffing from hiring to compensation and development.

Tourism Sector: refers to the industry and economic activities associated with travel for leisure, recreation, business, or other purposes. It encompasses a wide range of services, businesses, and organizations that contribute to the planning, facilitation, and enjoyment of travel experiences.

External Communication: the processes responsible for communicating with people and entities outside your organization. These include customers, businesses, suppliers, partners, investors, government agencies, and law enforcement. External communication refers to exchanging information between a company and external entities such as customers, suppliers, investors, media, and the general public. It involves conveying messages and information about the company, its products or services, and its values to the outside world.

Innovation: the practical implementation of ideas that result in the introduction of new goods or services or improvement in offering goods or services. Innovation is the use of new ideas, products or methods where they have not been used before.

Internal Communication: Internal communication entails the methods an organization uses to communicate among staff. Internal communications is defined as the process of aligning employees to company strategy by systematically informing, influencing, motivating, and engaging people at all levels of the company through the one-way and two-way channels—digital and physical—that are most relevant to each employee.

Small and Medium-sized Enterprises (SMEs): SMEs make up the majority of the businesses operating around the world. Generally, they are independent firms with less than 50 employees.

Chapter 13
Building A Robust Supply Chain for Religious Tourism

Kunal Purohit
https://orcid.org/0009-0001-5847-6103
Chetna's Institute of Management Studies and Research, India

Mohd Osaid Koti
https://orcid.org/0009-0000-4676-395X
Chetna's Institute of Management Studies and Research, India

Sandeep Nemlekar
https://orcid.org/0000-0001-9851-5720
Chetna's Institute of Management Studies and Research, India

ABSTRACT

Supply Chains for Religious Tourism will have to play a very important role in enhancing the overall experience and accessibility of religious tourism. This chapter deals with the essential skillset required for developing a robust supply chain in religious tourism while emphasizing its significance in human capital management and competitive advantage within the sector. The growing demand for authentic religious experiences and sustainable practices are challenges the tourism sector needs to rise up it.

DOI: 10.4018/979-8-3373-0071-9.ch013

1. FUNDAMENTALS OF SCM IN RELIGIOUS TOURISM/INTRODUCTION

1.1. Religious Tourism

Travel which is undertaken for spiritual or religious purposes is known 'Religious Tourism' or 'Faith Tourism'.

Figure 1. Religious tourism (Khoshkop & Nadalipour, 2016)

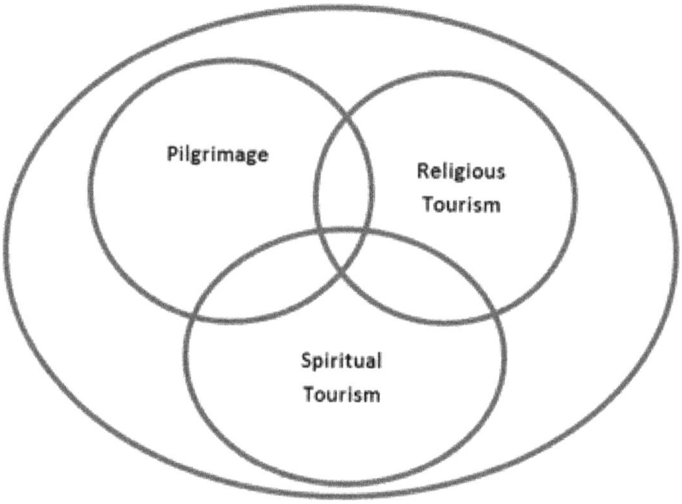

Millions of people undertake tourism around the world for any one of the following religious activities.

- Pilgrimages: Travelling to holy and spiritually significant sites, shrines or destinations
- Participating in religious festivals: Attending events like Hajj, Kumbh Mela
- Seeking Spiritual healing and enlightenment: Visiting retreats or ashrams for meditation, yoga or Ayurveda.
- Heritage and cultural tourism: Exploring historical and cultural significance of religious destination.

Religious tourism can be considered one of the oldest forms of tourism dating back to thousands of years. Although religious travel during ancient times did not have the convenience of modern logistics and connectivity, unwavering faith of humans made them endure severe hardships in their quest spiritual fulfilment. The most popular or concentrated tourist destinations are always the religious ones. Faith still remains a very strong motivator for human travel.

Pilgrims, historically have never been considered tourists in the conventional sense but they have always been of significant importance to the religious destinations they visit. These pilgrims need to eat, place to sleep, travel, shop just like any tourist would. Prominent destinations around the world are now putting pilgrims on the same pedestal as coveted tourists who contribute prominently to the economies of the religious destinations and the economies of the nations they belong to. Smaller destinations are also being provided with necessary infrastructure to take advantage of these religious tourists.

Some of the major Religious Tourism destinations are

1. Mecca & Medina -Saudi Arabia
2. Varanasi -India
3. Jerusalem-Israel
4. Rome-Italy/Vatican
5. Lourdes-France
6. Fatima-Portugal
7. Bodh Gaya-India
8. Ajmer Sharif- India

1.2. The Religious Tourism Industry

The faith-based tourism market is predicted to surge at a CAGR of 9.1% during the forecast period. The industry is standing at USD 16,066.1 million as of 2024 and is on its way forward to cross USD 38,384.8 million by 2034.

Many people today seek more meaning and purpose in their lives. As a result, more are traveling for religious affiliation, such as retreats and pilgrimages. This is the main reason for the growth in faith-based tourism.

The global religious tourism industry is large, with more than one-third of international tourists traveling for religious reasons. This translates to about 450 million international trips made for religious purposes.

Table 1. Global faith-based tourism industry analysis

Attributes	Description
Estimated Global Faith-based Tourism Market Size (2024E)	USD 16,066.1 million
Projected Global Faith-based Tourism Market Value (2034F)	USD 38,384.8 million
Value-based CAGR (2024 to 2034)	9.1%

Demographic changes like an aging population, a growing middle class, and greater mobility also boost faith-based tourism. Millennials, middle-class families, and older people all seek memorable trips that reflect their values and spiritual beliefs.

Religious tourism providers make money by offering accommodation, travel, food, and other services. This helps to boost faith-based tourism and economic development. For instance, the Hajj pilgrimage in Mecca is not just a religious duty but also a big boost for Saudi Arabia's economy. As a result, faith-based traveling is getting more attention and funding to stimulate the economy and help locals maintain their way of life.

Faith-based travelers seek unique experiences that match their spiritual beliefs. This demand has led to specialized faith-based travel programs like themed pilgrimages, health retreats, and cultural immersions. This offers many faith-based tourism market opportunities.

1.3. Role of Technology in Religious Tourism

The internet has changed how religious tourism is advertised and experienced. For example, virtual reality tours of the Vatican let visitors see sacred places without leaving home, creating new opportunities in technology.

Role of technology in faith-based tourism is irrefutable. Technology has made it easier to find information on faith-based tourist places, activities, and travel options. There's a chance to create online platforms for virtual tours, live streams of religious events, and online shopping for religious items.

Technology and innovation have changed how pilgrims experience sacred places and rituals. It's not just an emerging trend in faith-based tourism but a big change that makes pilgrimages more accessible, personal, and fulfilling. This includes things like mobile applications and social media that satisfy pilgrims' needs and inspire entrepreneurs in the travel industry.

The blend of technology, innovation, and spirituality is creating a new chapter in religious tourism

1.4. Country-Wise Insights

The following section discusses the faith-based tourism market regional tourism reports. The report provides information about key economies in Europe, Asia Pacific, and North America.

In North America, the United States is leading and is on its way to surge at 5.9% yearly until 2034. In Europe, Italy tops the chart in the faith-based tourism industry and is set to progress at 6.9% yearly until 2034.

In Asia Pacific, India is emerging as a leading market for faith-based tourism. It is on track to grow more rapidly than China, with a yearly growth rate of 16.3% compared to China's 19.2% until 2034.

Table 2. Country-wise insights

Countries	CAGR 2024 to 2034
United States	5.9%
Canada	13.4%
China	16.3%
Italy	6.9%
India	19.2%

1.5. Religious Tourism in India

Religious Tourism in India is rising rapidly. Religious tourism is a big part of India's tourism industry, with 60% of domestic tourists taking part in it. According to the Ministry of Tourism, this sector alone is expected to generate a revenue of USD 59 Billion by 2028 creating 140 million temporary and permanent jobs by 2030. The market is further expected to grow at a CAGR of 10% from year 2024 to 2032. Post COVID the religious inclinations of Indians have grown and this is translating into noteworthy increase in overnight journeys for pilgrimage and higher donations. More and more tourists in India are preferring to go on a' Pray-cation' instead of a Vacation.

The growth of spiritual tourism in places like Puri, Varanasi, Tirupati, and Shirdi is expected to play a major role in expanding India's religious and spiritual tourism market. The new Ram Temple at Ayodhya has also given a sudden rise in religious tourist numbers. Cities like Puri and Varanasi offer not only traditional religious experiences but also opportunities for people to relax and refresh through yoga retreats and Ayurvedic spas, attracting a larger number of visitors. Limited infrastructure and underdeveloped supply chains are struggling to catch up with this unprecedented demand. The Indian Government has started many infrastructure projects and schemes to keep up with this demand (Indian Religious and Spiritual Market Report and Forecast 2024-2032, n.d.).

2. SUPPLY CHAIN MANAGEMENT FOR RELIGIOUS TOURISM

2.1. The Journey of the faithful: Unravelling the Supply Chain for Religious Tourism

Envisage a spiritual journey to a popular sacred site where millions of pilgrims converge to seek peace and enlightenment. Behind this sea of spiritual souls lies an intricate network of stakeholders who work day in and day out to make this experience meaningful and emotionally satisfying for these travellers of faith. Welcome to the world of 'supply chain management for religious tourism'

2.2. Let the Journey Begin

Consider a devout Hindu devotee named Shravan undertaking a religious trip to the holy city of Varanasi. Shravan will first book his tour through a travel agency, which sets in motion a series or chain of activities involving several stakeholders

2.2.1. The Stakeholders in the Supply Chain

1. **The Tour Operator**: Shravan's travel agency will tie up with the local tour operators to arrange transportation, stay and local tours with tour guides
2. **Local Accommodation Providers**: Hotels, lodges, ashrams provide various stay options to Shravan.
3. **Transportation services**: Bus operators, taxi services, flights, trains to help pilgrims travel to Varanasi as well as local taxi, auto and rickshaw services.
4. **Food & beverage Suppliers**: local restaurants, cafes and food stalls for the benefit of pilgrims like Shravan
5. **Souvenir and Gift Shops:** These sell religious items such as religious beads, holy water, items symbolic of rich local culture, spiritual books, pictures and other articles
6. **Priests and Local Guides:** Priests provide religious knowledge and perform religious rituals and also explain the history and mythology associated with the destination. Local guides also play an important role in helping Shravan with local sightseeing and providing convenience due to their local connect

7. **The Local Authorities:** The Local Government Bodies have the responsibility of providing sanitation, amenities like good roads, efficient public transport, water supply, drainage, electricity while dealing with a massive floating population. This also gives rise challenges of crowd management and law and order.
8. **The Shrines/Temples:** The trusts managing shrines and temples at the religious destinations have the responsibility of upkeep of the shrines and providing convenience to the pilgrims while taking care of their various needs within the boundaries and even outside the boundaries of the venue.

We can see how the religious tourism supply chain comprising a gamut of stakeholders has seamlessly interconnected them to provide Shravan an everlasting spiritually enriching experience. It is important that each stakeholder works smoothly and in perfect synergy everyone else. This will ensure that millions of faith travellers like Shravan have hugely satisfying religious trips which will encourage him and many more like him to undertake religious tourism more often adding to their spiritual growth while economically benefiting stake holders and local and nation economies.

2.2.2. Religious Tourism Supply Chain: Challenges and Opportunities

Although this Supply chain is like any conventional supply chain as it objectives remain the same such as providing superior experience while maintaining efficiency in diverse resource management, it has its typical challenges and opportunities which make it stand out.

Unique Challenges:

- Crowd management and ensuring safety
- Balancing spiritual and commercial goals
- Cultural sensitivity
- Local environmental Concerns

Opportunities:

- Showcasing Local Culture
- Economic growth of the area and the stake holders
- Personal and Spiritual growth

2.3. Religious Tourism Supply Chains-Triple Bottomline Approach

Religious tourism supply chains must always endeavour to contribute to the triple bottom line (TBL) framework, which focuses on three key areas: profit, people and planet

2.3.1. Economic Impact-Profit

Religious tourism generates significant revenue for local economies through spends on accommodation, transportation, food, and souvenirs. Supply chains should attempt to keep this growing yoy. For example, major pilgrimage sites like Mecca during Hajj or Varanasi in India generate billions in tourism-related income. This boosts local employment, supports entrepreneurship, and ancillary industries like construction, hospitality, and retail.

2.3.2. Social Sustainability- People

Religious tourism promotes cultural preservation and social cohesion by fostering an understanding of religious heritage and traditions. It provides opportunities for local communities to showcase their customs and engage with diverse global visitors. Training programs for local guides and service providers enhance human capital, reducing poverty and improving quality of life in pilgrimage regions

2.3.3. Environmental Impact-Planet

Managing the environmental footprint of large-scale pilgrimages is critical. Religious tourism supply chains should incorporate sustainable practices like waste management, eco-friendly accommodations, and responsible water usage to minimize negative environmental impacts. For instance, the Saudi government's efforts to modernize infrastructure for Hajj include green technologies and smart city solutions aimed at reducing energy consumption and waste.

By aligning with the TBL framework, religious tourism supply chains should focus sustainable growth while balancing economic gains, social well-being, and environmental protection, ensuring long-term benefits for both local communities and global pilgrims.

2.3.4. Resilience in SCM for Religious Tourism

As in any supply chain there is a need for making religious tourism supply chain extremely resilient. Resilience refers to the ability of the supply chain to cope with or withstand, recover from and adapt to any sudden crisis or disruption which may adversely affect delivery of goods and services to the religious tourists, or obstruct their access to the religious destination and/or endanger their safety. A resilient supply chain in religious tourism is essential to ensure safety and comfort of the faith traveller while taking care of the interests of stake holders.

The following are the components of resilience in religious tourism supply chain

1. Robustness

It is the capability of the supply chain to withstand disruptions and maintain its utility and functionality

E.g. At the Hajj Pilgrimage in Saudi arabia there are 'waterproof canopies and tents' to provide shelter to pilgrims during sandstorms and heavy rainfall.

2. Redundancy

It is the availability and maintenance of back up systems, suppliers or logistics to ensure continuity of operations in case of disruptions

E.g. The famous Tirupati Temple trust in India has multiple sources of suppliers of food, water and other consumable to ensure uninterrupted supplies to pilgrims.

3. Flexibility

It is the adaptability of supply chain to changing circumstances such and unexpected events

E.g. The Umrah pilgrimage has scalable infrastructure including temporary prayer halls and waiting areas to accommodate large influx of pilgrims during peak season.

4. Rapid Recovery

It is the ability of the supply chain to quickly recover from any sudden shocks and resume normal operations

This will involve collaboration with emergency services such as ambulances, fire brigade, disaster management cells and police to ensure rapid response and recovery

5. Adaptive capacity

It is the ability of supply chains to learn from disruptions and have the capacity to overcome newer challenges

6. Collaboration and Communication

Every supply chain for religious tourism should enable its stakeholders to share information and collaborate effectively to effectively respond to unforeseen disruptions.

7. Risk Management

It is the ability of a supply chain to anticipate risks that may cause future disruptions to supply chain and take corrective actions to mitigate the same.

It is certainly desirable to enhance the resilience of supply chains for religious tourism by actively working on the above components while accounting for the following factors which will always make this quest a daunting task

- **Supply Chain Complexity:** The sheer number of stakeholders with their diverse objectives makes the supply chain too complex to be geared towards a common objective
- **Dependency on key suppliers:** It can be very difficult to shed over reliance on legacy key suppliers due to political or cultural reasons
- **Geopolitical Risks:** Terrorism and natural disasters can cause immense damage to pilgrims and stake holders while disrupting supply chains for long durations
- **Seasonal Fluctuations**: Religious tourism is more often than not seasonal in nature which can pose formidable challenges to its supply chain
- **Remoteness of Locations:** The remoteness of many religious destinations makes logistics and travel very challenging
- **Local sensibilities:** Religious tourism cannot be possible and its supply chain cannot be effective if local sensibilities and culture are not give their due respect.

3. CORE FACTORS FOR DEVELOPING ROBUST SUPPLY CHAINS FOR RELIGIOUS TOURISM

Supply Chains in Religion based tourism are usually tasked with managing thousands of daily visitors or millions of annual visitors in a relatively small district which has a meagre population of its own with limited resources. In such cases you have a perfect recipe for disaster.

On July 2, 2024 a stampede killed 121 people in Hathras, India at a Hindu religious gathering. The reason given was lack of personnel and poor crowd management.

Heat stroke is one of the major reasons of pilgrim deaths at the Hajj Gathering of Muslim pilgrims in Saudi Arabia. There are also problems such as poor transport facilities, garbage and waste management, sanitation, health, food and shelter as well as effective police control that almost religious destinations need to tackle.

We now have a fair understanding about what a supply chain for religious tourism broadly looks like. We know who are the stakeholders involved. We appreciate the importance of building resilience into this supply chain and the unique challenges that need to be overcome to ensure that religious tourism can sustain a thriving economy based on it while providing exceptional spiritual experiences to the faith travellers.

To put in place a robust supply chain interrelationship between various stakeholders and resulting complexities arising from such interrelationships must be carefully managed. The professionals involved in managing these supply chains should have a diverse skillset which includes

- Strategic Planning,
- Stakeholder Collaboration and
- Cultural Sensitivity.

3.1. Strategic Planning for Religious Tourism Supply Chains

Without proper Strategic planning, supply chains for religious tourism will be chaotic and mismanaged leading to compromise in pilgrim safety, experience and destruction of local economies.

Strategic planning or proactive approach enables authorities to anticipate potential shortcomings, minimize risks while ensuring optimal utilisation of resources. It helps putting in place crucial pieces of infrastructure to aid smooth management of mass pilgrim events.

Infrastructure Planning for Ayodhya: Recently a grand temple dedicated to Lord Rama, one of the most revered deities of the Hindus was constructed in Ayodhya, a small city in the state of Uttar Pradesh, India. It is projected to receive around 50 million religious tourists annually surpassing destinations such as the Vatican City and Mecca. This temple is expected to contribute hugely to the growth of the local, state and national economy. Tax collections could rise to the tune of 500 million USD in the year 2024-24. The Indian government along with the local authorities has undertaken numerous infrastructure projects to prepare Ayodhya to handle this massive tourist influx without being overwhelmed. This includes development of a new international airport at Ayodhya, revamping existing infrastructure like rail and bus transport. A plethora of new hotels and homestay options are being made available. Extensive Car Parking infrastructure is being created. It also involves creating new roads and upgrading existing ones. The city has been given a complete makeover. Internal roads have been widened while locals have been adequately compensated for relocating their homes and businesses. All in all, around 178 projects have been undertaken to convert Ayodhya into a world class pilgrim centre (Verma, 2024).

To have some idea how infrastructure requirements are anticipated for a pilgrimage centre, Let us have a look at some data on Ayodhya tourists projections and the room inventory projections for managing this footfall.

Figure 2.

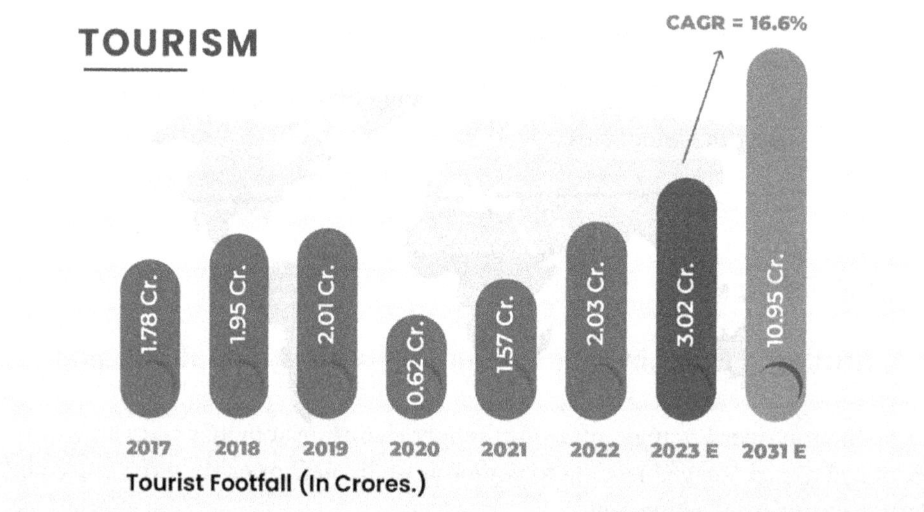

*Source: Ministry of Tourism / *E=Estimated*

Figure 3. Ayodhya: India's emerging religious tourism destination calls for increased infrastructure focus (Verma, 2024)

PROJECTIONS

	Conservative Scenario	Government Projections	Optimistic Scenario
Global Hindu Population (2020)	1,20,00,00,000	1,20,00,00,000	1,20,00,00,000
% of Expected Footfall	7.500%	9.125%	10.750%
Expected Footfall	9,00,00,000	10,95,00,000	12,90,00,000
Footfal per Day	2,46,575	3,00,000	3,53,425
% Requiring Branded Accomodation	5.00%	5.00%	5.00%
Hotel Demand	45,00,000	54,75,000	64,50,000
Guest Density	2.20	2.20	2.20
Length of Stay	1.00	1.00	1.00
Roomnights Required	20,45,455	24,88,636	29,31,818
Daily Roomnights Required	5,604	6,818	8,032
Marketwide Occupancy	65%	65%	65%
Required Inventory	8,622	10,490	12,358

3.2. Stakeholder Collaboration in Religious Tourism

The success and the smooth functioning of a tourism destination cannot be ensured by the government of that area alone. An active collaboration between various public and private stake holders is a must to make it thrive. Ultimately a supply chain cannot work if stakeholders who are a part of it are not in sync. Over many years the major religious tourism centres have seen the emergence of a semblance of some sort of stakeholder coexistence but it is always a challenge to convert this coexistence to active and productive collaboration. This coexistence is based on intricate power dynamics between competing stake holders.

A deep understanding of the same is important to get all stakeholders to work together while taking care of their individual interests. This will lead to larger economic gains for everyone involved and better spiritual experience for religious tourists. Strategic planning needs to take into account stakeholder dynamics and ensure a synergistic relationship amongst them.

In one such instance, the government collaborates with other stakeholders such as local cultural organizations and religious institutions to preserve the spiritual and cultural heritage of the destination. They may fund cultural events, exhibitions, and educational programs for visitors. At the Golden Temple in Amritsar, the government supports cultural programs that educate visitors about Sikh traditions and history. Local businesses, including artisans and guide services, profit from increased interest in the cultural and spiritual aspects of the temple.

On the other hand, some local businesses might attempt to exploit pilgrims by charging excessively for basic services like food, accommodation, or transportation, leading to negative experiences for visitors and potentially damaging the reputation of the pilgrimage site. Governments can implement and enforce regulations on pricing, ensuring that businesses offer fair, transparent pricing for services. At Shirdi, a prominent pilgrim destination in Maharashtra, India, local businesses are regulated by the government, which ensures fair pricing for services like accommodations and food. Pilgrims have access to government-approved service lists, helping them make informed choices and preventing exploitation.

3.3. Cultural Sensitivity in Religious Tourism

It is crucial that the cultural and faith element remain a centrepiece of any strategic planning for development and maintenance for religious destinations. Faith and culture are the only factors that draw religious tourists to such locations and provide each site its unique and rich identity. It is hence paramount to maintain cultural sensitivity to ensure that experiences are respectful, enriching and harmonious while supply chains are being upgraded to meet modern standards.

The first International Conference on Religious Tourism (ICORET 2006), organised by the World Tourism Organisation, which was an attempt to get together all stakeholders in religious tourism on a single platform came up with the following conclusions on cultural sensitivity at religious placcs

- Overcommercialisation must not be allowed to be compromise the religious and spiritual significance of the destination
- The integrity of religious spaces must be preserved and the significance of prevalent customs and traditions should be respected e.g. Adhering to the dress code and following prescribed rituals
- Benefits to the local community should be assured and their members should be give priorities in activities related to the site.
- The needs of different types of religious tourists must be met in such a way that conflicts do not arise between them e.g. There can be tourists who visit a religious tourist place only for its historical value, or for its beauty or only for their faith. Systems should be so designed that these tourists are sensitised to the needs of the others and eventually respect the coexistence without antagonising each other.

- Care should be taken to respect local customs and not cause damage to the ecosystem and environment of the religious

These aspects should never be compromised and always be given due importance by religious trusts, governments, pilgrims, local businesses and inhabitants to maintain the sanctity of the religious destination.

3.4. Role of Technology in Religious Tourism Supply Chains

The massive advances in technology have tremendously helped in strategic planning and stakeholder collaboration within supply chains serving religious supply chains. Digital tools such as predictive analytics, AI, and blockchain streamline decision-making, optimize resource allocation, and ensure transparency across the supply chain. Cloud-based platforms facilitate real-time communication among stakeholders, improving coordination and reducing delays. Internet of Things (IoT) devices enhance inventory management, ensuring timely delivery of essential goods for religious events and services. Use of technology has revolutionised crowd management in large religious gatherings ensuring safety and comfort of pilgrims. Technology is also used to promote ethical sourcing and compliance with religious guidelines, boosting trust and reliability. As a result, supply chains become more robust, efficient, and resilient in serving religious communities.

3.5. Role of Human Capital in Religious Tourism Supply Chains

Religious tourism is expected to create up to 200,000 job opportunities in India until 2030. It is also expected to strengthen opportunities for entrepreneurship in food services, consumer goods, hospitality, transportation handicrafts, logistics, warehousing, etc. (Hajj, 2023).

We can clearly see that human capital is a key ingredient of the religious tourism supply chain, ensuring its smooth functioning, resilience, and overall success. Skilled professionals which include logistics managers, tour operators, hospitality staff, and local vendors, law enforcers along with volunteer groups work collaboratively to meet the unique needs of religious travellers. Their expertise in cultural sensitivity, multiple languages, and customer service enhances the pilgrimage experience while fostering trust and satisfaction among tourists.

Thus, training and development of human capital is a must to improve operational efficiency, from managing accommodations and transportation to coordinating religious events and ensuring safety. Furthermore, local communities should be encouraged to contribute to the supply chain by providing authentic products and services, promoting sustainable tourism, and driving regional economic growth. By investing in human capital, religious tourism supply chains become more adaptable, responsive, and capable of delivering a seamless and enriching experience for pilgrims.

4. CASES: FOCUS ON SUPPLY CHAINS AT MAJOR RELIGIOUS DESTINATIONS

Let us now consider a few cases which demonstrate the integration of crucial aspects of strategic planning, stakeholder collaboration and cultural sensitivity along with the effective use of technology while harnessing human capital to ensure incident free experiences for faith travellers. In each case a good amount of thought has been given to planning for the future while giving due consideration current and past information.

4.1. Case: The Preparation for Hajj 2024

Hajj, the annual Muslim pilgrimage in Saudi Arabia is one of the five pillars of Islam. It is required to be performed at least once in the lifetime of every physically and financial capable individual who practices Islam (The New Arab, 2023). The Hajj is one of the world's largest religious gatherings. It covers a large region of around 68,000 sq kms with multiple activities being carried out simultaneously at many sites. The two main regions are the Mekkah region which comprises the Makkah city and its three holy sites and the region of Medina.

4.1.1. Strategic Planning

The authorities in Saudi Arabia were expecting an upwards of 2 million pilgrims in 2024. Almost 1.85 million pilgrims had arrived in Saudi Arabia for Hajj in 2018.

Strategic planning involved focusing on these the two main regions of Mecca and Medina along with multiple entry and exit points throughout Saudi Arabia have to be managed. As the Hajj was going to take place during summer, extreme heat was another important factor which Haj authorities have to take into consideration temperatures soaring beyond 50deg C

The Ministry of Hajj (MOH)- Organisation of Hajj & Co-ordination between Stakeholders

The Government of Saudi Arabia has a dedicated ministry for the Hajj pilgrimage in the country known as the Ministry of Hajj. It is responsible for smoothly conducting the hajj pilgrimage and ensuring the safety and wellbeing of pilgrims who visit the country from Islamic nations all over the world. It develops plans and coordinates between various stakeholders.

The MOH initiated an 'early readiness plan' which was initiated right after Hajj 2023. Under this plan every resource needed to ensure comfort and safety of pilgrims was made available and put to use. Over number of years a strong infrastructure has been put in place for the benefit of the pilgrims. This infrastructure is constantly reviewed and enhanced for each subsequent Hajj under the country's VISION 20230 to elevate services provided to pilgrims to a higher standard.

The Hajj Infrastructure

For 2024 Hajj the world's largest cooling station for the Grand Mosque (Masjid al-Haram) was installed and the Mashair Train which is designed to transport over 350,000 pilgrims between holy sites, was put in operation. Facilities at holy sites were upgraded with sunshades, misting fans, along with improvement of escalator efficiency and improvement had been carried out in the area surrounding the Sacred Monument or "the Hajj station of Muzdalifah" for easier movement. We will now also focus on the necessary arrangements which were put into place for this grand event

- **Pilgrim Accommodation:** 11 new buildings have been introduced to accommodate 37,000 pilgrims by the MOH. There are many options for accommodation for Hajj Pilgrims. These include a large number of hotels, apartment, rooms and tents. There are licenced Travel Agencies which enable pilgrims to book their preferred accommodation. The Mina Tent city is a shining example as to how respectable and comfortable accommodation can be provided to thousands of pilgrims

    The Mina Tent City: Mina is a very important site where arrangements are made for pilgrims stay during the days of Hajj. It is a city created specially to house a large majority of religious tourists. The city accommodates about 100,000 fire proof tents. Each tent can accommodate 20 to 40 people. These tents have cooking areas, toilets and shower areas. These tents are provided with air conditioning in recent years to give respite from the extreme heat (Patowary, 2014).
- **Food Arrangements:** For almost 2 million pilgrims there has to be adequate availability of good quality and easy availability of food and water. On a given day during Hajj, over five million loaves of bread are baked and nearly two million blocks of ice are produced. 289 companies and catering establishments have been geared up to serve up to 30 million meals, including breakfast, lunch, and dinner, along with snacks, juices, dairy products, water, fresh fruits, and both hot and cold beverages at the holy sites. Food is to be paid for by the pilgrims but the Saudi Government offers free packaged food to a

percentage of pilgrims. Arrangements are also made for pilgrims at camping sites to cook their own food. 78.5 million cubic meters of portable water will be made available for the pilgrims round the clock (Slurrp, 2023).

- **Logistics and Transportation**

  Buses: During Hajj, 20,000 buses are utilised to move pilgrims to and fro various sites like Mecca, Medina, Mina, Arafat, and Muzdalifah (SaudiPedia, 2024).

  Airlines: More than 100 airlines from around the world operate their flights to Jeddah and Medina during the Hajj. The government of Saudi Arabia coordinates with international airlines to manage the large volume of passengers.

  Mecca Metro: The Mecca Metro (also known as the Mina Metro) which was inaugurated in 2010, helps transportation of pilgrims between key locations It has the capacity to carry 72,000 passengers per hour and covers 18 km (around 11 miles) leading to reduced traffic congestion and better transport efficiency.

  Hajj Terminal in Jeddah: The King Abdulaziz International Airport in Jeddah is one of the primary points of entry for pilgrims. In 2019, it handled more than 2.5 million passengers during the Hajj season alone.

  Electric vehicles: Provision for E-Scooters has been made at the religious sites for the benefit of elderly and disabled individual.

- **Healthcare Facilities:** More than 35,000 healthcare workers (doctors, nurses, paramedics) offer superior medical services to Hajj pilgrims round the clock. Around 183 hospitals and health centres equipped with the latest medical technologies have been set up by the Saudi government at key pilgrimage sites, including Mina, Arafat, and the Grand Mosque in Mecca.

  Emergency Medical Services: 1,500 ambulances are deployed by the Saudi Ministry of Health during Hajj to ensure rapid response to medical emergencies.

  Preventative Healthcare: It is ensured that pilgrims are made to undergo health checks before the pilgrimage, including vaccinations for diseases such as Meningitis and, during the pandemic, COVID-19. This is done to prevent spread of communicable diseases (Saudi Gazette, 2024).

- **Security Measures**

  Security Forces: More than 100,000 security personnel are deployed every year to ensure the safety of pilgrims and maintain order. These include police, military, and civil defence personnel. Also a team of 500 multilingual personnel will be deployed for crowd management at the Grand mosque for the benefit of travellers from multiple nationalities.

Surveillance: The use of advanced technologies such as cctv cameras, drones and facial recognition systems helps authorities keep a watch on large crowds and look out for potential security risks. The Saudi government has also enhanced cybersecurity to protect against digital threats.

- **Accident Prevention:** Saudi Arabia has invested massively in a lot of effective accident-prevention measures which include improved roadways, better crowd management systems, and enhanced emergency response protocols (India Today, 2015).
- **The Holy Water: Zamzam**

  Zamzam water which comes from a historic well at Mecca holds deep significance in Islam. Zamzam water holds deep significance in Islam. It is considered a symbol of purity and a source of spiritual healing. Muslims have a strong belief that drinking Zamzam with a pure heart brings Allah's blessings, and many pilgrims drink it during their pilgrimage and take it home for family and friends.

  It is transported to the Grand Mosque and Prophet's Mosque by pumping at 360 cubic meters per hour through two giant pumps. The water is then transported to the King Abdullah bin Abdulaziz Zamzam Water Project for storage, disinfection, and distribution to the Zamzam tank station and King Abdulaziz sabil station.

  It is transported using a network of 4 kilometres of stainless-steel pipelines, equipped with air chambers, cleaning chambers, and control systems. 3,348 specially equipped tankers will also be put to service for water transportation around the religious sites during the Hajj. The authorities are geared up to provide around 60000 tonnes of Zamzam water during the Hajj. Arrangements have also been made to provide bottled water to the visiting pilgrims so that they can take Zamzam water back home for their own spiritual needs and share it with their close ones
- **Sustainability Efforts**

  Waste Management: Given the massive number of people, waste management is a critical challenge. The Saudi government manages around 50,000 tons of waste during Hajj. Recycling programs and waste diversion initiatives are in place to reduce the environmental impact.

  Water Usage: The pilgrimage generates enormous demand for water. The Saudi authorities provide millions of litres of drinking water every day, which is distributed at key sites.

  Sustainable Infrastructure: Many of the new buildings and facilities have been designed with eco-friendly and energy-efficient features. For example, the Haram Expansion Project includes solar energy panels and water-efficient systems.

4.1.2. Role of Human Capital at Hajj

For providing better overall experience to pilgrims the MOH encourages participation of volunteers. These volunteers are on boarded through the National Volunteer Work Platform and provided a certificate in recognition of their services. Hajj 2022 saw 100,570 volunteers who aided the pilgrims to comfortably perform their rituals. The number over volunteers increased by another 35,000 in the subsequent year. Training of over 120,000 workers and group leaders was carried out. More than 2,500 training workshops were conducted in various languages to provide assistance to over 10,000 volunteers

4.1.3. Technology at Hajj

The use of technology aids strategic planning tremendously and the hajj authorities have embraced it to the fullest to avoid repeating past mistakes and preventing new ones.

- **Establishing a command and control centre.** The Command and Control Centre, under the leadership of the Ministry of Interior, was developed to ensure the safety and security of pilgrims. This centre oversee the use of technology at the Hajj. Over 6000 cameras gave authorities complete surveillance of all locations. The centre was considered a place to control and collect the flow of information about Hajj
- **Hajj Apps:** In recent years, the Saudi government has launched official mobile apps that provide pilgrims with essential information, such as prayer times, rituals, maps, and real-time updates. These apps have become vital tools for helping pilgrims navigate the event.
- **Electronic Tracking:** Pilgrims are increasingly required to use electronic bracelets to monitor their location. This helps authorities locate lost pilgrims, manage health emergencies, and improve safety. The innovation was introduced in 2016 after the horrific and deadly 2015 Hajj season that killed more than 750 people
- **Crowd Management**

The above information provides us a snapshot of the herculean efforts that need to be put in by any planning authority for a religious event of such magnitude. We can appreciate the fact that no amount of preparation is enough as the scale of the event needs to increase with the passage of time to keep the pilgrims spiritually fulfilled and the stakeholders and local economy in good shape. An event like the Hajj not only boosts the economy of the host nation but also is important for its political clout and influence. Hence planning and arrangements need to improve and there can be no inertia or complacency. Despite all the efforts, resources and contingency plans in place Hajj 2024 faced an unprecedented human tragedy

4.2. Strategic failure: Tragedy at Hajj 2024

Being prepared for mega congregations such as Hajj involves careful planning and safety measures (Page, 2020). The Saudi Ministry of Health (MOH) made arrangements for shade, put in place water mist sprays, and distributed water bottles and numerous umbrellas to reduce heat stroke risks. Extensive screening processes helped to isolate and treat individuals at high risk, such as those senior citizens over 65 years or individuals with chronic illnesses, reducing heat-related incidents. Free health-care services were provided by the MOH to over 465000 pilgrims during Hajj 2024, including 141000 services to unregistered pilgrims. Also 29 open-heart surgeries, 720 cardiac catheterisations, and 1170 dialysis sessions for pilgrims were carried out. These numbers clearly demonstrate MOH's commitment to ensuring the health and wellbeing of pilgrims.

Despite these efforts, as many as 1300 fatalities due to heat strokes occurred do unprecedented extreme hot weather conditions. Mainly affected were unregistered pilgrims who faced prolonged sun exposure and avoided using official transportation in order to evade capture.

Unregistered pilgrims could not gain access to public facilities like air-conditioned tents, misting centres, transportation, or adequate drinking water for rehydration. The official Hajj costs are very steep and this is primarily why there is an alarmingly high number of unregistered pilgrims Many tour companies send pilgrims without Hajj permits on mandatory personal visit visas. It has been discovered that "83 percent of those of died did not have permits, meaning they were exposed to long distances and periods under the sun without shelter.

This means that the authorities were not prepared for unregistered pilgrims. These were not accounted for during planning and hence facilities could not be made available for them. These unregistered pilgrims with non-Hajj visas managed to infiltrate the Hajj areas and the system was not robust enough to prevent this from happening. The Hajj authorities have understood the need to ensure that such incidents are not repeated in the future.

5. CASE: SIZE DOES MATTER-THE MAHA KUMBHA MELA 2025 PRAYAGRAJ, INDIA

The Kumbh Mela in Hinduism is a religious festival or a mega religious fair ('mela' in Hindi) that is celebrated four times over the course of every 12 years. Interestingly the site of the pilgrimage keeps rotating between four pilgrimage places in India on four sacred rivers. The locations are Haridwar on the Ganges River, Ujjain on the Shipra river, at Nashik on the Godavari river, and at Prayagraj (earlier Allahabad) at the confluence of the Ganges, the Jamuna, and the mythical Sarasvati river which used to flow in ancient times. Each site's celebration is based on a distinct set of astrological alignments of the Sun, the Moon, and Jupiter. The Kumbh Mela at Prayagraj, in particular, attracts millions of pilgrims.

The Ardha (half) Kumbha, which falls between two Maha (Great) Kumbhas was held previously in Prayagraj in 2019 and was regarded as a huge success in terms of strategic planning and presence of effective infrastructure. It had a footfall of 250 million out of which a staggering 110 million faithfuls bathed in the confluence of the two rivers. Hindus believe that bathing at this confluence under a during a particular astrological event will cleanse them from their sins and free them from the cycle of birth and death (Pandey, 2019).

The Maha Kumbha spread across 4000 hectares, is a 45-day event scheduled to be held at Prayagraj between the months of January 25 to February 25. The preparations for the same have been undertaken at an unprecedented scale. This scale is warranted as a sea of 400 million pilgrims from India and all around the globe are expected this time. This number is greater than the population of United States and United Kingdom combined. The Maha Kumbha is expected to generate economic activity to the tune of INR 200,000 crores. The economic benefits will extend to nearby religious sites like Ayodhya and Varanasi. The Indian state of Uttar Pradesh has pumped in about 6990 thousand crore indian rupees (INR) which is almost double than what it had spent 6 years ago to organise the Ardha Kumbha. The last Maha Kumbha was organised in 2012 with a footfall of 120 million pilgrims and an expenditure of INR 1,152 crores. As we can see that every time this festival is held the scale almost doubles. Such massive growth in footfall can only be managed by hard core strategic planning which involves taking cues from past experiences and accurately projecting future requirements (Sharda, 2024).

5.1. Strategic Planning for the Maha Kumbha:

- **Creation of A New District**

The Uttar Pradesh Tourism Department wants the Mahakumbh 2025 to be a major global tourism attraction. To streamline the management and look after the administration of the Maha Kumbha festival the Chief Minister of the State of Uttar Pradesh decided to form a new Maha Kumbha Mela District. The Maha Kumbha District will comprise the world's largest 4000 hectare 'Tent City" specially created for the event. It will have 2000 tents and 25000 public accommodations to serve the pilgrims. It will be illuminated by 67,000 stretlights.

This district will have all the resources and the government machinery and decision making power which just as any district managing a full-fledged city in India. This strategic step was undertaken to enable better co-ordination between stakeholders and enhance administrative efficiency. The Maha Kumbha Mela District has been further subdivided into 25 administrative sectors to make crowd management easier. As an anti-climax, the district will cease to exist after March 2025, once the Kumbha festivities are over.

- **Transport arrangements**

The Railway Ministry will be arranging around 1000 special trains for Prayagraj during the great festival.

The Prayagraj Airport has been revamped by constructing a brand new terminal and expanding the parking area for planes.

The new 594 km six lane Ganga Expressway, which is one of the state's longest expressway is on the verge of completion and will connect Prayagraj to the important city of Meerut, while providing access to a number of small towns and villages in between.

The state roadways department is geared up to run 7,000 buses on different highways that connect to Prayagraj. It will also ply about 550 shuttle buses from Prayagraj to the Mela venue. As an eco-friendly move 20,000 e-rickshaws will be available for the benefit of pilgrims.

For making movement for pilgrims easier across the 'Tent City', the Public Works Department (PWD) is in the process of construction 400 kms of temporary roads and 30 temporary floating bridges over the river Ganga to provide access to the bathing sites.

A total of 120 temporary mass parking spaces, covering an area of around 1800 hectares have been created cater over 2 million private vehicles in addition to the buses

- **Electric Supply for the event**

The state power department will install 67,000 LED lights and 2,000 solar hybrid lights, besides two new power substations and 66 new transformers to ensure uninterrupted power supply during the 45-day event

- **Water Supply for the event**

The Uttar Pradesh State water undertaking is laying a 1,294 km potable water line to supply potable water across the Mela sectors while also installing around 200 water ATM stalls and 85 water pumps

- **Sanitation Arrangement for the event**

As many as 150,000 toilets have been planned to be installed before the grand pilgrimage across the grounds of the venue. Services of 55 vendors have been enlisted for installation and maintenance of these toilets. These toilets include soak pit, mobile toilets and FRP toilets with septic tanks. Advanced technology will ensure odours are eliminated within 10 minutes and waste is disposed within 24 hours. At least 10% toilets will be reserved for the disabled (Dixit, 2024).

- **Security Arrangements for the Event.**

Deployment of more than 37,000 police personnel across the venue is being planned for security purposes. These personnel will be supported by state of the art technology and tight co-ordination between security agencies.

1,378 women police have been appointed for the safety of women devotees. The seven-layer security system will be seeing an increase of around 10,000 personnel compared to event held 6 years ago making it one of the most secure Kumbh Mela organised ever.

To strengthen security further AI-enabled CCTV cameras for crowd monitoring, facial recognition, and data collection through Technical Service Providers (TSP) (Srivastava, 2024).

- **Healthcare facilities for the Event**

The authorities have decided to leave nothing to chance as far as the health care needs of millions of pilgrims is concerned. For this purpose, as many as 43 temporary hospitals with 238 beds are being set up and 305 additional beds will be reserved at existing hospitals in Prayagraj. There will be 407 doctors along with 182 nursing staff, 150 ward boys, 354 pharmacists and 60 lab technicians will be available to serve the health needs of the pilgrims round the clock. To take care of the needs of female pilgrims gynaecologists will be present and a labour room has also been set up. Funds have also been allocated to provide for 125 road ambulances, 20 river ambulances along with 1 air ambulance. Community health centres, primary health centres and a drug warehouse have also been set up on the way leading to the Mela area (Media Eye, 2024).

- **Fire Safety management at the Maha Kumbha 2025**

There were 612 fire incidents in the kumbha mela of 2013 with 6 fatalities and 15 burn injuries. This reduced to only 55 incidents in 2019 with zero fatalities or burn injuries. The target this time as a fire proof Mela. To ensure this, robotic fire tenders will be used for the first time to reach places which are difficult to access. 200 specially trained fire commandos will be stationed for managing fire related emergencies and protecting pilgrims. AI enable CCTV technology will be used to anticipate and spot any fire related hazard. 50 temporary fire stations will be set up, this number was 43 in 2019.Over 7000 fire hydrants will be installed along with 50 fire watch towers and 20 fire posts. Fire boats will be put to use to provide river water to extinguish fires. Daily fire audits have been planned to ensure prevention of any electrical or any other fire related hazard (Latest News India, 2024).

- **Lost & Found Centres**

At such large gatherings there are many incidents of children and elderly getting separated from their families. Prayagraj authorities are developing a hi-tech registration system with digital 'Lost & found" centres to reunite persons who go missing in the Kumbh Fair with their families or group. The high-tech lost-and-found centres will have digital registration for anyone who goes missing to help families and friends to locate them more easily. Every lost person will be promptly registered, and their details will be shared across other (lost-and-found) centres and social media partners such as Facebook and X. CCTVs equipped with face recognition technology will be used to locate missing individuals (The Week, 2024).

- **Sustainability efforts during the event**

This event is aiming to be environmentally friendly by banning single use plastic. Items like leaf bowls, leaf plates and earthen cups are being promoted instead of disposable plastic. No plastic bags will be available and cloth and jute bags will be made available through bag dispensers available throughout the site.

Green transport in the form of e-rickshaws, use of solar lighting and energy efficient led lighting, construction of eco-friendly toilets, deployment of thousands of eco-friendly waste bins and waste segregation at source are some of the many initiatives being undertaken for a sustainable event.

5.1.1. Use of Techonology at the Maha Kumba

- **The Integrated Control and Command Centre (ICCC)**

As we observed in case of the Hajj preparations, an Integrated Control and Command Centre (ICCC) has been set up at the Maha Kumbha to serve as the central hub for real-time intelligence and coordination. It was first set up in 2019 and is now being upgraded for a grander festival. The services of top engineering institute in the country have been enlisted for this purpose. The ICCC will monitor and control the 45-day festival with the help of around 1650 CCTVs, 24 Automated Number Plate Recognitions (ANPR) Cameras, 100 smart parking systems and AI tools for vehicle and crowd management. As discussed earlier cutting edge technology has also been put in place for fire related emergencies.

5.1.2. Involvement of Local Stake holders

The success of any religious event needs the wholehearted support of the local stakeholders comprising local businesses and individuals. Locals can be both, a hindrance as well as a massive support system for the organisation of a huge religious event depending how sensitively they are managed. A religious tourism supply chain will be well oiled only by the active participation of locals and this can be achieved by allowing them to partake economic benefits accruing from this tourist activity. All this needs to be done while taking care of their cultural sensitivities. Keeping these factors in perspective the organising authorities have set a target of creating employment opportunities for almost 45000 families in the region

These employment opportunities include street vending and other tourist supporting roles like tour guides, boatmen and taxi drivers. The tourism department is carrying out training programmes for these roles. Local stakeholders like hotels, lodges, restaurants, taxi and bus operators along with shop owners will also be sensitised about importance of customer service and cleanliness to improve overall experience of the religious tourists.

6. A GOVERNMENT'S ROLE IN HARMONIZING RELIGIOUS TOURISM

Religious tourism, is a harmonious blend of faith and travel. It is a complex supply chain that requires meticulous organisation and planning. Large-scale events as Hajj and Kumbh Mela would be significantly hindered if the role of the respective governments is inefficient or curtailed. As we can clearly see from the earlier discussed cases, Governments play a crucial role in ensuring a seamless experience for millions of pilgrims.

- **The Stage Setting:**

It is evident that only Governments can lay the foundation for this spiritual journey by developing robust infrastructure. They construct roads that lead to sacred sites, build bridges that connect pilgrims to divine grace, and establish airports that transport devotees from across the globe. They also ensure the availability of quality accommodation, from modest lodgings to opulent retreats, catering to the diverse needs of pilgrims.

- **The Safety Net:**

The safety and security of pilgrims are paramount. Governments establish robust security measures, including surveillance systems, checkpoints, and emergency response teams, to safeguard the sacred spaces and those who visit them. They also collaborate with healthcare providers to ensure medical facilities are readily available, particularly during large-scale religious gatherings.

- **Preserving the Heritage:**

Governments recognize the immense cultural and historical significance of religious sites. They invest in the preservation and restoration of these sacred spaces, ensuring that future generations can experience their spiritual power. They also promote cultural heritage and traditions, enriching the pilgrimage experience.

- **Facilitating the Journey:**

Governments streamline visa and immigration processes, making it easier for pilgrims to obtain necessary permits and travel documents. They also facilitate group travel, providing special arrangements for organized pilgrimages.

- **A Sustainable Future:**

Governments strive to balance the economic benefits of religious tourism with environmental sustainability. They implement eco-friendly practices, such as waste management and energy conservation, to minimize the impact on the environment. They also work with local communities to ensure that the benefits of tourism are shared equitably, fostering sustainable development.

By playing these pivotal roles, governments can elevate religious tourism to new heights, creating unforgettable experiences for pilgrims and contributing to the economic and social well-being of communities.

Governments are thus majorly to provide infrastructure and create framework for stakeholder collaboration at religious destinations but the smooth running of a pilgrimage site is equally dependent on the strategic management and organisational skills of the caretakers or trusts responsible for the day to day functioning of those religious sites.

6.1. Case: Langar-The Free Community Kitchen at The Golden Temple, Amritsar

The Langar or the community kitchen we are going to focus on is located at the Golden Temple in the city of Amritsar in the Indian state of Punjab. The Golden Temple complex houses the Harminder Sahab which is the holiest shrines of the Sikh faith.

On an average this community kitchen or Langar feeds as many as 50,000 people daily and this number can more than double on special days. It does not discriminate between individuals on the basis of their class, caste, community, religion or nationality. The service is completely free of cost and is run on donations.

The langar is a 24x7 operation on all 365 days of the year. It has been going on at the Golden Temple since centuries and is a testament of the Sikh philosophy of selfless service.

The Shiromani Gurdwara Parbandhak Committee (SGPC) is responsible for the management of the Goden Temple trust and oversees the working of the community kitchen. The community kitchen is one of the many important aspects of the management of Golden temple that the SGPC has to deal with. The langar functions with the crucial support of selfless volunteers who find spiritual satisfaction committing themselves to this duty.

- **The Volunteers**

Only 10 per cent of the people involved in the langar are employed by the Golden temple management. The major work load is handled by an army of volunteers. Almost 500 volunteers participate daily in the cooking and serving process of the Langar with the support of the Sikh community. The washing of utensils is also managed by the volunteers. Volunteers can be from nearby cities and villages of Punjab, other parts of India or from anywhere around the world

- **The Dining Halls**

The temple premises have two huge dining halls totalling 50,000 sq ft with a seating capacity of 5000 pilgrims at a time. These dining halls are cleaned every 15 mins to make them ready for the next batch of hungry devotees. Every pilgrim is supposed to sit down on the floor as equals to partake their food.

- **The Food**

The food served comprises dal, vegetables, roti, rice and a thick milky rice pudding called kheer. Each time the meal is served the raw material required is a huge 12,000 kgs of flour,1500 kgs of rice, 13,000 kgs of lentils and 2000kgs of vegetables. A lot of effort and planning is put into procurement of sourcing good quality ingredients from nearby locations. An effort has also been made to transition to pesticide free organic feed to inspire farmers of Punjab to take up organic farming. The SGPC has tied up with Punjab Agro Industries Corporation Ltd (PAIC) for replacing chemical fertilizers with organic fertilizers (Anand, 2019).

- **The Preparation**.

There are two kitchens in which the food is prepared. There are 11 hot plates, multiple burners, specialised machines for sieving and kneading dough, and several other utensils. Automatic vegetable washers are used to clean large quantities of vegetables efficiently. Industrial-scale peelers and choppers are employed to chop vegetables such as potatoes, onions, and carrots. On normal days, volunteers or sevadaars prepare all the food by hand. On holidays and religious occasions, a roti making machine which was donated by one of the devotees is used to churn out 25,000 rotis in an hour. One hundred gas cylinders are needed to cook the food. Cooking temperatures are carefully monitored and systems have been put in place to ensure water quality. Additionally, proper waste disposal measures are in place, and inspections for maintaining hygiene are conducted regularly to maintain sanitation standards. All the ingredients are hygienically store in the basement which also has a huge cold storage. of the kitchen area and

The Langar at the Golden Temple ensures that nobody ever goes hungry in the city of Amritsar. It is one of the prime attractions of the famed religious site as every visitor makes it a point to eat at the dining hall. The food at the langar has become an integral part of the spiritual experience for the faithfuls. The temple authorities put in every effort to provide all the resources and the logistics while actively involving many pilgrims as volunteers making them an integral part of the entire process.

- **Challenges**

The temple authorities face an ongoing challenge continuously rising footfalls. The additional problem faced is this number keeps fluctuating making forecasting difficult. Another challenge is an aging infrastructure which is in need for modernisation and space constrains. Volunteer management can also be difficult as their numbers are huge and most of them lack prior experience in the task assigned. Responsible disposal of vast quantities of food waste is a challenge. The SGPC which is responsible for the running of the Golden Temple needs to ensure that all the activities related to the langar should be run in a transparent and accountable manner while maintaining regulatory compliance. Even though the temple can currently boast of managing the world's largest community kitchen, the challenges are never ending and the use of better planning, modern technology and advance forecasting tools will have to be employed to keep the langar filling the stomachs and fulfilling the spiritual aspirations of millions of pilgrims in the times to come.

6.2. Case: Crowd management at The Venkateshwara Temple, Tirumala

Crowds in religious gatherings vary in multiple aspects, with a significant portion consisting of senior citizens and children. Providing comprehensive services to cater to such a diverse population is essential, with a particular focus on medical support, food, ventilation and sanitation facilities. The safety of the pilgrims is a huge responsibility of the governing bodies of the religious sites.

The Lord Venkateshwara Temple at Tirumala is situated in the Tirupati district of the Indian state of Andhra Pradesh. It is the most visited pilgrimage site of the Hindus. It is managed by the Tirumala Tirupati Devasthanams (TTD) which is an independent trust managed by the Government of the State of Andhra Pradesh. The total net worth of the organization in 2024 is US$36 billion making it the richest Hindu temple board in the world. It employs more than 21,000 people, which include 7000 permanent and 14000 contract workers.

Between 60,000 to 80,000 pilgrims visit the Lord Venkateshwara Temple every day. The temple is considered to be a shining example for efficient crowd management with the ability to manage as many as 400,000 pilgrims on special occasions. The temple employs mammoth queue complexes with facilities such as toilets, bathing and free meals.

- **Queue Complexes at the Tirumala Temple**

The first time that the temple management took a major step in managing pilgrim flow was 1983. This was when the construction of the first queue complex was initiated. The mammoth complex with 37 compartments was designed to accommodate 17,000 pilgrims.

As crowds continued to increase a second queue complex was constructed to accommodate another 10,000 pilgrims.

Pilgrims have the option of paid and free darshan or sighting of the deity. The old complex is used by the devotees who pay for the service while the second complex is used by devotees who avail the free service.

Construction of a third queue complex is being planned to accommodate the ever increasing crowds of devotees.

- **Facilities Provided at the Queue Halls:**

The Tirumala Tirupati Devasthanams (T.T.D.) has meticulously tried to ensure a comfortable and sacred experience for pilgrims. The queue complexes comprise spacious, well-ventilated halls equipped with ceiling fans, providing relief from the elements. Affordable food options are available through T.T.D. canteens and reasonably priced food packets. Additional amenities include first aid facilities, clean toilets and bathrooms, even within the queue halls. Pilgrims can also enjoy devotional programs and music via closed-circuit TV. Convenient cloakroom facilities are available at the Pilgrim Amenities Complex and Vaikuntam Queue Complex. Free shoe-keeping centers are strategically located near these areas. To maintain order and prevent malpractices, officers are stationed at the temple entrance (Mahadwaram) and within the Vaikuntam Queue Complex to oversee pilgrim comfort and facilities.

- **Online Darshan Tickets**

Online booking of darshan slots is available. This has eliminated the need of long physical queues and accommodation requirement. This online system has been successfully emulated by my religious sites across India.

- **The Three- Layered Queue system**

The authorities of the temple have set up wooden platforms of varying heights to form three layers in order to provide hassle free darshan to the pilgrims. The first platform is of a height of 16 inches, while the second is 7 inches high and the third one is on the floor level. These variations in platforms enables pilgrims to witness the deity without any visual obstruction from crowds at other levels thereby avoiding jostling between devotees and push and pull by the scouts & volunteers in the queue management area.

The expertise of the Tirumala Tirupati Devasthanams (TTD) in crowd management has made it the preferred advisor of the temple trusts of the newly constructed Ayodhya Temple and the very popular Shrirdi Sai baba temple so that best practices of the Tirumala templecan be adopted in these places

In fact, Kishore Biyani the head of the Future Group, which ran the very popular Big Bazaar stores all over India, has admitted during one of his latest interviews that he learnt crowd management from the Tirumala temple and replicated crowd management strategies at his stores when faced with immense crowds.

7. CONCLUSION

Religious tourism which is a rapidly expanding industry presents a unique opportunity for economic growth and cultural exchange. While the influx of pilgrims can significantly boost local economies, it is imperative to manage this growth responsibly to preserve the sanctity and cultural significance of religious sites.

To harness the potential of religious tourism without compromising its core values, a robust and adaptive supply chain is essential. This supply chain should involve collaboration among various stakeholders, including government agencies, religious institutions, local communities, and private sector businesses. By working together, these stakeholders can ensure high-quality services and provide robust infrastructure to accommodate the increasing number of pilgrims.

Furthermore, the integration of technology can play a crucial role in managing crowd flow, enhancing visitor experiences, and avoiding safety risks. By implementing advanced crowd management systems, real-time monitoring tools, and digital information platforms, authorities can optimize the use of space, reduce congestion, and improve overall pilgrim satisfaction. Additionally, the use of technology can help in preserving cultural heritage through virtual tours, digital archives, and interactive exhibits.

However, it is crucial to strike a balance between economic growth and cultural preservation. Overtourism can lead to the degradation of sacred sites, erosion of local traditions, and a decline in the overall spiritual experience. To safeguard against these risks, sustainable tourism practices should be adopted, including limiting visitor numbers, implementing responsible tourism guidelines, and promoting eco-friendly initiatives.

In conclusion, religious tourism offers limitless potential for economic development and cultural understanding. By carefully managing this growth, prioritizing sustainable practices, and leveraging technology, we can ensure that religious sites continue to inspire and uplift millions of people for generations to come.

REFERENCES

Anand, N. (2019, September 6). *Exploring The World's Biggest Community Kitchen Inside The Golden Temple | City On Pedals*. City On Pedals; City On Pedals. https://cityonpedals.com/blog/exploring-the-worlds-biggest-communal-kitchen-at-amritsars-golden-temple

Choubey, N. (2024, March 5). *Ayodhya Ram Mandir: What to Learn from Tirumala Tirupati for Effective Crowd Management*. Native Planet; Native Planet. https://www.nativeplanet.com/news/ayodhya-ram-mandir-inauguration-what-to-learn-from-tirumala-tirupati-for-effective-crowd-management-010547.html#goog_rewarded

Dixit, K. (2024, November 18). Maha Kumbh 2025: Ensuring Unmatched Sanitation and Safety for Devotees in Prayagraj | Prayagraj News - Times of India. *The Times of India*. https://timesofindia.indiatimes.com/city/allahabad/maha-kumbh-2025-advanced-sanitation-standards-set-to-ensure-clean-and-safe-experience-for-devotees-and-tourists-in-prayagraj/articleshow/115414356.cms

Khoshkhoo, M. H., & Nadalipour, Z. (2016). *Search of a Common Experience: A Comparative study on Tourists' Spiritual Experiences in Relation to the Various Types of Tourism*. International Journal of Tourism and Spirituality.

Page, M. (2024, June 25). *Deaths During Annual Hajj in Saudi Arabia Underscore Extreme Heat Dangers | Human Rights Watch*. Human Rights Watch; Human Rights Watch. https://www.hrw.org/news/2024/06/25/deaths-during-annual-hajj-saudi-arabia-underscore-extreme-heat-dangers

Pandey, G. (2019, January 14). *Kumbh Mela: How to plan a festival for 100m people*. BBC; BBC News. https://www.bbc.com/news/world-asia-india-46834335

Patowary, K. (2014, August 5). *Mina, The City of Tents*. Amuising Planet; Amusing Planet. https://www.amusingplanet.com/2014/08/mina-city-of-tents.html

Saha, S. (2024, June 1). *Faith-based Tourism Market*. Future Markets Insights Inc.; Future Marketing Insights Inc. https://www.futuremarketinsights.com/reports/faith-based-tourism-sector-overview#:~:text=The%20faith%2Dbased%20tourism%20market,and%20purpose%20in%20their%20lives

SaudiPedia. (2024, June 11). *Transportation During Hajj Season - Saudipedia*. Saudipedia; SaudiPedia. https://saudipedia.com/en/article/1254/religion/hajj-and-umrah/transportation-during-hajj-season#:~:text=Pilgrims%20arrive%20in%20Makkah%20al,buses%20or%20private%20transport%20vehicles

Seth, M. (2024, October 28). Preparing for Maha Kumbh: 15 departments race against time to wrap up 500 projects | Lucknow News - The Indian Express. *The Indian Express*. https://indianexpress.com/article/cities/lucknow/maha-kumbh-prayagraj-uttar-pradesh-projects-6000-crore-9642968/

Sharda, S. (2024, November 27). *Massive Economic Boost Expected from Mahakumbh 2025 with 40 Crore Pilgrims | Lucknow News - Times of India*. The Times of India; Times of India. https://timesofindia.indiatimes.com/city/lucknow/massive-economic-boost-expected-from-mahakumbh-2025-with-40-crore-pilgrims/articleshow/115708909.cms

Shukla, G. (2024, October 24). *TTD contemplating construction of third queue complex - The Hindu*. The Hindu; The Hindu. https://www.thehindu.com/news/national/andhra-pradesh/ttd-contemplating-construction-of-third-queue-complex/article68791386.ece

Srivastava, S. (2024, October 19). *Maha Kumbh Mela 2025 - Maha Kumbh Mela 2025: UP government plans 7-tier security, 37,000 policemen to be deployed - UP News | India Today* (M. Pandey, Ed.). India Today; India Today. https://www.indiatoday.in/india/uttar-pradesh/story/maha-kumbh-mela-2025-yogi-adityanath-uttar-pradesh-government-plans-security-policemen-deployed-cctv-2619712-2024-10-19

Tala, M., & Mihaela, P. (2008). DIMENSIONS OF RELIGIOUS TOURISM. *Amfiteatru Economic*, •••, 242–253.

Verma, R. (2024, March 7). *Ayodhya: India's emerging religious tourism destination calls for increased infrastructure focus*. Grant Thornton; Grant Thornton. https://www.grantthornton.in/insights/blogs/ayodhya-indias-emerging-religious-tourism-destination-calls-for-increased-infrastructure-focus/

ADDITIONAL READING

Chalishazar, M., & Thadani, M. (2024, February). *Ayodhya's Gold Rush: Hospitality Boom in the Offing*. Hotelivate; Hotelivate. https://hotelivate.com/hotel-development/ayodhyas-gold-rush-hospitality-boom-in-the-offing/

Chapter 14
A Bibliometric Approach to Examine the Future Trends in Digital Tourism

Sakshi Pandey
Pal College of Technology and Management, India

Anil Kumar
https://orcid.org/0009-0000-8565-9522
Graphic Era Hill University, India

ABSTRACT

The growth of tourism has piqued the interest of political leaders, prompting them to market their countries as popular tourist destinations. Recognizing tourism's potential as a significant economic engine, authorities in certain nations have begun to focus on international relations tactics to improve their country's image and earn a portion of global tourist income. The present study is a bibliometric approach to examine the future trends in digital tourism through a review approach using R tool. The study examines the contribution of top authors, institutions, journals and countries and also examined the top cited articles and authors. Scopus database is used to extract the dataset as it is the largest repository of published articles. The thematic map technique is used to examine the trends in digital tourism to pave the way for future research directions for academicians and researchers.

DOI: 10.4018/979-8-3373-0071-9.ch014

INTRODUCTION

Tourism has long been recognized as one of the world's most important economic industries. In 2018, it contributed both directly and indirectly to 10.4% of the global GDP (World Travel & Tourism Council [WTTC], 2019). This industry has contributed significantly to job creation, revenue generation in local communities, and the expansion and development of linked sectors. The growth of tourism has piqued the interest of political leaders, prompting them to market their countries as popular tourist destinations. Recognizing tourism's potential as a significant economic engine, authorities in certain nations have begun to focus on international relations tactics to improve their country's image and earn a portion of global tourist income (Shafiee et al., 2019).

The expansion of the tourist business has coincided with advances in information and communication technologies (ICTs), which have transformed the tourism experience (Xiang & Fesenmaier, 2017). ICTs enable visitors to make more informed decisions by providing better access to information (Gretzel et al., 2015). Many governments are making significant investments in smart city programs and smart tourist destinations (Gretzel et al. 2016). In many nations, the idea of "smart tourism" has become well-known as a calculated strategy to boost the growth of the travel industry. For example, countries in Asia are working on smart tourism initiatives, including South Korea, Taiwan, and China (Zhang et al., 2012; Zhu et al., 2014) (Hwang et al., 2015). Smart city projects are the source of many smart tourism efforts in Europe (Caragliu et al., 2011). Political leaders around the world recognize the revolutionary power of smart technologies, not just for their economic advantages but also for their capacity to improve the social and experiential elements of travel (Gretzel et al., 2015). The use of these technologies by the tourist sector encourages innovation and creativity as well as competitiveness among locations (Gretzel et al., 2016). Tourism destinations can improve the quality of their services, provide more pleasurable experiences for passengers, and attract tourists by utilizing smart technologies through the development of tourism-oriented information technology (Minghetti & Buhalis, 2010). Despite arguments that smart tourism technologies have greatly accelerated innovation in the travel industry (Tu & Liu, 2014), researchers have not thoroughly examined these technologies (Gretzel et al., 2015). There is a lot of promise for these technologies to help underdeveloped nations grow their tourism sectors. But since much of the research in this field has been conducted in rich countries, there is a knowledge vacuum about how smart infrastructures and technologies operate and are implemented in less developed areas. According to the World Economic Forum's (WEF) 2024 Travel and Tourism Development Index (TTDI), India is ranked 39th out of 119 nations. The report highlights India's advancements in three key areas: boosting tourism and travel, strengthening security and safety, and advancing sanitation and health. According to the UNWTO Barometer for May 2024, India accounted for 1.47% of the global inbound tourism sector in 2022, receiving 14.3 million of the 975 million foreign tourists globally. Additionally, India accounted for 15.66% of all international tourists to the Asia-Pacific region in that same year. (PIB, 2024). Technological innovations have had a considerable influence on the tourist business in recent years, with the use of smart technologies becoming more popular among numerous players in the sector.

Historically, travel has been defined as the process of discovering new or uncharted territory (Arthur & Nuenen, 2019; Ashcroft, 2015). But this viewpoint has been altered by centuries of technological progress, from steam trains to cars to airplanes, which have made travel considerably simpler and more accessible (Löfgren, 1999). According to Salazar (2010), the development in "cosmobility" or global movement can be attributed to the expanding middle classes in industrialized nations having more access to international travel in recent decades. We now live in a "world of flows" (Franklin & Crang, 2001), where tourism, labor migration, commuting, and the international exchange of commodities and services are all intertwined, as Franklin and Crang also note in Tourist Studies. Over the past two decades, mobility has emerged as a significant area of study in the social sciences, with tourism playing a major role (Hannam, 2009; Hannam et al., 2014; Sheller & Urry, 2004; Vannini, 2010). Mobility has become a normal aspect of life (Franklin & Crang, 2001). To uncover the publication trends in the field of Digital Tourism, this study aims to identify the most influential journals, authors, countries, and articles that are shaping academic work in this area. Additionally, the study seeks to explore emerging topics and themes within the academic literature related to Digital Tourism. By examining these aspects, the research will also aim to uncover the social network among authors, countries, and institutions actively contributing to the field of Digital Tourism.

LITERATURE REVIEW:

Role of Tourism In Fostering Growth

Despite ongoing technological advancements, the tourist business has grown to be a significant worldwide industry (Kontogianni & Alepis, 2020). Both wealthy and emerging nations must modify their approaches to remain competitive in the global market as the demand for tourism rises. As a result, tourist locations have a number of difficulties in keeping up with the quick changes in technology (Iunius et al., 2015). Technology is changing the travel industry, impacting the competitiveness of travel agencies and destinations, and changing their strategies (Buhalis,

2020). The tourism industry is now driven by information technology (Januszewska et al., 2015). Information and communication technology (ICT) has had a huge impact on tourism over the last 20 years, changing how travelers perceive their trip experiences (Xiang & Fesenmaier, 2017). ICT provides prospects for greater data and insights into travel behavior and allows travelers to access tourism products in new ways (Gretzel et al., 2015).

Technology and Tourism

E-tourism is a contemporary approach to travel product distribution in which service or product suppliers reach clients online, wherever they may be. It facilitates quicker customer service, increases profitability, lowers expenses, and lets travelers look up information about travel-related goods and locations. This procedure frequently promotes information sharing among travelers (Buhalis & Deimezi, 2004). E-tourism also makes it easier for people to share their thoughts and experiences about places on social media.

Modern communication technologies give tourists the means to become knowledgeable travelers. They can look up places to visit, weigh their alternatives, and gain insight from other people's travel experiences and choices (Wang et al., 2016; Snellen & de Hollander, 2017). Websites, travel blogs, advisory systems, online communities, and mobile technology are some of the platforms that enable this. Before, during, and after their travels, visitors' experiences are influenced by information and communication technologies (ICTs) (Wang et al., 2016).

Since 2010, the emergence of Web 2.0 and its focus on interaction, as well as developments in areas like search engines, social media, the Internet of Things (IoT), and mobile technologies, have made a more sophisticated framework for tourism management necessary. The collecting and analysis of data enabled by the integration of ICT infrastructure with interconnected systems facilitates better decision-making based on common knowledge. This approach improves quality of life and operational efficiency. The Internet of Things is crucial to building a smart technological environment because it connects digital and physical infrastructures (Atzori et al., 2010). People can work together and communicate toward common objectives thanks to technologies like mobile devices, sensors, and radio frequency identification (RFID). According to Miorandi et al. (2012), these Internet-connected technologies aid in bridging the gap between the real and virtual worlds. The growth of big data analytics has made businesses, cities, and organizations more capable of meeting the demands of their communities (Xiang & Fesenmaier, 2017). New networking and communication techniques made feasible by contemporary technology infrastructures have allowed for deeper insights into the travel experience (Xiang et al., 2015). Additionally, mobile communication has increased due to improvements in location-based technology, which influences passengers' behavior by encouraging freedom and creativity (Wang et al., 2012). According to researchers, these advancements mark the beginning of a new era of "smart tourism" (Gretzel et al., 2015).

Enhancing access to online sharing and interactive services is largely dependent on the use of mobile devices and the Internet of Things (IoT) for resource and information sharing (Wang et al., 2013; Dickinson et al., 2014), as well as smartphones and online platforms for information exchange (Wang et al., 2012; Dickinson et al., 2014). Furthermore, the accessibility of these services is greatly impacted by the value of utilizing social networks and content channels (Xiang & Gretzel, 2010; Leung et al., 2013; Zeng & Gerritsen, 2014). At tourist locations, promoting the availability of interactive services and online sharing might increase demand for digital solutions.

Digital tourism technology have advanced, yet there are still a number of unanswered questions. One major problem that underserves emerging economies is the unequal accessibility to tools like social networks, mobile devices, and the Internet of Things, which are mostly available in industrialized countries. Furthermore, there aren't many thorough research looking at how users' experiences with social networks affect their enjoyment and judgment. It can be difficult to integrate digital solutions with traditional tourism services, especially in locations with poor technology infrastructure, and little is known about how promoting digital tourism affects society and the environment, including concerns about digital equity, data privacy, and energy use. This study aims to fill existing gaps by analyzing the evolution of digital tourism research, identifying significant authors, and exploring novel subjects including sustainability and inclusivity. Another objective is to map the networks of cooperation among authors, institutions, and countries. By focusing on the effects of interactive and online-sharing services on the travel and tourism industry, the study seeks to provide significant insights into addressing current challenges while promoting innovation and furthering inclusivity.

RESEARCH OBJECTIVES

1. To uncover the publication trend in the area of Digital Tourism.
2. To uncover the most influential journals, authors, countries, articles shaping the academic work in Digital Tourism.
3. To identify the emerging topics, and emerging themes related to Digital Tourism within the academic literature.
4. To uncover the social network among authors, countries and institutions working in the field of digital tourism

MATERIAL AND METHODOLOGY

This study employed bibliometric analysis to visualize global research trends and future research directions in Digital Tourism. Bibliometric analysis is a quantitative method for analyzing scientific literature and identifying patterns, trends, and structures within a specific research field. The data was extracted from the Scopus database, one of the most comprehensive and widely used bibliometric databases.

Search Strategy

The search strategy was designed to identify relevant literature by using specific keywords and search terms related to Digital Tourism. The search terms included:

```
TITLE-ABS-KEY ("Digital Tourism" OR "E-tourism" OR "Elec-
tronic Tourism" OR "online tourism" OR "smart tourism" OR
"smart-tourism") AND PUBYEAR > 1999 AND PUBYEAR < 2025 AND
(LIMIT-TO (LANGUAGE, "English")) AND (LIMIT-TO (SUBJAREA,
"BUSI") OR LIMIT-TO (SUBJAREA, "SOCI") OR LIMIT-TO (SUBJAREA,
"ECON") OR LIMIT-TO (SUBJAREA, "ARTS")) AND (LIMIT-TO (DOCTYPE,
"ar") OR LIMIT-TO (DOCTYPE, "re"))
```

Data Collection

These terms were applied to the title, abstract, and keywords fields to ensure a comprehensive retrieval of relevant publications. The search period was set from 2000 to 2024 to encompass recent developments. The subject areas included Business, Management and Accounting, Economics, Econometrics and Finance, Social Sciences, and Arts and Humanities. Only articles and review papers published in English were considered to maintain consistency and quality. Initially, the search identified 2852 papers. Filtering by Year range the number remain 2845, by applying Language filter it came to 2754. subject area reduced the number to 1515 papers. Further refinement to include only articles and reviews resulted in 988 papers. The final count included in our study therefore is 988 articles.

Data Analysis

The extracted data was analyzed using bibliometric technique. The Bibliometric R tool was employed for data processing, visualization, and analysis. This software is widely recognized for its capability to handle large bibliometric datasets and generate insightful visualizations. Descriptive analysis was first conducted to outline the basic characteristics of the data, including publication trends over time, distribution by country, and leading journals in the field. Citation analysis followed, identifying highly cited papers, influential authors, and prominent institutions. Co-occurrence analysis of keywords was conducted to identify major research themes and topics, and thematic map and thematic evolution was used to uncover the trending theme whereas social network analysis was performed to uncover the collaboration network.

Table 1. Selection criteria and selection of article

Selection Criteria and article selection	**Exclude**	**include**
Filtering Criteria		
Search Engine- Scopus		
Search Date- 6 September 2024		
Search Term- TITLE-ABS-KEY ("Digital Tourism" OR "E-tourism" OR "Electronic Tourism" OR "online tourism" OR "smart tourism" OR "smart-tourism")		2852
Period of Publication2000-2024	7	2845
Language: English	91	2754
Subject area "Business, management and accounting, Economics, Econometrics and Finance, Social sciences and Arts and Humanities"	1239	1515
Document type: ''Articles'' and ''Reviews''	527	988

Source: Author Elaboration

DESCRIPTIVE ANALYSIS

Table 1 provides a brief summary of the dataset used for analyzing Digital Tourism in the academic scenario during 2000-2024. A total of 327 sources produced 988 documents during this period with an annual growth rate of more than 20 percent. The average age of document was 4.32 year with average citation per document being 35.77. A total of 53469 references were analyzed with 1433 keywords plus and 2991 author keywords. Total authors in our analysis were 2196 out of which authors who contributed as single author in a document were 94. The international co-authorship percentage was less than 30% which indicate that there is wide scope for foreign collaboration in this academic piece of work. Out of the 988 total documents, 937 were research papers while 51 were review papers.

Table 2. Summary of dataset

Description	Results
MAIN INFORMATION ABOUT DATA	
Timespan	2000:2024
Sources (Journals, Books, etc)	327
Documents	988
Annual Growth Rate %	22.03
Document Average Age	4.32
Average citations per doc	35.77
References	53469
DOCUMENT CONTENTS	
Keywords Plus (ID)	1433
Author's Keywords (DE)	2991
AUTHORS	
Authors	2396
Authors of single-authored docs	94
AUTHORS COLLABORATION	
Single-authored docs	101
Co-Authors per Doc	3.1
International co-authorships %	28.14
DOCUMENT TYPES	
article	937
review	51

Source: Author Compilation

Figure 1 Shows the annual scientific production or the article production over time in the context of Digital Tourism from the year 2000 till 2024. Figure 1 clearly reflects that there is an increasing trend in the publication pattern in this research area. This trend reflects the importance of this field in the academic literature. As we can see that from 2000 till 2006 there was constant rate of publication of one or three articles which triggered in the year 2007 from where we can see a constant increase in the annual publication with some dips in between in the year 2021. In the year 2023 the article production was highest with 175 articles. As we can see that till date in the year 2024 there are 119 articles that have been published in the field of Digital Tourism and we have more to come in the remaining time period.

Figure 1. Annual production over time

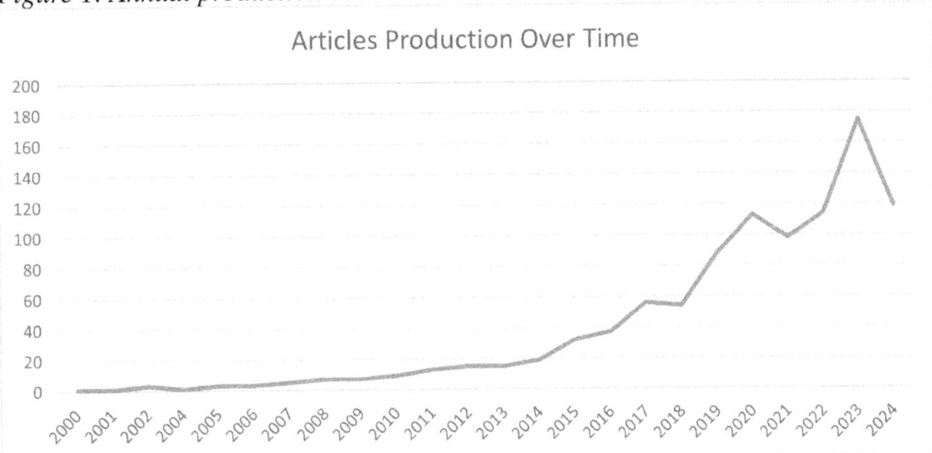

Source: Author Creation

Figure 2 represents "Average Citations per Year" plots the average number of citations received by scientific articles from 2000 to 2024. The y-axis measures the average citations, and the x-axis represents time in years. The figure 2 is showing ups and downs in the citation trend throughout the years from the very commencement in the Average Citations since 2000. In the year 2000 the AC was 0.6 which was 1.1 in 2001 and till 2005 there was an increasing trend. The first major decline came in te year 2006 when the average citation came to 0.7. the average citations reached highest in 2010 with AC of 15.9. following that there was sharp decline till 2015 when it reached second highest average citations of 15.3. there was a sudden fall in this and till date there is ups and down in this aspect reflecting that somehow digital tourism is being explored in some years and in some durations very less importance is assigned to this phenomenon. The graph shows that while there were periods of high citation impact, overall, there seems to be a downward trend in recent years.

Figure 2. Average citations per year

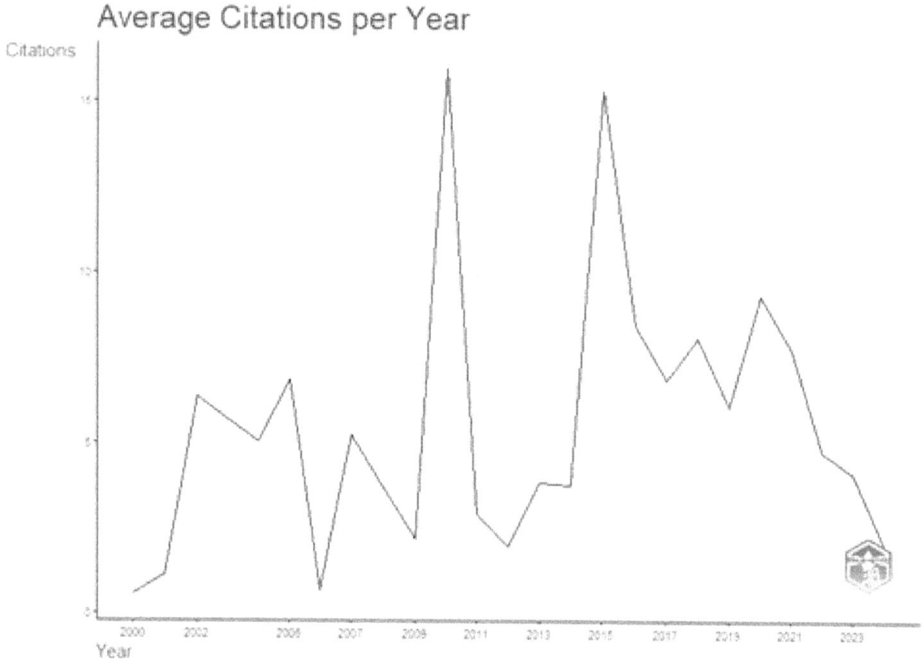

Source: Author Creation

Figure 3 is a three-field plot that visualizes the interconnections between countries, authors, and keywords within a body of academic literature. The leftmost column comprises of the most active sources working in context of Digital Tourism. The middle column comprises of most prolific keywords and the rightmost column comprises of the most active countries. We found that Smart Tourism, Tourism, E-Tourism, Smart Tourism Destination and Social Media were the prominent keywords in these years. Sustainability (Switzerland) is the prominent journal that is working on smart tourism and is highly promoted by Spain and Korea. Smart Tourism Destination is a major theme in Sustainability (Switzerland) that is explored in Italy and Spain the most. E-Tourism is a major theme in China, Italy and Spain which is published majorly by Information Technology and Tourism.

Figure 3. Three field plot

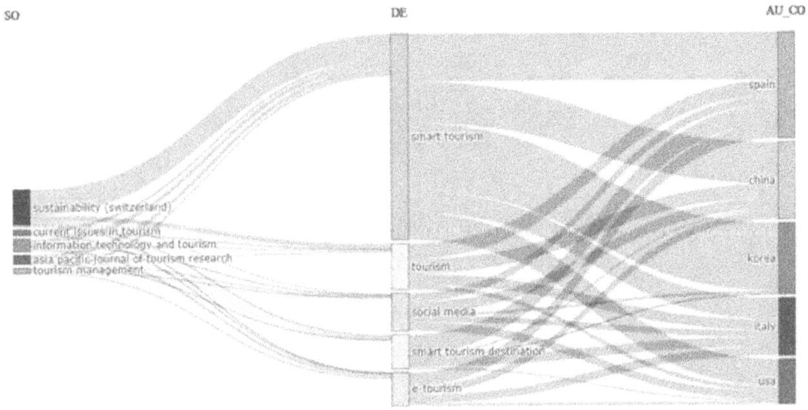

Source: Author Creation

Figure 4 presents a bubble chart titled "Most Relevant Sources," displaying the distribution of articles published across various academic journals and conference series within a specific field. The x-axis, labeled "No. of documents," indicates the number of articles, while the y-axis lists the names of the sources, such as journals and conference proceedings. Each bubble's size correlates with the number of articles published in that source.

Sustainability (Switzerland) is the most relavant source with highest publication of 101 articles, Asia Pacific Journal of Tourism Research is the second most productive journal followed by Current Issues in Tourism with 27 article each. These leading sources suggest a strong focus on Climate risk and financial resilience within the dataset. Figure 5 provides a list organized by Bradford's Law, categorizing sources into three distinct zones based on their productivity in a given field. Zone 1, the core zone, includes sources with the highest number of articles, such as "Sustainability (Switzerland)" with rank 1 and "Asia Pacific Journal of Tourism Research" holding rank 2 "Current Issues in Tourism" holding the rank 3, 'Information technology and tourism' holding 4th rank and "Tourism Management" ranked 5th in this law. Suggesting these are the most influential or most commonly referred to in the research area. These sources form the core or essential publications in the field.

Figure 4. Most relevant sources

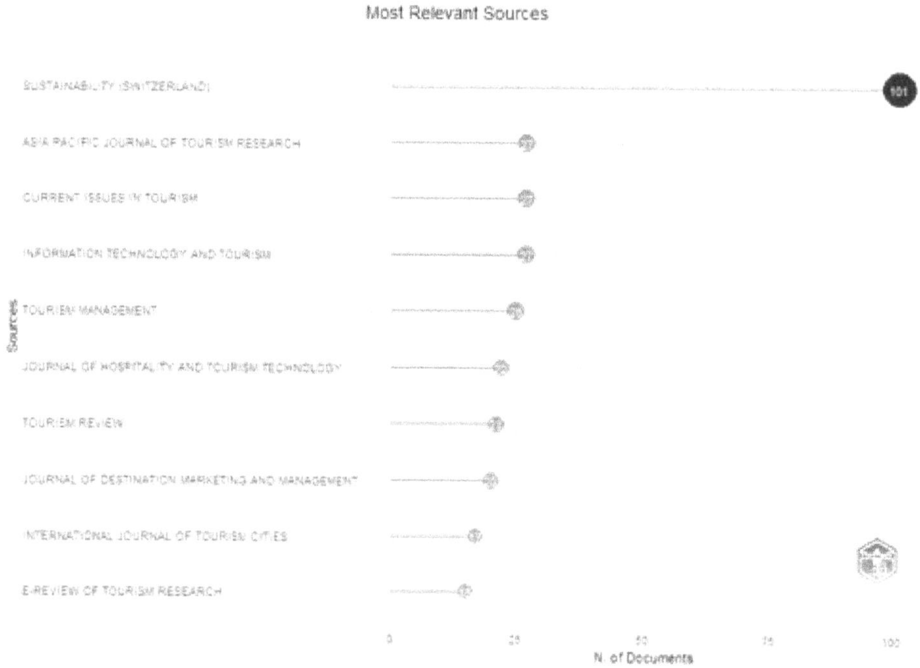

Source: Author Creation

As we move to Zones 2 and 3, the frequency of articles per source diminishes, which aligns with Bradford's Law, indicating that fewer articles are published in a larger number of sources. The distribution suggests a typical pattern where a few core journals publish most of the articles, and as one moves to less productive journals, the number of articles per journal decreases. This pattern is useful for identifying which journals are most central to a research area and guiding literature search strategies for researchers.

Source of Impact

Source impact is how impactful a journal is in context to the area of study and the h-index is a metric that aims to capture both the productivity and citation impact of the publications within these sources. Figure 6 depicts that Sustainability (Switzerland) is at the top in this list with an H-index of 32 followed by 'Tourism Management' with an H-Index of 22. Information Technology and Tourism is the third most impactful source with an H-Index of 17 followed by Asia Pacific Journal of Tourism Research, Current Issues in Tourism and Journal of Destination Marketing and Management with H-Index of 14 each.

Figure 5. Bradford's law

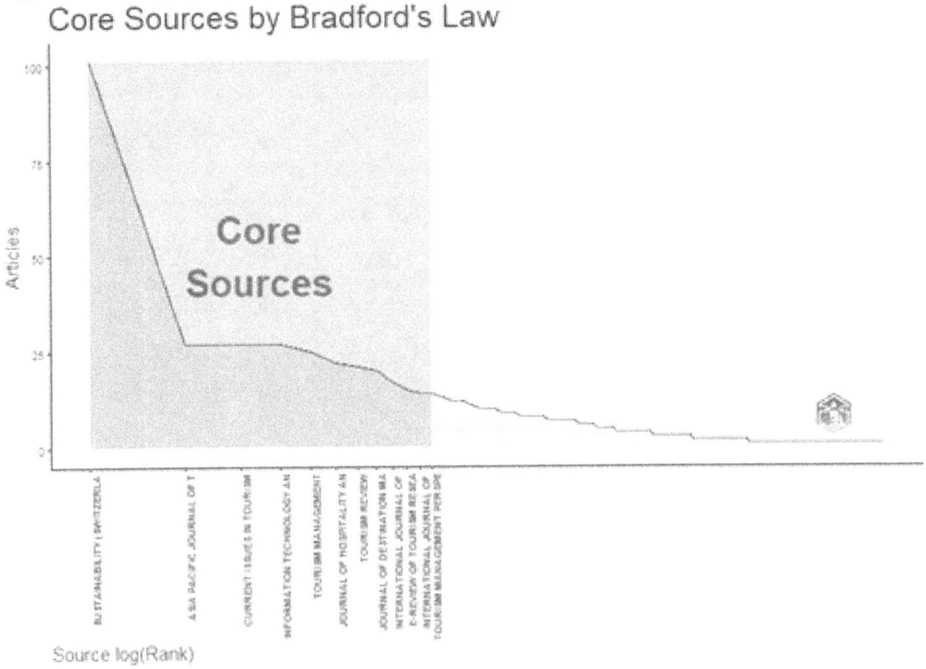

Source: Author Creation

Higher h-index values suggest that the publications from those sources are frequently cited and are influential in the field. 'Sustainability (Switzerland) stand out as the most impactful sources with the highest h-index values, indicating they are likely to be key outlets for research dissemination in the field. The variation in h-index among these sources helps researchers identify where to find the most seminal and potentially influential work in their area of study, and also to discern the key outlets for disseminating their own research to reach a broad and engaged audience.

Figure 7 shows "Sources' Production over Time" depicts the cumulative publications from different sources from around 2000 to 2024. Each line represents a different academic source, and the steepness of the line indicates the rate of publication over time. From the said graph, we see that "Sustainability (Switzerland)" is the leading source in context to Digital Tourism but the first article focusing on this aspect was published in the year 2002 in the journal "Current Issues in Tourism' and in 'Tourism Management' as per the data extracted. This was followed by 'Asia Pacific Journal of Tourism Research' and 'Information Technology and Tourism' which published their first article in this aspect in the year 2015. Sustainability (Switzerland) started publishing articles in Digital Tourism in the year 2016 and there onwards the productivity is the highest among all these top five sources.

Figure 6. Sources of local impact by H index

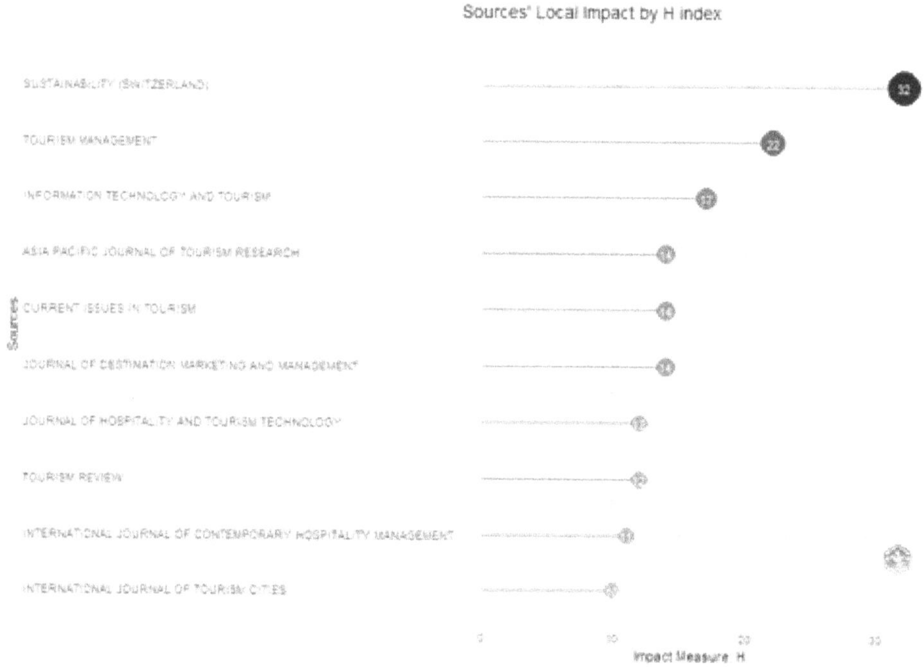

Source: Author Creation

Most Relevant Authors

The graph of "Most Relevant Authors" visualizes the academic output of various authors, measured by the number of articles published (Figure 8). The y-axis lists the names of the authors, while the x-axis likely represents the h-index or another metric of publication impact, though it's not labeled here.

Based on the number of publications by each author to find the most productive author figure 8 represents an idea to it Chung N is the most relevant author in the domain of digital marketing with 28 articles till date followed by Law R with 26 articles and Koo C with 19 articles.

Figure 7. Sources' local impact by H index

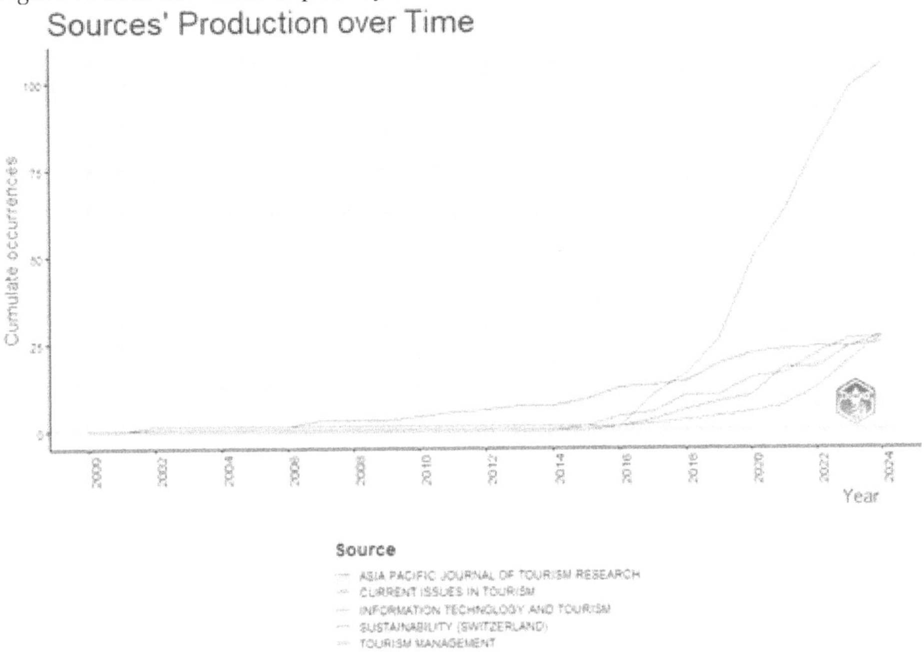

Source: Author Creation

The figure 9 shows the author's production over time. This analysis is important from various aspects. Firstly it talks about the journey of an author as when an author started producing articles in any domain and on the same time the citation the article got during specific duration of time. The bubble size reflects the total number of publication by any author and the color of the bubble represent the number of citation received by the article. The darker the circle the more the number of citation received by any article in the dataset analyzed in the study by the author.

Buhalis D first published in the domain of digital tourism in the year 2002 with an total citation per year of 17.78, the author is producing continuously over the years and the last work as per the data extracted is in the year 2023 with total citation per year of 46. The article produced by any author reflects the most prolific author as the author is contributing in the domain of Digital tourism, whereas the citation is reflecting the importance the article of the author has received in the academic literature as the citation is considered as getting recognition in academia. Law R is one of a consistent author with 26 articles produced over the year at increasing pace and the citation average per year is also increasing with highest as 114 in 2020. Chung N is one of the prolific author with 28 articles over the years with highest 6 articles in 2019 and last work in 2024.

Figure 8. Most relevant authors

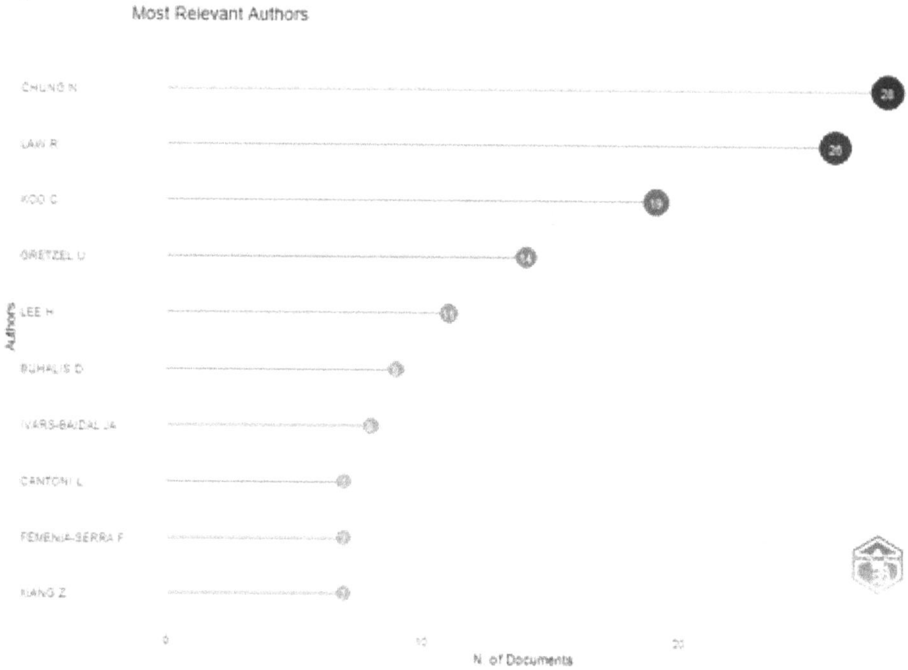

Source: Author Creation

Authors local impact is one of the measure to assess impactful author over the period of time. In this study H-Index is used as a measure to assess the author's impact. Chung N and Law R are the most impactful authors with H-index of 18 in the domain of digital tourism. Gretzel U is at third place with an H-index of 12 followed by Koo, C with H-index of 11. Buhalis D is at 5th Position with H-index of 9 followed by Ivars JA and Lee H with H-index of 8. The top ten authors are in the h-index range of 6 to 18 which is a good count as all authors included in this list are somehow impactful with their work in the domain of digital tourism.

Institutions relevance is reflected in figure 11 as it shows "Most Relevant Affiliations," each bubble represents an academic or research institution's contribution to the literature in terms of the number of articles published. The position of the bubble along the horizontal axis suggests the quantity of articles, while the vertical positioning corresponds to different institutions. The institution with the largest bubble appears to have produced 102 articles, indicating a significant level of research activity and output. This could suggest a leading role in the respective field, possibly due to robust funding, a large number of active researchers, or a focus on prolific publishing practices.

Kyung Hee University is the most prolific affiliation with 102 articles in the dojmain of digital tourism. The Hong Kong Polytechnic University is with 80 articles followed by University of Aucante and University of Sovi Nad is with 24 articles each. This reflects that South Korea, Hong Kong and Spain are promoting research in this domain as these universities are located in the respective countries.

Figure 9. Author's production over time

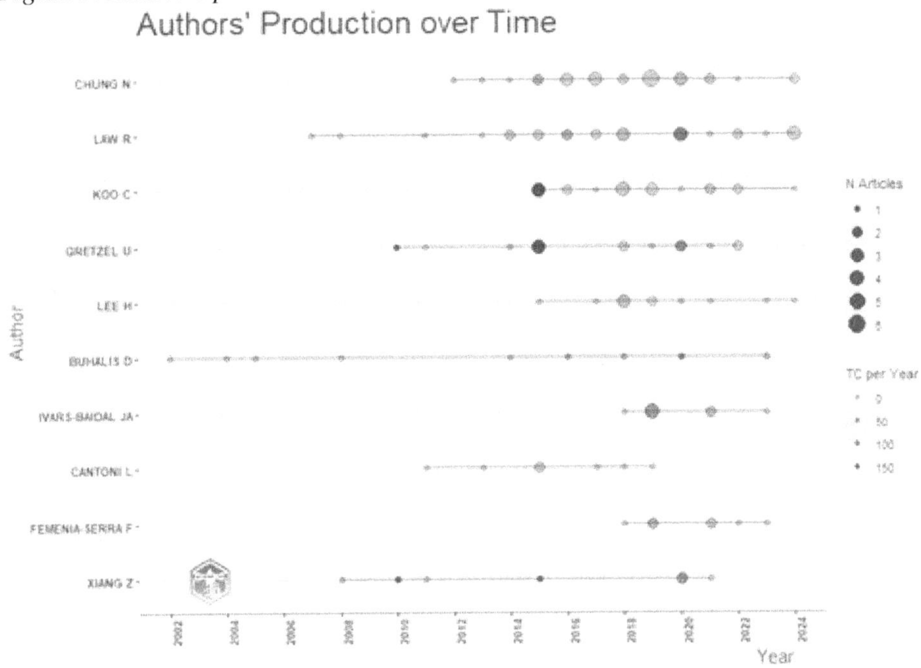

Source: Author Creation

In context to article production over time by the affiliations, The Hong Kong Polytechnic University published the first article in domain of digital tourism in 2008 and in 2024 it published 80 article till date. followed by Kyung Hee University of Spain which published first article in 2012 and in 2024 it has 102 articles till date. The Sun-Yat Sen University of China in 2014 published the first article and in 2024 it has 19 articles which shows that compared to the former ones, this university is publishing at a slower pace.

Figure 10. Author's local impact by H-index

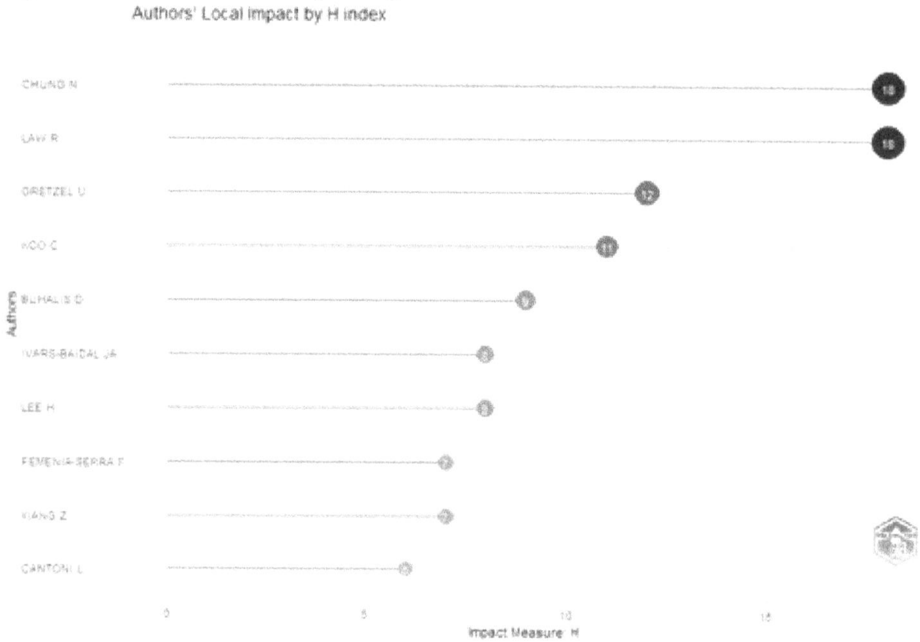

Source: Author Creation

Assessing the countries scientific production visualized that China is the most productive country in the domain of digital tourism as can be seen in figure 12 with 400 publication till date. It is followed by Spain with 296 articles, South Korea with 220 articles, USA with 168 articles and Italy with 164 articles as top 5 productive nations. India is also at 8th position with 94 articles in its name indicating that digital tourism is now being explored well by India.

In context to country's production over time to assess which country produced first and how the growth in the productivity emerged during the years, it can be seen from figure 13 that Korea published its first article in the year 2002 and till 2012 the publication rate was low but since 2013 there is a surge in the production and in 2024 it got highest publication of 220. USA published the first article in 2004 and since then the publication growth is rising upward with 168 publications as highest in 2024. Italy published first article in 2007 but till 2013 the growth was low and after 2014 there is an upward trend with highest publication of 164 in 2024.

Figure 11. Most relevant affiliations

Source: Author Creation

In context to most cited countries, USA is the most impactful country with 4348 citations followed by Korea with 4028 citations and is the second most impactful country. China is at third position with 3287 citations, Spain is with 2778 citation and is at fourth place in most impactful nation. UK with 2449 citations is the 5th place in context to most cited nation followed by Italy with 1964 citations followed by Hong Kong with 837 citations. This indicates that along with productivity these nations are also getting recognition as articles produced in these articles are getting good citations.

Global citation is used in figure 15 to analyze the most relevant document in the present study to study the academic literature of Digital Tourism. Global citations are the total citations received by any article from all domains in the total time span of the article which makes this an important aspect to consider while studying the most relevant document. The vertical axis consists of author name with year of publication while the horizontal axis consist of total global citation received. Xiang Z "Role of Social Media in Online Travel Information Search" which was published in 2010 is the highly globally cited article with 1950 Total Citation and an average annual citation of 130. The article examined the extent to which social media appears when someone search for travel related aspects. Study results indicated that social media appears frequently as travelers search for travel related aspects and indicate that social media and travel have a relationship. Lu J published article "Recommender System Application Development: A Survey" in 2015 that examined how users can get personalized services in travel. Results indicated that recommender service offers great assistance in this. The article received 1242 citations and average annual citation of 124.20. Gretzel U published article in 2015 which got 1154 total citation and titled "Smart Tourism: Foundations and developments". In this study smart tourism was defined with its various forms and it was found that being a new phenomenon this can assist travelers and industry to promote new form of tourism.

Figure 12. Country's scientific production

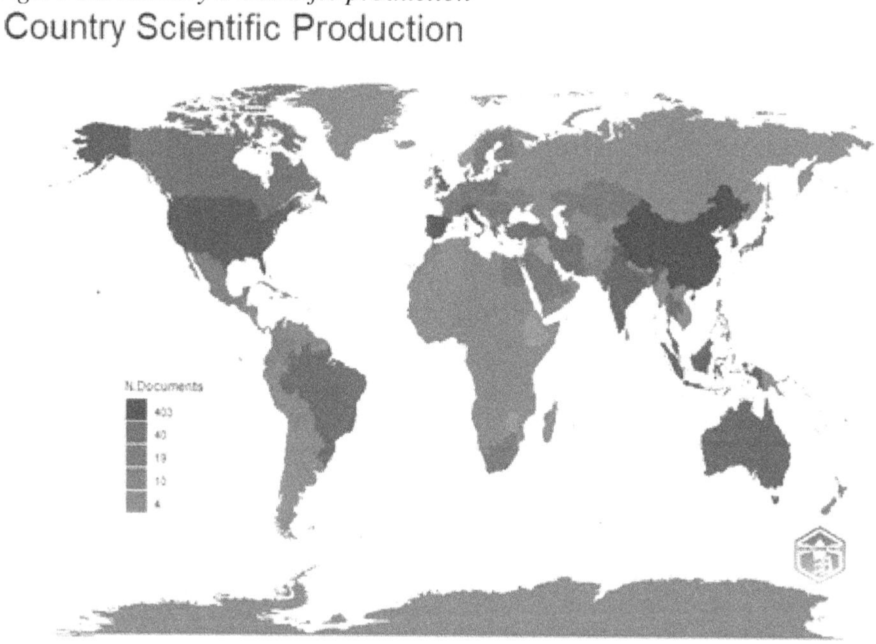

Source: Author Creation

Keyword analysis is one of the important tool to gain insight regarding trending topics in any domain. Author keywords refer to the keywords as specified by the author in their article while submitting the final manuscript for submission. The figure 16 (Most Relevant Words) likely plots keywords on a two-dimensional plane, with the x-axis representing the number of documents a particular keyword appears in (its occurrence), and possibly the y-axis representing the strength of the relationship between keywords (measured by a metric like the co-occurrence or a weighted occurrence score).

"Smart Tourism" appeared in 275 documents denoting the topmost relevance of the word in context of the present study and indicating that how this topic is in exploration in the academic literature. The word "e-tourism" occurred 108 times and indicate that digital tourism is one of the main theme that is/has emerged. This indicates a high volume of research and discussions for exploring new form of tourism and to fulfil the needs of modern day travelers is being synthesized and suggested by academic writers. These influential words are followed by "tourism", "Smart Tourism Destination", "Social Media", "Sustainability", "Smart City", "Covid-19", "Digital Tourism", "Smart Tourism", "Sustainable Tourism". This analysis highlights that sustainability and social media are some of the other major themes that are being explored in context to digital tourism.

Figure 13. Country's production over time

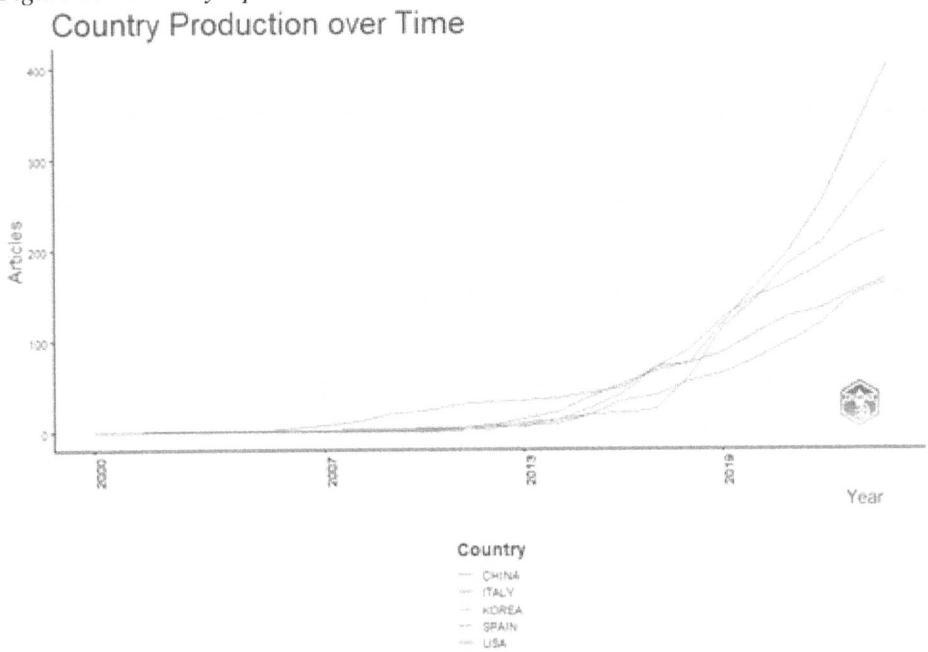

Source: Author Creation

Figure 14. Most cited countries

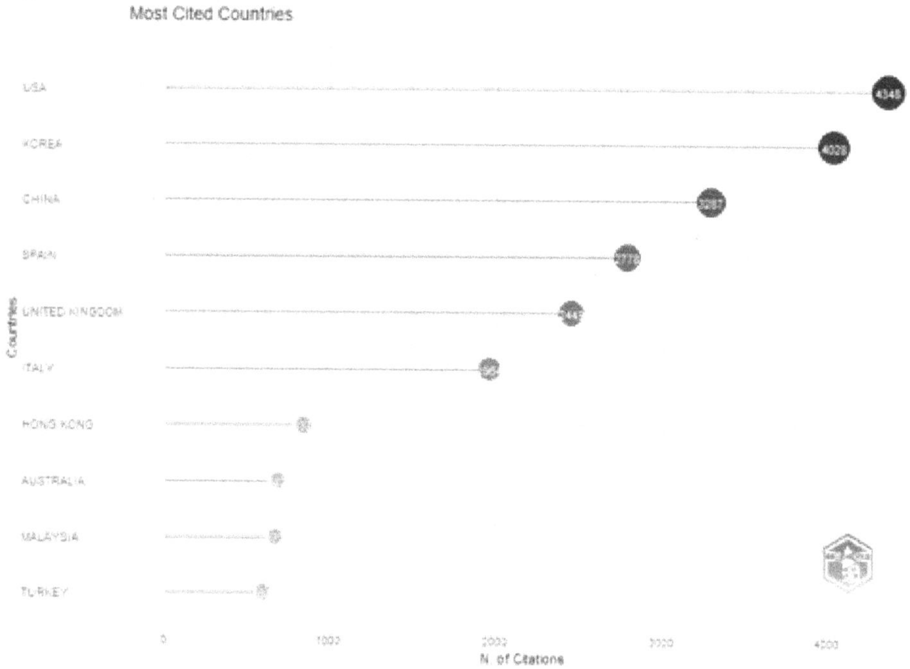

Source: Author Creation

Word Cloud

Word cloud is a feature in biblioshiny that allows to visualize the most frequent words by making them a central point in the visualization. In context of Digital Tourism by using author keywords and keeping 50 minimum keywords, word occurrence by frequency, it can be clearly noticed that "Smart-Tourism", 'E-tourism', 'tourism', 'Smart Tourism Destination', 'Sustainability', 'Smart Destination', and 'Social Media' are some of the major words that are being shown as the most impactful keywords in context to the research in Digital Tourism. This puts light in the fact that researchers in this domain are majorly working on these topics and also it highlights the future trending keywords. This also focuses as how various aspects of Digital Tourism is being explored by researchers in the academic front nowadays.

TreeMap graphically (figure 18) represents the relative frequency of various keywords in a dataset, likely from academic research or publications. In this treemap, each keyword is allocated a space proportional to its frequency, with 'Smart Tourism' being the most prominent, indicating it is the most frequently occurring or studied topic within the context of the data, occupying 38% of the occurrences.

Following Smart Tourism, the term 'E-Tourism' holds 15% visibility, suggesting significant attention towards various aspects of digital tourism aspects. 'Tourism', 'Smart Tourism Destination;, 'Social Media', occupy 12%, 6% and 6% visibility. 'Sustainability' and 'Smart City' occupy 5% visibility each followed by 'Covid-19', 'Digital Tourism' and 'Sustainable Tourism' holding 4% visibility each.

Figure 15. Most global cited documents

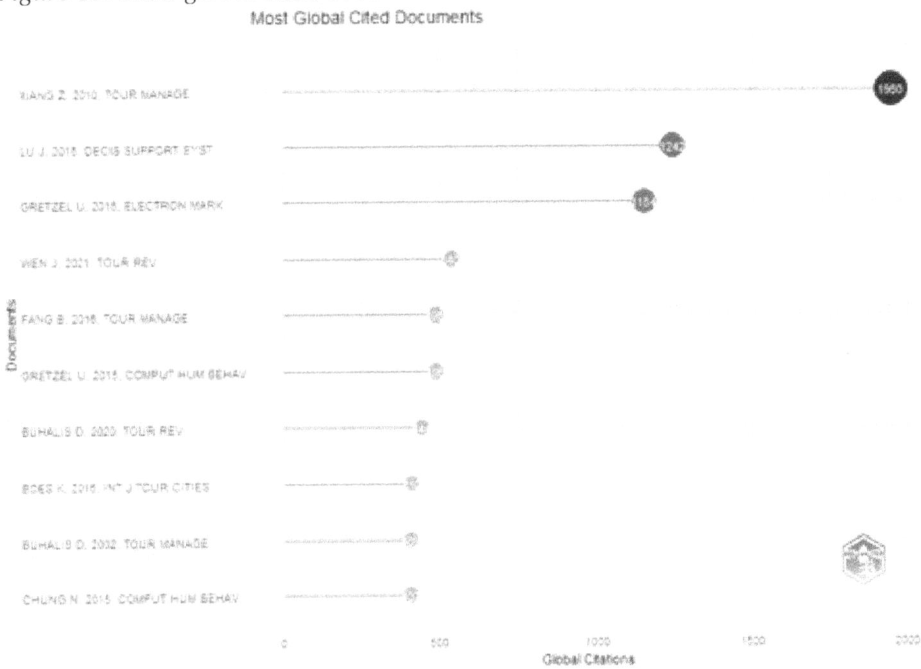

Source: Author Creation

There are some words that appear in an year and may sustain for long duration and some words may disappear from the academic literature. Figure 19 illustrates the words frequency over time which demonstrates as how these words are being evolved and sustained in the progressive course of action with many advancement in research in Digital Tourism. The graph demonstrates that 'Smart Tourism' firstly appeared in the year 2013 with 1 occurrence and since 2016 the graph has surged with an increasing rate with 275 occurrences in the year 2024 which is the highest till date. This shows that this aspect is being now explored and is a major theme today in the academic literature. The word frequency is a major technique in biblioshiny to explore the trend in words from its evolution in specific domain to know that what aspect is evolving at present in that domain. 'E-tourism' which occurred first in year 2004 evolved trough these years and has a continues occurrence in the academic literature over the years showing that this theme is still adopted by many researchers even getting 108 occurrences in 2024. 'Social Media' in context to tourism was first used in the year 2010 and since then there is a continues growth and in past five years this occurrence has got great surge. 'Smart Tourism Destination' which appeared for the first time in 2014 is one of the trending topic in the academic literature on digital tourism which is being promoted nowadays. 'Sustainable Tourism' appeared for the first time in 2007 which shows that this trend of sustainability in tourism evolved way back past decade and still one of the prominent topic.

Figure 16. Most relevant words

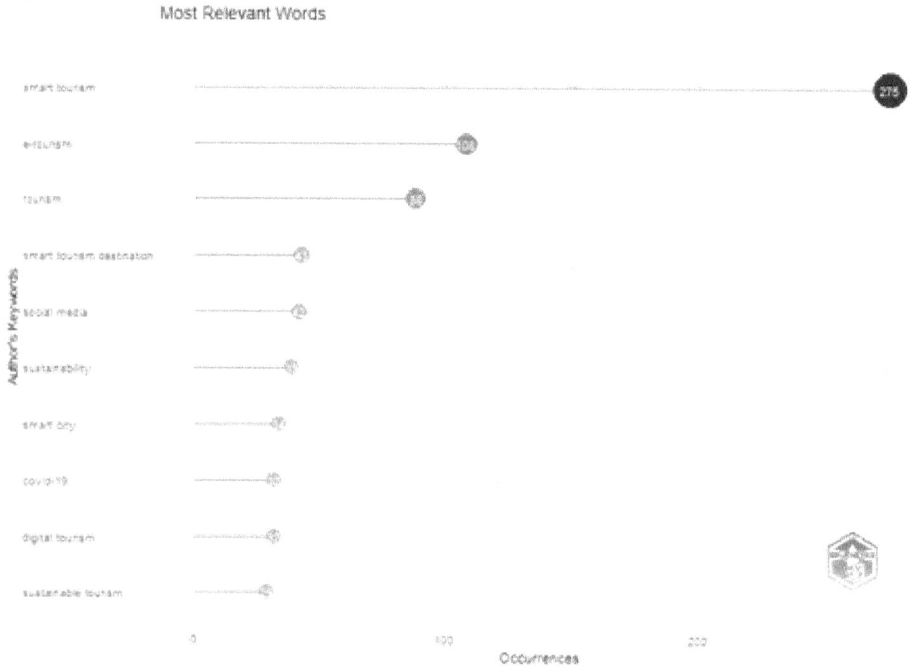

Source: Author Creation

To further examine the trending topics in the context of Digital Tourism, an analysis of author keywords was conducted with time span from 2000 till 2024. The size of the bubbles represents the term frequency, while their position on the horizontal axis indicates the time of occurrence, by setting timespan ranging from 2000 to 2024 considering minimum 5 occurrences and 2 words per year, the results indicates the various aspects. The term 'Semantic Web', 'User Experience', 'E-commerce', 'E-services' were trending topics between 2008-2013, 'e-tourism', 'ict', 'Recommender Systems', 'Technology acceptance model' were some of the trending topics between 2014-2019. 'Big Data', 'Smart Tourism', 'Sustainability',

‘Smart Tourism Technology’, ‘Artificial Intelligence’, ‘Digital Transformation’ are trending topic since 2019 . This indicate that now this topic is much explored.

Figure 17. Word cloud

Source: Author Creation

In addition, our study employs the keyword co-occurrence using author keywords to gain insights into the field of Digital Tourism. Keyword Co-occurrence Network (KCN) analysis draws the links between the keywords used in the literature that provides deep insights regarding knowledge structure (Esfahani et al., 2019). Notably, some keywords seem to have a greater impact on a network. For example, a close examination of these keywords from its color code suggests that a bigger keyword represented by their width are cohesively connected to other smaller keywords.

Figure 18. Tree map

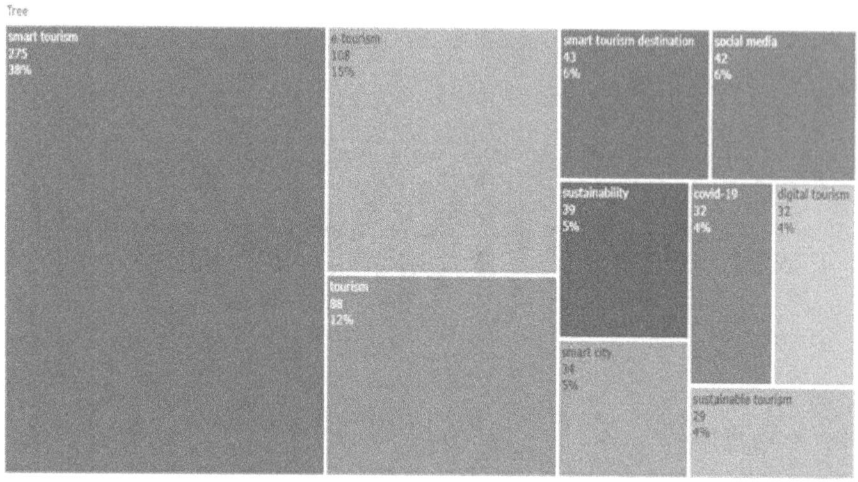

Source: Author Creation

Figure 21 shows node-link diagram, highlighting the interconnectivity between various terms related to Digital Tourism. In this network, the nodes (represented by dots or circles) stand for terms or concepts, and the links (the lines connecting the nodes) illustrate the relationships or associations between these terms. The figure represents direct as well as indirect linkages between various keywords that have been also a part of highly cited keywords or trending topics and here in the co-occurrence keyword network diagram they are linked to guide scholars towards some themes in which potential for exploration is there. The co-occurrence network diagram clearly showing that 'Digital Tourism' is directly linked with 'Big Data' and 'Smart Tourism Destination' as these co-occurred frequently as the bubbles are joined with a thick node. There we can observe five colors of bubbles (Red, Green, Blue, yellow and Violet). Cluster 1 (Red) consists of nineteen keywords which are interrelated to one another but the word 'Smart Tourism' is connected to all words and is the main or major theme in the cluster and closely with 'Big Data' and 'Sustainability'. Cluster 2 (Blue) consist of 13 keywords with 'E-tourism' as a main theme and major co-occurrence with 'Internet'. Cluster 3 (Green) consist of 8 keywords of which 'Tourism' seems to be the major theme linked with all other keywords and high co-occurrence with 'Technology'. Cluster 4 (Violet) consist of 7 keywords of which 'Smart tourism destination' is a major theme and the only direct link with 'Smart City'. The final cluster 5 (Yellow) consist of 3 keywords of which high linkage is between 'Smart tourism Technology' and 'Destination Image'.

Figure 19. Words' frequency over time

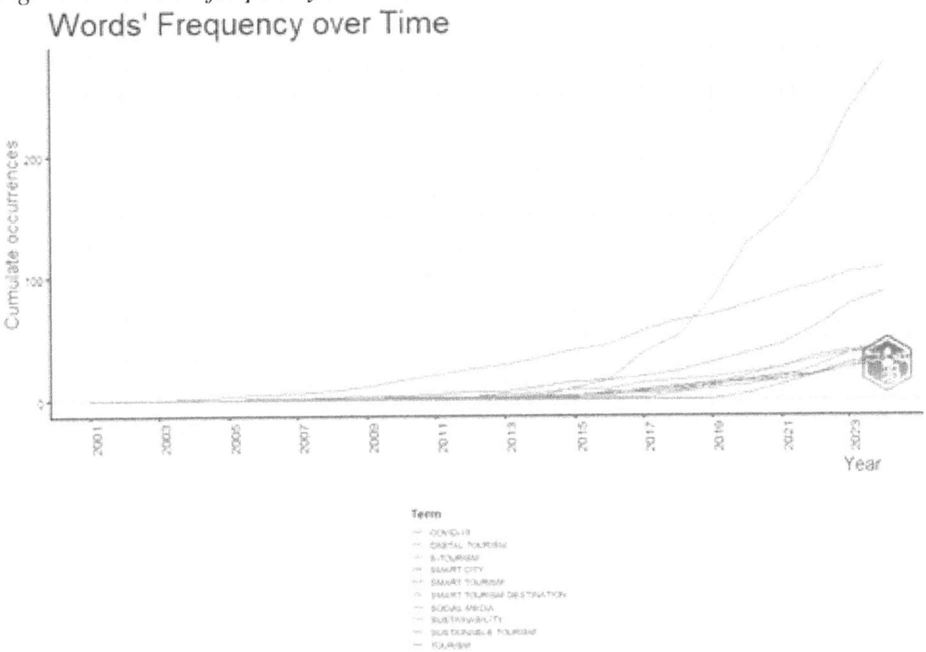

Source: Author Creation

Thematic Map: A Thematic map is a two dimensional plot which plots the typological themes on the basis of centrality and density (Cobo et al., 2011). In this, clusters are identified based on the co-word analysis and then the themes in each cluster is generated in research domain. These themes can be classified into four quadrants on the basis of density and centrality. Each theme is represented in the map with a bubble. Centrality is plotted on X-axis whereas the density is plotted on the Y axis. Centrality is a measure of inter-cluster interaction among the keywords and it denotes as to which extent one topic is connected or related to other topic in a domain. Density on the other hand refers to the intra-cluster interactions of keywords to develop a theme of that cluster. The top right quadrant contains motor themes with high centrality and density denoting to those themes that are well developed as well as are core to the research domain. The lower right quadrant refers to Basic theme with high centrality and low density denoting themes that are important and can impact other themes but are less developed internally. Themes in the lower left quadrant refers to emerging or disappearing themes as they have low centrality as well density and are less explored. The upper left quadrant consist of niche themes that are having high density but low centrality and are well developed internally but less discussed widely.

The upper right quadrant in the figure 22 consist of Motor themes that are highly discussed and are highly developed in the research domain due to which they are the core themes including 'Smart Tourism', 'Big Data', 'Artificial Intelligence'. The upper left quadrant that consist of the Niche themes that are well developed internally but have wide scope of discussion in the research domain consist of keywords such as 'Destination Marketing', 'Tourism 4.0', 'Tourism Motivation', 'Social Media', 'Online Reviews', 'Destination Image', 'Smart Tourism Technology', 'Text Mining', 'Satisfaction'. The lower right quadrant consist of basic themes which are of utmost importance for the development of the research field but are less developed internally and includes keywords such as 'E-tourism', 'Digital Tourism', 'ICT', 'Sustainability', 'Sustainable Tourism', 'Covid-19', 'Smart Tourism Destination', 'Smart City', 'Smart Destination'. The lower left quadrant consist of themes which are either emerging or which may disappear with time include keywords such as 'Tourism', 'Digitalization', 'Bibliometric Analysis'.

Thematic evolution. The thematic evolution demonstrates the evolution of themes in a broad manner over a time period by dividing the entire time span into time slices with various cut points. Thematic evolution assist scholars in exploring themes based on centrality and density. With 100-word count in author keyword field,, thematic evolution, over four time slices with cut points of 2006, 2012, 2018 and 2024 is shown in figure 23-26.

In the time slice 1 thematic evolution it can be seen that 'Digital TV' lies between niche theme and motor theme indicating that this topic was either a new aspect or a core theme for academicians while 'E-tourism' lies between emerging or basic theme which also indicate the same in 2000-2006. In the time slice 2 between 2007-2012, 'Satisfaction' and 'websites' were niche themes indicating work on tourist satisfaction and focus on website development for tourism as niche aspect. 'cultural heritage', 'e-services', 'electronic tourism', 'internet', 'search engine' and 'travel information search', 'e-tourism', 'e-commerce', 'semantic web' were the motor themes and core concepts. 'Destination Marketing', 'Tourism Marketing', 'ICT' lies between motor and basic theme indicating these topics as core as well as important. 'tourism' and 'mobile devices' were basic themes. 'Sustainable Development', 'Consumer Behavior' were emerging concept in this time slice. In the time slice 3 between 2013-2018 we can observe new themes growing such as 'User Experience', 'economic growth' related studies were focused using bibliometric analysis as these keywords also appear as niche theme. 'ICT', 'Satisfaction', 'Smart Tourism Destination', 'Smart City', and 'Big Data' were the core themes. 'Webometrics', 'Social Media', 'Destination Marketing' and Perceived Value' were emerging or disappearing themes along with 'Smart Tourism', 'Content Analysis', 'Technology acceptance model', 'e-tourism', 'recommender system', 'sustainability', 'sustainable tourism', 'trust', and 'Innovation' being the basic themes. In the time slice 4 between 2019-2024

‘Tourism Development’, ‘Cultural Heritage’, ‘Economic Growth’, ‘Social Media’, and ‘Digital transformation’ were the niche themes. ‘Smart Tourism’, ‘Big Data’, ‘Sustainable Tourism’, ‘E-tourism’, ‘Digital Tourism’ being motor themes. ‘Smart Tourism Destination’, ‘Smart Destination’, ‘Sustainability’, ‘Technology’ being basic themes. ‘Smart tourism technology’, ‘rural tourism’, ‘satisfaction’, ‘smart tourism destination’, ‘destination management’ in emerging or disappearing themes.

The three field plot captured the emergence of broad themes in context to Digital Tourism which is shown in figure 27. A closer look at the inter-linkages among the themes separated by four-time spans, namely period from 2000 to 2006, 2007–2012, 2013–2018 and 2019-2024 underscores the thematic evolution. In the time slice 1 there is only one concept which emerged as major themes namely ‘E-Tourism’. ‘Consumer Behaviour’, ‘Content Analysis’, ‘E-services’, ‘Social Media’, ‘Cultural Heritage; emerged as trending and evolving themes during 2007-2012. All themes except e-services and Cultural Heritage merged in e-tourism. ‘E-tourism’, ‘also merged in ‘Destination Branding’, ‘Destination Marketing’, and ‘E-learning’. ‘E-services’ merged in ‘Consumer Preference’ in the year 2013-18 and some new prolific themes ‘Trust’, ‘Smart Tourism’, ‘Sustainability’, ‘Perceived value’ emerged. In recent years in time slice 2019-2024 ‘Smart Tourism’, ‘Smart Tourism Technology’, ‘Online Tourism’, ‘Smart City’, ‘Social Media’, and ‘Smart Destinations’ are the major evolving themes.

SOCIAL NETWORK ANALYSIS

The social network analysis in bibliometric study assist in developing knowledge that which authors, universities or countries work together in the respective domain of study. Collaboration map of authors, countries and affiliation are shown in the figure 28 to figure 30 that reflect author, country and institution collaboration respectively. Law R, Chung N, Koo C are the major collaborating authors in this domain. ‘China’, ‘Korea’, ‘Spain’, ‘USA’ are the major collaborating countries in digital tourism. ‘Kyung Hee University’, ‘The Hong Kong Polytechnic University’ are the major collaborating universities in digital tourism.

Figure 20. Trending topics

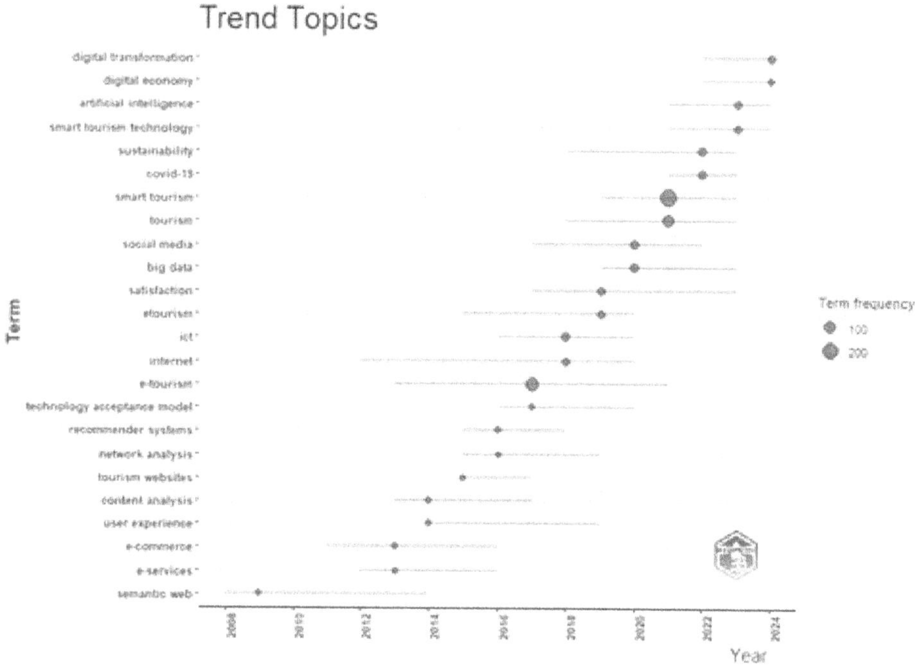

Source: Author Creation

Figure 21. Co-occurrence network of keywords

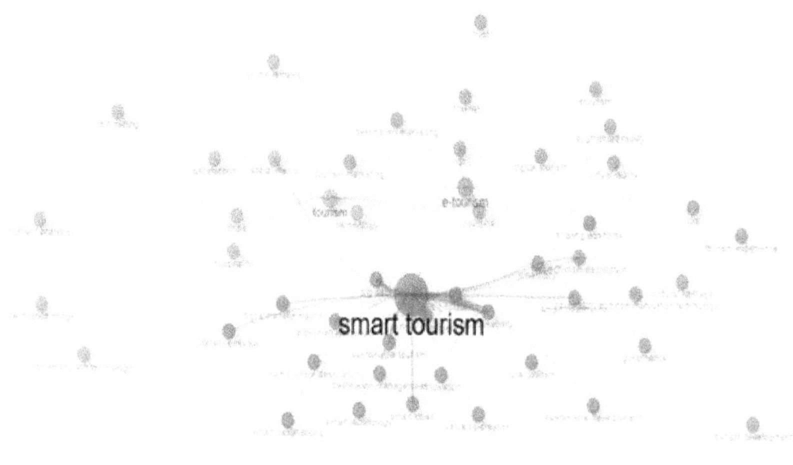

Source: Author Creation

Figure 22. Thematic map

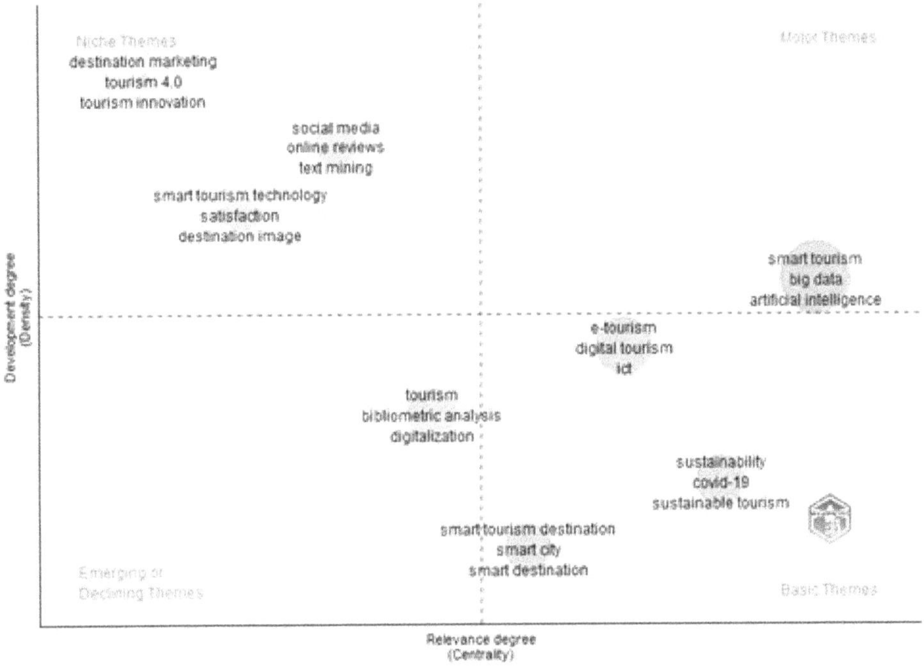

Source: Author Creation

Figure 23. Time slice 1: thematic evolution 2000-2006

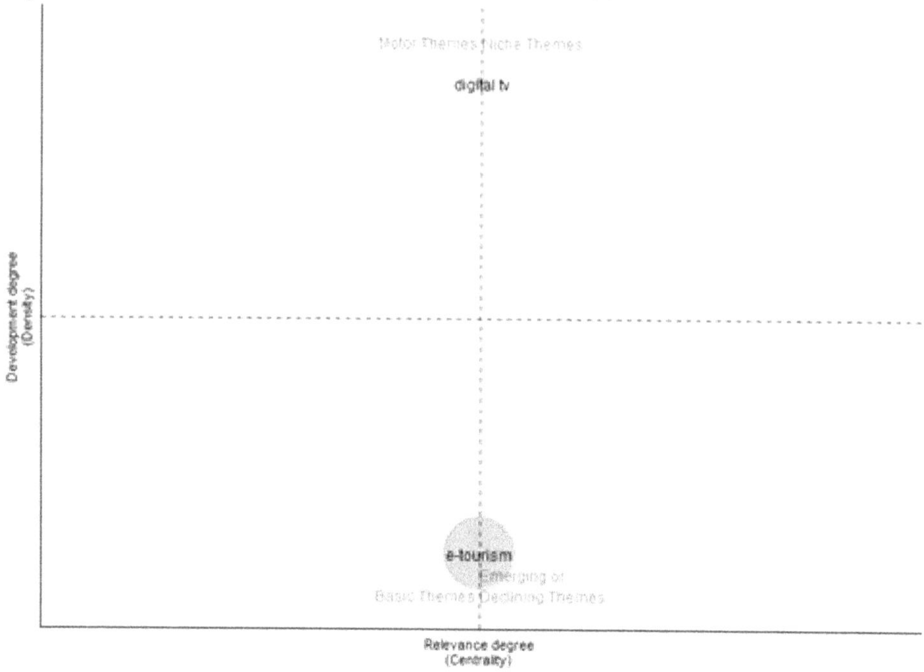

Source: Author Creation

Figure 24. Time slice 2: thematic evolution 2007-2012

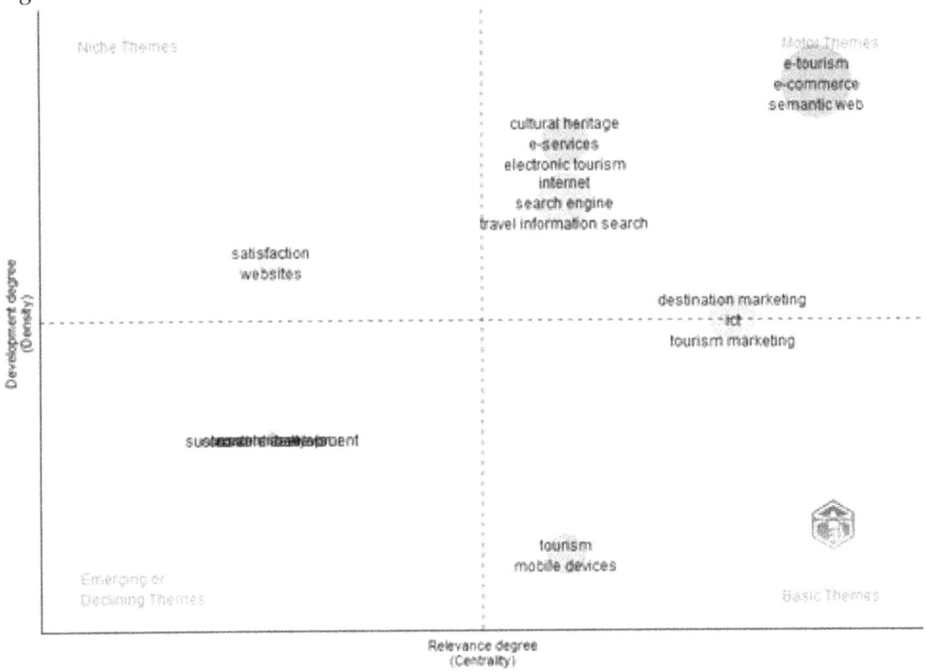

Source: Author Creation

Figure 25. Time slice 3: thematic evolution 2013-2018

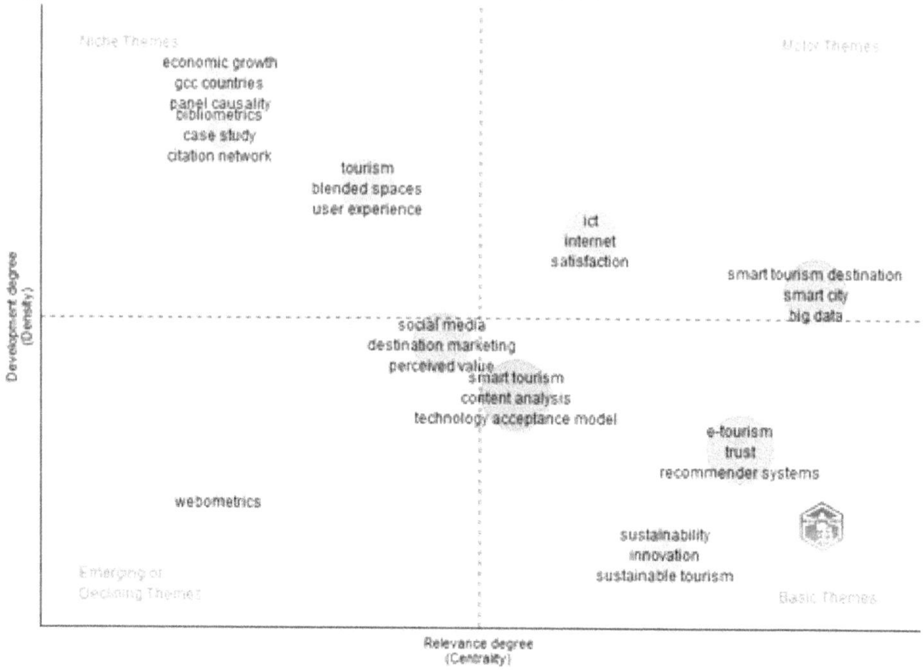

Source: Author Creation

Figure 26. Time slice 4: thematic evolution 2019-2024

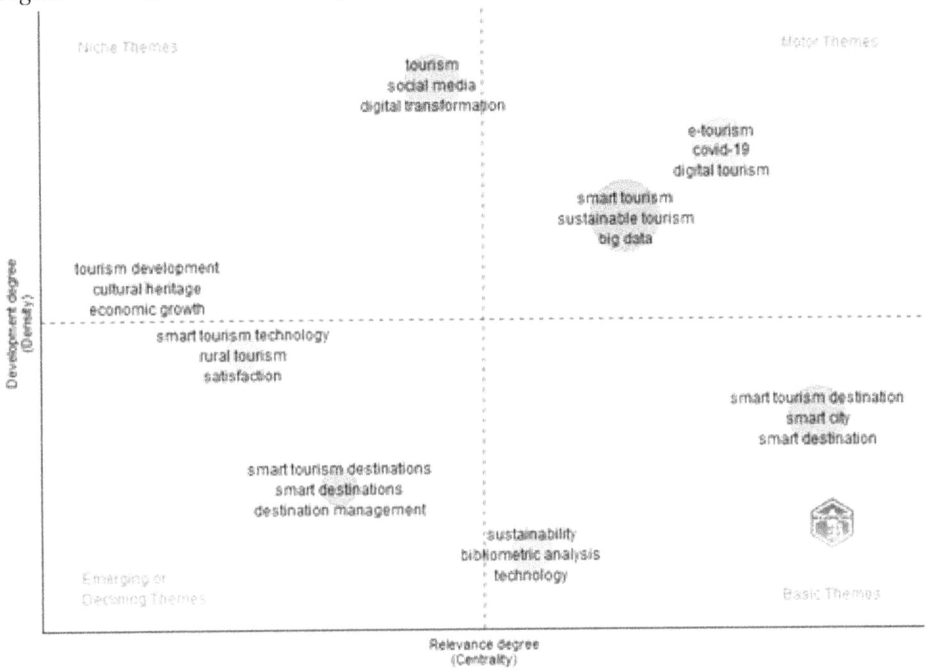

Source: Author Creation

Figure 27. Thematic evolution

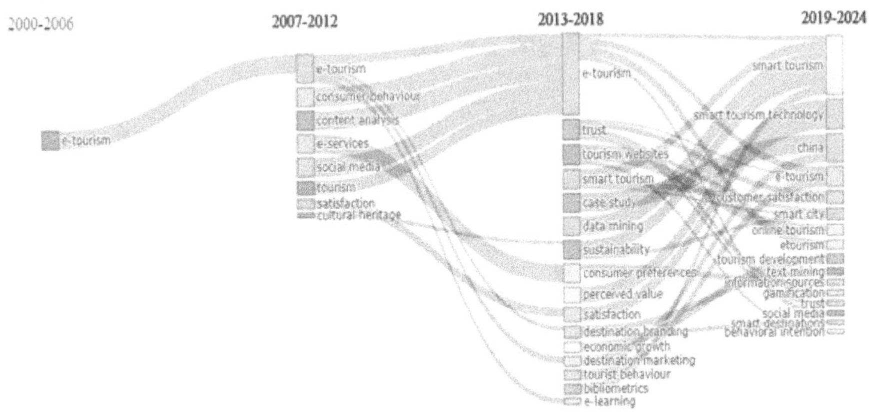

Source: Author Creation

Figure 28. Author collaboration network

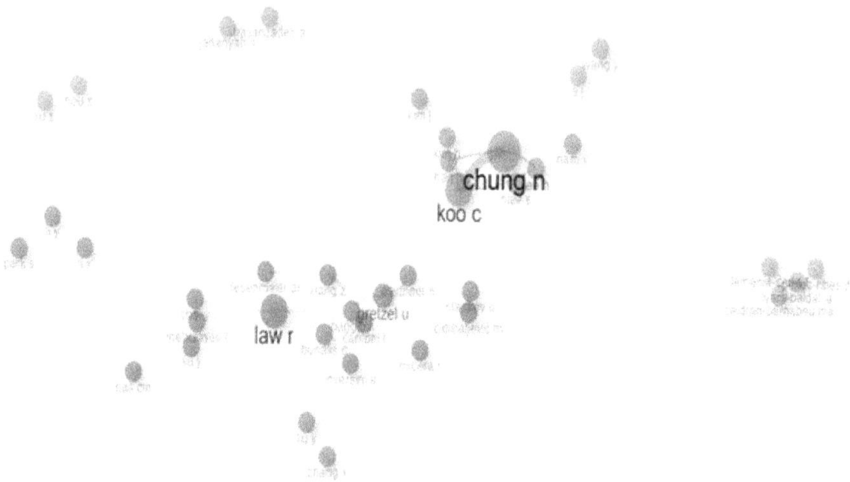

Source: Author Creation

Figure 29. Country's collaboration network

Source: Author Creation

Figure 30. Institutions collaboration network

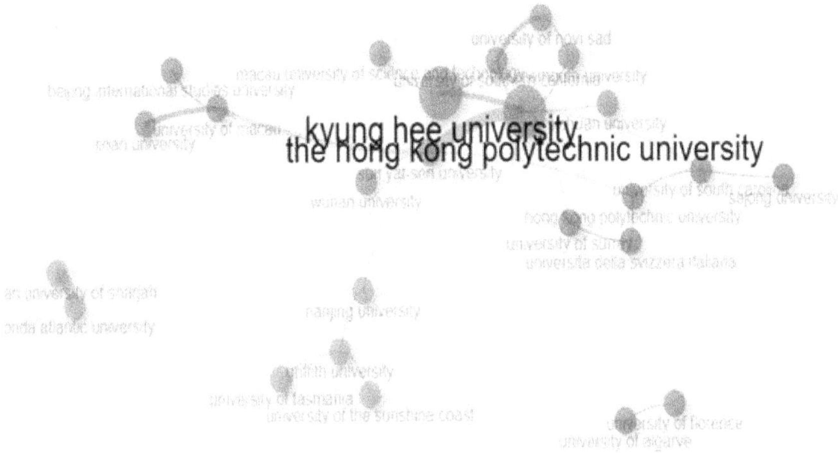

Source: Author Creation

DISCUSSION AND FUTURE RESEARCH DIRECTIONS

This study employed bibliometric analysis to visualize global research trends and future research directions in Digital Tourism. The search period was set from 2000 to 2024 to encompass recent developments. A total of 988 documents were included in performing the final analysis. The Bibliometric R tool was employed for data processing, visualization, and analysis. Descriptive analysis was first conducted to outline the basic characteristics of the data, including publication trends over time, distribution by country, and leading journals in the field. Descriptive analysis reflected that A total of 327 sources produced 988 documents during this period with an annual growth rate of more than 20 percent. The average age of document was 4.32 year with average citation per document being 35.77. A total of 53469 references were analyzed with 1433 keywords plus and 2991 author keywords. Total authors in our analysis were 2196 out of which authors who contributed as single author in a document were 94.

In context of annual scientific production there is an increasing trend in the publication pattern in this research area. The average citations recorded ups and downs in the citation trend throughout the years from the very commencement in the Average Citations since 2000. We found that Smart Tourism, Tourism, E-Tourism,

Smart Tourism Destination and Social Media were the prominent keywords in these years. Sustainability (Switzerland) is the prominent journal that is working on smart tourism and is highly promoted by Spain and Korea. Smart Tourism Destination is a major theme in Sustainability (Switzerland) that is explored in Italy and Spain the most. E-Tourism is a major theme in China, Italy and Spain which is published majorly by Information Technology and Tourism. Sustainability (Switzerland) is the most relavant source with highest publication of 101 articles, Asia Pacific Journal of Tourism Research is the second most productive journal followed by Current Issues in Tourism with 27 article each. In context of impact, Sustainability (Switzerland) is at the top in this list with an H-index of 32 followed by 'Tourism Management' with an H-Index of 22. Information Technology and Tourism is the third most impactful source with an H-Index of 17. Based on the number of publications by each author to find the most productive author figure 8 represents an idea to it Chung N is the most relevant author in the domain of digital marketing with 28 articles till date followed by Law R with 26 articles and Koo C with 19 articles. Buhalis D first published in the domain of digital tourism in the year 2002 with an total citation per year of 17.78, the author is producing continuously over the years and the last work as per the data extracted is in the year 2023 with total citation per year of 46. Chung N and Law R are the most impactful authors with H-index of 18 in the domain of digital tourism. Kyung Hee University is the most prolific affiliation with 102 articles in the domain of digital tourism. The Hong Kong Polytechnic University is with 80 articles followed by University of Aucante and University of Sovi Nad is with 24 articles each. China is the most productive country in the domain of digital tourism with 400 publication till date. It is followed by Spain with 296 articles, South Korea with 220 articles. USA is the most impactful country with 4348 citations followed by Korea with 4028 citations and is the second most impactful country. China is at third position with 3287 citations. Xiang Z "Role of Social Media in Online Travel Information Search" which was published in 2010 is the highly globally cited article with 1950 Total Citation and an average annual citation of 130. The article examined the extent to which social media appears when someone search for travel related aspects. Study results indicated that social media appears frequently as travelers search for travel related aspects and indicate that social media and travel have a relationship. "Smart Tourism" appeared in 275 documents denoting the topmost relevance of the word in context of the present study and indicating that how this topic is in exploration in the academic literature. The word "e-tourism" occurred 108 times and indicate that digital tourism is one of the main theme that is/has emerged. This indicates a high volume of research and discussions for exploring new form of tourism and to fulfil the needs of modern day travelers is being synthesized and suggested by academic writers. The term 'Semantic Web', 'User Experience', 'E-commerce', 'E-services' were trending topics between 2008-2013, 'e-tourism', ‘ict’, ‘Recommender Systems’, ‘Technology acceptance model’ were some of the trending topics between 2014-2019. ‘Big Data’, ‘Smart Tourism’, ‘Sustainability’, ‘Smart Tourism Technology’, ‘Artificial Intelligence’, ‘Digital Transformation’ are trending topic since 2019 . This indicate that now this topic is much explored. The co-occurrence network diagram clearly showing that ‘Digital Tourism’ is directly linked with ‘Big Data’ and ‘Smart Tourism Destination’ as these co-occurred frequently as the bubbles are joined with a thick node. There we can observe five colors of bubbles (Red, Green, Blue, yellow and Violet). Cluster 1 (Red) consists of nineteen keywords which are interrelated to one another but the word ‘Smart Tourism’ is connected to all words and is the main or major theme in the cluster and closely with ‘Big Data’ and ‘Sustainability’. Cluster 2 (Blue) consist of 13 keywords with ‘E-tourism’ as a main theme and major co-occurrence with ‘Internet’. Cluster 3 (Green) consist of 8 keywords of which ‘Tourism’ seems to be the major theme linked with all other keywords and high co-occurrence with ‘Technology’. Cluster 4 (Violet) consist of 7 keywords of which ‘Smart tourism destination’ is a major theme and the only direct link with ‘Smart City’. The final cluster 5 (Yellow) consist of 3 keywords of which high linkage is between ‘Smart tourism Technology’ and ‘Destination Image’. The three field plot captured the emergence of broad themes in context to Digital Tourism. A closer look at the inter-linkages among the themes separated by four-time spans, namely period from 2000 to 2006, 2007–2012, 2013–2018 and 2019-2024 underscores the thematic evolution. In the time slice 1 there is only one concept which emerged as major themes namely ‘E-Tourism’. ‘Consumer Behaviour’, ‘Content Analysis’, ‘E-services’, ‘Social Media’, ‘Cultural Heritage; emerged as trending and evolving themes during 2007-2012. All themes except e-services and Cultural Heritage merged in e-tourism. ‘E-tourism’, ‘also merged in ‘Destination Branding’, ‘Destination Marketing’, and ‘E-learning’. ‘E-services’ merged in ‘Consumer Preference’ in the year 2013-18 and some new prolific themes ‘Trust’, ‘Smart Tourism’, ‘Sustainability’, ‘Perceived value’ emerged. In recent years in time slice 2019-2024 ‘Smart Tourism’, ‘Smart Tourism Technology’, ‘Online Tourism’, ‘Smart City’, ‘Social Media’, and ‘Smart Destinations’ are the major evolving themes. Law R, Chung N, Koo C are the major collaborating authors in this domain. ‘China’, ‘Korea’, ‘Spain’, ‘USA’ are the major collaborating countries in digital tourism. ‘Kyung Hee University’, ‘The Hong Kong Polytechnic University’ are the major collaborating universities in digital tourism.

This study provided various results which indicated how digital tourism evolved and what future potential it provides. But along with this there are some limitations that exist. The search criteria and the keywords used in this study have determined the research's sample and consequently all the results. The study incorporated Scopus database to analyze the results, in future studies web of science can also be incorporated along with Scopus database to make the study results more reliable.

The future research work can also include systematic literature review along with bibliometric analysis to enhance the qualitative analysis. The study offers policy makers and practitioners a useful baseline for developing policies and strategies to promote tourism digitally through its various forms.

REFERENCES

Arbidane, I., Puzule, A., Znotina, D., Narkuniene, R., & Daubariene, J. (2023). Accessibility and smart tourism: Tourism for all and reducing inequalities: A tourism agenda 2030. *Worldwide Hospitality and Tourism Themes, 15*(5), 497–506. *Scopus.* Advance online publication. DOI: 10.1108/WHATT-06-2023-0078

Arthur, P. L., & Nuenen, T. (2019). Travel in the Digital Age. In Das, N., & Youngs, T. (Eds.), *The Cambridge History of Travel Writing* (pp. 504–518). Cambridge University Press. DOI: 10.1017/9781316556740.033

Ashcroft, B. (2015). Travel and Utopia. In Kuehn, J., & Smethurst, P. (Eds.), *New Directions in Travel Writing Studies* (pp. 249–262). Palgrave Macmillan. DOI: 10.1057/9781137457257_16

Atzori, L., Iera, A., & Morabito, G. (2010). The Internet of things: A survey. *Computer Networks, 54*(15), 2787–2805. DOI: 10.1016/j.comnet.2010.05.010

Buhalis, D. (2020). Technology in tourism-from information communication technologies to eTourism and smart tourism towards ambient intelligence tourism: A perspective article. *Tourism Review, 75*(1), 267–272. DOI: 10.1108/TR-06-2019-0258

Buhalis, D., & Deimezi, O. (2004). E-tourism developments in Greece: Information communication technologies adoption for the strategic management of the Greek tourism industry. *Tourism and Hospitality Research, 5*(2), 103–130. DOI: 10.1057/palgrave.thr.6040011

Caragliu, A., Del Bo, C., & Nijkamp, P. (2011). Smart cities in Europe. *Journal of Urban Technology, 18*(2), 65–82. DOI: 10.1080/10630732.2011.601117

Chin, W. L., & Pehin Dato Musa, S. F. (2021). Agritourism resilience against Covid-19: Impacts and management strategies. *Cogent Social Sciences, 7*(1). *Cogent Social Sciences, 7*(1), 1950290. Advance online publication. DOI: 10.1080/23311886.2021.1950290

Choi, I. Y., Ryu, Y. U., & Kim, J. K. (2021). A recommender system based on personal constraints for smart tourism city. *Asia Pacific Journal of Tourism Research, 26*(4), 440–453. *Scopus.* Advance online publication. DOI: 10.1080/10941665.2019.1592765

Chung, H. C., Chung, N., & Nam, Y. (2017). A social network analysis of tourist movement patterns in blogs: Korean backpackers in Europe. *Sustainability (Switzerland), 9*(12). *Sustainability (Basel), 9*(12), 2251. Advance online publication. DOI: 10.3390/su9122251

Dickinson, J. E., Ghali, K., Cherrett, T., Speed, C., Davies, N., & Norgate, S. (2014). Tourism and the smartphone app: Capabilities, emerging practice and scope in the travel domain. *Current Issues in Tourism, 17*(1), 84–101. DOI: 10.1080/13683500.2012.718323

Franklin, A., & Crang, C. (2001). The Trouble with Tourism and Travel Theory? *Tourist Studies, 1*(1), 5–22. DOI: 10.1177/146879760100100101

García, F. A., Dos Santos, A., & Hosseini, S. (2022). A transition towards a smart tourism destination: Analysis from perspective of stakeholders in Lisbon. *Journal of Tourism Analysis, 29*(2), 194–233. *Scopus.* Advance online publication. DOI: 10.53596/jta.v29i2.435

Gong, Y., & Schroeder, A. (2022). A systematic literature review of data privacy and security research on smart tourism. *Tourism Management Perspectives, 44.Tourism Management Perspectives, 44*, 101019. Advance online publication. DOI: 10.1016/j.tmp.2022.101019

Gretzel, U., Sigala, M., Xiang, Z., & Koo, C. (2015). Smart tourism: Foundations and developments. *Electronic Markets, 25*(3), 179–188. DOI: 10.1007/s12525-015-0196-8

Gretzel, U., Zhong, L., & Koo, C. (2016). Application of smart tourism to cities. *International Journal of Tourism Cities, 2*(2), 216–233. DOI: 10.1108/IJTC-04-2016-0007

Han, H., Park, A., Chung, N., & Lee, K. J. (2016). A near field communication adoption and its impact on Expo visitors' behavior. *International Journal of Information Management, 36*(6), 1328–1339. *Scopus.* Advance online publication. DOI: 10.1016/j.ijinfomgt.2016.04.003

Hannam, K. (2009). 'The End of Tourism? Nomadology and the Mobilities Paradigm', Philosophical Issues in Tourism 37: 101–114. Hannam, K., G. Butler and C. M. Paris (2014) 'Developments and Key Issues in Tourism Mobilities'. *Annals of Tourism Research, 44*(1), 171–185.

Hao, J.-X., Yu, Y., Law, R., & Fong, D. K. C. (2015). A genetic algorithm-based learning approach to understand customer satisfaction with OTA websites. *Tourism Management, 48*, 231–241. *Scopus.* Advance online publication. DOI: 10.1016/j.tourman.2014.11.009

Hossain, M. Z. (2023). A Modified Innovation Resistance Theory Approach to E-Tourism Resistance Intention in Bangladesh. *Journal of Technology Management and Innovation, 18*(4), 59–71. *Scopus*. Advance online publication. DOI: 10.4067/S0718-27242023000400059

Hung, N. T., Anh, L. H., Hien, D. T. T., & Hang, V. T. T. (2020). A studying on factors affecting decision to use smart tourism applications using extended TAM. *WSEAS Transactions on Business and Economics, 17*, 288–299. *Scopus*. Advance online publication. DOI: 10.37394/23207.2020.17.30

Hwang, J., Park, H.-Y., & Hunter, W. C. (2015). Constructivism in smart tourism research: Seoul destination image. *Asia Pacific Journal of Information Systems, 25*(1), 163–178. DOI: 10.14329/apjis.2015.25.1.163

Iunius, R. F., Cismaru, L., & Foris, D. (2015). Raising competitiveness for tourist destinations through information technologies within the newest tourism action framework proposed by the European commission. *Sustainability (Basel), 7*(9), 12891–12909. DOI: 10.3390/su70912891

Januszewska, M., Jaremen, D. E., & Nawrocka, E. (2015). The effects of the use of ICT by tourism enterprises. Zeszyty Naukowe Uniwersytetu Szczecińskiego. Scientific Journal. *Supervisory Management, 16*, 65–73. DOI: 10.18276/smt.2015.16-07

Jiang, C., & Phoong, S. W. (2023). A ten-year review analysis of the impact of digitization on tourism development (2012–2022). *Humanities and Social Sciences Communications, 10*(1). *Humanities & Social Sciences Communications, 10*(1), 665. Advance online publication. DOI: 10.1057/s41599-023-02150-7

Joo, J. (2002). A business model and its development strategies for electronic tourism markets. *Information Systems Management, 19*(3), 58–69. *Scopus*. Advance online publication. DOI: 10.1201/1078/43201.19.3.20020601/37171.8

Kontogianni, A., & Alepis, E. (2020). Smart tourism: State of the art and literature review for the last six years. *Array (New York, N.Y.), 6*, 100020. DOI: 10.1016/j.array.2020.100020

Koo, C., Joun, Y., Han, H., & Chung, N. (2016). A structural model for destination travel intention as a media exposure: Belief-desire-intention model perspective. *International Journal of Contemporary Hospitality Management, 28*(7), 1338–1360. *Scopus*. Advance online publication. DOI: 10.1108/IJCHM-07-2014-0354

Kwon, H.-J. (2022). A New Trend of Tourism in the Post-COVID-19 Era: Big Data Analysis of Online Tours in Korea. *Social Sciences, 11*(12). *Social Sciences (Basel, Switzerland), 11*(12), 574. Advance online publication. DOI: 10.3390/socsci11120574

Law, R., Chan, I. C. C., & Wang, L. (2018). A comprehensive review of mobile technology use in hospitality and tourism. *Journal of Hospitality Marketing and Management, 27*(6), 626–648. *Scopus.* Advance online publication. DOI: 10.1080/19368623.2018.1423251

Leung, D., Law, R., Van Hoof, H., & Buhalis, D. (2013). Social media in tourism and hospitality: A literature review. *Journal of Travel & Tourism Marketing, 30*(1-2), 3–22. DOI: 10.1080/10548408.2013.750919

Li, H., Nijkamp, P., Xie, X., & Liu, J. (2020). A new livelihood sustainability index for rural revitalization assessment-a modelling study on smart tourism specialization in China. *Sustainability (Switzerland), 12*(8). *Sustainability (Basel), 12*(8), 3148. Advance online publication. DOI: 10.3390/su12083148

Li, J., Peng, X., Liu, X., Tang, H., & Li, W. (2024). A study on shaping tourists' conservational intentions towards cultural heritage in the digital era: Exploring the effects of authenticity, cultural experience, and place attachment. *Journal of Asian Architecture and Building Engineering.Scopus.* Advance online publication. DOI: 10.1080/13467581.2024.2321999

Li, K. W., & Law, R. (2007). A novel English/Chinese information retrieval approach in hotel website searching. *Tourism Management, 28*(3), 777–787. *Scopus.* Advance online publication. DOI: 10.1016/j.tourman.2006.05.017

Lin, W.-R., Lee, S.-S., & Huang, W.-S. (2023). A scale for measuring tourists' technological competence. *Journal of Hospitality and Tourism Technology, 14*(5), 802–814. *Scopus.* Advance online publication. DOI: 10.1108/JHTT-09-2021-0276

Löfgren, O. (1999). *On Holiday: A History of Vacationing*. University of California Press. DOI: 10.1525/california/9780520217676.001.0001

Lu, A. C. C., & Gursoy, D. (2015). A conceptual model of consumers' online tourism confusion. *International Journal of Contemporary Hospitality Management, 27*(6), 1320–1342. *Scopus.* Advance online publication. DOI: 10.1108/IJCHM-04-2014-0171

Mehraliyev, F., Chan, I. C. C., Choi, Y., Koseoglu, M. A., & Law, R. (2020). A state-of-the-art review of smart tourism research. *Journal of Travel and Tourism Marketing, 37*(1), 78–91. *Scopus.* Advance online publication. DOI: 10.1080/10548408.2020.1712309

Menon, S., Bhatt, S., & Sharma, S. (2021). A study on envisioning Indian tourism–Through cultural tourism and sustainable digitalization. *Cogent Social Sciences, 7*(1). *Cogent Social Sciences*, *7*(1), 1903149. Advance online publication. DOI: 10.1080/23311886.2021.1903149

Mileti, F. A., Miranda, P., Langella, G., Pacciarelli, M., De Michele, C., Manna, P., Bancheri, M., & Terribile, F. (2022). A geospatial decision support system for ecotourism: A case study in the Campania region of Italy. *Land Use Policy, 118.Land Use Policy*, *118*, 106131. Advance online publication. DOI: 10.1016/j.landusepol.2022.106131

Minghetti, V., & Buhalis, D. (2010). Digital divide in tourism. *Journal of Travel Research*, *49*(3), 267–281. DOI: 10.1177/0047287509346843

Ministry of Tourism. (2024, August 1). *Press Release: Ministry of Tourism*. Press Information Bureau, Delhi. Retrieved from https://pib.gov.in/PressReleaseIframePage.aspx?PRID=2040132

Miorandi, D., Sicari, S., De Pellegrini, F., & Chlamtac, I. (2012). Internet of things: Vision, applications and research challenges. *Ad Hoc Networks*, *10*(7), 1497–1516. DOI: 10.1016/j.adhoc.2012.02.016

Ndou, V., Hysa, E., & Maruccia, Y. (2023). A Methodological Framework for Developing a Smart-Tourism Destination in the Southeastern Adriatic–Ionian Area. *Sustainability (Switzerland), 15*(3). *Sustainability (Basel)*, *15*(3), 2057. Advance online publication. DOI: 10.3390/su15032057

Peng, X., & Huang, Z. (2017). A novel popular tourist attraction discovering approach based on geo-tagged social media big data. *ISPRS International Journal of Geo-Information, 6*(7). *ISPRS International Journal of Geo-Information*, *6*(7), 216. Advance online publication. DOI: 10.3390/ijgi6070216

Reino, S., Alzua-Sorzabal, A., & Baggio, R. (2016). Adopting interoperability solutions for online tourism distribution: An evaluation framework. *Journal of Hospitality and Tourism Technology, 7*(1), 2–15. *Scopus*. Advance online publication. DOI: 10.1108/JHTT-08-2014-0034

Salazar, N. B. (2010). *Envisioning Eden: Mobilizing Imaginaries in Tourism and Beyond*. Berghahn Books., Available at https://books.google.nl/books?id=Vx85TX9T3h0C DOI: 10.3167/9781845457600

Sánchez-Rivero, M., Gutiérrez-Fernández, M., Fernández-Torres, Y., & Gallego-Sosa, C. (2024). A gender-oriented analysis of digital skills and ICT use intensity in tourism companies in Extremadura (Spain). *Gender in Management, 39*(2), 239–254. *Scopus.* Advance online publication. DOI: 10.1108/GM-04-2022-0147

Shafiee, S., Ghatari, A. R., Hasanzadeh, A., & Jahanyan, S. (2019). Developing a model for sustainable smart tourism destinations: A systematic review. *Tourism Management Perspectives, 31*, 287–300. DOI: 10.1016/j.tmp.2019.06.002

Shafiee, S., Ghatari, A. R., Hasanzadeh, A., & Jahanyan, S. (2021). A Study of Online Tourism Services in Iran: The Viewpoint of Tourists. *Tourism, 70*(1), 67–86. *Scopus.* Advance online publication. DOI: 10.37741/t.70.1.5

Shao, T., Yang, P., Jiang, H., & Shao, Q. (2023). An Analysis of Public Service Satisfaction of Tourists at Scenic Spots: The Case of Xiamen City. *Sustainability (Switzerland), 15*(3). *Sustainability (Basel), 15*(3), 2752. Advance online publication. DOI: 10.3390/su15032752

Sheller, M., & Urry, J. (2004). *Tourism Mobilities: Places to Play, Places in Play.* Routledge. DOI: 10.4324/9780203340332

Sun, Y., Ma, H., & Chan, E. H. W. (2018). A model to measure tourist preference toward scenic spots based on social media data: A case of Dapeng in China. *Sustainability (Switzerland), 10*(1). *Scopus.* Advance online publication. DOI: 10.3390/su10010043

Tu, Q., & Liu, A. (2014). Framework of smart tourism research and related progress in China. In A. Kong (Ed.), International conference on management and engineering (CME 2014) (pp. 140-146). Shanghai, China.

van Nuenen, T., & Scarles, C. (2021). Advancements in technology and digital media in tourism. *Tourist Studies, 21*(1), 119–132. *Scopus.* Advance online publication. DOI: 10.1177/1468797621990410

Vannini, P. (2010). Mobile Cultures: From the Sociology of Transportation to the Study of Mobilities. *Sociology Compass, 4*(2), 111–121. DOI: 10.1111/j.1751-9020.2009.00268.x

Villar-García, M., & Pereira-Moliner, J. (2024). Advantages and barriers to the creation of a tourism intelligence system in smart destinations. *Cuadernos de Turismo, 53*, 133–156. *Scopus.* Advance online publication. DOI: 10.6018/turismo.616421

Wachowicz-Pyzik, A., Sowiżdżał, A., Maćkowski, T., & Stefaniuk, M. (2024). A New Approach to the Development of Geothermal Water Utilization in the Context of Identifying and Meeting the Social Needs of Local Communities: A Case Study from the Mogilno–Łódź Trough, Central Poland. *Sustainability (Switzerland), 16*(1). *Scopus.* Advance online publication. DOI: 10.3390/su16010037

Wang, D., Li, X. R., & Li, Y. (2013). China's "smart tourism destination" initiative: A taste of the service-dominant logic. *Journal of Destination Marketing & Management, 2*(2), 59–61. DOI: 10.1016/j.jdmm.2013.05.004

Wang, D., Park, S., & Fesenmaier, D. R. (2012). The role of smartphones in mediating the touristic experience. *Journal of Travel Research, 51*(4), 371–387. DOI: 10.1177/0047287511426341

Wang, D., Xiang, Z., & Fesenmaier, D. R. (2016). Smartphone use in everyday life and travel. *Journal of Travel Research, 55*(1), 52–63. DOI: 10.1177/0047287514535847

Wang, X. (2023). Advanced Algorithmic Approaches for Comprehensive Evaluation of Utilization Efficiency in Regional Financial Environmental Protection Funds Using Big Data Analytics. *Journal of Commercial Biotechnology, 28*(1), 225–237. *Scopus.* Advance online publication. DOI: 10.5912/jcb1113

Werthner, H. (2022). A digital humanism view on e-tourism. *Information Technology and Tourism, 24*(3), 347–360. *Scopus.* Advance online publication. DOI: 10.1007/s40558-022-00237-6

World Travel & Tourism Council. (2019). Economic impact. https://wttc.org/Research/Insights

Wu, Y., & Wang, Y. (2024). An Empirical Study on the Tourist Cognitive Evaluations of Tourism Public Services in Xinjiang Province, China. *Sustainability (Switzerland), 16*(5). *Sustainability (Basel), 16*(5), 1712. Advance online publication. DOI: 10.3390/su16051712

Xiang, Z., & Fesenmaier, D. R. (2017). Big data analytics, tourism design and smart tourism. In Xiang, Z., & Fesenmaier, D. R. (Eds.), *Analytics in smart tourism design* (pp. 299–307). Springer., DOI: 10.1007/978-3-319-44263-1_17

Xiang, Z., & Gretzel, U. (2010). Role of social media in online travel information search. *Tourism Management, 31*(2), 179–188. DOI: 10.1016/j.tourman.2009.02.016

Xiang, Z., Wang, D., O'Leary, J. T., & Fesenmaier, D. R. (2015). Adapting to the Internet: Trends in travelers' use of the web for trip planning. *Journal of Travel Research, 54*(4), 511–527. DOI: 10.1177/0047287514522883

Yazdani, R., Taghipourian, M. J., Pourpasha, M. M., & Hosseini, S. S. (2022). A study of the key drivers of brand strengthening in e-tourism businesses: Ranking with ISM approach. *International Journal of Electronic Customer Relationship Management, 13*(4), 295–313. *Scopus*. Advance online publication. DOI: 10.1504/IJECRM.2022.126900

Zeng, B., & Gerritsen, R. (2014). What do we know about social media in tourism? A review. *Tourism Management Perspectives*, *10*, 27–36. DOI: 10.1016/j.tmp.2014.01.001

Zeng, D., Tim, Y., Yu, J., & Liu, W. (2020). Actualizing big data analytics for smart cities: A cascading affordance study. *International Journal of Information Management, 54.International Journal of Information Management*, *54*, 102156. Advance online publication. DOI: 10.1016/j.ijinfomgt.2020.102156

Zhang, L.-y., Li, N., & Liu, M. (2012). On the basic concept of smarter tourism and its theoretical system. *Luyou Xuekan*, *27*(5), 66–73.

Zhou, B., Dong, Y., Yang, G., Hou, F., Hu, Z., Xu, S., & Ma, S. (2023). A graph-attention based spatial-temporal learning framework for tourism demand forecasting. *Knowledge-Based Systems, 263.Knowledge-Based Systems*, *263*, 110275. Advance online publication. DOI: 10.1016/j.knosys.2023.110275

Zhou, X., Tian, J., Peng, J., & Su, M. (2021). A smart tourism recommendation algorithm based on cellular geospatial clustering and multivariate weighted collaborative filtering. *ISPRS International Journal of Geo-Information, 10*(9). *ISPRS International Journal of Geo-Information*, *10*(9), 628. Advance online publication. DOI: 10.3390/ijgi10090628

Zhu, W., Zhang, L., & Li, N. (2014). Challenges, function changing of government and enterprises in Chinese smart tourism. In Z. Xiang, & I. Tussyadiah (Eds.), Short paper proceedings of the ENTER 2014 conference on information and communication technologies in tourism. https://ertr.tamu.edu/enter-2014-volume-4-research-notes/

ADDITIONAL READING

Alghanayem, H., Lamberti, G., & López-Sintas, J. (2023). A dark side of retargeting? How advertisements that follow users affect post-purchase consumer behavior: Evidence from the tourism industry in Saudi Arabia. Innovative Marketing, 19(4), 234–246. *Scopus*. Advance online publication. DOI: 10.21511/im.19(4).2023.19

Balasubramanian, S., Sethi, J. S., Ajayan, S., & Paris, C. M. (2022). An enabling Framework for Blockchain in Tourism. Information Technology and Tourism, 24(2), 165–179. *Scopus*. Advance online publication. DOI: 10.1007/s40558-022-00229-6

Besbes, A., Legohérel, P., Kucukusta, D., & Law, R. (2016). A Cross-Cultural Validation of the Tourism Web Acceptance Model (T-WAM) in Different Cultural Contexts. Journal of International Consumer Marketing, 28(3), 211–226. *Scopus*. Advance online publication. DOI: 10.1080/08961530.2016.1152524

Birenboim, A., Bulis, Y., & Omer, I. (2023). A typology of tourism mobility apps. Tourism Management Perspectives, 48. *Tourism Management Perspectives, 48*, 101161. Advance online publication. DOI: 10.1016/j.tmp.2023.101161

Blöcher, K., & Alt, R. (2021). AI and robotics in the European restaurant sector: Assessing potentials for process innovation in a high-contact service industry. Electronic Markets, 31(3), 529–551. *Scopus*. Advance online publication. DOI: 10.1007/s12525-020-00443-2

Burgess, S., Sellitto, C., & Karanasios, S. (2012). A Model of ICDT Internet flows on mobile devices for the travel and tourism consumer. Tourism Analysis, 17(6), 705–719. *Scopus*. Advance online publication. DOI: 10.3727/108354212X13531051127140

Cao, Q., & Schniederjans, M. J. (2006). Agent-mediated architecture for reputation-based electronic tourism systems: A neural network approach. Information and Management, 43(5), 598–606. *Scopus*. Advance online publication. DOI: 10.1016/j.im.2006.03.001

Chakraborty, D., Polisetty, A., Mishra, A., & Rana, N. P. (2023). A longitudinal study on how smart tourism technology influences tourists' repeat visit intentions. Asia Pacific Journal of Tourism Research, 28(12), 1380–1398. *Scopus*. Advance online publication. DOI: 10.1080/10941665.2023.2293801

Chen, S.-H., & Tham, A. (2023). A crypto-tourism case study of agnes water/seventeen seventy, Australia. Tourism and Hospitality Research, 23(1), 108–112. *Scopus*. Advance online publication. DOI: 10.1177/14673584221085472

Elliot, S., & Joppe, M. (2009). A case study and analysis of e-tourism curriculum development. Journal of Teaching in Travel and Tourism, 9(3–4), 230–247. *Scopus*. Advance online publication. DOI: 10.1080/15313220903379299

Errichiello, L., & Micera, R. (2021). A process-based perspective of smart tourism destination governance. European Journal of Tourism Research, 29. *European Journal of Tourism Research, 29*, 2909. Advance online publication. DOI: 10.54055/ejtr.v29i.2436

Fazzolari, M., & Petrocchi, M. (2018). A study on online travel reviews through intelligent data analysis. Information Technology and Tourism, 20(1–4), 37–58. *Scopus.* Advance online publication. DOI: 10.1007/s40558-018-0121-z

Fiore, G. D., Mainetti, L., Mighali, V., Patrono, L., Alletto, S., Cucchiara, R., & Serra, G. (2016). A location-aware architecture for an IoT-based smart museum. International Journal of Electronic Government Research, 12(2), 39–55. *Scopus.* Advance online publication. DOI: 10.4018/IJEGR.2016040103

Gao, C., Xia, S., Liu, J., Tao, H., & Zhu, Z. (2024). Adaptive evolution and dynamic mechanism of resort socioecological system in tourism cities: The case of Qinhuangdao, China. Habitat International, 151. *Habitat International, 151*, 103138. Advance online publication. DOI: 10.1016/j.habitatint.2024.103138

Gelter, J., Lexhagen, M., & Fuchs, M. (2021). A meta-narrative analysis of smart tourism destinations: Implications for tourism destination management. Current Issues in Tourism, 24(20), 2860–2874. *Scopus.* Advance online publication. DOI: 10.1080/13683500.2020.1849048

Giménez Manuel, J. G., Giner Pérez de Lucia, J., Celdrán Bernabeu, M. A., Mazón López, J. N., Cano Escribá, J. C., & Cecilia Canales, J. M. (2024). Advancing smart tourism destinations: A case study using bidirectional encoder representations from transformers-based occupancy predictions in torrevieja (Spain). IET Smart Cities. *IET Smart Cities, 6*(4), 422–440. Advance online publication. DOI: 10.1049/smc2.12085

Happ, E., & Ivancsóné Horváth, Z. (2020). A study of digital marketing tools usage habits among Hungarian tourists. Geojournal of Tourism and Geosites, 32(4), 1283–1289. *Scopus.* Advance online publication. DOI: 10.30892/gtg.32414-570

Hlee, S., Yhee, Y., Chung, N., & Koo, C. (2019). #Service innovation by design thinking methods: A case of seoul children's grand park (SCGP). [Scopus.]. *Ereview of Tourism Research, 17*(2), 271–291.

Jing, F., Chakpitak, N., & Goldsmith, P. (2012). A knowledge supply chain: Reengineering e-tourism curriculum design. [Scopus.]. *Ereview of Tourism Research, 10*(2), 56–62.

Johnson, A.-G., & Samakovlis, I. (2019). A bibliometric analysis of knowledge development in smart tourism research. Journal of Hospitality and Tourism Technology, 10(4), 600–623. *Scopus*. Advance online publication. DOI: 10.1108/JHTT-07-2018-0065

Kolahkaj, M., Harounabadi, A., Nikravanshalmani, A., & Chinipardaz, R. (2020). A hybrid context-aware approach for e-tourism package recommendation based on asymmetric similarity measurement and sequential pattern mining. Electronic Commerce Research and Applications, 42. *Electronic Commerce Research and Applications*, *42*, 100978. Advance online publication. DOI: 10.1016/j.elerap.2020.100978

Križaj, D., Bratec, M., Kopić, P., & Rogelja, T. (2021). A technology-based innovation adoption and implementation analysis of european smart tourism projects: Towards a smart actionable classification model (sacm). Sustainability (Switzerland), 13(18). *Sustainability (Basel)*, *13*(18), 10279. Advance online publication. DOI: 10.3390/su131810279

Liang, S., Schuckert, M., Law, R., & Guo, X. (2017). A Retrospective Analysis and Future Trends of E-tourism Research in China. Journal of China Tourism Research, 13(3), 231–256. *Scopus*. Advance online publication. DOI: 10.1080/19388160.2017.1376728

Logesh, R., Subramaniyaswamy, V., & Vijayakumar, V. (2018). A personalised travel recommender system utilising social network profile and accurate GPS data. Electronic Government, 14(1), 90–113. *Scopus*. Advance online publication. DOI: 10.1504/EG.2018.089538

Madeira, C., Rodrigues, P., & Gomez-Suarez, M. (2023). A Bibliometric and Content Analysis of Sustainability and Smart Tourism. Urban Science, 7(2). *Urban Science (Basel, Switzerland)*, *7*(2), 33. Advance online publication. DOI: 10.3390/urbansci7020033

Martins, J., Gonçalves, R., Branco, F., Barbosa, L., Melo, M., & Bessa, M. (2017). A multisensory virtual experience model for thematic tourism: A Port wine tourism application proposal. Journal of Destination Marketing and Management, 6(2), 103–109. *Scopus*. Advance online publication. DOI: 10.1016/j.jdmm.2017.02.002

Melijosa, I. S., Pino, J. F. B., & Del Valle Tuero, E. (2022). An analysis of the research on smart tourism destinations based on bibliometric network visualisations. Investigaciones Turisticas, 23, 266–289. *Scopus*. Advance online publication. DOI: 10.14198/INTURI2022.23.12

Moradi, L., Yahya, Y., Mohamed, I., & Raisian, K. (2017). A study of factors influencing online purchasing intention within e-tourism setting. Journal of Environmental Management and Tourism, 8(4), 882–895. *Scopus.* Advance online publication. DOI: 10.14505/jemt.v8.4(20).18

Park, J. H., Lee, C., Yoo, C., & Nam, Y. (2016). An analysis of the utilization of Facebook by local Korean governments for tourism development and the network of smart tourism ecosystem. International Journal of Information Management, 36(6), 1320–1327. *Scopus.* Advance online publication. DOI: 10.1016/j.ijinfomgt.2016.05.027

Pilelienė, L., & Jucevičius, G. (2023). A Decade of Innovation Ecosystem Development: Bibliometric Review of Scopus Database. Sustainability (Switzerland), 15(23). *Sustainability (Basel), 15*(23), 16386. Advance online publication. DOI: 10.3390/su152316386

Prinsloo, A. S., & Fitchett, J. M. (2023). A nexus between airbnb and inequalities in water use and access. Environmental Development, 47. *Environmental Development, 47*, 100879. Advance online publication. DOI: 10.1016/j.envdev.2023.100879

Sahu, K. C., Das, A., Chary, T. P., & Mudhiraj, N. S. (2018). An empirical exploration of the success dynamics of online tourism aggregators in India. Journal of Social Sciences Research, 4(12), 769–776. *Scopus.* Advance online publication. DOI: 10.32861/jssr.412.769.776

Chapter 15
The Business of Wellness Tourism: Emerging Trends and Economic Impacts

Mohammad Badruddoza Talukder
https://orcid.org/0009-0008-1662-9221
International University of Business Agriculture and Technology, Bangladesh

Musfiqur Rahoman Khan
https://orcid.org/0009-0005-7416-2533
Daffodil Institute of IT, Bangladesh

Dil Afrin Swarna
https://orcid.org/0009-0000-9176-920X
National University, Bangladesh

Kuldeep Singh
https://orcid.org/0000-0002-7999-1585
Amity University, Haryana, India

Sanjeev Kumar
https://orcid.org/0000-0002-7375-7341
Lovely Professional University, India

Firoj Kabir
Daffodil International University, Bangladesh

ABSTRACT

The concept of wellness tourism has been steadily popular in the last decade and has factually emerged as one of the most rapidly growing segments in the travel industry. The author looks at the trends leading to the beginning of health and wellness tourism, the drivers of this industry, and the economic effects on several countries. The paper offers a rich perspective into the wellness tourism industry from the literature review and case studies of wellness destinations. This sector has adopted the notion of health and wellness as its primary focus of activity, and technology has opened up opportunities for making each person's improvement program unique. Consumers seek customization and quality and are more inclined to use sustainable tourism products characteristic of green destinations. The advantages of wellness

DOI: 10.4018/979-8-3373-0071-9.ch015

tourism depict the potential to promote productiveness to the local and international markets. Also, this study emphasizes cultural incorporation in tourism operations and calls for strategic responses to address the dynamic demands of customers in the tourism sector.

INTRODUCTION

As our world has become increasingly fast-paced, digitally dominated, and overwhelmed by stress, wellness tourism has become one of the most revolutionary movements in global travel. It responds to modern-day challenges like endless stress, sedentary lifestyles, and the pursuit of authentic experiences. As more people understand that well-being's physical, mental, emotional, and spiritual aspects are interwoven, wellness tourism has soared in the last decade. This chapter introduces the diverse scope, growing importance, and extensive impact of the experience of wellness tourism; at its core, wellness tourism is a different mentality on travel — no longer simply a form of recreation but a path to healing and self-betterment. Such a shift aligns with the evolving priorities of modern-day travelers who want more than physical rest but more mental clarity, emotional re-engagement, and spiritual growth (Kumar & Hussain, 2022).

Wellness tourism grows in appeal because it responds to diverse needs. From someone with a chronic illness to a person on a mission to be better overall, wellness travel caters to various needs, which include everything from traditional spa treatments and yoga retreats to more adventurous and culturally immersive activities. At its core, wellness tourism is journeying that creates a unique and meaningful experience to mirror the hopes and ambitions of each individual. This individualized emphasis distinguishes wellness tourism from other forms of tourism because it caters to a broad base of travelers seeking enrichment in their lives.

Key to this growth is the growing awareness of the detrimental impact of contemporary lifestyles. The increasing prevalence of sedentary work environments, poor eating habits, and constant screen time is generating rising demand for venues where individuals can physically, mentally, and emotionally recuperate. Unsurprisingly, travelers seek destinations to let them escape their day-to-day chaos, reflect on their lives, and give their bodies and minds a much-needed reset. Such sanctuaries are available in wellness tourism that combines natural beauty, therapeutic services, and cultural elements to provide places for self-reflection and self-care (Majeed & Gon Kim, 2023).

In addition to attracting individual travelers, wellness tourism has become a new economic engine for many destinations. You make large chunks of money, all the jobs it creates, all the people it gets to eat at a restaurant, and so on. Destinations can compete to be global wellness hotspots and attract tourist retreats by providing specialized services and infrastructures. As a result, the enormous economic potential has made many countries and regions spend heavily on wellness tourism infrastructure so that they do not miss the increasing demand for high-quality, holistic travel experiences. According to Krishna Pasupuleti (2024), wellness tourism is a strategic instrument for economic sustainability, generating robust continuous revenue without impacting unwanted damage to the local culture and resources.

The growing popularity of wellness tourism does, however, come with complications. To ensure the industry's sustainability, we should be responsive to the negative, such as over-tourism, the commodification of wellness practices, and cultural appropriation. However, over-tourism stresses the resources that a particular place has to offer, disrupting the peaceful and wellness intent of many destination approaches. Likewise, commercializing traditional wellness practices could dilute their authenticity and lessen their cultural heritage. To overcome these challenges, the wellness tourism sector must balance commercial imperatives with cultural and environmental preservation. Only by practicing sustainability and demonstrating proper reverence towards local customs can the industry thrive long-term by providing valuable travel experiences (Kumar et al., 2024).

This chapter outlines wellness tourism's trends, challenges, and opportunities. The research will examine what drives wellness travelers, the wellness experiences provided, and its hefty economic impact. Focusing on successful wellness destination case studies, the chapter aims to uncover successful strategies and practices that have enabled this evolving sector to flourish. All we want to achieve is a (new) definition of wellness tourism for a global audience and how it can change/transform the travel world.

THE RISE OF WELLNESS TOURISM

The rapid ascent of wellness tourism stems from the global trend towards living a healthy lifestyle and caring for one's health. With increasing awareness of holistic health, travelers increasingly seek travel experiences supporting their wellness goals. The COVID-19 pandemic has also accelerated this trend, highlighting the importance of physical, mental, and emotional wellness. For others, the pandemic also instilled a need for resilience, self-care, and care for others, which led many travelers to integrate a sense of wellness into their travel plans (Dimitrova, 2023).

A standout characteristic that makes wellness tourism so appealing is its variety. Some travelers like relaxing and relieving stress using spa treatments and yoga retreats, while others prefer physical challenges like hiking, trekking, or adventure sports. Another attraction within wellness tourism is cultural immersion, where travelers participate in traditional healing methods, food experiences, and spiritual rituals. Such variety makes wellness tourism attractive to many demographics, from millennials to retirees (Talukder et al., 2024).

The second trend is wellness tourism because its economic impact is just as potent. Recent studies have shown that wellness travelers spend more than the average tourist, resulting in higher earnings for destinations. Targeting premium offerings such as high-end accommodation, organic food, and personalized wellness programs all increase the amount of spending. Wellness tourism also aids tourism, hospitality, and local artisans in many areas. It also fosters Sudan's economic inclusiveness, creating chances for small and medium-sized businesses (SMEs) and local craftsmen (Nasiche, 2024).

Wellness tourism is also skyrocketing because of integrated technology. Wellness travel is being redefined with digital tools and platforms that improve the wellness experience via personalized recommendations, virtual consultations, and real-time health tracking. Things like wearable devices, mobile apps, and online wellness programs make it easier for travelers to keep their health on track, even on the go. Technology-enhanced integration enhances the wellness experience and improves accessibility and convenience (Krishna Pasupuleti, 2024).

Figure 1. Core components of wellness tourism: trends and economic dimensions

Source: Author Compilation

It illustrates the essential topics involved in wellness tourism, such as wellness retreats, Sustainable tourism, Health tourism, wellness travel, and Wellness tourism. This web of factors highlights the rising trends and the economic impact of our industry's rise. It describes how wellness tourism combines health-driven travel with environmentally sustainable lifestyles and cultural experiences to produce high-growth business opportunities. This framework highlights the role of this sector in promoting sustainable development, enhancing mental and physical health and overall well-being, and stimulating economic growth worldwide.

LITERATURE REVIEW

One burgeoning spatial practice in recent world travel is wellness tourism, which inspires many (Błotnicka et al., 2024) travelers to get physical and emotional alignments. This trend is a form of health tourism where concerns for health and travel replace health facilities and health seekers (Abdallah & Al-Hashmi, 2023). Wellness tourism is the product of a focused, impactful shift in global consciousness throughout cultures concerning body-mind-feelings-spirit interaction (Nair, 2020). This change signifies an increasing awareness of the interconnected nature of wellness, where various facets of health converge to provide a more meaningful life experience.

As the contemporary lifestyle has become rife with stress, inactivity, and ubiquitous digital devices, the need for environments to disengage and refresh is more significant than ever. Not only has the well-being of tourism risen due to these factors, but it has also transformed into a need rather than a want. According to Piccirillo (2024), we can break the cycles of intervention of modern forms of stress and monotony with wellness tourism. The real transformative power of wellness tourism comes from the capacity of the many to recover, ponder, and spiritually blossom. Elaborating on this, Rajapakshe and Arachchi (2024) note that spiritual growth constitutes an inherent dimension of the wellness tourism experience.

Wellness tourism encompasses various activities and caters to individual preferences and goals. Whether it be a spa and yoga holiday or an adventure-based or cultural experience, the diversity of wellness tourism makes it enjoyable for everyone. According to Alharethi and Kabil (2024), these activities are directed toward a range of clients—including clients with chronic health conditions and clients looking for general development in their well-being. This inclusivity is one of the main reasons for the sector's success. Wellness tourism has risen above traditional tourism models by providing personalized experiences that are deeper and more meaningful.

Wellness tourism is an industry that cannot be overlooked or underestimated in terms of economic value—the most reliable source of income generation for regions worldwide. Joson et al. (2024) reemphasize its influence on employment and local economic development. Its capacity to underpin financial performance and economic growth has made it a strategic priority for some destinations. Poland has resort destinations with a growing adult wellness focus, seeking experiences around transformation and being unique. Specialized strategies highlight how wellness tourism may respond to market evolution and consumer expectations to support continued growth.

Wellness tourism specifically appeals to authenticity and cultural engagement, making it unique. In many destinations, wellness tourism blends ancient customs and local culture, providing an exceptional experience for travelers to interact and blend into new cultures. It transforms the travel experience into a more rewarding and meaningful venture rather than merely a recreational activity. In this way, these cultural elements are not made an object of trade. The developments in wellness tourism and its future will heavily rely on its authenticity and well-being as a lifestyle, not a trend.

In summary, wellness touring is a big move within the national wellness travel circle. It meets the increasing demand for physical and emotional health balance with a broader range of activities suited to everyone. Due to its economic advantages and focus on cultural interaction, it is a relevant segment of the contemporary tourism markets. Wellness tourism will never run out of steam, with many people putting that first as part of their travel plans. Thus, the future of global travel will be shaped around wellness tourism.

The Expanding Scope of Wellness Tourism

Wellness tourism is a promising and integral part of the world travel market. Various age groups become ever more health-conscious and self-improvement-driven. It is a new industry comprising spa therapies, yoga vacations, adventure, and culture. They seek venues to unwind, revitalize, and expand their souls (Balcioglu, 2024). Wellness tourism is economically essential for the destination because it is oriented toward revenue, employment, and local business activity. As a result, more healthful consumers also want to indulge in travel experiences focused on wellness. This led to the creation of wellness resorts, spas, and even retreats, which offer many activities, including healthy meals, workout sessions, yoga, and others (Balcioglu, 2024). Greener tourism practices, digital detox holidays, and wellness holidays based on age are specific emerging trends that leave much to be desired for the future of wellness tourism. As the market for this space evolves, it is crucial to start tackling questions of sustainability, authenticity, and ethics to preserve the market for the future (Abdallah & Al-Hashmi, 2023).

Wellness Tourism: A Broad Perspective

Travel today is defined by wellness. It speaks of travel without physical, psychological, emotional, or spiritual metrics. The activities and experiences sought range from a straightforward unwind in a regional health facility and a yoga hideaway to a thrilling active sporting activity or a social occasion. So, tourists are in search of destinations that relieve stress and help them get work done (Manjula et al., 2024)

It generates income, employment, and development in the area, making it a very important social and economic factor for tourist destinations. These new priorities have caused people to be more intrigued toward an inclusive well-being journey that brings forth new inclusive costs associated with travel. In addition, wellness resorts, spas, or retreats with fitness, healthy fare, and other pampering but beneficial services have come into the fold due to consumer demand over the past few years (Kajornatthapol et al., 2024). Given all these new trends, from green tourism to digital detox retreats to wellness retreats appropriate for certain ages or other demographic groups, it does not have to state that the future of the wellness tourism market looks bright. As the industry matures, so should its guiding principles, including diversity, authenticity, and integrity, if this industry is to thrive in the long run (Balcioglu, 2024).

Economic Impact Wellness Tourism

The emergence of wellness tourism has become more than just a trend but a revenue source for most tourist destinations. In pursuing a wellness experience, travelers usually spend more on lodgings, spa treatments, ancillary medicine, wholesome nutrition, and workout facilities. It is thus an increase in spending, creates value locally, and can be taxed by the state authority. This revenue stream enables the deployment of other assets for the post-concrete establishment– urban planning and principles, education, and health into the territory (Talukder et al., 2020).

Well-being tourism not only provides work to people in various fields, including hospitality and tourism, health care, and wellness services (Khairullayev Abdulatif, 2024). Open in a new window, wellness tourism targets spa therapists, yoga trainers, tour guides, and hospitality laborers. Moreover, wellness tourism can benefit cultural and natural resource management practices. Therefore, wellness tourism positively impacts the environment and society by promoting these practices and properly utilizing available resources (Abdallah & Al-Hashmi, 2023a).

Changing the Face of Travel: Making Wellness Travel

Well, the movement of wellness tourism did not alter travel habits; instead, it modified tourism objects from sightseeing that were directed purely to travel for health. It gives room to learn more about the different traditions and practices while being fit in body, mind, and soul. This increasing trend mentioned above cannot be limited to the original scope of tourism, primarily leisure, if we also integrate awareness or self-improvement (Tran Thu Phuong, Vu Huong Giang, 2024). Through wellness practices, tourists rarely, or if at all, feel stressed while enjoying the atmosphere, wholesome food, sites, amusement, sports events, and relaxing at the location (Bimetric model, 2023; Dahanayake et al., 2023). This may be yoga, meditation, hiking, or even getting a massage. Now, picture the adventurers having adopted a well-being approach on the journey. In that case, everyone will return from such a trip filled with inspiration and vitality from the warm beaches where they vacationed (Lopes, 2022). Wellness tourism contributes to economic development in specific spaces through income generation, job creation, and economic growth and support (Błotnicka et al., 2024). Wellness tourism is becoming an increasingly significant market segment, while health seekers and spa tourists concentrate mainly on fountain health treatments. The rapid growth in mass wellness vacations, spas, and retreats (Wulandari, 2024) then soon followed.

Wellness Tourism: A Trip for Wellness

Wellness-oriented tourism is associated with the connections between the individual as a tourist and traveling as a method of recovering wellness. Travel is ostensibly to maintain physical, psychic, and spiritual well-being. Wellness centers will assist you in forgetting about the challenging core activities of life by filling your day with an environment full of comforts, refreshes, and self-improvement. Wellness tourism is defined differently by mild yoga retreats, demanding trekking tours, or abundant cuisines. Everyone who could book a trip of this nature went to browsing, players, or just sitting down more or much less deal with. Thus, this approach to the end traveler's well-being and how inequitable journeys do healthy travel when one returns fresh, energized, and happy (Makoondlall-Chadee et al., 2024). Moreover, wellness tourism also has a social impact as it creates income for the destination and employment and supports regional development. Health-conscious clients are already prepared to pay even more for their journeys when it pertains to wellness travel and extra facilities (consisting of lodging) (Chartrand et al., 2024). Such developments have created unique wellness trends, especially wellness resorts, and spas, including new services like fitness programs, healthy food, and complementary medicine.

As a lucrative investment sector, wellness tourism has brought enormous economic advantages to destinations worldwide (Talukder, 2021). Finally, consumers focus on health and well-being and invest in wellness travel experiences. This leads to money spent in communities: business income, job creation, and tax dollars. High-spender tourists choose wellness tourism destinations as they require a high level of services and experiences (Abdallah & Al-Hashmi, 2023). This encourages building luxury resorts, high-end spas, and private-style epicenters for wellness. Investing in wellness infrastructure and promoting wellness tourism can help the destination make an improved brand and convey an image to the customers of a highly professed and differentiated corporate clientele with quality services.

In addition, wellness tourism is one step, and word plays a role in sustainable community development. Wellness tourism can benefit the social and ecological side by supporting local businesses, keeping a cultural legacy, and decreasing the environmental footprint (Balcioglu, 2024). With the increasing demand for wellness experiences, investing in tourism with wellness target groups can provide enormous returns over the long term.

Meet the Wellness Traveler: A Snapshot of the Modern-Day Voyager

The wellness tourist of today is not just a focused 'vacationer' – they must be physically, mentally, and spiritually progressive to embark on such trips (Hritz et al. 2014). They are pretty challenged with their fitness and psychological and emotional readiness. These people have the means to transcend the ordinary. The seekers of health are not your regular visitors; they treat each trip as an opportunity to test the thresholds of body and mind (Musakin et al., 2024). They travel to quiet places, hoping to mend themselves in the stillness. Enjoy yoga and meditation classes, health spas, and rambling in forests? These activities help them regain attention, combat stress, and improve their physical well-being (Riashenkova, 2024). A wellness traveler is also a socially responsible tourist who aims to avoid the negative impacts of tourism. They constantly search for green lodgings, support local businesses, and try to be the least impact tourists (Kupcewicz & Bentkowska 2023). This encourages the preservation of the environment and culture.

TYPES OF ACTIVITIES, THE MOTIVATIONS OF WELLNESS WARRIORS

The increasing prevalence of wellness tourism locales is primarily the result of participants wanting to know much more about the forces that drive wellness tourism. A few main motivations behind this trend attract more and more travelers who want something meaningful and transformative:

Quest for Comfort: This is primarily because people use wellness tourism to escape daily life's problems and tensions. Warm Climate Flow, Peaceful Settings, and Tranquility draw the masses to escape when there are hot spots. As Hudson et al. (2020) explain, destinations of this type provide the conditions for relaxation and the opportunity to be free from the burden and constraints of everyday life in an ambiance promoting serenity, restoration, and peace.

Enhancing Physical Well-being: Wellness tourism typically includes physical health-oriented activities. Among them are leisure activities such as hill climbing, yoga classes, and health spas. These pursuits allow travelers to engage in goals that enhance their physical fitness. It is beautiful for clients who want to manage chronic health issues or change their lifestyle to be healthier so that they can arrange short-term benefits with long-term wellness approaches side-by-side.

Mental and Emotional Health: A substantial wellness travel motivator is the importance of a destination focused on cognitive and emotional recovery. This blend of beautiful views and well-being activities eliminates mental fatigue, enables relaxation, and reestablishes emotional balance. These experiences are essential as they allow individuals to recover holistically through enjoyment and normalcy, taking time to care for themselves and engaging in emotional responses in settings explicitly designated for comfort and contemplation.

Spiritual Growth: Many travelers view wellness travel as an opportunity for spiritual development. Hence, they visit meditation retreats, pilgrimage sites, or clubs that provide cultural and spiritual exchanges, and this motivation inspires them to visit these places. More travelers treat this type of growth as a key component of holistic wellness. It is essential to offer spiritual experiences that foster awareness of the self and perspective on life. They may include mindfulness, ritual, or traditional immersion that provides personal insight.

Affiliation: However, wellness tourism also focuses on community and togetherness, providing travelers with a sense of belonging and connection. But pricey group things like workshops, retreats, and wellness programs are another way travelers connect with others striving for the same thing. Such bonds cultivate and pave the way for lifetime companionship and better well-being.

SETTING EXPECTATIONS IN THE WELLNESS TOURISM SECTOR

First, the wellness tourism industry has developed several norms and practices to meet multiple client's demands. Without these norms, the industry's success would not be sustainable, and travelers would not be assured of experiences that fit their health, rest, and growth agenda. Wellness tourism shows some of the most popular experiences, such as:

Spa and Wellness Centre: A spa focuses on body treatments, massages, facials, and other therapies associated with exercise and good health. Wellness tourism focuses on spa and wellness centers, one of this industry's main components, offering limitless arrangements for clients' requirements (Leo Bentley, 2024). Apart from improving overall physical well-being, these services are also known to provide mental and emotional relief to detoxify from health conditions and stress.

Yoga and Meditation Retreats: Designed to help participants develop inner peace and spirituality, yoga and meditation retreats focus on physical and mental well-being. These retreats offer programs that cultivate mindfulness, emotional regulation, and self-awareness. Such intensive retreats are now becoming more in demand, and their rising popularity draws from the latter desire of people wanting experiences that cultivate calmness, clarity, and a more profound sense of connection with the self.

Wellness tourism interestingly blends adventure with wellness practices in adventure-based tourism involving physical activity and exploration, including hiking, trekking, surfing, and other outdoor activities. These activities improve physical fitness in exchange for great opportunities to experience nature and a few feelings of accomplishment. Adventure tourism has injected excitement into wellness travel, attracting those who look for relaxation and a physical challenge, shooting adrenaline to the adrenaline-seeking.

Cultural Exchange: A large number of wellness travelers prefer traveling to destinations where they can have the opportunity to learn about the culture of that place. Such involvement could involve taking native medication, having food experiences, or practicing cultural practices to get a broader perspective on varied cultures. Wellness tourism promotes personal enhancement and global outlook development by encouraging intercultural contact.

Health Tourism: Health tourism revolves around medical or preventive care and is based on exploiting people who travel long distances to obtain treatments or therapies for various diseases or conditions they cannot access in their countries. Such visits are part of a specific type of wellness tourism—those that involve travel to specialty clinics, hospitals, or resorts that provide cutting-edge medical services and conventional wellness activities. The evolution of health tourism reveals that wellness and medical care are interrelated, and maintaining health is ensured by treating the disease on the one hand and staying healthy on the other.

THE ECONOMIC IMPORTANCE OF WELLNESS TOURISM

Wellness tourism is a significant economic force for destinations across the globe — earning billions and serving livelihoods. As a profitable segment of the broader tourism market, it can generate employment, help bring about infrastructure development, and, with a realization of damage done to the environment by tourism, even contribute to sustainability in many areas. The economic impacts of wellness tourism have two types:

Job Creation: Wellness tourism creates jobs as travelers spend money on lodging, food and beverage, transportation, and wellness services. These expenditures [are] funding local economies and sustaining various sectors of the economy (Dimitrova, 2023). Wellness travel attracts high-value tourists who spend more than average, creating an even more significant economic impact.

Job Opportunities: Wellness tourism facilitates job creation across diverse segments such as hospitality, wellness services, healthcare, and local artisan activities. Careers directly supported by wellness tourism include spa therapists, yoga instructors, tour guides, and hospitality staff. Moreover, the growing demand for wellness products and services generates indirect jobs in ancillary sectors, contributing to economic development.

Local Economic Development: Wellness tourism fosters economic development by promoting SMEs and well-being infrastructure investments. Increased demand for authentic, locally grown, and sourced goods is also a way for local artisans and producers to benefit. Such economic inclusiveness guarantees that the advantages of wellness tourism are shared throughout communities, promoting sustainable development.

Wellness tourism sustainability: Current research, like Talukder (2023), focuses on wellness tourism, encouraging sustainability and respect for cultural heritage. If more of us followed the footprints the likes of Tenzing and Hillary left back in 1953 and moved onwards around the world, such as Big Mountain, the wellness tourism sector could match economic ambition with fundamental environmental and social responsibility by focusing efforts on sustainability measures that do the least harm and indeed benefit the local people and environment. It increases the liability for local people and creates difficulty for the responsible visitor.

More Substantial Listing for Brand of Destination: Wellness tourism offers successful branding for destinations, appealing to high-value tourists with a disposition to spend money on premium services and unique experiences. Such enhanced branding increases tourism earnings and niche destinations as sustainable and transformative travel leaders. Destinations can develop strong last impressions, leading to destinations being revisited and long-term economic gains by aligning offerings with their cultural and natural assets.

Looking ahead at the rationale behind the motivations of wellness travelers unmasks the diversified nature of wellness tourism. It unveils wellness tourism's role as an economic pillar in the sector. Whether through comfort and nurturing the body, mind, and soul or cultural and community engagement to find purpose and belonging, wellness tourism fills many different human needs and desires. Its economic impact also underlines its importance to the industry, with jobs, revenue, and sustainability. The sector must work to embrace the potential of wellness tourism to shape the future of travel with sustainable personal and community health gains alongside economic prosperity.

FUTURE TREND OF WELLNESS TOURISM

The wellness tourism industry is changing rapidly as consumer needs and global trends change fast. As we know, the story of wellness continues to unfold, and many new trends are emerging that are changing the landscape of wellness-focused destinations and service providers seeking to suit the new travel needs of consumers. These trends showcase the sector's resilience, focus on sustainability, and use of technology to improve the entire travel experience.

Technology Integration

The use of technology as part of wellness tourism has evolved as an essential requirement for providing bespoke and effective services. Digital Travellers — From swellable devices to mobile apps, the wealth of technological improvements allows tourists to tap into wellness offerings in a digital environment. According to Krishna Pasupuleti (2024), technology can provide customized experiences, from virtual consultations to monitoring health and providing feedback in real-time. For example, travelers may use applications to create itineraries, monitor their daily activity levels, or even engage in guided meditation sessions away from home.

Wellness tourism is being changed dramatically by virtual reality (VR) and augmented reality (AR). Using VR technology, people can explore simulated wellness, whether a sunrise over the Grand Canyon or a yoga class, from the safety of their own homes. On the other hand, AR augments the experience of traveling in the physical world by projecting digital information onto physical-world locations, which enables travelers to immerse themselves in wellness destinations more fully as they explore their surroundings.

Additionally, telehealth services have become part of the wellness tourism industry — allowing travelers to meet with health experts virtually before or during their trip. This enables seamless continuity of care and adds to the convenience of pursuing wellness tourism. With the ever-growing technological advancement, the features of wellness tourism are expected to diversify - facilitating more significant traveler demographics with more accessibility and personalization.

Green Wellness Tourism

Firstly, it has an appeal of sustainability in wellness tourism. Thus, travelers are increasingly interested in eco-friendly and socially responsible health tourism experiences. Eco-wellness tourism, or green wellness tourism, involves sustainable offerings in the travel sector as part of wellness tourism. This trend indicates a more significant intention to source environmental sustainment to deliver premium quality wellness experiences.

Green wellness tourism covers actions with the lowest impact on natural environments, including using renewable energy sources, limiting waste, supporting local economies, etc. At Eco-Friendly Accommodations Solar Energy-Based Resorts and Biodegradable Amenities, Wellness programs also focus on sustainable lifestyles from forest bathing and organic farming workshops to eco-tours — cultivating a connection to nature while learning to live gently on the planet.

Travelers are interested in environmentally non-harmful options for lodging and food, transportation, and wellness. More farm-to-table dining, eco-certified spas, and sustainable adventure tours are available at more destinations. These trends enable the wellness tourism sector to help solve some environmental issues and increase the number of more conscious consumers.

THE ADVANTAGES OF WELLNESS TOURISM FOR SENIORS

With aging populations in different parts of the world, the demand for wellness tourism products that suit older adults will increase. As a result, age-targeted healthcare programs and services are being established across the industry to cater to this changing demographic. Wellness tourism for seniors resonates with an audience that values holistic health and longevity, making it relevant to contemporary lifestyles for promoting physical fitness, mental well-being, and social connection.

Active and health tourism products directed towards older international travelers usually combine gentle physical activity or fitness programs with nutritional services and therapies for degenerative diseases. Destinations cater to experiences focused on accessibility with mobility-friendly hotels and transportation. For seniors, wellness retreats include mild yoga, hydrotherapy, and meditation to promote greater relaxation and well-being.

Another crucial element of wellness tourism for seniors is social connection. Programs that involve traveling in groups and wellness activities that cater to communities create a sense of belonging and lower the risk of isolation. As the number of older people increases, wellness tourism can be essential in serving those growing groups to promote a better quality of life where specific needs are taken care of.

Emotional Disorders And Luxury Travel

As the demands mounted on the travel industry and the increasing prevalence of mental health challenges became a necessity, wellness tourism unequivocally focused on emotional well-being started to take hold as travelers looked for destinations and programs that offered therapeutic solutions for stress, anxiety, depression, and other emotional disorders. This trend indicates a more significant societal move towards mental well-being, an integral part of holistic health.

According to Rajapakshe and Arachchi (2024), this sector, in turn, includes various services, such as mindfulness retreats, CBT sessions, art therapy, and wound healing workshops. Such programs help individuals build safe spaces to process emotions and develop coping mechanisms for inner peace.

Aside from conventional wellness therapies, destinations are adding novel therapies to their menu. Nature-based therapy—like hiking, forest bathing, or equine-assisted therapy—has become a sought-after treatment because of its soothing abilities for the mind and body. Similarly, digital detox retreats promote tech-free travel through mindfulness-based activities to improve clarity of thought and emotional fortitude.

Wellness tourism treats emotional disorders and emphasizes inclusiveness and accessibility. Intra-country destinations are creating programs that consider different cultural backgrounds and individual needs from where they come from, ensuring that all can enjoy its therapeutic benefits. Wellness tourism plays a role in achieving that happy middle ground by understanding mental health issues.

SUSTAINABLE, REAL AND PURPOSEFUL

With the increasing growth of the wellness tourism market, more focus is being paid to sustainability, authenticity, and ethicality. As travelers become more discerning, they're looking for experiences that align with their values and help the destination they visit. If you have been paying any attention to this trend, it sets up very high expectations for the behavior of travelers and service providers.

The sustainability initiatives within wellness tourism are the reduction of carbon footprints, the conservation of natural resources, and the support of local communities. From eco-certifications to community-based tourism models to waste management systems, destinations ensure that their supply meets environmental and social objectives.

The success of wellness tourism still relies heavily on authenticity. People are looking for authentic experiences that reflect the culture and traditions of the place. As a result, there has been a renewed focus on old wellness traditions. Promoting these practices also enables the industry to set itself apart from others whilst honoring the cultural diversity of its destinations.

However, responsible behavior also comes down to travelers. Fitness and wellness travelers are invited to engage in learnings and practices that reduce their impact on the environment and respect the destinations and cultures they are partaking in. It includes booking green hotels, engaging in sustainable practices, and shopping from local businesses. By taking ownership of the issues facing those involved, wellness tourism can flourish to benefit traveling consumers and the people and places hosting them.

WELLNESS TOURISM: TRENDS, OPPORTUNITIES AND ISSUES

For the past few years, wellness tourism has become more significant among the overall travel trends in real-world business applications, mainly the market segments interested in self-repair and personality change. This is the interrelationship between health and travel — the practice in which individuals intentionally travel to attend to and/or enhance their health condition and/or well-being (Wang et al., 2024). The connectedness of a health philosophy's physical, mental, emotional, and spiritual underpinnings as the basis for greater global transformative development awareness drives wellness tourism.

Emerging Trends

Some emerging trends are changing the landscape of wellness tourism as follows:

Tech Integration: Technology is changing how the wellness tourism industry revolutionizes personalized experiences, virtual consultations, and remote wellness programs. Mobile apps, wearable devices, and virtual reality can help enhance travelers' experience with customized recommendations tailored to the individuals, monitor their health metrics, and offer virtual wellness consultations (Sarkar, 2024).

Wellness Tourism with Sustainable Character: The demand for sustainable practices during wellness experiences is growing since these travelers are increasingly looking for eco-friendliness and social responsibility (Dimanche & Andrades, 2024). Sustainability also continues to integrate into wellness destinations, which are becoming more ecologically conscious by exploring approaches like minimizing carbon footprints, reducing trash, and engaging local communities.

The Elder Population and Wellness Tourism: An increasingly aging global population will generate a niche market for wellness tourism products and services. Wellness destinations provide bespoke experiences and are equipped with facilities to meet seniors' unique needs, emphasizing relaxing, gentle fitness, therapeutic services, and dietary counseling.

Wellness Tourism and Mental Health Mental health tourism is a new niche that is quickly becoming noteworthy as people seek treatment for mental health issues. From mindfulness retreats and CBT to counseling, destinations have several choices of mental health services to offer.

Wellness Tourism's Potential To Deliver

Opportunities for all levels and at all points of the wellness tourism industry Rapid growth is fuelled by growing global consciousness toward health and wellness, coupled with an increasing demand for more holistic travel experiences. Opportunities are diverse, including economic growth, innovation, and sustainable development. The key opportunities within wellness tourism are further explored below.

Economic Expansion

Wellness tourism is a lucrative, high-impact segment that contributes to the socio-economic development of locations. The industry earns significant revenue by offering spa services, wellness centers, yoga programs, lodging, food, and transportation. Wellness travelers are appealing because they spend nearly twice as much as the average tourist, which means big bucks for the destination that can provide this type of travel. Destinations can diversify the amounts of money coming in and create continuous income streams by giving unique wellness experiences.

Furthermore, wellness tourism creates jobs and employment across several business sectors, including hospitality, health, and other local artisans. Wellness travelers, for example, spend so much money on goods and services that a regional economy will benefit from the increased demand for things like health spa centers, yoga instructors, and wellness practitioners. Such an economic expansion benefits entire communities, especially in rural or underdeveloped regions, through sustainable sources of income, resulting in reduced economic disparity.

Wellness tourism generates both direct economic benefits and indirect economic impact. For instance, local farmers and producers of organic food for wellness resorts can grow their businesses significantly. Likewise, transportation and logistics services stand to gain as wellness tourists travel to a destination. Overall, in terms of a multiplier effect, the benefits of wellness tourism have a ripple effect that goes beyond the confines of the economy.

Destination Marketing and Promotion

This makes wellness tourism an optional tool for uniquely promoting destinations with aspirations of odysseys. As more global travelers focus on health and well-being, destinations can showcase their evolution as wellness centers for the body, mind, and spirit. Such positioning augments the image of the destination and appeals to the high-end traveler in search of a deluxe experience.

According to Jones (2024), wellness tourism is a means for a destination to build a competitive edge and distinguish itself in a saturated market. These destinations may entice a specific sector of health-conscious tourists by emphasizing their natural attractions, culture, and wellness facilities. A destination with great beaches and eco-friendly practices can be an oasis to relax and recover. Likewise, places famous for traditional healing practices can also take advantage of wellness tourists' need to utilize their cultural uniqueness, e.g., Ayurveda in India and hot spring therapies, etc. in Japan.

Part of wellness tourism marketing also necessarily includes establishing a solid digital footprint. They impact social media channels, wellness blogs, and influencer collaborations to connect with and target these audiences. A specific region using videos and photographs can make travel enthusiasts feel that a particular transformation can happen by visiting the destination, thus creating an emotional connection. These marketing strategies allow destinations to increase their visibility and draw a continuous flow of tourists.

Social Planning

With proper social planning, this form of tourism enables it to become a local, sustainable development. It encourages businesses and communities to promote cultural heritage and environmental conservation practices. Sustainability adds more value to the wellness tourism experience, which, in turn, gives a better future for the destination.

Social planning in wellness tourism typically involves facilitating green initiatives. Again, Destinations: Develop some sustainable initiatives, waste management programs, and conservation projects, resulting in a less harmful environmental impact. Destinations preserve natural resources and attract eco-conscious travelers by incorporating these practices into wellness tourism offerings.

Wellness tourism also helps maintain cultural identity. Traditional wellness practices include herbal medicine, meditation techniques, Indigenous rituals, etc. Such travel offers genuine and powerful experiences to travelers, making it easier for the local community to stay true to their forms and functions of culture. Talukder et al. (2020) On the other hand, the practicality/viability of wellness tourism as a lucrative solution to address the commercialization issue undermines calls to reconnect with the heart of wellness tourism, one that genuinely respects and preserves local culture, traditions, and practices (Panda et al. 2024).

Thus, social planning in wellness tourism should engage with and empower the community. Destinations can create ownership and pride through resident engagement in wellness tourism development and operations. Income generation opportunities can take the form of community-based wellness programs, yoga workshops, or organic farming tours while reinforcing social cohesion. This collaborative step ensures that all stakeholders equally benefit from wellness tourism.

Business Growth and Innovation

Radical innovation and entrepreneurship are natural features of the wellness tourism sector. It is fertile ground for new products, services, and business forms. With the consumer demand for wellness experiences on the rise, there is potential for creative answers to the ever-changing preferences of the consumer.

In wellness tourism, one such innovation is the infusion of technology. Mobile apps and wearable devices can offer personalized wellness recommendations, deliver fitness goals, and even provide virtual wellness programs. The squad will offer immersive experiences like VR guided meditations or AR wellness tours. These developments improve the quality of wellness products and services and increase their accessibility to a worldwide audience.

Wellness tourism can also mean entrepreneurship by creating niche markets. An emerging market, for example, is wellness tourism for seniors, which must offer relevant services like accommodations free of mobility barriers to other age-appropriate wellness programs. Likewise, mental health tourism, which is based on treatments for stress, anxiety, and emotional well-being, offers massive room for growth. Focusing on those niche markets allows entrepreneurs to design differentiation and unique selling points within the wellness tourism landscape.

The wellness tourism sector is also evolving due to the rise of key demand segments, including eco-sensitivity and responsible care, which are creating new business models. Wellness resorts with sustainable philosophies, from zero-waste policy to sustainable local materials, are being found increasingly. From pop-up wellness retreats to mobile wellness services, new ideas are taking shape for travelers looking for options that shift and change. These business models highlight the multitude of shapes and forms tourism can take to meet the unique needs of consumer population segments.

The scope of opportunities in wellness tourism creates enormous potential for economic growth, destination marketing, social planning, and innovation. Seizing such opportunities allows destinations and businesses to create unique and transformative experiences for travelers and enable sustainable development. The economic impacts of wellness tourism revenue generation, job creation, community empowerment, and local industry support. Effective marketing is the key to positioning destinations as distinct wellness hotspots that appeal to wealthy travelers.

By ensuring wellness tourism is driven by environmental and cultural sustainability, social planning plays a crucial role in safeguarding the integrity of destinations and, at the same time, improving them. The development of the industry through innovations and entrepreneurship in new products, services, and business formats that align with trends. The success of wellness tourism will need to adapt to changing consumer demands along with global challenges to ultimately dictate the future of this space as it continues to expand. The wellness tourism industry can build a healthier, more sustainable, and inclusive world by seizing these opportunities.

CHALLENGES

The wellness tourism industry, despite its possible growth, has several challenges that need to be addressed:

Overtourism: Increased interest in wellness tourism may lead to overtourism, causing detrimental effects on the environment and residents.

Commercialization: As with all trends, such commercialization of wellness will ultimately lead to an erasure of genuine experiences and tools (Nasiche, 2024c)

Sustaining: The economic function of wellness tourism and social and environmental sustainability seems daunting.

Competition: It's becoming more challenging to position and attract wellness travelers as there is an increase in competition in tourist destinations.

People are getting more «total wellness, so wellness tourism has matured into a mass leisure activity service. It covers a full range of services, from typical wellness getaways to safari tourism in the sense of most tourists. Sustainable development issues, native qualities, or social responsibility are topics common sense cannot recover in the gastronomy and wellness tourism industry development and healthy and organic fat nowadays.

RECOMMENDATIONS

Invest in Infrastructure And Tech Integration

Destinations must also invest in new wellness infrastructure and technology to stay competitive in the wellness arena. Modern wellness resorts, spas, and facilities — outfitted with technology (like wellness monitors, for example) can create new types of wellness experiences that meet the changing needs of wellness travelers. However, technology also has the potential to make the process more accessible as travelers can check all services, locate themselves, and manage their wellness journey during and after the trip. In this highly competitive landscape, destinations that embrace digital innovations such as virtual reality (VR) and augmented reality (AR) competitions to offer immersive wellness experiences will emerge as leaders.

Encourage Sustainability and Eco-Friendly Practices.

It highlights the importance of sustainability, especially given the increase in the market for green wellness tourism. Destinations must implement sustainable practices, eliminate waste, and utilize green energy and local organic products in wellness offerings. To target environmentally conscious travelers, you should provide eco-certified accommodations and activities. Encouraging travelers to use carbon-neutral modes of transport and partnering with local communities to conserve natural and cultural assets should also be a focus. Aligning wellness tourism with SDGs will ensure its long-term success and attractiveness.

Target Niche Markets And Personalized Experiences

By focusing on specific wellness sub-segments such as senior citizen programs, mental health retreats, or corporate wellness solutions, companies can choose from these niche markets to further diversify their offerings. Custom fitness programs, dietary programs, and stress management workshops can all be personalized to travelers, offering more personalized wellness experiences. Preferential anticipatory services offer customers a unique value that boosts their long-term loyalty and satisfaction through extensive data analysis and customer feedback collection.

Enhanced Branding and Marketing of Destinations

It's up to the destination to market itself as a wellness destination by offering unique selling points such as beautiful landscape options, culture, and traditional healing practices. Partnerships between government bodies, private businesses, and local communities can help a destination gain visibility through collaborative marketing campaigns. It must execute the digital marketing strategy to gain worldwide attraction using influencer, social media, and video content marketing. We must also attend international fairs and wellness tourism exhibitions, which enhance brand popularity and bring more affluent travelers to our services.

Boost Involvement of Local Residents and Heritage Conservation

Instead, they should involve local communities at all levels of engagement to ensure that the benefits and burdens of wellness tourism are enjoyed equitably, to make tourism 'communicative' and inclusive. Involving local artists, therapists, and wellness practitioners in tourism can deliver genuine experiences and help secure livelihoods. Maintaining traditional wellness practices such as Ayurveda, herbal medicine, or indigenous rituals will protect cultural heritage and set destinations apart. Developing ownership and sharing success through educational programs and workshops to involve local communities in wellness tourism.

Establish Partnerships and Collaboration

Buying Wellness Tourism will require the concerted joint effort of all industry stakeholders, government, private industry, and academia to advance. These partnerships can lead to the exchange of ideas, innovations, and resources. Encourage businesses to invest in wellness tourism with tax rebates for grants. University partnerships can also facilitate research on emerging trends, passenger behavior, and sustainable practices, resulting in decisions based on objective data. Partnerships with global wellness organizations can help destinations gain trust and attractiveness.

Then, focus on managing over-tourism to maintain international demand for high-quality destinations and rethink capacity management.

Capacity management should be in place at a destination to avoid over-tourism ramifications. In this way, it could reduce the pressure on popular meccas by limiting visitor numbers, advocating for off-season travel, and disseminating and diversifying the attraction about lesser visited sites. By implementing visitor management systems and quality infrastructure upgrades, wellness destinations can develop while ensuring the capacity to host travelers without diluting the quality of experiences and eco-cultural resources.

Pushing Research And Innovation

Ongoing research is to change traveler behavior — this makes adapting to trends necessary; governments and businesses must invest in research on the economic implications of wellness tourism, the impact of technology, and new business opportunities across wellness assets and services. There is a need to encourage innovation in wellness tech innovations, mental health tourism, and sustainability fine-tuned business models. Insights from research can inform and provide a competitive advantage to strategic planning at the destination level.

Encourage Accessibility and Inclusion

Wellness tourism should be open to travelers, persons with impaired physical abilities, older adults, and families. Develop mobility-friendly infrastructure in the destination that meets different customer needs, such as facilities dealing with mobility issues and family-focused wellness programs. Pricing strategies should also be inclusive and not exclusive to high-income travelers only. By providing tiered packages at different price points, more of us can experience varying levels of luxury silliness in our wellness.

Layout a Crisis Management & Resilience Plan

Revolutionary disruptions, including pandemics, natural disasters, or depression in the global economy, could always threaten the wellness tourism industry. Crisis Management PlansIncluding health and safety protocols, flexible booking policies, and communication strategies, businesses and destinations should develop plans to respond to a crisis effectively. With diversification, digital transformation, and sustainable practices paving the way to resilience, the industry will keep bouncing back and positioned for the uncertainties ahead of us.

By providing the following recommendations, the wellness tourism industry can take advantage of its significant growth opportunity while developing solutions to major challenges. With investments in building infrastructure, promoting sustainability, narrowing down niche segments, and encouraging collaborations, key stakeholders can make wellness experiences transformative and inclusive. Wellness tourism will remain one of the most vibrant and sustainable segments in the global travel industry when the focus is placed on research, innovation, and the safeguarding of cultures.

Figure 2. Strategic framework for wellness tourism and economic development

Source: Author Compilation.

The framework describes how wellness tourism can steer from well-being to economy through four key posts: a well-being tourism strategy, sustainable practices, technology mixing and growth, and learning & exercising. It highlights the space wellness tourism has in regaining and improving sustainable development, continental small opportunities, digital transformation, and workforce training to develop global economic mobility.

CONCLUSION

Wellness tourism has emerged as a significant force within the global travel industry, driven by a growing consumer awareness of health, well-being, and personal growth. This chapter has explored the multifaceted dimensions of wellness tourism, including its motivations, experiences, economic impact, and emerging trends. Key findings from this research highlight the diverse motivations of wellness travelers, ranging from stress relief and relaxation to spiritual growth and social connection. The industry offers many experiences, from traditional spa treatments and yoga retreats to adventure tourism and cultural immersion. The economic impact of wellness tourism is substantial. It generates revenue for destinations, creates jobs, and stimulates local economies. By prioritizing sustainability, authenticity, and personalized experiences, wellness tourism can continue to thrive and contribute to the well-being of travelers and host communities. However, the industry faces overtourism, commercialization, and environmental impact. To address these challenges, adopting sustainable practices, supporting local communities, and prioritizing the well-being of travelers and the environment is crucial. As the wellness tourism industry evolves, embracing emerging trends, such as technology integration, personalized experiences, and sustainable practices, is essential. By understanding the motivations of wellness travelers, the diverse range of experiences available, and the economic impact of this burgeoning sector, industry stakeholders can develop innovative strategies to meet travelers' evolving needs and ensure the industry's long-term sustainability. Future research should delve deeper into the specific needs and preferences of different segments of wellness travelers, the role of technology in shaping the industry, and the impact of wellness tourism on local communities and the environment. By fostering collaboration between industry stakeholders, governments, and academia, we can collectively shape the future of wellness tourism and create a more sustainable and fulfilling travel experience.

REFERENCES

Abdallah, A., & Al-Hashmi, B. (2023). Are Medical and Wellness the Future of Tourism in Qatar? *Études Caribéennes, 9*. DOI: 10.4000/etudescaribeennes.28020

Abdulatif, K. (2024). Theoretical Dimensions of Classification and Segmentation in Therapeutic Wellness Tourism. *Academic Journal of Digital Economics and Stability, 37*(4), 74–80. DOI: 10.51699/economics.v37i4.160

Alharethi, T., & Kabil, M. (2024). Charting the Sustainable Course: Navigating the Saudi Arabia Medical and Wellness Tourism Roadmap with Business Model Canvas (BMC). *Sustainability (Basel), 16*(9), 3856. DOI: 10.3390/su16093856

Balcioglu, Y. S. (2024). Exploring consumer engagement and satisfaction in health and wellness tourism through text-mining. *Kybernetes*. Advance online publication. DOI: 10.1108/K-12-2023-2721

Bentley, L. (2024). *The role of technology in enhancing health and wellness tourism experiences*. DOI: 10.5281/ZENODO.11403443

Biggs, T., Cuevas, A., Dahal, A., Pelser, M., Vansuyt, P., & Barbosa, B. (2024). Exploring the Potential of Wellness Tourism in the Wine Industry: Multiple Case Study Approach. In Castanho, R. A., & Franco, M. (Eds.), *Advances in Hospitality, Tourism, and the Services Industry* (pp. 161–178). IGI Global., DOI: 10.4018/979-8-3693-3158-3.ch007

Błotnicka, A., Górski, Z., & Jurasiński, D. (2024). Current trends in the wellness tourism market in light of selected reports analyzing the effects of the covid-19 pandemic. *Folia Turistica, 62*, 133–160. DOI: 10.5604/01.3001.0054.6890

Boulay, R., Hritz, N. M., & Ashton, C. (2013). An Exploratory Study of Wellness Travel: Differences Between U.S. and Non-U.S. Travelers. *Journal of Tourism Insights, 4*(1). Advance online publication. DOI: 10.9707/2328-0824.1036

Chartrand, M.-E., Bélisle, D., Patry-Beaudoin, G., & Cheikhrouhou, S. (2024). The retail wellnesscape: Conceptualizing consumer wellness in a health food retailing context. *Qualitative Market Research, 27*(4), 631–649. DOI: 10.1108/QMR-09-2023-0127

Chen, J. S., Prebensen, N., & Huan, T. C. (2008). Determining the Motivation of Wellness Travelers. *Anatolia, 19*(1), 103–115. DOI: 10.1080/13032917.2008.9687056

Dahanayake, S., Wanninayake, B., & Ranasinghe, R. (2023). Unveiling the essence: Constructs of memorable wellness tourism experiences. *Tourism and Hospitality Research, 14673584231223860*, 14673584231223860. Advance online publication. DOI: 10.1177/14673584231223860

Dimanche, F., & Andrades, L. (2024). Tourism Trends: Current Challenges for Tourism Destinations Management. In Andrades, L., Romero-Dexeus, C., & Martínez-Marín, E. (Eds.), *The Spanish Model for Smart Tourism Destination Management* (pp. 3–21). Springer International Publishing., DOI: 10.1007/978-3-031-60709-7_1

Dimitrova, B. (2023). Brain drain's economic impact on the development of wellness and spa tourism in Bulgaria. *Trakia Journal of Sciences, 21*(Suppl. 1), 9–14. DOI: 10.15547/tjs.2023.s.01.002

Hritz, N. M., Sidman, C. L., & D'Abundo, M. (2014). Segmenting the College Educated Generation Y Health and Wellness Traveler. *Journal of Travel & Tourism Marketing, 31*(1), 132–145. DOI: 10.1080/10548408.2014.861727

Jones, P. (2024). Wellness in the Global Hospitality and Tourism Industry. *Athens Journal of Tourism, 11*(3), 225–238. DOI: 10.30958/ajt.11-3-3

Joson, G. H. G., Pyke, J., Delacy, T., & Davidson, C. (2024). Wellness in the Spa Industry: An Investigation of Hot Spring Tourism in Australia. In Chhabra, D., Atal, N., & Maheshwari, A. (Eds.), *Sustainable Development and Resilience of Tourism* (pp. 63–79). Springer International Publishing., DOI: 10.1007/978-3-031-63145-0_4

Kabir, F., Talukder, M. B., & Kumar, S. (2024). Exchange of Cultures in the Field of Gastronomy Tourism: Evidence of Bangladesh. In Castanho, R., & Franco, M. (Eds.), *Cultural, Gastronomy, and Adventure Tourism Development* (pp. 142–159). IGI Global., DOI: 10.4018/979-8-3693-3158-3.ch006

Kajornatthapol, P., Siyaphat, S., Tarmthai, P., & Thumtheang, S. (2024). Exploring Interpersonal Dynamics in Wellness Tourism: A Reexamination of Intentions Through a Case Study of Generation X Citizens in Thailand. *Revista de Gestão Social e Ambiental, 18*(11), e09635. DOI: 10.24857/rgsa.v18n11-036

Krishna Pasupuleti, M. (2024). Sustainable Tourism and Digital Wellness: Shaping the Future of Recreation and Health. In *Digital wellness programs and sustainable tourism practices in recreation* (First Edition, pp. 29–48). National Education Services. DOI: 10.62311/nesx/17960

Kumar, S., & Talukder, M. B. (2025). Leadership's Role in Promoting a Culture of Learning in the Organization. In Derbali, A., Chaudhary, S., Sood, R., & Chandel, A. (Eds.), *Unleashing Absorptive Capacity and Unlearning for Organizational Excellence* (pp. 257–274). IGI Global., DOI: 10.4018/979-8-3693-3820-9.ch012

Kumar, S., Talukder, M. B., & Kaiser, F. (2024). Artificial Intelligence in Business: Negative Social Impacts. In *Demystifying the Dark Side of AI in Business* (pp. 81-97). IGI Global. https://doi.org/ DOI: 10.4018/979-8-3693-0724-3.ch005

Kupcewicz, E., & Bentkowska, A. (2023). Health and its significance in the modern concept of wellness and spa. *Journal of Education, Health and Sport*, *49*(1), 44–55. DOI: 10.12775/JEHS.2023.49.01.003

Lopes, M. (2022). Can Volunteer Tourism be a sub-segment of Wellness Tourism? *International Conference on Tourism Research, 15*(1), 208–215. DOI: 10.34190/ictr.15.1.300

Majeed, S., & Gon Kim, W. (2023). Emerging trends in wellness tourism: A scoping review. *Journal of Hospitality and Tourism Insights*, *6*(2), 853–873. DOI: 10.1108/JHTI-02-2022-0046

Makoondlall-Chadee, T., Ramasamy-Coolen, P., Naria, O., & Bokhoree, S. (2024). Mauritius as a Sustainable Island Destination: Opportunities, Implications, and Challenges for Sport Tourism. In Van Rheenen, D., Naria, O., Melo, R., & Sobry, C. (Eds.), *Sport Tourism, Island Territories and Sustainable Development* (Vol. 24, pp. 347–366). Springer Nature Switzerland., DOI: 10.1007/978-3-031-51705-1_21

Manjula, K., P, K., R, V., & Thirupathi, D. G. (2024). Yoga Tourism: A Journey towards Holistic Wellness. *International Journal of Advanced Multidisciplinary Research and Studies*, *4*(5), 514–518. DOI: 10.62225/2583049X.2024.4.5.3278

Musakin, A., Ruglova, L., & Vorontsova, G. (2024). Modern hotel profitability centers: Spa and wellness in the Russian hotel space. *The Eurasian Scientific Journal, 16*(1), 59ECVN124. DOI: 10.15862/59ECVN124

Nair, B. B. (2020). Heal and Revive: Emerging Trends in Wellness Tourism in Kerala. In Paul, S., & Kulshreshtha, S. K. (Eds.), *Advances in Hospitality, Tourism, and the Services Industry* (pp. 220–235). IGI Global., DOI: 10.4018/978-1-5225-9787-2.ch012

Nasiche, N. (2024a). The Role of Wellness Tourism in the Growth of the Hospitality Industry. *Journal of Modern Hospitality*, *3*(1), 53–64. DOI: 10.47941/jmh.1954

Phuong, T. T., & Giang, V. H. (2024). Some theoretical basis and experience for developing wellness tourism. *T p Chí Khoa H c Trư ng Đ i H c M Hà N i, 65*, 65. Advance online publication. DOI: 10.59266/houjs.2024.446

Piatto Clerici, A., Murphy, C., & Castanheira Almeida, N. M. (2023). The future of wellness tourism after COVID-19. *European Spatial Research and Policy, 30*(1), 103–122. DOI: 10.18778/1231-1952.30.1.05

Piccirillo, P. (2024). Bleisure Tourism and the Impact of Technology: The New Trends in Business Tourism. In Sharma, S., Kumar, N., Ribeiro Dos Santos, V., & Miranda-Fernandez, K. (Eds.), *Advances in Hospitality, Tourism, and the Services Industry* (pp. 45–60). IGI Global., DOI: 10.4018/979-8-3693-8377-3.ch003

Rajapakshe, R. L. T. D. S., & Arachchi, R. S. S. W. (2024). Ayurveda Wellness Tourism: An Overview of the Sri Lankan Context. In Sharma, A., & Arora, S. (Eds.), *Strategic Tourism Planning for Communities* (pp. 173–195). Emerald Publishing Limited., DOI: 10.1108/978-1-83549-015-020241014

Riashenkova, A. A. (2024). Creating a speech portrait of a modern Chinese teacher in online media. *Филология: Научные Исследования, 9*(9), 59–66. DOI: 10.7256/2454-0749.2024.9.71735

Sarkar, S. (2024). Prospects and challenges of the tourism industry in Gujarat- a geographical study. *vidya - a journal of gujarat university, 3*(2), 21–26. DOI: 10.47413/vidya.v3i2.417

Talukder, M. B. (2020). An Appraisal of the Economic Outlook for the Tourism Industry, especially Cox's Bazar in Bangladesh. *i-manager's Journal on Economics & Commerce,* 2(1), 23-35. DOI: 10.26634/jecom.2.1.17285

Talukder, M. B. (2020). The Future of Culinary Tourism: An Emerging Dimension for the Tourism Industry of Bangladesh. I-Manager's. *Journal of Management, 15*(1), 27. DOI: 10.26634/jmgt.15.1.17181

Talukder, M. B. (2024). Implementing Artificial Intelligence and Virtual Experiences in Hospitality. In *Innovative Technologies for Increasing Service Productivity* (pp. 145–160). IGI Global., DOI: 10.4018/979-8-3693-2019-8.ch009

Talukder, M. B., Hossain, S. E., Al Ferdous, F., & Khan, M. R. (2024b). Exploring the Rise of Wellness Tourism: Trends, Benefits, and Market Potential. In Jermsittiparsert, K., & Marzo, R. R. (Eds.), (pp. 351–378). Advances in Computational Intelligence and Robotics. IGI Global., DOI: 10.4018/979-8-3693-9158-7.ch013

Talukder, M. B., Kabir, F., & Mia, Md. N., & Khan, M. R. (2024). Application of Smart Technologies in the Development and Promotion of Religious Tourism Destination: In R. A. Castanho & M. Franco (Eds.), *Advances in Hospitality, Tourism, and the Services Industry* (pp. 71–88). IGI Global. DOI: 10.4018/979-8-3693-3158-3.ch003

Talukder, M. B., Kumar, S., & Khan, M. R. (2024). The Integration of Sustainable Practices in Cultural and Gastronomic Tourism. In Munuhwa, S. (Ed.), (pp. 467–484). Advances in Civil and Industrial Engineering. IGI Global., DOI: 10.4018/979-8-3693-3755-4.ch017

Talukder, M. B., Kumar, S., & Tyagi, P. K. (Eds.). (2024). *Impact of AI and Tech-Driven Solutions in Hospitality and Tourism*. IGI Global., DOI: 10.4018/979-8-3693-6755-1

Talukder, M. B., & Muhsina, K. (2024). The prospect of Smart Tourism Destination in Bangladesh. In Correia, R., Martins, M., & Fontes, R. (Eds.), *Advances in Hospitality, Tourism, and the Services Industry* (pp. 163–179). IGI Global., DOI: 10.4018/979-8-3693-2137-9.ch009

Talukder, M. B., Swarna, D. A., & Khan, M. R. (2024). The Allure of Tranquillity: How Less-Crowded Destinations in Bangladesh Captivate International Tourists. In Jermsittiparsert, K., Wekke, I. S., & Suanpang, P. (Eds.), (pp. 399–418). Advances in E-Business Research. IGI Global., DOI: 10.4018/979-8-3693-9230-0.ch020

Tashpulatova L. M & Suyunova F. B. (2024). Digital transformation in tourism: trends, challenges, and opportunities. *International Journal of Global Economic Light*, 1–8. DOI: 10.36713/epra17744

Wang, L., Damdinsuren, M., Qin, Y., Gonchigsumlaa, G., Zandan, Y., & Zhang, Z. (2024). Forest Wellness Tourism Development Strategies Using SWOT, QSPM, and AHP: A Case Study of Chongqing Tea Mountain and Bamboo Forest in China. *Sustainability (Basel)*, *16*(9), 3609. DOI: 10.3390/su16093609

Wulandari, L. W. (2024). Optimization of the Newa-Based Tourism Development Model (Nature, Ecotourism, Wellness, and Adventure) Through the Eco-Wellness Tourism Concept Approach. *Eduvest - Journal of Universal Studies, 4*(8), 6907–6919. https://doi.org/DOI: 10.59188/eduvest.v4i8.1742

ADDITIONAL READING

Andreu, M. G. N., Font-Barnet, A., & Roca, M. E. (2021). Wellness Tourism—New Challenges and Opportunities for Tourism in Salou. *Sustainability (Basel)*, *13*(15), 8246. DOI: 10.3390/su13158246

Arsić, M., Vujko, A., & Knežević, M. (2024). Development Perspectives on Wellness and Spa Tourism in the Context of Tourism Business Sustainability. *Sustainability (Basel)*, *16*(20), 8760. DOI: 10.3390/su16208760

KEY TERMS AND DEFINITIONS

Wellness Retreats: A wellness retreat is a planned trip where the focus is on physical, mental, and emotional well-being. They usually involve activities such as yoga, health, meditation, spa treatments, and nutrition. These activities offer detox and help the participants to relieve stress and improve health as a whole.

Sustainable Tourism: Sustainable tourism focuses on limiting the harm done to the environment and helping local communities as much as possible. It combines sustainability practices, cultural preservation, and sustainable behavior during the trip. The objective is to provide tourism with sustainable environmental and social welfare outcomes.

Health Tourism: Health tourism is traveling to receive medical treatments or health-promoting experiences, from spa therapies and wellness programs to surgeries and alternative medicine. This integrates health service and leisure; it can optimize health results and quality of life.

Wellness Travel: The specific focus of wellness travel is all on trips explicitly designed to improve health and wellness. It is for relaxation, fitness activities, or holistic therapies. According to Isha A. Bhatia, the head of corporate communication at ITM GROUP, wellness travel's ultimate purpose is to engender a rejuvenated body and mind whilst indulging in enriching travel experiences.

Wellness Tourism: Wellness tourism is travel that makes you stay in shape or enhance your well-being. It covers different sectors such as spas, yoga retreats, and eco-tourism. This rapidly growing industry is about living a healthy lifestyle, relieving stress, and creating sustainable travel experiences.

Chapter 16
Visualization of Global Research Trends and Future Research Directions of Sustainable Tourism and Sustainable Development Goals Using Bibliometric Analysis

Anil Kumar
https://orcid.org/0009-0000-8565-9522
Graphic Era Hill University, India

Aastha Jain
https://orcid.org/0000-0003-1081-9135
Vaish College of Engineering, India

Kuldeep Singh
https://orcid.org/0000-0002-7999-1585
Amity University, Haryana, India

ABSTRACT

This study employed bibliometric analysis to visualize global research trends and future research directions in sustainable tourism and its alignment with the Sustainable Development Goals (SDGs).The search strategy was designed to identify relevant literature by using specific keywords and search terms related to sustainable tour-

DOI: 10.4018/979-8-3373-0071-9.ch016

ism and the SDGs Scopus database was selected to collect the data. A total of 380 documents were collected from the Scopus database. The search period was set from 2000 to 2024 to encompass recent developments. The subject area included Business, Management and Accounting, Economics, Econometrics and Finance, Social Sciences, and Arts and Humanities. By applying various filters and data cleaning process 230 documents were included in performing the final analysis.

INTRODUCTION

Sustainable tourism has become an essential element in the global pursuit of sustainable development (Geng et al., 2024; Buhalis et al., 2023). Unlike traditional forms of tourism, which often result in environmental harm and cultural disruption, sustainable tourism is designed to reduce negative impacts while enhancing the well-being of local communities and ecosystems (Baloch et al., 2023). With continues growth in tourism, it is important to maintain a balance between Socio-Economic and Environmental integrity (Li et al., 2024; Baloch et al., 2023; Irawan & Hartoyo, 2022; Hall, 2019). As per the UNWTO, Green Tourism is a key that addresses the needs of both present travelers and host communities, while also preserving and improving prospects for future generations. It focuses on minimizing tourism's environmental and social impacts while maximizing its economic contributions and supporting the preservation of cultural heritage (Causevic & Neal, 2019; Streimikiene et al., 2020).

The 17 SDGs are aimed for global objectives introduced by the UN in 2015 (refer to Figure 1). These goals are designed to tackle Socio-Economic and environmental issues by the year 2030. They build on the foundation laid by the earlier Millennium Development Goals (MDGs) and emphasize the need for unified efforts to eliminate poverty, safeguard the environment, and foster peace and prosperity universally. However, a notable obstruction in achieving these goals is the lack of awareness among individuals and organizations regarding the SDGs (Özgit & Zhandildina, 2021). Sustainable tourism, however, can contribute both directly and indirectly to the achievement of all the SDGs (Mohan, 2022). By advocating for responsible travel practices and supporting local economies, "sustainable tourism can help reduce poverty (SDG 1) and promote decent work and economic growth" (SDG 8). Furthermore, "initiatives to conserve natural and cultural heritage support the protection of terrestrial ecosystems" (SDG 15) and the development of sustainable cities and communities (SDG 11) (Monroy-Rodríguez & Caro-Carretero, 2023; Pradhan, 2023; Zhao, 2022; Seraphin, 2021; Glass & Newig, 2019; Sachs et al., 2019; Spenceley & Rylance, 2019). The comprehensive nature of sustainable tourism enables it to intersect with multiple SDGs, offering a holistic approach to global development. Thus, sustainable tourism is not only a key economic force but also a vital contributor to the global effort to achieve the SDGs.

Figure 1. 17 global objectives of sustainable development goals

Source: United Nations Report, 2015

Although sustainable tourism is increasingly acknowledged as crucial for advancing the SDGs, a significant gap persists in fully comprehending global research trends and identifying future directions in this area. Earlier studies have examined various aspects of sustainable tourism and its impacts, there is a lack of systematic bibliometric analyses that map the evolution of research topics, identify influential publications, and highlight key areas for future investigation. Bibliometric analysis, a mixed method for evaluating academic literature, offers a powerful tool for mapping the development and trajectory of research fields (Aggarwal et al., 2022). By examining patterns in scholarly publications, citations, and collaborations, bibliometric analysis can provide insights into the precedent, current, and future trajectories of research (Moyle et al., 2020).

LITERATURE REVIEW

Sustainable Tourism and SDGs

Fauzi (2023) analyzed "the role of Sustainable tourism and SDGs in tourism and hospitality sector" and their findings revealed that through bibliometric approach managerial and theoretical implications were examined Due to large numbers of tourists and their activities there is a large impact on natural resources of the destination which results in the sustainable tourism concept (van Nuenen&Scarles, 2021). The role of sustainable tourism is to maintain equilibrium in the environment, Socio-Economic conditions and to reduce the negative impact on natural resources (Buckley, 2012; Hall, 2019). Some new concepts of sustainable tourism are green-hotels, green transport, green building and green resources which are the need for current generation (Pan et al., 2018).

Though the government, private sector, local community, tourists and various stakeholders emphasizing on sustainable tourism, still there is a death of current studies on this topic (Pan et al., 2018). Therefore, present work attempts to sort the gap while applying bibliometric techniques in the current trends of tourism and SDGs.

SDG in Tourism

According to Rasoolimanesh et al. (2020). SDGs are newer concepts which are accepted worldwide. The UN also declared 2017 as "an International Year of Sustainable Tourism" and its main focus is on sustainability and conservation of tourism resources (Bolu & Rasoolimanesh, 2022). Further, inclusive growth and equal distribution of resources concept was launched in first world tourism research conference held at Massey University New Zealand in 2019 (Scheyvens & Cheer, 2021). During this conference mostly countries discussed the link of SDG through tourism whether it has climate issues, water issues, land resources issues, technology issues etc. (Scheyvens& Cheer, 2021). In addition, Hall (2019) revealed that socio economic development in tourism sector needed sustainability with preservation of resources.

Magio et al. (2021) investigated sustainable practices in heritage of Mexico region and aligned it with SDG Goals. García et al. (2020) analyzed the association between tourism and sustainability in sports tourism. They applied bibliometric techniques to analyze the future trends of sports tourism and focused on key issues related to planning of the destinations and education. The main examples of sustainability are related to the field of tourism, business management, and corporate governance.

Soh et al. (2023) revealed that "there is a relationship between sustainability and competitiveness and to manage tourist destinations the role of sustainability has become very crucial". To sustain market position competitiveness strategies along with preservation of tourism resources required.

Abdou et al (2020) analyzed the green hotel practices in Egypt and focuses on the environmentally friendly resources which are aligned with SDG goals. Their findings mainly discuss the difference between four- and five-star hotels in which all SDG goals are incorporated.

Need of Sustainability and Green Practices

There are different views of sustainability in hospitality and tourism sector such as Kapera (2018) analyzed the current trends of sustainability and carrying capacity in the current scenario of hotels. Han et al (2018) focused on the perception of guest regarding conservation of water and waste management practices and analyzed that guest focus is shifted towards green practices and sustainability. Prud'homme and Raymond (2013) analyzed "the effect of sustainable development in tourism and hospitality sector of regions of Quebec in Canada".

The sustainable use of water in tourism sector and control of pollution with efficient technology are very crucial for the protection of resource" (Kasim, 2019). Most consumption of water energy and resources is spent on the hotel sector, and it can damage the environment due to its high utilization of resources. Therefore, the need for green hotels and preservation of resources required to manage the sustainability of hotels (Mensah, 2006). Recently many hotels and tourist destinations gave more stress on sustainable resources with green practices which can help to reduce pollution and maintain resources (Manaktola & Jauhari, 2007). Customers will also be attracted towards these hotels and destinations and the role of markets become crucial to focus more on green sustainability (Dodds & Holmes, 2016). Kang et al. (2012) claimed that sustainable issues in the hospitality and tourism sector should incorporate preservation of water and saving of energy through green practices. This approach will also help to combat the negative effects of climate change and reduce greenhouse gases.

This study seeks to address a significant gap by utilizing bibliometric analysis to map and visualize global research trends in sustainable tourism and the SDGs. Additionally, it seeks to explore the knowledge framework of the field by thoroughly reviewing key publications and emerging themes, with the goal of identifying promising future research directions. By doing so, this study provides valuable insights for policymakers, researchers, and practitioners on the current state and potential advancements in sustainable tourism in alignment with the SDGs. So, the objectives of this paper are:

1. To uncover the publication trend in the area of sustainable tourism and SDGs.
2. To uncover the most influential journals, authors, countries, articles shaping sustainable tourism and SDGs.
3. To identify the key research trends, emerging topics, and emerging themes related to sustainable tourism and SDGs within the academic literature.

MATERIAL AND METHODOLOGY

This study utilized bibliometric analysis to explore research trends and identify future policy directions in sustainable tourism with the SDGs. Bibliometric analysis, a quantitative approach, allows for the examination of scientific literature to uncover patterns, trends, and structures within a particular research domain. The data for this analysis was extracted from Scopus, recognized as one of the most comprehensive and widely utilized bibliometric resources.

Search Strategy

The search strategy was designed to identify relevant literature by using specific keywords and search terms related to "sustainable tourism and the SDGs". The search terms included:

```
TITLE-ABS-KEY ("ecotourism" OR "Eco Tourism" OR "eco-
tourism" OR "green tourism" OR "sustainable tourism" OR "nature
based tourism") AND ("sustainable development goals" OR "SDG"
OR "SDG's")
```

Data Collection

These terms were applied to the title, abstract, and keywords fields to ensure a comprehensive retrieval of relevant publications. The search period was set from 2000 to 2024 to encompass recent developments. The subject areas included- 'Business, Management and Accounting', 'Economics', 'Econometrics and Finance', 'Social-Sciences', and 'Arts and Humanities'. And to ensure consistency and quality, only articles and review papers published in English were included. Initially, the search identified 380 papers. Filtering by subject area reduced the number to 304 papers. Further refinement to include only articles and reviews resulted in 236 papers. Finally, limiting the dataset to English-language publications resulted in a final count of 230 papers.

Data Analysis

The extracted data was analyzed using bibliometric technique. The Bibliometric R tool was employed for data processing, visualization, and analysis. This software is widely recognized for its capability to handle large bibliometric datasets and generate insightful visualizations. A descriptive analysis was initially performed to highlight the fundamental attributes of the data, such as trends in publication over time, country-wise distribution, and the most prominent journals within the field. Citation analysis followed, identifying highly cited papers, influential authors, and prominent institutions. Co-occurrence analysis was performed to pinpoint major research themes and topics, while co-citation analysis revealed influential papers and research clusters; and thematic was used to uncover the trending theme.

DATA ANALYSIS AND INTERPRETATION

Descriptive Statistics

Figure 2 shows "Annual Scientific Production" charts the number of scientific articles published annually from 2000 to around 2024. The y-axis, labeled "Articles," tracks the count of publications, while the x-axis denotes the years. From 2000 to2024, the graph shows a consistently similar outputfrom 2000 till 2018 and thereafter there is an increasing trend till the year 2023. In 2024, the scientific production is less as only four month data is extracted till date, implying a high pace of scientific publication.

Figure 2. Annual scientific production

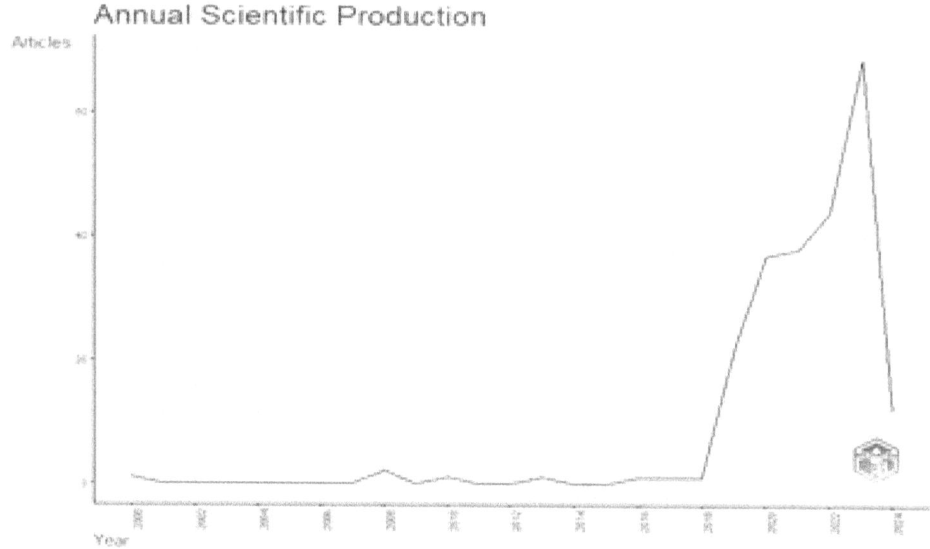

A remarkable shift can be seen in the figure 2 from the year 2018 onwards, with the number of articles rising from consistent annual scientific production of 1 to an increase of annual scientific production of 22 in the year 2019, ASP of 37 in 2020, 38 in 2021, 44 in 2022 and 69 in the year 2023. This clearly indicates the growth of scientific production in context to sustainable tourism and SDGs. This could reflect a period of intense research activity, potentially in response to a global event or a shift in scientific focus. Following this peak, there is continues growth till the year 2024. The graph suggests a period of heightened scientific activity followed by normalization.

Figure 3 represents "Average Citations per Year" plots the average number of citations by scientific articles from 2000 to 2024. The y-axis measures the average citations, and the x-axis represents time in years. Initially, there was a steep decline in the average citations from 2000, reaching a low around 2008.

Figure 3. Average citations per year

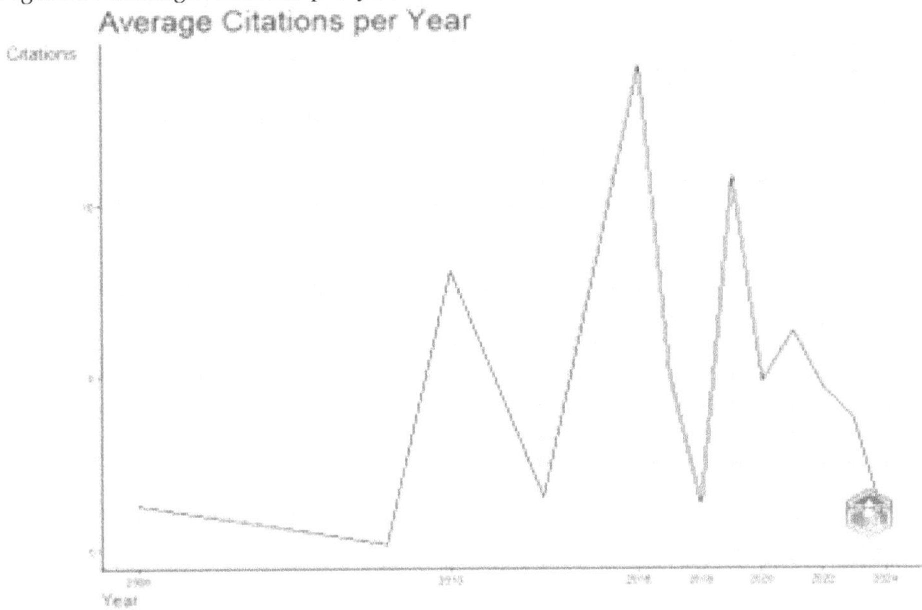

As in 2000 the ACP per year was 1.24 which came down to 0.12 in the year 2008. The reason for this could be the fact that from 2001 till 2007 there was no publication came in context of sustainable tourism and SDG. After this trough, the average citations per year increased till 2010 with an ACP of 8.07. In the year 2013, the ACP came down to 1.5 the reason being there was no publication in the year 2009, 2011, 2012. The figure shows a continues drift of ups and downs in the ACP till 2023. The graph peaks sharply around 2019 with ACP of 10.8, dips, rises again slightly in the following year, and then shows a dramatic decline towards the end of the graphed period. This pattern indicates a dynamic academic environment with changing impacts of scientific work over the years. There were periods of high citation impact, overall, there seems to be a downward trend in recent years.

Three Field Plot

Three-field plot (Figure 4) that visualizes the interconnections between countries, authors, and keywords within a body of academic literature. The leftmost column comprises of the most active sources working in context of sustainable tourism and SDGs, the middle column comprises of most prolific keywords and the rightmost column comprises of the most active countries. We have to focus on the height of the boxes and the thickness of the connecting lines. We found that SDGs and sustainable tourism are most occurred keywords and themes developed. “Journal of sustainable tourism” and “sustainability” are the most active journals in the topic and China is the most active country in context to SDG and sustainable tourism followed by Australia and USA.

Figure 4. Three field plot

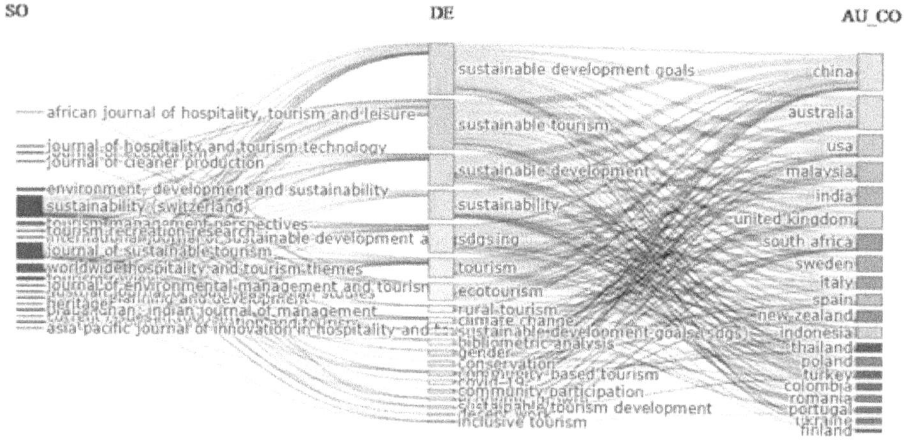

The top keywords “Sustainable Development Goals” and “Sustainable Tourism”,:- sustainable development”, “Sustainability”, “SDG” and “Tourism”. In consideration to the most influential journals as per the three field plot, “Sustainability”, “Journal of sustainable tourism”, “worldwide hospitality and tourism themes” are the most prolific sources. The visualization serves as a map to the landscape of academic inquiry, showing which authors are most active or influential in specific areas, which topics are receiving the most attention, and how these topics are interconnected within the broader research framework

Figure 5. Most relevant sources

Figure 5 presents a bubble chart titled "Most Relevant Sources" displaying the distribution of articles published in academic journals and conference series within a specific field. The x-axis, labeled "No. of documents," indicates the number of articles, while the y-axis lists the names of the sources, such as journals and conference proceedings. Each bubble's size correlates with the article publised in the source. The "Sustainability (Switzerland)" stands out with the largest bubble, indicating the source with most publication at 43 articles. This is followed by the "Journal of Sustainable Tourism" with 12 articles, and "Sustainability (Switzerland)" with 40 articles. These leading sources suggest a strong focus onSustainable Tourism and SDGs within the dataset. Other notable publications with smaller bubbles, such as Worldwide Hospitality and Tourism Themes, Tourism Review and Environment, Development and Sustainability indicate a moderate number of contributions, signifying their relevance but to a lesser extent. The spread of bubbles across the chart reflects a diverse range of sources that contribute to the field, yet the concentration of larger bubbles towards the higher end of the document count points to key sources that dominate the academic discourse.

Figure 6. Bradford's Law

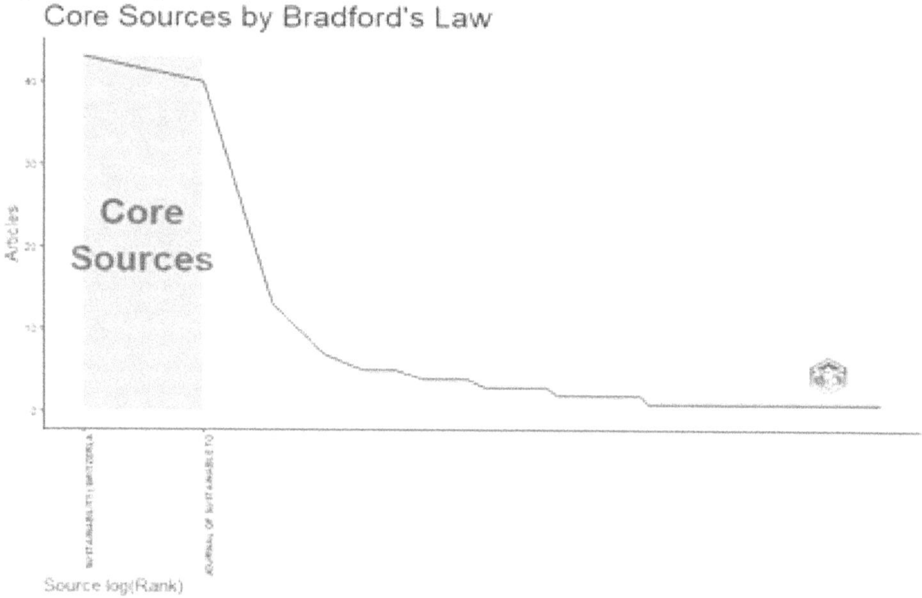

Figure 5 provides a list organized by Bradford's Law, categorizing sources into three distinct zones based on their productivity in a given field. Zone 1, the core zone, includes sources with the highest number of articles, such as "Sustainability (Switzerland)," and "Journal of Sustainable Tourism".Suggesting these are the most influential or most commonly referred to in the research area. These sources form the core or essential publications in the field. As we move to Zones 2 and 3, the frequency of articles per source diminishes, which aligns with Bradford's Law, indicating that fewer articles are published in a larger number of sources. The distribution suggests a typical pattern where a few core journals publish most of the articles, and as one moves to less productive journals, the number of articles per journal decreases. This pattern is useful for identifying which journals are most central to a research area and guiding literature search strategies for researchers.

Source of Impact

Figure 6 details out the impact of various academic journals and conference series within a specific research field as measured by the h-index. For instance, a journal like the "Journal of Sustainable Tourism" has an h-index of 21, indicating that it has published 21 articles that have each been cited at least 21 times. The chart plots these sources against their h-index values, demonstrating a range of impact from an h-index of 21 to 1.

Figure 7. Sources of local impact by H index

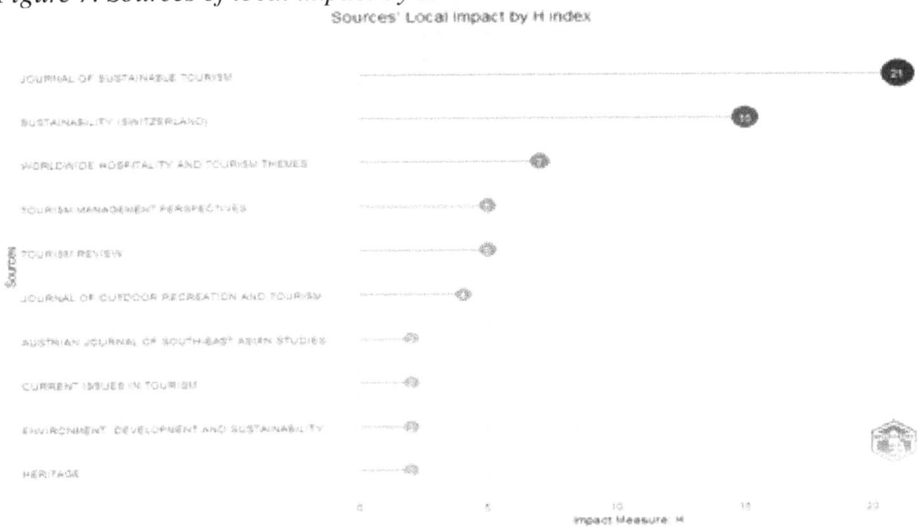

Higher h-index values suggest that the publications from those sources are frequently cited and are influential in the field. The "Journal of Sustainable Tourism," "Sustainability (Switzerland), stand out as the most impactful sources with the highest h-index values, indicating they are likely to be key outlets for research dissemination in the field. The lower h-index values for other sources do not necessarily indicate low quality but may suggest a more niche or emerging area of research, or a younger publication history. The variation in h-index among these sources helps researchers identify where to find the most seminal and potentially influential work in their area of study, and also to discern the key outlets for disseminating their own research to reach a broad and engaged audience.

Figure 7 shows "Sources' Production over Time" depicts the cumulative publications from different sources from around 2000 to 2024. Each line represents a different academic source, and the steepness of the line indicates the rate of publication over time.

Figure 8. Sources' production over time

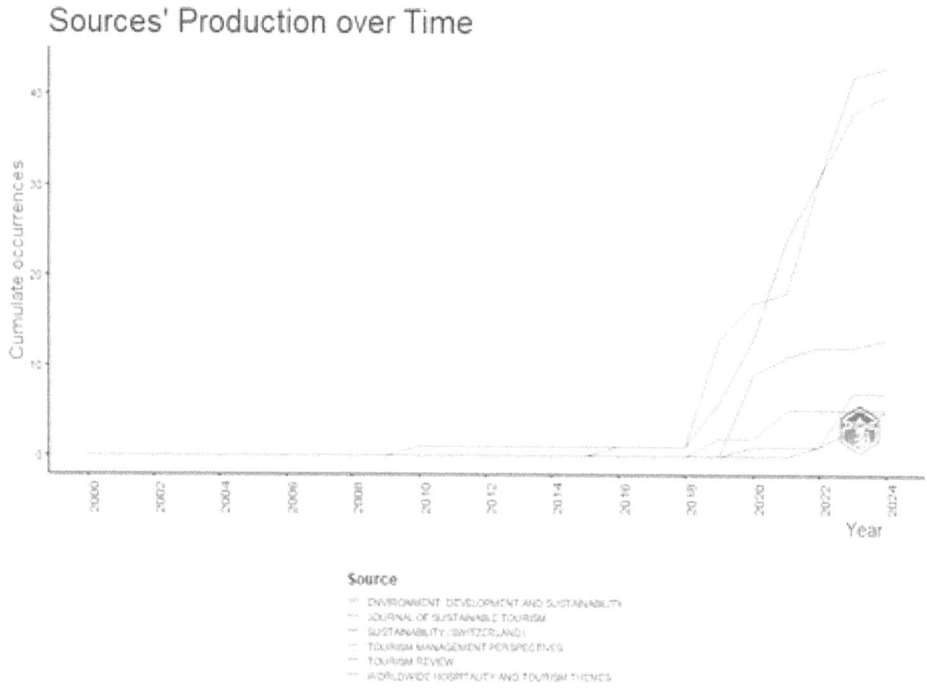

From the said graph, we see that"Sustainability (Switzerland)" has the most dramatic increase in publications, starting around 2016 and showing rapid growth thereafter. This suggests a significant surge in productivity or relevance in the field during this period."Journal of Sustainable Tourism" shows a more gradual but consistent increase over a longer period, beginning in the early years depicted and continuing to rise through to 2024."Worldwide Hospitality and Tourism Themes" shows a moderate and steady increase throughout, while "Tourism Management Perspectives", "Tourism Review" and "Environment, Development and Sustainability" has the least growth, indicating a smaller contribution to the field or a more specialized scope with fewer publications.

Most Relevant Authors

The graph of "Most Relevant Authors" visualizes the academic output of various authors, measured by the number of articles published (Figure 8). The y-axis lists the names of the authors, while the x-axis likely represents the h-index or another metric of publication impact, though it's not labeled here.

Figure 9. Most relevant authors

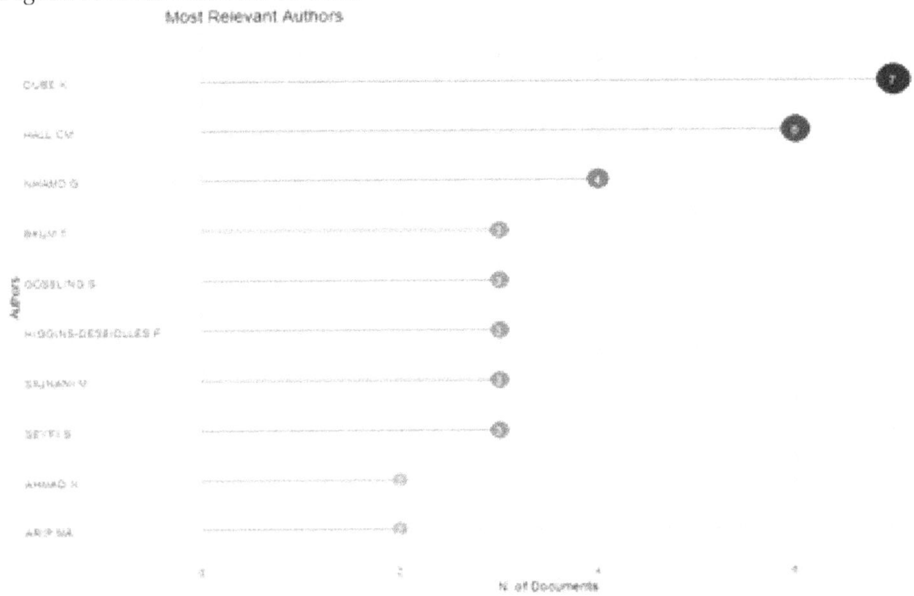

It visualizes the academic output of various authors, measured by the number of articles published. The y-axis lists the names of the authors, while the x-axis likely represents the h-index or another metric of publication impact, though it's not labeled here.

Author Dube K has the largest bubble with 7 documents in their name emerge as most productive author followed by Hall CM with 6 articles produced during this time on sustainable tourism and sustainable development goals.Nhamo G is the third most productive author with 4 articles in credit. Baum C, Gossling S, Higgings-Desbiolles F, Sajnani M, Seyfi S are closely following them with four article by each of these authors. Ahmad N and Arif MA are with two article each related to sustainable tourism and sustainable development goals. Their prominent positions suggest that their work is impactful and well-regarded in the academic community.

Figure 10. Authors' production over time

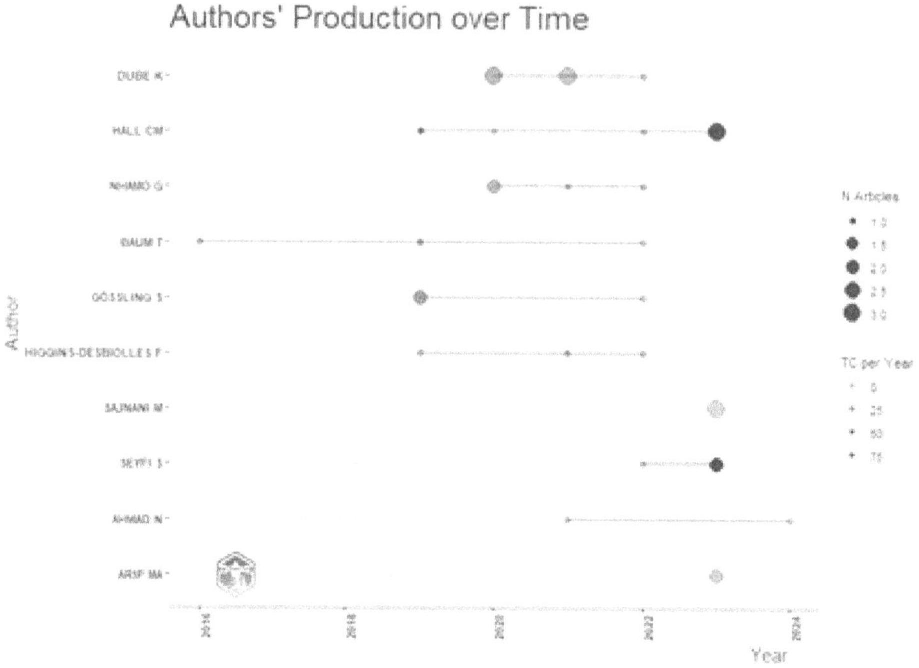

The figure 9 "Authors' Production over Time" illustrates the publication activity of several authors from 2016 to approximately 2024. Each horizontal line represents an author, with points plotted corresponding to the years in which they published articles. The size of each point reflects the number of articles (N. Articles) they published that year, with larger points indicating a greater number of publications. Additionally, the color intensity of the points suggests the total citations (TC per Year) those articles received within a year, serving as an indicator of the impact or influence of their work for that time period. For example, Dube K is the most productive author with seven publication over the period of time in context to sustainable tourism and SDGs followed by Hall CM with six articles published over this period of time followed by Nhamo G. Baum T is the seminal author with a constant publication from 2016 till 2022 even having less publication. In context of citation count Dube K and Hall CM are the most prolific authors with a good record in citation count pointing their articles as impactful in context to sustainable tourism development.

Figure 11. Authors' local impact by H index

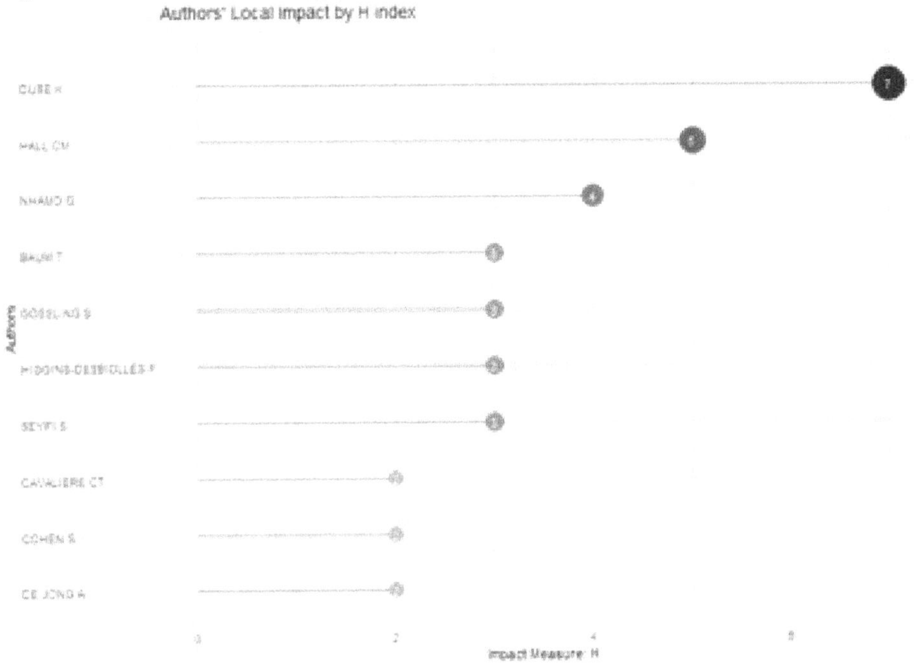

In the figure 10, each author is positioned along the vertical axis with their corresponding h-index displayed along the horizontal axis. The size of the bubbles associated with each author reflects the quantity of their publications.

From this graph, authors such as Dube K, Hall CM and Nhamo G can be seen with highest h-index of 7, 5, 4 respectively. Baum T, GosslingS, Higgings-Desbiolles F, Sajnani M, Seyfi S have a equal size bubble with h-index of 3. Cavaliere CT, Cohen S and De Jong A are with an h-index of 2. Dube K with h-index of 7 is behind Hall CM in citations as Hall has a citation of 618 as compared to Dube K with 224 TC. This shows that even the citation count of Dube K is less, the impact is more as per the h-index.

Figure 12. Most relevant affiliations

Figure 11 shows "Most Relevant Affiliations," each bubble represents an academic or research institution's contribution to the literature in terms of the number of articles published. The position of the bubble along the horizontal axis suggests the quantity of articles, while the vertical positioning corresponds to different institutions. The institution with the largest bubble appears to have produced 22 articles which is the Stockholm University, indicating a significant level of research activity and output in Sweeden. This could suggest a leading role in the respective field, possibly due to robust funding, a large number of active researchers, or a focus on prolific publishing practices.

Rey Juan Carlos University of Spain is at second position in context to contribution to sustainable tourism and SDG with 12 articles followed by University of Surrey located in England with 11 publications. Griffith University Australia and Vaal University of Technology at South Africa are with 9 publication each. Dali University China, University of Cadiz Spain, University of Johanessburg South Africa are with 8 publication each. At the lower end, an institution with 7 articles is the least represented among the groups visualized, which may indicate emerging involvement or a niche area of research specialization within the broader field.

Figure 13. Country scientific production

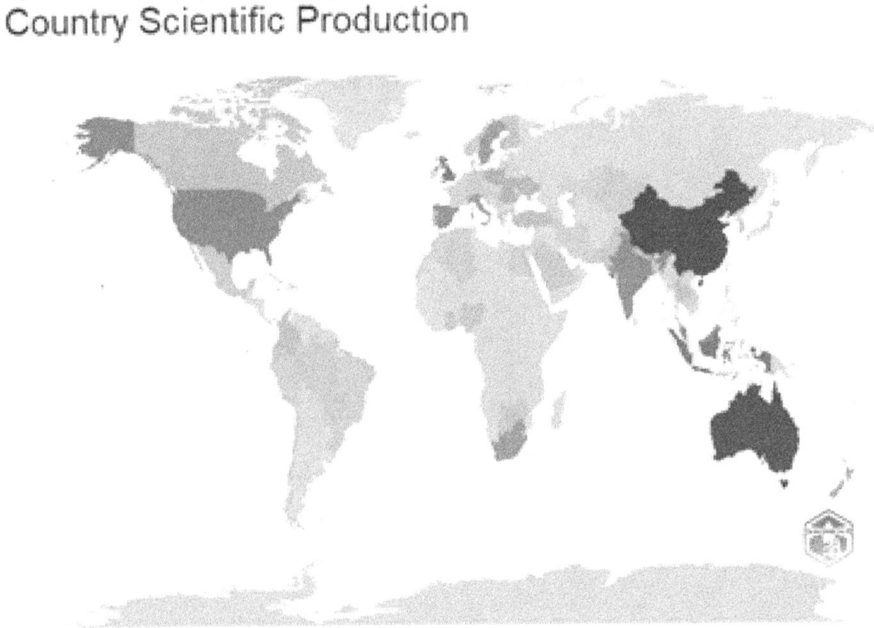

The map (Figure 12) visualizes the scientific production of various countries, highlighting the disparities and concentrations of research output around the globe. China leads significantly in this depiction, with a staggering 72 article outputs, underscoring its prominent position in global scientific research. Australia follows with a notable contribution of 69, while Indonesia closely tails with 50 outputs, indicating their substantial engagement in academic activities. The UK is also featured, contributing 47 outputs to the scientific community. USA, Malaysia, Spain, India and Sweden are with 39, 36, 36, 35, 29 article contribution in the field of sustainable tourism and SDGs. The map also notes single outputs from countries like Barbados and Cambodia. reflecting a diverse but less concentrated research production in these regions.

The figure 13(Most Relevant Words) likely plots keywords on a two-dimensional plane, with the x-axis representing the number of documents a particular keyword appears in (its occurrence), and possibly the y-axis representing the strength of the relationship between keywords (measured by a metric like the co-occurrence or a weighted occurrence score).

Figure 14. Most relevant words

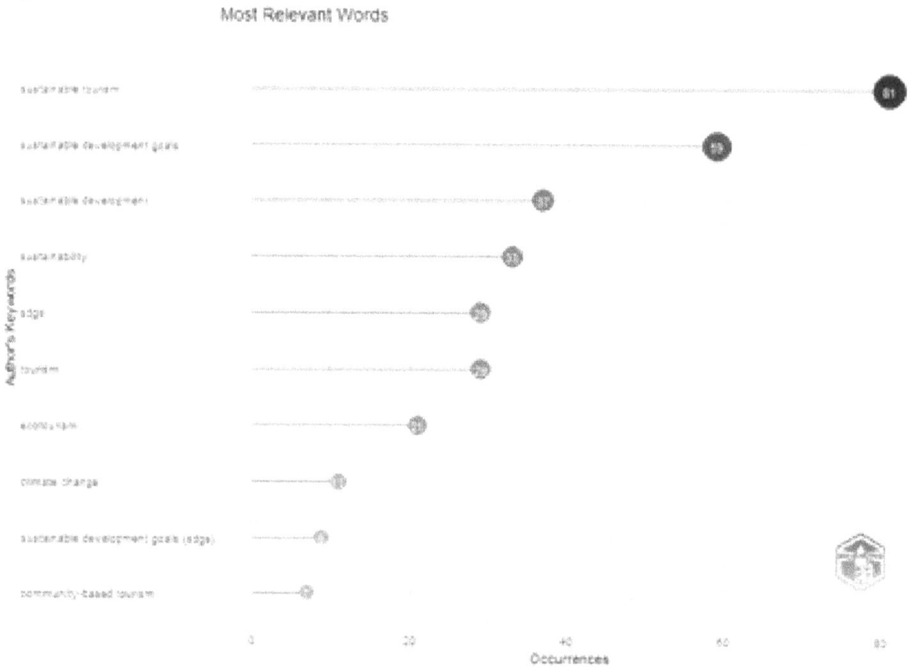

The figure 13 clearly demonstrates that "sustainable tourism" appeared in 81 documents denoting the topmost relevance of the word in context of sustainable tourism and SDGs. The word "Sustainable development goals" occurred 59 times. This indicates a high volume of research and discussions for achieving sustainable development goals through tourism promotion is happening in the academic literature. Followed by "Sustainable Development" which appeared for 37 times followed by "Sustainability" which appeared 33 times in the documents extracted from the database which were published in this context. "SDGs" and "Tourism" occurred for 29 times each. If another term like "Tourism" is also prominent and close to "SDGs" on the graph, it suggests a strong associative relationship between the two topics within the literature.

Word Cloud

Word cloud is a feature in biblioshiny that allows to visualize the most frequent words by making them a central point in the visualization. In context of sustainable tourism and sustainable development goals, it can be clearly noticed that "sustainable tourism", "sustainable development", "Sustainability", "SDGs", "Ecotourism" are some of the major words that are being shown as the most impactful keywords in context to the research in sustainable tourism and SDGs. This puts light in the fact that researchers in this domain are majorly working on these topics and also it highlights the future trending keywords. This also focuses as how sustainable development goals are seen by considering the aspect of sustainable tourism.

Figure 15. Word cloud

TreeMap graphically (figure 15) represents the relative frequency of various keywords in a dataset, likely from academic research or publications. In this treemap, each keyword is allocated a space proportional to its frequency, with 'Sustainable Tourism" being the most prominent, indicating it is the most frequently occurring or studied topic within the context of the data, occupying 18% of the occurrences. Following Sustainable Tourism, the term Sustainable Development Goals' holds 13% visibility, suggesting significant attention towards Tourism driven approaches to SDGs. 'Sustainable development' also has a substantial presence, with 8%, underscoring the focus on economic progress in relation to Tourism and SDGs. Other significant keywords include 'Sustainability' and 'Ecotourism', highlighting a research emphasis on long-term ecological balance and Sustainable development.

Figure 16. Tree map

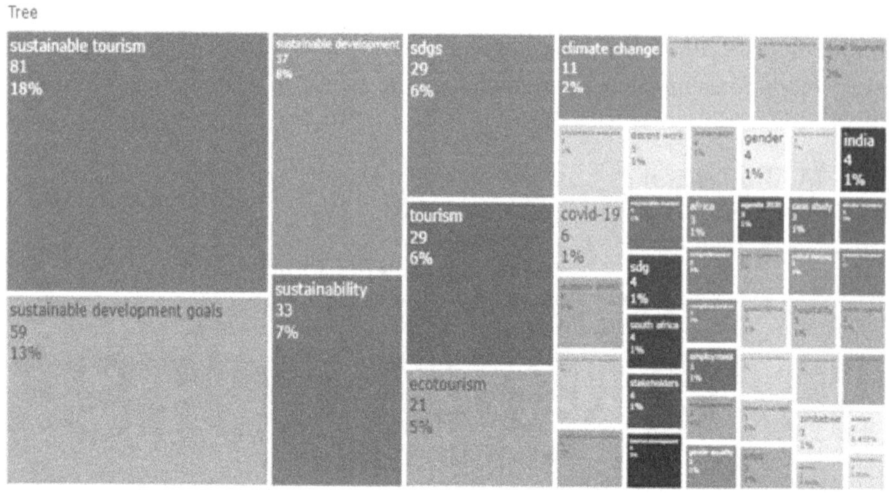

Figure 16 illustrates the words frequency over time which demonstrates as how these words are being evolved and sustained in the progressive course of action with many advancement in research in sustainable tourism and sustainable development goals. The graph demonstrates that 'Sustainable Tourism' evolved in the year 2000 and till 2010 there was a constant use of the word and thereafter it got some importance. From 2019 there is a drastic gain in the occurrence and 'Sustainable Tourism' reached its peak in the recent years showing a thematic trend in 'Sustainable tourism'. Word 'Sustainable Development Goal' evolve in 2008 but got first major importance in 2019 with 6 occurrences and thereafter it is emerging as a most important and trending word leading to develop a new theme to work out by the researchers and got highest count in recent years. 'Sustainability, Sustainable Development' evolved in 2016 and 2017 respectively and in recent years emerging as trending words reflecting their importance in the academic literature.

Figure 17. Word frequency over time

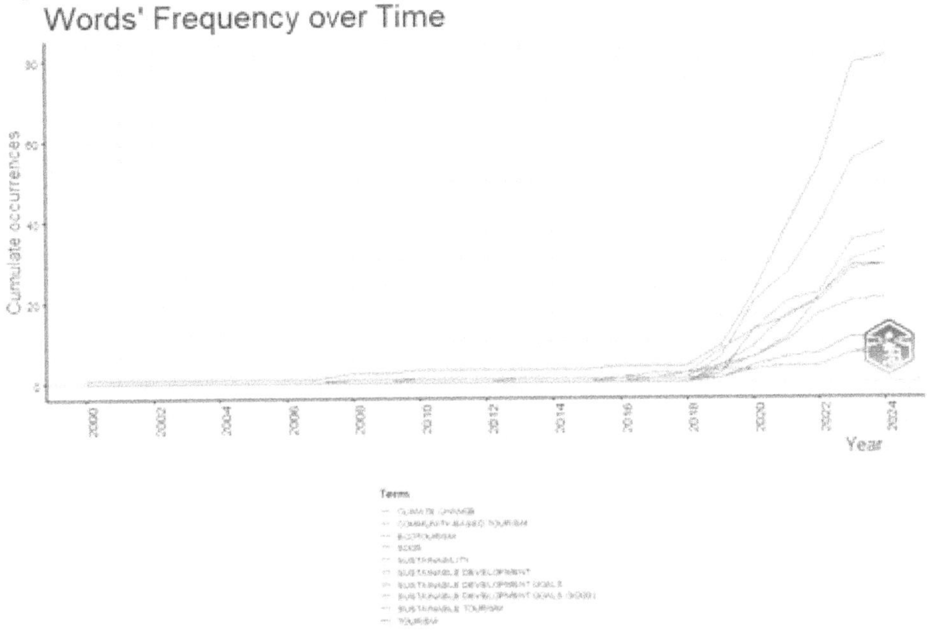

In addition, our study employs the keyword co-occurrence using author keywords to gain insights in SDGs and Sustainable Tourism. Co-occurrence Network analysis draws the links between the keywords used in the literature that provides deep insights regarding knowledge structure (Esfahani et al., 2019). In the analysis it can be seen that keywords with bigger size are high impactful and are closely connected with other keywords with less width or smaller keywords.

Figure 18. Co-occurrence network

Figure 17 shows node-link diagram, highlighting the interconnectivity between various terms related to Sustainable tourism and SDGs. In this network, the nodes (represented by dots or circles) stand for terms or concepts, and the links (the lines connecting the nodes) illustrate the relationships or associations between these terms. The co-occurrence network diagram clearly showing that 'Sustainable Development Goals' and 'Sustainable Tourism' are co-occurred frequently as the bubbles are joined with a thick node. There we can observe four colors of bubbles (Red, Green, Blue and Violet). All four colors reflects four clusters (Sustainable Tourism, SDG, tourism and Sustainability). The Red cluster is dominated by 'Sustainable Tourism', blue cluster is dominated by 'Sustainable Development Goals', Green cluster is dominated by 'Sustainable Development' and Violet cluster is dominated by 'Tourism'.

Thematic Map: A Thematic map is a two dimensional plot which plots the typological themes on the basis of centrality and density (Cobo et al., 2011). In this, clusters are identified based on the co-word analysis and then the themes in each cluster is generated in research domain.These themes can be classified into four quadrants on the basis of density and centrality. Each theme is represented in the map with a bubble. Centrality is plotted on X-axis whereas the density is plotted on the Y axis. Centrality is a measure of inter-cluster interaction among the keywords and it denotes as to which extent one topic is connected or related to other topic in a domain. Density on the other hand refers to the intra-cluster interactions of keywords to develop a theme of that cluster. The top right quadrant contains motor themes with high centrality and density denoting to those themes that are well developed as well as are core to the research domain. The lower right quadrant refers to Basic theme with highcentrality and lowdensity denoting themes that are important and can impact other themes but are less developed internally. Themes in the lower left quadrant refers to emerging or disappearing themes as they have low centrality as well density and are less explored. The upper left quadrant consist of niche themes that are having high density but low centrality and are well developed internally but less discussed widely.

Figure 19. Thematic map

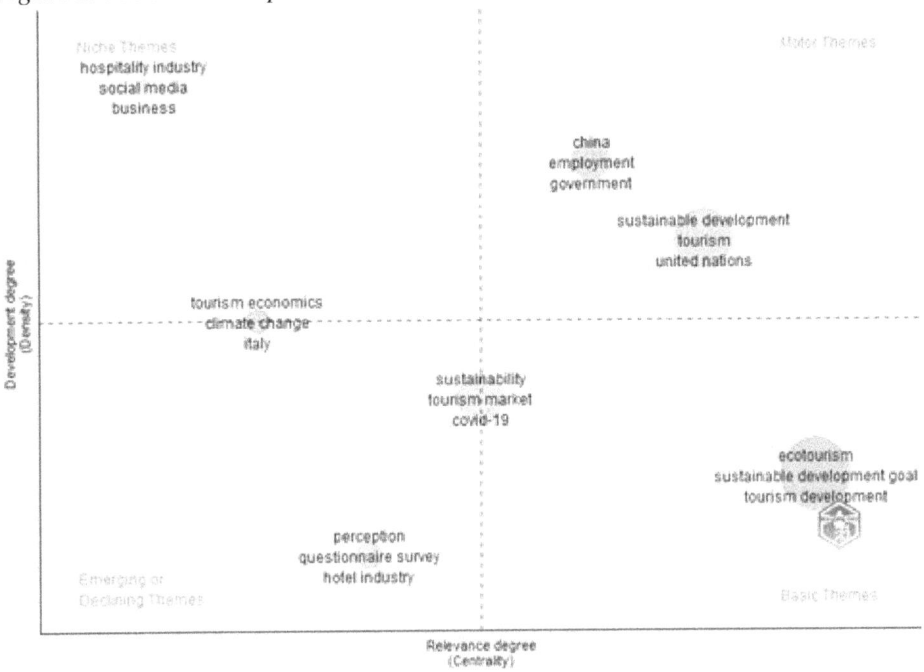

In figure 18 Motor themes that are highly discussed and are highly developed in the research domain due to which they are the core themes including 'China', 'employment', 'Government', 'Sustainable Development', 'Tourism' and 'United Nations'. The Niche themes that are well developed internally but have wide scope of discussion in the research domain consist of keywords such as 'Hospitality industry', 'Social Media', 'Business'. The basic themes which are of utmost importance for the development of the research field but are less developed internally and includes keywords such as 'Ecotourism', 'Sustainable Development Goals' and 'Tourism Development'. The themes which are either emerging or which may disappear with time include keywords such as 'Perception', 'Questionnaire Survey' and 'Hotel Industry'. The theme 'Tourism Economics', 'Climate Change' and 'Italy' are lying between niche and emerging/disappearing themes may have some potential to develop in the research domain. The keywords 'Sustainability', 'Tourism Market' and 'Covid-19' is lying between Basic and emerging/disappearing themes indicates that some of the work is still the foundation for the researches in sustainable tourism and sustainable development goals and some work are might be emerging or disappearing in recent years and thus researchers can work on these themes to find out the answers to the questions.

DISCUSSION AND FUTURE RESEARCH DIRECTIONS

This study was an attempt to analyze the relation between sustainable tourism and SDGs through bibliometric methodology. The search period was set from 2000 to 2024 to encompass recent developments. 230 documents were finalized in performing the final analysis. The Bibliometric R tool was employed for data processing, visualization, and analysis. Descriptive analysis was first conducted to outline the basic characteristics of the data, including publication trends over time, distribution by country, and leading journals in the field. Descriptive analysis reflected that a consistently similar output was there from 2000 till 2018 and thereafter there is an increasing trend till the year 2023. In 2024, the scientific production is less as only four month data is extracted till date, implying a high pace of scientific publication. The analysis of average citation per year reflected a continue drift of ups and downs in the ACP till 2023. This pattern indicates a dynamic academic environment with changing impacts of scientific work over the years. The result shows that while there were periods of high citation impact, overall, there seems to be a downward trend in recent years. The results of three field plot revealed that The highly frequent keywords "Sustainable Development Goals" and "Sustainable Tourism", "sustainable development", "Sustainability", "SDG" and "Tourism". In consideration to the most influential journals as per the three field plot, "Sustainability", "Journal of sustainable tourism", "worldwide hospitality and tourism themes" are the most prolific sources. The visualization serves as a map to the landscape of academic inquiry, showing which authors are most active or influential in specific areas, which topics are receiving the most attention, and how these topics are interconnected within the broader research framework. The Sustainability (Switzerland) stands out with the largest bubble, indicating the highest number of publications at 43 articles. This is followed by the "Journal of Sustainable Tourism" with 42 articles, and worldwide hospitality and tourism with 13 articles. The "Journal of Sustainable Tourism," "Sustainability (Switzerland), stand out as the most impactful sources with the highest h-index values, indicating they are likely to be key outlets for research dissemination in the field.

Author Dube K with 7 documents in their name emerge as most productive author followed by Hall CM with 6 articles produced during this time on sustainable tourism and SDGs. Nhamo G is the third most productive author with 4 articles in credit. Their prominent positions suggest that their work is impactful and well-regarded in the academic community. Dube K is the most productive author with seven publication over the period of time in context to sustainable tourism and SDGs followed by Hall CM with six articles published over this period of time followed by Nhamo G. Baum T is the seminal author with a constant publication from 2016 till 2022 even having less publication. The Stockholm University with 22 publications is the most productive affiliation followed by Rey Juan Carlos University of Spain is at second position in context to contribution to sustainable tourism and SDG with 12 articles followed by University of Surrey located in England with 11 publications.

The word analysis reflected that, "sustainable tourism" appeared in 81 documents denoting the topmost relevance of the word in context of sustainable tourism and SDGs. The word "Sustainable development goals" occurred 59 times. This indicates a high volume of research and discussions for achieving sustainable development goals through tourism promotion is happening in the academic literature. In context of sustainable tourism and sustainable development goals, it can be clearly noticed that "sustainable tourism, sustainable development, Sustainability, SDGs, Ecotourism" are some of the major words that are being shown as the most impactful keywords in context to the research in sustainable tourism and SDGs.

The co-occurrence network diagram clearly showing that 'Sustainable Development Goals' and 'Sustainable Tourism' are co-occurred frequently as the bubbles are joined with a thick node. There we can observe four colors of bubbles (Red, Green, Blue and Violet). All four colors reflects four clusters (Sustainable Tourism, SDG, tourism and Sustainability). The Red cluster is dominated by 'Sustainable Tourism', blue cluster is dominated by 'Sustainable Development Goals', Green cluster is dominated by 'Sustainable Development' and Violet cluster is dominated by 'Tourism'.

Thematic Map analysis was performed to identify major research themes and topics, A Thematic map is a two dimensional plot which plots the typological themes on the basis of centrality and density (Cobo et al., 2011). In this, clusters are identified based on the co-word analysis and then the themes in each cluster is generated in research domain. These themes can be classified into four quadrants on the basis of density and centrality. The top right quadrant in the Thematic Map consist of Motor themes that are highly discussed and are highly developed in the research domain due to which they are the core themes including 'China', 'employment', 'Government', 'Sustainable Development', 'Tourism' and 'United Nations'. The top left quadrant that consist of the Niche themes that are well developed internally but have wide scope of discussion in the research domain consist of keywords such as 'Hospitality industry', 'Social Media', 'Business'. The bottom right quadrant consist of basic themes which are of utmost importance for the development of the research field but are less developed internally and includes keywords such as 'Ecotourism', 'Sustainable Development Goals' and 'Tourism Development'. The bottom left quadrant consist of themes which are either emerging or which may disappear with time include keywords such as 'Perception', 'Questionnaire Survey' and 'Hotel Industry'. The theme 'Tourism Economics', 'Climate Change' and 'Italy' are lying between niche and emerging/disappearing themes may have some potential to develop in the research domain. The keywords 'Sustainability', 'Tourism Market' and 'Covid-19' is lying between Basic and emerging/disappearing themes indicates that some of the work is still the foundation for the researches in sustainable tourism and sustainable development goals and some work are might be emerging or disappearing in recent years and thus researchers can work on these themes to find out the answers to the questions.

This study provided various results which indicated the nexus between sustainable tourism and SDGs but along with this there are some limitations that exist. The study incorporated Scopus database to analyze the results, in future studies web of science can also be incorporated along with Scopus database to make the study results more reliable. The future research work can also include systematic literature review along with bibliometric analysis to enhance the qualitative analysis. The study offers policy makers and practitioners a useful baseline for developing policies and strategies to promote sustainable tourism for achieving the SDG's.

REFERENCES

Abdou, A. H., Hassan, T. H., & El Dief, M. M. (2020). A description of green hotel practices and their role in achieving sustainable development. *Sustainability (Basel), 12*(22), 9624. DOI: 10.3390/su12229624

Aggarwal, D., Jain, A., & Jain, P. (2022). A bibliometric analysis of the global tourism industry in the wake of COVID-19. *Journal of Tourism, 23*(2), 85–94.

Baloch, Q. B., Shah, S. N., Iqbal, N., Sheeraz, M., Asadullah, M., Mahar, S., & Khan, A. U. (2023). Impact of tourism development upon environmental sustainability: A suggested framework for sustainable ecotourism. *Environmental Science and Pollution Research International, 30*(3), 5917–5930. DOI: 10.1007/s11356-022-22496-w PMID: 35984561

Boluk, K. A., & Rasoolimanesh, S. M. (2022). Introduction to the special issue on "Deepening our understandings of the roles and responsibilities of the tourism industry towards the United Nations Sustainable Development Goals (SDGs).". *Tourism Management Perspectives, 41*, 100944. DOI: 10.1016/j.tmp.2022.100944

Buckley, R. (2012). Sustainable tourism: Research and reality. *Annals of Tourism Research, 39*(2), 528–546. DOI: 10.1016/j.annals.2012.02.003

Buhalis, D., Leung, X. Y., Fan, D., Darcy, S., Chen, G., Xu, F., Wei-Han Tan, G., Nunkoo, R., & Farmaki, A. (2023). Tourism 2030 and the contribution to the sustainable development goals: The tourism review viewpoint. *Tourism Review, 78*(2), 293–313. DOI: 10.1108/TR-04-2023-620

Causevic, S., & Neal, M. (2019). The exotic veil: Managing tourist perceptions of national history and statehood in Oman. *Tourism Management, 71*, 504–517. DOI: 10.1016/j.tourman.2018.10.001

Cobo, M. J., Lopez-Herrera, ´. A. G., Herrera-Viedma, E., & Herrera, F. (2011). An approach for detecting, quantifying, and visualizing the evolution of a research field: A practical application to the fuzzy sets theory field. *Journal of Informetrics, 5*(1), 146–166. DOI: 10.1016/j.joi.2010.10.002

Cobo, M. J., Lopez-Herrera, ´. A. G., Herrera-Viedma, E., & Herrera, F. (2011). An approach for detecting, quantifying, and visualizing the evolution of a research field: A practical application to the fuzzy sets theory field. *Journal of Informetrics, 5*(1), 146–166. DOI: 10.1016/j.joi.2010.10.002

Dodds, R., & Holmes, M. (2016). Is there a Benefit from being Green. *Assessing Benefits from Marketing Sustainability by North American Hotels.J Hotel Bus Manage*, *5*(145), 2169–0286. DOI: 10.4172/2169-0286.1000145

Esfahani, H., Tavasoli, K., & Jabbarzadeh, A. (2019). Big data and social media: A scientometrics analysis. *International Journal of Data and Network Science*, *3*(3), 145–164. DOI: 10.5267/j.ijdns.2019.2.007

Fauzi, M. A. (2023). Sustainable tourism and sustainable development goals (SDGs): A state-of-the-art review of past, present, and future trends. *Environment, Development and Sustainability*, *27*(2), 1–22. DOI: 10.1007/s10668-023-04077-0

Geng, Y., Zhang, X., Gao, J., Yan, Y., & Chen, L. (2024). Bibliometric analysis of sustainable tourism using CiteSpace. *Technological Forecasting and Social Change*, *202*, 123310. DOI: 10.1016/j.techfore.2024.123310

Glass, L. M., & Newig, J. (2019). Governance for achieving the Sustainable Development Goals: How important are participation, policy coherence, reflexivity, adaptation and democratic institutions? *Earth System Governance*, *2*, 100031. DOI: 10.1016/j.esg.2019.100031

Hall, C. M. (2019). Constructing sustainable tourism development: The 2030 agenda and the managerial ecology of sustainable tourism. *Journal of Sustainable Tourism*, *27*(7), 1044–1060. DOI: 10.1080/09669582.2018.1560456

Han, H., Lee, J. S., Trang, H. L. T., & Kim, W. (2018). Water conservation and waste reduction management for increasing guest loyalty and green hotel practices. *International Journal of Hospitality Management*, *75*, 58–66. DOI: 10.1016/j.ijhm.2018.03.012

Irawan, N. C., Hartoyo, E., Suswadi, , & Mustaqim, . (2022, November). Environmental management and stakeholder roles in sustainable tourism development: A feasibility study. [). IOP Publishing.]. *IOP Conference Series. Earth and Environmental Science*, *1108*(1), 012068. DOI: 10.1088/1755-1315/1108/1/012068

Jiménez-García, M., Ruiz-Chico, J., Peña-Sánchez, A. R., & López-Sánchez, J. A. (2020). A bibliometric analysis of sports tourism and sustainability (2002–2019). *Sustainability (Basel)*, *12*(7), 2840. DOI: 10.3390/su12072840

Kang, K. H., Stein, L., Heo, C. Y., & Lee, S. (2012). Consumers' willingness to pay for green initiatives of the hotel industry. *International Journal of Hospitality Management*, *31*(2), 564–572. DOI: 10.1016/j.ijhm.2011.08.001

Kapera, I. (2018). Sustainable development in the hotel industry: Between theory and practice in Poland. *Turyzm*, *28*(2 ENG), 23-30.

Kasim, A. (2009). Managerial attitudes towards environmental management among small and medium hotels in Kuala Lumpur. *Journal of Sustainable Tourism, 17*(6), 709–725. DOI: 10.1080/09669580902928468

Li, Y., Liu, Y., & Solangi, Y. A. (2024). Analysis of factors and strategies for the implementation of sustainable tourism in a green economic structure in China. *Journal of Cleaner Production, 434*, 140011. DOI: 10.1016/j.jclepro.2023.140011

Magio, K. O., Lizama Aranda, L. L., González, L., & Alpuche, C. (2021). Analysis and identification of sustainable public policy for management of cultural and natural heritage in the Maya Region in line with the sustainable development goals. *Heritage, 4*(4), 4172–4183. DOI: 10.3390/heritage4040229

Manaktola, K., & Jauhari, V. (2007). Exploring consumer attitude and behaviour towards green practices in the lodging industry in India. *International Journal of Contemporary Hospitality Management, 19*(5), 364–377. DOI: 10.1108/09596110710757534

Mensah, I. (2006). Environmental management practices among hotels in the greater Accra region. *International Journal of Hospitality Management, 25*(3), 414–431. DOI: 10.1016/j.ijhm.2005.02.003

Mohan, P. (2022). Sustainable tourism and the sustainable development goals in sub-national island jurisdictions: The case of tobago. *Island Studies Journal, 17*(2), 168–191. DOI: 10.24043/isj.183

Monroy-Rodríguez, S., & Caro-Carretero, R. (2023). Congress tourism: Characteristics and application to sustainable tourism to facilitate collective action towards achieving the SDGs. *Cogent Business & Management, 10*(3), 2286663. https://doi .org/. DOI: 10.1080/23311975.2023.2286663

Moyle, B., Moyle, C. L., Ruhanen, L., Weaver, D., & Hadinejad, A. (2020). Are we really progressing sustainable tourism research? A bibliometric analysis. *Journal of Sustainable Tourism, 29*(1), 106–122. DOI: 10.1080/09669582.2020.1817048

Özgit, H., & Zhandildina, D. (2021). Investigating stakeholder awareness of the sustainable development goals and tourism stakeholder collaboration: The case of North Cyprus. *Worldwide Hospitality and Tourism Themes, 13*(4), 498–509. DOI: 10.1108/WHATT-02-2021-0027

Pan, S. Y., Gao, M., Kim, H., Shah, K. J., Pei, S. L., & Chiang, P. C. (2018). Advances and challenges in sustainable tourism toward a green economy. *The Science of the Total Environment, 635*, 452–469. DOI: 10.1016/j.scitotenv.2018.04.134 PMID: 29677671

Pradhan, B. K., Yadav, S., Ghosh, J., & Prashad, A. (2023). Achieving the sustainable development goals (SDGs) in the Indian state of Odisha: Challenges and opportunities. *World Development Sustainability, 100078*, 100078. Advance online publication. DOI: 10.1016/j.wds.2023.100078

Prud'homme, B., & Raymond, L. (2013). Sustainable development practices in the hospitality industry: An empirical study of their impact on customer satisfaction and intentions. *International Journal of Hospitality Management, 34*, 116–126. DOI: 10.1016/j.ijhm.2013.03.003

Rasoolimanesh, S. M., Ramakrishna, S., Hall, C. M., Esfandiar, K., & Seyfi, S. (2020). A systematic scoping review of sustainable tourism indicators in relation to the sustainable development goals. *Journal of Sustainable Tourism*, •••, 1–21.

Sachs, J. D., Schmidt-Traub, G., Mazzucato, M., Messner, D., Nakicenovic, N., & Rockström, J. (2019). Six transformations to achieve the sustainable development goals. *Nature Sustainability, 2*(9), 805–814. DOI: 10.1038/s41893-019-0352-9

Scheyvens, R., & Cheer, J. M. (2021). Tourism, the SDGs and partnerships. *Journal of Sustainable Tourism*, •••, 1–11.

Seraphin, H., & Gowreesunkar, V. G. (2021). Tourism: How to achieve the sustainable development goals? *Worldwide Hospitality and Tourism Themes, 13*(1), 3–8. DOI: 10.1108/WHATT-08-2020-0086

Soh, A. N., Puah, C. H., & Arip, M. A. (2023). A bibliometric analysis on tourism sustainable competitiveness research. *Sustainability (Basel), 15*(2), 1035. DOI: 10.3390/su15021035

Stojanovska-Stefanova, A., & Dimitrov, N., &MagdincevaSopova, M. (. (2019). The significant role of the tourism in achieving the United Nations sustainable development goals. *Knowledge-International Journal. Scientific Papers, 34*(5), 1259–1264. DOI: 10.4337/9781788117104.00015

Streimikiene, D., Svagzdiene, B., Jasinskas, E., & Simanavicius, A. (2020). Sustainable tourism development and competitiveness: The systematic literature review. *Sustainable Development*. Advance online publication. DOI: 10.1002/sd.2133

United Nations. (2015). Transforming our World: The 2030 Agenda for sustainable development. New York: Division for Sustainable Development Goals. Retrieved from 21252030 Agenda for Sustainable Development web.pdf (un.org) 'UNWTO', Sustainable development (unwto.org) (accessed on 6 June 2024).

Zhao, W., Yin, C., Hua, T., Meadows, M. E., Li, Y., Liu, Y., Cherubini, F., Pereira, P., & Fu, B. (2022). Achieving the Sustainable Development Goals in the post-pandemic era. *Humanities & Social Sciences Communications*, *9*(1), 1–7. DOI: 10.1057/s41599-022-01283-5 PMID: 35967482

About the Contributors

Mario Silic, PhD, Professor, at the Swiss School of Business and Management SSBM Geneva. He has over 25 years of professional experience in various senior management positions. He worked for several international corporations. He achieved his master's degree in computer science in 1999 and post-graduate degree in Computer Networks and Telecommunications in 2001 from University of Lyon I, France. He is also holding an MBA. He is currently a Postdoc at the University of St Gallen, Switzerland. He is teaching various courses: Cybersecurity, Machine Learning/AI applied to the business context, Data Analytics and Decision Making, Programming, Project Management, Innovation Management, Web server, etc. He has received 2059 citations on Google Scholar with an H-index of 22 and i10-index of 33. Dr. Silic's scholarly contributions have significantly impacted the field of management and information systems, earning recognition from academics and professionals worldwide. His research has been published in some of the most prestigious academic journals, further underscoring the quality and relevance of his work. He recently published research on the (12-month longitudinal study) that investigated the role of gamification in Human Resource Management fostering job satisfaction and engagement. He has been appointed to the Editorial Team of the prestigious research journal "Frontiers in Computer Science.". Dr. Silic's dedication to research and his ability to address complex issues in management and information systems have not only advanced academic knowledge but also provided valuable insights for practitioners. His work continues to shape the discourse in these fields, demonstrating the practical implications of rigorous academic research. He utilizes his technology expertise in multi-disciplinary research. His passion for pushing the boundaries of knowledge is truly remarkable.

Mahesh Luthia PhD, is Professor and Area Chair, Human Resources at CIMR. A Ph. D. in management from NMIMS he is an ICF certified Transformative Leadership Coach. His doctoral research focussed on re-conceptualising Customer

Orientation in the contemporary Indian BFSI sector. He has taught various courses at national and international universities in areas of Strategic Management, Organisational Behaviour, Human Resources, International Business and Organisation Development. As a consultant and lead project manager in his previous assignment, he was involved in a wide range of consulting assignments, profit, and non-profit clients to help them achieve their goals and manage human resources. During his diverse career of over 27 years in industry and academia he possesses unique experiences of managing operations and working across different cultures. His research interest and contribution include topics covering comparative HR strategies, cross-cultural studies, leadership, digitalisation of business, sustainable business practices and change management. His research philosophy is based on Interpretivism, a research paradigm in social sciences that focuses on adding to the body of knowledge and making meaningful contributions to the industry. He has papers published in high indexed and peer reviewed National and international journals. For his research in management, he has collaborated with various international authors from different countries. He has presented papers in various international conferences and has chaired sessions in conferences. He is the editor for a forthcoming book on Innovation Management to be published by Cengage. He is also on the board of reviewers of national and international journals.

Faizan Ahmad is an Assistant Professor of Computer Science at the Cardiff School of Technologies, Cardiff Metropolitan University. He is a member of the Creative Computing Research Centre. With over 12 years of teaching and research experience in computer science, he has developed a strong background in various areas of the field. He has developed and led courses in Artificial Intelligence (AI), Human-Computer Interaction (HCI), Games, and Web and Mobile Application Development. His research interests lie in AI, HCI, Gamification, Metaverse, Internet of Things (IoT), and Machine Learning (ML) based solutions for Smart Learning, Assistive Technologies, Educational Technologies, Healthcare, and Industry 5.0. To date, he has published 30 high-quality research articles, with a total impact factor of 55.46 and over 700 citations (h-index: 7, i10-index: 5) in prestigious conferences and Q1 journals. In recognition of his contributions, he was awarded the Distinguished Foreign Student Award by Beihang University, China, and Fellow status by the Higher Education Academy, UK. Additionally, he is honored to be endorsed by the Royal Society, UK, as a Global Talent. He is also the guest editor for the Special Issue on Emerging Media and Technology Applications in Learning Sciences: Innovations, Impacts, and Future Directions in the Journal of Human Behavior and Emerging Technologies.

Partha Pratim Chakraborty, is a seasoned academic and industry professional with over two decades of strategic leadership experience across leading organizations such as Mahindra Holidays & Resorts, Sterling Holidays, Thomas Cook (India), and Everonn Education. He holds a Doctorate from the Swiss School of Business Management (SSBM), Geneva, and is currently pursuing a second doctorate—Fellow Program in Management (FPM)—at Chetana's Institute of Management and Research (CIMR), Mumbai (2024–2028). He has also earned an executive certification in Leadership and Digital Business Trends from The Wharton School, University of Pennsylvania. Dr. Chakraborty's research spans influencer marketing, digital transformation, AI ethics, the experience economy, and sustainable tourism. He has articles in European Economic Letters, IPE Journal of Management, Journal of Research, and Global Business and Interdisciplinary Studies , book chapters published by IGI Global.

***

Raed Awashreh is Professor of Management & Public Administration. He brings over 25 years of combined academic and industry experience, teaching undergraduate and postgraduate courses. Dr. Awashreh has authored 50 articles, several Book chapters, and 3 books spanning topics such as, human resources, governance, public policy, strategy, leadership, Entrepreneurship, Innovation, multidisciplinary linked AI, and management. In addition to his academic role, Dr. Awashreh serves as a consultant in business, management, governance, HR, and organizational development, working closely with government, private, and non-governmental sectors. He earned his degrees in Public Administration and Management from Flinders University, Australia, and Monterey, USA.

Saurabh Chandra is an accomplished legal scholar and currently serves as an Associate Professor & Assistant Dean at the School of Law, Bennett University, India. With a robust academic foundation, he earned his Bachelor of Arts and Bachelor of Laws (B.A. LL.B.) from the prestigious Aligarh Muslim University (A.M.U.). He further specialized in Business Laws, completing his Master of Laws (LL.M.) at the renowned National Law School of India University (NLSIU), Bangalore. Dr. Chandra's academic journey culminated in a Doctorate in Law (Ph.D.) from the esteemed National Law University (NLU) Delhi. In addition to his impressive legal education from some of India's most prestigious institutions, Dr. Chandra also holds a master's degree in Management with specialization in Human Resources in Management and another in Journalism and Mass Communication. With more than16 years of teaching experience, he has numerous publications to his credit. His expertise is complemented by a robust portfolio of scholarly publications. Throughout his career, Dr. Chandra has consistently produced high-impact research. His publications are widely recognized for their depth of analysis, innovative perspectives, and practical relevance. His publications not only reflect his scholarly rigor but also his dedication to addressing contemporary challenges faced by businesses and policymakers. By bridging the gap between theoretical insights and real-world applications, Dr. Chandra's work serves as a valuable resource for academics, legal practitioners, and industry professionals alike. Dr. Chandra brings a wealth of experience in Academic Administration, having successfully held various key administrative positions. His diverse qualifications and extensive experience make him a distinguished figure in the academic and legal communities.

Aastha Jain is an Assistant Professor in Department of Management Studies, Vaish College of Engineering, Rohtak, since 2021 (affiliated to Maharshi Dayanand University Rohtak, Haryana). She is B.Com (Hons.), M.Com, Ph.D. and UGC-NET (3-times in Commerce) qualified. She got her Ph.D. degree in Commerce from Maharishi Dayanand University in 2022. She has published many research papers in various National and International (Scopus/UGC Care listed/Peer reviewed) journals and edited books. She has also presented many research papers at various sponsored conferences and seminars. Her main research interests include Behavioral Finance, Entrepreneurship, Marketing, and Human Resource, etc. Her technical expertise lies in SPSS, AMOS, R-Studio.

Firoj Kabir is a researcher, Lecturer of the Department of “Tourism and Hospitality Management” at the Daffodil International University, Dhaka, Bangladesh, with a solid academic background in BBA and MBA majoring in Tourism and Hospitality Management from the University of Dhaka. His passion lies in exploring the intersection of travel and culture. His diverse areas of interest include archaeological tourism, sustainable tourism, and the unique characteristics of Generation Z travelers. Through extensive research and insightful writing, he sheds light on the intricate connections between historical sites, responsible tourism, and the evolving preferences of the next generation of travelers. His work not only enriches the field of tourism but also inspires readers to engage with the world around them in meaningful and responsible ways.

Musfiqur Rahoman Khan is an accomplished author and Teaching Assistant at the Department of Tourism and Hospitality Management at Daffodil Institute of IT (DIIT), Dhaka, Bangladesh. He holds a Bachelor's degree in Business Administration (BBA), majoring in Tourism and Hospitality Management, from the same institute. With a strong academic background and a passion for exploring the intersection of travel and culture, Musfiq's diverse areas of interest include Adventure tourism,

Cultural tourism, and Wildlife tourism. Through his teaching and writing, he strives to inspire others to discover the richness and diversity of the world through travel.

Mohd Osaid Koti A highly skilled and experienced professional with over fourteen years of expertise in academics, research, and analytics. Known for exceptional analytical abilities, capable of interpreting, summarizing, and forecasting data for meaningful applications. A management researcher with extensive knowledge of analytical and data handling skills, possessing a strong affinity for numbers, and a keen interest in business research.

Anil Kumar is working as an Assistant Professor in the School of Management Graphic Era Hill University Haldwani Campus He has academic experience of 2 year. He has qualified UGC- NET JRF in Commerce and UGC-NET in Management. Dr Anil completed his PhD from Kumaun University Nainital in the year 2023 in Commerce He has published various research papers listed in SCOPUS/ABDC/ UGC CARE listed journals Dr Anil has been a resource person in 3 FDP's on research methodology. His area of interest includes Sustainable Tourism, Behavioral Finance, Consumer Behavior and Organizational Behavior. His technical expertise are in software such as SPSS, AMOS, SMART-PLS, Eviews, VosViewer and R.

Sanjeev Kumar is a Professor in Lovely Professional University Punjab India. He received Undergraduate in Hotel Management from Osmania University, Postgraduate in Tourism Management from Madurai Kamaraj University. He completed Doctor of Philosophy in Hospitality Management in 2019 from Amity University Jaipur India. His research areas lies in food Service Industry, his research focuses on Alcoholic beverages, Event management and Sustainable Management Practices, Metaverse, AI Machine Learning and Artificial Intelligence. He published more than 60 research papers, articles and chapters in Scopus Indexed, UGC Approved and peer reviewed Journals and books. Dr. Sanjeev Kumar participated and acted as resource person in various National and International conferences, seminars, session chair, research workshops and industry talks and his work has been widely cited. Dr. Sanjeev also edited more than 12 books with various International Publishers such as IGI Global, Cambridge Scholars, Emerald, CABI, Bentham Science, Taylor & Francis. Dr Sanjeev is an active researcher and has published numerous research articles in prestigious national and international journals and books.

Archan Mitra is an Assistant Professor at School of Media Studies (SOMS), at Presidency University, Bangalore. He edited various publications and wrote "Cases for Classroom Media and Entertainment Business," an IIM textbook. "Environmental informatics and communication for sustainability" is his doctorate at Visva-Bharati

Santiniketan, West Bengal. He is also a qualified Science Communicator and Journalism from Indian Science Communication Society (ISCOS), Corporate Trainer with Amity Institute of Training and Development, and Social Media Network Analyst. He loves environmental communication. He received the Journalistic Club of Kolkata Medal of Honour and PRSI Kolkata Chapter Certificate of Merit. He was a World Bank research assistant at IIM Kashipur. He launched the World Bank's Green MBA MOOC. He publishes in prestigious emergency management magazines. IIM Kashipur, Alabama State University, Birmingham, USA, is his research partner. He used Developing Communities from Within (DCFW) to turn a West Bengal village called "Noachar" into an eco-village.

Sanchita Paul is a dedicated and accomplished content strategist with extensive experience in managing diverse content formats across different digital platforms. With a strong background in content strategy, editing, and UX writing, she has honed her skills in branding, social media management, and technical writing. Holding an MA in Communication and Journalism from Visva-Bharati University, Ms. Paul is proficient in tools like Google Analytics, Canva, and MS Office Suite, making her a versatile professional committed to producing high-quality, impactful content to improve brand visibility.

V S Sharada is a dedicated research scholar specializing in Organizational Behavior and Human Resources. She is currently pursuing a Post Graduate Diploma in Management at ASCI, Hyderabad, and working as a Research Intern at IIT Bombay. She has also interned at NIT Silchar and Goa Institute of Management, focusing on HR Analytics, workplace incivility, and employee engagement. Sharada has co-authored several book chapters and journal publications with IGI Global, Emerald Publishing, and Pearson, covering topics like AI in HR, well-being at work, and talent acquisition. She has presented research at IIM Jammu, IIM Trichy, IIM Shillong, IIM Sambalpur, IBS ICFAI, and Woxsen University, winning a Best Paper Award. Her research interests include employee well-being, incivility, mental wellness. Beyond academics, she is a skilled Carnatic Veena player, event host, and active contributor to academic forums. With strong analytical and leadership skills, she aims to contribute meaningfully to HR and Organizational Behavior research.

Kuldeep Singh currently serves as Assistant Professor in Amity School of Hospitality, amity university, Manesar, India. He completed his Ph.D. in tourism from Maharishi Dayanand University (Rohtak) in India in the year 2020. He is also a UGC (Net- JRF qualified). Dr. Singh has also served the tourism industry for couple of years and more than three years in academics. Dr. Singh has so far published more than 30 research articles in both international and national referred journals as well as in edited books in the field of Tourism. Currently, He is serving as an editor of book series in various reputed publications (Emerald, IIP series). Dr. Singh is passionate about the academic areas of Service Quality Management, Rural tourism, Ecotourism, and Sustainable tourism. He also won aspiring researchers welcome award from Indian Hospitality Congress. His credential may be verified on various research platforms like Google Scholar, SSRN, LinkedIn, Academia, and Research Gate.

Kuldeep Singh currently serves as an assistant professor at Amity School of Hospitality, Amity University, Haryana, India. He completed his Ph.D. in tourism from Maharshi Dayanand University (Rohtak), India, in 2021. He is also a UGC (Net- JRF qualified). Dr. Singh has also served the tourism industry for a couple of years and more than three years in academics. Dr. Singh has so far published more than 45 research articles in both international and national refereed journals as well as in edited books in the field of Tourism. Currently, He is serving as an editor of a book series in various reputed publications (Emerald, CABI, Routledge, IGI Global, Bentham Science, IIP series). Dr. Singh is passionate about the academic areas of Service Quality Management, Rural tourism, Ecotourism, and Sustainable tourism. He also won an aspiring researchers' welcome award from the Indian Hospitality Congress. His credentials may be verified on various research platforms like Google Scholar, SSRN, LinkedIn, Academia, and Research Gate.

Bhupinder Singh working as Professor at Sharda University, India. Also, Honorary Professor in University of South Wales UK and Santo Tomas University Tunja, Colombia. His areas of publications as Smart Healthcare, Medicines, fuzzy logics, artificial intelligence, robotics, machine learning, deep learning, federated learning, IoT, PV Glasses, metaverse and many more. He has 3 books, 139 paper publications, 163 paper presentations in international/national conferences and seminars, participated in more than 40 workshops/FDP's/QIP's, 25 courses from international universities of repute, organized more than 59 events with international and national academicians and industry people's, editor-in-chief and co-editor in journals, developed new courses. He has given talks at international universities, resource person in international conferences such as in Nanyang Technological University Singapore, Tashkent State University of Law Uzbekistan; KIMEP University Kazakhstan, All'ah meh Tabatabi University Iran, the Iranian Association of International Criminal law, Iran and Hague Center for International Law and Investment, The Netherlands, Northumbria University Newcastle UK,

Bruno Barbosa Sousa is Professor Coordinator of Marketing at Polytechnic Institute of Cávado and Ave (IPCA), Portugal and PhD in Marketing and Strategy in

Universidade do Minho, Portugal. Head of Masters Program - Tourism Management and Marketing Tourism (IPCA); CiTUR – Center for Tourism Research, Development and Innovation and UNIAG research member. He has published in the Journal of Enterprising Communities, Tourism Management Perspectives, Current Issues in Tourism, Journal of Organizational Change Management, World Review of Entrepreneurship, Management and Sust. Development, among others.

Dil Afrin Swarna is a renowned expert in education and research. She holds a research-based MBA in Human Resource Management (HRM) from the National University of Bangladesh. Swarna's passion for HRM drives her to explore various themes, showcasing her understanding of business dynamics and interconnections. Her research benefits both academia and industry. Swarna has delved into organizational behavior, employee development, and strategic management, demonstrating the critical role of HRM in corporate performance and offering practical solutions to current managerial challenges. She actively participates in conferences, publishes articles, and collaborates with other specialists in education and research. Her innovative approaches to HRM challenges are highly regarded and push the boundaries of existing knowledge. Through her dedication to research and teaching, Dil Afrin Swarna continues to make significant contributions to academia and her industry. Her work exemplifies how committed and insightful research can enhance organizational practices and deepen our understanding of human resource management.

Mohammad Badruddoza Talukder is an Associate Professor, College of Tourism and Hospitality Management, IUBAT - International University of Business Agriculture and Technology, Dhaka, Bangladesh. He holds PhD in Hotel Management from Lovely Professional University, India. He has been teaching various courses in the Department of Tourism and Hospitality at various universities in Bangladesh since 2008. His research areas include tourism management, hotel management, hospitality management, food & beverage management, and accommodation management, where he has published research papers in well-known journals in Bangladesh and abroad. Mr. Talukder is one of the executive members of the Tourism Educators Association of Bangladesh. He has led training and consulting for a wide range of hospitality organizations in Bangladesh. He just became an honorary facilitator at the Bangladesh Tourism Board's Bangabandhu international tourism and hospitality training institution.

Index

A

B

C

D

E

F

H

I

K

L

M

O

P

R

S

T

V

W

www.ingramcontent.com/pod-product-compliance
Lightning Source LLC
LaVergne TN
LVHW080613300926
849162LV00005B/1144

* 9 7 9 8 3 3 7 3 0 0 7 1 9 *